D0849649

THE PARTNERSHIP

George Marshall, Henry Stimson, and the Extraordinary Collaboration That Won World War II

EDWARD FARLEY ALDRICH

STACKPOLE
BOOKS
Guilford, Connecticut
Blue Ridge Summit, Pennsylvania

STACKPOLE BOOKS

An imprint of Globe Pequot, the trade division of
The Rowman & Littlefield Publishing Group, Inc.
4501 Forbes Blvd., Ste. 200
Lanham, MD 20706
www.rowman.com

Distributed by NATIONAL BOOK NETWORK

Copyright © 2022 by Edward Farley Aldrich

British Library Cataloguing in Publication Information available

Library of Congress Cataloging-in-Publication Data available

978-0-8117-7094-1 (cloth)
978-0-8117-7095-8 (electronic)

♾️™ The paper used in this publication meets the minimum requirements of American National Standard for Information Sciences—Permanence of Paper for Printed Library Materials, ANSI/NISO Z39.48-1992.

To Susie, the better half of our partnership.
And of course, JBT

CONTENTS

ACKNOWLEDGMENTS

First, I must thank Dave Reisch at Stackpole Books for taking a chance on a first-time author and providing the energy, creativity, experience, and confidence to bring this project home. I am also in debt to his talented colleagues at Stackpole (including Elaine McGarraugh and Stephanie Otto), and the larger Rowman & Littlefield publishing house to which Stackpole belongs.

As a lifelong devotee of American history, I had circled around Henry Stimson and George Marshall for years, but never as a team and generally in the background of someone else's story. My interest in Stimson grew over a ten-year period as a result of five outstanding books, one a 1938 biography of his principal mentor Elihu Root by Philip C. Jessup, and four others that covered one or more of his protégés written by prominent historians Kai Bird, David Halberstam, Walter Isaacson, and Evan Thomas. Wanting to learn more about this man held in such high regard by so many leaders of the postwar generation, I read Elting Morison's *Turmoil and Tradition*. This definitive biography on Stimson, which I borrowed from heavily for *The Partnership*, caused me to question Winston Churchill's famous post-World War II comment that it was George Marshall who had been the "organizer of victory." It seemed to me that the American general had a solid civilian partner in Stimson.

Digging deeper, I read Forrest C. Pogue, Jr.'s four-volume biographical masterpiece on Marshall published between 1963 and 1987. To research his book, one I also borrowed from liberally for mine, Pogue poured over 3.5 million pages of material and interviewed more than three hundred former colleagues of Marshall (as well as the reserved general himself). Although Pogue's efforts provided wonderful insight into Marshall and Stimson's working relationship, I knew there had to be something else out there that could further illuminate it. That something was Stimson's remarkable diary. In taking the time every night to record a full account of his day and general thoughts during his five years working alongside Marshall, Stimson left a treasure behind of over 4,000 pages from which I could gradually assemble a picture of how truly astonishing the two men's partnership was.

For providing me additional color on the relationship between Stimson and Marshall as well as information on various members of Stimson's staff and Roosevelt's cabinet, I must acknowledge Robert P. Patterson, Jr. and

Robert M. Morgenthau, both now deceased. Patterson's father was Stimson's under secretary of war Robert P. Patterson whom Robert Morgenthau served under as an aide after the War. Morgenthau was the son of Henry Morgenthau, Stimson's fellow cabinet member (he was FDR's treasury secretary). I am grateful to both men for the generous time they granted and their wealth of anecdotes.

Among the enjoyments of undertaking this project was spending time researching Stimson (at Phillips Academy at Andover, Yale, Harvard, and Woodley Mansion), and Marshall (at the George C. Marshall Foundation located on the campus of the Virginia Military Institute). Not only did I have the pleasure of strolling through the majestic and historic settings of these iconic institutions but was also welcomed by friendly, knowledgeable, and helpful staff (thank you Jeffrey Kozak, Melissa Davis, Jessica Becker, Darwin Walker, Allerton Kilborne, and Paige Roberts among others). A special thanks to Karen Sallick, a trustee of Phillips Academy, for assisting me in gaining access to the archives of Stimson's beloved alma mater and for her general enthusiasm for the project.

For general guidance during the publishing process, I owe authors Evan Thomas, Kai Bird, Walter Isaacson, Michael Beschloss, David Roll, Walter Stahr, Larry Haas, Herman Pirchner, Mimi Swartz, and Hilary Wyss as well as the renowned literary agent Esther Newberg. They all offered their support and encouragement and gave me hope that being an international commodity banker by trade would not preclude me from getting the attention of a reputable publisher.

I must acknowledge my only research assistant, Robert H. Aldrich (aka Dad). After accompanying me on my very first research outing in 2011 (to the Yale University Library) he decided to learn all he could about the decision to drop the atomic bomb. My father turned eleven years old the month Japan formally surrendered to the Allies aboard the USS *Missouri* in Tokyo Bay and, like many Americans his age, still has a strong emotional and intellectual connection to World War II. Given this and his passion for science (he studied chemical engineering at Princeton), I was fortunate to be able to run things by his annoyingly impressive intellect and grateful to be the recipient of his unwavering enthusiasm for the project.

My interest in history was sparked when I first walked into Ms. Kohn's second grade classroom at Rowayton Elementary School in Connecticut. When she saw that I was captivated by the individual portraits of the U.S. presidents on the walls, she recommended that I go to the library and take out a biography of Andrew Jackson. Once my mother introduced me to the celebrated, *We Were There* series of books a year or so later, history became a permanent part of my life and in the ensuing fifty years, I've been blessed with a supportive family who've enabled my obsession. For thoughtfully gifting me books or passing along recommendations, I am in debt to my parents, my siblings and their families, my three sons, and various members of the Scull, Short, and Ferrarese clans that make up my wife's side of the family. I have also been fortunate to have several friends over the years (Hunter Smith, Brien Horan, and the late Peter G. Diamandis most notably) who typically opened conversations with me by saying "hey, I'm reading a book I think you'd like."

Finally, I want to thank my wife, Susie for all her support over the decades. When my bank transferred me to Switzerland in 1990, she set aside a successful career in Manhattan. Moving with me again to London a few years later, towing along three boys under the age of five, Susie, an entrepreneur by instinct, became captivated by the beautiful gardens in England and pondered to herself why the English should have a monopoly on stunning landscapes. When we returned to Connecticut three years later, she started her own landscape design company pairing timeless English style with her own innovative flair. Her business took off, she created dozens of jobs, and—after nearly two decades—the landscapes and gardens from Greenwich to Westport will never be the same. A bundle of energy, Susie did all this while partnering with me to raise three incredible sons in a family environment that nurtured kindness, love, humor, laughter, compassion, music, sports, the pursuit of knowledge, independence, and a strong desire to share with each other, and celebrate, all our individual and collective passions. As a result, life in our home has always been both entertaining and fascinating in equal parts. Successful partnerships always yield fruitful results and ours produced Jack, Ben, and Tommy.

INTRODUCTION

It remains a mystery to me as yet unexplained how the very small staffs which the United States kept during the years of peace were able not only to build up the armies and air force units, but also to find the leaders and vast staffs capable of handling enormous masses and of moving them faster and farther than masses have ever been moved in war before.[1]

—WINSTON CHURCHILL, 1950

On May 8, 1945, just hours after the formal surrender of Germany to the Allied powers in Europe, a group of high-ranking American Army officers and senior War Department officials began gathering in a spacious office on the third floor of the Pentagon. Once assembled, a distinguished man in a dated business suit, four months shy of his seventy-eighth birthday, called in General George C. Marshall, chief of staff of the United States Army, and motioned him toward the center of the room. Referring to Marshall's extraordinary contributions since 1939 in building an army and air force from scratch and leading it to victory over Nazi Germany, the elderly gentleman said to him, "General, I have never seen a task of such magnitude performed by man." Continuing, he added in the serious tone that characterized him, "I have seen a great many soldiers in my lifetime, and you, sir, are the finest soldier I have ever known."[2]

Who was this elderly man dressed in the civilian threads of a long-retired Wall Street lawyer commanding the undivided attention of some of the top leaders of wartime Washington? It was none other than George Marshall's boss for the previous five years: retired Wall Street lawyer, former secretary of war, former secretary of state, and incumbent secretary of war Henry Lewis Stimson.

1

In what was arguably the greatest personnel decision with the most far-reaching consequences ever made by a United States president (with the possible exception being George Washington's appointment of Alexander Hamilton to his first cabinet), Franklin D. Roosevelt paired Stimson up with Marshall in the summer of 1940 in anticipation of the global war into which all three men knew the United States could be shortly drawn. From adjoining offices, where the door between them was deliberately left open at all times, Stimson and Marshall spent their first seventeen months together leading efforts to prepare an unprepared and reluctant America for possible war from a military, industrial, economic, and political standpoint. This included building an army and air force up from the skeletal levels to which each had fallen since the end of World War I, organizing the housing and training for both, and overseeing the design, testing, production, and distribution of the machines, weapons, and materials required to support them (the air forces were part of the Army both before and during the Second World War). Concurrently, the two men had to develop, revise, re-revise, communicate, and promote strategic military plans for whatever combination of events the future might hold in Europe and Asia. In order to succeed, order and structure had to be first introduced into an administrative environment that lacked both.

Stimson and Marshall had the immense burden of accomplishing all of this while delicately balancing two competing and conflicting pressures: time and isolationism. The urgency was brought on by the rapidly escalating events in Europe and Asia (when Stimson took over the War Department in July 1940, Denmark, Norway, Holland, Belgium, and France had already fallen to the Nazis). Isolationism, on the other hand, was a deeply entrenched American principle that drew greater strength during the thirties. By 1940, a majority of Americans, and their representatives in Washington, wanted to avoid the existing war in Europe and any future war in Asia. It took great skill by these two men, with more than a little help from President Franklin D. Roosevelt, to balance these two diametrically opposed forces, the former uncontrollable and the latter only slightly less so. Push too hard, and the three men risked giving up political control to the isolationists; move too slowly, and they risked leaving America unprepared to defend itself and its interests in case war came.

Although the severe weight of isolationism was lifted immediately following the Japanese attack on Pearl Harbor (allowing the two men to begin accelerating their preparedness initiatives), Stimson and Marshall were suddenly faced with the task of having to fight two wars on four separate continents against two extremely formidable enemies, all while managing the widely disparate opinions, personalities, and agendas of Roosevelt, Winston Churchill, Josef Stalin, their respective British and Soviet Union counterparts, the United States Navy, Douglas MacArthur, Congress, industrial and labor leaders, the media, and a great number of other parties interspersed between the Army, the Cabinet, and several administrative agencies set up to help assist with all aspects of war mobilization. Finally, the two men shouldered their responsibilities against a surprisingly diligent effort by civilian officials, from Roosevelt on down, to make sure the United States Army did not get too influential or powerful.

Considering these challenges, the success of Stimson and Marshall over the five years they worked side by side was nothing short of phenomenal, and arguably the greatest feat of management in the history of the world. Historians often credit Marshall—as Winston Churchill did—as the true "organizer of victory," but the triumph was a shared one between him and the secretary of war. Although they generally divided their responsibilities (Marshall focusing on military matters, Stimson on civilian ones), major problems were tackled together with both men blending the full breadth of their talents and experience to find appropriate solutions. Forrest Pogue, who spent thirty years writing the definitive multivolume biography of George Marshall, said of Stimson that he and Marshall were "so tied up" that you couldn't write about one without writing about the other.[3]

Aside from their exceptional working relationship, among the many reasons these two men overcame all the trials they faced during their shared service was the exceptional men each recruited to support them. Stimson's staff during the War was widely considered the most competent in Washington, and the four core subordinates who served him throughout it (Robert Patterson, John McCloy, Robert Lovett, and Harvey Bundy) were so highly respected that they were all recruited for important assignments in the postwar period. The childless Stimson took a paternalistic interest in his talented young subordinates, trusted them with considerable responsibility, and inspired and guided them to individual and collective greatness.

Marshall was equally proficient in finding the right men to assist him. Through a career-long practice of keeping a "little black book" filled with the names of officers who impressed him during his numerous Army assignments (along with the specific attributes he observed in each man), Marshall was able to almost flawlessly match the right individual to the right job at the right time. Arnold, Eisenhower, Bradley, McNair, Somervell, McNarney, Clark, Taylor, Collins, Smith, Ridgeway, Gerow, Middleton, and Groves were just a few of the outstanding officers Marshall placed in key positions leading up to and during the War. Like Stimson's men, several of Marshall's subordinates also filled critical public roles during the Cold War years, operating from within the Army or government (and in the case of Dwight Eisenhower, the Oval Office).

Remarkably, following their joint military triumph, the influence of these two men on U.S. foreign policy extended well into the second half of the twentieth century. Marshall is far better known today for the plan to economically rebuild Europe after the War launched by the United States while he served as secretary of state under Truman (the Marshall Plan) than for his contribution to winning World War II. Far less recognized is the longer lasting and more significant influence of Henry Stimson. Although he retired just after the War ended and died five years later, Stimson's deeply held belief that it was the moral obligation of the United States to reform the world was actively promoted by his influential wartime protégés and their successors throughout the second half of the twentieth century.

Many of the original "Stimsonians" were central figures in a group of men popularly referred to in the years following the War as the "the establishment" or the "wise men." Men like Lovett, McCloy, Dean Acheson, Charles Bohlen, James Schlesinger Jr., Averell Harriman, Clark Clifford, Paul Nitze, Dean Rusk, and McGeorge Bundy shuffled between private sector positions along the Northeast Corridor and public positions in Washington, and gave advice to presidents on foreign affairs—either individually or as a group—from the start of Harry Truman's administration through the end of Ronald Reagan's. Historian David Schmitz stamped Stimson as the "First Wise Man."[4] To these men coming from the same Northeastern prep schools, Ivy League universities, top law schools, and prestigious law firms or banking houses, Stimson was, in the words of Schlesinger, "a deity," and those who followed him carried his interventionist torch with great zeal.

As a result of the tremendous teamwork, unity of purpose, seamlessness, and common beliefs shared between Marshall and Stimson during World War II, several of these "wise men" could be considered protégés of either man. Robert Lovett, one of four key individuals on Stimson's staff during the War and someone who was later offered his choice of any cabinet position by President-Elect John F. Kennedy, said there were just three people in the world to whom he could never say no: Stimson, Marshall, and his wife.[5]

Much, but not enough, has been written about George Marshall, surprisingly little on Henry Stimson, and nothing specifically on the monumental partnership between these two giants of the twentieth century who, with the exception of FDR himself, were more responsible than any other Americans in contributing to the defeat of Hitler and his armies. One of the reasons for this oversight has to do with the specific positions they held during World War II. Few secretaries of war are well remembered today, even those who held the office during a major conflict; Edwin Stanton (Civil War) and Newton Baker (World War I) are cases in point. As far as the Army chief of staff position is concerned, it is a desk job, and the mantle of glory rarely falls on those who operate out of harm's way. This book looks to bring their massive joint accomplishment into its proper light.

Although they had spent time with one another during World War I and corresponded between the wars, the paths of Henry Stimson and George Marshall did not significantly intersect until July 1940, when they were brought together by FDR toward the end of their brilliant respective careers. Despite coming from entirely different worlds, Stimson and Marshall could not have been more perfectly suited, both individually and as a team, to the top military and civilian leadership positions in the U.S. Army at that critical time. Each man represented the very best that emerged from two unique but quintessentially American archetypes: the "Army lifer" and the "Wall Street lawyer." It was the former that had produced such military heroes as Scott, Lee, Grant, Longstreet, Stuart, Sherman, and Pershing, while the latter contributed public figures of the caliber of Webster, Seward, Stanton, Root, Brandeis, and Hughes (for the purpose of this book, the terms Wall Street lawyer and corporate lawyer are interchangeable. Not all these men practiced law on Wall Street or even Manhattan, as Stimson did). Although the qualities formed within these two distinct professions over several generations contrasted sharply, the United States always seemed to benefit when a specific attribute—found in one profession or the other—was suitably matched with a precise role at a particular moment in history.

For the positions of Army chief of staff and secretary of war in 1940, the country needed candidates with highly developed leadership skills, intelligence, experience, an international outlook, focus, gravitas, organizational skills, patience, frankness, courage, determination, sound judgment, and above all other traits, strength of character. It was this latter quality that set both Marshall and Stimson far apart from their peers and helped guide FDR in making his game-changing decision to pair them together. In a democracy, the quality of integrity can often yield enormous power (it was said of Marshall that he was the only general in the world Winston Churchill

ever feared).[6] That the country could find two men with unparalleled reputations in this respect was fortunate enough; that both men also placed
teamwork as a fundamental component of success seemed providential.

Like nearly all triumphant wartime leaders, the path to victory for Stimson and Marshall during World War II was not free from mistakes, controversy, and criticism. With Stimson, history will always associate both the
internment of Japanese American civilians shortly after the attack on Pearl
Harbor and the atomic bombing of Hiroshima and Nagasaki in 1945. In
both instances, the responsibility to make recommendations to the president was given directly to him. In the case of the Japanese Americans, Stimson acted against his better judgment by bowing to pressure from local
authorities, the public, and within the War Department itself to aggressively
deal with perceived but unproven internal threats from the Japanese American community. As for the decision to drop the atomic bombs, although
Stimson was administratively responsible for the Manhattan Project and
controlled all planning for the use of the bomb, his poor health, advanced
age, and the death of Franklin Roosevelt combined to significantly limit his
ability to influence President Truman's final decision. He has nevertheless
been given a fair share of the blame for failing to get the new president to
back off the policy of unconditional surrender for the Japanese first articulated by FDR. Stimson hoped that by doing so, the United States might be
able to end the War without having to either use the new weapon or invade
the Japanese homeland.

George Marshall has not escaped criticism either. Whether it was the
Army's role in the Pearl Harbor debacle, his system to individually replace
casualties on the front during the War (as opposed to by unit), or his insistence to cross the English Channel far earlier than his British counterparts (and ultimately Roosevelt) thought prudent, Marshall was attacked
during the War and in the retrospective histories that followed it. Not all
the criticism was undeserved, but when one considers the multitude of tasks
assigned to him against the severe pressure he faced, Marshall's record
stands up to any other American military leader serving before or after him.

Henry L. Stimson was born in 1867, just two years after the end of the
Civil War. He was not only a product of the nineteenth century, but he had
lived nearly half his life during it by the time FDR nominated him to run
the War Department in 1940. Born to a prominent New York family, Stimson
attended Phillips Academy at Andover, Yale, and Harvard Law School before
beginning an extremely successful legal career working for Elihu Root, an

established and connected New York lawyer and future secretary of war and secretary of state. Root, considered by many historians to be the most talented administrator in United States history, introduced Stimson to Teddy Roosevelt, and it was Roosevelt (just nine years older than Stimson) who launched the young lawyer into a career of public service by appointing him U.S. Attorney for the Southern District of New York in 1906. Stimson excelled in this first assignment, catching the public service bug in the process.

Guided initially by Root and Roosevelt, Stimson spent the rest of his life moving back and forth between the high-level government work he loved (secretary of war, global troubleshooter, governor-general of the Philippines, secretary of state, and secretary of war again) and his hugely successful legal practice (in 1946, *Time* magazine called him "one of the greatest living U.S. Lawyers"[7]). While making him wealthy, the practice of law never satisfied his desire to reform and bring order to the world, "do good," and "make a difference."

Although a committed conservative on social and economic issues like other Republicans of his era, Stimson was an unwavering internationalist when it came to foreign policy. He was certain the United States was destined to play a leading role in the world and was convinced its foreign policy had to be carried out on a bipartisan basis to be successful (although a longtime Republican, he was always issue-oriented and therefore unfazed in 1940 when the archenemy of his socioeconomic class asked him to serve in his administration).

If he was never appointed to run the War Department in 1940, historians would still recognize Henry Stimson as a highly accomplished and influential American public figure during the twentieth century due to the variety of contributions he made during each of its first four decades. But when one adds his service to the nation during World War II and his continuing influence on U.S. foreign policy beyond the grave in the decades that followed, one cannot help but stand in awe of a man who, historian Kai Bird wrote, "cast a longer shadow" over the twentieth century than any other single individual.[8]

That Stimson's crowning achievement took place between the ages of seventy-three and seventy-eight is even more striking. A predecessor of Stimson's, Newton Baker, secretary of war during World War I, was reflecting on his years at the helm when he wrote a friend it "was highly fortunate that I was as young as I was" as it would have "been difficult for a man of much greater age."[9] Baker was forty-six when World War I ended, *thirty-two years younger* than Stimson was at the end of World War II.

Perhaps because of his age and the reduced role he played in the closing days of the Second World War, many historians have undervalued Stimson's impact throughout it. They were mistaken. One Pentagon official during the War tried to summarize Stimson's influence: "You will never get it down on paper, but every day in the War Department people did not do certain things and did do certain other things in a certain way because Stimson was in the office of the Secretary."[10]

George C. Marshall was a difficult man to figure out. He was remote and cold, yet famously generous; explosively temperamental by nature, but a master at controlling it; fiercely ambitious, yet unyielding in his refusal to lobby for advancement; stubborn and self-assured, yet insistent on hearing all dissenting views; and a military professional to his core, but with remarkable insights into civilian values and perspectives. There was nothing puzzling about Marshall's integrity; it, too, was his greatest strength and, along with Stimson's, unmatched by any military or political figure of the War. After the War, Winston Churchill said that Marshall was "the greatest Roman of them all" and that he was the single greatest figure produced by the War.[11]

Although born more than eighty years after George Washington's death, Marshall was Washingtonian in almost all aspects of his character. Both men were supremely disciplined, deliberate, poised, efficient, and principled with personalities meticulously self-designed and controlled in order to command respect. Like Washington, Marshall's formality in dealing with others was legendary, yet both men were revered by those above and below them in rank. Neither man was intellectually brilliant nor exceptionally creative, yet both were intelligent, practical, competent, productive, and wise. They were also leaders of the highest caliber.[12]

Marshall was born in 1880 in Uniontown, Pennsylvania, into a family with Virginian roots. Attending the Virginia Military Institute, Marshall proved to be average from an academic standpoint but peerless when it came to military discipline and leadership. He was commissioned into the U.S. Army as second lieutenant in 1902.

Marshall's career in the Army was characterized by a curious dichotomy between his service record and the pace of his promotions: The former was consistently and unusually exceptional, the latter painfully slow (the long-established system of promotion by seniority and bad timing put brakes on Marshall's ascent).

During wartime, the normal conventions of seniority are tossed aside, and performance on the battlefield in the command of troops is the leading path to promotion for an officer. Ironically, it was Marshall's out-standing record of success that handicapped his chances of getting his first star during World War I. Since the top brass knew Marshall's talents as a staff officer were unmatched, they rejected his numerous requests to get field command assignments and instead gave him a leading role on General John Pershing's staff (Franklin Roosevelt used essentially the same rationale for declining to give Marshall command of the Normandy invasion twenty-five years later). As a result of his stunning success in planning and organizing a mass movement of troops and supplies to the main offensive in 1918, Marshall emerged from World War I as a logistics superstar. But when it came to promotions, men who had done well on the battlefield (like Douglas MacArthur) were given priority consideration.

It was fortuitous to America that patience and optimism were among Marshall's attributes; otherwise he might have given up and accepted one of the attractive offers made available to him outside of the Army following the First World War (in 1918, he was offered a highly lucrative senior position at J. P. Morgan by a partner of the bank who worked as a civilian aide for Pershing during the War). Marshall must have believed or hoped he was destined for high command, because he instead accepted an offer from General Pershing to be his aide-de-camp for five years, a position that gave him insight into the chief of staff position he would later occupy.

After Pershing's retirement in 1924, Marshall spent the next fifteen years moving back and forth between teaching assignments and troop command duties, earning the respect of everyone he met, including President Franklin Roosevelt's closest advisor, Harry Hopkins. With another global war in Europe looking likely, Hopkins sat down with Marshall to get a sense of America's level of preparedness. So impressed was Hopkins that he (along with several others) prodded FDR to appoint Marshall to the top Army job in 1939. He was officially sworn in as chief of staff on September 1, by sheer coincidence the day Germany invaded Poland to start World War II.

When Marshall took over the Army, it had been less than twenty-one years since World War I ended. Not only was the nation opposed to being drawn into another war, but it also had little desire to even prepare for one, believing the very act of doing so could lead the country into it. As such, he received little support to raise the Army up from its global ranking on the day he took office (seventeenth, right behind Romania).

The fall of France to the Nazi blitzkrieg nine months later changed some minds. Within a few weeks, Marshall had a new boss in interventionist Henry Stimson and a reasonably healthy war chest from Congress. On June 27, 1940, Marshall visited Stimson at the latter's vast estate on Long Island to begin the first of countless conversations between the two men that only ended five years later after America achieved victory in both Europe and Asia.

Dwight Eisenhower once remarked, "The supreme quality for leadership is unquestionably integrity." There can be no doubt he was reflecting on both his former boss and Henry Stimson when he made this general observation, because on the subject of greatness, Eisenhower also said Marshall possessed "more of the qualities" of it than any other American he had met in his life, with Stimson a close second.[13] Working side by side for more than five years, from July 1940 through the end of World War II, the partnership of Henry Stimson and George Marshall represented genuine greatness by any historical standard.

I

TRAINING

1

The Education of a Wall Street Lawyer (1867–1899)

"Finis Origine Pendet." (The end depends upon the beginning).

—FOUNDING MOTTO OF PHILLIPS ACADEMY AT ANDOVER

Unlike many American patricians of his era from families long established in the new world, Henry Lewis Stimson seemed to have only a passing interest in genealogy and appeared not to boast or even discuss with others the deep roots his family held on the East Coast of the United States (branches of his family had been living in America for over two centuries). In fact, it is hard to find evidence of Stimson discussing his ancestors at all outside a brief paragraph he devotes to them in his memoirs, where he states simply they were "sturdy, middle-class people, religious, thrifty, energetic and long-lived" and included enough clergymen and deacons to maintain the "moral standards of the stock."[1] It is not that Stimson did not care; it is more likely he was simply too busy during his life to spend much time thinking about it, particularly in his later years, when men of his age, social status, and pedigree might be more inclined to begin looking backward.

Moving the well-worn path westward from Massachusetts, Stimson's ancestors put down roots in Albany, New York, before Stimson's great-grandfather—after serving in the Revolutionary War—became the first person to settle the town of Windham, New York, in the Catskills Mountains. Although Windham soon became an active hamlet, Henry Stimson's grandfather (Henry Clark Stimson) decided to leave and made the first in a series of moves that ultimately brought the Stimson family to New York

City. Seeing opportunities in the rapidly growing city after the Civil War and taking advantage of a small inheritance from his wife, Henry Clark Stimson purchased a seat on the New York Stock Exchange, where he earned a reputation as an honest and competent broker.

With clients including Cornelius Vanderbilt, James Gould, and Leonard Jerome (Winston Churchill's maternal grandfather), the firm Henry C. Stimson & Sons did extremely well until the Panic of 1873, at which time the company took a considerable hit. Although he lost a lot of cash, Stimson's grandfather had prudently saved money. Adding it to his wife's inheritance, he retired to his home on East 34th Street in Manhattan and spent more time with his wife and seven children, including his second son Lewis, the father of the future secretary of war.

Lewis Stimson, after attending Yale and serving the Union cause during the Civil War, joined the family brokerage firm in New York. A man who apparently knew what he wanted and how to attain it, Lewis followed a young woman to Europe after becoming enamored with her at a party in New York in the fall of 1865. The woman, Candace Wheeler (Henry Stimson's mother), had gone there with her well-to-do parents for a year. Candace was raised by a family active in the intellectual, artistic, and social circles of New York City. Her mother has been credited with changing the course of textile and interior design in the nineteenth century (she partnered with Louis Comfort Tiffany in an interior design business), and her younger sister Dora was a distinguished portrait artist whose works hang today at the Met, the National Portrait Gallery, and in other prominent collections. Candace, encouraged to develop a wide variety of interests, could sing, paint, and converse on any number of subjects. To her suitor, raised in a more mercantile environment, she was captivating.

What might be labeled stalking today paid off for Lewis Stimson as he arrived in Europe unannounced, pursued Candace relentlessly, and finally managed to convince her to marry him in the U.S. Embassy in Paris in November 1866. Mission accomplished, he moved back to New York City with his bride, settled into his father's brokerage business, and began raising a family. Candace delivered two children over the next three years, the first being the future secretary of war on September 21, 1867.

Even more so than his father, Lewis Stimson disliked the stockbroking business. After five unhappy years, the twenty-seven-year-old sold his seat on the Exchange and took his family to Europe. Making this big change easier to justify was the fact that his wife was not well. Candace had been sick since shortly after her daughter was born (a few historians have speculated that she had diabetes).

While traveling within Europe, Lewis Stimson took up the study of medicine. Whether this was done to gain a better understanding of his wife's condition or simply to begin a new career is not certain. Regardless, he found his life's calling. He spent the better part of three years tirelessly studying surgery in Zurich and Paris (where he worked with Louis Pasteur for a year), before coming back to New York in 1873, getting his degree, and beginning his new life as a surgeon.

Despite his proficiency as a doctor and solid contacts within the medical community of New York, there was little Lewis Stimson could do to help his wife. Candace continued to suffer until her death in 1876, at the age of thirty. Henry Stimson was just eight years old at the time.

The death of his wife shattered Lewis Stimson. He quickly determined that the best way to recover was to focus all his efforts on his new profession. He sold his house, rented an apartment for himself, and placed Henry and his six-year-old sister with his parents at their East 34th Street brownstone, visiting them once a week. With his children in safe and loving hands, Lewis Stimson went on to become a prominent surgeon and an accomplished author of several standard works on surgery.[2] Eschewing a lucrative private practice, Lewis Stimson preferred the greater good he could accomplish by working in hospitals with the poor, which he did until the end of his life. He never remarried.

For the eight-year-old Henry Stimson, the combination of his mother's death and his father's manner in coping with it must have had a profound emotional effect on him. Making the pain a little more tolerable was the fact that he and his sister were taken in by a devoted Stimson family and put directly under the wing of an unmarried aunt (Mary, Lewis Stimson's sister). "Minnie" Stimson took great care to give her nephew and niece the love she felt they needed and was helped not only by her parents but also by a great number of cousins, uncles, and aunts who gathered regularly in the family's spacious brownstone.

For five years, Henry Stimson lived with his aunt and grandparents, until his father abruptly decided in the fall of 1880 to send him away to Phillips Academy in Andover, Massachusetts. Although sudden, the decision grew out of a growing frustration Stimson's father had with the quality of education Henry was receiving in New York. The result was that the thirteen-year-old unexpectedly found himself two hundred miles away from the familiar streets of Manhattan. His years at the Academy ended up having a profound influence on his life, allowing him to develop his mind, habits, ethics, drive, and personality.

Phillips Academy at Andover
(October 1880–June 1883)

When Stimson arrived in Andover, Massachusetts, to enroll at Phillips Academy in 1880, it was not the nationally recognized school it became a generation later, when it was referred to as the "American Eton" (after the world-famous British boarding school founded in 1440). It aspired to be thus, but it was still in the development stage more than a hundred years into its existence.

Changes that began seven years prior to Stimson's arrival with the naming of a new principal accelerated during the three years Stimson matriculated at the Academy, helping set the school on track to achieve the prominence it coveted and the reputation it soon acquired as one of the best of America's elite private schools. During this time, the school grew, the curriculum was modernized, the quality of teachers was upgraded, and the conservatism dominating the campus since its founding was pushed aside in favor of a more progressive spirit. Being part of this large-scale transformation was exciting to the young New Yorker and led to an intellectual awakening within him.

Stimson would come to warmly embrace the memory of his three years at Phillips Academy, and he maintained extremely close ties to the institution for the rest of his life. Serving on the Board of Trustees for forty-one years, he always considered the campus a second home. His loyalty to the Academy extended beyond his life; he and his wife left a sizable portion of their fortune to the school along with the deed to Woodley Mansion, the impressive and iconic Washington, D.C., estate he purchased in 1929, when he became secretary of state.[3]

Back in the fall of 1880, Phillips Academy was small. The entire faculty consisted of only eight members who taught approximately 250 boys between them. The students were largely drawn from rural Massachusetts, although the school had boys from most of the other thirty-seven states existing at that time as well.

Known on the Andover campus as "Kid," given he was the youngest member of his class and small for his age, Stimson was too frail to do well in athletics, but he had a brilliant academic record (standing second in his class by the time he graduated). He was shy and relatively inactive during his years in Andover (understandable, given that most of his classmates were two years older than he was and many were three and even four years older), but he was respected enough to be chosen as an officer of one of the largest and most important student organizations on campus (the Society of Inquiry).[4]

When he wasn't studying, writing letters home, or enjoying the outdoors in and around Andover, Stimson could be found participating in the religious activities of the school. Although the new principal was weaning the student body off the rigid strictures of Calvinism, the school was still very pious, and Stimson opened his arms to this aspect of student life as well. He joined a weekly prayer group that was far more inspiring to him than the sermons he sat through on Sunday.

When reviewing Henry Stimson's time at Phillips Academy, one can see how his three years there (from ages thirteen to sixteen) could have played a significant part in developing what nature bestowed on him. Stimson certainly believed so; in later years he credited the Academy for bringing about the "revolution worked into" his character.[5] Throughout his life, Stimson was known for his righteousness, independence, discipline, diligence, respect for authority, loyalty, and integrity. One can make an argument that each of these attributes was forged into his constitution during his three years in Andover.

When it came to his morals, Stimson was hardly a blank slate upon arriving in Massachusetts. Commenting on his first week in school, Stimson explained to his aunt in a letter that he did not have any friends yet, as he was still working out "the good boys from the bad."[6] But what nature and family instilled in him in this regard grew at Andover.

As for independence, the experience of being sent two hundred miles away to a boarding school at the age of thirteen as the youngest member of the school must have provided Stimson with the major building blocks that would later characterize his independent persona throughout his public and private careers. Additionally, the students were generally expected to be fully self-supporting while staying current with the typical curriculum of a late-nineteenth-century high-end boarding school (math, Greek, Latin, etymology, history, English, science, etc.).

From a discipline and diligence standpoint, arriving at the school three weeks into the semester and academically behind his fellow students forced Stimson to acquire early habits of self-control and hard work. He was provided some level of guidance from his aunt (who suggested Stimson study four hours per day "by the watch"),[7] but most of the work habits he carried with him throughout his life emanated from the three years he spent in the northern hills of Massachusetts figuring out what he needed to do by himself. A prime example can be seen in the decision he made promptly in his first year to rise from bed early every morning and get as much work undertaken at the start of the day (habits he maintained for a lifetime). This decision revealed Stimson at his most pragmatic; he simply did not feel sharp at night.

With respect to Stimson's integrity, it was partly inherited; both his father and grandfather were well known for it. The former greatly valued this quality, counseling his son in a rare letter to Andover to "show no shame on the account of any honest thing you do."[8] But Stimson's reputation for honesty and integrity was so exceptional that one would have to assume his experiences at Phillips Andover played a vital role in strengthening it.

Having a respect for authority can come from any number of circumstances or be learned from any combination of early mentors. But for the teenage Stimson, it seems he developed a love of order at Phillips Academy that stayed with him for the rest of his life. He respected the entire program, the people who offered it, and the rules that guided it. It was likely at the Academy where he first observed that chaos could quickly fill the void created by recalcitrant students who failed to show respect for authority and follow the established rules. In fact, if one substitutes "unruly nations" for "recalcitrant students," one can recognize a core belief of Stimson's that guided his general philosophy and approach to the problems he encountered nearly a half century later as America's top diplomat.

Yale (September 1884–June 1888)

Stimson's independent nature was further revealed following his graduation from Phillips Academy. Like many alumni of the school during this era (and for many years after), Stimson observed that the road leading from Andover to New Haven, Connecticut, was smooth and well-traveled. As class salutatorian, getting accepted to Yale would have been easy. But Stimson wanted to enter his college years without having to face the issues he experienced at Phillips Academy as a result of being the youngest in his class.[9] He used this argument when appealing to his father to be allowed to take a year off before attending Yale. Succeeding, he spent the next several months getting further prepared by taking courses in New York and at Phillips

Academy. Revealing the quiet but single-minded ambition he carried with him throughout his life, Stimson wanted to hit the ground running upon his arrival in New Haven to take up new challenges and "struggle" for the honors and prizes awarded at the college.[10] He arrived on campus in the fall of 1884, still one of the youngest students, and did just that.

In his memoirs, Stimson gives credit to several institutions and individuals for helping shape his personality, but he describes his experience at Yale as "the most important in my life, both in the character developed and the friendships formed." Like Phillips Academy, Yale was undergoing major changes at the time Stimson arrived on campus; it had only just adopted the elective system all other top colleges were using. The academic courses offered were standard for the times but taught—in Stimson's words—"rather less effectively" than the same subjects at Andover. Stimson bemoaned the lack of opportunities inside the classroom for original thinking, stating in later years that the general academic exercise at Yale was simply reciting back what one heard or read.

What happened outside of the classroom was a different story. Stimson became captivated with the extracurricular activities led by students. He believed their importance to the overall collegiate educational experience was unique to Yale and helped develop successful, confident, and independent graduates.

Of these outside activities, by far the most important to Stimson was his membership in the Skull and Bones organization, a secret campus society whose list of alumni reads like a Who's Who of America's political, business, and educational elite during the nineteenth and twentieth centuries (including U.S. presidents, Supreme Court justices, secretaries of state, secretaries of war, senators, governors, university presidents, and prominent financiers). Stimson was chosen to become part of "Bones" because of his academic standing within the classroom (he ended up third in his class) and his successes outside of it (Stimson sought out competition wherever he could find it, whether it was in the form of seeking office, entering various contests,or gaining a position on an athletic team).[11]

Everything about the Skull and Bones organization appealed to Stimson: It was elite (each year the senior members of the society selected just fifteen members of the junior class who had evidenced leadership, intelligence, and high achievement); it was steeped in tradition (following rituals dating back to the founding of the society in 1832, the members were initiated into the secret organization in an elaborate ceremony); it was a lifelong brotherhood that stressed honesty (Skull and Bones strongly encouraged

members to be themselves and to share their deepest thoughts and feelings
with each other, knowing they would receive support, discretion, and loyalty
from all other members for the remainder of their lives).

Most appealing to Stimson was the promotion of service to the community encouraged by the organization. "Doing good" and contributing
to society were unmistakable parts of the genetic makeup of Stimson reinforced through Skull and Bones. For these reasons he described the organization as the most important educational experience of his life.[12]

As important as Skull and Bones was to his overall college experience,
Stimson partook in a number of other extracurricular activities during his
years in New Haven. After going out for football his first year despite weighing just 120 pounds, he turned his sporting ambitions toward rowing. He
wrote little about his experience on crew, but it was not without its exciting
moments. In the middle of February of his junior year, his scull collided
with a large cake of ice two hundred yards from the Yale boathouse, knock-
ing everyone on board into the Housatonic River. The eight boys were
trapped by numerous blocks of ice and were only rescued when other boys
at the boathouse heard their shouts. By the time all the youths got to shore,
a couple of them were unconscious. Although everyone recovered quickly,
the team decided to keep a lid on the entire ordeal so that nobody would
try to prevent them from continuing their training. Despite their efforts, it
was in the newspapers the following day.[13]

For a young man who liked to think of himself as decisive and independent, Stimson was at a loss as to what he wished to do with his life following graduation from Yale in 1888. For inspiration, Stimson set out for the
wilds of Colorado with a couple of guns and a selection of books. For each
of the previous three summers, he had made similar trips to either Colorado or Canada. He was completely taken in with the excitement, beauty,
and remoteness the untamed frontier offered and the independent challenges it presented to him. Such excursions became a lifelong passion (for
over twenty consecutive years, he spent time during the summer in one or
the other region) and helped bond him a few years later with another New
Yorker who loved the Wild West: Theodore Roosevelt.

Prior to his trip, Stimson narrowed down his career choices to the min-
istry, medicine, and law (the latter being the profession he claimed to be
least interested in). Despite the vast time he had out West to narrow down
his choices, he was still undecided upon arriving back in Manhattan. He
only determined that he wished "to do good in someway."[14] Gathering his

father and two uncles together to discuss the advantages and disadvantages of each option, Stimson reluctantly chose to pursue the law after the elder Stimson assured him it was a noble profession. He headed to Harvard Law School in the fall of 1888.

Harvard Law School
(September 1888–June 1890)

As an individual considered one of the nation's most talented corporate lawyers during the first half of the twentieth century, Stimson's path to the top did not start off promising. During most of his first year at Harvard, Stimson expressed a dislike for Boston, Harvard men, and the general study of law. He was also uncertain as to whether a law degree would lead to anything worthy of the ideals he acquired at Yale.

It was not that he was unchallenged; on the contrary, Harvard Law School had only recently undertaken the changes that put it at the forefront of the case method of instruction. Introduced by Christopher Columbus Langdell, who became dean of the law school in 1870, the case method replaced one characterized by rote memorization that had been in existence since the school's founding in 1817. Langdell believed that students needed to understand how laws evolved over time from specific cases. By trying to reason through the major issues, he believed one could better retain the key principles behind the relevant laws. While the work was interesting for Stimson, it was also challenging. The kind of quick thinking required to stand out and succeed at Harvard Law School during those years was contrary to the deep and philosophical bent that characterized Stimson's mind and served him so well at Yale.

But what Stimson lacked in an agile mind, he more than made up for in sheer diligence, a trait that distinguished him for the rest of his career in law and public service. His competitive nature, along with a powerful, if not quick mind, drove him to master each and every pertinent fact in a case prior to going up against his classmates (and teachers). Through sheer effort, he began to lift himself up into the elite status of students as his second year got underway.

With success, the young New Yorker gradually began to realize that Harvard guys were okay, Boston society was not so bad, and the law had an intelligent logic that was greatly appealing. He also began to gain a better appreciation of the positive role that law could play in society. Although

Yale gave Stimson a "greater faith in mankind," Stimson credits Harvard with the greatest "revolution" in his power of thinking. He felt blessed at getting the best each institution had to offer and spent the rest of his life believing there was no combination that better prepared men for public service and the law than a Yale undergraduate and Harvard law degree.

Following graduation in June 1890, Stimson began his career as a "Wall Street lawyer," quite literally as he accepted a job working in the law offices of a former Yale graduate located at 52 Wall Street in Manhattan.

Wall Street Lawyer

Working in New York was not a given for Henry Stimson. In his final semester at Harvard, he contemplated heading west after graduation to make his mark, but since his father strongly urged him to return to New York, his plans never got too serious. It is also likely that Stimson weighed the feelings of a young woman he had met in New Haven a few years earlier. Mabel White was a member of a large, respectable, and established New Haven family of four brothers, all of whom were lawyers. One of the brothers had four daughters, Mabel being the second oldest. She and her sisters were popular with the students at Yale, and Stimson met Mabel at one of the various parties the family held for groups of students from time to time. He proposed to her during his last semester at Yale, and she accepted.

Stimson's father did not think it right one should be committed to a woman prior to being able to support her financially, and he tried convincing his son, just before he headed off to Harvard, that releasing Mabel from the commitment was the right thing to do. Stimson took his father's advice, much to the disappointment of Mabel. Despite this relationship setback, the couple remained committed to one another, and their courtship—conducted largely from a distance through letters—held steady during his two years at Harvard and for the three additional years he spent establishing himself financially in New York (it was customary in those days to spend the first year out of law school as an unpaid clerk before gaining admission to the bar).

In his informative biography of Stimson published in 1960, Elting Morison talked to members of the White and Stimson families in an effort to piece together the saga of the five-year post-engagement relationship between Henry Stimson and Mabel White. He concluded that Stimson was torn between his desire to get married to White and his longing to please his father and establish a meaningful relationship with him. One will recall that Stimson saw little of his father after being dropped off to live with his grandparents at the age of eight following the death of his mother. Morison speculated that Stimson wanted to see if the reserved nature generally held by Stimson men could be moderated a bit and whether the remote relationship the two had with one another might evolve into something greater, perhaps resembling the open and candid relationships he enjoyed with his fellow Skull and Bones members.

Complicating matters further was that Stimson's father was highly motivated to establish his son in the right circles of New York by introducing him to its most highly connected families (e.g., the Astors, Whitneys, Danas, and Delafields). Unspoken, but certainly considered by the elder Stimson, was the possibility these connections would lead to a more favorable marriage for a young man on the rise in New York—more favorable than a marriage to a young woman from a middling town like New Haven.

Henry Stimson was wise to his father's machinations but balanced his deeply felt need to bond with him with his commitment to marry Mabel. Ultimately, he was successful, but it was not without a cost: The five-plus years were difficult for Mabel (and therefore Stimson). But despite the pain, she sensed Stimson could be trusted to live up to his promises. She was correct, and their fifty-seven-year marriage was a happy one by all accounts.

During the three years leading up to his marriage, Stimson buried himself in his work. The job he first accepted with the Yale alumnus was frustrating to him. It was not because it was unpaid or that the tasks assigned to him were menial. It was because the firm was focused on small-time law. Stimson was impatient and ambitious and wanted to get involved sooner than later in larger and more important cases.

After expressing these feelings to his father, who shared them with his well-connected friends, the twenty-four-year-old Stimson got the break that changed his life: an interview with Elihu Root. Root would be one of three men who exerted the greatest influence on Stimson during his life (his father and Theodore Roosevelt being the other two).

Although Root is little remembered today, he is still considered by many historians as a leading figure in the progressive movement, the greatest administrator in U.S. history, and the most influential peacetime secretary of war the country has ever had. To understand Stimson, his legal career, his administrative talents, and his view of the world (and the role of the United States within it), one must know something about Elihu Root.

Root began life in 1845 as the son of a mathematics professor at Hamilton College in Clinton, New York. At the age of nineteen, he graduated first in his class there. After teaching a year to earn money for law school, he left for New York City, where he attended and received a law degree from New York University. He was admitted to the bar in June 1867 and a year later formed a partnership. By the time he reached his thirtieth birthday, he was a highly prominent corporate lawyer in Manhattan, handling cases largely involving banks, railroads, and municipal governments.

Root's success owed itself to an uncommon intelligence, a powerful memory, clear logic, a great sense of timing, a love for the law, and a hard-core approach to preparing for trial. Through the law, Root loved nothing more than bringing order to the world of business, particularly when he began noticing how the growing complexity of industry and commerce began to negatively impact society in late-nineteenth-century America. Attempting to reorganize American capitalism was an intellectual challenge to Root, one he relished and at which he excelled. Root, like Stimson after him, felt that just as in business, there were few problems in America that could not be solved with hard work, talented people, and applying the logic of law.

Through the elevated contacts he made among the corporate, financial, legal, and political elite in New York, Root got involved in politics. A high position at the New York bar during that era led to increasing political demands, and Root's involvement grew accordingly, from making speeches and drafting resolutions to serving as a delegate to conventions.

As a member of the Republican Party, Root had contacts with many leading Republicans of New York, and one of them, U.S. President Chester Arthur, asked him to serve as the United States Attorney for the Southern District of New York in 1883 (the same position Stimson would hold twenty-three years later). Root served successfully for two years and oversaw several high-profile cases before resigning when the Democrats took over the White House.

For the next fifteen years until appointed secretary of war, Root became the most sought-after lawyer in the country, representing and advising governments, corporations, and many of the men who ran them. For the last eight of these years, Henry Stimson worked side by side with him.

It was the single largest client of Root's, William Whitney, who introduced Stimson to his forty-six-year-old lawyer. Whitney was a friend of a friend of Stimson's father and apparently believed Root needed more assistants. The interview went well, and Henry Stimson started working as a clerk for Root & Clarke in November 1891 at the Liberty Mutual Building in downtown Manhattan (present day 32 Liberty Street). He practiced law in this building, on and off, for the next fifty years.

Like Phillips Academy, Yale, and Harvard Law School during the years Stimson was in attendance, the corporate law business in New York was beginning to undergo a transformation at the time he joined Root's firm. Among the changes included the growing importance of law firms to American corporations as opposed to simply one specific lawyer. Law firms in New York were small at this time (few, if any, had more than five partners, and Root & Clarke had just three on the day Stimson started), but given the rapid growth of industry, transportation, and finance in the late nineteenth century, they needed to grow accordingly.

Further, the Second Industrial Revolution that rapidly accelerated after the Civil War brought greater complexity to the economy, forcing law partners to take on new responsibilities. Many began spending an increasingly greater proportion of their time advising their corporate clients rather than simply advocating for them at court or otherwise dispensing with the routine legal requests that were then the purview of a successful practice (e.g., writing wills, collecting debts, or executing standard corporate documents). This trend paralleled not only the general growth of the U.S. economy but also the increasing tendency of firms to achieve growth through acquisition.

Equally important to lawyers, the era also saw a greater step-up by the U.S. government in its effort to control and regulate against corporate excesses. The Sherman Act, signed just over a year before Stimson began with Root & Clarke, created several legal and organizational challenges for large corporations. Increasingly they looked to their law firms for guidance on how to manage them all.

As senior lawyers began focusing on these new activities, more was expected from their clerks. With greater expectations, greater talent was required, and the smart law firms did not take long to figure out that if one wanted higher-quality clerks, it made sense to start paying them. Stimson was a beneficiary of this trend, earning a starting salary of $750 per year, which at the time was $750 more than most clerks were earning.

The income was nice to have, but all clerks knew that the real value in a clerkship was in the education and mentorship one received at the firm from the experienced senior partners. In the case of Henry Stimson, there was no better place to begin his career. From Root, he was able to get the training he needed to be a successful lawyer in New York involved in large and meaningful cases.

Elihu Root led by example, and his success was rooted in an extreme work ethic, particularly when it came to preparing himself for a trial. Although his contemporaries credited him with a powerful brain and crystal-clear logic, it was the mastery of all the facts of a specific case—from the perspective of both sides—that set him apart. He simply made it a point to know more at his trials than any other person in the room. Stimson took careful notes.

Next to his father, Stimson would attribute Root with the greatest influence in developing both his intellectual growth and his moral advancement. Stimson spent eight years under the celebrated lawyer's tutelage until President William McKinley appointed Root secretary of war in 1899. During this time, he assisted him on many of the high-profile cases that Root fielded in the last years of his law career before taking his talents to Washington, D.C.

Although greatly indebted to Elihu Root for the broader lessons learned at the bar, it was a fellow clerk named Bronson Winthrop who helped Stimson master the technicalities of the law. Winthrop joined Root & Clarke straight out of Columbia Law School on the same day Stimson started. Both men became partners of the firm three years later and senior partners after Root left for Washington in August 1899. They remained law partners and close friends for life, giving their names to Winthrop & Stimson (later Winthrop, Stimson, Putnam, & Roberts), one of New York's most prestigious law firms throughout the twentieth century.[15]

Winthrop, a direct descendent of John Winthrop, first governor of Massachusetts Bay, was born in Paris and educated in London. He was an urbane intellectual who dazzled Stimson with his command of history, his taste in literature, and his overall refinement. Like Stimson, Winthrop was also dedicated to the law (in fact far more so) and became an expert in the finer points of it, which he happily shared with Stimson. This allowed the younger Stimson (by four years) time to focus more closely on litigation, his specialty.

Gifted with intelligence, a great work ethic, and excellent mentorship, the two young lawyers performed well enough to earn the respect and trust of Root. In fact, despite just eight years working with them, he felt comfortable enough to place his entire practice—one of New York City's best—in their hands when he went to Washington to join President William McKinley's cabinet.

For the next seven years, Stimson added to the solid reputation he had acquired the previous eight working as a partner under Root. His clients included notable utilities, railroads, banks, and industrial companies. His reputation at the bar grew with each new case he took on.

2

Uniontown, Pennsylvania, to the U.S. Army (1880–1903)

When I was begging to go to VMI, I overheard [my brother] talking to my mother; he was trying to persuade her not to let me go because he thought I would disgrace the family name. . . . The urgency to succeed came from hearing that conversation; it had a psychological effect on my career.[1]

—GEORGE MARSHALL

As thirty-one-year-old Henry Stimson began adjusting to his new role as a senior law partner in New York (after Elihu Root headed to Washington in late 1899), nineteen-year-old George Catlett Marshall Jr. was 350 miles south, beginning his third year at the Virginia Military Institute located in Lexington, Virginia.

A military life was not destined for George Marshall. There were some soldiers in his family tree, but his ancestors were largely made up of farmers, lawyers, politicians, and businessmen long established in Virginia (and those territories of Virginia that became part of Kentucky). Like Stimson, Marshall seemed to have no interest in his ancestors despite hearing about them often when he was a child. Marshall's family was particularly attentive to its heritage because one of its relatives was the great chief justice of the United States, John Marshall. Although a distant relation, John Marshall cast a long shadow.

William Champe Marshall, the future general's grandfather, was a successful lawyer in Augusta, Kentucky. An ambitious man, he married the daughter of the town's leading merchant, became mayor of Augusta, and remained a major political figure in Bracken County throughout his life.

He and his wife had nine children, the fifth of whom, George Catlett Marshall (George Marshall's father), was born in 1845 (he will be referred to as George Sr. going forward).

Augusta was a pleasant town to grow up in for the large and established Marshall family, until the long-simmering disputes between the North and South eventually came to a boil when George Sr. entered his teenage years. Although his parents were Southern sympathizers like many of their immediate neighbors, Kentucky was a border state. Like other border states, there were deep divisions between its counties, communities, and even families (when one reads about brothers fighting against brothers during the Civil War, they were typically residents of either Missouri, Maryland, Kentucky, or those other sections of states that spread southwest and then west from Delaware to Kansas).

Although officially residing in a neutral state, the two eldest sons of William Champe Marshall served in the Confederate Army. But he and his youngest son, George (who was sixteen when the war started), served in the Augusta Home Guard, a group of one hundred or so men officially committed to the Kentucky state policy of neutrality (even though its commander was in sympathy with the Union cause).

In the fall of 1861, the Confederates attempted to take control of Kentucky when Major General Leonidas Polk occupied Columbus in the southwest corner of the state. This violation of neutrality ultimately led the Kentucky government to declare its allegiance to the Union (after which a shadow government was formed by Southern sympathizers who soon declared secession). It was in this environment that Marshall's father and grandfather got caught up in a small engagement between North and South that took place in August 1862 as both sides continued to vie for territorial advantage. The battle, which left twenty-eight dead and thirty-three wounded, was won by the Confederates, who took both father and son as prisoners.

For seventeen-year-old George Sr., the episode proved a blessing in disguise because he was paroled shortly after being taken prisoner (under the condition he did not fight again). Given that over ten thousand soldiers from Kentucky died for the Union Army by the end of the Civil War, it is likely he was not too troubled by the terms of his release. Following the war, he entered Augusta College and then began a career in business.

With the increase in the number of railroads following the Civil War, the general business prospects of river port towns like Augusta were in decline. Aware of this, George Sr. decided to try his luck in the iron business in Pennsylvania.[2] He joined the Dunbar Iron Company as a clerk in the small town of Dunbar.

Like many companies during that era, the Dunbar Iron Company exploited the famous Connellsville coal vein located in and around the small town of Connellsville, Pennsylvania, thirty-six miles southeast of Pittsburgh. It was the high-quality bituminous coal from this vein that fed the great steel mills owned by Andrew Carnegie in the late nineteenth century. Such was the wealth created from this coal that at one point, Connellsville had more millionaires per capita than any other place in the world.

After learning the business for three years, George Sr. and a friend of his started a company producing firebrick for the growing steel mills. The business took off immediately, and with the increased financial comfort it brought, he married his former childhood sweetheart, Laura Bradford, in 1873. Bradford, also of Virginia roots, was the niece of George Sr.'s former commander of the Augusta Home Guard.

George Sr. and his wife were well-established in Pennsylvania by the time their fourth and last child, the future General George C. Marshall Jr. was born on December 31, 1880, in Uniontown, a village of 3,500 sitting alongside the Monongahela River less than fifty miles south of Pittsburgh and twenty-five miles north of the West Virginia border.

George Marshall's childhood was standard for someone growing up in a rural town during that era. Much of it was spent with friends exploring the countryside and streams surrounding his neighborhood. A poor student generally, Marshall later blamed an overly aggressive great-aunt for turning him against academic pursuits. Eliza Stuart, who lived with the Marshall family, forced Marshall from the age of five to sit with her for long hours of study on Saturday mornings, a time he normally reserved for playing with his friends. Considering such training only lasted a year before Marshall was old enough to go to school, it seems the aunt's efforts were a convenient excuse; Marshall was a proud man and did not like people to think he was at all challenged when it came to academics. Regardless of why he received only average grades, school was simply not enjoyable for Marshall from the beginning. In fact, it was painful.

By nature, George Marshall generally sought to reach the top in everything he did. It therefore embarrassed him when he fell short from an academic standpoint, particularly when those shortcomings were public knowledge (grades were posted in his school). Nobody likes to be made fun of, but Marshall was particularly sensitive to it as a child. Listening today to

Marshall's taped interviews with his biographer, Forrest Pogue, it is evident that his memories of school in Uniontown—specifically those moments when he was humiliated in public—still grated on him sixty years later.

The only academic subject Marshall liked and excelled at was history. From a young age, he was fascinated with the history surrounding Uniontown. His own house was on the National Road, which passed directly through town as it moved west toward West Virginia and into Ohio and Indiana. Countless pioneers and many famous men of the nineteenth century traveled the road, including Lafayette, who spent the night in Uniontown in May 1824 after being honored there during his famous return-to-America tour.[3]

More significant to Marshall were the several notable battles of the French and Indian War fought near his town, including the opening skirmish in May 1754 (on land that became Uniontown when it incorporated in 1776). Two months later, the first major battle of the war was fought at Fort Necessity, nine miles from Marshall's home.

In both these engagements, twenty-three-year-old George Washington was in command of the troops fighting for the British. A year later, and less than a mile away from Fort Necessity, British general Edward Braddock died from his wounds after being taken off the field by Washington (his senior American aide), who buried him on the road to keep his body from being desecrated by the Native Americans. Marshall and his father often visited the battleground and General Braddock's grave (moved off the road after the war) during hunting and fishing trips. The love of history, along with the more common love of fishing and hunting, were shared bonds between father and son.

Although Marshall enjoyed some wonderful moments with his father during these years, later in life he would occasionally reveal a certain level of dissatisfaction with George Sr. that went beyond what generational differences normally explain. He was embarrassed, for example, about his father's excessive enthusiasm for Chief Justice John Marshall. Marshall recalled thinking that it was "about time for somebody else to swim for the family."[4] This feeling likely reflected his disappointment in his father's business failings.

For a man who was singularly driven to succeed and whose entire professional career was characterized by outstanding achievement at every level, it did not sit well with Marshall that his father suffered a major financial setback in 1890, when Marshall was ten years old. A year earlier, George Sr. and his partners sold most of their assets to Henry Frick, who was building up a sizable monopoly in the coke business. The profit was substantial, and George Sr. decided to put his entire share of it into real estate speculation in the Shenandoah Valley. Buying at the high, Marshall's father saw the market crash within a year, taking most of his investment and much of his overall fortune with it. Almost overnight, the family's financial condition went from comfortable to uncomfortable.

George Sr. still owned land and an interest in a mining company, and his wife had property from which she earned income, but in aggregate there was not enough cash flow to maintain the lifestyle to which the family had become accustomed. Public school replaced private school, servants were dismissed, and there was a general tightening of the budget. Marshall was embarrassed and blamed his father.

Notwithstanding the financial downturn, the seventeen years Marshall spent in Uniontown seemed on balance to be happy ones.

Virginia Military Institute (September 1897–June 1901)

After finishing his high school education, Marshall expressed an interest in attending the Military Academy at West Point. Both parents were opposed to the idea, despite the benefits a free education would have had on their overall financial situation. Aside from believing that there were few prospects accompanying a career in the military, Marshall Sr. also thought it would be difficult to secure an appointment for his youngest child, given he was a prominent local Democrat and the congressman who represented Uniontown was Republican, as were both of Pennsylvania's senators. There was also the matter of the entrance examination; Marshall had only a mediocre academic record and would have needed a strong performance to overcome any of the political disadvantages he might have faced as the son of a Democrat. These considerations caused the son to shift his focus to the Virginia Military Institute (VMI), a school his brother had graduated from three years earlier and several other Marshall relatives had attended over the years. His parents agreed to let him apply despite the strain it would put on their finances.

By the very name of the college, it sounds as if Marshall's parents yielded to the idea of their youngest son becoming a soldier. On the contrary, although the VMI had its roots as an arsenal and contributed a few distinguished soldiers to the country (most notably one of its former professors, Thomas "Stonewall" Jackson), it was a school focused on military-style discipline, not military training. Although the students lived in barracks, the courses they took were not unlike other colleges during that era. As such, its graduates enjoyed no distinct advantage in obtaining a commission in the U.S. Army. The year Marshall's older brother Stuart entered VMI, not more than ten VMI alumni were serving with the regular army (Stuart became a chemist upon his graduation in 1894).[5]

Located in Lexington, Virginia, some 150 miles directly south of Uniontown, VMI's campus was originally occupied by a state arsenal. Local citizens frustrated by the off-duty activities of its soldiers decided that offering them an education would keep them better occupied during those hours when they were not protecting the store of arms. In 1839 the school was launched with twenty-three cadets. Its golden era occurred a generation later during the Civil War, when, under the leadership of Professor Jackson, the Cadet Corps trained recruits, supplied officers for the Confederate Army, and fought with distinction as a unit.

Following the death of Jackson at the battle of Chancellorsville in 1863, the Cadet Corps was honored with the job of escorting the body of the legendary general to his grave in Lexington. It was at the start of that battle that Jackson famously said, upon seeing so many VMI alumni around him, "The Institute will be heard from today!"

A year after Jackson's death, the entire Cadet Corps fought together and honored the school with its bravery at the Battle of New Market, where ten of its members were killed and forty-four wounded after they charged the retreating Union Army and took approximately one hundred prisoners. The school would go on to honor the fallen each anniversary of the battle with great ceremony and reverence, a tradition that continues to this day.

The description of such a college, as Marshall would have surely heard in detail from his brother, had to appeal to a boy who loved history in general, had been raised on stories of the battles fought in and around Uniontown, and harbored dreams of a soldier's life.

Fortunately for Marshall, his academic record was no hurdle to admission. The superintendent at that time weighed the family background of a candidate far greater than his scholastic record. The Marshall name was famous in Virginia and prominent at VMI (a Marshall cousin was among those cadets who had fought at the Battle of New Market). There is no record Marshall even took the exam normally given by the superintendent himself.

Sixteen-year-old George Marshall arrived on campus by train in September 1897 with, according to Marshall, a newfound burning drive to distinguish himself brought on by an incident at home before he left. Marshall overheard his brother appealing to his mother one day not to let him attend the VMI, believing he would "disgrace the family name." Sixty years later, Marshall told his biographer that hearing his brother's protestations that day had a profound psychological effect on his overall career and provided him with a distinct urgency to succeed over and above his natural desire to excel.[6]

There were 122 first-year cadets (referred to as Rats) on campus when Marshall began his four years at the VMI. That number began to shrink from attrition within a few weeks (forty of the boys left before the year was out and another forty-nine before graduation). An attrition rate of approximately 70 percent over four years was typical for a class at the VMI. A life of strict discipline and spartan conditions was clearly not everybody's cup of tea, and Superintendent Scott Shipp did little to make life comfortable for cadets.

Shipp, who had led the Cadet Corps on the field at the Battle of New Market and was among the wounded that day, was only the second superintendent of the school, having replaced the first one seven years earlier. For Shipp, the school was all about discipline. Drills, parades, inspections, spartan barracks, and dreary food were all designed to instill obedience, self-restraint, and self-respect. Throughout the school year (early September to late June), very few hours were unaccounted for. The week ended at 1:00 p.m. on Saturday, after which the boys were given two hours to go into downtown Lexington (provided they had no penalties assessed to them during the week). On Sundays, after attending church together, they could go into the country for a few hours before dinner was served. During the school year, there were only four days they had off: Christmas Day, New Year's Day, Washington's birthday, and May 15 (the anniversary of the Battle of New Market).

Marshall did not pretend to enjoy the austere life, but more than most he understood the purpose of it. As such, he was able to deal stoically with the long hours and discomforts during his first year, as well as the hazing from upperclassmen. The hazing did nothing to improve attrition rates, and it was relentless for Rats starting from when they first woke up. Rats were required by tradition to sleep next to open windows. During winter, this meant having to brush snow off the end of the bed when preparing it for inspection and fetching breakfast for upperclassmen and delivering it to their rooms.

For Marshall, the close proximity of his room to where the class ahead of him bunked (since he was the last of his class to arrive on campus) was an additional burden for him. On one occasion during the first month of his arrival, a few members of the class ahead of him forced Marshall to squat over a bayonet placed on the floor. It was a typical hazing practice at the VMI known as "sitting on infinity" that for Marshall almost ended tragically. The upperclassmen generally allowed the victim to stand up once it became clear he could no longer safely hold the position. Marshall, who was still recovering from a case of typhoid fever that left him weak (and was the reason he was late arriving at school), slipped prior to being released from the position, suffering a deep and bloody wound on his backside. Given that hazing was officially banned from the school under penalty of expulsion, the fate of Marshall's tormenters was in his own hands as he went off to the surgeon. Despite the pain and lengthy recovery period, Marshall was silent on the cause of his wound, gaining gratitude and respect from the upperclassmen (as well as an exemption from additional hazing for both himself and his roommates for the remainder of the year).[7]

Like Henry Stimson at Phillips Academy, and to a lesser extent at Yale, Marshall had to overcome another obstacle not shared by other cadets. For Stimson, it was his age and size that set him apart; for Marshall, it was his accent. In a school that worshiped Stonewall Jackson and Robert E. Lee, his Pittsburgh accent labeled the cadet from Uniontown early on as a northerner. It had only been thirty-two years since Lee—buried a literal stone's throw away from the VMI campus—had offered his sword to Ulysses S. Grant, ending the Civil War. The feelings were still fresh. Many of the cadets would have had fathers, grandfathers, or uncles who had served and perhaps died for the Confederate cause. Marshall, like Stimson at Phillips Academy, overcame this disadvantage by winning the respect of the cadets through excellence and through the natural leadership skills he was developing on campus. He made no attempt to change his accent.

More than offsetting the spartan conditions for Marshall was the great ceremony, pageantry, history, and traditions that characterized the VMI and drew him there in the first place. It was more than just the legend of Jackson, the shrine that was Lee's nearby grave, or the oft-told stories of the Battle of New Market. There was a pride that came with joining the Cadet Corps. And for Marshall specifically, there was the still-greater satisfaction about being a respected leader among his peers. He earned this not through academic achievement—Marshall was still only an average student—but through sheer excellence in military subjects and discipline. With respect to discipline, Marshall did not get a single demerit in four years. By comparison, the class mean was well over one hundred demerits per cadet *each* year. This was an astonishing accomplishment. By the end of his first year, when the list of cadet officers for the following year was listed, Marshall stood at the top as first corporal. He would be first on the list the following year as well when first sergeants were appointed.

Despite these honors and the passion he held for life at the VMI, Marshall did not commit himself to a career of soldiering until the summer between his second and third year. He was in Uniontown in late August 1899, joining huge crowds in welcoming home the local troops returning from the Philippines after fighting in the Spanish-American War. Past countless flags, and under specially made arches, the soldiers paraded down Main Street (painted red, white, and blue) to great adulation. Marshall would say later of the event that there was a moment when he experienced his "first great emotional reaction," one that had a "determining effect" on his career choice.[8]

Strongly motivated from the excitement felt by the parade, Marshall stepped up his efforts to an even greater degree in his third year, focusing his efforts on the goal of being named first captain for his final year, an honor that required hard work, discipline, and—as Marshall cleverly deduced—a certain detachment from normal social relationships with fellow cadets.

Marshall began to realize at the VMI that to command one's peers effectively required keeping a certain distance from them. Many otherwise capable men are either never able to grasp such a concept or, more likely, are unwilling to make such a sacrifice. The instinct to be liked is natural, but it does not correspond to being respected. Close friendships—particularly in an environment as stern and potentially lonely as VMI—are simply too valued by most young men to jeopardize for the sake of gaining the respect necessary to lead.

No so for George Marshall. Much like a natural athlete who can dominate his peers on the gridiron or baseball diamond, Marshall possessed the personality, natural abilities, and strong desire to command men. It was the reason Dean Acheson, who later served under Marshall at the State Department during the Cold War, once said that the name by which everybody called Marshall ("General Marshall") fit him "as if he'd been baptized with it."[9]

Given this approach to acquiring respect and leadership, it followed that outside of his two roommates, Marshall had no intimate friends at the

VMI. By nature, he was reserved, so it was less of a sacrifice for Marshall than it would be for other boys to maintain the proper distance he believed was required between himself and those he would lead. But Marshall took this tactic to an extreme; he insisted on a rigid George Washington–like formality when it came to dealing with superiors, peers, or subordinates. He began working on this skill in Lexington and honed it to perfection over the course of his career.

Although Marshall credited the VMI with helping him to develop the ability to manage men, such skills are not easily taught; the school simply gave Marshall the opportunity to test his own theories on how to effectively lead. What the VMI could take credit for was grinding into Marshall the concepts of self-control and discipline. Considering his future profession and the importance of these two attributes for a career in the military, the overall experience at the VMI had a profound influence on Marshall. "This institution," Marshall once commented, "gave me not only a standard for my daily contact among men, but it endowed me with a military heritage of honor and self-sacrifice."[10]

For all his sacrifice and meticulousness in following the strict rules set up for cadets, Marshall did break them on more than a few occasions in his last year, and he did so at great risk (demotion in rank, if not expulsion from the school). The excuse for each transgression was one even the most obedient of nineteen-year-old males might use under similar circumstances: It was about a young woman.

On the edge of the school's southern gate lived Elizabeth "Lily" Carter Coles. Five years older than Marshall, Coles lived with her widowed mother and was by all accounts a good-looking and charming woman (with an excellent Virginian pedigree). Marshall met her in the beginning of his final year at the VMI. He heard music coming from a piano within her house while walking one afternoon and stopped on the street to listen. He returned from time to time and sat on the side of the road to enjoy the music wafting out through an open window. One day he was invited in by Lily's mother and introduced to Lily, the person responsible for the melodies. Marshall began to see her on a regular basis.

With his time limited by the demands of school, but wanting to see more of her, Marshall often saw Lily outside of the area he was restricted to during certain hours. At an even greater risk, he would "run the block" to spend time with her (cadet speak for leaving the barracks at unauthorized times). Fortunately for Marshall, he always got away with it.

Lily Coles dated several cadets over the years, including Marshall's older brother Stuart six years earlier. It is surprising no Marshall biographer has commented on any possible link between his choice to date Coles and the conversation he overheard a few years earlier when Stuart tried to warn his mother that George would disgrace the family name if they let him go to VMI. Given the sting of Stuart's appeal, perhaps in at least his initial decision to date Coles, he was sticking it to his older brother.

It is surprising Marshall took such great risks to see Lily Coles during his last year at the VMI given the challenge he knew he faced in securing a commission in the United States Army, a goal he fully set for himself two summers earlier. Even with the additional demand for officers brought on by the Spanish-American War, it remained a long shot for any graduate of the VMI to become commissioned. Priority for the appointments went to West Point graduates, followed in order by men applying from within the ranks, former officers who led volunteers during the Spanish-American War, and civilians. VMI graduates were considered civilians.

As spring arrived during his final year at the VMI, all but the civilian positions were filled, leaving 142 open spots for which there were more than ten thousand applications on file. His position as first captain and his excellent military and discipline record at VMI would not likely be enough to offset his weak academic standing (Marshall stood fifteenth in his class of thirty-four). He therefore lobbied hard for a spot, leaving nothing left to chance in his quest.

Superintendent Shipp had already written letters (including one to President William McKinley) praising Marshall as "fully equal to the best." Believing more was needed, Marshall rallied his father to the cause. George Sr., if not enthusiastic with his son's career choice, was at least resigned to it and agreed to help. Interestingly, prior to making the effort and spending whatever political capital he possessed, he wrote to Superintendent Shipp asking if his son had what it took to be an officer. Shipp more than satisfied George Sr., claiming his son was "as well qualified for officer of infantry as any man who has been turned out here."[11] Once satisfied, the father was as relentless as the son in taking the necessary steps to obtain a commission. He arranged for some of his contacts to write additional letters to McKinley in support of his son.

More importantly, George Marshall Sr. persuaded, either directly or indirectly, both of Pennsylvania's senators (Matthew Quay and Boies Penrose) to write letters of recommendation directly to the War Department. Their letters alone would likely have been enough to seal the deal, given that quotas for the positions were assigned to each state. But wanting to cover all bases, the elder Marshall also asked a strong political supporter of McKinley in 1896 (and graduate of the VMI) to write the president a letter on behalf of his son.

Still not satisfied that all possible angles had been explored, both father and son decided the latter should personally lobby for himself in Washington. Marshall headed there in April 1901 with several letters of introduction. He first visited Attorney General Philander Knox, a friend of his father's, hoping that one cabinet officer might influence another. Marshall also dropped in uninvited on a reception to see the chairman of the House Military Affairs Committee, a distant relative by marriage of his mother's. To each man, Marshall made his case.

Showing a boldness that seemed surprising for someone of such reserve—but would become a trademark characteristic throughout his career—Marshall took one more step to make certain his future was in the U.S. Army: He went to the White House to confront President McKinley himself. Having no appointment and told by the White House usher it would be impossible to see the president without one, Marshall waited in the reception area for over two hours as one scheduled visitor after another paraded by him on their way in to meet with McKinley. Finally, and amazingly, the impatient and determined twenty-year-old jumped behind a couple and their daughter as they were heading into the president's office for their appointed meeting. After what must have been a few awkward minutes of standing there while the family presented themselves to McKinley and then left the room, the president was nice enough to ask Marshall what he wanted. Marshall got straight to the point and asked for a commission. McKinley was noncommittal, but later in life Marshall believed this brief encounter in the White House could have been the contributing factor that finally got him the appointment. Although an attractive story, it seems more likely the White House visit was overkill; the key factor would have been the support of the two Pennsylvania senators.

In any event, Marshall got what he wanted. After passing a relatively easy examination, he received his commission on February 3, 1902, in Uniontown. It was signed by President Theodore Roosevelt (McKinley had been assassinated five months earlier). The newly minted second lieutenant was immediately assigned to the 30th Infantry in the Philippines. He was given orders a few days later to report to Ohio to pick up recruits on the way to San Francisco, where they would then ship out.

Having ten days to report to duty, Marshall decided it was more than enough time to get married. The marriage took place in Lexington at the Coles's house eight days later. From there, the couple spent what they thought would be a one-day honeymoon at a fancy hotel in Washington. A sympathetic officer gave him an extra five days to report to duty, after which Marshall began his journey to the Philippines and Lily headed back to Lexington. He was out of the country for two years and would not see Lily again for closer to three.

The Philippines (May 1902–November 1903)

Life in the U.S. Army at the turn of the twentieth century was tough, particularly if one was a second lieutenant like Marshall, and a junior one at that. Since the Civil War ended a generation earlier, Americans remained generally hostile to war, soldiers, and anything associated with the military. This predominant attitude gave Congress little incentive to support the Army during the thirty-three years between the end of the Civil War and the start of the Spanish-American War.

The Army was given an opportunity to turn public opinion around when the Spanish-American War broke out, but corruption, red tape, general incompetence, and an appalling lack of coordination between the Army bureaus during the conflict outweighed the glory Teddy Roosevelt and his Rough Riders achieved on San Juan Hill. Morale, which should have shot up after a quick victory over a once-formidable European power, fell as the shortcomings of the Army began to be publicized. Before any young officer during this time even laced up his first standard-issue boots, he was generally aware of the negative perception to which his profession was held.

A newly commissioned officer's spirits were further lowered when he began to look at the fine print related to his compensation and benefits. The pay was not terrible for the times (Marshall earned the standard starting salary for a second lieutenant of $116.67 per month),but not everyone was aware they had to buy their own revolver, saber, binoculars, bedding roll, mess kit, and food upon entering the service.[12] Further, when an officer was asked to move (and officers moved constantly), he had to pay most of the costs (and if an officer was married, this included the expenses of moving his wife or family). When adding up these costs, as Marshall did quite regularly, the reality came as quite a shock. That he could recall to his biographer the exact costs of a spring hat and suit he considered purchasing fifty years earlier is testament to the tight budget Marshall was on during these years. He remembered keeping track of his expenses "down to the last dime."

Considering the financial burden, one might expect job satisfaction was something a young officer could at least count on. Not quite; the life of a career soldier at the turn of the century was largely unchanged from how it was since the Civil War ended thirty-five years earlier: It was an exercise in monotony. Moving regularly between one or another of the approximately fifty different army posts located in twenty-five or so different states was the fate of most soldiers.

The garrisons, selected many years earlier based on their proximity to hostile Native Americans, were generally located in isolated parts of the country. With the threat from the Native Americans largely a thing of the past by the start of the twentieth century, boredom was the common enemy. The inspections, drills, and duties that made up the daily routine at such army outposts offered little help, given they were generally completed by midday. This left the men with a lot of free time on their hands.

If Marshall was aware of any of this on his way to the Philippines, he might have hoped that things would be a little different on the other side of the world, where he began his first assignment. In most respects, he would have been mistaken.

Even before officially obtaining the colony from Spain in late 1898 following the Spanish-American War, the United States was having trouble with Filipino revolutionaries. The islanders declared their independence during the fighting between the Spanish and American naval forces. The American government, with no naval bases of its own in the Far East, had no interest in giving up its new possession. Thus, the Philippine-American War ensued, and although it officially lasted three years (Theodore Roosevelt declared peace in July 1902), sporadic fighting went on for several years in the more remote sections of the country.

Marshall spent much of his eighteen months in the Philippines moving between these remote locations, but never faced any combat. It was therefore a relatively boring assignment, broken up only occasionally by unique experiences such as getting caught on a small boat in a typhoon, dealing with a massive cholera outbreak among the natives, and guarding a particularly dangerous group of enemy prisoners.

But it was in the Philippines that Marshall began to put into practice many of his core beliefs about managing men, an art that for him began with establishing and maintaining discipline. Within any operational unit from a squad (up to ten soldiers) to a field army (up to 450,000), there is nothing more valuable for a leader to instill in his troops than discipline, and Marshall believed early on in his career that it could not be accomplished by simply issuing rigid and random orders. He was convinced men must be kept active, interested, and engaged. And although a strict disciplinarian, he also was of the view that men responded best to fair, thoughtful, and calm leadership (he rarely raised his voice).

Marshall also continued to present himself in front of others as unusually reserved and businesslike. Since this trait had worked out for him well at the VMI, he figured he would maintain it as a professional solider.

Ironically, for all his focus on practicing the art of command so that he could increase his command responsibilities, Marshall had no way of knowing as he left the Philippines in 1903 that twenty-nine years would pass before he was given a posting that gave him a greater command experience than the one he was leaving.

3

Wall Street Lawyer to Public Servant (1899–1911)

The leading rule for the lawyer, as for the man of every other calling, is diligence.

—ABRAHAM LINCOLN

Law, Charity, Politics, and Soldiering

While Second Lieutenant George Marshall was slowly making his way back to the United States from the Philippines in 1903, Henry Stimson was in New York City living a comfortable life as a senior partner of a highly respected law firm that carried his name. It had been four years since Elihu Root had bequeathed his law business to him and Bronson Winthrop to take a position in President William McKinley's cabinet as secretary of war. During those years, Stimson further enhanced the reputation he acquired under Root's tutelage as a top litigator.

Like other leading New York law firms at the time, Winthrop & Stimson began to focus more heavily on international business law. Just as New York had the nation's busiest port and was the gateway for European products into the United States, it was also the financial heart of the country and gaining greater importance each year as a global financial center of power. European investors who needed legal advice financed much of the growth of the American economy during this era. Additionally, European corporations were setting up offices in New York to assist in gaining greater access to both exporters and importers.

All these trends led to a greater demand for legal guidance, and Winthrop & Stimson positioned themselves perfectly to capture the business. During these years, Stimson's exposure to Europe, its economy, its leading corporations, and its problems grew exponentially, as did his understanding of global trade flows and how closely the world's major economies were connected. The procurement of this knowledge ultimately led him to become the leading internationalist in the country, and a valuable addition to the presidents he served.

As historian Godfrey Hodgson pointed out in his 1990 study of Stimson, it was the greater experience of New York lawyers in international business and finance that distinguished themselves from lawyers in other parts of the country during this era and made them more attractive candidates for high-level government posts in Washington. With the wealth a partnership of a successful corporate law firm in New York generated, Manhattan-based lawyers could also more easily afford to accept the paltry salaries public service offered. It was for all these reasons, Hodgson concluded, that so many "Wall Street lawyers" ended up serving in senior government positions in Washington starting in the late nineteenth century.

Unlike a number of these men, Henry Stimson was not motivated by the longing for public fame or the wish to be an important person. His ambitions—which were considerable—were driven by his sincere desire to use his skills and experience to make the world a better place. As a young man, Stimson was often burdened with the thought that he was not "doing good" or "making a difference." These were two distinct aspirations, although certainly linked. The need to "do good" was anchored in the conventional charitable traditions of Christianity taught to Stimson throughout his life. The need to make a difference, perhaps a less-common obsession among men of that era driven by the accumulation of wealth, seemed native to Stimson's character; he desperately wanted to be involved in important things. Both ambitions predated his legal career and his association with Skull and Bones (an organization that strongly pushed its members to contribute to society). As a friend of Stimson's at Yale observed, Skull and Bones only "enlarged" his "already lopsided concern for the pure forms of earnestness and the good."[1] In his memoirs, Stimson wrote that his law work at this stage of his career was not giving him the opportunity to get closer to the "problems of life." Only through public service, he believed, could he find such problems and work on fixing them. He began to do just that.

There were always opportunities in New York at the turn of the century to satisfy an individual's need to "do good," and Stimson involved himself in a variety of them. Initially, he took a direct approach by visiting poor families two or three times a month to provide them with decent company (and money). But it did not take him long to realize his efforts were better spent using his talents as an administrator and organizer of charitable organizations. He therefore began serving on the boards of several such institutions and acting as legal counsel for others.

Although these charitable activities allowed the young attorney to better satisfy the "ethical side" that he felt was taking a backseat to his professional career, making a difference at a higher level was still a hunger that charity work could not quite satisfy. So, within a year of becoming a partner in Root's law firm, and only four years after graduating from Harvard Law School, he began to address that need as well.

Stimson noticed almost immediately upon commencing his legal career an obvious and frustrating truth: When there was a conflict between public and private interests, the latter was nearly always better represented in court due to the greater resources it had available to attract more high-quality legal talent. No less obvious, but equally vexing to Stimson at the time, was the less-than-ethical practices of the local Democratic Party in New York, which also worked against the public interest. Both of these realities moved him to take the first small steps in 1895 toward what would become a life largely devoted to public service.

Like most people of his socioeconomic class in New York City at the turn of the century, Stimson might have looked down upon politicians. It was a profession many in his class believed was beneath them. If Stimson harbored such thoughts, spending time with Elihu Root changed his opinion quickly. He learned from Root that participating in the political process could not only be effective, but it was also a responsibility that capable citizens should assume if they could afford to.

Although born into a family of Republicans, Stimson revealed early on in his career both his independence and lack of partisanship by voting for Democrat Grover Cleveland in the presidential election of 1892, one year after joining Root & Clarke. It was a single issue for Stimson (reducing the tariff) that motivated him to join other Mugwumps in opposing the candidacy of Republican James G. Blain. Two years later, having moved back into the Republican Party after the Democrats largely rejected Cleveland's policies, Stimson began working within its lowest levels to reduce the power and abuses of the political machine that dominated New York City in the late nineteenth century.

Starting by working as a captain in his local election district responsible for three hundred voters, Stimson spent the next ten years giving speeches, holding forums, printing handbills, and pushing hard to bring general transparency to the local registration and voting process.[2] Victories were small and hard won, but when added together were visible: Honest and capable politicians started winning local and state offices; the power of the local political boss was reduced; and bills were passed that made primary elections more democratic in nature.

Encouraged by real progress, Stimson stepped up his efforts and was soon rewarded with greater responsibilities. By 1901, he was president of the 27th Assembly District Republican Club, and two years later he was elevated to the New York County Republican Committee. The political lessons learned during these years were valuable to him in later life, and his success confirmed to Stimson, yet again, that no matter what task one was involved in, diligence yielded results. He never wavered from this conviction.

Success is a wonderful motivator, and the time Stimson spent on political activities increased proportionately with every noticeable gain his efforts helped produce. He decided during these years he was not going to be held back from "making a difference" by waiting to achieve a major fortune from the legal profession; competing for wealth among the New York elite did not motivate him any more than fame did. That is not to suggest he was uncomfortable financially; on the contrary, he was doing quite well. But Stimson earned far less than his peers at other law firms given the time he was devoting to pursuing goals of a larger purpose. Although these extracurricular activities reduced his billable hours, they did not prevent him from consolidating his position as one of the top corporate lawyers in the country.

As if his legal, political, and charitable activities were not enough to keep him busy, Stimson also developed a passion during this time for soldiering and the military life. This interest took off when he enlisted in the National Guard at the start of the Spanish-American War in April 1898. Stimson was angry with himself for not anticipating the conflict so that he could be better prepared to take part in it. To be ready for the next war, or in case the war with Spain dragged on, Stimson joined the National Guard. Although the war lasted less than four months, he remained in his squadron for almost nine years, meeting weekly for drills and taking part each summer in military exercises. He loved it all: The military drills appealed to his sense of order, hard work, and preparedness; the exercise allowed him to take respite from the symptoms of lumbago and rheumatism that started to cause him trouble; and the camaraderie of young like-minded men was something Stimson reveled in at that time and for the rest of his life.

United States Attorney for the Southern District of New York (February 1906–April 1909)

Through his various legal, political, and military activities, Henry Stimson became well-known during this time to both the business and political elite of New York. Among those who took notice of the young lawyer was Theodore Roosevelt, the rising scion of a long and well-established Manhattan family who made a name for himself in New York State; New York City; Washington, D.C.; and Cuba (during the Spanish-American War). In 1900, the forty-two-year-old was elected vice president of the United States under William McKinley. Less than a year later, McKinley was assassinated, and Roosevelt became the twenty-sixth president of the United States.

Stimson and Roosevelt knew one another principally through their common membership in the Boone and Crockett Club, a wildlife conservation organization founded in 1887 by Roosevelt and George Bird Grinnell. Stimson recorded in his diary that they first met in 1894 and quickly discovered they shared a love for adventure, hiking, hunting, and the vast unoccupied lands of the American West. As they had homes only a few miles from one another in Long Island, the two men saw each other regularly, often over lunch and occasionally accompanied by their wives.

Given their friendship, Stimson found nothing unusual in an invitation by Roosevelt to come to the White House for lunch in December 1905. Although they periodically discussed local politics, Stimson assumed Roosevelt was simply looking to temporarily escape the pressures of his office by discussing with him any number of topics, such as how best to take down a bear, climb a difficult mountain, or deal with Native Americans. He took the train down to Washington to indulge his fellow outdoorsman.

Prior to his lunch with the president, Stimson paid a courtesy call to his old boss, Secretary of State Elihu Root. Root immediately set Stimson straight as to the reason for the president's invitation: Roosevelt wanted to appoint him as the United States Attorney for the Southern District of New York, a big job for which the president wanted and needed a man with legal talent, high energy, and unquestioned integrity. Minutes later, Stimson was in the president's office and jumped at the offer.

The job of United States Attorney for the Southern District of New York was little known to the general public back in 1906 (and still is to an extent today). In fact, it was the single most important law enforcement position in the United States, given it was located not only in the nation's most populated district, but also its most important one from the standpoint of commerce.

Stimson understood he was taking the position at a particularly critical time. Large corporate entities, not even in existence for much of the nineteenth century, were beginning to leverage their considerable weight in an attempt to get around, avoid, or otherwise ignore the checks on them legislated by the federal government, going back to the Sherman Act fifteen years earlier. By accepting Roosevelt's offer, Stimson became the nation's primary enforcer of these laws. If successful, his chances of making a difference were considerable.

Stimson was sworn in on February 1, 1906. In his memoirs, Stimson summarized that day as one where he "crossed forever the river that separates private citizens from public men." He was thirty-eight years old and had been practicing law for less than sixteen years.

Prior to officially taking office, Stimson met with Roosevelt's attorney general, William Moody, to get briefed. Moody, unhappy in general with the organization of all the districts under the Department of Justice, decided the times required a new model for the office Stimson was to inherit.

For starters, Moody wanted the top job to be a full-time one; it had previously been a requirement that the attorneys only show up to the office every day for "part of the time." In addition, Moody wanted to restructure how the position was compensated. All of Stimson's predecessors (including Elihu Root) continued their private practice while serving and operated under a fee system where they got to keep part of the sums recovered from a successful litigation (mostly customs cases). Such fees added up to approximately $100,000 annually in the years before Stimson took over. Finally, Moody was not impressed with the tradition of Stimson's predecessors handing big cases over to outside counsel.

The attorney general therefore gave Stimson straightforward instructions: Reorganize the office, get a decent staff, and try important cases yourself. He offered Stimson a decent salary of $10,000 per year (putting an end to the fee system for good) and explained that going forward, the job would require a great deal more time than it had required in the past. Stimson wasted no time in taking up the challenge.

Getting a decent staff was easier said than done. To do battle with big corporations and the finest legal talent their riches could procure, Stimson needed to level the playing field with talented lawyers of his own. The problem was that Uncle Sam was not known to be generous when it came to compensating employees; the eight assistants Stimson inherited were earning an average salary of $2,750 per man (and with few exceptions, Stimson believed the government was getting what it paid for). Stimson himself had earned $20,000 in private practice the year before his appointment, and many of his peers in other New York law firms earned far more. He knew there were few experienced and competent lawyers in New York earning less than $10,000 per year. Since the chances of getting an increase in the budget were impossible, Stimson needed another solution.

His approach was simple but shrewd: He targeted young brilliant students a year or two out of the very top law schools along with the brightest students in the country who were about to graduate from the same schools. In either case, he wanted people who were the number-one- or number-two-ranked students in their class. What a lawyer lacked in experience, Stimson figured, could more than be offset by a first-rate brain exposed to a high-quality curriculum.

Through correspondence with law school deans and conversations with peers in other law firms, he got candidates. In pitching the job to them, his goal was to appeal to the excitement of working for a popular and young president in carrying out efforts to reform the excesses of capitalism; he knew such an appeal would have caused him to sign up fifteen years earlier. Essentially, he was selling an opportunity to "make a difference" to people he assumed were like himself.

His strategy worked. Stimson hired sixteen men during his three years leading the office, half of them straight out of law school. They were an exceptional group of individuals who went on to be founders of major law firms, leaders in existing law firms, senior counsel to major corporations, solicitor generals of the United States, judges to the highest court in New York State, and colonial administrators in the newly acquired islands of the Philippines and Puerto Rico.

The most illustrious of this group was Felix Frankfurter, hired by Stimson less than two years after finishing first in his class at Harvard Law School (where he allegedly earned the highest academic ranking since Louis Brandeis thirty years earlier). Frankfurter excelled as an assistant to Stimson and went on to become a highly influential member of the United States Supreme Court from 1939 through 1962, as well as a close advisor to

Franklin Roosevelt (it was Frankfurter who formally introduced Henry Stimson to the newly elected president in 1933 and aggressively pressed FDR to appoint his old boss secretary of war seven years later).

Stimson prided himself on his ability to recruit, judge, and place men in appropriate positions, and give them enough space, responsibility, and accountability to shine. It all started with the selection process. Merit was the first and only consideration for Stimson when choosing his staff. From his first public job in Manhattan to his last in Washington, D.C., Stimson resisted all pressure from the outside to hire people with political, social, or familial ties no matter who was lobbying him (in 1908, he brushed aside Teddy Roosevelt, who was pushing a candidate on him by noting that the man in question did not "seem to have made quite the record for force and efficiency" required to get further consideration[3]). The staff Stimson assembled to support him as United States Attorney for the Southern District of New York was, he believed, "equal in their combined talents to any office anywhere, public or private."[4]

Stimson's achievement in forming this team was the first of many examples of his talent in assembling extraordinary individuals to work for him. It was an essential element to his success as a public servant. Equally critical, but more impressive, was his ability to get so many highly intelligent and competent men working together as an efficient team. This was his true gift as a manager, and there were several reasons why he was so successful: First, Stimson was able to command the respect of his staff through his dedication to mentoring them, treating them fairly, and giving them his full loyalty; second, like many great managers, he led by example, revealing to his charges a strong work ethic, an exceptional ability to focus on the task at hand, the highest of ethical standards, and teamwork; third, he always clarified and repeatedly drove home to his staff the larger common goals of the group.

But there was another management technique Stimson threw into the mix that helped earn him lifelong reverence and loyalty from so many of the accomplished and impressive men who worked for him over the years: He established a true family-like environment in and outside the office. If management experts today examined the career of Henry Stimson, they would see he was years ahead of his time in how he related to and motivated his staff. Long before "team building" became a popular management exercise in corporate America, Stimson undertook it on a regular basis. He promoted the "work hard, play hard" maxim to his staff (though not using those words exactly). Stimson's idea of playing hard involved sailing, baseball, hiking, riding horses, shooting skeet, running races, and tennis. But it also included intellectual pursuits such as play readings, amateur theater, and popular games of the era. All these activities, taking place at or near Stimson's Long Island estate, encouraged rest, relaxation, and fun with the ultimate goal of building a strong, close, and happy team (notwithstanding the fact that Stimson always found time during or after the activities to discuss cases with his subordinates and debate the merits of different legal strategies).

Once Stimson's posse of high achievers was in place, there was no shortage of bad guys to go after. Although the nature of the position often required (as it does today) working on the low-level transgressions and schemes that every generation of capitalists seems to contrive, Teddy Roosevelt did not hire Stimson to bring small-time cheats to justice; he wanted to reel in the big fish, and he directed Stimson to go hard after any corporation that was breaking the laws established by either the Elkins Act passed in 1903 or the Sherman Act passed thirteen years earlier. There had been no cases successfully brought to trial in the Southern District of New York under either of these measures, and the aggressive president was hell-bent on having his new man reverse that record.

With a clear mandate, a gifted staff, and corporate targets that became complacent over the years in disguising their infractions, Stimson was able to achieve considerable success during his three years at the helm. Initially, his targets were those entities involved in railroad rebates, a long-practiced scheme that the government particularly detested. Large companies with dominant positions in a specific trade essentially dictated the price at which their goods were transported by railway. This was done by insisting on getting a rebate back from the railroad companies equal to the difference between the published rates established by the Interstate Commerce Commission and the rates they wished to pay the railroad companies. By lowering their transport costs, large companies could more easily drive out competition, giving them a more dominant market share, which ultimately led to higher overall costs to the consumer. The Elkins Act gave prosecutors the ability to go after the shippers *as well* as the railroad companies and levy far larger fines on both.

Stimson was able to win several convictions against perpetrators of this practice.[5] The biggest victory—and the most important of any category during his time as United States Attorney—came against American Sugar Refining Company and nine different railroads. The relentlessness at which Stimson's office pursued this case and others, along with the ensuing publicity each victory produced, essentially ended the activity.

Another important case Stimson won during his tenure as United States Attorney fell under the category of customs abuses. Import duties were something corporations commonly tried to avoid, and many became quite sophisticated in dodging them. For close to ten years, a combination of sugar companies rigged scales to underestimate the weight of imported sugar, thus avoiding the full duties required by law. They did this by inserting wires through small holes bored into the government's scales. The fraud was spotted in 1907, but it took the painstaking efforts of Stimson and his team to show there were significant differences between the amount of sugar sold by the companies over the years and the amount on which it paid duties. Eventually, $3,500,000 in back duties was recovered.

Goldthwaite Dorr, one of Stimson's assistants during this time, said Stimson himself interviewed close to a thousand people relating to this specific case and examined in great detail the history of each cargo of sugar as it made its way from the Caribbean Islands, to the scales, into the books (one column with the fake weight, one with the real), and out to the customers.[6] Stimson wrote in his memoirs that he spent "the better part of two full years of his life" on this case and similar ones involving customs abuses.

Following these and other successful prosecutions, Stimson resigned his office in April 1909 after three years. Teddy Roosevelt had left the White House a month earlier; he was anxious to rebuild his net worth, and he believed he had accomplished his goals. He left with a strong sense of pride about "setting a new standard of effectiveness" for the office.

Not only was Stimson able to win cases, but he did so with carefully crafted arguments that could serve as precedents for future prosecutors. More remarkable was that he could win victories without going too far in condemning large American corporations who, despite their less-than-honorable conventions, were still popular within the country and driving its dramatic economic growth. As a corporate lawyer, Stimson was aware of their importance to the economy and understood their role as well as anyone in linking the United States to the rest of the world. His attacks were therefore focused against the practices, not the companies themselves.

Stimson later said that his three years in office were the most enjoyable and meaningful of his career. He knew well before he walked out the door that he wanted to spend the rest of his life serving the public in one capacity or another, but he needed to get his finances in order so that he could permanently be available when opportunities arose.

There would be no shortage of opportunities; Stimson's reputation was made as a result of the judgments he secured during his term as United

States Attorney in New York, particularly among progressive Republicans. He successfully took on not only the largest corporate interests in the country, but also many of the top corporate lawyers who represented them. It was not just Stimson's victories that impressed people, but the great effort and shrewd tactics he used in getting the verdicts. They admired the countless hours he spent contemplating how exactly to present a case and how precisely to define the charges in order to tie them to specific laws. Although he consulted with the Attorney General's office and with his own staff on these topics, it was understood that the cases were his responsibility to consider and resolve. He made the big decisions.[7]

To as much as anything, Stimson's success during these three years could be attributed to what one leading lawyer at the time (who'd been on the losing side of one of the cases) described as "absolutely perfect preparation." Stimson took this considerable ability—and his elevated reputation—back with him to the law offices of Winthrop & Stimson.

"Wise Man" in the Making

Setting what would become a regular pattern for himself for the rest of his life, Stimson's return to the private sector in April 1909 was brief. Over the next two years, he was selected to run for mayor of New York City, nominated as the Republican candidate for governor of New York State, and appointed as secretary of war by President William H. Taft. Before the term was coined for a later generation of men after World War II, Stimson was slowly transforming himself during these years into a "wise man," a highly successful lawyer or banker, typically based in New York, often sought by his government for advice, and called to high-level service when needed. He would define this role for the next thirty-six years.

Stimson's journey toward becoming a "wise man" began five months after returning to private practice when a special committee was formed in New York City made up of members of the Republican Party, the Independence League (run by William Randolph Hearst), and another prominent group to select a New York City mayoral candidate under a fusion ticket to take a shot at breaking up the power and corruption of Tammany Hall. After he was selected, two representatives of the committee tracked Stimson down on one of his hunting trips in the Canadian wilderness north of Quebec to offer him the nomination. He reluctantly accepted, but only after consulting Root and his father, each of whom advised that duty demanded it.

For a variety of reasons, none of which involved Stimson, Hearst withdrew his support, and both the committee and effort broke apart.[8] But nine months later, Teddy Roosevelt began pitching him on the idea of running for governor of New York in November 1910.

Stimson's relationship with Roosevelt—politically and personally—was rock solid. Although they had known each other for fifteen years, the two men grew closer during Stimson's three years as United States Attorney of New York. They shared several common political views: Both believed in a strong central government and a liberal interpretation of the constitution; both were ardent reformists and committed internationalists; both considered that it was the duty and destiny of the United States to drive the moral progress of the world; and each man also understood that force was often required against those who interfered with that destiny.

From a personal standpoint, they had even more in common: Both came from prominent Manhattan families led by bighearted and charitable fathers whom they revered; both grew up undersized and frail in comparison to their peers, which drove them harder to make a name for themselves; both held duty, honor, and service among the highest of values; and both shared the love of highly vigorous recreational activities, what Roosevelt famously branded as "the strenuous life."

In fact, when it came to physical activities, their interests were practically indistinguishable; they shared an incurable passion for the great outdoors. Hiking, fishing, riding, hunting, exploring, and regularly roughing it in the Far West, Canada, or the Adirondack Mountains of New York State were activities closely associated with Roosevelt but equally engaged in by Stimson. For both men, such activities were relaxing and a form of escape from the intellectual but sedentary rigors inherent in their professional lives. It was a curious form of relaxation they shared. On their independent trips to the West, both men sought thrills, entertained real danger, and acted with a fearlessness that often crossed the line into recklessness.

Both men also fully enjoyed exhibiting these qualities to one another. On a frigid day in January 1902, President Roosevelt and Secretary of War Root were together on their horses in Rock Creek Park in Washington, D.C., when Roosevelt spotted Stimson across a wide creek atop his horse. Because the water of the swollen creek was freezing and moving with force, Roosevelt yelled to Stimson in jest to cross the water to join them. Stimson naturally hesitated until Root, following up on the president's good-natured humor, yelled, "The President of the United States directs Sergeant Stimson of Squadron A to cross the creek and come to his assistance by order of the Secretary of War."

Picking up on the joke, Stimson saluted and immediately headed for the creek with the intention to cross it. His horse slipped while negotiating the bank and plunged into the freezing water with Stimson in the saddle. Moving downstream quickly, both Stimson and the horse were submerged at times and could neither get to the other side of the creek nor find a good place to get back up on land on their side of it. Getting caught in the branches of a submerged tree farther downstream, Stimson dismounted and somehow led himself and the horse to an easier section of the bank to climb up. Still on the opposite side of the creek from his two friends, Stimson then swiftly rode farther downstream to a nearby bridge despite having wet clothes that were beginning to stiffen in the icy temperatures. He galloped across and rode back up to where a shocked Roosevelt and Root had been watching him. "Ready for duty," Stimson announced nonchalantly to both men. When Roosevelt embarrassingly expressed his surprise that Stimson bothered to make the attempt, Stimson responded by saying that orders were to be followed, not questioned. All three enjoyed a good laugh, and Roosevelt regaled the membership of the Boone and Crockett Club later that night with an account of Stimson's exploits.[9]

In June 1910, Roosevelt twice invited Stimson to "Sagamore Hill," his home in Oyster Bay, New York, approximately eight miles west from "Highhold," Stimson's one-hundred-acre estate in West Hills just outside Huntington. On these two visits, the main subject was politics, specifically the state of the factionalized Republican Party in New York State. Roosevelt, fifteen months out of the White House, was quietly champing at the bit to become relevant again.

At the first meeting, Roosevelt casually suggested to his neighbor that Stimson might be called to run for governor later in the year. At the second, he was a bit more direct and suggested to Stimson that he would make a great governor and should think about whether it was an office he wished to pursue.

Roosevelt was scheming and taking the first steps toward regaining the White House in 1912 from William Howard Taft, the man Roosevelt handpicked to replace him but who now was a disappointment to the ex-president. Taking care of his home state was a priority for Roosevelt, and he knew a respectable reformist on the ticket for governor could help his cause in unifying the Republicans under his leadership. As the New York State Republicans were preparing for their state convention in September in Saratoga, Roosevelt was elected to be temporary chairman of the convention. Appealing to Stimson's sense of duty, Roosevelt convinced him to run for governor.

If Stimson's five-week campaign for governor in 1910 proved anything, it was that campaigning was not his strong suit. Although organized, well-prepared, and concise in his message, he was remote by nature, a poor orator, and reluctant to toot his own horn. Roosevelt, one of the greatest campaigners in United States history, good-naturedly lectured Stimson after one specific speech he made. Addressing him by the nickname used by Stimson's friends, Roosevelt said, "Darn it, Harry, a campaign speech is a poster, not an etching!"

Even with Roosevelt's strong support, there was little Stimson could have done to win the election; it was a Democratic landslide in New York and throughout the country, and one of the worst defeats for the Republican party in its history. The Democrats gained fifty-six seats in the U.S. House of Representatives, gained nine seats in the U.S. Senate, and took over most of the governors' mansions throughout the country. Voters in Dutchess County, New York, sent a Democrat to the State Senate (the first in thirty-two years) when they elected twenty-eight-year-old Franklin Roosevelt. Within New York, as around the country, the Democrats were unified while the Grand Old Party was hopelessly divided between its progressive and conservative wings. It split two years later when Roosevelt formed a third party in an attempt to oust Taft from the White House.

It was agreed by all those close to Stimson that his loss did no apparent damage to his reputation. On the contrary, he created a lot of goodwill among many Republicans by taking one for the team in a good cause. He went back to Winthrop & Stimson with no regrets and felt in debt to Roosevelt for the opportunity given to him. His return to private practice would once again be brief.

For better or worse, Henry Stimson was now labeled a "Roosevelt man," and it was partly for this reason that President Taft asked him six months later to be his new secretary of war. Taft—two years into his first term—believed that by placing a few men in the cabinet who were politically close to Roosevelt, the ex-president would be less likely to challenge him for the Republican nomination for president in 1912. Although considered an unlikely event to many observers at the time, Taft was convinced Teddy

Roosevelt wanted his old job back. Taft also knew enough about Stimson to be confident he would make an excellent War Department head.

While honored, Stimson was conscious of the deteriorating relationship between Taft and Roosevelt and wanted to first make clear to the former that he was loyal to the latter. He got assurances from the president that this would not be a problem; Taft viewed Stimson as a "middle-of-the-road progressive,"[10] lying politically between himself and the other titular head of the Republican Party. Satisfied, Stimson advised the president that before accepting, he needed to consult with Roosevelt, his father, Bronson Winthrop, and his wife. Winthrop, despite the continued sacrifice Stimson's absence from the firm would cause, encouraged his close friend and partner to accept any call to public service that gave him an opportunity to accomplish something good. His wife and father gave him essentially the same advice.

More important was getting the blessing from the former president. To do so, Stimson headed out once again to Sagamore Hill. He opened his meeting with Roosevelt by making it clear that joining the current administration would be difficult given the loyalty he felt toward him. Seemingly untroubled, the ex-president, according to Stimson, strongly encouraged him to accept the appointment for the sake of Stimson's own career and to "help make Mr. Taft's administration a success." In his diary, Stimson claims he left Sagamore Hill with the feeling he "virtually carried his [Roosevelt's] commission" to take the job and perform it well.

Stimson was fooling himself. Knowing Roosevelt and after listening to his complaints about Taft over the past few months, a more objective man might have understood exactly how the ex-president felt about an old friend serving his new enemy. Roosevelt was an excellent politician and did not go lightly into battle, but he was not advertising his intentions regarding 1912 at the time Stimson came to see him and would therefore have no obvious rationale to advise Stimson to decline the offer from Taft.

If Stimson contemplated any of this, he kept it to himself. It is clear from a letter he sent to Roosevelt eight months earlier that he was worried about Roosevelt forming a new political party.[11] Regardless, the opportunity for Stimson was incredible; it was a high-level cabinet position that gave him command over an institution he greatly admired and an office his mentor, Elihu Root, had exited only seven years earlier. Root served in the office to critical acclaim, and it led him to the more prestigious office of secretary of state just eighteen months after leaving office. Surely Stimson had this same career path in mind when he chose to take Roosevelt's words of support at Sagamore Hill literally.

Stimson accepted the appointment as soon as he returned home. At the age of forty-three, he was heading to the nation's capital to take the third most prominent position in the cabinet. He excelled at the job during the remaining two years of Taft's presidency, but at a cost; his new position drew him into the center of the escalating quarrel between Roosevelt and Taft, one that spiraled during Stimson's tenure at the War Department into one of the greatest political feuds of the twentieth century.

4

The Making of an Army Legend (1903–1919)

There is a man near genius and if war comes again, which it is going to come, and it will probably be in your time, you can do no better than try to tie yourself to George Marshall.[1]

**—MAJOR GENERAL FOX CONNER's advice to
Dwight Eisenhower shortly after the end of World War I**

When Henry Stimson began winding up his affairs in New York before heading off to Washington to take over the War Department in May 1911, thirty-year-old First Lieutenant George Marshall was between assignments, having spent most of the previous four years in Leavenworth, Kansas, some 1,200 miles west of lower Manhattan and considerably further by just about any other measure.

With each assignment completed by Marshall since leaving the Philippines in 1903, his reputation soared. Whether organizing one of the largest maneuvers among professional soldiers since the Civil War ended (in Texas) or the largest maneuvers ever among militia (in Massachusetts), officers of all ranks were beginning to talk about the special talents the young soldier from Pennsylvania possessed. But the nation was at peace, and during peacetime, promotions in the military proceed at a glacial pace.

Fort Reno (December 1903–August 1906)

After completing his first assignment in the Philippines in November 1903, Marshall spent the next three years based in Fort Reno, an obsolete outpost located in present-day Oklahoma. The fort, founded thirty years earlier to keep an eye on two nearby Native American tribes, was as isolated as many of the places he had been stationed in the Philippines (Oklahoma City, with its ten thousand–plus citizens, was thirty or so miles east of the fort). The new posting was made worse for Marshall given that his wife would spend only a short amount of time with him during it. It is not clear from the historical record when exactly Lily joined him at Fort Reno; what is known is that after Marshall's ship docked in California, he was ordered to go straight there despite having not seen his bride for over two years. It appears she spent little time at the fort for a couple of reasons: First, she suffered from a heart condition (mitral regurgitation), which prevented her from undertaking even mildly strenuous activities; and second, Fort Reno was not exactly an assignment coveted by Army wives. The consequence was that the couple spent less than a week together during their first three years of marriage. Somehow, their regular habit of correspondence, acquired during their first two years apart, kept the relationship going.

Most of the time spent at Fort Reno was routine for Marshall. He served as ordnance officer, engineering officer, commissary officer, and quartermaster at one point or another during his three years there. Although he had a boss who was "exceedingly difficult" to please, the duties were straightforward, giving Marshall a lot of extra time. He typically spent that time hunting.

When soldiers of that era were not spending their time drilling, polishing their boots, or cleaning their barracks, they hunted. Marshall and his colleagues sometimes spent up to ten days at a time camping out on one of the nearby Native American reservations where the game was particularly plentiful. Marshall was an excellent shot, and it only improved during his days in the Oklahoma Territory. Although he found the work from this second posting mostly mundane, Marshall was assigned to one special duty he later claimed to his biographer was the "hardest service" he ever performed in the Army.

In June 1905—halfway through his assignment at Fort Hood—Marshall and a few other selected officers from different locations around the country were asked to help in a mapping exercise the Army was undertaking in southwest Texas. Two thousand square miles were to be mapped by different groups over a three- to four-month period. Arriving at Fort Clark, approximately one hundred miles due west of San Antonio, Marshall was provided with two horses, five men, a wagon pulled by four mules, and twenty-four additional pack mules to take with him as he headed to his assigned starting location thirty miles farther west (close to the border of Mexico).

The area Marshall was responsible for was like a desert, with little if any water and no decent foraging prospects. The temperature, Marshall claimed with doubtful accuracy, rose to as high as 130 degrees Fahrenheit in July as he walked along the railroad tracks counting the sections of rails in order to get an exact measurement. Adding that detail to measurements gained by an odometer on the wheel of the wagon and through the measured pace of his riding, Marshall managed to average ten to fifteen miles per day. When their rations ran out, the men lived off canned meat and bacon. During one stretch, he was without water for eighteen straight hours and had to travel close to fifty miles. Marshall lost thirty-three pounds during the adventure (20 percent of his body weight).

Despite the hardship, his efforts paid off. Superiors told him that his map was not only the best one turned in, but also the only one fully completed. His reward was a four-month leave. He immediately left to see Lily. After reacquainting themselves with one another, the couple returned to Fort Reno in January 1906. A few months later, he was fortunate to be given the opportunity to attend the Infantry and Calvary School at Fort Leavenworth in Kansas. He arrived at the fort in August to begin the most influential assignment of his life.

Fort Leavenworth (August 1906–January 1911)

What Harvard Law School was to Henry Stimson, Fort Leavenworth was to George Marshall. Stimson credited Harvard with revolutionizing his power of thinking. Marshall would say much the same about the Staff College at Fort Leavenworth. It was there that he "learned how to learn."[2] The fort, founded in 1827 on a bluff above the Missouri River in northwestern Kansas, was originally built as an outpost to keep tabs on the Native Americans. It first established itself as a military school for higher education in 1881 under the direction of William T. Sherman of Civil War fame. Sherman was commanding general of the Army at that time and believed officers needed a place to learn and train in a high-quality program. He named it the School of Application for Infantry and Calvary.

Despite Sherman's intentions, the school remained as uninspiring as its name, and, like most Army schools of that era, it was still ruled by the old guard. As such, the program rarely strayed far from the customary practice of routine drills and the memorization of regulations. Mercifully for the students, the school was closed during the Spanish-American War in order that both students and teachers could join the effort. It was Stimson's old boss and mentor, Elihu Root, who reopened the fort as a Staff School as part of the Army War College in 1902, while serving as Teddy Roosevelt's secretary of war. Root was convinced after the poor showing by the Army during the Spanish-American War that the Army needed a general staff, and he pushed a bill through Congress creating one along with an educational system capable of supplying its future members with competent officers.

Root wanted the Army War College used as a training course for those young officers in the Army considered as future candidates for higher command. Although the school was still falling short of Root's full aspirations for it when Marshall arrived in 1906, it had been transformed into a serious training ground for young talent in the discipline of tactics, logistics, and strategy. More importantly, the program focused on solving present problems, not past ones. Root figured if one put a group of highly intelligent officers together, the collective results of their brainstorming could provide novel and useful approaches to overcoming hurdles like those the United States faced when fighting Spain. Understanding Napoleon's tactics at the Battle of Ulm was important, but not as crucial as solving the problems of typhoid, logistics, and coordination that plagued the American Army both on its way to Cuba and once it got there.

The success of Root's vision was largely due to the efforts of three forward-thinking and erudite officers: General James Franklin Bell, Colonel Arthur Wagner, and Major John Morrison. These three men fought against the conventional wisdom of the old guard Army conservatives who believed too much thinking and writing was neither proper for American soldiers nor beneficial.

Bell arrived at Fort Leavenworth in 1903 to take over the responsibilities as commandant. He was a highflier who possessed both a Medal of Honor (for his bravery in the Philippines) and a law degree (picked up while working as a professor of military science). He immediately set out to upgrade the quality of officers coming into the different programs, the instructors there to teach them, and the overall curriculum. One instructor he kept on was Arthur Wagner, a colonel who had taught there for fifteen years. Wagner was a military scholar and a dedicated teacher who, under Bell's leadership, would become critical in shaping the future of how officers were trained.

Morrison, who arrived in 1906, left a huge mark on Army tactics and taught a generation of worshipping students how to solve problems by using common sense and keeping things simple. He changed the teaching paradigm at Fort Leavenworth away from one that relied heavily on straight memorization to one focused on finding practical solutions to problems in realistic situations. Years later, Marshall said of Morrison, "He taught me all I will ever know of tactics."[3]

Together, the three men worked to put in place the type of institution that would raise the quality of Army officers to the high level imagined by Elihu Root. And it was hard to find a young officer better suited to the program than George Marshall. By a combination of fate, timing, and luck (often requisites for success in the military), Marshall was at the right place at the right time when he arrived in Kansas during the summer of 1906.

Getting into the school as a first lieutenant was the first stroke of luck for Marshall. When Bell was promoted to chief of staff in April 1906, he kept a close eye on his special project and, in a continuing effort to improve the school, mandated that only officers with the rank of captain or above could attend the program going forward. Marshall, still eleven years from that rank, was appointed to the school at Fort Leavenworth just months before this edict and was grandfathered in. Had he missed that window, his career path might have gone in a different direction. Characteristic of Marshall, he took full advantage of the good fortune that befell him.

Although Marshall claimed that his ambition was long driven by the derisive remark about him he overheard his brother say to his mother years earlier as they discussed his prospects at the VMI, one might suspect the passage of time would have reduced that incident's motivational powers by the time he arrived at Fort Leavenworth. Whether it did or not, his determination was even further incited shortly after classes began. Apparently, Marshall was quite the eavesdropper, because it was yet another private conversation that he overheard that further stoked his resolve to succeed. Two students were speculating among themselves a few weeks into the program as to which of their classmates were likely to be invited back for a second year (the rule was that only the top half of the class were eligible). To his surprise and consternation, Marshall's name did not come up. This just added fuel to the fire lit by his older brother. He began to study with great intensity and determination, leaving nothing to chance in his quest to attain the top spot in his class. It wasn't enough to be in the top half or even in the top five; he wanted to be number one, and he would say in retirement that he never worked harder in his life than he did during that first year at Fort Leavenworth to achieve that goal.[4]

Marshall did finish first in his class, then repeated the feat the following year. He was beginning to gain a reputation not only among his immediate superiors, but also among his fellow officers. They recognized in Marshall a future leader who was serious, smart, efficient, and driven. General Bell took notice as well and would remember him in the future.

At the end of his two years in the Staff College, Marshall and four other officers were asked to stay on as instructors. This was an honor for all the men, but particularly for Marshall, since as a first lieutenant (he was promoted toward the end of his second year), he would be teaching officers ranked higher than himself. Special permission was required as a result of this unusual situation, and General Bell thought enough of Marshall to grant it. Marshall might not have realized it at the time—or later—but he possessed a unique aptitude for teaching. Alongside judging and managing talented officers, it was perhaps his most impressive skill.

Marshall's distinguishing attribute as a teacher was that he could both teach and inspire men simultaneously. Recalling his own boredom with many subjects as a student, Marshall took extra steps to make sure the subject matter he taught was always interesting. The feedback Marshall received was overwhelmingly positive from students and superiors alike. It was not simply that he could teach and inspire; the students came to recognize that he was also an encyclopedia of military information. Morrison himself said of Marshall that he had "one of the best minds I know."

In nearly every walk of life, good teachers are difficult to find and great ones nearly impossible. Senior brass took notice of Marshall's talent and made sure it was put to good use. Although flattered by the attention he was getting, Marshall had concerns about this. His ambition, like those of other officers, was to command men, not teach them. He was becoming a victim of his own success, and this remained a problem for him right up to the start of World War II.

New York, Texas, Massachusetts, Arkansas, Minnesota, Texas (January 1911–June 1913)

After more than four years anchored at Leavenworth, Marshall requested and was granted a three-month leave to tour Europe with his wife. He extended that leave for a month while there. The couple visited London, Paris, Vienna, Florence, Greece, and Algiers, among other places, enjoying all the sights Lily's health would permit and their budget would allow. Upon their return to America, Marshall spent the next two and a half years float-ing between assignments in Texas, Arkansas, New York, Florida, Minnesota, and Massachusetts.

Of note during this period were the maneuver exercises Marshall helped put together for General Tasker Bliss in the spring of 1912. They involved over seventeen thousand National Guard members from Maine, Vermont, Massachusetts, Connecticut, New York, and New Jersey, along with two thousand–plus regulars. It was during these exercises that Marshall's unique aptitude for planning on a large scale was first noticed. It was also during this assignment that Marshall's name was first brought to the atten-tion of then Secretary of War Henry Stimson (who showed up to observe the last of the maneuvers).[5]

The lessons learned during this massive exercise in moving men and equipment would prove invaluable to Marshall and the country six years later during the First World War, when he helped plan the Cantigny Opera-tion in May 1918, followed by the St. Mihiel and Meuse-Argonne Offensives later that same year. For the remainder of his career, Marshall fought hard for funds to support such large maneuvers during peacetime, recognizing the immense value they brought to the nation during times of war.

Second Assignment in the Philippines (June 1913–May 1916)

After ten years in the United States, Marshall was sent back to the Philip-pines in May 1913 for three additional years under more peaceful and less strenuous circumstances. Despite worries over her health, Lily joined her husband, and the couple experienced a wonderful three-year stay. Although he and his wife enjoyed all the perks and social benefits an officer of his rank were provided during his second assignment to the Philippines, Mar-shall characteristically made the most of his working days by aggressively pursuing any knowledge that could help make him a better leader in the future. He studied all the Filipino battlefields of the recent war with Spain, bringing along with him the official histories, reports, and maps from the United States. Whenever Marshall could enhance his knowledge about best practices in tactics, strategy, or supply line management, he would. There was hardly any information, no matter how trivial, he did not pursue in case there was a chance he might need to understand it in a future war. Marshall was not only the Army's finest teacher; he was also among its best students. His observations covered every aspect of Army life.

Like most great students, Marshall was keenly observant. There is a story William Frye related in his 1947 biography of General Marshall that reveals this quality in him, along with the contempt he felt for anyone who favored form over substance. The story was given to Frye by Johnson Hagood, who, while serving in the Philippines in 1913 as a major, heard a story being passed around about Marshall (whom he did not know) waging and winning an unusual bet involving the outcome of an inspection report. Disbelieving it, but not certain, Hagood headed out to the fort where Marshall was serving to question him about it directly. When confronted with the rumor, Marshall confirmed it and gave him the full version of the episode.

The company Marshall was responsible for was due for an inspection. In discussing with a fellow lieutenant how predictable inspections had become and how useless they were, Marshall made a bet with him that he could predict in advance three faults the inspecting officer would cite in his report. He further bet the lieutenant that he (Marshall) would intentionally make three serious errors in the field exercises (a standard part of the inspection) and none of them would be noticed. His colleague accepted the bet, assuming it was easy money. Marshall then handed him a sealed envelope within which he detailed the three faults the inspector would find along with the three basic tactical blunders he would make that the inspectors would miss.

When the inspection was over, Marshall's colleague unsealed the envelope and compared its contents to the official report. He was astonished. Marshall had correctly identified the three faults that appeared in the report: One soldier was cited for being unshaven; another for having two buttons unbuttoned; and a third for forgetting his bayonet. Further, not one of the three tactical mistakes Marshall intentionally made in the field (which were by no means subtle) appeared in the report.

Hagood, later selected by General John "Black Jack" Pershing to plan and organize the line of communications and service of supply for the Army in France during World War I, was notably impressed and took away two lessons from the episode: First, senior officers should focus on the essentials; and second, George Marshall was someone to keep an eye on. As for Marshall's recollections of the episode, he told biographer Forrest Pogue years later that he regretted the incident. Despite winning the bet and making his point, he had embarrassed a U.S. Army officer, something he was not proud of doing.[6]

Marshall's three years in the Philippines ended in 1916. His service record during this time was brilliant, and his reputation was further elevated after another exercise in maneuvers, this one organized to plan for an attack by the Japanese on the Philippines (something that would actually occur twenty-eight years later). Marshall was named second in command to a detachment of approximately five thousand men asked to carry out an amphibious attack followed by a march on the city of Manila (in reality, he was given command responsibilities by General Bell, given the incompetence of the actual man in charge).

The unit Marshall was attached to was instructed to attack another unit responsible for defending the city. Just before the maneuvers were to begin, the chief of staff of Marshall's detachment got sick. Marshall was asked to formally take over that role, too, even though there were higher-ranked and more senior men available. The man who made the decision was familiar with Marshall and recognized he not only knew the plans better than anyone else, but he was also the right guy for the job. His instincts proved correct; Marshall performed brilliantly.

Henry "Hap" Arnold, who later served under Marshall and was one of four members (including Marshall) of the Joint Chiefs of Staff during the Second World War, was a lieutenant at the time of the maneuvers assigned to the same detachment as his future boss. He had yet to meet Marshall and never forgot his first impression of him when he arrived on the field as Marshall began giving orders to his unit commanders. Lying on his back, staring up at a map pinned on to a tree, Marshall dictated to the men gathered around him the complete orders for the offensive. It was an elaborate plan with multiple components and several distinct sets of instructions for the different commanders in charge of specific tasks. The directives were clear, decisive, and to the point, according to Arnold. More impressive, Marshall delivered them without the use of any notes. When he was finished, no questions were asked, the group went off to their assignments, and the plan was executed just as Marshall designed it. Arnold said to his wife after the exercises ended that he had just met a future chief of staff.[7]

Henry Arnold was not the only person impressed; General Bell, the senior officer in the Philippines at the time (the same General Bell from Leavenworth), told his staff several days after the exercises ended that George Marshall was the greatest potential wartime leader the Army had in its service and he might become "the greatest military genius since Stonewall Jackson."[8] He had only just turned thirty-three years of age.

Utah, California, and New York
(May 1916–June 1917)

Not surprisingly, General Bell named Marshall as his aide-de-camp two years later, when he was named commanding general of the Western Department headquartered in San Francisco. His own experience, coupled with glowing reports from General Hunter Liggett (who took over from Bell in the Philippines and brought Marshall to Manila to serve as his aide), convinced Bell that the second lieutenant would be invaluable to him. Marshall and his wife left the Philippines for California in May 1916.

Bell wanted Marshall to help him prepare the country for war. Although America had successfully avoided the conflagration in Europe for nearly two years, many thought it was only a matter of time before the nation would be drawn in (the *Lusitania* was sunk by the Germans over a year before Marshall left the Philippines).

The first assignment Bell gave to Marshall was to run one of the citizen training camps provided by the National Defense Act of 1916. Modeled after the successful camp opened in 1915 by General Leonard Wood in Plattsburgh, New York (as part of the Preparedness Movement led by Wood, Teddy Roosevelt, Elihu Root, and Henry Stimson), the camp was responsible for preparing and training civilians in the essentials of warfare (Stimson himself spent a month training at the Plattsburgh camp in 1916 at the age of forty-nine). Bell knew there was nobody better suited to the job than Marshall from the standpoint of temperament, experience, and pure competence.

The only problem was that Marshall was still too junior; too many feathers would be ruffled if he was given the job against long-established Army protocol. Bell therefore summoned Lieutenant Colonel Johnson Hagood to his office in San Francisco with a plan in mind. Hagood, one may recall, was the officer who went to visit Marshall in the Philippines to inquire about his inspection report wager. Bell and Hagood knew and liked one another and were both aware how the other felt about Marshall. Bell told Hagood he was not going to put some useless general in charge of one of his camps and he wanted him to command instead. Hagood was unable to suppress his excitement until Bell continued by commenting that Hagood should not be "too much puffed up about that," because he was sending Marshall along to be his adjutant. Bell then said to Hagood he had chosen him to run the camp "because I knew you had sense enough to let Marshall run it." Both men laughed, realizing it was a perfect way around the problem of putting a second lieutenant in charge of a major training camp.

Marshall reported to the camp (Fort Douglas in Utah) in August 1916, shortly after getting promoted to captain. His job was to train a group of eight hundred men between the ages of twenty-one and forty, most of whom were successful enough in their professions (law, medicine, finance, education, business) to be able to take off a month of work at their own expense.

These men were in for a treat. Captain Marshall gave them the best of what he had absorbed from Superintendent Shipp at the Virginia Military Institute; Bell, Wagner, and Morrison at Fort Leavenworth; and his own experiences. Despite the intensity of the program, the men remained enthusiastic to learn more and formally requested further instruction. When told there was not extra time in the program, the men insisted they receive it after hours.

As Hagood was filling out the annual efficiency report on Marshall after the first year, he came to the standard question asked toward the end of such reports during that era: "Would you desire to have him under your immediate command in peace and in war?" In what one historian speculated could be the greatest tribute ever made in the United States Army from a senior officer to a junior one, Hagood answered:

> *Yes, but I would prefer to serve under his command. . . . In my judgment there are not five officers in the Army as well-qualified as he to command a division in the field. . . . He should be made a brigadier general in the Regular Army and every day that this is postponed is a loss to the Army and the nation. [He is] the best officer in the Army below the grade of major, and there are not six better in any grade.*[9]

It was not the first time one of Marshall's superiors answered that question by similarly turning it around. His commander in the Philippines, Captain E. J. Williams, replied to the same question in his report on Marshall for the year 1914 by stating he "would be glad to serve under *him*." It is hard to overstate the impression Marshall made on his superiors, and it once again begs the question of how it was possible that such a high-quality soldier in the United States Army with Marshall's experience and record could not be fast-tracked to a higher rank. If there was even a remote resemblance of how the Army promoted its superstars in comparison to the corporate, banking, or law fields, Marshall would certainly have been—at the age of thirty-six—among the top guys in late 1917, a few short months before America entered World War I. But as we learned earlier, seniority was nearly the sole driver of promotions in the United States Army during peacetime. It took Marshall fourteen years from the time he entered the Army to when he attained the modest rank of captain in July 1917. This frustrated him; he believed he was wasting his most productive years. In 1914, Marshall considered leaving the Army, but he was talked out of it by one of his mentors.

When General Bell was transferred to run the Eastern Department in January 1917, he brought Marshall with him, and like every ambitious young officer at that time, Marshall became focused on one objective: to make sure he'd have a role to play in Europe in case America entered the Great War. He was confident that if given the opportunity, he would excel and gain a promotion that otherwise might elude him in peacetime.

President Woodrow Wilson gave him a shot. Angered with Germany's resumption of unrestricted submarine warfare in early 1917 and shocked by that nation's attempted machinations with Mexico (learned when he received a copy of the Zimmermann Telegram), Wilson asked Congress to declare war on Germany in April. Two months later, Marshall was assigned to Major General William Sibert, who commanded the 1st Division. Days after receiving his orders, he was on the first ship of the first convoy carrying American troops to Europe. In fact, of the two million–plus Americans who made their way to Europe over the next two years, Marshall would be the second man ashore in Europe after General Sibert.

World War I (June 1917–April 1919)

When one studies the American entry into the Great War (as World War I would be referred to until the start of World War II), it is hard to believe how unprepared the United States Army was for it. As Marshall said years later, 80 percent of the men in service were not soldiers by any definition of the word.[10] There were no weapons awaiting the men upon their arrival to France, and when they did finally arrive, many of the officers were unfamiliar with them.

The euphoria of the French people greeting the Americans upon their arrival was embarrassing to General Pershing and the rest of the top brass since they realized it would be a long time before their troops would be able to add any real value to the overall effort. Massive training had to be undertaken to teach the men the essentials of soldiering learned by the French and British over the previous three years of fighting. Digging and living in trenches, throwing hand grenades, manning machine guns, and defending against poisonous gas would be new concepts not only to the soldiers but also to their officers. It took nearly nine long months from their declaration of war on Germany before the Americans felt they were finally ready to fight.

Once in Europe, Marshall took complete charge of the training for the 1st Division, picking up where he left off at Fort Douglas a few months earlier, but obviously with an increased intensity. The stakes were high for Marshall given that the 1st Division would be the first to see action against the Germans and its performance was critical in reinforcing Pershing's arguments with the French and British that American soldiers should only be fighting under the command of American officers.

Marshall trained the soldiers relentlessly in the months leading up to their initial engagement (January 1918). Pershing, commander of the American Expeditionary Forces, kept a close eye on the training, not only because the 1st Division would be the first to fight, but also because he suspected Marshall's boss, General Sibert, was incompetent (an opinion Marshall did not share).

It was during one of Pershing's reviews in October 1917 that Marshall revealed that rare combination of courage, conviction, confidence, and competence that added immeasurably to his legend. Pershing had been reviewing a demonstration Marshall arranged of a new technique for attacking entrenched troops. Upon completion of the demonstration, Pershing asked General Sibert to critique the exercise. Almost as soon as Sibert opened his mouth, Pershing proceeded to harshly criticize him and the division's general lack of preparedness in front of all the other officers. This went on for several minutes. Once Pershing finished his tirade, Marshall began to protest, incensed at the injustice shown by the commanding general. When Pershing ignored him and started to walk away, Marshall grabbed his arm and said with authority, "General Pershing, there is something to be said here, and I think I should say it because I have been here longest." Pershing stopped suddenly, glared at Marshall, and curtly asked him to say what was on his mind. In what Marshall would later say was an "inspired moment," he quickly and concisely detailed a long list of facts in defense of the 1st Division and its commanders, explaining the numerous difficulties they had encountered and the realities they faced.

Marshall's fellow officers were stunned by what they were witnessing and believed he had abruptly thrown away his career. But he wasn't even finished. While contemptuously walking away from Marshall, Pershing grumbled under his breath that everyone should appreciate the troubles the Army was having. Marshall, still hot under the collar, did not let Pershing get in the last word, replying tersely, "Yes, General, but we have them every day and they have to be solved before night."[11]

Fortunately for George Marshall, he had picked the right commander to stand up to; Pershing would become well-known during the First World War for his ability to seek and accept constructive criticism. Doubtlessly impressed with Marshall's command of both the situation and the problems facing the 1st Division, Pershing took special notice of Marshall from that day forward and sought him out whenever he made his rounds.

Pershing's opinion of Sibert did not change, and he replaced him two months later with General Robert Bullard. Marshall reacted strongly once again by making it generally known to Pershing's staff that Sibert's dismissal was unjust. This time he paid for his outburst; upon hearing about Marshall's comments, Bullard decided that such a quality was not consistent with what he wanted in a chief of staff, a position he was more than likely going to give to Marshall. Although he never mastered his temper, Marshall understood the need to control it and learned over time to deliver more measured responses when his dander was up. He continued his role as head of operations, and both Pershing and Bullard insisted that he double his efforts to get the men ready. The 1st Division was going to begin fighting in January 1918.

For the next six months, Marshall carried out his own duties along with those that were the responsibility of General Bullard (who was suffering from a painful case of neuritis in the shoulder that prevented him from taking an active a role in the War). Marshall worked tirelessly as the 1st Division assisted the French in holding back a German assault in March and then undertook an offensive of its own in May in the tiny French village of Cantigny (the first major offensive by the Americans during the War). The effort proved successful, and although it provided little strategic value to the overall Allied effort, it boosted morale. It also gave the French confidence that the Americans could be trusted to hold the line against the Germans. Marshall was largely responsible for planning the offensive at Cantigny, drawing heavily on his training experiences in Massachusetts and later the Philippines.

St. Mihiel and the Grand Offensive

After a year with the 1st Division, Marshall was ordered to report to General Headquarters in July 1918 to work in the Operations Division. He was not pleased; everyone knew that promotions were prioritized for those who distinguished themselves on the battlefield. He tried hard to get such an assignment (making a formal request),[12] but he failed. The top brass knew Marshall's talents as a staff officer were rare and believed that the greater good of the Army would be served if he took a leading staff role. Marshall arrived as ordered to General Headquarters in the French city of Chaumont in mid-July just as the last major German offensive of the war stalled.

With a weakened German Army slowly retreating and enough American troops ready to fight on the southern flank of the Western Front, the French and English wanted to quickly launch a major offensive but couldn't agree with Pershing on an overall plan. Marshal Ferdinand Foch, in command of both the French and English armies since the spring of 1918, proposed a swift and broad attack northeast from the Meuse-Argonne sector and wished to embed American troops in with the French. Pershing, ever sensitive to the independence of the American Army and fully cognizant of the increasing leverage his growing army was giving him, rejected the request. He wanted instead to personally lead his troops in attacking a sizable force of Germans in Lorraine that held gains in an area that protruded out from an otherwise flat front (referred to as the St. Mihiel salient).

Attacking the St. Mihiel salient was an idea Foch had supported earlier, but under different circumstances, when the Germans appeared stronger. Sensing German vulnerability, Foch now thought it better to strike across a broader front. Unable to gain Pershing's acceptance, Foch had little choice but to forge a compromise. He agreed Pershing could go ahead with the St. Mihiel attack, but as soon the salient was reduced, he wanted him to move his forces to an area between the Meuse River and the Argonne Forest and then join the general Allied offensive across all German lines. Foch wanted this attack to begin by the end of September 1918 (the start of what would be referred to as the "Grand Offensive" or the "Hundred Days Offensive"). Pershing agreed, and the arrangement between the two men was finalized on September 3, 1918. The major offensive was scheduled for September 26. In the twenty-three days between those dates, the Americans had to plan their assault on St. Mihiel, execute the plan, win the battle, and then immediately move sixty miles to reorganize their positions along the sector assigned to them by Foch.

The American planners at Chaumont were burdened with the thankless task of quickly producing two full sets of offensive battle plans along with a plan on moving the Army from the St. Mihiel salient—once the German bulge was successfully reduced—to the twenty-four-mile sector of the front assigned to them by Foch.

Marshall, promoted to colonel just days earlier, went into overdrive, working closely with Brigadier General Fox Conner, considered to be among the great thinkers of the Army during the twentieth century (and a major influence on both Marshall and Dwight Eisenhower). Although Marshall made valuable contributions to both the planning of the St. Mihiel Offensive and the primary offensive, it was his work on the hugely complex movement of troops from the first sector to the second that helped further cement his reputation as a logistics genius and earned him the wartime nickname "Wizard." If he left the Army after World War I, Marshall would still be remembered today by military historians for this logistical triumph.

The American Army's strike on the St. Mihiel salient was more successful than is indicated by the thirteen thousand casualties it suffered during it. The German Army might have been demoralized and weakened, but they could still fight. By the time the Americans accomplished their goal and finished securing the last of the sixteen thousand captured prisoners, there were exactly ten days before the Grand Offensive was to start. Before then, Marshall had to move no less than four hundred thousand tired troops, ninety thousand exhausted horses and mules, three thousand guns, and forty thousand tons of ammunition to their assigned position sixty miles away.

The troops who had just fought on the line would be aggregated with reserves that had stayed behind them and a few others from nearby parts of France. There were three roads Marshall could send them on, but they had to be shared with French and Italian troops moving in the opposite direction. This further complicated an already trying task.

Naturally, much of the planning by Marshall was done prior to the start of the St. Mihiel battle, but the fortunes of war seldom allow plans to be realized perfectly, and this was one of those occasions. As the first battle evolved, new plans and orders had to be drawn up by Marshall and issued to the men detailing how and when they would move from their position when the first battle ended to where they should be when the larger offensive started.

Even though both Foch and Pershing strongly doubted the maneuver could be pulled off before the start of the main battle, Marshall managed to get every man, animal, weapon, and crate of ammo in place one day earlier than Foch thought was even possible. It was a prodigious effort, and to anyone who previously dismissed the rumors attributed to Marshall's unusual logistical talents as hyperbole, his feat proved otherwise. His earlier performances in planning the New England peacetime maneuvers of 1912 and the mock invasion of the Philippines in 1914 were no fluke; Marshall was a master planner and organizer.

The exalted thirty-eight-year-old captain was recognized and rewarded for his efforts by earning the position of chief of operations for the First Army. Working closely with Colonel Hugh Drum, chief of staff of the First Army, Marshall spent the remainder of the War advising General Pershing and handling the complex logistical problems created by the American Army's rapid advances on the front.

The Great War ended quickly once the Grand Offensive kicked into high gear, a little too quickly for Marshall's sake. Pershing had placed him on a list for promotion to brigadier general a month before the armistice was signed, but Congress decided to wait until the main offensive ended before acting on any promotions. But when it did end, so, too, did the War, along with the desire of Congress to award any more temporary promotions. Pershing gave the bad news to Marshall on November 29. Where his timing and luck had been often good in the past, it failed Marshall on this occasion. He would have to wait eighteen more years to become a general. Worse for Marshall was the fact that many of his peers, including those who entered the war junior in rank to him, got their stars during the War by commanding troops in the field.

Marshall was crushed. He enjoyed the attention he was receiving in France, the important responsibilities given to him following the armistice, and the high regard Pershing and the other top brass had for him, but seeing stars sewn on other men's shoulders cut him to the core. When one considers the number of men with lesser records who were given promotions ahead of him, it is shocking that he even decided to stay in the Army.

But Marshall did stay, and following the armistice he was given a variety of assignments that varied between training men, planning for an invasion of Germany (if negotiations broke down in Paris), preparing Pershing's formal report on the war, and building up the morale of the many disgruntled troops still waiting to get home. In this latter task, Marshall had to address the complaints of men not only impatient to leave Europe, but also frustrated at having to endure unnecessary training, paperwork, and inspections given by overzealous Army bureaucrats. The lessons he learned during this period helped guide him years later when the United States was demobilizing after World War II.

After five months helping solve these and other problems stemming from the end of the War, Marshall and members of Pershing's immediate staff were invited by the national hero of France, Marshal Petain, to Metz to receive the French Legion of Honor of Distinguished Service (one of several honors Marshall received from European governments). It was while in Metz that General Pershing asked Marshall to be his aide-de-camp. Given the high honor of the offer, Marshall immediately accepted. He spent the next five years in this role (one of the longest assignments of his career).

Although he would become the principal advisor and right-hand man to the most celebrated hero in America since Ulysses Grant, had opportunities to meet with many of the world's political and military leaders, and was an active participant at the highest level of discussions in the Army, Marshall would later insist that this five-year assignment handicapped his career due to the time it took him away from direct command experience. Perhaps this is true, but the hand of fate plays a role in any profession, and the career path Marshall followed for the next twenty years ultimately led him to the highest post the Army had to offer at the most critical time one could possibly assume it. It seemed to work out for him.

5

Secretary of War to Colonel in the Artillery (1911–1918)

I told him that I preferred to use a big gun rather than a little gun. When I had to deal a blow, I believed in striking hard.[1]

—SECRETARY OF WAR HENRY STIMSON on how he planned to court-martial Adjutant General Frederick Ainsworth in 1912

Every man owes to his country not only to die for her, if necessary, but also to spend a little of his life in learning how to die for her effectively.[2]

—HENRY STIMSON, address before the Republican Club, February 15, 1915

As the First World War wound down, fifty-one-year-old Henry Stimson was a colonel in charge of the 31st Artillery at Camp Meade in Maryland. He had returned from France three months earlier after commanding a battalion at the southern end of the front. How it came to be that a leading Wall Street lawyer and former secretary of war on the back side of fifty ended up commanding an artillery regiment during World War I speaks to the general character of Henry Stimson, his need to serve his country, his love for the Army, and his desire to continually challenge himself and make a difference.

Five years earlier, in 1913, Stimson's term as the nation's forty-fifth secretary of war came to an end when Woodrow Wilson moved into the White House following his victory over President Taft and third-party candidate,

Teddy Roosevelt. Given the contributions Stimson made to the War Department during the Taft administration, and the overall lessons he learned and successfully applied years later during his second stint as secretary of war, it is worth exploring the position in detail, its evolution leading up to Stimson's first appointment, and some of the figures who had the greatest impact in collectively shaping it—and by extension, the U.S. Army—up to the time Stimson first took it over in May 1911.

The Office of Secretary of War

The secretary of war was one of just four department heads named to the original cabinet by President George Washington at the start of his first term in office in 1789 (the other three headed the Departments of State, Treasury, and Justice). The concept of having a cabinet was only alluded to briefly in the Constitution in Article II, Section 2, which stated the president "may require the Opinion, in writing, of the principal Officer in each of the executive Departments, upon any subject relating to the Duties of their respective Offices." Nowhere did the Constitution cover any further details on the size, functions, or leadership of any of the executive departments.

There were forty-four secretaries of war before Henry Stimson was appointed in 1911. Few of them stood out. In the defense of those who failed to make an impact, they did not have much support. Americans up to that point had long been averse to war, the military in general, and any type of standing army in peacetime.

Even during times of war, the nation has looked upon the Army and its leaders with a healthy degree of suspicion. This distrust, inherited from the British and promoted by the great philosophers of the seventeenth and eighteenth centuries, was evident during the Revolution and following it, when the founders began framing a new constitution. When James Madison was speaking to his fellow Virginians during the ratification process, he expressed doubt that there was a single member of the Federal Convention who felt anything but "indignation" at the thought of a standing army (he somehow failed to consider the convention's president, George Washington, who definitely thought that having at least a small one was desirable).[3]

There were two other factors that worked against the establishment of a standing army after the Revolutionary War: The first derived from the mistaken belief that citizen soldiers were largely responsible for beating King George III's troops and could be called up again to defend the nation in a time of need; the second was that Americans generally felt safe from a political and geographical standpoint. Few feared Canada or Mexico, and nearly everyone believed that the oceans on either side of the continent formed an adequate first line of defense against any real threats (which is why the Navy was generally given priority when it came to military resources).

As a result of all these factors, the War Department did not attract the "great men" of the day who preferred the prestige of the State Department or the power of the Treasury Department. George Washington, deeply cognizant of the precedents he set daily while serving his first term as president, helped dictate the general pecking order of the four departments by naming Thomas Jefferson and Alexander Hamilton to lead the State and Treasury Departments respectively, while appointing lesser-known Henry Knox to the War Department.

Three occupants of the office prior to Stimson's first appointment in 1911 have been more recognized by history than others based on the merit of their contributions; two in the nineteenth century, and one in the twentieth; one who presided during a war, and two others who left their mark during peace. It is worth summarizing their accomplishments.

John Calhoun (served from 1817 to 1825)

John Calhoun is best remembered today as part of the "Great Triumvirate," a trio of statesmen (the other two being Daniel Webster and Henry Clay) who dominated the U.S. Senate during the first half of the nineteenth century.

Serving primarily as a senator from South Carolina, with stints as a congressman, secretary of war, vice president, and secretary of state, Calhoun was known as a brilliant intellectual with intense focus, great vision, a notable work ethic, impressive organizational skills, original ideas, and legendary inflexibility. Calhoun practiced law before coming into the House of Representatives in 1810, just shy of his twenty-ninth birthday. Within a couple years, he became nationally famous as a leader of the "War Hawks," a group of congressmen who demanded war against Great Britain as a point of honor (given the way the British were generally treating the United States at that time). James Monroe appointed him secretary of war shortly after the end of the War of 1812, a war that revealed far more weaknesses in the Army than strengths.

Calhoun was just thirty-five years old when he took over the War Department, and he knew nothing about war or soldiering. But he knew the Army needed urgent reform (it was little changed since the end of the Revolutionary War), and he went to work immediately educating himself on all matters pertaining to the military profession in general and the U.S. Army specifically. With as sharp an intellect as any politician of his era and working up to fourteen hours a day with his staff of approximately thirty-six clerks, Calhoun became enough of an expert in the field within three months to begin confronting the multitude of problems, both large and small, unaddressed since Yorktown.[4]

Calhoun had two primary goals: first, to rid the nation's reliance on the militia by creating an army of professional skilled soldiers capable of protecting the frontiers of the country as well as its seacoasts; and second, to centralize control over the operations of the Army in a manner that formally separated the duties of the fighting men (the line) from those who supported them (the staff). The challenges he faced in pursuing these goals and the results he secured are worth exploring, as the changes he implemented influenced all his successors, including Stimson.

To get the country and its leaders to accept the need for a professional army, Calhoun stressed the multitude of advantages to America that one would have: a standardized training program for soldiers; an army more skillful at fighting wars; and a potential boost to the nation's economic growth during peace by having the Army building the roads and canals that could carry the country's goods. Calhoun also aggressively promoted the concept that regardless of absolute size, a larger proportion of the Army should be made up of professionals. It would be these soldiers who could train and manage the citizen soldiers quickly pouring into the ranks during a time of war (this concept, first promoted by Alexander Hamilton, was eventually adopted).[5]

Calhoun moved on a parallel basis to push other initiatives designed to accomplish the same goal. Certain that West Point needed to be vastly improved (when many in Congress wanted to shut it down), Calhoun appointed Sylvanus Thayer, an engineering expert, to the post of superintendent. Thayer, known today as the father of the U.S. Military Academy, went on to reinvent West Point, turning it into a nineteenth-century engineering juggernaut that helped realize Calhoun's dream of having the Army assist in building up the country's infrastructure during peacetime while constructing the fortifications and coastline defenses necessary to defend the nation during war.

Calhoun also spearheaded several other major changes to further his larger goal of professionalizing the U.S. military. Special training schools were first set up under his watch, schools that taught specific skills (such as artillery) to entire units. He also believed a professional army needed a clear chain of command at the top, and so he created the position of senior officer of the United States Army, a job that eventually evolved into the chief of staff position held by George Marshall during the Second World War. The senior officer, Calhoun determined, would lead the Army in the field during war.

While creating the beginnings of a professional army, Calhoun also started the process of separating the "line" versus the "staff" functions within the Army. The general staff organization, largely unchanged since the Revolutionary War, was hopelessly disorganized and proved incompetent when it most mattered (there had been a breakdown in the supply system during both the War of 1812 and the First Seminole War). This, coupled with a failure by civilian contractors to adequately supply rations to the troops on the field during these conflicts, led Calhoun to conclude that the Army could only rely on itself to properly support its soldiers in an efficient and timely manner. The reorganization he undertook to accomplish this task remained largely unchanged through the balance of the nineteenth century, until Elihu Root's reforms at the dawn of the twentieth.

The general theory behind Calhoun's proposed changes was simple: The skills of a good fighter were different than those of a competent administrator. Toward this, he reorganized the department into a system of six bureaus, each created for a specific aspect of logistical support: for example, the quartermaster general was responsible for clothing, equipment, transportation, and housing; the commissary general for food; the chief of ordnance for weapons and ammunition; and the surgeon general for health-related services. Through the rest of the nineteenth century, other bureaus were added, each to provide a specific support function to the fighting men in the field. The chiefs of each bureau were to remain in office permanently.

As visionary as Calhoun was, he failed to predict that the new structure would lead to as many problems as it solved and become the bane of future War Department heads for a century. During Stimson's first assignment as secretary of war, he sought to ensure that Calhoun's legacy was largely put to rest after it somehow managed to survive Elihu Root's attempt to kill it in 1903. Even so, elements of it managed to survive until the start of World War II.

The ambitious Calhoun left the Department in 1825 and remained a powerful figure in the United States as the spiritual and intellectual leader of the pro-Southern, pro-slavery, states rights wing of the Democratic Party until his death in 1850.

Edwin M. Stanton (served from 1862 to 1865)

Abraham Lincoln appointed Edwin Stanton to the position in January 1862, nine months into the Civil War. Lincoln chose the forty-seven-year-old Stanton for the same reasons FDR chose Henry Stimson eighty years later: He was among the most talented lawyers in the nation, with a prodigious work ethic and unquestioned integrity. Stanton was also a Democrat, and Lincoln, like FDR in 1940, wanted to send a message to Americans—and Europeans—that the effort to save the Union was bipartisan. Although Stanton acquired plenty of critics during his tenure at the War Department (and historians have had mixed opinions of him since), he more than met the challenge and was extremely well thought of by the man he reported to in the White House.

Interestingly, the parallels between Stanton and Stimson go beyond their professions, competence, integrity, and diligence: Both had fathers who were successful physicians and absent during much of their childhood; both served as prosecuting attorneys; both were involved in some of the greatest corporate legal cases of their respective eras; and both believed the law was sacred, was critical to a civilized world, and should reflect divine law as closely as possible.

As for their public careers, both Stanton and Stimson had previously been strong critics of the presidents who eventually appointed them, occasionally let the high stakes and urgency of war take precedence over the constitutional rights of individuals, and could be blunt to the point of being rude.

Stanton, raised in Ohio, had a meteoric rise to prominence in the legal field through raw intelligence, a take-no-prisoners approach, and an insane work ethic. As the reputation of the Pittsburgh-based lawyer grew (he moved there in 1847 after practicing for a dozen years in Ohio), so did the importance of his cases. Soon, the Midwest became too small for his ambitions, prompting him to move to the nation's capital to take on the legal profession's elite in arguing the big cases of the day, many of them in front of the Supreme Court.

After enhancing his reputation further in Washington, President James Buchanan appointed him attorney general. Buchanan hoped Stanton could come up with a few creative, last-minute legal solutions that could save the Union (it was a little late; on the day he took over the Justice Department, South Carolina seceded). Other than keeping Lincoln briefed to help him prepare for his presidency, there was not much Stanton could do in the final ten weeks of the Buchanan administration. Lincoln, both grateful to and impressed by the patriotic lawyer, named him secretary of war in January 1862 after his first pick failed to impress.

Stanton wasted no time in prosecuting the war. During his first thirty days, he dispensed with incompetent and corrupt military leaders; dealt with the mess left behind by his predecessor regarding contracts for clothing, supplies, and weapons; and urged Lincoln (who needed no arm twisting) to issue General War Order No. 1 ordering the military to move on the enemy by February 22, 1862.[6] This latter order was aimed directly at George McClellan, commanding general of the Army of the United States, who, despite being a brilliant organizer, a master of logistics, and extremely popular with his men, was hesitant to engage the enemy.

Stanton's tenure as secretary can be best characterized as one of focus and energy. From a stand-up desk, Stanton labored punishing hours with no regard to his health and even less regard to the feelings of others (including Lincoln). His overall conduct during the Civil War, particularly how he worked with Lincoln to prosecute it, set a precedent for his wartime successors, including Henry Stimson.

After the war ended, Stanton remained in office under President Andrew Johnson for three years. Although Stanton made considerable efforts during this time to bring about organizational changes in the Army, the timing was not right, as the energies of the country were focused on healing and rebuilding. It would take thirty years, another war, and another respected corporate lawyer to finally bring about the sweeping changes required.

Elihu Root (served from 1899–1904)

Elihu Root's reputation as an expert in organizing a modern army spread well beyond the borders of America after the turn of the twentieth century. A newly appointed war secretary in the British government remarked to a friend in 1906 that his own qualifications were immaterial to his new assignment given that Root's reports written as secretary of war for the United States were the "very last word concerning the organization and place of an army in a democracy."[7]

Between Stanton and Root, thirteen men served as secretary of war. Just one is remotely remembered today and only because he was the sole living child of the martyred sixteenth president. To be fair to Robert Todd Lincoln and the other twelve men, once the Civil War ended, the chances of bringing about change to an increasingly disorganized army were slim. After losing six hundred thousand men during the conflict, the American people were hostile to anything associated with the military. Even Congress during the postwar era, despite being flush with veterans from both sides, had surprisingly little interest in supporting the Army. The disdain to which their constituents held the military generally trumped any sentimental or loyal attachment they themselves had to the armed forces.

This attitude began to change by the time President William McKinley asked Root to be his secretary of war in the summer of 1899. The abysmal performance displayed by the Army during the Spanish-American War was highly publicized and awakened many legislators to the problems inherent in its current organization. McKinley must have thought that having a sharp lawyer in the office would benefit the Army as it sought to reorganize itself.

Root was such a man, and the impact he made by establishing the General Staff alone was such that a later successor (Newton Baker, secretary of war during World War I) called the move the "outstanding contribution by any secretary of war from the beginning of history."[8] To appreciate Root's true impact, one has to appreciate the state of the Army in 1899. It had little changed since the Civil War.

As with the end of most of the major wars fought by the United States, demobilization after the Civil War was both quick and substantial. Within eight months of Lee's surrender to Grant, the Army reduced its numbers by more than 95 percent from over one million men to fifty thousand (further cuts in 1876 left an authorized force of just twenty-seven thousand, a number that remained in place until the Spanish-American War twenty years later).

It was not just the general antimilitary and antiwar sentiment that kept the Army small; the country continued to believe that given its geographical position, there was little justification for a large standing land force in the late nineteenth century. The Army therefore went back to its peacetime management structure, the one established by Calhoun after the War of 1812. Calhoun's structure evolved poorly following the Civil War and was bifurcated and rudderless by the time Root inherited the War Department in 1899.

There were three separate bases of power within the Army during the second half of the nineteenth century that evolved since the Calhoun reorganization in the 1820s, each of which struggled for authority with the others: At the top, in theory, stood the secretary of war; below him was the commanding general (referred to prior to 1821 as the senior officer of the United States Army and after 1903 as the chief of staff); and then there were the heads of the bureaus who also reported directly to the secretary of war.

Unique to the United States during the nineteenth century was that during war, authority and control over the Army shifted dramatically. The commanding general, largely a figurehead during peace, became the center of power when the fighting started. But once the time of war ended, his position reverted to one lacking any authority outside of training, discipline, and a few other specific military matters. There were no administrative and supply responsibilities and no planning function residing in the office.

Real power during peacetime belonged to the bureau heads. Former officers, these men became career bureaucrats once they were assigned to the tenured jobs within the various Washington-based bureaus (Quartermaster, Commissary, Pensions, Ordnance, Paymaster, etc.). Although the secretary of war was responsible for the bureau heads on paper, he held little influence over them from a practical standpoint. This was because the bureau heads had control over supply contracts and the location of bases, critical to politicians who fought for the benefit of their constituents to secure such contracts and to play host to such bases. Moreover, being permanently assigned to Washington gave the bureau heads plenty of time to gain further influence with key congressmen leaving the shorter-tenured secretary of war politically neutralized.

Elihu Root, like the others before him, understood these realities and took on the thankless task of overhauling the entire structure. For the veteran New York lawyer, the challenge was akin to a new case, albeit one from what he referred to as the "greatest" of possible clients, the U.S. government.[9] Root brought his Wall Street work ethic to a War Department accustomed to a considerably more relaxed environment. Driving his staff equally hard, Root began an elaborate and brilliantly conceived campaign to bring about major changes in small but forceful steps. Gathering dust-covered papers written by forward-thinking U.S. officers over the years detailing the best practices from Europe, Root buried himself in research. He interviewed as many experts as he could locate. At the same time, he lobbied senators, congressmen, and the press, explaining clearly the problems of the Army and how they could be solved.

Four months into the job, Root laid out his core philosophies in the Annual Report that was delivered each year by the secretary of war to Congress. Up until Root released his first report in December 1899, such reports were extremely dull and predictable papers. Root set out to make his first one not only readable and interesting, but also revolutionary. In it, Root promoted meritocracy over seniority regarding promotions, an Army War College for advanced training, a formalization in the way plans were made for war, and more large-scale war games. More importantly, he dropped the first of what were several strong hints about the creation of a General Staff in charge of planning, strategy, and policy execution controlled by a newly created chief of staff. Root knew it was too soon to move on these latter two initiatives, but he wanted to plant the seed.[10]

Eventually Root was able to persuade the government that the U.S. Army needed a centralized organizational structure under one chief of staff reporting through the secretary of war to the president. The chief of staff would be responsible for planning, training, and overseeing the various bureaus that provided all the requirements of a modern army. Henry Stimson believed the passage of the General Staff Act (the act that launched Root's restructuring) was one of the two or three great achievements of the "ablest man he ever knew."

In their biography of Secretary of the Navy James Forrestal, historians Townsend Hoopes and Douglas Brinkley credited Root with cementing and instilling within the Army—through his effort at reorganizing it—the philosophy of civilian over military control. By establishing a chief of staff subordinate to the secretary of war by law, Root laid down a foundation that was gradually accepted throughout the Army by the time World War II began. By contrast, the authors pointed out, the U.S. Navy never had such a reorganization. As a result, there was tension between the civilian and military authorities within the Navy during both World Wars.[11]

Although Root's major accomplishment of centralizing the leadership of the Army in the chief of staff did not translate to a complete change in the Army in the years following his departure, his protégé and former law partner would make sure to finish the job when he became secretary of war seven years later.

Stimson Enters the War Department

On May 22, 1911, Henry Stimson officially took over the War Department, moving into his office at the State, War, and Navy Building (now called the Eisenhower Executive Office Building). This French Second Empire–style building, located approximately one hundred feet from the West Wing of the White House, was less than twenty-five years old when Stimson became secretary of war (to give some perspective to the longevity of Stimson's public career, the building was designated a National Historic Landmark less than twenty-five years after he concluded his second stint at the War Department in 1945).

Although Stimson's public career continued for another twenty-eight years between leaving the War Department in 1912 and reentering it in 1940, the lessons he learned during his first stint were critical in preparing him for his second. He learned how an army works within a democracy and how to achieve the proper balance between civilian and military authority while making sure the former ultimately prevailed. He also got to test his skills in working with powerful figures both within and outside the military and—more importantly—learned when and how to take them on when he believed it was necessary. Above all, he familiarized himself with the challenges of how to lead a huge and complex organization.

Despite the prodigious efforts of Elihu Root a decade earlier, the army Stimson inherited in May 1911 was still disorganized, wasteful, inwardly focused, and plagued by internal power struggles. The three men who occupied the office between Root and Stimson were neither strong nor interested enough to hold the ground taken by Root, much less advance it. When the first of these (William H. Taft) began turning his attention to matters of the Department, he fell under the spell of Major General Fred Ainsworth, the powerful and well-connected adjunct general. To keep the peace between the General Staff and bureau heads, Taft restricted the activities of the General Staff to purely military matters and instructed the bureau heads to report directly to the secretary of war on non-military matters. With no pressure from the top to see that Root's hard-fought achievements remained in place, the bureau heads found it easier to circumvent the General Staff Act and retain their long-held powers.

To be fair to Taft and Stimson's other two predecessors, trying to effect change within a peacetime army is near impossible. President Ulysses Grant, making general comments about the War Department a decade after the Civil War ended, wrote that the only time it was at peace was "when it was at war."[12] During war, a common enemy exists against which everyone can rally. In peacetime, the energies and talents of many officers require an outlet, and they are usually directed toward non-military affairs, particularly in a democracy, where peace brings retrenchment and internal battles over reduced resources. Such an environment creates a breeding ground for all the negative characteristics of bureaucracies. They spread like a mold, and the longer peace lasts, the more difficult they become to remove. Except for the four-month conflict with Spain thirteen years before Stimson took over the War Department, America had been at relative peace for over forty-five years. Lethargic bureaucracies are created in far less time, and their worst features become more institutionalized with every passing year. For this principal reason, the objectives Root fought for in creating the general staff and the position of chief of staff were not fully realized in the years between his exit and his protégé's arrival. Henry Stimson would change things.

The Ainsworth Affair

Leading all others in defending the status quo as Stimson entered the War Department was the adjunct general, Major General Fred Ainsworth. Despite Ainsworth's long tenure in office, formidable power, considerable achievements, and well-connected friends, Henry Stimson immediately put him in his crosshairs. He was aware that Ainsworth opposed nearly every progressive measure going back to Root's term as secretary of war, and if he stayed in place, nothing could be achieved.

Such was Ainsworth's power that Stimson knew he needed a convincing excuse to take him on and force him out of the Army. He therefore waited patiently for an opportunity. Ainsworth himself provided one not long after Stimson's arrival. The story behind Stimson's victory over Ainsworth is worth touching upon because it reveals much about the former's strength, courage, fearlessness, and overall abilities.

Ainsworth, a former surgeon, was put in charge of the Bureau of Records and Pensions during Grover Cleveland's first administration (when Henry Stimson was still an undergraduate at Yale). Within a year of his appointment, he revolutionized the way information was collected in his department using a brilliant card index system he devised. The impact was impressive; his office could respond to a request from a congressman about a specific veteran inside of a single day where it previously took months. The rest of his career was a study in how to skillfully acquire and retain immense power, one that would be worthy of historian Robert Caro's treatment.

Through his abilities and his monumental ambition, Ainsworth worked his way up to the office of adjunct general (the chief administrative officer of the Army), an office where most of the records and correspondence of the Army passed. By controlling the flow of paper, and through the additional gift of skillful networking within Congress, Ainsworth managed to effectively control the Army, and there was little the rotating secretaries of war or chiefs of staff could do to diminish his power. By the time Stimson took over the War Department, most of Taft's cabinet, most members of Congress, and many within the Army itself thought of Ainsworth as indispensable.[13]

Stimson was going to make his own judgment. His first objective was to learn as much as possible about the Army. Like Calhoun and Root before him, he spent his first few months gathering and pouring over information with his predictable approach to preparation (preparation being a relative term as it related to Stimson since few men of his era assembled and digested information as diligently or skillfully as he did).

What Stimson discovered was disheartening; he presided over an army that was not only at war with itself but was unprepared to fight against any first-rate rival. He also came to more fully appreciate that all the bureau heads, led by Ainsworth, had been resistant to the efforts of the incumbent chief of staff to make those changes necessary to remedy the situation. The chief of staff was the well-known, respected, and forceful Leonard Wood, appointed a year before Stimson took over the Army. Wood was a legend; he fought in the last campaign against Geronimo in 1886 (at which time he was awarded the Medal of Honor) and together with Teddy Roosevelt, formed the Rough Riders under his command during the Spanish-American War. Taft named him chief of staff in April 1910, a year before Stimson took over the War Department.

Wood was effective in the position but made a lot of enemies both within and outside the Army—including Ainsworth. Stimson was aware of this upon entering the War Department. By the time he completed his initial research efforts and submitted his first Annual Report to Congress in December 1911, he saw that the rancor between the two military heads was only intensifying. Although he would inevitably be drawn into the middle of the fight, there is no doubt which man he backed. He and Wood liked one another, had much in common, and saw eye to eye on the major issues of the day involving the direction of the Army. Stimson knew that the challenges he faced in accomplishing his goals would be far less daunting with Ainsworth out of the way.

As a trial lawyer, Stimson had been trained to be watchful for any mistake made or weakness revealed by the opposition and to quickly make a judgment concerning the appropriate response, taking into consideration timing, leverage, risk, and reward. There were occasions when it made sense to build a case slowly on the foundation of such mistakes, and there were moments when it was better to strike swiftly. Less than nine months after Stimson took over the War Department, Fred Ainsworth presented him with an opportunity to take the latter course of action.

The subject was of a minor nature and involved paper; specifically, Ainsworth's response to a letter from Wood suggesting that Ainsworth, in order to save on the cost of paper, should take specific efforts to consolidate the database he kept on soldiers into another one kept by a different bureau (this suggestion did not come out of the blue; The Commission on Economy and Efficiency appointed by President Taft had just concluded, among other things, that the Army used too much paper).[14] Two months after ignoring the letter—and a follow-up one sent by Wood—Ainsworth responded to Wood in an overly condescending reply suggesting that the idea was stupid and encouraged by "incompetent amateurs" (implying not only Wood, but Stimson himself). Ainsworth went on to say that Wood was either "unmindful of consequences" or "uninformed of the needs of government" and he would only reconsider the proposal if "wiser" counsels suggested it.

After reading the contemptuous letter, Stimson seized the moment and informed the judge advocate of the Army that he wanted to court-martial Ainsworth for insubordination since Ainsworth was by law the subordinate of Wood (wisely, Stimson had earlier warned Ainsworth against insubordination, thus making it easier to recommend a court-martial).

Fearful of the consequences, the judge advocate proposed a lighter punishment, but Stimson explained to him that his preference was to use "a big gun rather than a little gun." After briefly consulting both President Taft and Elihu Root, Stimson relieved Ainsworth from active duty. Initially defiant, Ainsworth quickly realized the game was up after several friends (including a close ally in the Senate) advised him he ought to resign rather than face a court-martial. Taft and Stimson were agreeable to this, and within eleven days of writing the explosive letter, Ainsworth was gone, and a major step had been taken to transfer the power of the Army into the hands of the chief of staff, where it properly resided by law.

Even with Ainsworth out, this would not happen overnight, such was the long-standing strength he and the bureaus had built up. So ingrained was that power that major turf wars between the chiefs of staff and bureau heads continued during Stimson's two-year term beginning in 1911, Newton Baker's term before and during the First World War, and to a lesser extent, until Marshall and Stimson were teamed up in 1940. Nevertheless,

Ainsworth's fall was a critical victory for those favoring the general staff concept and ensured that the chief of staff would have final authority under the secretary of war and the president as commander in chief.

The most important consequence of the Ainsworth affair was that it set a precedent and established more firmly the dominant power of the office of secretary of war at the top of the Army chain of command, something that had historically existed only during wartime. Stimson took on a long and firmly established arrangement of intertwined relationships between bureau heads and congressmen—a previously immovable bureaucratic monster nourished by the twin forces of politics and money—and nudged it just enough to prevent it from ever returning to full strength. This allowed his successors (including himself, twenty-eight years later) to maintain the civilian control over the military that the Founding Fathers had worked so hard to establish.

With Ainsworth gone, Stimson went to work on two other major goals: establishing the concept of an organized reserve made up of trained soldiers, and consolidating the far-flung army posts. Accomplishing the latter task proved to be a unique challenge. When Stimson took office in 1911, he presided over an army of approximately seventy-five thousand troops spread out among fifty different posts located in twenty-four different states across the country (a quarter of the forces were located in American territories such as Hawaii, Alaska, the Canal Zone, Puerto Rico, and the Philippines). A great majority of the garrisons were originally selected for their proximity to Native Americans, and the average one held only seven hundred men.[15] They remained in place long after the Native American threat disappeared, because removing an army base in the early part of the twentieth century was as politically difficult as it is today. Congressmen from the twenty-four pertinent states, along with their influential friends, created a formidable fighting force against which the War Department had to battle.

The main issue was that the current dispersion of the troops made it impossible to quickly mobilize any reasonably concentrated force. This had been proven just before Stimson took office, when an exercise took place to see how fast a certain quantity of men of division strength (between fifteen thousand and twenty thousand) could be assembled in one location. Not since the Civil War had such a concentration of soldiers been attempted. Ninety days after orders were issued to men from different posts around the country, only 75 percent of the soldiers made it to the assigned location (thirty-one-year-old First Lieutenant George Marshall being one of them). Even after this high-profile failure, the collective political power of congressmen and other interested parties was too strong to overcome. Stimson and Wood's proposal to reduce the number of forts from forty-nine to eight failed.

Despite the setback, Stimson found another way to accomplish much of his goal by reorganizing the Army along a divisional structure. If the divisions could not physically come together through the closing of bases, they could at least share a commanding general, common training, and a common purpose. Stimson did not devise the change (it came out of a War College exercise), but he and Wood built up support for it within the higher ranks of the Army by appealing to the sheer logic of it. The result of this reorganization was that the Army had for the first time in its history—other than during a time of war—a permanent tactical structure larger than a regiment (three thousand to five thousand men). It flattened the organization and eventually led to the physical coming together of division-sized forces, Stimson's original intention. He believed it to be his greatest achievement during his two years under Taft. Through this tactical reorganization, the Army was now organized such that the command of units during peace reflected the probable command of them during war.

Not many individuals in American history have served in the same high-level cabinet position more than once in their careers; Stimson was the only secretary of war to do so.[16] The two years Stimson served in the position from 1911 to 1913 proved invaluable to him a generation later, when Franklin Roosevelt recruited him for the same post. He learned that for the United States Army to be effective, it had to be made up of highly skilled professionals who could effectively teach civilians how to fight; he determined where the boundaries of military power were in a democracy; he got to understand how Congress thought and acted collectively; and he figured out how to negotiate and compromise with individual congressmen. Most importantly, Stimson gained an understanding of the power and limits of the presidency. This lesson was reinforced to him when he later served as secretary of state under Herbert Hoover. By the time he returned to the War Department in 1940, this knowledge assisted him greatly as he teamed with George Marshall to arm the country in the run-up to war and to successfully defeat the Axis powers during it.

Stimson's success in accomplishing change within the Army during peacetime reaffirmed his long-held conviction that a group of people with a combination of brains, passion, diligence, and focus can make things happen under the most difficult conditions. That his accomplishments occurred during the middle of what became one of the great schisms in the history of any American political party is a tribute to the focus and sense of purpose for which Stimson was famous. That the rupture of his Republican party was the responsibility of his close friend and mentor Theodore Roosevelt is further testament to Stimson's abilities to avoid distractions when working on important problems.

Presidential Election of 1912

As we learned in chapter 3, Stimson was aware of Teddy Roosevelt's dissatisfaction with President Taft before taking over the War Department based on his conversations with the ex-president in Long Island.[17] But he was unaware of how actively Roosevelt was scheming to get his old job back. Speculation and rumors began to emerge about Roosevelt's intentions from the time Stimson arrived in Washington to take his post. Stimson proactively made attempts to convince Roosevelt that Taft was supportive of him, and there were few issues of importance that the twenty-sixth and twenty-seventh presidents differed on.

When the rumors escalated at the start of 1912, Stimson decided to take another trip to Sagamore Hill with a like-minded and mutual friend of Roosevelt's, Secretary of the Navy George Meyer. The two men wanted to confront the restless Roosevelt, ascertain his intentions, and attempt to dissuade him in case he was harboring serious thoughts of tossing his hat back into the ring. Explaining to Roosevelt what should have been obvious to him (that the Republican Party would suffer if he challenged Taft), Stimson and Meyer also suggested that Roosevelt's own reputation would be damaged if he ran since people would generally believe that he had treated Taft unfairly. Roosevelt dismissed the rumors and sent both men back to Washington believing he had no desire to be president again.[18] Six weeks following this visit to Sagamore Hill, Roosevelt announced he was a candidate.

So just nine months into his tenure as secretary of war and seven months prior to the Republican convention, Stimson was faced with making a choice between his friend, who had launched his public career six years earlier, and his current boss, who had put him in charge of the War Department. The choice was clear if not painful to Stimson: He would support Taft because doing so was in the best interests of the Republican Party.

Stimson reached out to Roosevelt with a thoughtful and friendly letter explaining how he sincerely believed it was a mistake for him to run and that he had little choice but to support Taft. Two weeks later, he received an equally friendly reply from Roosevelt explaining that he understood Stimson's position. Comforted by Roosevelt's reply, Stimson came out publicly for Taft in the first week of March 2012. In a carefully prepared statement, Stimson stated that he had entered public life under his "sincere friend" Roosevelt and shared his political beliefs, but he thought that those who were "forcing him" to run against his "original intentions" were doing a disservice to the cause of reform in America.[19]

Despite approving Stimson's carefully crafted statement before its publication and claiming their relationship would be unaffected by Stimson's support of Taft, Roosevelt was quoted by journalists shortly thereafter saying that Stimson's choice revealed his "ingratitude." The two men did not speak for three years.

Stimson was devastated by the breach in his eighteen-year relationship with the ex-president; he devoted over twenty thoughtfully written pages of his personal diary summarizing the election, and several more on specific events surrounding it. Although their friendship recovered in 1915 and flourished in the remaining four years of Roosevelt's life, the episode would remain a painful memory to Stimson for the rest of his life.

Practicing Law and Reforming Government

Following Woodrow Wilson's inevitable victory over Roosevelt and Taft in the fall of 1912, Stimson once again prepared to return to private practice. But true to both his bipartisan approach to politics and his concern for the country, he first reached out to the president-elect through a mutual friend in order to brief him on the state of the Army and to impress upon him the need to hire a competent man to head the War Department. Stimson knew that only a forceful and energetic replacement could prevent the still powerful and well-supported bureau heads from reversing the changes initiated by Root and kept alive by himself.

Wilson sent an emissary to Stimson, who spent two hours with him getting a complete overview of the situation. Stimson described the emissary as throwing his hands up "every few minutes" during the meeting and exclaiming, "Great heavens! Wilson knows nothing of it." Stimson believed Wilson's appointment of the capable Lindley Garrison to succeed him would not have happened without such an initiative. After Garrison took over, Stimson graciously spent five days with him at the War Department, bringing him up to speed on all the department's activities. The two established a friendship and kept in close touch during Garrison's three-year tenure in the office.

Feeling confident he had left the War Department in good hands, the forty-five-year-old Stimson headed back to New York and the offices of Winthrop & Stimson. After battling with generals and congressmen for two years in Washington and dealing with all the political and personal aspects of the fallout between Roosevelt and Taft, the challenges of corporate law for Stimson must have seemed a welcome relief when he arrived back at his Liberty Street offices and the comforting presence of his law partner and dear friend, Bronson Winthrop.

It was also nice for Stimson to get back to his long-established New York routines. His father and sister continued to live in the townhouse adjoined to his on Lexington Avenue. It was essentially one household given the daily contact they all had with one another. Continuing in the tradition of his grandfather (with whom he had lived while growing up), Stimson regularly played host during the week to a variety of relatives representing all generations on both sides of the family. Unable to have children himself (likely due to a bout with the mumps shortly before his marriage), Stimson was a devoted uncle to his nieces and nephews.

At the end of every workweek, Stimson and Mabel made a quick exit from Manhattan to "Highhold," the Long Island estate he had acquired in 1903. Located just outside the town of Huntington in a village called West Hills, Highhold was where the Stimsons spent most of their summers and weekends for the rest of their lives, until retiring there permanently after the end of World War II. Stimson had everything he wanted at Highhold to satisfy his physical, intellectual, and emotional needs. His "farm" consisted of one hundred acres of rolling hills, fields, and woods where he could ride his horses on the high grounds overlooking Long Island Sound a few short miles to his north and the Atlantic Ocean twenty-five miles to the south. (Jayne's Hill, the highest natural point on Long Island, is just east of where Stimson's house stood.) Cows, chickens, and gardens dotted his property, and he employed a competent man to look after them. A cook on weekends and a few other full-time staff during the summer provided Stimson plenty of time to read, ride, and relax.

The house he built, and added to over the years, was neither ostentatious nor designed by any famous architect of the day (a cousin of his drew up the plans).[20] But it was comfortable and large enough to entertain relatives during the summer and, from time to time, several members of his staff for work weekends and/or team-building exercises. Stimson had no desire to mingle with the other wealthy New Yorkers who were building Gatsby-like mansions a few miles away on the Long Island Sound; he chose his property because of its remote and rural nature.

Over time, Stimson and his wife became attached to the small village of West Hills and the people who lived there. They attended the local Presbyterian Church and got involved with a variety of community issues throughout their lives. Stimson's love for the village was best exemplified by the annual "Highhold Games" he and his wife hosted for the entire town each Thanksgiving. Resembling a town fair, approximately a thousand villagers looked on as Stimson formally opened the games by firing his double-barreled shotgun into the air, after which a variety of events were held for all ages mixed in with rounds of cider, sandwiches, and donuts.

Although Stimson was most relaxed and comfortable around his family, if strenuous exercise was involved, he could be as socially active as any man. One activity that occupied him for over twenty years with several of his neighbors was fox hunting. For Stimson, the chase was thrilling and physically challenging as the foxes led the riders over fences, walls, open fields, and woods on his and adjacent properties.

Exercise in general was an obsession for Stimson; he believed it was the only way he could get relief from the various ailments that had begun bothering him at the turn of the century. Lumbago and rheumatism plagued him to the point where it was difficult for him to stand in the courtroom. Since walking to and from work in Manhattan was not enough during the week to combat these ills, Stimson became what today is commonly referred to as a "weekend warrior." Riding one of his horses hard for approximately twenty miles over the fields and woods in and around Highhold was an activity Stimson relied on to keep his health in check and to clear his mind. The older he got, the more exercise he required on a day-to-day basis in order to stay, as he regularly put it, "fresh."

When Stimson resumed the life of a Wall Street lawyer in March 1913, he had much to be thankful for. He was wealthy, happily married, and highly thought of nationally as both a public servant and a corporate lawyer. As neither wealth accumulation nor the practice of law for its own sake were primary drivers for Stimson, he kept far more reasonable working hours than the typical downtown lawyer. He got into the office rarely before 9:30

a.m., and he left normally at 5:30 p.m. Both he and his partner, Bronson Winthrop, were of like minds, believing there was more to life than hustling for clients and making money. They did not aggressively market their services and tried to manage their case flow to fit with their lifestyles.

By all appearances Stimson seemed content as he picked up where he left off at Winthrop & Stimson, but his partner and others who knew him best were highly doubtful whether the law alone could keep him satisfied during the workweek. They were correct; Stimson still craved consequential work and wanted to be in a position of influence where he could make a significant difference on the public issues he cared about.

A part of what drove Stimson to address reform and other public issues was the tortured style he brought to working on legal problems for his clients; he believed the extreme physical and mental effort he shouldered on behalf of his clients would be far better off spent toward a higher purpose. Stimson's approach to any specific case was legendary among those men who worked for him; he seemed to expend all his intellectual energy focusing on one problem or issue at a time. This method both fascinated and frustrated his colleagues in equal parts. Stimson shuttered himself in his office taking copious notes and deliberating for hours on a single issue, often at the expense of other issues linked to the one on which he was focusing. If anyone in the office, from senior partner down to clerk, needed to speak to Stimson during these hours Felix Frankfurter described as his "time of concentration," it was at his own peril; he generally greeted each interruption, justified or not, with an angry outburst that included the worst words the decorous Stimson could conjure up: "Confound it!" or "Damn!"[21]

This was Stimson's approach to work throughout his life, regardless of what type of work it was. Shortly after becoming president of the Board of Trustees of Phillips Academy, the headmaster of the school described him as follows:

> An excellent presiding officer, but with a completely one-track mind which tolerated no wandering from the main issue. He hated interruptions and bluntly ignored irrelevancies. Dignified austerity. His reserve was temperamental, not deliberate and he did not encourage the advances of strangers. By nature he was serious-minded, with no levity in his nature, and his attempts at humor were awkward, even when they were sincere.[22]

Once Stimson emerged from his "time of concentration," he would bring his associates into the room. He would then pace the floor, either talking to himself or asking questions of his staff, sometimes the same questions repeatedly. It often took Stimson several explanations before he finally understood a concept that one of his staff was trying to get across. Those who witnessed these struggles believed his intelligence—although formidable—was of a slow-moving nature.

Stimson was by no means the smartest lawyer in the office when working for Winthrop & Stimson, far from it. He surrounded himself with men of exceptional intelligence, just as he did as a U.S. Attorney in New York ten years earlier and as he ran the War Department twenty years later. Felix Frankfurter and Alfred Loomis were the most notable examples. First in his class at Harvard Law School during each of his three years there, Frankfurter was brilliant by anyone's assessment and went on to serve twenty-three distinguished years on the U.S. Supreme Court after working for Stimson when he was the U.S. Attorney in New York and later, albeit briefly, at Winthrop & Stimson. Alfred Loomis, a first cousin and protégé of Stimson's, measures up against almost any American during any historical era when it comes to diverse accomplishments. He was a top Wall Street lawyer (working for cousin Henry), a legendary investment banker, a masterful investor, and a brilliant scientist, who pioneered the use of radar for military use during World War II and invented LORAN (the long-range radio navigational system that enabled ships and aircraft to determine their position and speed from low-frequency radio signals).

What most struck younger colleagues like Frankfurter and Loomis about Stimson was the utter transformation Stimson undertook once he left the offices of Winthrop & Stimson and entered a courtroom. Where there was confusion and frustration at the office when working on a case, there was order, composure, and confidence in the courtroom when presenting it. He was simply dominant, and his preparation was, as a leading peer once described, "absolutely perfect."

While there was ample success for Stimson in the courtroom, there was rarely joy. He wore himself out after each big case and did not see what it bought other than money, a grateful client, and an elevated reputation in a narrow circle. So he began to spend a greater amount of his free time on his pet projects, so much so that he estimated to a friend three years after he rejoined his law practice that 75 percent of his time in the previous year was spent on such "non-professional work."[23]

At the time Stimson made this estimate, the country was in the middle of the Progressive Era, a period that began toward the end of the nineteenth century and was characterized by efforts at federal, state, and local levels to reform the political, social, and economic systems; reduce corruption; and minimize the influence of political bosses. It was only natural that Stimson took a lead in the movement given that both of his mentors (Teddy Roosevelt and Elihu Root) were principal figures in the Progressive Era's earlier years. There were plenty of opportunities to get involved, and Stimson went after them as soon as he left the War Department, stepping up his activity each year.

Realizing that working within the two-party structure was the best way to effect change, Stimson simultaneously tried to build up the Republican Party, which was a shell of its former self following the debacle of 1912. It is not that he was a diehard Republican; on the contrary, Stimson was by nature bipartisan, and he explained to Republicans without hesitation that unless the Party reorganized under the banner of Progressivism, he would leave it.[24] Using whatever influence he possessed within the Party, he gave speeches, wrote letters, and buttonholed other Republicans, explaining that inefficiency, waste, and excessive spending were the reasons republics collapsed historically and that the same could happen to America.

His activism and stature within the GOP got him a ticket to the New York State Constitutional Convention of 1915 chaired by Elihu Root. Held for almost five months beginning in April, the Convention served as an opportunity for progressive politicians to push through all the changes they had been debating for over thirty years. At Root's request, Stimson played a major role in the preparation for the Convention by learning all he could from the leading experts on government in the country, merging that knowledge with the ideas he and his colleagues discussed over the years, and educating others in the Party about the required changes needed and the rationale behind them. Stimson took the study of government and his role in the Convention seriously. The importance to him of his work at the Convention is suggested by the fact that he devoted almost twice as many pages in his memoirs toward it than he did his three years working as the United States Attorney of the Southern District of New York.

Preparedness Movement

As if he did not have enough on his plate during this period of his life, Stimson was also one of the major figures in the Preparedness Movement. Once again, it was Roosevelt and Root, along with former Army Chief of Staff Leonard Wood, leading the charge in this effort. Their goal was to prepare the

Army in case the war in Europe, which began in the summer of 1914, threatened the United States or its interests abroad. Stimson joined these three men in recruiting other lawyers, bankers, doctors, and businessmen who also thought America should adopt a far more active approach to international affairs befitting a country with the economic might it had acquired since the Civil War. This group believed the United States needed a larger and more professionally trained army capable of taking on any other army in the world.

To move forward on these goals, a National Service Program was proposed by which all men turning eighteen years old would be required to train for six months and then be assigned to a unit that could be assembled quickly when needed. Under such a plan, the regular Army would oversee training the young men.

Stimson worked hard to promote this concept and was maniacal on the subject, believing that every American man should not only be willing to die for his country, but also "spend a little of his life in learning how to die for her effectively." Ultimately, the National Service Program failed to gain traction. Although politics played a role in killing it (Democrats were in power, and it was a Republican-led effort), it was the ubiquitous presence of isolationist voters throughout the country that left it dying on the vine; few politicians felt that the need for preparedness was strong enough to risk their displeasure.

Unbowed, Stimson and other leading internationalists organized a series of privately run summer training camps beginning in 1915 for reserve officers in Plattsburgh, New York. Run by Leonard Wood and attracting college-educated men of the upper classes (who could afford to take the time off work and pay their own expenses), the "Plattsburgh Movement" trained over forty thousand men, many of whom were called upon to lead troops in the field two years later, when America was drawn into World War I.

Stimson himself spent a month at the Plattsburgh camp in 1916 at the age of forty-nine. These camps were officially sanctioned by the National Defense Act of 1916, signed into law by Woodrow Wilson, who changed his mind about preparedness after the Germans sank the *Lusitania*. It was at one such camp in Utah, modeled after the one at Plattsburgh, that George Marshall cemented his reputation as the Army's finest trainer of soldiers.

World War I

Stimson was on a speaking tour of the Midwest promoting preparedness when Woodrow Wilson asked Congress to declare war on Germany in April

1917. Stimson rushed home, applied for and received a commission, and reported to duty at the War College in Washington on June 1. Since Stimson had no intention of serving his country in an administrative capacity, he immediately began lobbying for a position in the Field Artillery, citing his service in the National Guard since 1898, his month of training at Plattsburgh, and the fact that all his ancestors had been "in the fighting branch" when called to service.

Unlike most other prominent men seeking an appointment based on their political or social positions, Stimson put in serious hours of training to further justify consideration. Before work began each day at the War College, he drilled with artillerymen at a local fort. After work, he hunkered down for further study of the duties of an artillery officer. That is not to say he failed to leverage his political weight and reputation to get what he wanted; on the contrary, he lobbied both Secretary of War Newton Baker and Army Chief of Staff Hugh Scott. The combined results paid off. It took Stimson nearly three months, but he finally got an appointment as a lieutenant colonel in the Field Artillery of the National Army (formed earlier that year). In early September, he reported to Long Island to train with the 305th Field Artillery attached to the 77th Division. Just before Christmas 1917, he was transferred to France to train with the British Army. He was fifty years old, twice the age of the average enlistee.

Beginning in January 1918, Stimson spent a month with a British artillery unit a few miles behind the lines. He was able to visit the front on several occasions to make observations. With a British guide, Stimson also had the opportunity to cross the entire Somme battlefield, which, two years earlier hosted the bloodiest fighting the world had ever seen. Between the destruction he witnessed there, the constant shelling during his stay, and the "never-ending darkness and dampness," the overall experience was enough to remove any previous beliefs he might have shared with Teddy Roosevelt about the glory of war.[25]

In February, Stimson was sent to the General Staff School in Langres for two months of further training while awaiting the arrival of the 305th to France. He described his work there under various instructors as the most rigorous he had done since leaving Harvard Law School, and "even there we didn't do it except before exams."[26]

The instructor who most challenged him in Langres was a thirty-seven-year-old captain in the Army named George C. Marshall, who had spent nine days at the General Staff School during Stimson's stay before going back to his duties with the 1st Division. Stimson knew who Marshall was; he remembered his role in planning the successful maneuver exercises in New England six years earlier when Stimson was serving as secretary of war. He had thought enough of the captain to put his name on a list Teddy Roosevelt asked him to prepare when Roosevelt was looking for good men to form a division in 1917.

While at Langres, Stimson was determined to better acquaint himself with the young Army instructor. The two men went horseback riding together and shared meals during Marshall's time there. Not surprisingly, Stimson was impressed with Marshall (few people weren't), and he remembered him a decade later when he offered him a job as an aide to assist him as Governor General of the Philippines.[27]

Stimson's training at Langres ended in May 1918 with the arrival of the 305th Regiment in France. For the next six weeks, Stimson passed along to other officers in the regiment all he had learned in France over the previous five months. In June, the 305th was assigned to replace a French division in a relatively quiet sector in Lorraine. Stimson was put in charge of the First Battalion, consisting of roughly half of the 1,300 men in the regiment. Their location put them close enough for Stimson's men to fire their guns at the enemy, but far enough away to avoid the endless bombardment faced by more seasoned troops closer to the action.

Before he had a chance to get into the thick of the fighting, Stimson was promoted and ordered back to the United States to command and train a new regiment of artillery. His war was over, and it was with mixed feelings that the newly minted colonel left France. He missed his wife and the comforts of home, but he felt he was abandoning his men just as they were about to face greater trials. He also believed his character and skills were better suited to leading prepared men on the front lines than training raw recruits behind them.

Words his old friend Teddy Roosevelt sent to him several months earlier made it easier for Stimson to accept the transfer. Roosevelt, writing to Stimson in March after the latter had spent a month on the firing lines with the British, advised him that "having been on the front in danger," he could now "accept any position" his commanding officer gave him going forward. From anyone but Roosevelt, the words would have meant little; coming from the man who had charged up San Juan Hill, they must have been reaffirming. Perhaps it was time another younger man be moved up to make his own mark.

Henry Stimson faced danger in France, worked himself to exhaustion, and proved he was a strong and capable military leader. The lessons he took home served him well twenty-two years later, when he was once again called to take over the War Department.

The newly promoted colonel spent the next three and a half months training men at Fort Meade in Maryland while dealing with the horrendous consequences of the flu pandemic in October 1918. The pandemic, which ended up killing between twenty million to fifty million people globally, killed 21 of Stimson's men and hospitalized approximately 40 percent of the 1,250 men he was training at Fort Meade.[28]

One month after the Armistice was signed on November 11, 1918, "the Colonel" (as he would be referred to for the rest of his life by close friends and colleagues) was once again sitting behind his desk on Wall Street.

6

The Slow Climb (1919–1939)

Although I do not write often, you are in my thoughts frequently and I am hoping that some of these days you will come into your own. Everybody that I meet who knows you always speaks in the highest terms, of course, and I think it is only a question of time when you will be repaid for your patience.

—GENERAL OF THE ARMIES JOHN PERSHING
to George Marshall, February 28, 1930[1]

As Colonel Henry L. Stimson closed out his World War I duties at Camp Meade in Maryland, Captain George C. Marshall was in Europe helping to demobilize the U.S. Army while preparing to take up his post as the right-hand man of General John "Black Jack" Pershing, the most celebrated military hero in America, if not the world. Not surprisingly, the five years spent with Pershing between 1919 and 1924 proved to be a pivotal learning experience for the future chief of staff. He brought to the assignment, as he did with every posting, his practice of diligently observing and absorbing everything he experienced: Incompetence was studied as closely as competence; waste as thoroughly as efficiency; complexity as carefully as simplicity; and the wrong way of doing things with equal weight to the right approach.

If Henry Stimson was famous for the methodical and torturous preparation he undertook before each of his law cases, Marshall's general preparation for a future war was no less intense. The difference was that it was something he seemed to undertake daily. While most officers spent peacetime enjoying a generous balance between work and play, Marshall occupied his days thinking about and planning for the next war. He believed it was his duty.

As part of that duty, Marshall spent his entire career constantly scrutinizing officers he met along the way in order to determine exactly how best he could employ the more capable ones if he found himself in a position of authority during a future war. As one who instructed top officers at the Army's highest-level colleges and training schools, he was well-positioned to make such observations, and he spent much time and effort doing so despite knowing that two scenarios needed to take place concurrently before he could make use of the information he so meticulously gathered: The United States would have to be at war; and he would have to be near the top of the Army hierarchy. After the end of World War I, neither scenario seemed probable. That both might occur seemed extremely unlikely, certainly at the time Marshall was beginning his new assignment as aide-de-camp to Pershing in the spring of 1919.

Aide-de-Camp (May 1919–July 1924)

After the Armistice, there was still a tremendous amount of work to be done winding down the affairs of the immense American Army in Europe (close to 1.5 million men). Once assigned to Pershing in May 1919, Marshall returned to Chaumont to assist him with this effort.

By this time, Marshall's growing reputation had spread beyond the Army. It was while working at Chaumont that Marshall was approached by Dwight Morrow of J.P. Morgan & Co. with an offer to join the bank at a starting annual salary of $30,000. Morrow, a future ambassador to Mexico (and the future father-in-law of Charles Lindbergh), was in France during the War serving as Pershing's top civilian advisor, and he had the chance to observe Marshall closely. In making the generous offer, Morrow was not looking for a rainmaker who could bring his fame and contacts to the bank in exchange for a nice office and a cushy salary; Marshall was not famous, his contacts outside of the Army were limited, and his personality was hardly suited for such purposes. Morrow wanted a talented and decisive leader. J.P. Morgan was the nation's most powerful bank, and its management had begun to think about the vast postwar opportunities that America would be given to increase its trade and wealth. Any man with leadership and organizational skills sharp enough to manage the movement of half a million men over sixty miles within a ten-day period during the chaos of war could be very useful to a bank with high aspirations to maintain its top position in the postwar world.

Without a single star on his shoulder, or much of a savings account, as he approached the age of forty and anticipating a long period of peace, Marshall must have given Morrow's offer serious consideration. In 1919, a salary of $30,000 a year would have made him a relatively wealthy man. How much thought he gave to the offer is not known, but he politely rejected it. There was a lot of work to be done. But first, it was time to celebrate.

After the Treaty of Versailles was signed in late June 1919, Pershing's team relocated to Paris and spent much of the next two months preparing for and participating in the unprecedented festivities and ceremonies organized for the senior representatives of the victorious Allied armies in various cities. The victory tour kicked off in Paris in July, where Marshall could be seen riding a horse in a massive parade up the Champs-Élysées just behind Pershing and Pershing's chief of staff (and in front of thirty American generals). The tour continued in London (where Marshall first became acquainted with Winston Churchill, spending a day serving as his official escort) before heading to France, Italy, and then back to France. On September 1, 1919, the proud but tired heroes boarded a ship in Brest and sailed for home. Landing in New York a week later, the celebrations resumed with an immense parade down Fifth Avenue starting on 107th Street and ending in Washington Square. When the dust finally settled on all the celebrations, Marshall took an office next to Pershing's in Washington, D.C.

Following the Armistice, War Department leaders immediately began planning the future of the Army with a focus toward correcting the mistakes of the recent past (the primary one being the general lack of preparedness). They had to approach their efforts carefully; as we learned earlier, American politicians historically ignored major postwar reforms, particularly any that called for an expansion in the number of professional soldiers. After the carnage of the First World War, most Americans saw no reason to ever get involved again in a European conflict. With two oceans protecting them, two nonthreatening neighbors to the north and south, and airpower still a generation away from being taken seriously, most Americans still believed the country had little to fear from foreign enemies.

Additionally, increasing the size of the Army was expensive. Although it was Calvin Coolidge who stated a few years after the First World War that "the chief business of the American people is business," he was only echoing Frenchman Alexis de Tocqueville's observation about Americans a century earlier: They were a people driven to acquire and maintain wealth. A large army would mean having to give some of it back.

Although aware of the challenges, the War Department was hopeful that the end of such a horrific war might actually bring about a shift in the attitude of isolationists. Such hope was misplaced; a bill to authorize a standing army of five hundred thousand men organized by Chief of Staff Peyton March and Secretary of War Newton Baker in 1919 went nowhere. In 1920, Congress decided that 280,000 was a more appropriate number, but it cut that a year later to 125,000 (and then cut it further two years later).

With a broad retrenchment inevitable, Pershing was asked by Secretary of War Newton Baker to go around the country visiting Army camps and weapons plants to help determine which ones could be closed. Marshall, who would join Pershing, immediately got to work preparing an itinerary down to the smallest of details. Once the tour began, he and two other members of Pershing's staff were required to present briefs to the general before each stop along the way and accompany him to all the events set up for him in various cities spread around the thirty-two states visited over three months (only taking a break for Christmas). For Marshall, the experience was invaluable. It not only gave him a unique insight into all the strengths and weaknesses of the U.S. Army, but it also introduced him (or reintroduced him, in many cases) to several of the officers who would later serve under him during the Second World War.

In July 1921, Pershing was named Army chief of staff by President Warren Harding and served in the position for just over three years. Major Marshall (he was promoted a year earlier) took on progressively greater responsibilities as other members of Pershing's entourage began taking on new assignments. In his new role, Pershing was often away either touring Army colleges and training schools or representing the Army overseas. Known around Washington as the person who best represented Pershing's views, Marshall was given a great deal of power and responsibility.

Marshall used this power to seek improvements in the Army based on what he observed over the course of his career and what he learned during the three-month tour with Pershing. Whether it involved the overall promotion system or the coordination between the Army and the Navy, Marshall strived to make a difference at a time when he could leverage his unique position as Pershing's proxy. But most of his efforts during the three years were consumed in the great struggle he and all of Pershing's team waged to prevent the Army from falling into a worse state of preparedness than in the years leading up to World War I. They were swimming against a strong current in this regard.

As budget cuts continued to reduce the size of the Army in 1923, Marshall did all he could to ensure that the training for officers was at a level high enough to offset the disadvantages brought on by the cuts. The concept he and other officers promoted was straightforward: When war came, all highly trained officers would share in the responsibility of training the huge influx of citizen soldiers into the ranks. As we learned earlier, the idea was not original; Alexander Hamilton first promoted this concept of an "expansible army" in the late eighteenth century, and John Calhoun pushed hard for it a generation later, when he was secretary of war. But the notion of dramatically increasing the level of training for professionals in the Army was Marshall's idea.

To get there, more money was needed than Congress was willing to provide. Marshall wanted more officers, housing, and facilities. He also wanted funds to stage more large-scale maneuvers, the kind he was able to participate in earlier in his career in New England and the Philippines. He knew that without taking part in such past maneuvers, he would not have been able to pull off the massive movement of troops, equipment, and guns from the St. Mihiel attack zone to the principal Allied line of attack in September 1918.

Despite his efforts, and those of his more influential boss, Congress would not budge. Its isolationist disposition, reflecting the nation's mood, remained largely unchanged from when Marshall left Pershing's side in July 1924 to the fall of Paris to the Nazis in June 1940.

Although his efforts did not produce the results he would have liked, and despite maintaining in later years that his assignment to General Pershing derailed his career, Marshall's years with Pershing proved to be an indispensable part of his overall education. His exposure to politics and politicians, business and businessmen, and the Army and officers at a variety of levels and in different regions gave him as clear a view as anyone what attributes were necessary in a leader to effectively run an army in a democracy. He made use of it when he was given the top job in 1939.

Particularly beneficial to Marshall was the time he spent with individuals who contributed significantly to America's efforts during World War I. Ever the student, he was able to learn from such men as financier Bernard Baruch (who managed the economic mobilization for the country as chairman of the War Industries Board) and Secretary of War Newton Baker what worked and what did not work during the War.

No time was more valuable than that which he spent with Pershing himself. Through direct observation, Marshall ended up learning a great deal about leadership during the War. Years later, when *Time* magazine was looking for input about a cover story it was writing about Pershing for publication in November 1942, Marshall took the time to write down his thoughts despite all that was going on during the Second World War. He wrote that Pershing's greatest contribution during World War I came in the fall of 1918. At that time the Americans were taking a beating in the Meuse-Argonne, and many senior officials were advising Pershing to suspend activities. Marshall commented that in brushing aside such advice, Pershing displayed the "determined, aggressive, offensive spirit" that came to define the Americans in France. Although Marshall was not one to blow his own horn, the implication was clear that the observant student was following in his teacher's footsteps.[2]

There was something even more unique about Pershing that Marshall greatly respected and noted during his years with him: He was extremely thick-skinned. Writing to a former superior shortly before Roosevelt appointed him chief of staff in 1939, Marshall remarked on this great strength of Pershing's, emphasizing his "complete tolerance towards all discussions regarding the matters in which he was considering." More than anyone Marshall had ever known, Pershing not only welcomed feedback but accepted criticism without taking it personally.[3] For the rest of his career, he successfully sought to emulate his mentor in this regard.

Fort Benning, Georgia (November 1927–June 1932)[4]

With Pershing set to retire and Marshall due for a transfer, the latter requested to be sent to China, an assignment he had long coveted. Marshall was an adventurer, and just as the advent of the safety bike during his childhood gave him greater access to the lands of southwestern Pennsylvania, the Army gave Marshall the opportunity to explore the world. He and his wife set sail in July 1924. The assignment lasted three years. Although it was relatively uneventful for Marshall from a professional standpoint, his experience there gave him an insight into the problems of the country that allowed him to better understand the complexities of dealing with the Chinese both during and after the Second World War.

As the assignment was coming to an end, Marshall was asked to teach at the Army War College in Washington. Although he would have much preferred to teach at the Infantry School at Fort Benning (which had requested him in 1924 and 1925), his availability and the school's open positions could never seem to align properly. He set sail for the United States with his wife in May 1927. Classes were to begin in September. Less than a month into his new assignment, Marshall became a widower.

American history is filled with examples of men who have driven themselves to substantial heights following a personal tragedy. Unmitigated labor, serving as an escape from heartache, led certain individuals to new levels of productivity, creativity, and accomplishments. Thomas Jefferson, Andrew Jackson, Abraham Lincoln, Teddy Roosevelt, and John Pershing are a few examples of American political and military figures who emerged from the depths of mourning to achieve great things. George Marshall proved to be another example.

Shortly upon returning home from China, Lily fell ill with a diseased thyroid gland that required an operation, one that her doctors predicted would be challenging given her heart condition. It ended up being more than her body could handle; she died on September 15, 1927, three weeks after her surgery. Marshall was pulled out of a lecture and given the news over the telephone.

With no children, few close friends, and the lack of a core support group, a devastated Marshall felt completely alone. Writing to Pershing, who had lost his wife and three of his four children in a fire twelve years before, Marshall wrote that Lily's death left him "lost in my best effort to adjust myself to future prospects in life." He poured his soul out to Pershing, explaining it would be even more difficult for him to recover since he was not "given to club life" or "other intimacies with men." He believed he would be better able to cope if there were a "campaign" or some other "pressing duty."[5]

There wasn't one, of course, but Marshall believed if there was an assignment for him more challenging than lecturing at the Army War College, he could lose himself in the work and reduce the amount of time he was left alone in grief. The month following Lily's death, he was offered a position at Fort Benning that had just opened. Marshall headed to Georgia in November to take up the assignment. Training in the U.S. Army would never be the same.

Upon his arrival in Georgia, Marshall immediately threw himself into his work as if it were indeed a campaign. In a sense it was, given Marshall's core philosophy that it was the sacred duty of a U.S. Army officer to continually and urgently prepare for the next war. He spent the next five years completely revamping the way the United States Army trained its officers. Marshall's work ethic had always been impressive, but the anguish brought on by his wife's death drove him to new levels of productivity without which the dramatic changes he desired could not have been accomplished. Those changes would help the United States win the next war.

During his stay at Fort Benning, Marshall was responsible for the instruction of hundreds of officers, approximately 150 of whom would later serve as generals during World War II (including Omar Bradley, Joseph Stillwell, J. Lawton Collins, Walter Bedell Smith, Charles Bolte, and Matthew Ridgway). It was the Duke of Wellington who allegedly said more than a century earlier that the Battle of Waterloo was won on the playing fields of Eton. A far stronger case can be made that America's victories over the German Army during the Second World War were won in the classrooms and on the training fields of Fort Benning.

Fort Benning was established as Camp Benning just outside of Columbus, Georgia, in late 1918 to provide basic training for soldiers headed to Europe during World War I. It became an infantry school in 1920 and was renamed Fort Benning shortly thereafter. Its principal purpose was to train infantry officers how to lead small units of men in battle, but it also provided courses to higher-ranked officers and members of the National Guard looking to update their general knowledge base. Marshall's job, as assistant commandant, put him in charge of the academic and training program. He grasped immediately upon arriving that he had the opportunity to revolutionize the training of combat officers, incorporating all he had learned and absorbed over the past twenty-five years.

That Marshall could so confidently contemplate creating a new paradigm for infantry training was partly because the commandant he reported to (General Edgar Collins) fully trusted Marshall and gave him carte blanche when it came to the curriculum. Given this freedom and the high stature of Fort Benning among Army War Colleges, Marshall realized he had the opportunity to change not only the way Fort Benning students were taught but the way the entire U.S. Army trained its officers. Although he was not commanding troops, this was a dream opportunity and just the type of challenge he needed to distract him from Lily's death.

As Marshall began his quest to transform the methods of teaching and training Army officers, he reflected on what he had learned from John Morrison twenty years earlier at Fort Leavenworth. It was Morrison, one will recall, who captivated Marshall and others with his passion about keeping things simple and using common sense. Despite Morrison's popularity among those who learned under his tutelage at Fort Leavenworth between 1905 and 1912, the Army's teaching philosophy had stubbornly remained centered on what Marshall believed was an overemphasis on the rote memorization of complex techniques and elaborate planning at the expense of straightforward tactics.

Marshall was a committed disciple of Morrison in theory after leaving Leavenworth, but it was not until World War I and the subsequent training exercises he carried out in China that he fully appreciated how much the Army needed to adopt Morrison's teaching practices and bury the current methods. During his time in France and China, Marshall saw with his own eyes how well-trained American officers stumbled when conditions on the battlefield or training ground turned out differently than anticipated. He once observed a young officer during a training exercise in China attempt to draft a formal order for seventy men to attack a flank. Marshall was aware this particular officer had stood first at Fort Benning and was "no fool," but by the time it took him to write the standard five-paragraph field order then taught in the U.S. Army, all opportunity for success had passed.[6] The "absurd system" taught to the young man was fully to blame, and Marshall decided "then and there . . . to get my hands on Benning."[7] American soldiers were extremely well trained on how to do things, Marshall believed, but not on how to efficiently solve unexpected problems. Success in any battle required this skill.

Marshall also understood that the U.S. Army would likely remain an army of citizen-soldiers. Given this, he believed the training requirements currently in place were "too complicated for anything but a professional Army."[8] Thus it was even more imperative to impart on his charges the same importance to the basic and simple concepts of tactics Morrison had passed on to him years earlier.

Partly to escape the loss of his wife, partly because it was his approach to work, and partly because of the importance to which he assigned the task, Marshall threw every ounce of energy he possessed into overhauling the Army's long-established practices. In an approach he came to rely on when attempting to commence great changes, Marshall initially moved slowly in order to get the appropriate buy-in from those in the Army opposed to change and who believed the performance of the officers leading the doughboys during World War I was evidence enough that nothing needed to be fixed.

Marshall knew better. By the time America began to actually fight in early 1918, the Germans were too beat up after nearly four years of brutal trench warfare to take advantage of the many mistakes made by U.S. Army officers. He knew the Americans had more confidence, energy, and initiative than the Germans in the final year of the war, and they enjoyed the great luxury of time to make elaborate plans and issue "highly paragraphed" orders before going to battle.[9] But it was a delicate task to make these arguments firmly without depreciating either the men who led the American war effort (including Pershing) or those lower-ranked soldiers on the front who fought, bled, and died for the cause. He needed another angle, and the one he found was simple. He emphasized that the next war would be far more sophisticated than the last one, and therefore a general reassessment of how the Army trained its infantry was required.

Change is always hard to sell within a large organization, and to successfully indoctrinate new ideas into the student officers required continuous reinforcement from Marshall and his staff. One morning Marshall asked his class to make a detailed map of the route they had each just taken to get to class, including any and all information that could be of use to them in the event a battle was to be fought on the same ground. As he expected, the results were weak, but the exercise drilled home the importance of being continually observant of one's surroundings. By creating such habits during a time of peace, he hoped they would become second nature during war.

One device Marshall used to highlight the need for officers to respond to the unexpected was to send them out to the school's training grounds with troops to attack an "enemy force" led by other officers. But unbeknownst to the officers, the enemy force had been earlier instructed by Marshall to retreat away from the training ground. Once the attacking officers got comfortable the exercise was ending, Marshall sent a third force to attack them from the opposite direction.

Anything Marshall could do to get his officers closer to the chaotic conditions of an actual war, he would do. During maneuvers or exercises, he rarely handed out up-to-date maps. Instead, he provided old maps, foreign maps, small-scale maps, or no maps at all, because that was often the experience of officers during World War I. The ability to improvise was highly undervalued in the Army, and through such training techniques, Marshall was able to teach it and—just as importantly—find out which officers had a knack for it.

Once drills on the training ground were concluded, the instructors and students gathered in sessions (often led by Marshall) to analyze in detail what was done right, what was done wrong, and what lessons could be carried over to wartime situations. Marshall encouraged a healthy debate during these postexercise sessions, insisting the rank of a soldier should never prevent him from speaking out if he disagreed with an opinion or an idea held by a superior (not a surprising attitude coming from the man who had famously confronted and lectured Pershing during World War I).

What Marshall most wanted to develop in his officers at Fort Benning was creative thinking, more popularly referred to today as "thinking outside of the box." Innovation was the key, and no novel approach to a problem would ever be ignored at Fort Benning as long as Marshall was in charge. In fact, he ordered that any solution to a problem that was "radically" different to the school's solution or showed "independent creative thinking" should be published for the benefit of other students.[10]

Certain officers felt he went too far in valuing the unorthodox and those officers who showed a proclivity toward original ideas. By doing so, they believed, Marshall may have occasionally overlooked better solutions and the men who advocated them simply because they were more conventional. Perhaps this was true on occasion, but Marshall must have assumed that the risk was more than offset by the creative environment he was successful in fostering.

That the students selected to train at Fort Benning were earmarked to be the future leaders of the Army fit perfectly with Marshall's views on another obvious element of success in battle that he thought was particularly underrated: strong leadership skills at the command level. As a steadfast believer in the need for a proper chain of command during battle, Marshall insisted that the commander of any unit, regardless of its size, be able to make quick decisions with limited information and be able to communicate those decisions to his subordinates in a clear and concise manner. It helped to have a pool of strong candidates to train.

To be able to teach these select students how to make quick decisions, Marshall weaned officers and instructors off the traditional aim for perfection that had been part of the training culture in American Army Colleges for decades. With enough time, Marshall felt, one could always come up with a better plan, but time was not a luxury an officer in the field normally enjoyed during war. Marshall always set up his exercises to limit time. To succeed, one had to come up with solutions quickly, even if the solutions decided upon were not optimal.

Even a quick decision would be pointless unless a commander was able to quickly convey it to those serving under him. Therefore, communication was another on the list of qualities Marshall was convinced was both underrated and in short supply in the Army. This, too, he observed during the First

World War, and it was not necessarily the fault of the officers. He believed the skill to communicate concisely had not historically been prioritized by the Army Colleges. Marshall insisted it could be taught and should be.

To help focus his students on acquiring this competence, Marshall insisted that all lectures and presentations (a traditional part of Army training) be brief and given without notes. Marshall practiced what he preached when it came to this style of communication; it was natural for him and something he prided himself on. There is a great story told by one of Marshall's students that demonstrated his ability to be concise. It had been an established practice at Fort Benning that lengthy papers were presented each semester by students on some aspect of military history. Marshall insisted on two changes to this tradition: Papers had to be presented orally; and individual presentations could not exceed twenty minutes. When some of the students complained to Marshall that twenty minutes was not enough time to properly address all the pertinent issues of a military problem, he immediately responded by giving them a complete history of the American Civil War in less than five minutes.[11]

Naturally, Marshall could not change so many long-prevailing methods and philosophies all by himself. He staffed the college with men who shared his vision. Joe Stillwell (known later during the Second World War by the moniker "Vinegar Joe"), Lieutenant Colonel M. C. Stayer, Omar Bradley (eventually the ninth and last five-star general in the history of the United States), and Major Edwin Harding were part of what Marshall would later describe as the "most brilliant, interesting, and thoroughly competent collection of men I have ever been associated with." Aside from their talents, it did not go unnoticed by Marshall that each of these men possessed a high level of energy and a robust work ethic. Although the other traits Marshall valued could be taught, those two could only be found. Anytime they were, he made notes.

As serious and hardworking as Marshall was at Fort Benning, he was also devoted to making it a fun place to be posted. Like Stimson, Marshall also subscribed to a "work hard, play hard" philosophy and believed there was a strong correlation between the overall morale at a specific post and the quality of work it achieved. At Fort Benning, he stepped up his efforts in this regard and improved the physical, social, cultural, and intellectual activities for both the men under his command and their wives.

Twice a week, from October through April, Marshall hosted foxhunts on the expansive acreage of Fort Benning for sixty or more officers and their spouses. In lieu of formal military reviews, which Marshall found boring, he organized pageants for the benefit of visiting dignitaries. At these pageants, resembling modern-day suburban Memorial Day parades, soldiers marched by in groups arranged by the various activities undertaken at the post (tennis players marched together with their rackets, ball players with bats and gloves, polo players with their ponies, etc.). Marshall also regularly organized plays to entertain the soldiers.

And then there were the parties he hosted. Although enjoyable, they were hardly Gatsbyesque. Shortly after they began, Marshall would suggest playing intellectual games. He not only enjoyed them, but he also thought they kept the mind honed. It is doubtful that everyone present welcomed these amusements, and not surprising that such initiatives, along with Marshall's generally puritanical nature, gave rise to the nickname "Uncle George" bestowed upon him by the men stationed at Fort Benning (but only used when referring to Marshall behind his back).

It is possible that "Uncle George" was overscheduling himself and the men during these years as a result of the void created following Lily's death. Fortunately for Marshall, his loneliness came to an end two years into his assignment at Fort Benning, when mutual friends at a dinner party in nearby Columbus, Georgia, introduced him to a recent widow.

Katherine Boyce Tupper Brown was by all accounts an attractive, tall, humorous, and interesting woman, and Marshall had completely fallen for her by the end of the evening. The daughter of a distinguished Baptist minister from Kentucky, Brown shocked her father by pursuing an acting career after completing her university studies. After a few years touring with companies in England, Australia, and the United States, health issues caused her to give up her dream and return to America, where she got married and started a family.

A year before she met Marshall, Brown lost her husband (a successful Baltimore-based lawyer) after he was shot by a disgruntled law client. She was left with three children between the ages of eleven and fifteen. After taking roughly eight months off with relatives in Connecticut to recover and a few more months with her daughter in Hawaii, Brown was on her way back to Baltimore to resume her life when she stopped in Columbus to visit a friend. During this stay, she was invited to the dinner where she met Marshall.

Not one to ever let the knock of opportunity go unanswered, Marshall was as aggressive in pursuing Brown as he was in pursuing his first wife back when he was a student at the VMI. Taking up Marshall's offer to give her a ride home after dinner on the night they met, Katherine Brown was driven around for an hour by Marshall before his car finally pulled into the driveway of the house she was staying in, only a few minutes from where they had dinner. In response to her question inquiring why he was not more familiar with the roads of Columbus after serving two years at Fort Benning (a few miles away), Marshall responded self-assuredly that he was quite familiar with them, and it was just such keen knowledge of the roads that had enabled him to drive for an hour without once crossing the street where she was staying.[12]

After several months of correspondence and a second meeting in Columbus the following spring, Brown agreed to marry Marshall under the condition that her three children consented to the idea. She owned a summer cottage on Fire Island in New York and invited Marshall to join other friends of hers for five weeks in the summer of 1930. Marshall easily won over the children, and the couple married later that fall. General Pershing served as his best man. As classes were about to resume at Fort Benning, the two went straight from the altar to the train station. They remained happily married for thirty years until Marshall's death in 1959.

Fort Screven, Fort Moultrie, and the CCC (July 1932–October 1933)

Since the length of assignments in the Army was highly regulated during the years between the wars, Marshall's time at Fort Benning was up in the spring of 1931. But there were always loopholes to be exploited. Marshall was asked, at the specific request of the post's commandant, to join the 24th Infantry, which just so happened to be garrisoned at Fort Benning. This move gave Marshall another year to transform the nation's training methods.

A year later, Marshall felt he had accomplished a lot, and he accepted an assignment to command a battalion of troops at Fort Screven in Georgia, 275 miles east of Fort Benning on a small island near Savannah. He was thrilled; as rewarding as his five years as assistant commandant at Fort Benning had been, he needed and wanted command experience. Despite being just a lieutenant colonel at the age of fifty-two, Marshall did not give up hope that his time would come. There is no evidence he lowered his professional standards during this period or slowed down his resolve to reach the top—quite the contrary, in fact.

His second wife provided a wonderful anecdote in her memoirs about Marshall's ambition and his attention to detail at this stage of his career.

Shortly after they were married, Marshall and his wife were to be honored at a huge reception at Fort Benning by the fort's commanding general. The newlyweds were required to greet close to a thousand individuals in a reception line, including many men Marshall had known at various stages in his career (along with their wives). Katherine—new to the Army—was extremely nervous, but Marshall told her to relax, explaining he would whisper to her single code words, such as "China" or "flowers," as the various guests approached. If, for example, he said the word "China," she was supposed to say something like, "Oh, you served with Colonel Marshall in China, didn't you?" If he said the word "flower," she was to greet that individual or couple by saying, "Thank you for the lovely flowers" (Marshall had committed to memory the name of each guest who had sent flowers to the house). Either way, he explained to his wife, "It will be most flattering to them."[13] That evening, his wife stood in awe of her new husband as he shot off these two code words and others without hesitation as each of the guests moved rapidly through the line. A man more pessimistic about his future might not have bothered to stay on top of his game at this juncture in his career.

This optimism, along with his genuine devotion to the Army, made it easier for him to turn down two more attractive opportunities presented to him during the five years he served at Fort Benning. The first came again from Dwight Morrow, the J.P. Morgan partner who had offered Marshall an annual salary of $30,000 to work for the bank after World War I. Morrow had been asked to serve as governor general of the Philippines in 1929 and was looking to recruit some talented men to join him. The secretary of state at that time (Henry Stimson) suggested Marshall's name to Morrow for the prestigious and lucrative post of chief of the constabulary. Morrow, of course, remembered Marshall from a decade earlier and jumped at the suggestion, inviting him to Washington to talk it over.

Marshall toyed with the idea, as anyone his age and rank would (he went down to Washington to meet with Morrow), but Pershing gave him the moral support to turn it down by writing to Marshall that his future was with the Army. Although it was a decision Marshall was likely to have made anyway, Pershing's advice might have helped him get comfortable with it. If the World War I hero thought his protégé had little chance of reaching the top, he might have advised him otherwise. Although Pershing had been retired for five years, he remained a powerful and well-connected man in Washington. It made sense for Marshall to seek and consider his counsel.

Shortly after declining the offer from Morrow, Marshall turned down an opportunity to be superintendent of his beloved alma mater. It was not the first time the VMI had reached out to its former student; it twice tried to get him assigned as commandant in 1909 and 1912, but on each of those occasions, Marshall's superiors believed the time away from line duty would hurt his prospects. The opportunity at the VMI had to be tempting, but as fond as he was of the school and the state of Virginia, he would not easily leave a profession to which he had devoted thirty years, particularly when he had achieved great success and a sterling reputation, if not the star on his shoulder that he coveted.

The roads not taken were behind Marshall when he arrived to take over command of Fort Screven in July 1932. Marshall came to the post at a time when America's Great Depression was reaching its high-water mark. The month he took command, the Dow Jones Industrial Average and the Industrial Production Index sank to the lowest points they would reach during the Depression, and U.S. unemployment was closing in on its peak level of 25 percent. Also taking place that month was the Democratic National Convention in Chicago, where a popular governor from New York was chosen to represent the Democrats in the presidential election in November. Franklin D. Roosevelt began the tradition that year of accepting the nomination in person at the convention, and during his speech he outlined a plan that included the concept of putting thousands of the unemployed to work around the country to reverse soil erosion and revitalize overused agricultural land. FDR was elected four months later, and the plan, referred to as the Civilian Conservation Corps, or CCC, was signed into law the month he was inaugurated. Marshall had no way of knowing it at the time, but this law would have a far-reaching impact on his career.

The CCC was part of a larger New Deal program ushered in by FDR to stimulate the economy and get Americans working. Marshall spent a greater part of the next seven years using his leadership skills to help make the CCC a success. His efforts did not go unnoticed. When FDR needed to replace his Army chief of staff in 1939, Marshall's file was well known to a few members of the president's inner circle who were aware not only of his overall stellar service record but also of his great accomplishments with the CCC.

Why Marshall and the Army got involved in the CCC was simple: Once the logistical realities of the New Deal caught up with its idealistic aims, Roosevelt realized the Army was the only institution capable and equipped to both organize and run the various work camps being set up around the country. As a result, it was put in charge of essentially all aspects of the camps save the technical and scientific supervision of the projects themselves. The Army had no objections; the work required was entirely consistent with what it was largely trained to do: mobilize, organize, administer, and motivate a large number of civilians toward a common goal.

Although the first hundred days of the Roosevelt administration were most notably remembered for the unprecedented pace of lawmaking that occurred, the execution of those laws was equally if not more impressive. FDR took the oath of office on March 4, 1933, and got the CCC bill passed on March 31st; three months later, there were close to 1,500 CCC camps operating around the country with over 250,000 enrollees.

Almost overnight, Marshall went from supervising the routine duties of training men and keeping his post looking respectable, to an aggressive program of building camps in and around the swamps of Georgia and Florida. In early June, he was formally named a commanding officer of one of the CCC districts and charged with setting up and operating nineteen camps located in South Carolina. Marshall organized the effort from a new base at Fort Moultrie, three miles outside of Charleston. It was there where he took command of the 8th Infantry. Along with the added responsibility came a scheduled promotion to colonel that became effective later that summer.

Marshall could not have been more pleased at the turn of events. He was one promotion away from brigadier general, he was commanding large numbers of men toward what he believed was a noble purpose, and he was, as usual, getting results and plaudits for his efforts. Plus, Marshall always loved a challenge; he wrote an Army colleague about his experience in South Carolina, describing it as the "most interesting problem of my Army career."[14]

The men welcomed to the camps by the newly minted colonel were generally from rural areas. Many brought with them questionable habits. This was particularly difficult to manage given that whenever a new camp opened, there immediately appeared entrepreneurs wanting to sell liquor to the men. Ever the pragmatist, Marshall decided that curtailing supply would be far easier than demand. If the local officials he spoke to failed to stop the trade, Marshall made appointments with businessmen, bankers, and merchants in the community. He told them that if the liquor trade did not stop by the end of two weeks, he would move the respective camp. During the Depression, having a camp in one's town was meaningful to the local economy as the men and officers spent a portion of their paychecks purchasing goods and services from local merchants. Following Marshall's threats, the liquor trade generally ceased.[15]

Even with improved levels of sobriety, it was still a huge challenge to turn the men into a healthy collection of spirited, disciplined, and motivated workers. Marshall relished the opportunity and couldn't wait to see results. Therefore, it came as a great disappointment and shock to him when he got word, just three months after arriving at Fort Moultrie, that he was being reassigned to yet another teaching position. Douglas MacArthur, three years into his stint as Army chief of staff, recommended Marshall for the position of senior instructor with the Illinois National Guard. Marshall was distraught. He was sure such an assignment would kill any chances he had for a senior command position in the future, something he felt he needed for his next promotion. A direct appeal to MacArthur, the first of such kind Marshall ever made while in the Army, was rejected, and Marshall promptly left for Chicago.

Marshall and MacArthur had a bit of history, going back to the First World War. Long after the fighting ended, the latter remained suspicious of any member of the "Chaumont crowd" (that group of officers who served under Pershing at the American headquarters in France). Not only did MacArthur look down upon any officers who spent the War behind the front lines (including Pershing himself), but he also felt that the men surrounding Pershing had been jealous of him and conspired to discredit him or reduce his role during the War. As Marshall was Pershing's principal protégé and emerged from the conflict as a superstar within his own right, it was inevitable the ambitious MacArthur looked upon him as a potential rival to be thwarted. This can't be discounted when one considers MacArthur's role in transferring Marshall to Chicago.

Chicago and the First Star
(November 1933–August 1936)

Few who knew Marshall's abilities were surprised when the troops under his command in Chicago began receiving the highest inspection grades they'd seen in years. He put forth his usual effort by arranging maneuvers, teaching talented National Guard officers to take over the training done by Army officers, and even editing the official Illinois National Guard newspaper himself. Although Marshall still felt strongly that the transfer to Chicago would derail his chances for a top job, teaching and molding officers was something Marshall genuinely loved doing, and there was nobody in the Army better at it.

In August 1936, after nearly three years in Chicago, Marshall was rewarded for his performance with a new assignment commanding troops in Washington State (MacArthur was no longer chief of staff). He was also advised—at long last—that he was to become a member of the general officer ranks by receiving the promotion that gave him the coveted first star of a brigadier general.

It took over thirty-four years for Marshall to achieve the rank (Douglas MacArthur, although born in the same year and joining the Army a year *after* Marshall, took approximately half as many). Marshall was obviously pleased but felt the promotion was long overdue and possibly too late. He certainly had time to think about it as he headed west across the country to his new assignment. If during that journey Marshall began playing out in his mind possible scenarios for a top job in the future, he would have reminded himself that although politics always played a role in the selection of high command positions, timing and luck were equally influential factors. By the time he reached Washington State to take up his new command assignment, he might have been content to know that at the very least, he was positioned to benefit from either or both. And it was not just any senior job he set his eyes on; it was the one at the top, chief of staff. Marshall always aimed high.

Despite years of seeing other men with weaker records advance more quickly to the general officer ranks, Marshall did not give up hope he could reach the apex. In this case, timing was the most critical factor. Even at the highest command levels, there were rules strictly followed when considering top contenders. The specific one that made timing so important for Marshall was that any candidate for the chief of staff position (and a few other high command posts) had to be able to serve four full years before hitting the mandatory retirement age of sixty-four. This was a curious paradox considering the general convention of seniority that dictated most promotions in the Army; when an officer finally reached a high enough position of seniority to be considered, he was often too old to be eligible.

This established convention limited the overall pool of candidates for chief of staff, which naturally meant there were fewer talented choices for a president to consider when the position needed to be filled. For Marshall, the numbers worked as follows: He was just shy of fifty-six years old when he received his first star in 1936. He therefore had four years of eligibility for the chief of staff position. During that time, he believed he needed to receive the second star of a major general if he were to have any realistic chance of being appointed. Working against Marshall's chances was the fact that several men of the same rank—or higher rank—had received their first or second stars earlier than he did.

From the time he was promoted to colonel three years earlier in September 1933, Marshall had been keenly aware of this math. From that moment, he knew that each year he remained a colonel was going to make his chances for the top spot that much more difficult. At about that time, two senior generals wrote to Marshall unsolicited that they had asked Secretary of War George Dern to place his name on the list of candidates for promotion to brigadier general. When Marshall received the letter, he forwarded it to Pershing and asked him to speak to the secretary of war on his behalf to see if he could get on the next list for promotions to brigadier general.

The note Marshall penned to Pershing (written in November 1934) opened matter-of-factly:

> *Dear General: I am enclosing two letters which are self-explanatory. Two or three BG vacancies now exist. I want one of them. As I will soon be 54, I must get started if I am going anywhere in the Army.*[16]

Perhaps sensing that this was too aggressive, Marshall then asked Pershing to simply mention his name to the secretary of war and suggest he send for his record; he knew there were no colonels in the Army who could touch it. Pershing had no reservations about advocating on behalf of Marshall, and he did so directly with Dern and Chief of Staff Douglas MacArthur on more than one occasion.

During peacetime, promotion by seniority rarely gets challenged, and Douglas MacArthur did not see any benefit in appearing to favor certain officers over others. Several historians have speculated that MacArthur held up Marshall's promotion due to the differences the former had with members of Pershing's inner circle. Although there is no evidence of this, MacArthur knew Pershing never liked him, and everyone in the Army knew how close Pershing was with Marshall. Military brilliance aside, MacArthur was both political and petty, and it is highly unlikely he would have lifted a finger to assist Marshall.

Surely sensing this, Pershing appealed to Roosevelt directly. The president agreed to get involved and asked both Dern and MacArthur if Marshall could be considered for his first star, given Pershing had "asked very strongly" that he be placed on the next promotion list.[17] The president was given the same run-around Pershing had received. Despite all the pressure exerted by men of influence on his behalf, the peacetime practice of advancing men strictly based on seniority prevailed. Marshall was forced to wait it out for two more long years before getting his first star.

Vancouver Barracks and the CCC (August 1936–July 1938)

After his formal promotion in October 1936, the newly minted brigadier general drove from Chicago to the northwest to take over command of Vancouver Barracks located in Vancouver, Washington, for another CCC assignment. Accompanied by his wife and stepdaughter, he took his time along the way (about three weeks) to tour historical sites and other places of interest.[18]

Vancouver Barracks was less than ten miles north of Portland, Oregon, just over the Washington border. It was established in 1849 and had hosted several legendary Civil War soldiers, including Ulysses Grant, Phil Sheridan, George Pickett, and John Pope. The post was in a physically beautiful location, and Marshall was thrilled to be back in a position of command. Like all the posts Marshall ran during his career, Vancouver Barracks soon benefited from the "Marshall treatment" (physical improvements to both the grounds and fort, military pageants, an improved post newspaper, community engagement, etc.). Building up morale was always on the forefront of Marshall's mind. Napoleon famously believed that in war "the morale is to the physical as three is to one." Marshall did not break it down mathematically but spoke of its importance incessantly and knew that without it, wars could not be won.

There was no war, of course, when Marshall was in command at Vancouver Barracks, but his strong beliefs in the correlation between high morale and success carried over to his work with civilians assigned to the twenty-five-plus camps in Oregon and southern Washington for which he was directly responsible. It was his main concern throughout his stay in the Northwest.

Marshall's love and respect for the CCC program only grew during this period. He was dazzled by its potential to develop American men who could lead productive lives and contribute to society. He later said that a dream job for him would have been to lead the entire CCC program, and he wrote to a friend in late 1938 that his work with the CCC program was "the most instructive service" he ever rendered for his country and the "most interesting."[19]

Despite the long working hours Marshall put into overseeing both the CCC camps and Vancouver Barracks, his stay in the Northwest was as enjoyable and relaxing from a personal standpoint as any previous assignment undertaken in his career. The geographical disbursement of the various camps required Marshall to spend a lot of his time traveling throughout the beautiful outdoor spaces of Oregon and Washington. During his visits, he found time to fish and hunt and often brought his wife with him as a traveling companion. They spent the weekends together between camp visits in various remote cabins either on the coast or in the mountains, often inviting guests. In the summer of 1937, the two drove 1,400 miles through eastern Oregon visiting various camps and enjoying the scenery. Marshall's wife wrote in her memoirs that their two years in the Northwest were "two of the happiest years of our life."[20] When the assignment ended, neither Marshall nor his wife could have guessed that the two of them would have to wait another thirteen years until they were able to spend as much time together.

War Plans Division, Washington, D.C. (July 1938—September 1939)

As busy and happy as Marshall was in the Northwest, he was keeping an increasingly close eye on the deteriorating situation in Europe and Asia. The Spanish Civil War, which started a few months before he arrived in Vancouver, served as both a barometer of the general condition of political affairs in Europe and a demonstration of how warfare had evolved since the end of World War I. Adolf Hitler, who tested his newly manufactured weapons and planes in Spain in support of the Nationalists, also began testing the political mettle of the other European powers. Emboldened after reoccupying the Rhineland in early 1936, Hitler arranged the takeover of Austria and then began making noise about the Sudetenland in Czechoslovakia. In Asia, the Sino-Japanese War started a year into Marshall's assignment, making several prominent Americans (Henry Stimson most notably) equally uncomfortable about Japan's aggression in the Pacific.

One man who was particularly uneasy about the prospects of a global war was Army Chief of Staff Malin Craig. Believing it was inevitable, he wanted the best men helping him plan for it. Like many senior officers at that time, Craig greatly respected Marshall and wanted him by his side in the War Department; in fact, he wanted to bring him in two years earlier but was advised by a few officers that Marshall needed to bolster his résumé with more experience commanding troops. With aggression around the world accelerating in the early part of 1938, he no longer could afford to wait and ordered Marshall back to Washington in May to serve as assistant chief of staff in charge of the War Plans Division.

Following the announcement, there was immediate talk in Washington that Marshall would soon be appointed deputy chief of staff, which, in turn, would lead to the chief of staff position upon General Craig's retirement the following year. Despite these rumors and the precarious state of international affairs, Marshall remained certain that staff work, planning, or teaching could only hinder him. He knew his path to the top required a second star, and he believed his greatest chance for this lay in continued troop duty. Therefore, he was in no mood to begin celebrating his appointment.

It was not only Europe and Asia that were experiencing hostilities in the summer of 1938 when Marshall began his new assignment; the War Department itself was the scene of an open and all-out battle between Secretary of War Harry Woodring and Assistant Secretary of War Louis Johnson. The former was a cautious Midwestern isolationist, the latter an aggressive West Virginian interventionist. Roosevelt appointed Johnson in 1937 to mollify interventionists who were out for Woodring's head. In addition to their diverging political views, Woodring and Johnson also happened to dislike one another immensely and were not on speaking terms.

About the only thing the two men could agree on was that they both admired George Marshall. But Johnson, the more ambitious of the two men, wanted to accelerate Marshall's appointment to deputy chief of staff. In October, he took advantage of Woodring's absence to order—in his capacity as acting secretary of war—the chief of staff to name Marshall to the position of deputy chief of staff. Malin Craig's only objection was the one normally felt by senior officers who wished to respect the custom of seniority; he did not wish to slight other more senior officers in the Army by naming Marshall so quickly to the post. Johnson was unsympathetic to such arguments and ordered Craig to make the appointment immediately. Marshall began his duties on October 15, 1938, only three months into his new position.

The rumors circulating throughout Washington that Marshall would succeed General Craig in August 1939 only increased after Marshall was appointed his deputy. Marshall was not happy at the talk, believing it could hurt his cause by angering any combination of Craig, Woodring, or the president. At the same time, he certainly knew his chances of reaching his goal had increased due to Johnson's machinations.

If the decision to replace the retiring Craig was made strictly by the book, Marshall was fifth in line with respect to seniority after eliminating thirty-one officers more senior to him who would exceed the age of sixty-four by the time the four-year assignment ended. Of the four who were more senior to Marshall, only one had a résumé rivaling his: General Hugh Drum, a friend and colleague of Marshall's for many years. Drum's record was excellent, and he had already been twice considered for the job (in 1930 and 1935).

The decision, of course, rested with the president, and FDR was rarely someone who went by the book. Roosevelt could have easily decided to ignore the age limit if there was a candidate he wished to appoint. Alternatively, if there were men further down the ranks who stood out and caught his attention, he would not have hesitated to appoint one of them. Marshall, like most Americans observing President Roosevelt over the five previous years, was aware he was not averse to skirting convention. But having no control over the matter, he simply went about his work, comfortable in letting the quality of it, along with his excellent record, determine his fate.

The one thing Marshall would not do was lobby for the appointment or request others to do so for him. Despite the substantial efforts he made to get his commission thirty-eight years earlier, and his recruitment of Pershing in 1934 to assist him in getting his first star, it was not Marshall's style to campaign for advancement. In fact, following his request for Pershing's help, Marshall went out of his way for the rest of his career to avoid even the perception of seeking favor.

As deputy chief of staff, Marshall did have one distinct advantage over other rivals seeking the top spot: exposure to Roosevelt. Considering how swiftly the state of the world was deteriorating in 1938, this advantage only increased with time. Hitler was showing no sign of tempering his aggressive behavior, and reports were coming in to the White House from a variety of sources in Europe about the massive buildup of airpower Germany had been undertaking.

It was against this background that the newly appointed deputy chief of staff was invited to a meeting at the White House in November 1938, hosted by Roosevelt and attended by a dozen high-ranking military and civilian officials. The subject was aircraft; specifically, the president wanted to announce to those gathered his plan to dramatically boost production in the United States to a level exceeding ten thousand planes per year. Roosevelt suggested that with such a massive output, America would not only be able to deter the German leader from any future hostile intentions he had on the Americas, but the United States also could prevent or delay any attacks by Germany on England or France.

Roosevelt's plan was characteristically grand in scale but light in details. Marshall did not think it was well thought out (it did not address the need for pilot training nor properly weigh the importance of ground forces as a deterrent to a German strike on America). But as the new kid on the block, he remained silent during the meeting while everyone else in the room gave the president enthusiastic feedback and support. Taking notice, Roosevelt asked Marshall toward the end of the meeting what he thought of the plan. Marshall bluntly told him he disagreed with it. This startled FDR, so much so that he abruptly ended the meeting without even asking Marshall to clarify his answer.

Twenty years earlier, Marshall had famously grabbed the arm of General Pershing and lectured him on a field in France about unjust criticism of his division and its top commander. Although his fellow officers at that time thought his career was through, Marshall quickly went on to be a Pershing confidante. Similarly, after the meeting with Roosevelt ended, several men around the room assumed Marshall's days were numbered and wished him well accordingly. These officers were similarly mistaken.

Roosevelt, like any president, had no shortage of yes-men surrounding him. By contrast, Marshall presented himself that day (and in many other heated meetings to follow) as a straight shooter with no apparent personal agenda. Notwithstanding Marshall's excellent record, by appointing Marshall a few months later to the top job, the president revealed—to his everlasting credit—that the quality of candor in a military advisor was one he valued as highly as Pershing did years earlier.

FDR's feelings aside, there were several individuals who made it their business during the following months to promote Marshall as the next chief of staff. These men did so not because it benefited their own careers, but because they had all worked with Marshall and knew there was no other candidate as capable to take over the position. First among Marshall's advocates was General of the Armies John Pershing, the most respected and celebrated military man in the country. Although such a reference from a national hero could not have hurt Marshall's cause, it is doubtful it helped much; Pershing was an octogenarian more than two decades past his peak fame and not particularly close to the president.

But FDR was extremely tight with Harry Hopkins, and without the strong support of this remarkable individual, Roosevelt could have easily gone in a different direction. Hopkins, Roosevelt's principal advisor, had not known Marshall long, but he was favorably impressed with his overall knowledge of the Army and specifically its deficiencies toward the end of 1938. With Hopkins pressing the merits of Marshall to the president, his appointment might have been assured.[21] In any event, FDR made up his mind and advised Marshall in April 1939 that he would become chief of staff in September when General Craig retired.

It was a remarkable turn of events for the fifty-eight-year-old who, only two years earlier, was still a lieutenant colonel. But based strictly on his unparalleled record, the breadth of his experience, and the esteem in which he was held within the Army, nobody had a better claim to the job.

George Marshall had reached the top. He unofficially took up the duties of chief of staff in June, became acting chief of staff on July 1, and was formally sworn into the position on September 1, 1939 (which, by pure coincidence, was the day World War II began with the German invasion of Poland).

When a reporter asked Roosevelt that day if the nation could stay out of the war, he answered that he believed the country could, that he hoped they would, and that every effort would be directed toward avoiding it. He knew better. So, too, did Marshall; based on letters he wrote during the first week of September, he hinted it was just a matter of time before America was drawn into the conflict. His job was to get the Army prepared as soon as possible.

Chief of Staff

The chief of staff position was created, along with the General Staff, as part of the reforms initiated by Secretary of War Elihu Root through the General Staff Act of 1903. Root placed all administration, supply, and planning functions under the position. Despite his efforts, it took years and fierce battles (several led by Henry Stimson during his first stint as secretary of war) to get Root's vision and the reality of command in the Army more closely aligned. Only when Marshall began to settle in as chief of staff was the overall environment promising enough to secure all of Root's original goals. His own stature within the Army, the existing global conflicts in Europe and Asia, and the realization among many that a new paradigm was needed to take on a dictator like Hitler silenced any remaining holdouts to change.

According to the Army regulations in effect at the time Marshall succeeded to the job, the chief of staff was the "immediate advisor to the Secretary of War on all matters relating to the military establishment" and was charged by him with "the planning, development, and execution of the military program." The responsibilities included recruiting, mobilizing, organizing, supplying, equipping, and training the Army. As far as command during war, the regulation stated the chief of staff had it unless the president chose someone else.

FDR added another twist to the job through an executive order in early July 1939 permitting direct contact between the president and chief of staff relating to "strategy, tactics, and operations." This order, made after Marshall had informally taken over the responsibilities of the position, essentially cut out the secretary of war as it related to war strategy. This change reflected both Roosevelt's low opinion of the secretary of war at the time (Woodring) and his desire to maintain control over such matters.

With Marshall firmly in place, the question of whether he was reporting directly to the president or the secretary of war on such matters was the least of his concerns. He needed to get the country prepared for war. This undertaking proved to be the most challenging of his life.

Going to Work

When Marshall was sworn in as chief of staff, the United States Army barely made it onto the list of the top twenty armies of the world (it stood at nineteenth, between Portugal and Bulgaria). Even though Congress had authorized a standing army of 280,000 two decades earlier, it provided only enough funding to maintain the level at an average of between 130,000 and 190,000 men during the ensuing twenty years (it was approximately 170,000 when Marshall took over). Worse, the soldiers were scattered in approximately 150 small garrisons.[22] This made training for any reasonably sized group of men impossible, given that there were no effective means to move men and equipment from various garrisons to a concentrated point. Maneuvers, a key practice for any serious army, were held every four years, and even then, for only two weeks (just five days of which involved any type of field action). The United States Army was nowhere near ready for war.

The principal cause for the nation's lack of preparedness was isolationism. Congress generally reflects the will of the people, and a sizable majority of them during that era were isolationists, still angry that America had sacrificed blood and treasure during World War I for no obvious gain. None of their arguments had changed over the years: The Atlantic and Pacific Oceans continued to offer the nation adequate protection against its enemies even with the advent of airplanes, and America would once again be able to rely on its citizen soldiers to carry the day on the field with the support of a workforce at home that would unleash the strength of the nation's industrial capabilities to quickly produce enough weapons and supplies to overwhelm the enemy.

Both hopes relied in part on two continuing myths: First, that it was the American citizen soldier who was principally responsible for America's successful track record in war; and second, that the country had the ability to rapidly retool her powerful industrial capacity from a peacetime to a wartime footing. The former myth has been discussed in earlier chapters; the latter was born after the victory of World War I (for all the country's industrial efforts during that era, the actual number of weapons making it from the United States to Europe before the end of the war was small). The belief in both misconceptions condemned the country to a level of preparedness in 1939 that Marshall later estimated lengthened World War II by a full year, added billions of dollars to its cost, and added one hundred thousand to its total U.S. casualties.[23]

But wasn't fighting a war and preparing for it two unrelated notions? Not to the isolationists. Despite attempts by Marshall and others to convince the American people there was a difference, most isolationists were against building up the nation's military strength, believing the very act of doing so would lead the country to war.

To Marshall, this thinking was absurd. Ever cognizant of history, he regularly reminded Americans during this period of two realities: First, the country had been extremely lucky in the past to overcome its habitual unpreparedness; and second, it takes a long time to build up an Army and an even longer time to provide it with weapons.

The history lessons Marshall delivered in speeches and private conversations predated his appointment to the top job by FDR. In November 1938, in remarks to the American Legion, Marshall carefully reviewed the state of the American military at the start of the War of 1812, the Mexican-American War, the Spanish-American War, and World War I. What was not covered in schoolbooks, Marshall explained to his audience, was how woefully unprepared the nation was for each of those conflicts. He concluded that it was only larger armies, luck, incompetence of the enemy, and (in the case of WWI) the assistance of allies that prevented disasters of the highest order.

As for weapons, Marshall knew it took eighteen months generally to manufacture one from start to finish. With the world on high alert and war a distinct possibility, he warned the audience that "no matter how many billions of dollars Congress places at our disposal on the day war is declared, they will not buy ten cents worth of war material for delivery under twelve months." In case those listening missed the obvious, Marshall continued by stating, "In other words, whatever your son and my son is to use to defend himself and to defend us and the nation has to be manufactured in time of peace." In less than 2,200 words, Marshall delivered a set of arguments seemingly impossible to ignore.[24] Still, most Americans seemed content to discount his advice and wave off his observations.[25]

The intense desire of Americans to avoid war stemmed from something other than simply abhorrence to the loss of life and treasure. There has always been another deeply rooted worry permeating the nation's collective psyche: War was a threat to freedom. Tocqueville observed in 1835 that anyone who wished to "destroy the liberties of a democratic nation ought to know that war is the surest and shortest means to accomplish it." This fear in the United States predated Tocqueville's *Democracy in America* but became more fervent following the swift and brutal rise of fascist governments in Germany, Italy, and Spain.

In such an environment, progress for Marshall was practically impossible to attain. Although Roosevelt was smart and surrounded by many capable people who understood the sensible course of action vis-à-vis preparation, he was keenly mindful of how his constituents felt. At the time Marshall formally took the chief of staff position, FDR faced a potentially difficult election in just over a year. No president had ever sought a third consecutive term—a difficult enough challenge—and Roosevelt could not win without some level of support in the Midwest, a region where isolationism was most strongly rooted. Therefore, against his better instincts, the president generally proceeded with caution when it came to preparedness. Marshall, serving at the president's pleasure, had little choice but to be generally patient.

But on some subjects related to preparedness, Marshall would not sit by. Training was one of these, specifically the need for the Army to undertake large-scale maneuvers. He said he did not know of any "single investment which will give this country a greater return in security and in the saving of lives."[26] One will recall that Marshall made a name for himself early in his career through his performance during maneuvers in New England and the

Philippines in 1912 and 1914 respectively. Responding to questions from a subcommittee of the House Committee on Appropriations in late November 1939, Marshall politely but firmly defended the need for the Army to build up its technique of command, control, and leadership on something other than a theoretical basis. Citing the experience of the Army during World War I, Marshall commented, "Fortunately the AEF had allies to protect itself for more than a year." The implication was clear; without undertaking the type of training that most closely replicates battlefield conditions, this might not be the case in the future.[27]

Until France capitulated to the German blitzkrieg in June of 1940 (one year after Marshall took over the duties of chief of staff), it was an uphill battle to persuade Congress to loosen up the purse strings for much of anything, much less maneuvers. Marshall's first budget request was cut by 10 percent in early April 1940 despite his assertion to Congress that the budget was "modest" (which was a huge understatement). At that time, Congress did not see a lot of fighting going on in Europe (there had been little engagement between the main forces) and wanted to send a strong message to the Roosevelt administration about where it stood on the issue of building up the military. A week after the cuts were made, the invasion by Germany of Denmark and Norway gave Marshall the excuse to seek a restoration of the reduction. When this effort stalled, he asked the influential Bernard Baruch (the czar of civilian war production during World War I) to arrange meetings for him with key members of the Senate Appropriations Committee.

Baruch contacted Senator Jimmy Brynes, the powerful senator from South Carolina, who arranged a dinner with over a dozen other important senators. Outlining where the Army stood and where it needed to go in order to properly defend the nation, Marshall spoke until nearly three o'clock in the morning and displayed his usual full command of facts and statistics. By the time he was finished, most of the senators were convinced the situation was serious. Marshall rarely spoke with notes during his career, and his ability to impress people in such a manner with logical arguments supported by specific data had long been his strong suit. Baruch believed the meeting was a turning point in the administration's efforts to appeal to isolationists.

Although restoring the cuts was important, America was still far short of what Marshall believed was required. He knew he had to go back to Capitol Hill to ask for additional resources and he had to do it quickly. But he first needed to get President Roosevelt on board.

Six months prior to an election, a politician of the caliber of FDR generally assumes a heightened level of intensity and focus. In 1940, it was simply not good politics to be seen advocating any step that could get the country involved in the war. To gain Roosevelt's support, Marshall needed assistance. He went to Treasury Secretary Henry Morgenthau, a close friend of the president and a powerful member of his inner circle. Morgenthau had been in the cabinet for six years and had known FDR for over twenty-five. Marshall quickly persuaded him that far more was needed than the increased aircraft production Roosevelt discussed. Impressed, Morgenthau set up a meeting between Marshall and Roosevelt on May 13, 1940.

Joining the three men at the meeting were Secretary of War Woodring, Assistant Secretary of War Johnson, and the Director of the Bureau of the Budget, Harold Smith. Marshall made his pitch to FDR about needing to expand the Army to 280,000 men by the end of September and requested that enough equipment and armament be purchased for 750,000 men in case America did get drawn into the conflict. Before Marshall even finished presenting his case, the meeting broke down. Roosevelt seemed unmoved by the arguments and began arguing with Morgenthau; Johnson did not agree with Marshall on several aspects of the proposal; and Secretary Woodring sat silent. When Roosevelt attempted to end the meeting after snidely dismissing Morgenthau's plea to let Marshall continue, the chief of staff walked calmly but directly up to the president's desk and quietly asked him for three minutes of his time. FDR concurred, and Marshall proceeded to describe—as only he could—all that was needed and why. Standing up and looking down on the president for effect, Marshall spoke with efficiency (although he might have taken longer than the three minutes because Roosevelt was forced to cancel his next appointment with an influential Democratic senator).[28] He put his textbook style of persuasion on display, reciting relevant facts and figures from memory and covering them in the authority and credibility he brought to all high-level meetings. He closed his arguments by forcefully warning Roosevelt, "If you don't do something and don't do it right away, I don't know what is going to happen to this country."

Roosevelt got the point, just as General Pershing had over twenty years earlier when Marshall had grabbed his arm and lectured him in France. He asked Marshall and the others to come back at the same time the following day with a detailed list of what was required. Although he did not agree to support all Marshall asked for, he sent a healthy request to Capitol Hill shortly thereafter. Marshall would later say it was this meeting that helped break the "log jam" that had prevented anything substantial from moving forward the previous eleven months.

Even with the president's endorsement, the battle to convince Congress was difficult. Interestingly, considering the desperate state of America's armed forces at the time, Marshall was cautious when dealing with Congress over the weeks that followed and advocated for a more restrained military buildup than he believed was needed. His goal in doing so was to gain credibility with moderate isolationists on the Hill. By asking for less now, Marshall believed he could get more later.

Within a month of Marshall's breakthrough meeting with the president, everything changed. The Germans took Paris on June 14, and France, considered to have among the best armies in Europe, surrendered eleven days later. Great Britain, under the leadership of Winston Churchill since May, now faced Germany and Italy alone (Italy officially joined Hitler on June 10).

Roosevelt could no longer afford to have an isolationist running the War Department. Normally loath to fire people, FDR got rid of Secretary of War Woodring less than a week after Paris fell and replaced him with a seventy-three-year-old Republican known for his integrity, intelligence, strength of character, and strong desire to support Great Britain. Appointed on June 22, 1940, and confirmed by the Senate on July 9, Henry Lewis Stimson arrived at the War Department a day later, taking the office adjacent to Marshall's. Earlier that same day, the first phase of the Battle of Britain began as Germany sent planes to bomb British shipping in the English Channel and the dockyards in South Wales.

7

Wise Man (1918–1940)

I had rather a restless night because I was thinking of Manchuria and so I got up early in the morning at six o'clock with my mind rather clarified on what I wanted to do. I went down to my library and there wrote out in long hand a short note to the Chinese Government and to the Japanese Government, based largely upon the note of 1915. Previously we had been thinking of a longer note, with a resume of what had taken place. Thinking it over during the night I made up my mind not to do that but make it as brief as possible and that was the result.

—STIMSON, describing how he came to formulate
the Stimson Doctrine (HLS diary, January 3, 1932)

Henry Stimson was fifty-one years old when World War I ended. He would be just shy of seventy-three when President Franklin Roosevelt asked him to run the War Department after the fall of France. In the two decades in between, "the Colonel" steadily reached a position that, in the early nineteenth century, might have earned him the nickname the "Sage of Highhold." But since such sobriquets were no longer in style, Stimson was simply referred to as an elder statesman (as *Time* magazine described him after his appointment to secretary of war).[1] Stimson earned this title through the competence he displayed in each public service opportunity presented to him since first recruited by Teddy Roosevelt in 1906. Solid work, unquestioned patriotism, the highest level of integrity, and proven bipartisanship allowed Stimson to build on his unique reputation during the years between the world wars.

Unlike the frustrations he had with the business of law shortly after leaving the War Department in 1913, Stimson was reawakened to its challenges upon his return to civilian life at the end of the First World War. It had been thirteen years since he had worked full-time as a New York corporate lawyer, and his standing in the legal profession had consequently fallen (memories on Wall Street were as short back then as they are now). Stimson was surprised some of his younger professional peers did not realize he had been at the top of the heap at the turn of the century. The competitor in him responded; he would remind the younger generation of exactly who he was.

Pride was not the only thing driving him; Stimson also wanted to fill his bank account up quickly so that he could take on any new assignment his government might recruit him for in the future without having to consider his financial resources. With hard work, he believed he could achieve true financial independence (relatively speaking, of course) sooner than later.

A greater attention toward the law did not mean deserting politics; on the contrary, Stimson was active following the end of World War I on several fronts: government reform; the 1920 presidential election; and the much-debated League of Nations. But his political involvement was far less intense than it had been previously; there were several interesting and diverse legal cases that landed on his lap requiring his attention. His success in handling them put him comfortably back among the top trial lawyers in the country and helped him achieve the financial independence for which he was looking.

Among the first cases he handled were two relating to antitrust matters, a subject quite familiar to Teddy Roosevelt's former enforcer in this realm. After these were over, Stimson was approached by a committee formed by President Warren Harding to make recommendations to the United States Coal Commission to ensure that the country had a reliable supply of coal. The committee, formed due to the shortages of coal due to strikes, asked Stimson to represent them and help prepare a brief. Stimson's job was to determine a way to stabilize the relationships between management and labor in the coal industry. It was a case Stimson could hardly refuse given the great public interest involved. He agreed to take the job in December 1922 and spent the next six months studying all aspects of the industry and reviewing its evolution over the previous seventy-five years. The overall exercise gave Stimson the opportunity to take a deeper dive into the relationship between labor and management in a critical industry from all angles. The lessons Stimson took away served him and the nation extremely well twenty years later, when he was in Franklin Roosevelt's cabinet and in charge of procurement for the Army as secretary of war.

For the next three years, Stimson continued practicing law and rebuilding his net worth. But real wealth came to him only through the skillful management of his assets by his extremely successful first cousin and former law partner, Alfred Loomis.[2] Loomis, a bona fide financial genius, helped his mentor and personal hero attain complete financial independence.[3] By the end of the 1920s, Stimson no longer had any need to practice law and wished to spend the rest of his productive life serving the United States, the entity his former boss and mentor Elihu Root referred to as the "greatest of all possible clients."

The client called again in 1926. President Calvin Coolidge asked Stimson to come down to Washington to give him advice. A dispute between Chile and Peru over some provinces lying between them had been going on for almost fifty years. The Coolidge administration had been trying to resolve it without success and felt the problem needed a "detached mind."[4] Stimson was more than happy to oblige and submitted opinions on the matter to Secretary of State Frank Kellogg. Not long after, Stimson was asked to give his advice on the Philippines, and after a five-week visit there, he returned to brief Coolidge on the trip and offer helpful recommendations.

Impressed by the lawyer's suggestions, commitment, and availability, Coolidge—at the suggestion of Kellogg—invited him to Washington six months later to offer him a new and far more important assignment. Sensing Stimson could deliver more than just good advice, Coolidge asked him to end a particularly bloody civil war in Nicaragua and essentially left it up to Stimson to determine how to do it. He set sail for Nicaragua on April 9, 1927, and was back the following month with peace in hand. He wrote later there was "hardly any single month" in his life better spent. Following this achievement, Stimson officially became a Republican troubleshooter.

Governor General of the Philippines (December 1927–February 1929)

The story of how Stimson secured peace in Nicaragua, one that included having to travel to a remote province to meet with a rebel general under a thorn tree by an isolated river, would normally have made great copy. Unfortunately for him, Charles Lindbergh grabbed all the headlines in the United States and around the world during the same week for his transatlantic flight from New York to Paris. But if the public was ignorant of Stimson's accomplishment, Calvin Coolidge was not; shortly after returning to the United States, Stimson was once again summoned by the president. Following the death of Leonard Wood in August 1927, there was a vacancy in the prestigious position of governor general in the Philippines. Having spent five weeks there a year earlier, Stimson was familiar with the territory's problems. He was also the favored candidate of the top Filipino leaders. Coolidge formally announced Stimson's appointment to the post in December 1927. Stimson was honored and felt it would be a "last short adventure" before old age (he was sixty at the time) and a "welcome addition to his memories."[5] He also looked forward to taking on the considerable challenges awaiting him; it was another occasion to bring order to a part of the world lacking it.

Always certain that the key to success in private or public life was having exceptional men assisting him, Stimson reached out to someone who had impressed him a decade earlier in France. Through the adjutant general of the Army, he sent a telegram to Lieutenant Colonel George Marshall serving at Fort Benning in Georgia inviting him to join him in the Philippines as his aide. Marshall immediately but politely turned down the offer, explaining to Stimson that becoming his aide after serving Generals Liggett, Bell, and Pershing in the same capacity might mark him forever within the Army as "only an aide and never a commander." Marshall was confident Stimson would understand. Stimson wrote back that he "appreciated perfectly" Marshall's rationale.[6]

Arriving in Manila in March 1928, Stimson immediately began a series of meetings with all those who could provide him with the information he needed to enhance the overall welfare of the Filipinos and bring better government to the country. Through frank dialogue, the articulation of clear goals, the avoidance of overpromising, and his lifelong gift of acquiring people's trust, Stimson managed to establish instant credibility on the islands. He backed this up by making small but important decisions: meeting Filipinos alone without a white aide present (as his predecessor required); opening social events at the Malacañan Palace to Filipinos (as opposed to Americans only); and leaving the church he was attending when he found it refused membership to Filipinos.[7]

The trustworthiness gained by these actions made it easier for Stimson to get his larger goals accomplished. He brought back key functions to the executive branch and improved the working relationship between it and the legislative branch. Although it had been almost ten years since Stimson was a delegate to the New York State Constitutional Convention of 1915, in solving some of the problems in the Philippines, he was able to bring solutions formulated during the convention. It was incredibly satisfying work to him.

In late January 1929, after having spent just ten months in the Philippines, one of Stimson's law partners cabled him that President-Elect Herbert Hoover was considering placing him in the cabinet as head of either the State Department or the Department of Justice. Stimson cabled back that he was only interested in the former, explaining that his interest in legal problems was "not so great as twenty years ago."[8] Hoover promptly offered him the post. After accepting, he wound up his professional and personal affairs in the Philippines and sailed for home. Arriving in Washington on March 26, 1929, the sixty-one-year-old Wall Street lawyer–cum–public servant took the oath of office two days later, becoming America's forty-sixth secretary of state.

Secretary of State (March 1929–March 1933)

With his two previous assignments from Calvin Coolidge in faroff locations with little if any formal instruction or interference, Stimson now had to get used to sitting in Washington working for a radically different boss.

Whatever Herbert Clark Hoover had touched during his lifetime leading up to the presidency had turned to gold (quite literally in the early part of his career), and he was one of the most accomplished individuals ever to be elected president. After an astoundingly successful career as a global mining engineer, he gained national recognition by arranging the evacuation of over 120,000 U.S. citizens from Europe at the outbreak of the First World War. He then went on to become an international hero when he organized and ran a commission to provide food to starving Belgian victims caught between the major World War I combatants. Using his considerable intelligence, energy, confidence, organizational and business skills, contacts, and persuasive abilities, Hoover ran an organization with sovereign-like status that literally saved millions of lives.

His accomplishments and popularity landed him an invitation to serve in the Coolidge administration, where he quickly became the most important and productive member of the cabinet by turning the previously weak position of secretary of commerce into a force of influence on all aspects of the American economy. His fame and track record of success earned him the Republican nomination for president in June 1928. He won 84 percent of the electoral vote against Democrat Al Smith that November.

Once Stimson arrived stateside to take up his duties, Hoover decided to invite him to the White House for ten days so that each man could get to know the other and discuss the major international issues of the day. Although generally uncomfortable in his presence during the visit, Stimson could not help but be astonished with Hoover's agile mind and level of energy. Stimson later wrote that he had never met anyone with a "greater capacity to assimilate and organize information" nor someone who was as "capable of more intense and prolonged intellectual effort."[9] Coming from someone who worked closely with Teddy Roosevelt, Elihu Root, Felix Frankfurter, and Alfred Loomis, among others, this provides an indication of Hoover's raw intellectual abilities and energy.

Stimson began tackling the large issues of the day in Europe, internal disputes over the Philippines, and revolutions in Argentina, Peru, and Bolivia, while simultaneously facing the general grind that defined the position during that era (which included having to suffer through "Diplomatic Hours," an endless string of appointments lasting between fifteen and twenty minutes each).

One of the first decisions made by Stimson as secretary of state ended up having a lasting impact on his legacy and furnished the quote for which he is best remembered. He learned shortly upon entering office that the War Department maintained a crew of code breakers since World War I who had been reading coded messages sent to and from various ambassadors and foreign representatives. To his further surprise, he learned the State Department had been financially supporting this effort. In cutting off its funding in the summer of 1929, Stimson effectively disbanded the group, sending a signal to those both within and outside of the country that the United States was going to lead by example with respect to how nations dealt with one another.[10] By famously stating, "Gentlemen do not read each other's mail," Stimson was trying to mirror the goodwill and efforts toward peace the major powers of the world were trying to exhibit after the First World War.

Stimson would be mocked for this quote in later years (and the lost intelligence due to his decision), but he claimed in his memoirs he had no regrets making the decision. Quick to adopt the best practices of espionage when he took over the War Department a decade later, Stimson did not believe he flip-flopped on the issue as much as followed the best course of action for the times (i.e., what he felt was improper during peacetime was perfectly acceptable during a time of war). He would use the same logic on a few key decisions during World War II.

Stimson's first sixteen months on the job were largely occupied with the situation in the Philippines, improving relations with Great Britain, and leading a major international naval disarmament conference. The latter two tasks were linked, given the tension existing between the former comrades-in-arms over what constituted adequate naval ship requirements. The disarmament conference, held for three months in London between January and April 1930, proved to be one of the great challenges of Stimson's life. Although the agreement reached at the conference fell apart within a few years, the overall experience was crucial in helping him a year later, when he undertook even more complex negotiations on a more important subject in the same city with most of the same players.

The London Conference (July 1931)

The London Conference of July 1931 was arranged hastily to deal with the potential fall of the European economies arising from the overall breakdown of the global economy and the twin issues leftover from the wreckage of World War I: German reparations, and debt payments due from France and England to the United States. Although the achievements at the conference ultimately failed to prevent the collapse of the European economies (and did nothing to improve the overall financial condition of America), an immediate political crisis in Germany was resolved. The experience was a continuation of the education of Henry Stimson and confirmed to him yet again how intertwined the economies of the world were.

Although the economic situation in Europe unraveled for several reasons in the spring of 1931, it was actions taken much earlier by France and England that set in motion the ripples that eventually overwhelmed it. Fearing a German revival and needing money to pay back the debts they had incurred from the United States during World War I, the two countries insisted at the Treaty of Versailles that Germany be obligated to pay what many believed was an inordinate amount of reparations (against the wishes of President Woodrow Wilson).[11]

Over time, France, England, and the United States began extending loans to Germany so that it could grow economically and make the required reparation payments (so that England and France could repay their debt to the United States). There was logic to this, but only if each of the victorious powers created an easy path for German goods to be imported into their respective countries. This was not the case because of forceful American tariff policies and a general reluctance by England and France to import German goods.

A run on European banks in 1931 jeopardized the entire plan, causing President Hoover to announce a one-year moratorium on debt payments in mid-June.[12] After visiting Europe to confer with all the relevant leaders in an attempt to calm the markets, Stimson concluded that not only was a one-year moratorium insufficient, but also that Germany needed new money. A conference was quickly organized for mid-July to discuss the steps in making this happen.

Accompanied by Secretary of Treasury Andrew Mellon, and coordinating closely with Hoover back in Washington, Stimson did his best in London to help guide the conference participants. He was called on to use his legal talents to focus the parties on the most important goal (keeping existing credit lines flowing to Germany) while limiting any discussions that had political overtones significant enough to crater potential progress. He undertook this responsibility even though the president was strongly against any new loans to Germany from either public or private sources.[13] More frustrating to Stimson was Hoover's insistence that the debts owed to the United States by France and England be ultimately honored following the moratorium. Stimson was a "cancellationist," believing that the gain to America by canceling the debts owed to it by England and France (meaning, an increase in world trade and goodwill) would far outweigh the cost.

Given Hoover's position, the best Stimson could do in London was to make certain that the current level of working capital loans made to Germany be maintained. He believed his work to secure even this achievement was among the "neatest and most successful" of his career. But it was not enough; Germany needed a longer-term solution. Adolf Hitler would eventually provide it.

The Stimson Doctrine

As if the challenges in Europe were not difficult enough, Stimson faced another crisis only two weeks after arriving home from London on September 3, 1931. This one was on the other side of the world, where Japan was executing the first steps of a plan that would ultimately lead it to war with the United States. It began when the Japanese army staged an incident on the South Manchurian Railway in order to justify an excursion by their troops into Chinese-held territory. Japan continued to take over additional territory in Manchuria while keeping a careful eye on the general reaction from the United States and the rest of the world (including the recently formed League of Nations). With few countries willing or able to do anything more than condemn the aggression in letters to the Japanese, the emboldened Japanese military spent the next few months taking town after town until they occupied the entire northeast region of China.

The actions did not sit well with Stimson, who, like his old boss Elihu Root, believed lasting peace could only be achieved if nations followed the rule of law and respected international borders. But Stimson was occupied with so many other pressing issues, largely related to Europe and the debt crisis, that he could give only limited attention to the events in Manchuria when the crisis began. When he did focus on it, he became incensed. But given the strong isolationist leanings of the country and Hoover's reluctance to get involved, there was little he could do outside writing letters of protest to the Japanese government and encouraging the League of Nations to take an active role against the aggression.

The League of Nations was generally weak and not focused on the problems in Asia (from where just four of its fifty-eight member countries were located). Tired of war and economically frail, its members (America was only present as an observer) could only manage to collectively issue resolutions condemning the aggression and send notes of appeal to the Japanese to withdraw their forces from Manchuria.

Three or four months into the crisis, Stimson became concerned with the continued resolve of the Japanese and tried to convince Hoover to apply economic sanctions on them. The president was dead-set against sanctions, believing that when applied to large nations, they would lead to war (considering what happened a decade later, Hoover's concerns were merited).[14] In later years, Stimson said his hands in the State Department were tied by virtue of working under a "pacifist" president (coming from a protégé of Teddy Roosevelt, this was as harsh a word as one could apply to an individual). Understanding that Hoover's views mirrored those held by most of the American people did not absolve Hoover in Stimson's mind; he believed presidents were paid to make the big decisions without first sticking their fingers in the wind.

Following news in January 1932 that the Japanese had taken yet another important Chinese city, Stimson decided something more was needed. Losing patience (and sleep) and wanting to put an end to the back-and-forth correspondence between himself and the Japanese, Stimson began drafting a final letter the following morning that he intended to send to the Japanese government stating essentially that the United States would not recognize any treaty compromising the sovereignty of China nor any gains made by the Japanese through the use of force.[15]

These simple but candid statements would become the Stimson Doctrine, a principle surviving today as a generally accepted rule of international law justifying non-recognition of conditions, occurrences, or circumstances created in violation of international law (the United Nations later adopted it in both its charter and in several of its resolutions). After running the concept by the president, who fully supported the initiative, Stimson sent his letter to both the Japanese and Chinese governments.

For all the longevity of the Stimson Doctrine, the letter first articulating it did not have the desired effect; less than three weeks after the note was delivered, Japan launched an attack on Shanghai and a few weeks later created the puppet state of Manchukuo out of their conquered territories. But the thought-provoking letter remained controversial. There was little subtlety in Stimson's words; they were forceful, and the message behind them was immediately recognized for what it was: a doctrine.[16]

Although critics made the argument that without the commitment to use force, the Stimson Doctrine was not only ineffective but counterproductive, others less devoted to realpolitik credited Stimson with introducing morality into international relations following the post–World War I era. As is so often the case when there is a sharp contrast between viewpoints, the value of the Doctrine lies somewhere between the two views: It did nothing to stop Japan, Germany, and Italy during the thirties; on the other hand, it helped clarify to the community of nations—in certain circumstances—what is right from wrong.

Stimson was the leading American interventionist of his era, and the letter he wrote to the Japanese was certainly not his favored choice of action. But he was fated to contend with a president who viewed things differently. As he did with Franklin Roosevelt a decade later, Stimson tried to nudge Hoover to take a more aggressive posture, but Hoover would not move from his belief that stronger actions would lead to war. This applied all over the world, and Stimson began to see a dark road ahead. In a discussion with the German chancellor in the last year of the Hoover administration, Stimson remarked, "The situation in the world seemed to me like the unfolding of a great Greek tragedy, where we could see the march of events and know what ought to be done, but [seemed] to be powerless to prevent its marching to its grim conclusion."[17] This was seven full years before Hitler attacked Poland to begin the Second World War.

The Presidential Election of 1932

Herbert Hoover was not a man to be envied going into the election of 1932. As difficult as the problems were in Europe and Manchuria, it was the ongoing economic depression that was crushing him. America's GNP decreased by over 13 percent during the year and had fallen 30 percent since he took office. Worse still, the unemployment rate was about to peak at 25 percent.

To have any chance of winning, Hoover needed to pull out all the stops, and he turned to Stimson, one of the most respected Republicans in the country, to give him a hand by making some speeches attacking his fellow New Yorker Franklin Roosevelt. Initially, Stimson was dead-set against it; he generally disliked making negative speeches and thought an attack speech would not only reflect poorly on him, but it would be bad for Hoover as well. Two years earlier and against his better wishes, Stimson had agreed to say negative things about FDR during the New York gubernatorial campaign. The episode left a bad taste in his mouth, and he did not wish to repeat the experience.

It was not just an attack speech Stimson wished to avoid; he also believed it was inappropriate for a serving secretary of state to stump for a serving president. But loyalty dictated that he do something, so he agreed to give a couple of speeches on foreign policy praising Hoover while generally going after the Democrats (he said nothing stronger against Roosevelt than that he was "extremely reckless").[18]

In the end, it was a hopeless cause; Americans demanded a change, and Roosevelt won all but six states in taking the White House.

One will recall that when Stimson left the War Department twenty years earlier, following Taft's defeat by Woodrow Wilson, he was committed to a smooth transition and worked closely with his successor, Lindley Garrison, in effecting one. Keeping true to his bipartisan nature, Stimson spent much time and effort over the four months following the election of 1932 trying to ensure that the international affairs of America would not suffer for want of cooperation between the outgoing and incoming administrations. This proved to be a challenge; not only was there a lot going on, but the relationship between Hoover and Roosevelt was among the most tense between any two presidents during any transition period in history.

Looking back, the transition period did not reflect well on either man. Hoover, stubborn until the end, insisted the debt payments from the British and French be honored, not only because he still believed they should be, but also because he had campaigned on the promise they would be. For his part, Roosevelt played the political games for which he later became famous, claiming that although he was happy to discuss the debt issues, all decisions until March 4 should be made by those constitutionally in charge.

Stimson took it upon himself to work with Hoover, balancing his own views with the president's, who insisted on linking the overall debt issue with a global economic plan and his long-sought goals regarding disarmament. The debates between the two men, both of whom by this time were tired of one another, got extremely heated during the remaining weeks of Hoover's presidency. Given that Hoover was under a tremendous strain due to the Great Depression and was demoralized by the overwhelming rejection he had received at the voting polls in November, Stimson could have been more sensitive to Hoover's state of mind. On the contrary, he was all business and kept pressure on Hoover, urging him to loosen up—if not abandon—his stubborn positions vis-à-vis the debts owed to America.

When another attempt by Hoover in late December to recruit Roosevelt to work together failed, Felix Frankfurter, an old protégé of Stimson's who also happened to be a great friend of Roosevelt's, was meeting with the president-elect in Albany. During the meeting, according to Frankfurter, Roosevelt suggested it would be a good idea to meet with Stimson. It is more likely that Frankfurter—a master at matching men with tasks—came up with the idea himself, concluding that the state of the country and the world required a base level of cooperation between Roosevelt and Hoover. He believed Stimson was the one man who could be trusted to make this happen. Frankfurter called his old boss, who agreed to a meeting, but only after getting the blessing of Hoover. Initially opposed to the idea, Hoover finally agreed.[19]

Stimson headed to Roosevelt's Hudson River estate in Hyde Park, New York, in early January 1933, and met the president-elect for nearly six hours, discussing not only the subject of debt payments, but also the entire range of issues around the globe. The conversations went very well. Stimson was the perfect candidate to brief the president-elect, not only due to his position as the steward of American foreign relations for the previous four years, but also because his legal background and skills allowed him to efficiently summarize in less than six hours all the major issues Roosevelt would inherit two months later.

The two men had not spent time with one another prior to this meeting, which was surprising given they were both prominent politicians from

New York State, had several mutual friends, spent a lot of their time in New York City, and had been close to Teddy Roosevelt. Roosevelt must have been impressed, because he sent a member of his extended "brain trust" to talk further with Stimson at Highhold the following day and requested another meeting himself with Stimson ten days later.[20]

Aside from liking and respecting Stimson, Roosevelt needed him because he detested both Hoover and Ogden Mills (Hoover's secretary of the treasury). Following these meetings and until the inauguration, Stimson acted as the intermediary between the thirty-first and thirty-second president on any important matter.[21] Although Stimson was completely transparent with Hoover about this arrangement, it naturally led to even greater tension between the two men. Since a smooth presidential transition period by its very nature benefits the incoming administration more than the outgoing one, Hoover's frustration with Stimson was understandable. As for Stimson, it seemed that he truly believed he was being loyal to his boss; by fulfilling his duty during the transition period, it would benefit both the country and Hoover's legacy.

Understandably, Stimson felt a great sense of relief when Inauguration Day arrived on March 4, 1933. Despite his vast differences with Hoover on the major issues and their antithetical temperaments, his respect for the much-maligned president never wavered; he thought he was one of the most distinguished Americans of his time who was handed challenges even his prodigious talents could not overcome. Stimson would go on to defend Hoover for the rest of his life. He thought it a shame that the animus between FDR and Hoover prevented the latter from playing any prominent role during the twelve difficult years that followed. As soon as Roosevelt died in April 1945, Stimson suggested to President Truman that he take advantage of Hoover's world-class talents and experience to assist with postwar problems in Europe. Truman placed a call to Hoover immediately.

Becoming Secretary of War

Tired, but feeling too young to call it a day, the sixty-five-year-old Stimson walked out of the State, War, and Navy Building and settled back into his role as a "wise man." Such a person needed a base of operations, and although Stimson contemplated setting up a law office in Washington, his natural bearings steered him back to the Liberty Street offices of Winthrop & Stimson, where he first began practicing law with Elihu Root

forty-two years earlier. Bronson Winthrop, in welcoming his old friend
back to the firm, assumed the aged Stimson had likely rendered his final
service to his country. Stimson was not so sure; he knew he could still
make positive contributions to the country's foreign affairs given his experience and the fact he had "just as many good friends among the Democrats as among the Republicans."[22]

To stay current on what was happening in Washington, Stimson decided
to keep "Woodley Mansion," the Federal-style estate he purchased there
four years earlier. Built in 1801, Woodley was a grand white mansion located
on twenty acres on a hill not far from the National Cathedral and less than
two and a half miles north of the White House. It had a notable history;
Martin Van Buren and Grover Cleveland had lived there, among other
Washington luminaries. Stimson and his wife loved the house and decided
to spend part of each winter and spring there before heading back to New
York in late May.[23]

Most of Stimson's time during the next seven years was spent in New
York practicing law. Initially, he tried to keep his schedule light, giving him
time to pursue other projects (he wrote a book on the Far Eastern crisis),
stay current on world affairs, and fulfill his duties as president of the Board
of Trustees of Phillips Academy (beginning in 1935).

But the lighter pace did not last; as much as he claimed his interest in
legal problems was "not as great as years past," he could not resist jumping
back into cases, particularly important ones.[24] It is also possible that after
over a quarter century of comings and goings at Winthrop & Stimson, he
felt an obligation to do a bit of steady work for the firm.

But at the same time, Stimson's advice was still in demand from the government. His successor in the State Department (Cordell Hull) reached out
to him often, and Franklin Roosevelt continued to seek out his views on
certain issues for the first two years of his presidency. Aside from periodic
letters and calls, FDR invited Stimson to the White House twice in 1933 and
again in 1934 to discuss global and domestic affairs. Their face-to-face meetings ended after 1934. A minor misunderstanding between the two was the
principal cause, but Stimson's objections to FDR's New Deal might have also
played a part. Additionally, Stimson was gradually becoming more outspoken about his anti-isolationist sentiment at a time when Roosevelt was presenting to the public an opposite viewpoint for political reasons.

None of these issues prevented friendly correspondence going back and
forth between the two. They continued to see eye to eye on most subjects
relating to international affairs. They had also established a bond during

their earlier meetings over their mutual belief that the Japanese were up to no good. Roosevelt's views on the subject were influenced as far back as his days at Harvard after a classmate from Japan gave him a detailed description of a one-hundred-year plan his country had created in 1889 to form a dynasty in Asia. The young Roosevelt was impressed enough with the step-by-step plan that he could still recount it, more than three decades later, to Stimson in full detail.[25]

When he was not working on legal cases or corresponding with the Roosevelt administration on international affairs, Stimson made it a point during these years to share his opinions publicly on issues important to him through letters, radio speeches, and published articles. The subjects he chose to speak about were generally tied to foreign affairs either directly or indirectly. The state of the world dominated his thoughts from the time he left the State Department in 1933 to the time he arrived at the War Department seven years later.

In 1934, he gave a radio address coming out in favor of a Democratic bill to reduce tariffs. Although a domestic issue on the face of it, Stimson saw high tariffs through the prism of internationalism; they promoted economic isolationism and reduced foreign trade. If nothing else defined Stimson's thinking during this era, it was that the United States should be increasing its connections with the rest of the world, not reducing them.

Disillusioned with his own party for promoting high tariffs and upset with the Democrats over the New Deal, Stimson stayed out of domestic politics during the 1936 election. His attention was drawn toward Europe, where war seemed inevitable as the Nazis were about to begin their fourth year in power. Long before other leading figures in America, Stimson warned of the dangers of Hitler. As much as he was frustrated by European leaders' unwillingness to confront the German leader, the concentration of Stimson's deepest wrath during these years was saved for those officials who promoted isolationism in the United States. He periodically warned the country through his writings and speeches that isolationism was a dangerous policy that actually increased the chances of American involvement in war. Starting in 1935, he began to speak out against it with more regularity.

With each new belligerent act committed by Germany or Japan, Stimson stepped up his anti-isolationist rhetoric and began publicly prodding the president to exercise the moral leadership his position demanded of him by taking a stand against it. At the very least, he believed Roosevelt should push for trade embargoes against the hostile countries. But anyone promoting such actions was swimming against a strengthening current. Fearing America would be dragged into another European war just as it had been twenty years earlier, isolationist members of Congress began to think of new ways to reduce the chances of getting involved in another war. In 1935, they redefined the concept of neutrality through a legislative act and got it extended and revised in 1936 and 1937.

Those who believed that international bankers and munitions makers were responsible for America's involvement in World War I pushed hardest for the Neutrality Acts. By preventing America from trading with any belligerents, the isolationists believed they were mitigating the risk of this happening again. Not satisfied, the more radical among them proposed an amendment in late 1938 requiring a national referendum to determine whether or not Congress could declare war. The Ludlow Amendment ultimately failed to get the necessary two-thirds vote in the House of Representatives, but the fact that 209 votes were cast in favor of it against 188 opposed stunned Henry Stimson. He reacted by stepping up his public statements, despite the fact that he was already the most outspoken interventionist in the country. But like Churchill's in England, Stimson's voice remained a lonely one shouting into the wind.

Looking back today at Stimson's speeches during this time, his opinions and predictions seem obvious. Only when one places them in the context of the times can one fully appreciate them. In a letter to the *New York Times* on October 5, 1937, after Japan went to war against China, Stimson wrote that taking a neutral stand between right and wrong would not work for the United States. "Such a policy of amoral drift," he wrote, "would not save us from entanglement." On the contrary, he continued, history had proven it makes "entanglement more certain." Six months later, in a speech to a business group, Stimson explained to the audience that the world was now interconnected far more than in the days before "steam and electricity," and therefore it was pointless to even debate isolationism.

When Stimson wasn't publicly preaching during this period of time, which he referred to as the "Ostrich Era," he was taking on a few legal cases, including the largest single lawsuit of his career (the Blaustein case). Initiated in March 1937, the Blaustein case pitted Stimson as counsel to Jacob Blaustein against John W. Davis, representing Standard Oil of Indiana. Davis, loser to Calvin Coolidge in the presidential election of 1924, was among the most accomplished lawyers of his era. The case was the biggest ever tried at the common law in the United States up to that time and one of the most challenging of Stimson's career.[26] Preparing for the trial, set for late 1939, took much of Stimson's time in 1938 and 1939.

But even the sheer size and importance of the case could not keep Stimson quiet on those occasions when a new turn in world events tore at his gut. In January 1939, he wrote another letter to his successor, Cordell Hull, urging him to lift the embargoes imposed by Congress against providing arms to the loyalists fighting the German-backed Nationalists in the Spanish Civil War. That same month he wrote a letter to the *New York Times* pointing out the evils of fascism and using Lincoln's "a house divided cannot stand" quote to suggest that democracy and fascism could not coexist on the planet. Stimson pushed hard for American intervention in the Spanish Civil War and privately expressed dismay that the United States ultimately had done nothing.

Commenting on the fascist powers in his diary during this time, Stimson wrote, "We do not see the end of the evil by a long shot." Stimson was certain war was coming, and when the British committed to supporting Poland at the end of March 1939, he believed it would come "at any moment." So certain was he after this event that he sent a cable to his sister in Europe and advised her to return to the United States.

When the Germans invaded Poland six months later, launching the Second World War, the news came as a relief to Stimson; he was sick and tired of the endless concessions given to Hitler and, like many, assumed Britain and France would win. But as the German blitzkrieg tore into one country after another, it was clear that he and the world had greatly underestimated that Nazi strength. As France was on the verge of falling in early June 1940, Stimson felt the strong need to speak again. Fortunately for him, he had invitations to talk about compulsory military training at Yale during the commencement exercise weekend and make a radio address from New Haven, Connecticut, the following night. He would have much to say.

The speech at Yale essentially summarized his earlier positions, but with more forceful warnings about the consequences of inaction. The radio speech the following evening was titled "America's Interest in the British Fleet." Stimson went well beyond this modestly titled subject matter to give a powerful and impassioned talk specifically laying out a series of steps he believed the country should immediately take in order to save freedom around the world. Besides the adoption of compulsory military service, these included repealing the Neutrality Act, opening America's ports to French and British ships, and sending arms to both countries (even if such shipments had to be escorted by the U.S. Navy).

It was a bold speech that articulated precisely what was at stake for the United States and which side the nation should support. It was also well publicized, even by the standards of the day when such nationally broadcast addresses attracted a lot of press attention and a large listening audience. Among the listeners was Franklin Roosevelt. The following afternoon, June 19, 1940, Stimson was back at his office at 32 Liberty Street when he received a call from the White House. The president asked him to take over the War Department.[27]

The call took Stimson by surprise. Although he had heard that his name had been mentioned to Roosevelt as a possible candidate for the post, he did not suspect that the president would ever appoint a seventy-three-year-old interventionist Republican who had blasted so many of his domestic policies over the previous seven years.

The idea of putting Henry Stimson in charge of the War Department had been pitched to FDR in early June by Felix Frankfurter, who had been approached by Grenville Clark, a prominent Wall Street lawyer and political advisor long influential in Washington, D.C. Clark was a huge proponent of universal military training and believed Stimson (with whom he had worked in developing the Plattsburgh training camps before World War I) was the only man who could successfully sell the concept to Congress. Frankfurter liked the idea, thought highly of Stimson, and was someone who had Roosevelt's ear. Although Clark and Frankfurter are generally credited by historians with first suggesting Stimson's name to the president, Stimson was hardly an unknown entity, and it is likely that others floated his name to FDR at one time or another in the first half of 1940 in reaction to the deteriorating situation at the War Department.

In considering Stimson, FDR was picking an extremely qualified and experienced public servant who was well respected by Democrats and Republicans alike and who generally shared his own thinking on the situation in Europe. If the new war ended up entangling America, FDR also saw the benefits of having a Republican or two in the cabinet to bring a sense of unity to the war effort.

Whether the advantage of Stimson's political affiliation, stature, and experience could overcome his age and health was the question FDR put to Frankfurter. After checking with Stimson's doctor, this issue was put to rest, but to hedge against any lingering concerns, Frankfurter and Clark suggested that a capable assistant be assigned to work closely with Stimson. They recommended Robert Patterson, a U.S. Circuit Court judge. Roosevelt liked the paring of Stimson and Patterson, but—true to character—he was hesitant in dumping either Woodring or Johnson and procrastinated for a few weeks. Only when France fell and he heard Stimson speak on the radio did he place the call to 32 Liberty Street.

After discussing the offer with his wife and two former law partners, Stimson agreed to the take the job under four conditions, all of which Roosevelt accepted: He would take no part in domestic politics; he would push hard to obtain universal military training; he would not have his speeches cleared through the White House; and he would get to choose his own subordinates (Stimson already agreed with Frankfurter and Clark that Patterson would be an ideal assistant secretary). Roosevelt asked Woodring for his resignation the following day and immediately announced both Stimson's appointment along with Frank Knox's (another Republican interventionist) to run the Navy.

If Stimson was surprised by Roosevelt's decision to choose him, Washington was stunned. How could it be that a senior member of the Republican Party, a protégé of both Teddy Roosevelt and Elihu Root, a member of the conservative white-shoe law firm that carried his name, and a leading figure of the moneyed elite of New York City was going to work for Franklin Roosevelt? As shocking as it was, it was even more controversial. Roosevelt's nomination of Stimson, the interventionist's interventionist, seemed to isolationists as simply the first step in a series that would lead to a declaration of war against Germany. Their reaction was swift; the chairman of the Republican National Committee read both Stimson and Knox out of the party, and Roosevelt was castigated for angling the country into war.[28]

Stimson could not have cared less; he immediately began settling his affairs in New York and preparing for the confirmation hearings. He needed to get fully up to speed on all the issues facing the Army. The Senate Military Affairs Committee (through which Stimson's nomination had to pass) gave Stimson less than two weeks to prep for a reception he knew would be hostile. It was time for him to sit down with George Marshall. He asked the chief of staff to fly up to visit him at Highhold.

Marshall was delighted to hear the news of Stimson's appointment; he was sick of dealing with the ongoing chaos brought about by the fallout between Secretary of War Woodring and Assistant Secretary of War Johnson.[29] Although he had spent time with Stimson in the past, it had been years, and Marshall wanted this meeting with his new boss to go well. He wrote a close friend, asking him to call him as soon as he could to provide "tips" on the best way to approach the new secretary of war.[30]

The chief of staff arrived in Long Island in the late afternoon of the following day. After touring Stimson's "farm" (which Marshall thought was "charming"), and dining with Stimson and his wife (both of whom he described to his wife as delightful), Marshall stayed up until nearly midnight talking with "the Colonel." They continued their conversation over breakfast at 6:30 a.m. before Marshall headed back to Washington. Stimson was fully satisfied after these discussions that in Marshall he had the best man in place for the most critical of positions. The chief of staff's typical command of all the facts impressed Stimson, and what he learned that day served him well as he prepared for the hearings.[31]

Confirmation Hearings

Stimson never had qualms about going head to head with angry politicians; on the contrary, he usually looked forward to it. The initial questioning from the senators, however, was fair if not firm; such was the respect that so many of them had for the elder statesman. This changed when Robert Taft (a Republican from Ohio and son of former president William H. Taft) was given the floor. Stimson was both disappointed and surprised that Taft, the brilliant fifty-year-old first-term senator, grilled him in a prosecutorial fashion that crossed well over the border into hostility. Given how well he knew, respected, and loved his father, Stimson felt the senator's behavior and political views were "not worthy" of a son of the former president.

Robert Taft was not even on the Committee but sought special permission to join the questioning of Stimson, which was granted to him due to his stature in the Republican Party (he had lost out to Thomas Dewey for the Republican nomination for president just days before the hearing) and his well-credentialed isolationism.

During his questioning, Taft tried to trap Stimson into making controversial statements. Was Stimson prepared, he asked among a string of questions, to risk war to "prevent the defeat of England and the destruction of the British fleet?" Stimson replied that if going to war was in the best interest of defending America's interests, then he would be in favor of taking the risk.

After addressing several more questions from Taft and the other senators, Stimson believed he had "more than held his own" during the two-plus hours of interrogation. He managed to remain steadfast to his own principles without politically damaging the president. With the election coming up in less than six months, Roosevelt was walking a fine line between his private interventionist beliefs and his far more nuanced views as a candidate. Stimson needed to answer questions truthfully while dialing down any particularly aggressive rhetoric. He did this with great skill.

Ultimately, the committee voted 4-3 in favor of recommending him. A week later the Senate confirmed the appointment by a 56-28 vote. Despite Stimson's interventionist views, it would have been difficult for the Senate to turn down a man who also had a reputation for integrity surpassing anyone in Washington. On July 8 (the day before he was confirmed by the Senate), Stimson returned to Washington to take up his duties. He knew this would be his best and last chance to do something profoundly meaningful not only for his country, but for the world.

On the same day, he had a second and far longer discussion with George Marshall under the trees outside Woodley Mansion. For the next five years, these two men, acting seamlessly, would put on a professional performance that stands second to none in the military history of the United States. As the duo settled firmly into their adjoining offices, where the door between them would always be deliberately left open, Roosevelt could not have realized how critically important his decision had been to pair the two men. As the president's focus pivoted toward getting reelected to a third term, Stimson and Marshall began preparing the Army for a possible war.

II

PREPARING

8

Together in Washington

A democracy has a very hard time in a war, particularly at the start of a war. They [democracies] can never get ready in advance.[1]

—**GEORGE C. MARSHALL**

There are three people in the world that I could never say no to, my wife, General Marshall, and Colonel Stimson.[2]

—**ROBERT A. LOVETT, assistant secretary of war for air during World War II**

Henry Lewis Stimson was sworn in as the nation's fifty-fourth secretary of war on July 10, 1940, more than twenty-seven years after leaving office as its forty-fifth. Earlier that day in Europe, the first phase of the Battle of Britain began.

It is a remarkable testament to both Stimson's longevity and the era in which he lived that when he first took over the War Department under Taft in 1911, he was responsible for an army that had one airplane and was still fighting Native Americans; by the time he left office after his second stint in 1945, America was the world's first nuclear power. The contrast must have dawned on Stimson as he walked into the War Department his first day, but he would not have dwelled on it for long. He knew the nation was headed for war and understood how difficult it was going to be for him and Marshall to get it properly prepared.

The gloomy briefings Stimson had previously received from the chief of staff on the current state of the Army did not come as a complete surprise to Stimson; he was familiar with the insufficient appropriations provided to the Army over the previous twenty years, as well as the chaotic environment that characterized the War Department at the time he took office. What he did not fully appreciate was just how far the morale of the Army had fallen. The challenges he and Marshall faced were difficult enough. To make any progress in such an environment, the two men would need all the help they could get from the Executive Branch.

Roosevelt, the Cabinet, and the Inner Circle

As Marshall continued to brief Stimson during the latter's first few days on the major issues within the Army and his progress in addressing them over the previous year, he would have also given him his opinion as to who was helpful within the Administration and who wasn't. While Stimson would have valued Marshall's observations, he was anxious to sit down himself with all the key players in the Roosevelt administration to size them up, and he would have wanted to start at the top.

One will recall from the previous chapter that Stimson spent quite a bit of time with Roosevelt during the transition period following the 1932 election and had corresponded with him on more than a few occasions since. He had been impressed with FDR, praising his versatility, his outstanding ability to "reach the kernel of a problem," and the "speed and clarity" with which he could make a decision.[3] But their face-to-face meetings had ended six years earlier, the world had changed, and Roosevelt was now his boss.

Although both men descended from established and wealthy Northeastern families; attended exclusive New England prep schools, universities, and law schools; practiced law in New York City; shared a number of mutual friends and acquaintances (not the least of whom was Teddy Roosevelt); and were most happy when relaxing at their respective country retreats, they had little else in common. Roosevelt's gregariousness contrasted sharply with the serious, reserved, and socially less comfortable Stimson; the president's chaotic management style clashed with one defined by order and logic; and his love of politics—and the high level of competence in which he practiced it—was antithetical to Stimson's sentiment and skill set in this field.

There was also a generational divide between the two men (as there was between the seventy-three-year-old Stimson and nearly everyone in the administration); Stimson was fifteen years older than the president. This was something the secretary made light of with his staff from time to time; when he was upset with some decision or statement made by the president, he often said, "I'll have to go over and talk to that young man." But there was some truth behind the humor; Stimson believed he had the right by age, experience, and acquired wisdom to speak candidly with Roosevelt. He also felt it was his solemn duty to do so as secretary of war and a senior member of the Cabinet, particularly on matters related to foreign affairs.

International matters, Stimson believed, required a more robust leadership in the United States than issues of a domestic nature due to his long-held view that Americans were "as ignorant as babies" about the former.[4] Given this, he constantly pressed the president in his first year to lead the people aggressively in this sphere. On more than a few occasions during one-on-one meetings with FDR, Stimson warned him he was going to be speaking "very frankly" on the subject before vigorously lecturing him, albeit respectfully. Several months into the job, after properly assuring the president of his loyalty and affection, Stimson rode FDR for his lack of overall leadership relating to the situation in Europe. He also advised Roosevelt that considering the great emergency the country was facing, he should stop joking around during press conferences and should instead reveal to the public a more appropriate level of gravitas.

In May 1941, he fired off a letter to Roosevelt begging him to step up as a leader to America and to that half of the world looking for him to take a stand against the "evil leaders of the other half of the world." Americans, Stimson wrote, should go to battle, not because of some "accident or mistake" made by the enemy in firing on them, but instead because it was the right thing to do.[5] The prose was vintage Stimson, and he even went so far as to offer up a draft resolution that he thought Congress should issue authorizing the president to fight after laying down the justification for it.

Stimson's pugnaciousness with the president was not confined to bilateral discussions or memorandums. Although it was rare, and although he inevitably regretted it afterward, Stimson sometimes ripped into the president during cabinet meetings. Less than a month before the attack on Pearl Harbor, Stimson was leading efforts to prepare the Army to take over several coal mines set to strike at the order of John L. Lewis, president of the United Mine Workers of America. Stimson spent the better part of two weeks addressing this potential strike, working alongside Marshall to develop a detailed plan on exactly when and how the Army would operate the mines in the event of a strike. He had sought and received the enthusiastic support of Roosevelt on the plan and was therefore taken aback when Roosevelt began to advocate for a softer, less aggressive approach to labor. In Stimson's words, the ensuing debate was "the hardest and hottest" of any cabinet meeting he had attended up to that date, and he never "talked out" to the president as much as he did during it. After cooling off by playing deck tennis (an almost daily ritual for Stimson after work), he called to apologize to FDR, explaining that his preference was to take up such issues alone with him.[6]

Aside from the stature and experience Henry Stimson brought to his administration, why did the president put up with a man who treated him this way? The answer was simple: He trusted the secretary of war, knew he was a loyal team player, and was certain he had the nation's best interests at heart. In speaking about Stimson with Democrat Sam Rayburn one day, Roosevelt explained, "When I disapprove [of] his recommendations, I don't have to look over my shoulder to see if he is going to the Capitol to lobby against me."[7]

George Marshall's personality was even more in contrast to the president's than Stimson's was. He was more reserved, more formal, and even less comfortable in social gatherings than the secretary of war. Marshall refused to be on a first-name basis with all but a handful of individuals in his life (before appointing him as chief of staff, Roosevelt once made the mistake of calling him by his first name during a meeting, only to receive in return an icy glare back from the general; FDR never tried again).

The contrast between Marshall and Roosevelt also reflected the overall differences between soldiers and civilians. Marshall spent thirty-seven consecutive years in the Army prior to taking over its leadership. Accustomed to a clear chain of command and an overly structured organization, he was shocked when he first observed how FDR ran the White House. Aside from the president's disorganized and scattered approach to management, Marshall was also dumbfounded that he retained subordinates who had questionable loyalty to him, were incompetent, or both. The chief of staff initially saw these traits as a sign of weakness in Roosevelt, and they colored his views on his decision-making skills during the prewar period.

Early on, Marshall also observed that although Roosevelt was easily bored with conventional presentations and could not focus on many topics for any length of time, he possessed exceptional curiosity for certain subjects. In preparing a brigadier general for a visit by the president to Fort Benning in November 1939, Marshall counseled him to keep both language and diagrams simple and to an absolute minimum emphasizing that with FDR, "you have to intrigue his interest, and then it knows no limits."[8]

Although the civilian in Henry Stimson might have been better able to appreciate Roosevelt's style, he, too, was irritated by it. Like Marshall, Stimson chafed at the president's unpredictable nature and chaotic handling of both personnel issues and administrative problems. His criticism of these traits remained consistent in his diary throughout the War. He railed against FDR's "government on the jump" in the fall of 1940 and declared a year later that two-thirds of his own troubles were due to Roosevelt's "topsy-turvy, upside-down system of poor administration."[9] Between these two dates and following them, there were many other occasions when Stimson unburdened himself to his diary about the president as an administrator. While acknowledging FDR's "flashes of genius," "wonderful memory," and "penetrative shrewdness," Stimson believed he fell short of the qualities required to "work out a hard problem in a short time."[10] As such, he concluded it was the job of cabinet members to assist him.

Although the secretary had numerous bilateral meetings with the president during the run-up to Pearl Harbor, there were times Stimson was exasperated he could not get more time with him, particularly since he was aware that FDR booked much of his calendar with people "who were not his regular assistants." Both he and Marshall were frustrated that Roosevelt sought and accepted military advice from far too many individuals. This predilection of their boss would cause no end of troubles for both men during the months prior to Pearl Harbor.

Offsetting many of the differences between Stimson and Marshall and the president was the fact that all three men were firm internationalists and of like minds when it came to their opposition to Hitler and their deep-seated concern about Japan's ambitions in Asia. But there was a major difference in their respective approaches to managing these threats during the summer of 1940, brought on by a political reality: Roosevelt's continuation in office had to be sanctioned by the electorate in November 1940. As such, he was reluctant to push the country in the interventionist direction he favored.

Stimson's job security was also tied to the presidential election, but his name was not on the ballot and his ambitions at seventy-three years old were obviously different from Roosevelt's at fifty-eight. As for the job of chief of staff, it had its own rotation and did not normally change with a new administration, but Marshall had determined from the start of his tenure that the best approach for him was to act as a loyal member of Roosevelt's team.

He understood that if the American economy was pushed too aggressively toward a wartime footing, the consequences could be fatal to his goal of building up the Army.

Neither Stimson nor Marshall displayed patience for politics and were frustrated whenever it interfered with their plans to prepare the nation for war. But it was a reality they were forced to accept while working with Roosevelt, not only during the five months leading up to the presidential election of 1940, but also during the thirteen months following the election leading up to the attack on Pearl Harbor.

What was equally difficult to manage was the president's insistence on making sure, one way or another, that he maintained ultimate power over all military matters, not just in theory but also in practice. Whether it related to domestic, military, or international affairs, the president's management style generally reflected his desire to have complete control. He demonstrated creative ways of achieving this throughout his first seven years in office by creating an environment where no single job, person, committee, or agency could develop too much power or influence. As this quality pertained to military affairs, it was even more prevalent given Roosevelt's strong belief in the importance of civilian control over the military. Both Stimson and Marshall were equally passionate about the need for civilian control over military matters, but that was not their major issue with the president in 1940; ambiguous job descriptions and proper authority levels were.

Marshall's issues with respect to his own job description predated both his appointment to chief of staff in 1939 and FDR's tenure in the White House. The chief of staff position, one will recall, was poorly defined in the General Staff Act of 1903 despite Elihu Root's best intentions. Full authority over several key subordinates was one of the legacy issues Marshall was compelled to confront. Only his stature in the Army, his leadership skills, and his direct access to Roosevelt allowed him to overcome this difficulty as the country moved closer to war.

With respect to Marshall's direct access to the Oval Office (as opposed to going through the secretary of war), this was FDR's idea, one he put into effect through an executive order in July 1939 permitting direct contact between the president and chief of staff relating to "strategy, tactics, and operations." Prior to this executive order, the secretary of war was the chief advisor to the president on military affairs. For this reason and others, Stimson's ability to grasp his exact role during the summer of 1940 was even more challenging. Considering the enhanced anxiety within the administration after the fall of France, clarity around the organization, strategy, and goals of the War Department was critical. But clarity was neither a goal nor a strength of the president. Ambiguity was not so much a natural trait in Roosevelt as it was a defined strategy used throughout his presidency to keep his options open, keep people guessing, and keep his power secure. Stimson and Marshall dealt with this problem—as they did with most of their problems with Roosevelt—by having frank discussions with one another to find a common position and strategy before taking it together or separately to the White House.

Another major concern for Stimson also predated his arrival to the War Department. When the bickering between Woodring and Johnson started to have negative consequences, FDR moved certain War Department responsibilities over to both the Treasury Department (run by Roosevelt's trusted and loyal friend Henry Morgenthau) and a new independent commission he formed (the National Defense Advisory Commission). The transferred responsibilities were hugely significant and included the task to procure munitions and equipment to supply the Army, overall plane production, and the coordination of airplane sales to Great Britain and France.[11] But as with most things related to Roosevelt's delegation practices, nothing was particularly clear.

Given this ambiguity, coupled with the "perfectly horrible" state of affairs left behind by his predecessor, it took Stimson less than two weeks from taking office before his frustration grew into despair. He wrote to Felix Frankfurter describing the overall situation and the dilution of the powers belonging to the War Department by right, and seriously questioned whether he was up to the job given the chaos existing everywhere.[12]

It did not help matters that Roosevelt was out of Washington for much of Stimson's first month at the helm (either cruising various waters or in Hyde Park).[13] He was able to meet with FDR on July 10 (the day he was sworn in), 11 (for a cabinet meeting), 12, and 19, but never alone for more than fifteen minutes at a clip. Although they spoke on the phone, they did not meet again in person until mid-August.

On top of every other frustration, the secretary was tired and hot. It was, after all, summer in a city Stimson once described as "this infernal hole they call Washington." Stimson mentioned several times in his diary in July 1940 that he had never experienced more oppressive heat in the nation's capital. Between the temperature, the loose job description, the Blaustein case (which he was transitioning to a Winthrop & Stimson colleague), and the excessive workload, he was exhausted, and his frustrations poured out in his letter to Frankfurter.

Although the uncertainty of the job continued to frustrate Stimson during the summer, things began to pick up for him within days of writing the letter. Perhaps it was no coincidence that Stimson installed air-conditioning in his bedroom and sitting room at Woodley Mansion in late July,[14] but his change in attitude was more likely due to his positive conversations with FDR in early August, the warm welcome he was receiving from other cabinet members, and the greater number of issues on which he was asked to advise. Stimson was always more productive and content when working on important matters.

As the summer of 1940 passed, Stimson's advice was sought out, not only by the president but by other members of the administration on issues both within and outside of his formal responsibilities. This energized him and brought him quickly up from the depths. He and Marshall spent the next five years working closely with these colleagues on some of the largest, most complex issues the United States faced during its history. Both men worked well in a team environment, and in Roosevelt's cabinet, it was an excellent team they joined.

The Cabinet and FDR's Inner Circle

In his memoirs, Henry Stimson criticized Roosevelt for not being a "good chooser of men." But this judgment is inconsistent with earlier reflections he made about key figures in the administration appointed by Roosevelt. In his diary, Stimson offered a great deal of praise for various cabinet members and advisors individually and collectively with respect to their cooperation and their collective awareness of the threats facing America during the summer and fall of 1940. Like most presidents, Roosevelt appointed his share of duds (he had more years in office than any other of his predecessors to make such mistakes), but for the key assignments, particularly as the nation geared for a potential war, FDR's record was commendable, and Stimson should have given him far more credit for his recruiting skills (after all, Roosevelt had chosen both him and Marshall).

Upon entering the administration as the "new guy," and a Republican to boot, Stimson was quite taken by the warm welcome he received, specifically from the key men who ran the Departments of State, the Treasury, and the Navy (Cordell Hull, Henry Morgenthau, and Frank Knox respectively), and with key presidential advisors Harry Hopkins, Major General Edwin "Pa" Watson, and Felix Frankfurter. These men were all given the highest marks by Stimson and credited for their contributions to both preparing the country for war and fighting it. Marshall's opinions of these men generally coincided with those of Stimson. To understand Stimson and Marshall's success, one must appreciate the value each member of Roosevelt's cabinet and inner circle brought to the table.

Frank Knox, Secretary of the Navy

Henry Stimson met Secretary of the Navy Frank Knox almost three decades earlier when the latter showed up at Stimson's office in the War Department with a letter of introduction from Teddy Roosevelt stating, "He is just our type." Frank Knox was a bipartisan interventionist and strongly believed the United States should aid Britain. Stimson was delighted he and Knox were coming into the cabinet together.

The mutual respect Stimson and Knox held for one another made it far less difficult for both to deal with the ever-present strain between the Army and the Navy. This tension had been an ongoing issue during nearly all of America's wars and would prove to be the case during both the run-up to World War II and throughout it. But to have the two civilian heads of each service on the friendliest of terms and working largely as partners for the common cause made it much easier to keep the friction manageable at lower levels. Besides the weekly meeting of the "secret three" Stimson organized between himself, Knox, and Secretary of State Hull shortly after joining the War Department, Stimson regularly met with Knox alone to go over all the issues they faced together as respective heads of the Army and the Navy.

As helpful as Knox wanted to be, he was limited in his powers for a few reasons: First, Roosevelt tended to act as his own secretary of the navy. Whether he was "swapping yarns" with other seamen, studying depth charts, or discussing the caliber of naval guns, Roosevelt was in his comfort zone when it came to naval matters and the sea; second, just as the position of secretary of war was historically weak, so, too, was that of secretary of the navy; finally and critically, Knox did not have a person like George Marshall as head of the Navy, someone who consistently bent over backward to keep his boss informed. Marshall's counterpart during the War, Admiral Ernest J. King, maintained an altogether different view regarding how civilian and military heads should work with one another.[15]

Cordell Hull, Secretary of State

Stimson had already established a good relationship with Secretary of State Cordell Hull during the transition period between the Hoover and

Roosevelt administrations. It only strengthened after Stimson joined the cabinet. Hull was four years younger than Stimson, closer in age than any other cabinet member. This would have provided Stimson a generational bond he shared with so few other people in the cabinet (the average age difference between Stimson and the other members in the summer of 1940 was approximately seventeen years).

Stimson did not always agree with Hull and often expressed frustration during the prewar period about his pessimism (in May 1941, he went so far as to suggest that the secretary of state was a defeatist).[16] Despite this and many other differences, their friendship was genuine, and it lasted until Stimson's death in 1950. Having such a friend and ally representing the State Department in the cabinet proved generally beneficial to Stimson in the beginning of his tenure in the War Department, but once the secretary of war found his own voice, Hull often became more of a professional hindrance than an ally.

Henry Morgenthau, Secretary of the Treasury

Heading the Treasury Department was the formidable Henry Morgenthau. Morgenthau, an early and strong supporter of Marshall, set up the critical meeting between the general and Roosevelt in May 1940 after hearing from the former how desperate the situation was regarding the Army's preparedness. It was this meeting that broke the eight-month logjam the chief of staff experienced in getting even the most basic requirements met. Two months later, Morgenthau welcomed Stimson and Knox with open arms. Morgenthau's first impression was that Knox was the stronger of the two, but he rapidly came to the realization that Stimson was the man who "made a difference in Washington."[17]

Although Morgenthau gave Stimson generous advice during his first few years in the War Department, the two men fought plenty of battles and often traded "warm words" with another. Stimson would inevitably feel guilty after such exchanges and follow up with a telephone call or personal visit to smooth things over (a trademark of Stimson's).

Having been asked by his close friend Roosevelt to involve himself in several areas of responsibility belonging to the War Department before Stimson arrived, Morgenthau could have proved difficult to work with, but he wasn't. He thought highly of Stimson's capabilities and shifted much of what Roosevelt handed over to him back to the War Department once Stimson joined.

Toward the end of World War II, Stimson and Morgenthau held starkly contrasting opinions on the future of postwar Germany, but as heated as their exchanges were over this particular issue (Stimson was violently opposed to Morgenthau's proposal to turn Germany's economy into one primarily agrarian in nature and devoid of heavy industry), neither man appeared to let the issue interfere with the great mutual respect each held for the other.[18]

Harry Hopkins, Diplomatic Advisor and Troubleshooter

More important to Stimson and Marshall than any other member of Roosevelt's cabinet was the indefatigable, brilliant, forceful, and wise Harry Hopkins. To both men, Hopkins was indispensable. Marshall called on him whenever he hit a "tough knot I couldn't handle," and either Hopkins or the two of them together would then speak to the president. After the War, Marshall wrote that the service Hopkins rendered to his country during it would "never even vaguely be appreciated."[19] Stimson wrote in his diary nine months before Pearl Harbor that having Hopkins in the White House was a "godsend."

Many historians and major figures of the era place Hopkins among the most influential of men during the Second World War. Churchill, in speaking after the War about the man he referred to as "Lord Root of the Matter," said that whenever the discussion "flagged" at major conferences, Hopkins would "rap out the deadly question" and ask, "Are we going to face it or not?" Edward Stettinius, U.S. secretary of state toward the end of the War, said of Hopkins that he had never worked with anyone whom he had respected more.[20]

As admired as he was within the administration, Hopkins had been a polarizing figure outside of it, resented by many during much of Roosevelt's prewar presidency due to his high-profile association with the New Deal and the influence he appeared to have over FDR. The fact was that FDR needed Hopkins. When asked by 1940 Republican presidential candidate Wendell Willkie during a friendly postelection meeting in early 1941 why he kept Hopkins "so close," FDR replied that he (Willkie) might one day sit in the White House and face an absolute onslaught of people coming into his office who wanted something out of him. "When that happens," Roosevelt continued, "you'll discover the need for someone like Harry Hopkins."[21] Hopkins enjoyed the complete confidence of the president and was used liberally by Stimson and Marshall both individually and collectively to advocate on their behalf to FDR on matters of the highest importance.

Hopkins did far more than simply act as a liaison; he gathered information, ideas, and requests for the president, separating the wants from the needs, and brought to Roosevelt's attention only those matters he believed to be important along with his own opinions on each one. Hopkins knew Roosevelt better than anyone else within the administration, was keenly aware of his strengths and weaknesses, and counseled him accordingly. He knew, for example, that FDR tended to take advice from too many people, and when Roosevelt began to display this tendency in regard to military matters in the spring of 1941, Hopkins stepped in insisting to the president that he limit the number of his military advisors to six. Stimson and Marshall were delighted. Until Hopkins intervened, Marshall joked that any man who had "slept in a tent during the last war" was considered by Roosevelt to be a "military authority" and one worth listening to.[22]

Other members of the cabinet or inner circle whom Stimson and Marshall respected and admired were Secretary of Commerce Jesse Jones and advisors Major General "Pa" Watson and Felix Frankfurter. Jones was a strong supporter of Stimson within the cabinet, and Watson and Frankfurter served both Stimson and Marshall as reliable bridges to the White House, regularly and effectively used throughout the War and during the critical months leading up to it.

Staffing

To make any progress in raising, training, and equipping an army in a nation deeply entrenched in isolationism, Stimson and Marshall needed more than a sympathetic White House and a cooperative cabinet during the summer and fall of 1940; they each needed a first-rate staff. Both men were nearly flawless in putting their respective teams together.

A modern scholar of management, looking for a different take on the subject, would be well served by examining the professional careers of both Henry Stimson and George Marshall. There is enough material for an instant classic in the field of management and leadership studies with concrete examples in practice of all the leading theories taught at business schools since Harvard first offered the MBA in the early twentieth century: Both men inspired others through their strength of character and their allegiance to the concept of teamwork; they led by example and demanded as much from their subordinates; they understood that productivity and sound decisions could only be achieved if morale was high; they were organized, efficient, and decisive but not at the expense of careful deliberation; they could draw from past experiences, but were forward thinking; they carried a vast knowledge of small details, but only to support the solving of larger issues; and they were direct and sometimes ruthless, but fair.

Like most great leaders, Stimson and Marshall were both extremely self-confident, but this was softened by the exceptional level of gravitas each man possessed, along with the one quality each was principally known for and that distinguished them above all other leading figures of the Second World War: integrity. It was this attribute, commented on by so many major figures of the era, that made those who worked for them want to perform at their very best.

Both men delegated responsibilities liberally, but prudently. Although their respective positions during the War gave them little choice but to do so, other historical figures, given similar responsibilities during times of war, had failed in this regard. Critical to their success was that they picked the right people for the right jobs, defined the overall mission, and cemented the concept of teamwork firmly in place from the beginning.

Stimson's Staff

Few leaders in any field of endeavor could match the success of George Marshall in finding, judging, and placing talent. Henry Stimson happened to be one of them. But his recruiting style contrasted with that of Marshall, reflecting the differences in both their professions and their personal styles. Throughout his career, Stimson asked people he knew and trusted to recommend the smartest and most productive people they could find to support him (ideally successful lawyers who had graduated at or near the top of their class from Harvard or Yale). He then interviewed the candidates and hired them only if they passed his character test. If his strategy was a bit more sophisticated than this, it was not significantly so.

The team Stimson chose to assist him as FDR's secretary of war was universally thought of in Washington as the most competent of all staffs during the War. It was likely the greatest staff of any cabinet member in American history.

One will recall that Stimson's strong recruiting track record went back to his first public-sector job in 1906. Faced with strict budget restrictions at that time, he corresponded with law school deans and peers at the New York bar, requesting the names of the top law students who were about to graduate or those who had graduated in the past two years (the top two of a class were his preferred candidates). Many of the sixteen men he hired to the U.S. Attorney's office went on to prominence in the field of law and public service (none more so than Felix Frankfurter).

With larger personnel budgets available to Stimson in later assignments, experience naturally came into play as a hiring consideration, but a first-rate brain remained the first prerequisite. His appointment of Joseph Cotton to serve as his undersecretary of state in 1929 was a case in point. Although Cotton was a highly respected fifty-year-old corporate lawyer, it was no coincidence that he was also considered one of the brightest minds ever to come out of Harvard Law School.

Since his strategy had worked well in 1906, 1911, and 1929, Stimson went back to the same well when he became secretary of war in 1940; all five of his top advisors during World War II matriculated at Harvard Law School, and three of those men received undergraduate degrees from Yale.

While brainpower never guarantees success, Stimson was confident he could get the best out of any subordinate's high intellectual capacity by appealing to that person's sense of duty and highlighting both the importance and the excitement of the work he would be undertaking.

Unlike the Army, where Marshall's goal was to train and then test his staff for greater responsibilities in the various theaters, the War Department was the first and final battleground for Stimson's team during the War. He planned on having members of his lineup in the same jobs for the duration of the crisis, and the four men who made up his principal staff from the beginning all served together under Stimson until the War ended (George Harrison, the fifth key member of the team, joined in the summer of 1943).

Of Stimson's numerous contributions to America's victory in World War II, his staff was thought by many to be among his greatest. Although his hiring decisions were exceptional, Stimson's greater contribution was in how he organized the responsibilities of each member and then challenged, guided, inspired, and supported them both individually and as a team. Newton Baker, secretary of war during the First World War, once reflected on the job by stating, "No one human being ever was born that could have a very intimate contact with or knowledge of many of the details of the vast business going on under his eye and in his name."[23] Delegation was required, and a competent staff was crucial.

One of his underlings said after the War that Stimson ran his team like a group of talented lawyers assisting him on a critical case; tasks were divided up, and there were never any secrets between the team.[24] Trust was the vital ingredient. One of Stimson's most oft-cited quotes came from a diary entry of his in 1932. He wrote that he had "found in life that the best way to make a man trustworthy is to trust him."[25] Although he was commenting at that time on negotiating with foreign counterparts, this sentiment served him well in his relations with superiors, peers, and subordinates. Morale—so essential for any team—was a by-product of trust and was established by the boss from the first days.

Stimson gave his staff unwavering support, demanding in return only great effort, teamwork, and loyalty. In this respect, Robert Patterson, John McCloy, Robert Lovett, Harvey Bundy, and George Harrison rarely let him down.

Robert Patterson

Active for his age, energetic, fond of outdoor sports, and obsessed with his physical and mental fitness, Henry Stimson would have been well suited to have had children of his own. But as he and his wife were childless, he made do by spending time with the younger men who served on his staff over the years. As his career lengthened, so naturally did the age differences between himself and his subordinates. Felix Frankfurter and most of the others who worked for Stimson in his first public sector job in 1906 were approximately fifteen years younger than their boss. Upon joining the War Department in 1940, the differences in age between Stimson and his four key assistants ranged between twenty-four and thirty years, the range one would expect in that era between a father and his children. Several of Stimson's biographers have pointed out the paternal relationship that Stimson seems to have had with his staff during the War. In most ways, they were right; Robert Lovett once said Stimson effectively adopted him and John McCloy.[26]

Of all the men who worked for Stimson over the years, it was Robert Patterson who most resembled his chief. He shared Stimson's substantial moral power, desire for action, passion for the army life, untouchable integrity, and outsized sense of patriotic duty. George Marshall described Patterson after the War as "the perfect citizen," and he could have just as easily been speaking about Stimson as well.

Born and raised in Glens Falls, New York, Patterson acquired his undergraduate degree less than forty miles south, at Union College in Schenectady, before heading off to Harvard Law School. At Harvard, he graduated second in his class, was named president of the Law Review, and was elected to the honorary position of marshal of the class of 1915. After graduation, Patterson's preference was to practice law in upstate New York, but at the urging of Frankfurter (one of his professors at Harvard), he headed to Manhattan instead and joined a firm run by Elihu Root's son.

Patterson loved the firm, the work, and the challenges the law business provided him. Outside of the office, Patterson joined the New York National Guard, principally for the exercise, just as Stimson had done years earlier. The weekly training kept him fit, but he also fell in love with the entire experience of being a member of the Guard. When his regiment was called to Mexico to help John Pershing in 1915, the adventure and camaraderie he experienced cemented his admiration for the United States Army.

Returning to practice law only briefly, Patterson left again to serve in the First World War (with the 306th Infantry Regiment of New York's 77th Division). He served on the front lines, seeing plenty of action, including one early morning when he and two other men came upon a shell crater in an open field full of a half-dozen Germans. Killing one from twelve feet away, Patterson then ran back toward his lines along with his companions, only to come across another crater full of more Germans. Patterson provided cover (killing another two Germans) to allow his colleagues to escape before taking off himself. Facing impossible odds as he drew fire from the men in both craters, he collapsed as if shot and lay flat on his stomach within sight and sound of the enemy. After approximately fifteen hours of lying perfectly still, he crawled his way to safety during the night.[27]

After the First World War ended, Patterson returned to the law, eventually starting his own small firm with a couple of friends from Harvard. The sterling reputation he built as a corporate lawyer during the next decade caught the attention of Herbert Hoover, who appointed Patterson a federal judge in New York in 1930. Over the next nine years, Patterson served the office with great distinction, earning a reputation for writing opinions that were short, to the point, and without any pretension (they were also inevitably affirmed by the higher courts at a greater percentage than his peers). In 1939, President Roosevelt appointed him a circuit judge, putting him on the nation's second highest court.

Although Patterson and Henry Stimson served in the same division during the First World War, the two did not get a chance to know one another. After the War ended, the two Wall Street lawyers became better acquainted due to their respective standing in the New York legal and military circles, but the twenty-four years separating their ages would have limited their professional and social contact.

The story of how the Stimson and Patterson "package" was sold to FDR by Grenville Clark and Felix Frankfurter was discussed in the previous chapter. Stimson, of course, had to buy into the plan first. He did not need much of a pitch. In Patterson, the important boxes could be checked off: second in his class at Harvard Law School; successful Wall Street law-yer; decorated war hero; aggressive, smart, and pragmatic (Stimson was apparently willing to forgive Patterson for not attending Yale). If these qualities were not Stimsonian enough, Patterson had also requested a few months earlier to be recommissioned into the infantry so that he could help serve the country in any capacity. Patterson was forty-nine, the age Stimson was when he received his commission to fight during World War I. That Patterson was willing to give up the lifetime job security of a circuit judge to serve at a time he felt the country was in real danger was simply icing on the cake for Stimson. He was, as Teddy Roosevelt might have said to Stimson in an earlier era, "one of us."

Despite the agreement between Roosevelt and Stimson regarding Pat-terson, the president took his time in removing the incumbent assistant secretary of war, Louis Johnson. Stimson, in a state of panic regarding the work to be done after getting fully briefed by Marshall, had no patience for the delay. After two weeks on the job, he took pen to paper and wrote, "*I hereby appoint Robert P. Patterson Assistant Secretary of War,*" leaving a blank space for FDR's signature. He sent it over to the White House, instruct-ing the messenger to wait for a response. This was not how members of his cabinet generally treated Roosevelt, but getting the message loud and clear from the "new guy," Roosevelt signed the paper, and it was back on Stimson's desk within an hour.[28]

Patterson joined Stimson toward the end of July as assistant secretary of war in charge of all procurement (he was sworn into the newly created office of undersecretary of war by the end of the year). Although the under-secretary of war was, by law, directly in charge of procurement, Patterson and other members of Stimson's staff thought the law was "ridiculous," and it was understood by Patterson that he served under the direction and supervision of the secretary of war.[29] Stimson ended up delegating most of the responsibilities related to procurement to "Patterson's department," not only because procurement was Patterson's job (and he was excellent at it), but also to preserve himself for the larger questions related to his responsi-bilities as the civilian head of the Army and as a member of the cabinet.

Patterson retained this responsibility through the end of the War, after which Truman named him to succeed Stimson as secretary of war. Contrib-uting greatly to the difficult and thankless job of unifying the military after the War, Patterson was then asked by Truman to be the nation's first secre-tary of defense in 1947 (the position that combined the secretary of war and secretary of navy positions). Patterson turned down the job, believing he had accomplished all he could for the military and went back to practicing law. Sadly, he died five years later in a commercial plane crash in New Jersey.

Patterson was relentless in his approach to the job (Stimson described him as "ruthlessly determined"), and he valued teamwork as much as his boss. His excellent working relationship with General Brehon Somervell, head of Services and Supply, mirrored that between Stimson and Marshall. Like Stimson, he was also fanatic in his belief that every citizen should share the sacrifice of war. This put him at odds with a great number of public figures, both before and during the War, who did not think people on the home front should be too "inconvenienced" by what was happening in Europe and Asia. Believing that in a democracy "all citizens have equal rights and equal obligations," Patterson led by example, working at a punishing pace few if any in Washington could match before or during the War.[30]

Given the nation's massive and unprecedented industrial output during the War (an amount that eventually exceeded the aggregate output of all the other participants on both sides combined) and the quality of those supplies brought to the two major fronts, Patterson's performance certainly places him among the greatest individual contributors to victory in Europe.

John J. McCloy[31]

The second member to join Stimson's staff was John J. McCloy, a man who would later become most identified with America's postwar "Establishment," serving as its unofficial chairman while holding a string of posts, including president of the World Bank, U.S. High Commissioner for Germany, chairman of Chase Manhattan Bank, chairman of the Ford Foundation, chairman of the Counsel on Foreign Relations, and trustee of the Rockefeller Foundation. Before, during, between, and following these assignments, the bipartisan "wise man" advised presidents from Franklin Roosevelt to Ronald Reagan.

Born, as he liked to frequently remind people, on the "wrong side of the tracks" in Philadelphia, McCloy got a scholarship to Amherst College on the strength of his academic and athletic record (he was a top tennis player). Not naturally brilliant, McCloy relied on a relentless work ethic to keep up with the students he felt were brighter and better educated than he. His effort paid off when he was accepted to Harvard Law School.

Arriving on campus in the fall of 1916, World War I soon interrupted McCloy's studies, and he served for two years seeing only limited action in France during the last two months of the War. He returned to Harvard in the fall of 1919. After graduating with decent marks, the twenty-six-year-old

McCloy went to practice law in Manhattan. Becoming a partner at Cravath Henderson & Gersdorff (now Cravath Swain & Moore) in 1929, McCloy was soon introduced to a case that eventually led him to his job at the War Department under Stimson.

The case, known as "Black Tom," stemmed from a massive explosion of ammunition in 1916 at a terminal in lower Manhattan. The explosion, heard as far away as Philadelphia, inflicted damage to the Statue of Liberty along with a million dollars' worth of windows in downtown Manhattan. Similar explosions at other plants led authorities to believe that German sabotage was involved. The case had essentially hit a dead end when McCloy took it up in 1930. He spent the next ten years methodically chasing down leads in the United States and Europe. He was ultimately successful in proving German culpability and soon became recognized as the country's leading expert on German espionage.

Back when Stimson was secretary of state, he met briefly with McCloy to discuss Black Tom. He also ran into him from time to time at the Ausable Club in the Adirondacks, a private hunting and fishing club to which both men belonged. In September 1940, Stimson asked McCloy to formally consult him on counterintelligence activities.[32] So impressed was Stimson that he hired him full-time in October 1940 as his special assistant. For the next five years, McCloy (who succeeded Patterson as assistant secretary of war in the spring of 1941) handled nearly everything nobody else on the staff happened to be working on. Since wars tend to create a multitude of unexpected issues and problems, he was a busy man in this regard and one whose activities were so varied, according to Stimson, that they "defied summary."

McCloy's competence, breadth of activities, strong work ethic, and winning personality gave him an enormous network of contacts. He became an unparalleled trader in information and soon gained the reputation around town as the "man who knew everything." George Marshall often sent visitors seeking information from him to "go speak with McCloy." It was not just information people were seeking from him; they also sought advice. Stimson sometimes wondered if anyone ever made a decision in Washington without first discussing it with his able assistant.

Judging solely by Stimson's daily diary entries made during his stewardship of the War Department, nobody seemed to impress him more than McCloy. Besides acting as his key advisor on the Lend-Lease Act, McCloy functioned as his principal counselor on matters relating to international relations and served as his personal envoy to foreign leaders. He represented the War Department when war plans were drawn up, when office space was required, when military government issues needed to be discussed, when generals needed to be put in place, and when the private sector needed prodding.

Aside from being unequaled at acquiring and dispensing knowledge, McCloy was a fixer extraordinaire (Robert Lovett called him the greatest negotiator he ever met). McCloy's exceptional competence in this and other regards meant that his services were in extremely high demand outside of the War Department. Although he fought against this throughout the War, Stimson did occasionally agree to lend his young staffer out. In January 1943, Dwight Eisenhower asked Marshall to ask the secretary of war if he might consider "loaning" McCloy to him for up to two months to deal with the civilian problems he was having in North Africa. Stimson was aware of the problems but would only agree to send McCloy for a month and only under the condition that he was not to be considered "attached" to Eisenhower's staff.[33]

One risk that McCloy presented for Stimson (that anyone managing a talented fixer might also face) was that in the rush to solve the increasing number of problems put on his plate, McCloy was sometimes willing to overlook certain legal or moral considerations. For the most part, this was a risk worth taking (e.g., McCloy was instrumental in providing the creative legal arguments to support the arming of Great Britain through the Lend-Lease program before the United States got into the War). But there were times when this quality in McCloy did not serve Stimson well; his leading role in persuading Stimson to support the internment of Japanese Americans after Pearl Harbor (discussed in chapter 12) is the most obvious case in point.

McCloy let few things stand in the way of his objectives, and this approach brought results. Not surprisingly, success and power got to his head on occasion. Robert Morgenthau, who worked for Robert Patterson after the War, provided an anecdote about McCloy when asked to contrast both men. Patterson was at Penn Station with Morgenthau, waiting to board a train at midnight behind a line of approximately twenty people, when he spotted McCloy come into the station and head obnoxiously toward the front of the line. Patterson waited a moment and then called out from behind, "Hey, Jack, you in a hurry?" to which the surprised McCloy replied sheepishly that he did not notice Patterson. "That's okay," Patterson joked. "I know that if you were not in a big hurry, you would be back here with me."[34]

Robert Lovett

A month after McCloy joined the War Department, Robert Lovett was appointed by Stimson to be his assistant on all matters related to airpower. As highly regarded as McCloy was after the War, Lovett's reputation was even stronger. Like McCloy, Lovett spent the postwar years as a "wise man," going back and forth between Wall Street and Washington. His government jobs included chairing the Lovett Committee (that ultimately recommended the formation of the CIA), and serving as both undersecretary of state (under George Marshall) and secretary of defense (during the Korean War). When John F. Kennedy began forming his cabinet after winning the presidency in 1960, he offered Lovett his choice to run either the Department of State, the Treasury, or Defense. Lovett declined all three positions on account of his health, but, further evidencing his stature at that time, each of the three recommendations he made to Kennedy for the respective positions were taken by the young president.

Born to wealth in Texas (his father was the right-hand man to E. H. Harriman and eventually chairman of the Union Pacific Railroad), Lovett was a Yale graduate (a member of Skull and Bones), and a decorated World War I Navy bomber commander. After taking postgraduate courses in both law and business at Harvard, he chose banking as a career and ended up joining Brown Brothers in New York, an established private bank formed in the early nineteenth century. He quickly flourished and became a partner within five years. Known as the "success boy," Lovett was instrumental in merging the firm with Harriman Brothers, the new but aggressive private bank formed by his friend Averell Harriman.

Responsible for the firm's international banking and foreign currency activities, Lovett traveled twice a year to Europe for up to six weeks at a time.[35] On these trips, he spent a lot of time in Germany and took notice in the 1930s of the focus Hitler was devoting to strengthening the nation's air capabilities. Lovett became concerned and undertook a private study of what it would require for the United States to catch up. He spent two years on the project, visiting every aircraft manufacturing facility in the country. Lovett was passionate about the potential of the nation's airpower in war, and the comprehensive report he created got into Stimson's hands at the War Department soon after he joined.

Stimson had known Lovett's father for several years. The son's background (Yale, Skull and Bones, Harvard, Wall Street, World War I) and great success were reasons enough for Stimson to offer him a job, but the paper he wrote on the state of aircraft production in the United States showed initiative, energy, intensity, and a thoroughness that spoke to the secretary of war. It also revealed a first-class expertise about airpower, which Stimson knew would be decisive during the coming war. He hired Lovett toward the end of November as his special assistant for air affairs. The following spring, his job was upgraded to assistant secretary for air.

Just as the Wall Street Lawyer/Army Lifer dynamic worked so well for both Stimson and Marshall and Patterson and Somervell, so, too, did it with Lovett and Henry "Hap" Arnold, commanding general of the U.S. Army Air Forces and member of the Joint Chiefs of Staff. Working from adjacent offices like their bosses, the two men teamed up to build the greatest air force the world had ever seen.

Lovett and McCloy together were referred to by Stimson as the "Heavenly Twins" or, when in a less charitable mood, the "Imps of Satan."[36] Both men seemed to be everywhere at all times but could—like their boss—apply laser focus on any specific issue at any given moment. They were deeply loyal to Stimson but did not hesitate to speak back at him. And they were both determined to challenge bureaucracy wherever and whenever it reared its head. Most importantly, they took on complex jobs, freeing Stimson, as was his want, to concentrate on the major issues.

Harvey Bundy

The last of Stimson's four core subordinates to join his staff was Harvey Bundy, the one he was closest to personally and had spent more time with outside of office hours. Bundy served ably as Stimson's assistant secretary of state during the last eighteen months of the Hoover administration and became close to both Stimson and his wife during that period. When Stimson was asked to run the War Department by Roosevelt, he immediately offered Bundy a job in Washington but was turned down (Bundy did not think America would be drawn into the global war). Only when the war in Europe grew more desperate in April 1941 did Bundy agree to serve as special assistant to the secretary.

Like Stimson, Bundy graduated from Yale (where he was also tapped by Skull and Bones) and Harvard Law School (first in the class of 1914). He then clerked for Oliver Wendell Holmes before practicing law in Boston. Turned down by the Army due to his bad eyesight, Bundy spent World War I with the Justice Department and as one of four assistants to food administrator Herbert Hoover. Although not someone who favored outdoor activities nearly as much as Stimson (according to his grandson), Bundy had much in common with his boss, and Stimson greatly enjoyed his company.

Put into the position as point man in the War Department on science and technology (as well as intelligence work), Bundy was Stimson's representative to the Office of Scientific Research and Development. In this capacity, he served as Stimson's emissary on all matters related to the atomic bomb (something both he and Stimson first heard about a month before Pearl Harbor).[37] As old as he was during the War, Stimson was a surprisingly firm believer, far more so than Marshall, that new technology would make the difference between winning and losing the war. He and Bundy pushed the chief of staff and other high-ranking military men, skeptical about innovative weapons, to support and embrace developments in innovations such as radar, detonators, guided missiles, and early warning systems.

Although extremely important to Stimson and an influential contributor to the Allied victory in Europe, Bundy was not pursued to the same degree after the War as were Patterson, McCloy, and Lovett. He went back to practicing law and advising the wealthiest of individuals of New England. As Kai Bird, a prominent chronicler of the postwar Establishment wrote, "If Henry Stimson was the grand patriarch of the American foreign policy establishment, Harvey Bundy was its preeminent clerk."[38] Although he went on to become the president of the board of trustees of the World Peace Foundation and later chaired the Carnegie Endowment for International Peace, it was his two liberal anticommunist sons, William and McGeorge Bundy, who had greater influence in the second half of the twentieth century through their positions with the CIA, the Pentagon, the State Department, and the Executive Office of the president during the Kennedy and Johnson years. Both brothers, who were like grandchildren to Henry Stimson, played major roles in planning and escalating the war in Vietnam.[39]

George Harrison

Although not part of the original core four, Special Assistant George Harrison became an indispensable part of Stimson's staff by the summer of 1943 after working as a consultant for three months. A longtime president of the Federal Reserve Board, Harrison was recruited by Stimson from the New York Life Insurance Company where he joined as president in 1941.

Although a Californian by birth, Harrison had the predictable pedigree of a Stimson staff member (Yale, Skull and Bones, and Harvard Law). But it was the fifty-six-year-old's background at the Federal Reserve that most attracted Stimson. Having his new subordinate work initially on a study of how best to take aircraft production to the next level from an economic standpoint, Stimson quickly put him in charge of addressing the issues of inflation and demobilization. Although the war was still two years from ending, Stimson wanted someone with the breadth of Harrison's experience and knowledge to begin contemplating such things as contract terminations and the disposition of war stocks and plants once the fighting ended.

By February 1944, Harrison began to take over some of McCloy's portfolio (as it grew beyond even his capabilities) and supported Bundy on matters related to the atomic bomb project. As the War progressed, and postwar issues began to occupy Stimson's mind, Harrison's importance to him grew proportionally.

After the War, Harrison went back to the New York Life Insurance Company, becoming its chairman in 1948.

Marshall's Staff

As mentioned earlier, among the peculiarities attributed to George Marshall during World War II was his devotion to the "little black book" he kept close at hand, where he had jotted down the names of impressive officers he crossed paths with during his career. Although the book was never found among Marshall's papers, and many historians now believe stories about it were apocryphal, Marshall certainly took careful note throughout his career of those men who caught his attention and the specific qualities that attracted him to them.

Recognized early on for his outstanding teaching ability, Marshall was consequently given far more opportunities than others to observe officers during his numerous assignments at Army schools. By scrutinizing talented individuals through the years—both inside of classrooms and on the training fields—Marshall developed an ability to visualize exactly how certain men might be used for specific wartime tasks. Such a disciplined practice allowed him to greatly enhance his chances of getting the right people into the right roles in any future assignments that he was in the power to give. Many of the men who went on to achieve fame on the battlefields of World War II were names of which Marshall had previously taken notice.

What were attractive attributes to the general? Not long after the First World War, Marshall was chatting while riding horses with a colleague, when he casually described the qualities he believed were critical for an officer to possess in order to achieve success in the United States Army. Impressed, the officer later asked Marshall if he would put them in writing for him. Marshall agreed and wrote that there were four key requirements, "assuming that you possess good common sense, have studied your profession, and are physically strong": An officer must be (1) cheerful and optimistic; (2) energetic; (3) loyal; and (4) determined (particularly when things are going poorly).[40]

It is not surprising Marshall placed common sense as the first prerequisite attribute; as a disciple of Major John Morrison during his four years at Fort Leavenworth, Marshall believed it was the single most essential trait for a leader of men in battle.

As for the other qualities, Marshall explained to the officer that several of them were determined by the unique characteristics of the American Army, specifically its historically poor level of unpreparedness going into wars. He placed great value on those traits he believed could help overcome this specific handicap.[41] Such thinking was characteristic of Marshall's thoughtful approach to organizing and operating the Army; he made it a point to remember that whatever decisions he made, they needed to be consistent with realities and the values, history, and democratic ideals of the country.

Initially, what Marshall needed most from his staff was help in managing the massive volume of correspondence that came with the job and dealing with his numerous direct reports (approximately sixty before he reorganized the Army in 1942). For these tasks, he selected three men: Orlando Ward, Omar Bradley, and Stanley Mickelson. This first group of officers, and those who followed them in the rotation system Marshall established, were referred to as "the secretariat." Bradley went on to achieve the most success among this group, eventually leading all U.S. ground forces in Europe from the Normandy landings through V-E Day and earning a fifth star in the process (one of just nine awarded by the U.S. military during the War).[42] Marshall had greatly admired Bradley at Fort Benning ten years earlier when Bradley reported to him as an instructor in tactics. After Marshall was appointed chief of staff, Bradley was one of the first men he brought over to join him.

Among other notable men who rotated in and out of the secretariat during the War were Maxwell Taylor (who went on to command the 101st Airborne Division and later became chief of staff), Lawton Collins (who commanded VII Corps from the landings of Normandy and became chief of staff during the Korean War), and Walter Bedell Smith (Eisenhower's right-hand man during the War and later ambassador to the Soviet Union and undersecretary of state).

Aside from the workload it took on, the secretariat served two additional purposes for the chief of staff: It was both a teaching and a testing ground for promising officers. Being part of the secretariat was not for the meek. Marshall was an incredibly demanding boss, the workflow was immense, decisions had to be made quickly, and those decisions had to be right. By evaluating the full upward flow of information into the chief of staff's office, summarizing it, deciding which matters were worthy of Marshall's attention, and then presenting them to him with recommendations, members got to witness a highly efficient method of processing large amounts of work that they could each take with them to their next assignment.

After each summary was submitted to him, Marshall asked direct and challenging questions before giving the presenter specific instructions or telling him to simply "take care of it." Omar Bradley recalled in later years that if Marshall's questions were answered properly, the general simply grunted and nodded; if they could not be answered, the presenter was rewarded with the "cold stare" for which Marshall was renowned, a stare Bradley believed was a far more effective management technique than yelling or screaming.[43]

By observing Marshall, the men who went through the secretariat learned how to lead effectively, delegate, demand accountability, and make decisions. As Bradley described in his memoirs, he learned the "rudiments of effective command" working with Marshall: "avoid intervening in a subordinate's duties; if an individual performed, let him go about his business, if he hesitated, try to help him, and when he failed, relieve him."[44]

Speed was another quality of Marshall's that impressed his charges. A number of people believed he possessed a photographic memory, and most thought his mind worked at an unusually rapid pace (his dictation speed was 150 words per minute).[45] The general's goal was always to make good decisions quickly. Once he was confident of his subordinates, this was easier to accomplish. Walter "Beetle" Smith interrupted Marshall one day during an important meeting he was hosting with other generals in early 1941 to tell him that a man from a small auto firm had just come in to see him about a proposal to build a new vehicle that was simple, mobile, and resilient. Although it had been rejected by the Ordnance Department, Smith had been impressed enough to disturb Marshall, urging him to meet the gentleman with any eye toward offering him a contract. Marshall looked up, asked Smith a couple of questions, and, having full trust in him, quietly told him to "go ahead and do it." This quick decision ultimately led to the building of 650,000 *Jeeps* during the War.[46]

When Marshall believed a specific member of the secretariat had absorbed the key lessons, he shipped him out of Washington to an important command assignment and replaced him with another strong candidate he either drew from his "little black book" or from the recommendation of a trusted colleague.

Concurrent to establishing his office staff (rounded out by the appointment of Brigadier General Lorenzo Gasser as deputy chief of staff), Marshall needed to find men capable of building and training an Army. Lesley McNair was someone he had targeted years before as an officer who could organize and train troops. As soon as he was appointed in April 1939, Marshall put McNair in charge of Fort Leavenworth and asked him to revise its training methods, particularly as they related to the Air Corps. Believing three months was enough time to make the necessary changes, Marshall then brought McNair to Washington to create full divisions from the disparate troops who made up the Army in late 1939 (regular officers, national guardsmen, reservists, and untrained men). McNair was a driven man, and Marshall gave him considerable credit for the work he carried out during his two years on the job. A few months after Pearl Harbor, Marshall put McNair in charge of training and preparing the divisions he had so skillfully organized.

Another protégé of Marshall's served as McNair's right-hand man until given a command assignment in Europe once the War started. Mark Clark impressed Marshall back when the latter oversaw Vancouver Barracks and Clark was stationed at nearby Fort Lewis in Tacoma, Washington. The chief of staff took notice of Clark's quality work in planning maneuver exercises in Monterey, California. When it was time to get someone to help McNair, Marshall brought Clark to Washington.

Preparing for War

Pleased with their personal relationship, satisfied with their partners in the Executive Branch, and highly confident of their respective staffs, Stimson and Marshall began to strategize together on how to best make up for lost time in building, training, and equipping an army. Although both men gained reputations during their careers as forward thinkers and open to new ideas, they were smart enough to take advantage of any lessons history could offer them. It had been less than twenty-five years since the country had gone through a similar exercise under somewhat comparable circumstances, and although America had ultimately triumphed in World War I, there were an abundance of mistakes made in preparing for it. To avoid repeating them, both Stimson and Marshall filled any gaps in their knowledge by consulting with those who had held positions of responsibility when the country was preparing to take on the Central Powers in 1918.

One man from whom they could not get advice was Newton Baker, Woodrow Wilson's secretary of war. He passed away in 1937. Although historians have given Baker mixed reviews, his contemporaries within the Army thought he was an extraordinary individual. General Pershing and Douglas MacArthur, among others, rated him as the best secretary of war in American history.[47] In his later years, George Marshall went even further in his praise of Baker; during an interview, he referred to him as "the greatest American—or I will put it, the greatest mind—that I ever came in contact with in my lifetime" and a man "I admired beyond any other man I had ever known."[48] Given how strongly Marshall felt about Baker, and the latter's influence on both Marshall and Stimson during the Second World War, it is worth briefly noting his accomplishments during World War I.

Baker, a lawyer who achieved national prominence as a successful reformist mayor in Cleveland, took over the War Department a year before the United States declared war on Germany. As America entered the war, he realized the United States would not only have to provide money, weapons, and supplies to their allies, but also furnish a great quantity of soldiers to replace the huge manpower losses suffered by the British and French. Despite this desperate need, his proposal for a draft was not met with great enthusiasm. Prominent men such as ex-President Teddy Roosevelt felt strongly the nation was better off with volunteers. But necessity quickly trumped this sentiment and a draft was instituted that led to the near-immediate registration of ten million men.[49]

Baker then quickly turned his attention toward building camps to house and train the massive influx of soldiers. Under his direction, thirty-two new camps were built within a year, each one able to house fifty thousand men. Like Henry Stimson a generation later, Baker recruited intelligent and driven men to assist him. No expert on military matters, he saw his role as almost purely managerial in nature. Through his intelligence, honesty, and hard work, he succeeded in getting the right balance between the wartime need for centralized control within the Army (through the chief of staff) and the general desire within America for a decentralized approach to making war (which included an active and dominant contribution by civilian stakeholders).[50] Baker deserves much of the credit for raising four million men over eighteen months, housing them, equipping them, and shipping them across the Atlantic to Pershing. He made some mistakes along the way, but his achievements were notable and greatly appreciated by the senior ranks of the Army.

With Franklin Roosevelt sensitive to the ever-present winds of isolationism blowing east from around the country, Marshall had one hand tied behind his back during his first year as chief of staff. Any sense of urgency brought about by the German invasion of Poland in September 1939 evaporated when Hitler paused to regroup in the fall and winter. The "phony" war, as it was called in Congress and in the press, led even members of Marshall's own War Plans Division to conclude that the Western Hemisphere was safe.[51]

Marshall wanted to be sure, but he knew he could not be too aggressive. Even though his April 1940 budget request was kept modest in order not to frighten Congress, it was still cut by 10 percent. This attitude changed when France fell two months later and the first faint signs of weakening could be seen among moderate isolationists. Roosevelt and Marshall felt they could now move a bit less cautiously in their general approach to preparation. This was easier to do once Stimson took charge of the War Department; the president and chief of staff would always come across as restrained by comparison.

9

Playing Catch-up

There is little to tell you except that each day is a repetition of the previous one, only the pressure seems to increase and the necessities become more imperative.[1]

—GEORGE MARSHALL, July 23, 1940

If you are going to try to go to war, or to prepare for war, in a capitalist country, you have got to let business make money out of the process or business won't work, and there are a great many people in Congress who think that they can tax business out of all proportion and still have businessmen work diligently and quickly. That is not human nature.[2]

—HENRY STIMSON, August 26, 1940

The defeat of France by Germany in June 1940 took nearly everyone in Washington by surprise. For Stimson, asked to take over the War Department just days after Paris fell, it was a further sign that American involvement in the fight against Hitler was a matter of when, not if. The ease to which Hitler's blitzkrieg tactics brought the French to their knees suggested that it could be sooner rather than later, which was just fine for Stimson. General Marshall feared it would be sooner, but desperately hoped it would be later. More of a pragmatist than Stimson, he did not wish to get involved in the fighting until his army was fully prepared. For this reason, he held reservations about entering the War right up until the autumn of 1941.

Following his second and longer briefing from Marshall under the trees at Woodley Mansion on the day he took up his duties in early July,

Stimson immediately began addressing the Army's shortage of officers, soldiers, barracks, training, weapons, ammunition, planes, trucks, and general supplies brought on by two decades of neglect from the government. This monumental task fully occupied both men for the next seventeen months, right up to the Japanese attack on Pearl Harbor on the morning of December 7, 1941.

Although the fall of France helped loosen the purse strings of the United States Congress, it did nothing to address the one shortage by which Stimson and Marshall were most distressed: time. With so little of it seemingly available, particularly now that England stood alone against the Nazis, every other shortage and problem needed to be addressed concurrently. Reading through Stimson's daily diary entries during the prewar period, one senses the great quantity and variety of issues both he and Marshall needed to tackle during the course of any given day. Attempting to prioritize any one over another seemed pointless; they all required attention in order to get the Army prepared to fight.

For the seventy-three-year-old Stimson, long recognized among his colleagues for his ability (and long-standing preference) to focus on one issue at a time, these were difficult days of adjustment. The sheer volume of problems exhausted him, and rarely a week went by when he did not allude to some level or another of fatigue in his diary. Newton Baker, reflecting on his years running the War Department before and during World War I, wrote that it "was highly fortunate that I was as young as I was," as it would have "been difficult for a man of much greater age."[3] Baker was forty-five when America entered World War I, twenty-eight years younger than Stimson was when he took over the War Department in 1940.

To stay effective and sharp during these days, Stimson treated his body and mind with the same discipline—relatively speaking—that a modern-day professional athlete might display; exercise and rest were twin obsessions. Stimson managed to satisfy the former religiously as he had ten years earlier when he was secretary of state and before that when he served in the Philippines. Nearly every weekday night (except Fridays, when he flew to Long Island), Stimson noted in his diary whether he had gone horseback riding in the morning or hosted a game of deck tennis with colleagues during the early evening at Woodley Mansion, his twenty-acre estate in Washington, D.C.

Deck tennis was a sport first played on the decks of passenger ships moving between the United States and Europe in the late nineteenth century. The game involved throwing a rubber ring back and forth over a net (approximately the height of a volleyball net) on a space similarly shaped but smaller in size to a tennis court. The sport became popular after World War I, and Stimson, likely having learned it on various overseas voyages he took, built an outdoor court at Woodley when he was secretary of state.[4] Stimson played singles or doubles, right-handed or left-handed, and kept track in his diary not only whether he played but how and with whom (and sometimes the game's results and how he performed). Stimson no doubt loved the camaraderie of the game and valued the chance to discuss work in a less formal setting over drinks after it ended, but those were just ancillary benefits to the workout he received, which he believed was crucial in order to successfully undertake his great responsibilities.

Throughout his tenure as secretary of war, Stimson always pushed other members of his staff and senior members of the Army to take time to exercise. While Marshall needed no prodding, others did. After General Arnold suffered a heart attack in May 1943, Stimson approached Marshall with the suggestion of forcing senior members of the Army to exercise in or around the Pentagon. Marshall was sympathetic to the idea; he regularly encouraged his subordinates to look after their bodies, as well and, like Stimson, took notice when his subordinates were showing the effects of long hours of deskwork.[5]

A good night's sleep and general rest and relaxation were the other components considered by Stimson to be essential to high performance. If he did not manage to find partners to play either deck tennis or lawn bowling (a satisfactory but less physical alternative exercise), or if he was simply too tired at the end of a working day, it was more than likely a masseur was waiting for him at his house. This form of rest had been an acceptable substitute for exercise for Stimson going back to his days as secretary of state, although definitely not a preferred one. Still on other evenings, he cleared his mind by asking his chauffeur to drive him and his wife twenty miles south to Mount Vernon and back.

Regardless of what he did once he left the office, dinner for Stimson often involved guests. Members of the cabinet, members of his staff, or old friends often joined Stimson and his wife at Woodley for a meal. Even when he wasn't hosting dinners, Stimson often received visitors at night, usually members of his staff who dropped by unannounced to run something by him, or more likely, to "cheer him up."

On Friday evenings throughout the year, Stimson and his wife nearly always flew to Long Island. Once there, he spent the weekend riding his favorite horse (often twice a day and usually for over two hours at a time), swimming in Long Island Sound (in the summer or early fall), walking with his wife, or hunting for small game in the woods within or surrounding his estate. Between these physical activities, he read work-related documents, napped, got caught up with old friends (Bronson Winthrop was a weekly visitor for tea), or conferenced with certain individuals who would come out to Highhold to discuss important issues. Unless the weather was too dangerous, he and his wife flew back on Sunday nights.

Stimson was a proud man and was pleased he could still maintain a busy schedule during the workweek. When *Time* magazine ran a story on him suggesting that people were passing along anecdotes in Washington about his inability to work more than a few hours a day and his habit of "dozing off" during important conferences, the secretary of war seriously considered suing the publication for libel, claiming in his diary he had never once fallen asleep during a conference in his entire life.[6]

For all the rest and exercise, a decent night's sleep was still a challenge for Stimson; his lifelong difficulties in this area were only getting worse as his age advanced. But he carefully improved his chances of getting one by avoiding as many formal social responsibilities as he could, eating carefully, and going to bed early.

Those working closely with the secretary of war were attuned to Stimson's requirements and took great care to avoid overworking him. Early in his assignment, Stimson refused to take a military plane to Long Island each weekend, given that there was a rule in the Army against wives flying on military aircraft with their husbands. Immediately recognizing the inconvenience to his partner, Marshall successfully lobbied President Roosevelt to order Stimson to use an Army plane and bring his wife along for his trips to and from Long Island, knowing that nothing less than a direct order from the president could change the old statesman's mind.[7]

As for Marshall, perhaps an entire career spent in the Army, as opposed to one devoted to law, gave him the training not only to sleep better (when one considers some of the places soldiers slept in those days), but also to work on a multitude of tasks simultaneously. Whether calibrated by training or simply its nature, Marshall's mind seemed better equipped than Stimson's to move seamlessly between the volume and variety of issues that besieged them both each day (to be fair to Stimson, when he celebrated his seventy-third birthday in September 1940, Marshall had yet to turn sixty).

Interestingly, during an era when the benefits of exercise and rest were generally less appreciated and men were not as consciously active as in later generations, Marshall shared Stimson's compulsion both to stay physically fit and to keep his body well rested. It was not out of vanity that he exercised, but simply a means to stay healthy and be more productive. Writing to one of his protégés Matthew Ridgway in 1936, Marshall expressed his concern that the forty-one-year-old major was going to burn out. "I know you have enough brains to perform your military duties," Marshall warned Ridgway, "but I doubt very much whether you have enough sense to take care of the human machine."[8]

Marshall was obsessed with productivity and knew that both his output and the quality of his work deteriorated when he was tired and short of exercise. Knowing that there were hours in the late afternoon when he was not at his best, he made it a rule to avoid making any important decisions after 3:00 p.m. To stay physically fit, he got into the saddle most mornings at 6:00 a.m. and rode in either Rock Creek Park or an area of land that today makes up part of Arlington National Cemetery (close to Quarters One, the redbrick home for chiefs of staff at Fort Myer).

On warmer evenings when the light allowed, Marshall packed a picnic dinner into a canoe and paddled approximately two miles up the Potomac River to Chain Bridge, with Katherine seated in the bow. The couple would then dine as the boat drifted slowly back.[9] During the cooler seasons, he spent time relaxing at home. True to the habits of a lifelong soldier, lights-out came early.[10]

Although Marshall and his wife purchased a beautiful house near the Blue Ridge Mountains in Leesburg, Virginia, in 1940, they leased it during the early part of the War from September 15 through early June.[11] Even during those months the house was free to him, he rarely had the time to travel the forty miles to get there. When he did manage, he would work in the garden, praying that a phone call did not interrupt him. Unlike Stimson, Marshall found it difficult to relax away from Washington once he became chief of staff.

Despite his efforts and good habits, Marshall suffered from overwork and stress in the months leading up to the War. It did not help matters that he was spending nearly half of his time on an airplane.[12] Just as Marshall concerned himself with Stimson, Stimson felt the need to step in to ensure that his chief of staff stayed healthy and fit. In October 1940, Stimson received word that Marshall, despite being tired and sick, was loyally planning on attending a party Stimson was hosting for the War Department staff and their spouses. He promptly fired off to Marshall the following written order:

The President of the United States directs that General George C. Marshall during the period between Friday, October 11th, and Monday, October 14th, shall visit the city of Charlotte, North Carolina, for the purpose of making a report upon the comparative akin and valor of the football teams of Davidson and Virginia Military Institute. During said period he shall be under the exclusive control and direction of Mrs. George C. Marshall and shall be protected against all interruptions, particularly of members of the Department and of the Congress. During said period the War Department shall be relegated to the tender mercies of the Secretary of War, the Assistant Secretary of War, and the Deputy Chief of Staff, General Bryden.

By order of the Secretary of War.[13]

Notwithstanding this light exchange, the elevated stress levels for both men reflected the worsening global situation and their knowledge that the Army remained woefully unprepared. Surprisingly, and to their great annoyance, there were many in Washington who did not share their sense of urgency. Most notable among them was their boss in the White House. Nearly two decades after this prewar period, Marshall was still unable to hide his frustrations. In the nearly thirty-one hours of taped interviews he gave to Forrest Pogue, at no time did the former chief of staff get more worked up as when he described his difficulty conveying to Roosevelt in the spring of 1940 how desperate the situation had become. Both he and Stimson repeatedly told the president during this time that for the Army to be adequately prepared, it needed everything, and all of it at the same time.

Munitions and Supplies[14]

Those men who made the greatest contribution to mobilizing America's resources during the First World War were immediately fearful following Armistice Day that the great difficulties they faced in turning America's industrial capabilities from a peacetime to a wartime footing would be largely forgotten in the euphoria over victory. Bernard Baruch, who chaired the influential War Industries Board during World War I, and Benedict Crowell, who served as assistant secretary of war, must have winced when Woodrow Wilson famously commented a few months before the Allied victory, "The highest and best form of efficiency is the spontaneous cooperation of a free people." In making this statement, the idealistic Wilson was misleadingly giving credit to American industry for turning out the supplies and weapons needed to help defeat the Central Powers. Although such a notion was pleasant to consider and inspirational for Americans, Wilson knew the actual experience was not as stirring; U.S. troops in Europe during World War I relied largely on France and Great Britain for their planes, tanks, and heavy munitions (the doughboys did bring their Springfield rifles with them). U.S. production eventually caught up, but the Great War ended before it could hit its stride.

Baruch, who counseled Stimson and Marshall on mobilization issues a generation later, was a late-nineteenth-century finance wunderkind who made a vast fortune on Wall Street before the age of thirty. A committed patriot and public servant, he accepted the challenge from President Wilson to use his considerable skills and contacts to help convert the nation's market-oriented economy into one that could quickly meet the demands of the military. But he soon discovered that the rapid mobilization of industry and labor in a freedom-loving democracy was problematic. Vast fortunes had been created during the fifty years following the Civil War, and American capitalists did not easily agree to give up profitable lines of business to supply the military with the weapons to fight a war in Europe.

Until Baruch took up the task assigned to him by Wilson, the effort to supply the troops was not well coordinated. The sudden and explosive demand for resources drove prices up accordingly and created an environment favorable to profiteering, fraud, and waste. The struggles Baruch and Newton Baker encountered to fix this are not within the scope of this book to detail, but it is worth summarizing the efforts made by the U.S. government and the War Department during the twenties and thirties to learn from their experience.

The first of these resulted in the National Defense Act of 1920, signed shortly after World War I ended. The Act included legislation calling for the War Department (under the leadership of the assistant secretary of war) to develop a mobilization plan during peace that could be quickly implemented in an emergency. As a result, a plan slowly evolved over the next nineteen years that called for several task-specific temporary agencies to be formed under the control of a War Resources Administration ("WRA") led by one individual who would be given far-reaching powers.

While the Act addressed many of the problems encountered by Baruch and Baker during the First World War, it failed to address others. An increasingly obvious flaw in the plan revealed as the 1930s progressed was its failure to consider that Americans might not agree on what constituted an "emergency." It would be one thing if the nation was attacked, but anything short of that scenario would be subject to a lengthy debate given the vast isolationist sentiment blanketing a large portion of the country. A greater defect still was that the plan neglected to consider that a man with the working style, general inclinations, and overall personality of Franklin Roosevelt might one day occupy the Oval Office during a time of crisis.

As previously mentioned, Franklin Roosevelt was what one might refer to today as a "control freak." Giving another individual power rivaling or exceeding his own was simply anathema to him. He largely ignored the final version of the mobilization plan completed in 1939, believing he could handle any international emergency in much the same manner as he had addressed the nation's massive economic problems during the Great Depression: creatively and informally, one issue at a time, assisted by the efforts and advice of many, through trial and error, and ever mindful of any and all political consequences.

Roosevelt was famous throughout his presidency for providing more than one group or individual overlapping responsibilities for certain tasks. This not only gave him access to a greater quantity and variety of ideas but also enabled him to retain ultimate control. Stimson and Marshall, opposed to this style of management, could only try to ensure that the War Department remained in the point position when it came to linking the nation's industrial and business community with the numerous civilian agencies assigned by FDR to assist in the great effort to rebuild the Army.

And what an effort it would be. Given the struggles Marshall faced during his first ten months on the job on account of isolationism and the dysfunctional War Department that he had to work with, he and Stimson were practically starting from scratch in July 1940. Outside of a cache of forty-year-old Springfield rifles (only enough to equip the regular Army, which stood at approximately 275,000), there were severe shortages of just about everything an army would need if drawn into war. These included planes, tanks, modern rifles, machine guns, mortars, antitank weapons, and light artillery.

It was not simply a matter of restarting the production of existing weapons. Given the phenomenal success of the German blitzkrieg in Europe, the Army knew it needed significant quality upgrades across the board, and it needed them soon. But technological improvements do not occur overnight. For every weapon or machine under consideration, a tradeoff had to be determined between the item's quality and the speed in which it could be assembled. America certainly possessed the ability to produce a world-class tank, but it would be useless if the war ended before it could be positioned on the battlefield.

Such issues had to be researched, analyzed, and debated for everything from small items (helmets, backpacks, and shoes) to major components (aircraft and tank engines). Consensus was almost impossible to come by, and there was pressure to choose between various options from a variety of sources, including congressmen representing suppliers in their home state, the national press, numerous self-described experts, and even the president (typically after having spoken to one of the other sources).

The late Keith Eiler, an authority on the mobilization efforts of the Second World War, wrote in detail about the substantial effort by the War Department to move forward on the mass production of the Garand rifle in the summer of 1940 to replace the bolt-operated Springfield rifle used during World War I. No sooner was the decision made by the War Department to go with the Garand rifle than critics of the gun (along with proponents of other rifles) began to lobby against it. U.S. senators, the NRA, prominent men in the National Guard, the Marines, *Time* magazine, and other organizations or individuals expressed surprisingly strong opinions about the choice. *Life* magazine called it "one of the greatest military squabbles in U.S. history."[15]

There was no right or wrong answer when it came to choosing a rifle. Between objective individuals, opinions differed, depending on how much significance one placed on each of the key variables that made for a quality one: consistency, durability, precision, rate of fire, ease of use, weight, ease of manufacturing, and cost. Although the War Department put a priority on how quickly large quantities could be produced when it chose the Garand, it happened to be a rifle of exceptional quality. (General George S. Patton famously commented that the Garand was the "greatest battle implement ever devised.")

Similar debates were carried out on multiple other weapons and supplies at a variety of levels (right up to Stimson and Marshall), depending on the importance of the item. All decisions were coordinated between Marshall's military men (who voiced strong opinions as to how each piece of equipment needed to perform) and Stimson's civilian staff (determined to efficiently organize the industrial resources required to produce it). The former group tended to underappreciate the consequences of trying to design the perfect weapon and the effects of making frequent changes to the design after the blueprints and specifications had already been approved and sent off to the manufacturers. This led to many disagreements.

Complaints from his civilian staff came into Stimson's office on these issues as soon as he joined the War Department. Both he and Patterson, veterans themselves and strongly sympathetic to the soldier, understood the Army's insistence on perfection; lives often depended on it.[16] But given the Nazis' lengthy head start, both men felt a greater emphasis should be given to getting the wheels of production moving quickly. Toward this, they asked Army officers only to suggest changes that were "absolutely necessary."[17] These problems persisted throughout the period leading up to Pearl Harbor and required Stimson's involvement on several occasions. In July 1941, after hearing about continuing delays of Boeing's 4-Engine bombers brought on by design requests from the Army Air Forces, Stimson demanded that any proposed change to the aircraft going forward had to be personally approved by him.[18]

Raw Material Shortages and Bottlenecks

Unfortunately for Stimson and Marshall, there were far worse problems than design changes that held up the procurement efforts; there was a shortage in basic raw materials, and there were bottlenecks throughout the production chain that made many design discussions moot.

Beginning in the fall of 1940, Stimson started to receive reports about aluminum shortages. Similar intelligence concerning steel arrived toward the end of the year, followed by shortage reports on zinc, copper, nickel, lead, rubber, and silk.

Given the lack of exhaustive and reliable economic data and sophisticated metrics the world takes for granted today, it was harder in 1940 to nail down the reasons for the shortages and structure possible solutions. The War Department initially believed it was a simple matter of adjusting priorities from civilian to military needs given that the former did not seem to be suffering from any lack of want. It soon became apparent, however, that the cause had more to do with the general chaos created by the massive ramp-up of production. The scale was unprecedented, and it should not have been a shock to anyone that shortages might quickly emerge.

It was not just a scarcity of raw materials coming out of the ground holding up progress; bottlenecks began to spring up at several places along the supply chain between where various inputs or raw materials were originated to where the finished products were delivered. The potential number of locations where logjams could occur was immense. The aluminum industry, for example, had four stages of production before factories even began using it to assemble their war-related products. Used for big items (planes, ships, and trucks), small items (mess kits), and countless other weapons and supplies in between, aluminum began its life in the ground as bauxite (a sedimentary rock). Once the bauxite was mined (much of it outside the United States), it was transported to a different location and processed into alumina (a crystalline substance). The alumina was then moved to a plant that used tremendous amounts of electricity to smelt it into pure aluminum foundry ingots. Depending on the final product to be manufactured, these standard-sized ingots needed to be either further processed or hot-rolled into different shapes before being sent to the appropriate weapon or supply factory. Only then were the finished products produced and prepared for shipment to wherever the Army needed them. During this entire process, storage and transportation had to be available at or between each location. And if the workers at any particular section of any specific site lacked anything they needed to perform the precise task assigned to them, the entire production could come to a halt.

During the buildup phase in 1940 and 1941, problems within the aluminum production chain ranged from those that were predictable (electrical power in the South required to run the smelters), to those harder to anticipate (a shortage of special heavy hammers used on aluminum ingots), to those that simply slipped through the cracks (too few facilities that could produce engine crankcases). It was up to the War Department to determine exactly where and why something was getting held up and then work to fix it.

Political Hurdles

Aside from logistical difficulties, there was a complex array of other issues that created a gap early on between the overall production goals set by the War Department and the results achieved. Many of them were political in nature. For example, since the War Department was regularly accused of trying to create monopolies when handing out contracts to those companies that could most quickly and capably fill them, it was forced to give business to smaller companies that were less efficient. It also lost crucial time dealing with politicians who lobbied to have plants built within their districts or contracts assigned to their constituents.

Such pressures frustrated Stimson to the core. As a bona fide trustbuster going back to 1906, he was sympathetic with those who worried about creating or enabling monopolies, but he made it clear to everyone that current national defense concerns should take a priority over this particular social goal. When aluminum shortages in the winter of 1941 threatened the aircraft production numbers, Stimson came down hard on those in the cabinet who believed the Aluminum Company of America (now Alcoa) was becoming too powerful and should be curbed.[19]

As frustrating as it was to deal with raw material shortages, bottlenecks, politics, and antitrust concerns during this period, what most angered Stimson and Marshall was the criticism by people both within and outside the government that too many raw materials were being steered toward military production at the expense of civilian use. Leading these critics were industry executives who placed the needs of their traditional customers over the needs of the government. Although this attitude was reasonable during normal times, Stimson and Marshall were astonished at how much of their effort was required trying to convince everyone there was nothing ordinary about the times. They continually emphasized that there were profound external threats in both Europe and Asia that could easily escalate to the point that America and its interests were seriously at risk. Therefore, an all-out production effort must take place in America to compete with the ones that had been successfully directed by Hitler in Germany and the Japanese military in Japan.

Their voices fell largely on deaf ears. There was complacency within the country, likely stemming from the victory just twenty-two years earlier against the Germans. Even individuals who were part of the Defense Commission created by FDR in May 1940 were initially unsupportive. Men like William Knudsen, Edward Stettinius, and Secretary of Commerce Jesse Jones tended to ignore the threat from Asia in 1940 and were hopeful the European war might end before the United States had to get involved. Believing this, they desired as little disruption to the economy as possible.[20] To get fully prepared for what *could* happen required a significant sacrifice from the American people, a sacrifice that these men and their president were not yet willing to fully support.

More than anything, the concept of civil sacrifice for the benefit of military preparedness was the missing thread that tied together so many problems related to the shortages Stimson and Marshall faced. Only through collective sacrifice could the country's realized industrial output match its potential. Both men believed the country was asleep in this regard and thought Roosevelt, more than anyone else, was to blame. They understood that it was only political considerations preventing him from sounding out the proper alarm. Although Stimson took FDR to task regarding this on more than one occasion, he could only move the needle so far.

Given the nature of the fighting taking place in Europe in 1940 and 1941, the deficiency felt most keenly by the War Department was related to aircraft. The terror brought to Europe by the offensive exploits of the Luftwaffe frightened everyone.

There were less than three thousand planes in the Army when Stimson joined the War Department, a great majority of which were adequate for training purposes only. General Henry "Hap" Arnold, responsible for the air forces within the Army, estimated that only 10 percent of them—just three hundred planes—were worthy of taking on an enemy.[21] Although Roosevelt had already set in motion plans to build eighteen thousand aircraft by the time Stimson got to Washington, there was still an enormous amount of work to do in order to convert plans to planes. Once again, the predominant problem was the nation's lack of urgency. This radically changed after Pearl Harbor, but until that day, indifference was the reigning attitude and was shared by most of the shareholder class, their management representatives, and Labor. In other words, nearly everyone.

Although the Nazi juggernaut awakened a number of public officials in Washington to the nation's need for preparation during the summer of 1940, those who ran the companies capable of turning out planes, ammunition, and weapons still did not see a threat great enough to withhold products from their existing customers or cause them to rush into building new factories that, in their minds, could be obsolete as soon as the "crisis" ended.[22] These business leaders had waited a long time for the nation to break out of the Depression, and they had no desire to take an economic step backward.

As a longtime provider of advice and legal services to many of these captains of industry, Stimson understood their concerns; he defended companies who lost money gearing up for military production during the First World War only to see the fighting end abruptly. He and his staff therefore carefully put together structures that reduced such risk in order to entice big business to join the effort. The various incentives given by the War Department slowly helped bring industrial leaders around.

But if corporations were going to be given downside protection, Congress insisted that their upside be limited as well. There were winners and losers among American companies during the First World War, and the memory of excessive profits from some companies was still relatively fresh in Washington. As both a public servant and patriot, Stimson was also sympathetic to this concern. Finding the right balance was challenging in such an environment; finding it quickly, even more so. There were those in government who believed, Stimson wrote in his diary, that one could "tax business out of all proportion and still have business men work diligently and quickly."[23] Noting that this went against human nature, the longtime supporter of capitalism added that in a country like America, one could not possibly prepare for war unless capitalists could make money in the process. He understood businessmen, having counseled them his entire career. He knew what was necessary to incentivize them. Although he was frustrated that it took six weeks to address the potential for excess corporate profits in the new tax law, he was satisfied the right balance was finally achieved.

To each new problem related to either a choking bureaucracy or insufficient incentives, the talented lawyers and finance specialists hired by Stimson and Patterson worked out numerous solutions to stimulate the production of weapons and supplies: Contracts were structured that provided various options for companies to buy out the interests of a specific plant from the government under certain conditions; letters of intent were provided to prospective bidders essentially guaranteeing them reimbursement for expenses they procured working up a bid; and when the conventional practice of opening any project to competitive bidding became too time-consuming, the War Department convinced Congress to pass a law allowing them to simply begin negotiating contracts instead (taking into consideration factors other than simply the lowest price per unit). For every problem one could encounter, there were seasoned lawyers or businessmen working in the War Department to solve them.[24]

Congress also passed two other laws during this period to accelerate production: One allowed for cost-plus-fixed-fee contracts and advance payments without interest; the other granted the president the power to require contractors to give priority to military orders and to take over plants when necessary for national defense.

All these efforts helped Stimson and Marshall, but there was one problem nearly impossible to overcome: greed. A reality in any economic environment, but particularly present when unprecedented amounts of public money are about to be spent, greed manifested itself quickly during the prewar period through the hiring by companies of nefarious lobbyists to obtain contracts, the relentless peddling by congressmen for the benefit of their constituents, and straight-up fraud. In battling greed, Stimson and his colleagues were required to balance the need to get things done quickly with the fiduciary responsibilities inherent in the job. Beginning in March 1941, they began to receive support in the fight from the Truman Committee (officially the Senate Special Committee to Investigate the National Defense Program), organized to be an all-purpose watchdog over every aspect of the rearmament program. The Committee's head, Senator Harry Truman from Missouri, proved a formidable investigator, and his efforts helped mitigate the risk of fraud and excess profits. After some early conflicts, Stimson and Marshall developed strong personal relationships with Truman, and this kept the Committee from going too far in the other direction, thus hampering progress.

Labor

Although corporate "fat cats" tend to take the brunt of public criticism when it comes to putting their interests ahead of the nation's during a war, labor leaders deserved as much scrutiny for their aggressive and selfish demands during the prewar period. Having won hard-fought gains against industrialists during the 1920s and 1930s, labor had no interest in turning back the clock for the sake of the nation's military production goals, particularly considering the United States was at peace and wished to remain so. On the contrary, the nation's attempt to rapidly rebuild its defense capabilities seemed to embolden labor leaders to greater efforts. By sheer habit, increased ambition, or both, labor pressed for further gains during the preparedness crisis perpetuating their never-ending battle with management and giving the War Department yet another giant challenge to overcome.

Shortly after Stimson took office, the chief commission appointed by Roosevelt to help advise on matters of procurement came out with a statement, supported by the War Department, that the gains made by labor over the previous years would be respected and maintained when it came to the nation's accelerated effort to rebuild its military strength. As much as the former Wall Street lawyer distrusted labor leaders, it seemed prudent to get them on board by assuring them that their hours, wages, and safety would not be compromised as the nation's factories began operating at highly elevated levels. On paper the statement sounded good, but it was not a law, and a great debate soon developed as to whether the War Department could or should sign contracts with firms that did not follow the principles outlined by the commission. Lawyers from all relevant parties weighed in on the subject and their opinions varied between the extremes. As with so many issues during this prewar period, Stimson and his staff carefully considered all aspects of the problem to determine the best course of action while keeping their focus, appropriately, on the ultimate objective of rebuilding the nation's defenses.

It was a tricky issue. Stimson knew the country needed labor fully on board to get prepared for war (nothing puts a dent in productivity like disgruntled workers), yet both he and Patterson were firm in their belief that sacrifice was something that should be shared by the entire country, labor included.

Further complicating the balancing act he faced was that in deciding how and whether to draft language into defense contracts that protected labor, he had to anticipate opposition from powerful companies. Chief among them was Ford Motor Company, which had spent years successfully fighting off labor. Ford had no intention of adopting what its weaker rivals might have given up during the same period for the sake of national defense. Given the sheer size of Ford and its potential importance to the overall procurement program, Stimson and his staff could not simply ignore the company. More than often, Ford's bids were the lowest and their anticipated deliveries the quickest. Exceptions therefore were made for Ford throughout this period and during the War.

As previously mentioned, Henry Stimson hired smart and competent men with views occasionally contrary to his own. To his credit, he was astute enough to realize that his opinions on any specific issue could be wrong or outdated, and therefore he often let his younger subordinates make the decisions they believed were the right ones. In Robert Patterson, Stimson had a man who happened to share many convictions with his boss but who was far more liberal on the important social issues of the times, including the rights of labor. While Stimson admired the working class for its patriotism (and respected its power), he did not trust its leaders. Patterson, probably by nature but also influenced during his years on the bench, went against the opinions of several of his own staff and many in the Army in deciding in late 1940 that procurement contracts should indeed contain protections for labor consistent with what it had gained during the first half of the twentieth century. There was nobody in government more passionate about the need for all Americans to sacrifice during this time, but Patterson was also pragmatic and was quite sure the production goals he was trying to meet would be much easier to achieve if the average working man on the factory floor was happy.

At the same time, Patterson realized that exceptions to the "labor rule" would be required to ensure that the production of planes, trucks, and tanks moved steadily forward. Ultimately, Stimson believed Patterson's approach was the best way forward. No matter how the War Department came out on the issue, Stimson reasoned, it would be criticized; such was the historical division within the nation between labor and management. To keep it in check and to avoid tarnishing the reputation of the Army directly, Stimson tried to stay out of disputes as much as possible by pushing them off to other civilian agencies better equipped to resolve them and better able to take the heat. Both he and Marshall thought it was in the best interests of the War Department and the Army to stay publicly impartial on the issue.

As the crisis in Europe escalated, greater pressure was placed on industry leaders to perform, and this stress was promptly passed on to the workers. When the workers felt they were being taken advantage of, they relied on a time-honored method to attract attention: the strike. There were twenty major strikes in the last three months of 1940, and fifty-seven in the first quarter of 1941.[25] With the economy beginning to crank on all cylinders, workers had little to lose by striking; demand for their services far outweighed supply.

Through strikes, the attention the workers sought was achieved, but too much so for their own good, as the country's attitude toward labor began to sour with each well-publicized walkout. This swing in sentiment made it progressively easier for the Army to navigate through each new crisis. When workers went on strike in early June 1941 at one of the nation's top aircraft manufacturing companies, Stimson was able to convince the president to take over the plant using troops.

The plant, located in California, produced approximately twenty planes per day, including B-25 bombers and B-51 fighters. When it went on strike, Stimson called for and chaired a meeting of the newly established Office of Production Management. It was unanimously decided at the meeting to suggest to the president he take over the plant under the powers granted him as commander in chief. Stimson got Roosevelt's support to threaten striking workers with a waiver of their military service deferments if they did not go back to work and got him to agree to protect the families of those who returned to their jobs. By the first week of July, the government handed control of the plant back to the company after the workers agreed to the terms laid out by a mediation board. At the time, Stimson believed his contribution ending this specific strike might end up as the most important one he'd make as secretary of war. It helped set an important precedent.

Attempts to Centralize
Procurement Responsibilities

The heightened pressure to swiftly rearm the nation in the face of labor problems and reluctant industrial leaders placed the overall procurement exercise in a permanent state of chaos during the prewar period. It soon became apparent to everyone involved that Bernard Baruch and others were right when they said America needed one formidable man to coordinate the entire effort.

Well, almost everyone; Franklin Roosevelt chose instead to spread out the responsibility in a characteristically haphazard fashion, ensuring the ultimate power remained with himself. An entire book could be devoted to the resulting assortment of agencies organized, reorganized, ignored, disbanded, merged, and ignored again during the War and the months leading up to it. There was little method to FDR's madness, and it tried the patience of Stimson, Marshall, and nearly all their respective colleagues.

The genius, or folly depending on one's point of view, of Franklin Roosevelt's management style was the continuous tinkering and sustained action characterizing his approach to governing during a crisis. His handling of the Great Depression was a prelude to how he managed the industrial mobilization of the country in the months leading up to December 7, 1941. There were scores of officials who felt his reluctance to put someone fully in charge of coordinating the entire industrial effort to rebuild the military was inefficient, if not irresponsible. Both Stimson and Marshall were in this camp.

The president's first major attempt to move closer to replicating the success of Baruch's War Industrial Board during the First World War was the appointment of the National Defense Advisory Commission ("NDAC") in June 1940. Despite the presence of the extremely capable industrialist William Knudsen (president of General Motors) as its head, and notwithstanding the energy, ideas, and experience brought to the overall effort by the other talented committee members, the NDAC was still a loosely structured committee of seven individuals with equal votes and an undefined role. This was the major problem. Another, according to Stimson, lay in the number of ambitious young men brought in to help the NDAC. "This crowd" Stimson remarked at the time in his diary, "is trying to make itself useful by proposing all kinds of theoretical red tape."[26]

Stimson did not limit his critical remarks to his diary; when given the chance, he let Roosevelt know that it was "bad administration" to have divided authority for such a task. Stimson made such statements to FDR both in private and during cabinet meetings. Always sure of himself, Stimson's age and experience gave him further justification to speak his mind when others may have hesitated. Approaching his mid-seventies, he knew this would be his last job in public service. With the stakes so high, he felt no reluctance to hold back.

The secretary of war did not want to give up his statutory responsibility for procurement within the War Department, but neither did he wish to stymy "the progress and light that might come to it from outside." He believed it was his duty to "say what weapons we want—the designs—the number—and the time when they are to be ready, and to sign the contracts." Once that was done, a strong coordinator was needed to help clear all the obstacles and establish priorities.

Although Stimson appeared to be the most outspoken opponent to the structure as it stood in the fall of 1940, he was hardly alone. It became increasingly clear to many in Washington that consensus was hard to come by, decision-making was slow, and there were mushrooming turf disputes. Something had to give. In December 1940, Stimson took the initiative to effect change. After talking at length with Bernard Baruch to obtain his views, Stimson joined Patterson and recruited their respective counterparts in the Navy (Knox and Jim Forrestal) to advise FDR to put Knudsen in *sole* charge of the effort.

With the 1940 election behind him, Roosevelt became more flexible on the matter, but only partially so; he offered a compromise. He established the Office of Production Management ("OPM") with Knudsen as director, labor leader Sydney Hillman as associate director, and Stimson and Knox as the other two members of the board. The other NDCA commissioners would continue to counsel the War Department, but through the OPM. This new group was responsible for prioritizing what munitions should be produced, getting them produced, and then purchasing them.

The OPM was an improvement, but still far from ideal. Many of its responsibilities already existed within the procurement organizations of each branch of the military along with the Army and Navy Munitions Board, a group jointly run by Stimson and Knox. As a result, compromises had to be once again brokered between the OPM and the War Department as to who would do what. Despite the best of intentions, uncertainty and chaos still reigned, and the limited human resources available to the OPM left the group with the frustrating choice of either rubber-stamping requests from the War Department or delaying a response in order to properly study it.

For most of 1941, officials within the War Department and officers within the Army remained frustrated with the great degree of effort required to overcome the flawed procurement structure. With no single agency willing or able to take the bull by the horns, progress was slow. Stimson and Marshall both lost confidence in the OPM, realizing that any success achieved up to that date was the result of hard work done by the War Department on its own. When this also became evident to Roosevelt, his instinct was simply to create additional agencies. The National Defense Mediation Board, the Office of Civilian Defense, the Office of Price Administration and Civilian Supply, and the Office of Defense Housing Coordination were all set up to deal with one issue or another. To Stimson, the additional agencies or appointments created only further work, as he had to organize a meeting for all those affected to "work out the various things that could make trouble."[27]

It was not the people Roosevelt put in place on top of these organizations that were the problem. On the contrary, they were run by outstanding individuals who had been at the top of some of the largest commercial and financial concerns in the world (Knudsen ran General Motors; Eberstadt was a leading investment banker; Stettinius was chairman of U.S. Steel; Ralph Budd ran the Chicago, Burlington, & Quincy Railroad: and Donald Nelson was a top executive at Sears, Roebuck). The problem was the environment into which each of these men was brought. In corporate America, the buck had always stopped at one individual. As the new appointees began their specific assignments, they soon found out this basic principle of American capitalism was missing for what was gearing up to be the greatest coordinated industrial effort in the history of the world. Like Stimson, they all did their best to work around the structural problems but were greatly frustrated at having to do so.

It was not until July 1941 that Roosevelt finally urged Stimson and Secretary of the Navy Knox to accelerate the conversion of the consumer-driven economy to one focused on military products. Writing to both of them less than three weeks after Hitler attacked the Soviet Union, he asked that they start calculating the overall production requirements to enable the country to "exceed by an appropriate amount that available to our potential enemies."[28] Stimson received the letter one day short of his first anniversary on the job. It is indicative of his struggles and Marshall's that it took a full year before the president formally asked for an estimate of the Army's requirements.

It took another month before Roosevelt established the Supply, Priorities, and Allocations Board ("SPAB") and put it in charge of determining how best to allocate the resources of the United States between its civil and military needs. FDR appointed Donald Nelson to run SPAB and named many of Washington's heavy hitters to its membership, including Stimson, Knox, Hopkins, and the newly appointed head of the Office of Price Administration, Leon Henderson. Although OPM and a few other agencies still had various administrative responsibilities, there was finally one individual responsible for at least "coordinating" the multitude of activities related to the procurement of the instruments of war.

Although it was a big step, it did not help much; Nelson's powers were still limited, and he tended to be weak. Only the Japanese attack on Pearl Harbor three months later created the conditions necessary for the nation to begin a focused effort. As for Stimson's struggle to convince Roosevelt to concentrate true powers in a single individual, it would continue for another two years, until FDR created the Office of War Mobilization under James Byrnes in the spring of 1943.

Army Manpower

Weapons could not fight wars alone, of course; men were required to operate them. Even before attempting to right the wrongs of America's twenty-plus years of neglect in maintaining adequate weapons and supplies, Stimson and Marshall had to address another of the Army's equally distressing shortages: manpower. When George Marshall took over as chief of staff in September 1939, the American Army (which included the air force) consisted of approximately 170,000 soldiers, ranking just seventeenth in the world.[29] The German army, by comparison, had between five and six million men (*excluding* airmen).

Following the aforementioned May 1940 confrontation between Marshall and Roosevelt in the Oval Office—the meeting during which Marshall blurted out to FDR, "If you don't do something and don't do it right away, I don't know what is going to happen to this country"—increased support from the president got the ball rolling on allowing the Army to increase its size to 375,000 men. But having a license to recruit a certain number of soldiers and achieving that defined level were two different matters. The Army soon realized they could not rely on volunteers to reach its goal given the glacial rate at which they were signing up. The same issue that stalled the procurement of munitions was holding up the volunteer efforts: Men who had suffered through the Depression and finally had steady work were not interested in giving it up for a war in Europe that might never involve America.

The only way to accelerate the tempo was through a formal draft, something Americans had never experienced except during a war (and even then, they had not embraced it). Given this history and considering the country's overall negative sentiment toward war after World War I, Marshall believed the initiative for such an effort should come from civilian as opposed to military leaders. He felt strongly that those Americans sitting on the fence separating isolationism and interventionism might fall to the side of the isolationists if the Army was seen as too proactive or "militaristic" on the issue of manpower. When it came time to supporting the effort, Marshall was happy to jump in, but he insisted that civilians launch the effort.

Since Roosevelt was uninterested in jeopardizing his chances for a third term in November 1940, there was a void in leadership on the issue of manpower before Stimson's arrival to the War Department. Interventionist civilians filled this quickly. Leading this effort was Grenville Clark, the active and influential New York lawyer. Clark lobbied relentlessly for compulsory military service. He found supporters in both the House and Senate and helped them quickly frame legislation that was placed in the docket just before Stimson was appointed secretary of war.

Stimson, well noted for his support of compulsory military service, immediately began lobbying for the bill's enactment upon joining the administration (one will recall that one of his conditions for accepting the offer from FDR to run the War Department was that he be allowed to push hard for it). Aware that Americans historically opposed conscription, he nevertheless believed that if the story were properly told, the country would step up and embrace the idea. In any event, he thought there was nothing to lose by making the attempt. Taking his views to the House Committee on Military Affairs and to individual congressmen, Stimson drove home the message on behalf of the administration with all the considerable passion he held on the subject.

As promised, Marshall stood by ready to fully back Stimson in supporting the Selective Service Act (also referred to as the Burke-Wadsworth Bill). He was soon summoned by Congress to give the Army's views on the legislation. There was no one in the entire military establishment who could better outline the needs of the Army in the clear, concise, commanding, and factual style that was required for the occasion and for which the chief of staff had become renowned. Speaker of the House Sam Rayburn once noted that of all the men he ever heard testify in front of a committee during his long career, nobody exceeded Marshall's ability to influence congressmen (Rayburn served in the House for nearly half a century).

The general appeared before the Senate Committee on Military Affairs on July 12, 1940, and provided compelling arguments in favor of a draft. He calmly and skillfully tied the need for it largely to the need for training. "If you are in actual war," Marshall told the senators, "you can get almost any quantity of men you want in the United States Army. The trouble is we do not have time to prepare them for the things they have to do."[30] Again drawing lessons from history, Marshall explained that World War I would have had a far better outcome if the Army was given sufficient time to train its men. "No one has ever really told the full truth of what might have been," Marshall said in describing "the great tragedy" that occurred in France in the First World War.

Even with the Army's biggest gun pitching Congress, Stimson wanted to leave no stone unturned and pushed the president to provide stronger support. This had to be proposed carefully as Roosevelt's backing on any issue during these years was a double-edged sword; it helped procure votes from those who represented his vast supporters around the country, but it also had the potential to turn away other congressmen who could not stomach helping him in any way, even if they were in agreement with his views. Stimson believed that for current purposes, the president's support would bring more votes than it would turn away. With the 1940 election only a few months away, Roosevelt was not inclined to go overboard in his endorsement of the bill, but by applying steady pressure, Stimson believed he was able to get him to "come down firmly on the right side."[31]

Although it was difficult to get the nation enthusiastic about making the sacrifices required to manufacture the necessities of war, Stimson and Grenville Clark correctly predicted that it would be willing to get behind a draft. That this support existed surprised many others, including Roosevelt and Marshall. But with it, proponents of the measure had an easier time overcoming the considerable efforts by the isolationists to kill or significantly water down the legislation.

The Selective Service and Training Act was signed into law on September 16, 1940. With the stroke of a pen, sixteen million men between the ages of twenty-one and thirty-six became eligible for service in the Army (the Navy relied on volunteers until later in the War). Although opponents of the bill in Congress did manage to insert a few conditions into the legislation (including a nine hundred thousand limit on the number of men who could be trained at any one time), the new law ensured that Stimson and Marshall could begin the wide-scale training of men they believed was essential. In late October, days before the presidential election, Stimson was blindfolded at a highly publicized ceremony in Washington and then drew the first capsule out of a goldfish bowl (the same one used for the draft in 1917). It was a major accomplishment.

African Americans and the Draft

Getting the new Selective Service legislation translated into real boots on real training grounds was made easier since the Army was extremely well prepared from an administration standpoint (by following the successful model adopted during the First World War). What the Army was not prepared for was the pressure put on it by the president to treat African Americans on an equal basis to Caucasian Americans.

Early in the 1940 presidential campaign, Republican candidate Wendell Willkie began courting African American voters by offering an end to their discrimination in government and in the military services. When prominent African American newspapers began coming out for Willkie, FDR took notice and put his staff to work on countering the Republican's platform. Less than two months before the election, Roosevelt asked the War Department to put out a statement announcing that African Americans would be given "an equal opportunity with white men" when it came to the activities of the Army. Unconvinced by this and other overtures from the president, African American leaders requested a meeting at the White House in late September. Stimson was asked to join but sent Patterson in his place, suggesting he had too much on his plate.

Stimson was doubtlessly busy, but he generally made it his business to show up when significant issues were discussed. It is more likely he wanted no part of the discussion. Despite frequent protests both before and during the War that all his "instincts were in favor of justice to the Negro," the secretary of war held prejudices against African Americans and did little to conceal his feelings on the subject. Writing in his diary on the day of the scheduled meeting, Stimson discussed their failures during the First World War when Wilson "yielded to the same sort of demand." He went on to write, "Leadership is not embedded in the Negro race" and "disaster and confusion" would follow any attempt to put them on the field without white officers to guide them. Stimson did not attempt to counter any efforts to give African Americans a "fair shot in every service," but he privately believed that integration would cause trouble and hoped Roosevelt would not pursue it.[32]

Henry Lewis Stimson was not only a product of the nineteenth century but spent his first thirty-two years living in it. Like his mentors Teddy Roosevelt and Elihu Root (and a great many other major figures of that era), Stimson believed the Caucasian race was superior to other races. For someone who often defied conventional wisdom and stood open to new ideas, new technology, and new ways of thinking, Stimson was stuck in the past (or in this case, the present) when it came to his views on race. He continued to believe that the United States and Great Britain needed to assume what English novelist Rudyard Kipling had earlier coined the "white man's burden."[33]

It was not only the African race Stimson felt was inferior; his attitude toward the Filipinos was little different. His hero Root once described Filipinos as "little advanced from pure savagery" with "many characteristics of children."[34] Although not nearly as harsh as his mentor, Stimson did not think of the Filipinos as equals, even if he was determined to treat them as such.

Although he held these general convictions, Stimson knew the younger generation did not share them, and he was also aware that there were valid political considerations involved when it came to FDR's request. As such, he did nothing to stop the president's efforts. On the contrary, in deputizing Robert Patterson to fill in for him when it came to such matters, he was sending a well-known proponent of civil rights and a great friend to the African American. Patterson's son, a United States District Judge in New York for nearly thirty years, commenting about the relationship between his father and the secretary of war, said that when it came to dealing with "union relations, Eleanor Roosevelt, and African Americans," Stimson knew that Patterson was the better and more appropriate man and agreed to have him handle such matters.[35]

Although not as candid on the subject—or as staunch—George Marshall also harbored the racist tendencies typical of the era and was against integrating the Army. His principal concern was with the defense of the nation, and he argued that it did not make sense the Army should be called on to solve a social problem that had "perplexed the American people" throughout its history. He believed that any gains made in the initiative would be at the expense of discipline and morale, two things he had devoted a career trying to build and protect. In this regard, even Patterson sympathized with the chief of staff, believing it unfair that the Army, desperate to build the nation's defenses up after years of neglect, would be further tasked to accelerate social changes that went against the existing social order. With war on the horizon, it did not seem to be the right time to experiment.

Given Marshall and Stimson's views on the subject, the Army would only go so far in promoting true parity between the races. On those occasions when faced with a decision that required balancing racial justice with the defense needs of the nation, both generally came out for the latter. Although the times were indeed stressful and the stakes historically high, more enlightened men in this respect should have absolutely done more to promote equality between the races—even if only relative to the times.

Extension of the Selective Training and Service Act

The signing of the Selective Training and Service Act in September 1940 was a giant step in the right direction toward solving manpower issues. But built into the Act was one glaring hitch: Each man was required to serve only twelve months. During discussions on the bill, supporters of it treaded lightly around the issue of how long the Army could keep each draftee enlisted. Marshall's preference was for eighteen months, but he settled for twelve with language added allowing for an extension if Congress declared a national emergency. It was the best Marshall could have hoped for under the circumstances. When the Draft Bill was promoted to congressmen, and then publicized to the nation, the Army highlighted the twelve-month term, thinking it would be an easier time horizon to absorb for those uncomfortable with the draft in general. This came back to haunt Stimson and Marshall during efforts to extend the Act the following summer. Opponents (and there were many) argued that the administration had acted in bad faith when emphasizing the twelve months.

Regardless of the intent or the final agreed language of the bill, War Department planners assumed the Army would be keeping selectees longer than twelve months given how events were unfolding in Europe, North Africa, and Japan. Any large release of men after a year of training would set back whatever progress any single division might have made in the previous twelve months (given that the selectees were spread out evenly between the divisions). If war were to come after any such release, America would be heading into it with largely untrained soldiers.

Stimson and Marshall could not simply wait around hoping that events in Europe and Asia would reach a level of crisis severe enough to cause Congress to declare that the national interest was imperiled (thus triggering an automatic extension). Congress could not be trusted to make that declaration unless U.S. interests were visibly under threat. Therefore, both men concluded during the spring of 1941 that it was time to start gathering support to extend the term of service.

Unfortunately, neither Roosevelt nor the Congress was anxious to reopen the debate for political reasons. As of the beginning of May 1941, the Army had 1,225,000 men.[36] A lot of political capital was spent by the administration to achieve this level, and nobody was sure how voters would view extending the length of time soldiers served. With all the headway made during the previous twelve months, it was felt by many that this issue could derail further progress in others. With no apparent middle ground, there would have to be a battle.

In June 1941, after discussing the issue with the president, Marshall and Stimson determined that the initiative in pushing for an extension should come once again from the head of the War Department. But they also concluded that more was needed; after a year in office, Stimson acquired an even greater reputation in Congress as a warmonger. Among other aggressive supporters of the Selective Service Act, Stimson was singled out, given both the bellicose statements he had made since his appointment and his advanced age (as a former protégé and close associate of Teddy Roosevelt, it was difficult for him to avoid being labeled a jingoist). Therefore, using the tag team approach the two men so often deployed during their five years together, Stimson began the effort, understanding it would be up to Marshall to take the "laboring oar."[37]

Taking the first step, the two men went to see Speaker of the House Sam Rayburn on July 11, 1941, to gain his support. Inviting other congressional leaders to join him, Rayburn listened as first Stimson and then Marshall presented their arguments. Rayburn was sympathetic but told them the leadership of the president was required given the difficulty he expected to face among his colleagues in the House. He asked for a meeting with FDR. Stimson set it up for the following Monday. Although the meeting went better than expected, Stimson still believed success required all of Marshall's creativity and talents.[38]

He would not be disappointed; Marshall indeed got creative. He decided to reinstate the tradition by which the chief of staff submitted an annual report to Congress on the state of the Army and use the occasion to emphasize the importance of extending the Act. These reports, traditionally full of boring statistics and charts, were typically as dry as anything delivered to Capitol Hill (Marshall had not even bothered to prepare one the previous year). But given the escalating tensions in Europe and the absolute necessity to extend the Selective Service Act, he believed the timing was perfect to not simply reintroduce the tradition, but to do so with his own signature style of clarity and simplicity. It would not only allow Marshall to pitch for the extension but also provide him an opportunity to educate Congress on the Army's accomplishments in the two years since he took over the duties as chief of staff. More critically, it was a platform from which to explain what more was required.

Marshall knew that to be successful, he needed to explain in clear terms why the Army—eight times larger than two years earlier—needed to keep newly trained men in uniform. He wanted to warn Congress that any release of officers and enlisted men would leave America unprepared for war. The report Marshall delivered was the first successful step in the process to get the Act extended, but it did not immediately gain as much traction as he had hoped for.

Once again, it was politics; the country was still deeply divided on what the proper role of the United States should be in relation to the fighting in Europe. A few months earlier, Harry Hopkins summed up the American viewpoint to Winston Churchill in London. He told the prime minister the country could be divided roughly into four basic groups: a small one, including "Knox, Stimson, and most of the armed forces," who wanted to go to war immediately; another (whom Hopkins described as Nazis and Communists), who wanted a negotiated peace and a German victory; a third, led by Joseph Kennedy, who wished to help England but "stay the hell away from war"; and the majority, who wanted to assist England to the maximum.[39] This informal survey by Hopkins indicated that although public opinion was changing, it was still divided. This made it difficult for Roosevelt, Stimson, and Marshall to extend the terms of service for the initial draftees.

Another reason why Marshall's annual report did not have the impact he expected was due to his own lack of sophistication when it came to public relations; he failed to get the report properly covered by the press. Having positive coverage from the media on any proposed legislation would provide cover to congressmen asked to vote on it. It was a mistake he vowed not to repeat again. Similarly, Marshall neglected to brief leaders of Congress prior to the report's distribution on Capitol Hill, revealing a less-than-polished approach to managing relations with that critical branch of the government. He would learn quickly from that miscalculation as well.

Despite this latter failure, those leaders sympathetic to the cause quickly forgave him, most notably Sam Rayburn. The strong support given to Marshall by the Speaker of the House was suggestive of Marshall's elevated stature in Congress. It had risen considerably during the previous twelve months among leaders and members alike. Men who would not consider making any vote at the request of Roosevelt could more easily support a measure if the general were its leading advocate; defending one's vote to constituents back home by citing Marshall's views was far more politically prudent than referencing Roosevelt's. Marshall helped his cause immensely with congressmen by remaining apolitical. He long believed members of the Army should stay out of politics (he never once voted[40]).

Only during the summer of 1941 did the chief of staff finally begin to fully appreciate the excellent reputation he had acquired among members of Congress and leveraged it to the fullest of his capabilities for the benefit of the draft extension. Appearing before them, he used all the arguments in his arsenal, drawing on history, facts, logic, patriotism, and fear to persuade as many members as he could that unpreparedness was foolish.

Despite his efforts, there were still many members (Republicans mainly) who could not be moved by any force of logic. Extreme isolationists and Roosevelt haters continued to use old arguments to oppose the Act's extension: The war was in Europe (and moving farther away following the Nazi invasion of the Soviet Union on June 22, 1941); the Atlantic Ocean provided ample protection to the nation; and the Navy could buy enough time for the country to mobilize if the Germans were arrogant enough to attack. Since Marshall knew every single vote was going to be meaningful, he wanted to appeal to this faction directly.

He asked one of his Republican supporters in Congress to bring together as many of these men from his party as he could to the Army and Navy Club so that he could present his case to them personally. Starting at 7:00 p.m., Marshall spoke in a private dining room of the Club to approximately forty Republicans who agreed to hear him out. While carefully moving through his arguments and receiving initial feedback, Marshall realized there were a few members who were not interested in facts. One of the congressmen complimented him on his presentation but in the same breath said he would "be damned" if he was going to support Roosevelt. Marshall glared at the congressman and asked him sharply but calmly, "You're going to let plain hatred of the president's personality dictate to you to do something that you realize is very harmful to the interests of the country?"[41]

When the meeting ended at 2:00 a.m., Marshall believed he turned close to a third of the audience during the seven hours. While this was progress, he soon learned there were defiant Democrats who needed convincing as well (in early August, the majority leader concluded there were forty-five Democrats opposed to the extension and another thirty-five yet to make up their minds). Marshall was stunned. Given what was going on in Europe, the general could not for the life of him understand how any individual from any party could be opposed to extending the draft. If war were to come, America's only possible chance to win was to have trained men ready to fight. He continued to lobby aggressively.

Marshall was not the only one fighting. Opponents of the extension were just as aggressive in their pursuit to kill it. Sending out a million postcards under the congressional franking privilege, the printing of which was financed by the influential America First Committee, Senator Burton Wheeler explained that a vote for extension was a vote to go to war. Quite a number of these postcards found their way to selectees and members of the National Guard who were currently in training. To many of these young men, already disgruntled for having to serve for twelve months with limited equipment and an insufficient explanation for being there, these postcards added fuel to their fire. The letters these men sent home to their family and friends got forwarded to their congressmen, putting additional pressure on them to vote against the measure. When this happened, Stimson became apoplectic, stating during a press conference that Wheeler was getting very "near the line of subversive activities against the United States—if not treason." When Wheeler later proved none of the postcards were intentionally sent to soldiers, Stimson apologized, but the choice words used by the secretary of war reveal the passions that went into the debate.

Had the draft extension been looked at by Congress on a stand-alone basis, it would have required less of a sales effort from Marshall and Stimson; the arguments were logical, and their merit could be effectively sold to the public and Congress, particularly when Marshall was the primary pitchman. But those who were inclined to support the extension (or those sitting on the fence) were also reading about increased military and equipment needs from Great Britain as the summer of 1941 progressed, along with newer requests from the Soviet Union.[42] If they factored this information into their decision on the extension, it was harder to support.

When Stimson first heard about the requests from the Soviet Union, he was justifiably worried that when the extension vote finally came up on Capitol Hill, Congress would weigh in on these and other issues and say "to hell with you."[43] His concerns sharpened in August 1941, when he heard from White House Press Secretary Stephen Early about the estimate given to him from the House majority leader on renegade or undecided Democrats. Early begged Stimson to make another speech, but the secretary of war maintained that words from him would only hurt the cause. The vote was going to be too tight for Stimson to take that risk.

In the end, it was largely the extraordinary effort by General Marshall that got the legislation passed. Both his and Stimson's instincts had been correct; each meeting, speech, presentation, and paper was worth it. On August 14, the measure passed the House by a single vote (203 to 202). The administration was able to convince twenty-one Republicans to vote in favor of the measure. The Senate passed it a few days later by a far more comfortable margin.

The Draft Extension Act provided that the terms of service for the selectees, National Guardsmen, and Reserves could be extended for a period not to exceed eighteen months. Stimson wrote in his memoirs that getting the draft and its extension approved was one of the "two or three most important accomplishments of the American people" in the period leading up to the War. Marshall believed that had the vote gone the other way, it could have been a "fatal point" in the nation's military history.[44]

Running Out of Time

I feel confident that we cannot permanently be in a position of toolmakers for other nations which fight and sooner or later I feel certain from what I know of young American men that when they once appreciate this issue between right and wrong they will be not satisfied unless they are offering their own bodies to the flames and are willing to fight as well as make munitions.

—HENRY STIMSON diary entry, December 29, 1940

The efficiency of any army depends on many different things but one is outstanding—and that is morale. You can have all the material in the world, but without a morale it is largely ineffective.[1]

—GEORGE MARSHALL, Speech to the Chamber of Commerce in Washington, D.C., April 1941

Training and Leadership

Having men in place with weapons and machines was one thing; training them properly quite another. Marshall stressed this obvious but underappreciated point whenever he could. The strength of a fighting force, he explained to an American Legion convention two months before Pearl Harbor, "cannot be measured in mere numbers. It is based on a high state of discipline and training."[2] Stimson was on the same page. Both enthusiasts of American history, he and Marshall would likely have known of and strongly supported Alexander Hamilton's contention, written down in

Federalist No. 25, that "war like most other things is a science to be acquired and perfected by diligence, by perseverance, by time, and by practice."[3]

As previously mentioned, Marshall went out of his way after becoming chief of staff to remind Americans how lucky the country was to have won past wars given the lack of preparedness existing at the start of each one. He used the same statistics repeatedly to emphasize that wars were won on training grounds. The United States, Marshall told one audience, "enrolled nearly 400,000 men in the Revolutionary War to defeat an enemy that numbered less than 45,000" and "employed 500,000 during the War of 1812 against an opponent whose strength never exceeded 16,000 at any one place." These advantages in numbers were necessary, he emphasized, because British troops had been far better trained on both occasions.[4] Stimson was equally aware of the importance of training (he had worked tirelessly to prepare himself and others for World War I). Together, he and Marshall did all they could to ensure that the massive inflow of men coming into the ranks would be properly prepared to take on the well-trained German and Japanese soldiers if America was drawn into battle with either of these potential enemies.

The success of any military training program generally depends on three components: time; method of instruction; and quality of instructors. Any rapid increase in soldiers must be accompanied by a proportional increase in skilled officers to train them. Long considered the final authority in the U.S. Army on training men, Marshall was confident he knew what to teach, how to teach it, and the time that it would take for the training to stick. But during the summer of 1940, he was not comfortable that the Army had the right leadership in place to ensure there would be high-quality instructors who measured up to his exacting standards. He needed to clear the deadwood that naturally stacks up within peacetime armies in order to advance younger and abler officers with more energy. Like all things he attempted before Pearl Harbor, this, too, proved challenging.

Marshall relayed his concerns to the House Military Affairs Committee a few months earlier, explaining that stamina and vigor far outweighed acquired wisdom when it came to the performance of officers in battle. Citing statistics, he said the single largest factor for relief of field officers above the rank of captain during the First World War was for physical reasons.

Despite his compelling arguments, Marshall could not find enough support to initiate a purge; older officers enjoyed close ties to congressmen, making it politically difficult to remove them. Hoping the turn of events in Europe in June and July 1940 could change some minds, Marshall approached Jimmy Byrnes, the influential senator from South Carolina who was a confirmed interventionist. After hearing Marshall out, the crafty Byrnes creatively slipped language into a general appropriations bill that gave Marshall the ability to promote younger officers into higher positions. When the bill passed, Marshall created a group of six retired officers led by former chief of staff Malin Craig and charged them to review the files of older officers in order to justify culling the worst ones. Within six months, this "plucking committee" removed 195 officers.

It was an awkward and painful period of time for Marshall, one he later claimed was among the most difficult he bore as chief of staff. Many of the men he removed were old friends who had excellent service records and often pleaded their cases directly with him. But Marshall, confident that the force of youth outweighed nearly every other factor when it came to effective leadership, summoned the ruthlessness to jettison many otherwise capable officers with strong records. He told his wife that he "could not afford the luxury of sentiment . . . mine must be cold logic." This attitude also carried him through a more significant officer purge he instigated in September 1941.

Henry Stimson was equally concerned about leadership within the Army at this time but believed talented civilians should be brought in to join existing officers to train and lead the incoming flood of recruits. As detailed in chapter 5, Stimson had been a leader of the Plattsburgh Movement organized and supported twenty-four years earlier by Leonard Wood, Teddy Roosevelt, Elihu Root, and Grenville Clark during World War I. One will recall that approximately forty thousand men, generally college educated, were trained (at each man's own expense) at a variety of camps set up for such purposes. Many of those who went through the program successfully led doughboys in France during the First World War.

Having spent over a month at one of the Plattsburgh camps himself, Stimson believed it was an excellent method for finding and developing strong leaders. In July 1940, Grenville Clark drew up a plan to have his group (the Military Training Camps Association) handpick thirty thousand similarly styled men to begin training. His idea was that when war came to America, leaders would be chosen equally between these men who had proved themselves in a variety of civilian fields and those currently serving in the Army.

Naturally, Stimson was on board with the plan. It broadly followed the same blueprint he used to recruit people to work for him at his law firm or in the various public positions he held over the years: hire the smartest men from the best schools or firms with proven success, mentor them, inspire them, support them, and allow them to get on with the job. Although he claimed the greatest lesson he learned during World War I was that there was no class or group of Americans with a monopoly over another with respect to strength of character, courage, or spirit, he apparently thought leadership qualities were more abundant among successful civilians than army lifers.[5] Stimson also felt strongly that such camps would have the ancillary benefit of sending a signal to the general population that every citizen must be prepared to die for America if war came.

It was not only Stimson who got behind Clark's initiative. Patterson, Lovett, McCloy, and Bundy had all spent time at the Plattsburgh camps prior to World War I and fully supported the effort. Patterson, in particular, was convinced the Army should be led by the best men America could produce and thought more of them could be drawn from the civilian population.

Although General Marshall seemed to accept the concept before the First World War and did nothing to discourage it between the wars, once Congress approved the draft, his attitude concerning Army leadership shifted considerably. During their five years working together from 1940 to 1945, he and Stimson had several serious disputes but managed to settle them after a healthy and frank exchange of views. By far the strongest disagreement they ever had was on this issue of where to source leadership for the Army. The two men began discussing it seriously in August 1940.[6]

From their initial conversations, Marshall gently but firmly expressed doubt to Stimson about the necessity for the camps.[7] There were three principal reasons he opposed the Plattsburgh model: First, he believed there was enough talent between the Army and the National Guard to satisfy all the demand for officers; second, officers capable of training men in the proposed civilian camps were in short supply, and diverting them would throw off the precise training schedule Marshall and his men had worked out for the Army; and third, he was of the opinion that officers would be more effective in all aspects of Army leadership if they had some inkling of what it was like to be a private in the U.S. Army. "Leadership in the field," Marshall once explained to a congressional committee, "depends to an important extent on one's legs, and stomach, and nervous system and one's ability to withstand hardships, and lack of sleep, and still be disposed energetically and aggressively to command men, to dominate men on the battlefield."[8] This leadership, he insisted, was more likely to come from men who had suffered such hardships throughout their careers. It is one thing to slave away for a client on a legal case in a plush office in downtown Manhattan, but it is quite another to spend three months—as Marshall had done earlier in his career—leading five men on a mapping exercise of two thousand square miles in scorching heat.

George Marshall was proud of his standing as the finest trainer of men within the Army. Having paid a dear price for that reputation in sacrificed promotions (given the long-standing preference within the Army to promote officers with command experience), Marshall might have felt even stronger that he had earned the right to have the last say on the matter. The outcome also had larger implications regarding who generally determined the policies of the Army on such issues: Stimson and his civilian aides, or Marshall and the Army. It was not an ego issue for the chief of staff (Marshall was renowned for his ability to set his ego aside); it was a matter of sound administration.

The general was initially patient in explaining the rationale behind his position to Stimson, but the secretary and his staff continued to promote the selection of officers based on their educational or professional accomplishments as opposed to leadership skills demonstrated on the Army's training grounds. Eventually, Marshall's patience ran out; in late March 1941, during a pivotal discussion with Stimson on the subject, he threatened to resign if the secretary of war insisted on moving forward with his plans. Stimson backed off quickly, surprised Marshall felt so passionately about the matter. Although Marshall greatly regretted resorting to this "reprehensible" tactic with Stimson, he explained years later that "nothing else could stop the thing."[9]

Although Stimson surrendered to General Marshall on this matter, his subordinates continued to push for a compromise. Patterson was hearing from his friends various accounts of college-educated selectees demoralized on account of the incompetence of those officers who were responsible for training them. But any further suggestions to the chief of staff fell on deaf ears.[10] The matter was settled.

Stimson did not relish losing arguments, but he was more than happy to be proven wrong on this issue, and he stated emphatically after the War that Marshall had been right. There were still plenty of incompetent officers, Stimson believed, but expanding the existing training programs already in place within the Army was not only more efficient, but it was also a fair and democratic way to build an officer corp. Although solid arguments were made by both sides, if one assumes leading men in battle is a skill acquired and perfected over time, one can understand why Marshall dug his heels in so deeply on the subject.

The ability of Stimson and Marshall to eventually work through this substantial difference of opinion, leaving their relationship no worse for the wear, is a tribute to the respect and admiration each man had for the other. There were several more notable disagreements in the future between the two men, but after each occasion their relationship seemed to only strengthen. They were brothers in arms from the very start of their partnership.

Housing

In addition to needing skilled officers to train the expected flood of enlistees, Marshall and Stimson were forced to scramble to make housing available to them as well. Consistent with the general lack of attention given by Congress to the Army during the 1920s and 1930s, the barracks that were quickly and cheaply built by Newton Baker to temporarily quarter soldiers training for the First World War were uninhabitable by 1940. In anticipation of the growth in the size of the Army, Marshall addressed this issue during his first year on the job but got nowhere.

It was not for lack of a plan; the Army knew which facilities needed to be demolished, which needed to be restored, where new facilities should be built, and exactly how the new structures should be laid out. It was instead a matter of funding—there was none. This abruptly changed only at the time the Selective Service and Training Act was signed into law in September 1940, a year after Marshall took over as chief of staff. Within three days of the signing, the House quickly approved $338 million in funding for housing for the newly expected draftees. Although there were still many isolationists in Congress, the attitude among those less passionate ones was shifting as the Germans continued to drop bombs down on London and the Italians invaded Egypt. The "ostrich era," as Stimson coined the years leading up to the War, was coming to an end. The shift in thinking by no means suggested Congress was ready to enter the War, but it did want the country prepared just in case it was forced into it.

George Marshall often commented on the great irony around the juxtaposition of money and time that fell upon the Army during the months leading up to Pearl Harbor in contrast to the two prior decades. For twenty years, he noted, the Army had insufficient funding but all the time in the world; by the end of 1940, it had little time, but all the cash it could possibly need. Shelter was required for one million soldiers by February

1941 (less than four months after Stimson drew the first capsule from the goldfish bowl launching the draft[11]). For Marshall and the War Department, the housing shortage was among the greatest challenges they faced together during the winter and spring of 1941. Barracks could simply not be built fast enough.

Delays and cost overruns, inevitable in any large construction project, were compounded by the short timetable and poor winter weather. As easy as it was to get the original outlay from Congress granted, there were still congressmen around to make the task of answering for overruns difficult. Marshall often made his way to Capitol Hill not only to ensure that he received the additional funds, but also to fully explain to legislators the problems he was facing. He made sure to take blame when blame was due, but he also explained to congressmen that it was their failure to respond to earlier requests that had caused many of the problems now being faced. By emphasizing this, he wanted Congress to more carefully consider the consequences of any further delays going forward relating to preparation in general.

It was not only Congress that needed educating on the issue of housing; the public did as well. Both Stimson and Marshall made radio broadcasts to support their efforts (during an era when radio broadcasts commanded a significant number of listeners). In January 1941 Marshall talked about living conditions in the Army. During the broadcast, he explained how the Army was "building from the ground up what amounts to forty-four new and complete cities for populations ranging from ten thousand to sixty thousand citizens."[12] Long a favorite tactic of Marshall's, the use of simple statistics and facts were presented to awaken Americans about the realities of building a trained army from scratch.

The efforts were not in vain. By the summer of 1941, housing had been built for over 1.2 million men in approximately 250 different locations. This was a remarkable accomplishment.

Morale

Once trainees arrived with places to sleep, food to eat, competent officers to instruct them, and weapons and equipment with which to train, one might have thought the problems and worries for Stimson and Marshall with regard to preparation would have started to diminish. This was not the case; both men knew from personal experience that taking randomly selected men out of a civilian environment and placing them into a military one was going to have negative consequences related to morale, particularly in an economy that was finally getting back on track. And they also knew the situation would be worse than it was during the First World War. Stimson summed up the problem in a speech at a conference of public relations officers when he explained, "The children of today are more used to luxuries than their fathers were."[13] He went on to tie the success of an army to the morale of its soldiers, which in turn was partially tied to the morale of the people at home supporting them. That support, he said, could only be earned if the Army was transparent with its recruits and the general population.

Although there have been complaints throughout American history from citizen soldiers relating to low pay, difficult training schedules, unfair and unkind superiors, insufficient communication, poor food, ill-fitting clothes, and inadequate entertainment during downtime, professional soldiers have generally accepted these and other difficulties as part of the life they've chosen. Stimson's comment to the public relations officers was correct; even to those who stepped forward on their own volition, army life in 1940 was a greater shock than it had been to their fathers a generation earlier. Considering the Army was gathering together a large number of civilians during peacetime, many selected by the hand of fate (or more accurately, the hand of a blindfolded Stimson), it was not surprising there was a significant step up in both the quantity and severity of complaints. Such grievances, like water down a stream, eventually make their way to congressmen. To stay ahead of this, both Stimson and Marshall spent a lot of time familiarizing themselves with all aspects of training camp life. As an army lifer, Marshall led the way.

The chief of staff strongly believed that a successful army was more than simply a "war machine" made up of powerful weapons, bombers, tanks, and shells. When speaking at Trinity College in June 1941, Marshall said, "Unless the soldier's soul sustains him he cannot be relied on and will fail himself and his commander and his country in the end."[14] Throughout his entire career, Marshall was well known for going out of his way to build up the morale of his troops or students. As chief of staff, his goal was to constantly strive to appeal to a soldier's heart, spirit, and soul across all activities.

What stood partly in the way of achieving this was cultural within the Army itself; after twenty years of forced penny-pinching, it was hard to reeducate the Army bureaucracy when it came to spending money to keep the soldiers properly provided for from a morale standpoint. Cost-cutting policies and procedures put in place since World War I slowed down the process of getting specific requests filled. These procedures had developed over time, often a reaction from the criticism of one congressional committee or another charged to investigate the spending habits of the Army. Ultimately, it required a complete reorganization to fully address this problem (something Marshall undertook immediately after Pearl Harbor). Until then, the chief of staff, with the support of the secretary of war, did his best to keep recruits engaged and satisfied.

Aside from the more obvious requirements of decent food, clothes, and shelter, Marshall believed having appropriate recreational facilities was essential for maintaining morale at an Army camp. This was a major concern of his going back to his first command assignment in the Philippines at the turn of the century. Since military posts were typically built in remote locations, Marshall felt the Army should be responsible for ensuring there were things for the men to do each day after training and on the weekends. Besides building morale, providing activities had the additional benefit of reducing the opportunities for soldiers to explore more unseemly pursuits.

To satisfy himself that proper conditions existed around various camps, Marshall traveled extensively across the country visiting them. On occasion, he dressed in civilian clothes and discreetly walked around whatever small town stood nearest to an Army base. He wanted to see what life was like for a soldier taking a deserved break. If it did not meet his standards, he held the unit commander accountable.[15]

Prior to the draft, Marshall ordered recreational facilities built for various camps around the country. Although they were a hit with the men and their representatives in Congress, the number of them built was a fraction of what would be needed when enlistments began pouring into the Army in early 1941. Made aware of the problem, Stimson acted quickly by appointing a War Department Community Service Committee and forming with the Navy a Joint Committee on Welfare and Recreation (which eventually grew into the enormously successful USO made famous by Bob Hope and other celebrities who entertained American troops on its behalf throughout the twentieth century). Marshall further demonstrated to the officer corps his stance on the subject by considerably upgrading the rank of the morale officer of the Army to a brigadier general (from assistant to the adjutant general).

As a career-long soldier, General Marshall also believed it crucially important that recruits fully understand the reasons they were in camps in the first place. By keeping them abreast of current events, by reflecting on the heritage of America, and by discussing the value the Army plays in defending the nation's interests, Marshall hoped to provide the men with a legitimate raison d'être. Initially, the message delivered to the recruits was only as strong as the local commanders who delivered it. Only when the professionals in Hollywood were commissioned by the War Department to produce films for the Army did Marshall's vision get fully realized in this regard (film director Frank Capra was the most notable of his recruits).

Stimson, equally passionate on this issue, believed the Army not only needed to give soldiers the reason they were fighting, but also the progress they were making toward achieving their goals. Nothing undermined the morale of soldiers so quickly or deeply, Stimson felt, as the feeling that their superiors were not giving them "the real facts about their progress and the progress of the cause which they are preparing to defend."[16]

On the overall subject of morale, Marshall, Stimson, and the men who worked for them were of like minds. Marshall estimated he spent on average twenty minutes a day reading summaries of letters from soldiers or their families.[17] He typically answered a half dozen of them personally. Once war came and the common enemy could be identified, it was far less of a challenge to motivate men. But until Pearl Harbor, the effort required constant attention.

Reorganization

Upon becoming chief of staff in September 1939, Marshall was well aware that the Army needed reorganizing, but he carefully weighed any initiative against the greater need for the Army to expand. He determined his best bet at achieving rapid growth was doing so within the existing organization he inherited; a major overhaul would not only be difficult and controversial but would more importantly delay needed progress.

That decision did not stop Marshall from occasionally shifting people around or removing them outright (as he did through the aforementioned "plucking committee"). When the impact of those changes fell short of his expectation, he accelerated the process in September 1941 by beginning a general officer purge. It was the first step toward the major reorganization he launched shortly after Pearl Harbor.

Attending the War Council meeting when Marshall announced the purge, the experienced Stimson immediately anticipated trouble for himself. Sure enough, Senator Tom Connolly of Texas, chairman of the

Committee on Foreign Relations, charged into Stimson's office shortly after the meeting with his "hair standing up on end" complaining about two generals of the Texas National Guard who were early victims of the purge. Checking with Marshall, Stimson was told one was old and the other incompetent. Stimson, never inclined to let politics interfere with sound management practices, carefully explained the situation to Connolly, making it clear to the senator that the decision was final.[18]

Several weeks later, both men had to deal with an unrelated plan hatched in Congress to make the Air Force an independent branch of the military outside of the control of the Army (as it was in Great Britain). Rumblings had gone on regarding this subject since Stimson joined the War Department. Facing criticism that the Army was not progressive enough and too turf-conscious, Marshall countered that this option had been studied closely. He explained that the Army was keenly aware of the lack of coordination between air and ground forces in Great Britain over the previous two years and believed that it caused disasters in "virtually every operation it had undertaken." Further, Marshall pointed out publicly in September 1941, the German Air Force was not—contrary to popular belief—independent of the ground services but was closely coordinated by "a system of command and staff over and above all civil departments" (a structure, he added, that would not be acceptable in the United States).

Marshall remained far more concerned than Stimson that Congress might get their way on this initiative. As late as a month before Pearl Harbor, he expressed his concern to the secretary of war about hearing that Robert Lovett was in favor of an independent Air Corps. Stimson "cooled him down" by explaining that Lovett felt exactly as he did on the subject.[19] The matter did not come up again.

On the same day that the secretary of war assured Marshall that the Air Force would not be spun out of the Army, he heard that the Japanese were sending a man to Washington to work out the differences between the two countries.

Stimson was pessimistic about the envoy's odds of accomplishing anything. His gut told him war was coming soon. He closed his diary entry of November 9 writing, "Everything looks as if we were getting into the war pretty fast now and everybody is pretty sound about it." A few days later, the House of Representatives voted to repeal key provisions of the Neutrality Acts. The vote was close (212–194) but a victory for interventionists. It was time to begin finalizing war plans.

Strategic Planning

While addressing all the critical issues around munitions procurement, manpower, housing, leadership, training, and morale during their first seventeen months together, Stimson and Marshall also needed to consider developing a strategic operating plan for the Army in case war came. Although they saw eye to eye on most of the issues they faced together during the prewar period, their views on planning varied and reflected their respective outlooks on both the prospects of war and the advisability of American involvement.

Stimson, of course, was the administration's most extreme and visible interventionist. So much so that it became somewhat of a running joke in the first year he served given the number of times he spoke out in favor of some form of intervention. At a cabinet meeting in the spring of 1941, the president was discussing a few ideas about his plans to patrol the Atlantic in order to support Britain and closed his comments by stating it was a "step forward." To the amusement of both Roosevelt and the rest of the cabinet members, Stimson—not known for his sense of humor—blurted out, "Well, I hope you will keep on walking, Mr. President. Keep on walking."[20]

Stimson's comment was not meant to be funny; he was disappointed with FDR and every other high-ranking official who did not take a more proactive approach to preparing for war from a strategic standpoint. Surprisingly, this included Marshall. Stimson believed that the chief of staff should pay more attention to working out specific plans to assist the British. Marshall, on the other hand, felt precise planning was a bit premature, considering he still needed to raise an army, supply it, and train it.

That is not to suggest there were no plans in the till. Following the First World War, the Army and Navy periodically updated their strategy to stay current with the geopolitical conditions of the world. As such, there were detailed plans made around the possibility of a war with Japan and a variety of blueprints drawn up on the chance the United States would again be drawn into a war in Europe (each one of them dealing with a different set of presumed enemies). As events unfolded in Europe and Asia in the late 1930s, a planning committee made up of Army and Navy planners also agreed upon a framework in the event war broke out in different regions simultaneously. Plan Dog, written by Chief of Naval Operations Harold Stark in November 1940, contemplated the United States and the United Kingdom at war against Germany, Italy, and Japan. Marshall thought these plans (referred to as the "Rainbow Plans") were adequate considering the state of the Army; Stimson wanted to fine-tune them and bring them up to date.

Further complicating such matters was the divergent theory held by each man as to who should be the principal advisor to the president on strategic planning. Although Stimson believed matters of strategy should properly originate with the chief of staff, he felt the secretary of war was entitled to review and pass judgment on them before relaying them on to the commander in chief. To Stimson, this was simply a matter of sound administrative practice and had nothing to do with how he felt about Marshall's judgment (which he highly valued). He accepted the president's right to directly consult with the chief of staff but believed the default hierarchal structure placed him between the two offices.

Marshall, for several reasons, thought the chief of staff should have the ability to raise issues directly with the president. This opinion also did not reflect any lack of respect he had for the secretary of war, but Stimson was a Wall Street lawyer–cum–public servant, not an Army lifer, and Marshall believed career Army officers were more capable than the civilian heads in not only determining proper military strategy, but also presenting it. As a man preoccupied with efficiency, Marshall thought the extra step required to get signoff from Stimson was inconsistent with his ideas of best administrative practices.

The men debated this issue shortly after Stimson took office. Both quickly agreed direct access by the chief of staff to the president was necessary. Their differences were over what specific topics could be discussed during such meetings. After forming a general basis for agreement, they ultimately realized the debate was moot while FDR remained in the Oval Office. The president marched to the beat of his own drum and was famous for casting his net far and wide when it came to gathering military advice, or advice of any kind for that matter. Although his two subordinates figured this out soon enough, they probably needed to flush out their own overall working relationship by discussing the major ground rules early on in their partnership. It was not a wasted exercise. Their candid exchange of views on such critical matters at the start of their partnership helped build an unbreakable foundation of trust between the two men.

As with so many issues Stimson and Marshall faced together, when it came to crucial decisions on strategy, this mutual trust allowed them to ultimately exploit the unique management style of their president. Throughout their partnership, both men went out of their way to share any and all information with each other, almost as if it was a competition between them. This practice was an effective counterweight to Roosevelt's habit of giving bits of different information to different people. The president believed that by flattering individuals through the sharing of choice information, they would likely keep the details to themselves in order to play their own power games, ultimately leaving him with the total control he coveted. What FDR did not realize—at least not initially—was that between his secretary of war and his chief of staff, there were no secrets.

Having identical information from which to work, as well as shared principles, the two men were better able to press their demands on the White House. When Marshall ran into trouble with Roosevelt on bigger issues around strategy, he called upon Stimson to lend his formidable weight to whatever point he was trying to get across. Just as frequently, it was Stimson who took advantage of Marshall's high standing in the White House to push for strategic initiatives about which he was passionate. On any given issue, Stimson and Marshall could—by instinct or through trial and error—call upon some combination of individual and collective pressure to ensure that the president at least understood their point of view, if not directly followed their advice. In late 1940 and throughout 1941, it was strategic issues that they were increasingly discussing with the president.

Assisting Great Britain

The big strategic debate in Washington was whether or not America should assist Great Britain. Absent a fringe group who wished for a German victory, the sympathies of the nation were with the British, who had bravely stood up to the relentless bombing campaign by the Luftwaffe. That consideration did not translate to tangible support, however; a sizable majority of the U.S. population was still fully committed to maintaining neutrality in 1940. Public opinion began to shift only toward the end of the year, but it varied depending on one's views of how long the British could hold out against the Germans and whether the United States could afford to provide them the instruments of war it was desperately short of itself. For key figures within the administration, the question of whether to assist Great Britain quickly evolved after the fall of France in June 1940 into a debate on how, and how much. The United States was in a massive rebuilding stage; every item coming off the factory line sent to the British was one less for the Americans. Congress understood this and decided in June that it would not allow the sale of surplus arms to the British unless the chief of staff and chief of naval operations certified that it was not essential for the protection of the United States.

Marshall struggled with the ensuing decisions and Roosevelt's increasing pressure to support the British. When his partner saw evidence of the strain in mid-September, he invited Marshall to Woodley to talk about how best they could manage the competing interests between the two countries. The following day, an inspired Marshall walked into Stimson's office to suggest that a survey of all requirements of the Army, Navy, and British services be made. Both men agreed that careful consideration in such matters must be made so that emotions of the moment could be removed from the decision-making process.

As the Battle of Britain picked up in intensity, Stimson spent a considerable portion of his time working with a team of other high-level officials from the military and all three branches of government in figuring a way to get much-needed destroyers to Britain. Since joining the War Department, Stimson had received calls from British, Canadian, and Australian officials, all of whom stressed the need for destroyers. Prevented by the neutrality laws from *selling* any destroyers to a belligerent power, the administration came up with the idea of *exchanging* them instead for the right to establish naval or air bases within various British possessions. The agreement was signed in the first week of September 1940.

Shortly after the destroyers-for-bases agreement was concluded, the Navy delivered a paper to Roosevelt proposing a general strategy for the armed forces to follow. It proposed that the United States should focus on defending the Western Hemisphere while preparing detailed plans to offer full offensive support to the British in the future.

Marshall supported this proposal, but insisted that the United States should take care of its own essential requirements as a hedge against a British defeat (as he and many of his colleagues predicted).[21] As for Stimson, everyone in Washington knew where he stood: He appreciated the limitations of the support that could be given by the Army to the British, but he strongly believed that in helping them, the United States would be helping itself. At a particularly long cabinet meeting on December 19, 1940, he told the president it was high time the country intervened directly to stop the German submarines from destroying more British merchant ships. The Battle of the Atlantic, Stimson pointed out, was a "terrific loss to civilization and to commerce."[22] This was a full year before Pearl Harbor.

Although Roosevelt told Stimson that the timing was not right for direct intervention, the general strategy of supporting England ultimately carried the day; the president confirmed it ten days later when he gave his "Arsenal of Democracy" speech. Stimson would have preferred a declaration of war, but he believed the president went "as far as he could at the present time." Two months later, the United States Congress approved the Lend-Lease Bill, which permitted the president to provide aid to any country whose defense he considered vital to the defense of the United States. It was an even bigger step forward, but Stimson knew that America could not limit itself to the role of "toolmaker" for long without getting into the fight.[23]

In looking at Stimson's diary during the two months prior to the enactment of the Lend-Lease Bill on March 11, 1941, one can sense the consuming effort he made in covering all angles to ensure its passage. As if handling an important legal case, America's number-one interventionist familiarized himself with all the facts and statistics, fully flushed out the opposition's opinions, and painstakingly prepared his arguments and counterarguments. But instead of presenting the case to a jury of twelve random people, Stimson faced Congress and the politics that divided it. Working with him step by step was the chief of staff. Never as aggressive as Stimson, Marshall was nevertheless fully on board with assisting the British during this period. The approval of Lend-Lease would be a monumental break from the Neutrality Acts originally passed in 1935 and updated or expanded almost annually for the balance of that decade.

When the likelihood of passage seemed certain after the vote in the House of Representatives in early February, Stimson, Marshall, and their respective staffs met almost daily to discuss exactly how Lend-Lease should be carried out once approved by the Senate. Prioritizing British needs and mapping those against production schedules and domestic requirements took up much of their time in February and March 1941. During these months, the situation in Europe was becoming so dire that the president ordered the U.S. fleet in April to begin patrolling the western part of the Atlantic in order to alert the British to the presence of German boats in the area. This move was consistent with the Lend-Lease Bill.

From March through June 1941, bad news from Europe streamed into Washington with increasing regularity. That the Germans were advancing in Greece and Libya and threatening Egypt added to the stress brought on by the continued heavy losses of British merchant ships at the hands of German submarines. The losses at sea were so appalling that U.S. Chief of

Naval Operations Harold Stark thought only a strong military intervention by the United States could save the British.

The Army was no less pessimistic. While regularly predicting Britain's collapse, Army intelligence officers also took aim at Churchill, criticizing him in general and accusing him of incompetence in relation to specific actions (e.g., pulling troops out of Libya to aid Greece). Stimson could tolerate neither the defeatist attitudes nor the specific vitriol directed at the prime minister. After hearing one of the intelligence officers make particularly histrionic statements against Churchill's ineptitude in April 1941, Stimson ordered Marshall to make sure there were no more negative comments from anyone in the Army made against the man who was standing up to Hitler. In making this request, he explained to Marshall that the success of the United States depended on the safety of the British fleet, which in turn hinged on Churchill's continuation at the helm because he was the only leader in England who fought the Nazis at every turn of events. He felt so passionately about this that he even suggested to Marshall on more than one occasion that he replace the naysayers in the intelligence units in favor of men with "broader vision."[24]

Placement of Resources between Europe and Asia

The rapidly deteriorating news coming from Europe during 1941 forced the administration to address another related critical strategic question: how to balance U.S. naval resources between the Atlantic and Pacific Oceans. This was part of a larger question related to the general allocation of resources if the country had to fight in both Europe and Asia simultaneously, a scenario that increased in likelihood with each passing month.

Back in November 1940, Stimson and Secretary of State Cordell Hull supported the Navy when it declared it was in America's best interests to avoid conflict with Japan so that the nation's military resources could be concentrated in Europe. Stimson was never fully comfortable with this position, however. He did not want the country's military assets dispersed in the event war broke out in Asia, and he did not wish to go easy on Japan. On the contrary, he was certain the Japanese only responded to "clear language and bold actions" and wanted badly to get up in their grill.

Stimson's attitude toward the Japanese was in part emotionally driven; they had been a thorn in his side since the Manchurian Incident in

September 1931 and through the balance of his term as secretary of state under Hoover. When he thought harder and with less emotion about the Japanese as secretary of war, he recognized Europe was the greater fire to put out. With a heavy consensus around that general belief within the Executive Branch and military, Stimson supported moving a major part of the fleet from Pearl Harbor to the Atlantic theater of action to provide aid and encouragement to Britain while sending a clear message to the Germans.

Although Marshall approved of this strategy as well, his reason for supporting it was different. For Stimson, it was yet another way to get involved; if he could not mix it up with the Japanese, he was steadfast in his desire to do so with the Germans. The chief of staff's rationale was more pragmatic: With too few men and an insufficient quantity of weapons, the U.S. Army was unable to assist Britain. Only the Navy could make a proper impression on Germany, and he believed the psychological benefit to the British in seeing the U.S. fleet in Atlantic waters outweighed the disadvantage of moving the fleet out of the Pacific, which could encourage the Japanese to make moves on Singapore or other regions of strategic interest to them.

In early June 1941, Stimson was invited by FDR to a meeting with Knox and Hull at the White House, where, according to Stimson, Roosevelt finally made the "vital decisions" as to "what shall be done in the Atlantic and as to the reinforcement of the Fleet."[25] Stimson was ecstatic. Although it was the cumulative buildup of bad news coming from the Atlantic and the Mediterranean that forced Roosevelt to shift naval resources to the Atlantic theater, he didn't care. The result was what mattered, and he felt much better that the United States was finally making a statement.

As Stimson began his second year on the job, Roosevelt was relying on him more frequently, not only for the interventionist voice he brought to the administration, but for the legal advice and overall judgment he dispensed as well. The president did not easily come to trust those who worked for him, but in Stimson he found someone who could marshal his own talents, and those of his staff, to solve the tricky prewar issues that seemed to arise daily. On issues large and small, Stimson was proactive and careful to consider all the consequences of any specific action he was considering. He was quick to make decisions and confident in his recommendations. Roosevelt greatly valued these qualities and continued to appreciate the lack of any political agenda behind his actions.

Stimson also provided Roosevelt great cover for the increasing political risks the president was taking, whether it involved assuming control of the aircraft production facilities, trading destroyers for bases, "lending" munitions to the British, dealing with subversive elements among the labor pool, or otherwise figuring out ways to support Churchill's efforts to stop the Germans. Stimson's sterling reputation and his lifelong affiliation with the Republican Party provided a meaningful degree of political support for every step Roosevelt took toward war.

German Invasion of the Soviet Union

Two weeks after Roosevelt declared his intentions to Stimson, Knox, and Hull regarding the fleet, the pressure that led Roosevelt to do so suddenly and dramatically eased; Hitler invaded the Soviet Union on June 22, 1941. To Marshall the invasion was a gift; to Stimson it was "almost providential." Both men were intent on taking full advantage of it.

They immediately conferred with one another, Harry Hopkins, and their respective staffs. It was decided that Stimson should draft a letter to the president encouraging him to leverage the "precious and unforeseen period of respite" by making prompt moves to shore up the nation's strategic position in the Atlantic.[26] Knowing the Germans would have their hands full for at least the next ninety days, Stimson sent off the letter to Roosevelt the day after the invasion. He urged quick action.

The sense of relief was only temporary; the quick success of the Germans in Russia raised the level of anxiety back up. Within ten days from the start of the German eastern offensive, bad news from that front brought Stimson to comment in his diary that he felt "more up against it than ever before." Although he privately questioned whether the United States had the power, sincerity, and devotion to take on the Germans, he penned and sent another memorandum to FDR on July 3 advising him to speak to Congress as soon as possible and explain that despite great efforts to avoid war, it was time for the country to step up to assist those "free nations who are still fighting for freedom" or risk having the greater task of fighting alone if they fell.[27]

A few days later, Stimson laid out a more specific argument to FDR for securing Iceland. He suggested if the Germans were to get there first, they would command Greenland, which would allow them to control Newfoundland and the eastern coast of Canada. From there, the Northeast, mid-Atlantic, and even parts of the Midwest could be vulnerable. Behind every success of Germany since the War began, Stimson wrote the president, a similar stepping-stone strategy was used, so controlling Iceland meant much more than simply protecting the North Atlantic sea-lanes.

On July 7, Roosevelt did deliver a message to Congress, and although greatly watered down from Stimson's recommendations, it did address the need to protect the sea-lanes. Stimson was satisfied, but still felt Roosevelt was waiting for the Germans to "fire the first shot," which he thought was a mistake. He believed Lincoln had made the same error prior to the Confederate shelling of Fort Sumter eighty years earlier and thought the consequences would be even greater for Roosevelt.

Despite Stimson's entreaties, it was another two months before the president announced in another of his fireside chats that the United States would shoot any German submarine or raider venturing into the "waters of self-defense" (an area in the North Atlantic defined by the United States). It was time, he said, for Americans to "stop being deluded by the romantic notion that the Americas can go on living happily and peacefully in a Nazi-dominated world." Stimson ended his diary that night (September 11) by expressing the "great sense of relief" he felt after hearing the president's speech.

Following the attack on his country by Hitler, a panicked Josef Stalin immediately bombarded Roosevelt with requests for munitions. Increased Russian demands were simply a new piece of the larger strategic munitions puzzle the secretary of war and chief of staff had long been trying to solve. Both men pressed their colleagues to give an update as to what America could afford to give the Russians based on production forecasts, British needs, and what the U.S. Army thought it needed to defend itself. Stimson was so concerned about the ability of the country to meet all the requirements that he told Roosevelt he saw two alternatives for America: join the war in order to light a fire under the country to reach its full industrial output potential; or risk that it would be over before it could meet the various demands.[28] A couple weeks later, a request for four hundred planes and four hundred tanks per month passed from Stalin to Churchill to Roosevelt to Stimson, further validating the secretary's warning.

Final Months of Preparation

Figuring out how to arm Stalin's troops was just one of several dozen critical issues Stimson and Marshall were handling concurrently as summer turned to fall in 1941. Issues that would be considered momentous in almost any other environment were seemingly dealt with as minor matters by the two. During the battles they faced getting the Draft Extension Act approved in the summer of 1941 while simultaneously trying to build an army, step up deliveries to the British, protect the shipping lanes of the North Atlantic, assist the Soviets, and keep Japan from extending its influence in Asia, Stimson devoted only a short paragraph in his diary about signing off on the construction of what would become the largest single building of any kind in human history. Stimson rationalized the decision of green-lighting the Pentagon that day in his diary by writing simply that it "probably would be a good thing" before devoting the rest of his entry to additional requests from the British and aircraft production problems caused by constant refinements and remodeling from engineers.[29]

Heading into the last two months of 1941, a greater proportion of Stimson and Marshall's time together, and their time with the president, was spent discussing military strategy. The secret meeting between Roosevelt and Churchill in early August on the USS *Augusta* off the waters of Newfoundland made it clear to Marshall (who attended) that the United States was embarrassingly behind the British when it came to planning efforts. This was understandable, of course, since the British had been at war for almost two years, but it nevertheless caused both men to focus much more closely on what the Army would do if suddenly thrust into war. They concluded that to do anything, they needed more of everything. Therefore, Stimson focused on making sure the country did not give away too many weapons to the British and Russians. As desperately as he wanted to see these countries succeed against Hitler, he now felt more strongly that it was his duty as secretary of war to ensure that when war came to the United States, the nation could properly defend itself.

His efforts in this regard were directed primarily toward the president, who tended to offer more to Churchill and Stalin than the War Department thought prudent. Toward the end of October, Stimson sent a three-page letter to Roosevelt in response to a request for advice on prioritizing the distribution of the four-engine bombers coming off the line between the United States, Great Britain, and the Soviet Union. Stimson used his response to relay his and Marshall's broader views on air strategy, explaining general concepts that eventually became doctrine. Stressing the importance of being able to quickly move substantial air assets to where power was needed, Stimson reminded his boss that since such areas of conflict changed constantly, a static distribution of planes between the three countries would be counterproductive.

Echoing a past lecture from Marshall to the president, Stimson also emphasized to FDR that a plane is not a "finished element" of power; only a trained crew and experienced mechanics can bring out its potential. Likening the commissioning of a plane to the commissioning of a ship, a comparison he knew Roosevelt would appreciate, Stimson suggested planes would go to waste in the hands of well-meaning but unprepared Allies.[30] Stimson closed the letter by explaining the various possibilities in each theater and how the United States would be better prepared to exploit such possibilities if it had the minimum requirement of bombers previously outlined a month earlier.[31]

With each passing week during late 1941, as news from the Eastern Front and Asia grew more ominous, the general atmosphere around the War Department grew tense, and the relative patience long extended to isolationists by both Stimson and Marshall began to wither. Less than two months before the attack on Pearl Harbor, Stimson was asked to appear before the House Committee on Foreign Affairs to answer questions related to the proposed repeal of the neutrality laws. He arrived in the committee room while Secretary of State Cordell Hull was getting badgered by a few of the isolationists on the Committee. The longer Stimson listened as he sat there, the angrier he became. In his diary that evening, he explained what happened next:

> So I sat about thirty minutes watching this performance and getting hotter and hotter all the time, making up my mind as to what I would do to those men when they turned on me—and frankly I did it up. I did so. I did them up. I didn't get on until about twenty minutes to one . . . when those pettifoggers turned on me, I ripped them up from end to end.[32]

Although Stimson thought highly of himself and was not above bragging in his diary or criticizing isolationists and other people he believed to be on the wrong side of an issue, this passage was unique in its fury. He and Marshall were fighting hard each day to strengthen the Army so that it could save the world from Nazi domination. After fifteen months on the job, his anger and disbelief with the isolationists peaked. In reacting to those men, Stimson seemed to be channeling Teddy Roosevelt. Although Roosevelt had died twenty-two years earlier, there was a part of him still present in Washington through his protégé. It is no wonder Franklin Roosevelt enjoyed having "Harry" around on occasion; the president had worshipped his distant cousin when he was a younger man, and it is likely he recognized a few of the former president's characteristics in his combative secretary of war.

Japanese Attack on Pearl Harbor

On November 25, 1941, Stimson and Marshall were in the White House along with their Naval counterparts to meet with the president at his invitation to discuss several issues related to the war in Europe. Putting the specific agenda aside, Roosevelt explained to the men that he believed the Japanese were going to attack United States interests as soon as December 1. Describing the Japanese as being famous for surprise attacks, FDR wished to discuss what could be done in general and how specifically he could "maneuver" them into firing the first shot without "allowing too much danger to ourselves." Nothing was decided, but Roosevelt's prediction seemed validated when Stimson got back to his office and heard from his intelligence sources that a Japanese expeditionary force of between forty to fifty ships was spotted leaving Shanghai and were currently south of Formosa. The countdown began.

When presented with more concrete evidence about the expeditionary force three days later, Stimson insisted on delivering it to Roosevelt in person first thing in the morning. After getting briefed by Stimson in his bed, the president said there were three options: do nothing; give a strong ultimatum to the Japanese; or attack them at once. Characteristically, Stimson replied to FDR that only the latter two were options and he personally favored fighting at once.[33]

The president suggested sending a note of warning to the emperor of Japan instead, but Stimson did not think this was a good idea ("one does not warn an Emperor," he told the president). He suggested an address to Congress instead, outlining the situation and the administration's intentions. FDR liked the idea, but he still wanted to keep open the option of sending a secret note to the emperor. The president then rushed off to Warm Springs, Georgia, to maintain a promise he had made to have Thanksgiving dinner with his fellow polio victims. Stimson took charge in organizing a team to draft an address over the weekend for FDR to deliver to Congress when he returned on Monday, December 1.

To Stimson's chagrin, the president took no action on the matter upon his return other than attempting to gather more intelligence about where and when the Japanese might attack. It was guesswork, and the list of potential locations could not be narrowed down to less than six. Stimson and Marshall continued to work on regular business for the rest of the week with an emphasis on making sure General MacArthur and his troops in the Philippines got the supplies that were currently en route to them.

The only thing that satisfied the secretary of war during this critical week was the "very warlike" atmosphere that hung over cabinet meeting on Friday, December 5. Staying in Washington for the weekend, Stimson got a horseback ride in on Saturday and wrote in his diary it might be "the last time I get one for some time." Both he and Marshall knew the Japanese were due to meet with the secretary of state the following day (Sunday, December 7), bringing along with them a reply to a series of questions and demands from the United States government. Both men also understood (from the United States having cracked the Japanese code) that the visit was timed precisely so that Japan could accomplish whatever plans it had been making.

Shortly after 1:30 p.m. on Sunday, December 7, General Marshall got a call at home from an excited colonel in the General Staff who said Pearl Harbor was under attack. After Marshall directed him to verify the information, the colonel received another more official message confirming the news. Marshall was in his office within ten minutes.

Earlier, Stimson had met with Hull and Knox from 10:30 a.m. until lunchtime, reviewing the latest intelligence (which had the Japanese advancing in the Gulf of Siam). The three men spent time discussing various potential scenarios and the actions that should follow each. The Japanese diplomats were due at the State Department at 1:00 p.m. but informed Hull they were going to be late. Stimson went to Woodley for lunch. Shortly after he arrived, he received a call from FDR asking if he had "heard the news." Stimson assumed FDR was referring to the latest Japanese movements in the Gulf of Siam and replied he had seen those reports. Roosevelt responded, "Oh, no, I don't mean that. They have attacked Hawaii. They are now bombing Hawaii!"[34]

III

FIGHTING

11

Pearl Harbor and the First Ten Weeks

I have been in constant conference with Marshall as to what we could send to the Philippines by air or before the Japanese had actually blockaded the islands. We have met with many obstacles, particularly because the Navy has been rather shaken and panic-stricken after the catastrophe at Hawaii and the complete upset of their naval strategy which depended upon that fortress. They have been willing to think of nothing except Hawaii and the restoration of the defense of that Island. They have opposed all our efforts for a counter-attack, taking the defeatist attitude that it was impossible before we even tried.

—HENRY STIMSON diary entry, December 14, 1941

I am convinced that there must be one man in command of the entire theater— air, ground, and ships. We can not manage but by cooperation. Human frailties are such that there would be emphatic unwillingness to place portions of troops under another service. If we make a plan for unified command now, it will solve nine-tenths of our troubles.[1]

—GEORGE MARSHALL to the British High Command, Arcadia Conference, December 26, 1941

Pearl Harbor

Henry Stimson's initial reaction upon hearing the news from Hawaii on December 7 was one of relief; the long period of "indecision" was over. Long the nation's most prominent interventionist, he was thrilled the country would at last be fighting for a just cause unified by a common goal. Referring to the procurement efforts to date, Stimson noted it had been an "awful task" trying to produce on a "wartime scale with a peacetime attitude." This would change immediately. In his diary that night, he wrote that with a unified country, America "has practically nothing to fear. . . ."

By contrast, George Marshall was shattered.

Considering Stimson and Marshall had been working side by side for seventeen months sharing any and all information with one another related to the war in Europe, Japanese aggression in Asia, and preparedness at home, the difference in their respective reactions seems counterintuitive. But when one factors in the differences in their personalities and professional experiences, it makes more sense.

In addition to being a more aggressive interventionist, Stimson was also more of an optimist than the chief of staff. But it was Stimson's deeper knowledge of the relative strengths of the Japanese, German, British, and United States economies (sharpened while serving in Hoover's cabinet) that provided him greater confidence than Marshall on December 7 about the ultimate outcome of a war with Japan (Germany did not declare war on the United States for another four days). After a half century representing and advising large industrial corporations in America, Stimson was able to foresee far more clearly than his partner could the rapid and massive industrial buildup that was about to take place within the country. It was a combination of these factors that explains why there is no evidence Henry Stimson panicked on December 7 or in the days immediately following.

Marshall, having little knowledge about global economic matters, was stunned into what his wife described as a "grim and gray" expression.[2] He said nothing to her when he came home that night except that he was tired and was going to bed.

To be fair to Marshall, the pressure on him was enormous; the buck stopped at his desk when it came to the military affairs of the Army. And it could not have helped his spirits that he had been convinced that Pearl Harbor was sufficiently defended. More crucially, he was now in charge of a wartime army still far from prepared. His nightmare had become a reality.

In one capacity or another, George Marshall had spent the previous twenty-three years (since the end of World War I) trying to keep the Army prepared for a war General Fox Conner warned him twenty years earlier would certainly come. The news from Pearl Harbor was a final blow to any hope he might still have clung to that his Army would be ready.

President Theodore Roosevelt's informal "tennis cabinet" on the White House lawn, March 1909. Stimson, who was a protégé and good friend of TR since 1894, is seventh from left. *Courtesy of the Library of Congress.*

In 1903, Stimson acquired "Highhold," a one hundred acre estate in a remote and rural part of Long Island approximately eight miles east of 'Sagamore Hill', his mentor Teddy Roosevelt's house just outside Oyster Bay. Stimson wanted no part of the Gatsby-style mansions the wealthy were building along the Long Island Sound. A cousin of his designed the large but unostentatious house and he and his wife spent most weekends there for the next forty-two years until he retired there after World War II. *Courtesy of Yale University Library.*

Henry L. Stimson turned forty-three years old in 1910. Educated at Yale and Harvard Law School, he had been a U.S. Attorney for the Southern District of New York and would run for governor of New York that year. Thirty-five more years of influential service to his country lay ahead. *Courtesy of the Library of Congress.*

Despite initial reluctance out of loyalty to Theodore Roosevelt, Henry Stimson agreed to become secretary of war to President William Howard Taft. He served from 1911 to 1913, during which time he was caught in the middle of the dramatic fallout between Taft and Roosevelt that split the Republican party. *Courtesy of the Library of Congress.*

George Marshall earned wide acclaim within the U.S. Army for his staff work during World War I and earned the great respect of Gen. John "Black Jack" Pershing, for whom he served as aide-de-camp for the five years following the war, the longest assignment of his career until World War II. *Courtesy of the George C. Marshall Foundation.*

Stimson was in the Midwest promoting preparedness when Congress declared war on Germany in April 1917. He rushed home, received a commission, and reported to duty on June 1. Through hard work and connections, he was appointed to the Field Artillery and sent to France before Christmas to train. He was fifty years old. Prior to being sent towards the front to fire shells at the enemy, his most challenging instructor at the General Staff School in Langres he attended was a 37-year-old captain in the army named George C. Marshall. The two rode horses and lunched together for the nine days Marshall taught at the school. *Courtesy of Yale University Library.*

Stimson served as secretary of state for the four years of Herbert Hoover's administration. Here he is pictured with the president and Secretary of the Navy Charles F. Adams III (second from right) around the time of the London Naval Conference. *Courtesy of the Library of Congress.*

Woodley Mansion, the Washington, D.C., home of the Stimsons from 1929 to 1950. Previous residents included Martin Van Buren, Grover Cleveland, and Gen. George S. Patton. Today it still stands within the grounds of the Maret School. *Courtesy of the Library of Congress.*

General Marshall is sworn in as U.S. Army Chief of Staff on September 1, 1939, by sheer coincidence the day World War II began in Europe. *Courtesy of the Library of Congress.*

During his first two years as chief of staff (until Pearl Harbor was attacked), one of Marshall's primary responsibilities was seeking greater defense spending. Here he appears with a member of Congress responsible for House appropriations. *Courtesy of the Library of Congress.*

George Marshall called Dodona Manor in Leesburg, Virginia, home from 1941 until his death in 1959. But during the War, he and his wife spent precious little time there (it was forty miles from Washington, D.C.), living instead at Quarters One, the residence for chiefs of staff at Fort Myer in Virginia, less than three miles from the Pentagon. *Courtesy of the Library of Congress.*

Partners in command Marshall and Stimson standing between the doorway that was always left open between their offices at the Pentagon. *Courtesy George C. Marshall Foundation of Lexington, Virginia.*

Flanked by Lt. Gen. Jacob Devers, commander of the U.S. Army's European theater of operations, and Maj. Gen. Ira Eaker, head of the U.S. Eighth Air Force, Stimson reviews bombing photographs at the Eighth's base in England, July 1943. *Courtesy of the National Archives.*

Stimson meets with the legendary Maj. Gen. James Doolittle, commander of the Northwest African Strategic Air Force, 1943. *Courtesy of the National Archives.*

General Marshall and Gen. Carl Spaatz, at the time commander of the U.S. Twelfth Air Force, chat at the Quebec Conference. *Courtesy of the Harry S. Truman Library and Museum.*

At the Cairo Conference in late 1943, American military commanders meet to debate and develop strategy. Adm. William Leahy, chief of staff to the commander in chief and head of the U.S. Joint Chiefs, sits at the head of the table while Marshall and Adm. Ernest King, chief of naval operations, have a back-and-forth. *Courtesy of the Harry S. Truman Library and Museum.*

Field Marshal Sir John Dill headed the British military mission in the United States during World War II and had an unusually close relationship with Marshall. It was Dill, seen here with Marshall in 1944 receiving an honorary degree from William & Mary, who acted as a critical bridge between the Americans and British during the War. The degree was one of several arranged by Marshall to impress Winston Churchill of Dill's importance to the Americans. *Courtesy of the National Archives.*

Marshall and other Americans leaders, including President Roosevelt at Yalta in February 1945, just two months before FDR's death. It was not until shortly after Pearl Harbor that Marshall concluded Roosevelt was a great man. *Courtesy of the Library of Congress.*

Gen. Dwight Eisenhower returns to the United States for a hero's welcome, June 1945. Marshall accompanies him in a Jeep in Washington, D.C. *Courtesy of the Harry S. Truman Library and Museum.*

Stimson, Secretary of State Edward Stettinius, and Secretary of the Navy James Forrestal at the White House after meeting with President Truman a week after the death of Franklin Roosevelt. *Courtesy of the Harry S. Truman Library and Museum.*

Stimson and General Eisenhower part on the tarmac in Germany, July 1945. Stimson was on his way home from the Potsdam Conference after having failed to convince Truman to reconsider the unconditional terms of surrender demanded by the Americans of the Japanese. *Courtesy of the National Archives.*

Stimson (right) reviews the 2nd Armored Division during the Potsdam Conference. Left to right are Maj. Gen. Floyd Parks, Gen. George Patton, Stimson's aide Col. William Kyle, Assistant Secretary of War John McCloy, and Stimson's special assistant Harvey Bundy. *Courtesy of the Harry S. Truman Library and Museum.*

Depending on his mood, Stimson referred to Robert Lovett and John McCloy, two of the four core Stimson advisors during World War II, as either the "Heavenly Twins" or the "Imps of Satan." Both men were highly regarded in Washington during the War and each became, like their mentor, a "Wise Man" in the post-war period advising presidents from Truman to Reagan when they were not serving in various high level government or private positions. *Courtesy of Yale University Library.*

The second week of August 1945 was a pivotal one for the War, with the dropping of the atomic bombs and waiting for Japan's surrender. Here, an exhausted Stimson, a month from turning seventy-eight years old, arrives at the White House for a meeting with President Truman. *Courtesy of the National Archives.*

President Truman displays the Japanese surrender documents while Forrestal, Stimson, and Marshall look on, September 1945. *Courtesy of the Harry S. Truman Library and Museum.*

On Stimson's last day as secretary of war (his seventy-eighth birthday), Marshall surprised him by gathering together 120 generals, Stimson's staff, and an Army band to greet Stimson and his wife as their car pulled onto the tarmac for their flight to their home on Long Island. Stimson would later write that he was at that time "on the eve of an emotional and coronary breakdown." *Courtesy of the Harry S. Truman Library and Museum.*

Truman congratulates Marshall on his retirement as chief of staff in November 1945 and awards him the Distinguished Service Medal at a ceremony in the courtyard of the Pentagon attended by an estimated twenty thousand military and civilian War Department officials. The entire ceremony lasted just fourteen minutes before Marshall and his wife happily drove off to their home in Leesburg to enjoy a long planned retirement. Later that same day, Truman telephoned Marshall and recruited him for an assignment in China. He would later serve as Truman's secretary of state and secretary of defense. *Courtesy of the Harry S. Truman Library and Museum.*

RETIRED STATESMAN Henry L. Stimson turned 80 on Sept. 21 and celebrated by giving a buffet supper at his Huntington, N.Y. estate for 19 close friends, who helped direct top U.S. strategy in World War II. As they gathered for this historic portrait their host, who served in three U.S. Cabinets between 1911 and 1945, announced that for once in his life he was free of protocol, placed his friends where he wanted them. The arrangement: (*seated, left to right*) Air Force Chief of Staff Carl Spaatz; General Eisenhower; Secretary of the Army Kenneth Royall; Secretary of State Marshall; Mr. Stimson; Secretary of Defense Forrestal; ex-Secretary of War Robert Patterson; Under Secretary of State Robert Lovett; Lieut. General Courtney Hodges; (*standing*) Major General Alexander Surles (ret.); Stimson War Aides Harvey Bundy and William Kyle; Major General Norman Kirk (retired Surgeon General); wartime Supply Chief Lieut. General Brehon Somervell; Atomic Engineering Consultant George Harrison; Far East Expert Major General Frank McCoy (ret.); Wartime Civilian Consultant Arthur Page; Manpower Expert Goldthwaite Dorr; former Stimson Law Partner Allen Klots, and McGeorge Bundy, Mr. Stimson's present secretary.

Knowing he was on borrowed time due to a shaky heart, Stimson invited a highly select group of his former colleagues to Highhold for his eightieth birthday. For the photo, he specifically put Marshall on his right, the place of honor. *Courtesy of Yale University Library.*

Irrespective of their contrasting emotions on that Sunday morning, both men had valid reasons to be depressed by the events in Oahu and other regions of the Pacific. The strategy Stimson and Marshall jointly agreed to for protecting American interests in the Pacific relied on the U.S. fleet. With a good portion of it destroyed on Battleship Row, both men knew their plans to defend the Philippines—plans they had worked on feverishly during the weeks prior to the attack—were severely if not fatally jeopardized. Any hope that the military and diplomatic consequences of losing the Philippines could be avoided went up in smoke when half of Douglas MacArthur's planes were destroyed on the ground shortly after the air attack on Pearl Harbor.

Compounding the distress of every ranking military official that Sunday, but particularly George Marshall, was the stark realization that the Japanese had caught the Army sleeping. Marshall was a deceptively proud man, and any potential blow to his legacy would have hit him hard. It was his army that was caught by surprise, and he must have punished himself thinking back to what he could have done differently.

That the Japanese attacked the United States without warning was not surprising; they drew up the move from a well-thumbed playbook familiar to American planners (the Japanese undertook surprise attacks on Russia in 1904 and Manchuria in 1931). Stimson worried for over a decade Japan might pull off a surprise attack on the country.[3] *When* the Japanese attacked was not unexpected, either; for over a week before the first wave of Zeros was launched in the direction of Pearl Harbor, the feeling in both the White House and the War Department was that an attack could take place at any moment.[4] But *where* the attack took place—that was quite a shock.

For several years, the Army had considered Pearl Harbor a possible Japanese military target worthy of focused study. In early 1938, the War Department concluded a survey by stating that in the event hostilities broke out with Japan, "there can be little doubt the Hawaiian Islands will be the initial scene of action."[5] Given this, Marshall paid close attention to the risk throughout 1940, even issuing a specific warning to his staff eighteen months before the attack that Oahu could be a likely target. Eight months later, he instructed the new Army commander in Hawaii that "the fullest protection of the fleet is *the* rather than *a* major consideration for us."[6]

But not long thereafter, the chief of staff and other military and civilian officials became increasingly convinced that any surprise strike from the Japanese would take place in the Far East instead. Japanese intelligence did an excellent job in steadily shepherding Marshall's planners, intelligence, and others toward that conclusion. Thailand, Singapore, Malaya, the Philippines, and the Dutch East Indies became greater areas of concern. When it was learned in late November 1941 that a Japanese force was heading by sea in a southerly direction from Shanghai, it only strengthened their conviction.

Speculation aside, Marshall had assured himself during these months that Pearl Harbor was safe. He did not believe the Japanese would ever risk attacking a target so far from home knowing the U.S. Army Air Forces would put up a substantial fight with its heavy bombers and its quality pursuit planes. Additionally, he was given further comfort a month prior to the attack when he received a report revealing that the radar system established on Oahu was working perfectly.[7] In case of an attack, troops would have time to prepare themselves.

The Navy had once feared a raid on Pearl Harbor as well. In the fall of 1940, Admiral James Richardson (then commander in chief, United States Fleet) risked his command by aggressively arguing with Roosevelt and other politicians against FDR's decision to redeploy the Pacific fleet from San Diego to Pearl Harbor. Richardson, an acknowledged expert on naval battles in the Pacific and Japanese warfare strategies, was convinced Pearl Harbor was not only the logical target for the Japanese to attack, but also, due to the physical layout of the harbor, impossible for America to defend.[8] But Roosevelt insisted that America's first line of defense be moved farther west from San Diego and fired the stubborn Richardson in February 1941. His replacement, Admiral Husband Kimmel, did not seem to share his predecessor's concerns.

Obviously, the successful strike on Pearl Harbor by the Japanese was the result of a major U.S. intelligence failure, and it did not take long before government officials began asking questions. When FDR finally got around to briefing a select group of congressional leaders in his office late on the night of December 7, Tom Connally, chairman of the Senate Foreign Relations Committee, broke a long silence that followed the president's description of the day's events by asking the question Henry Stimson believed was on the mind of everyone else in the room: How was it possible the United States was caught napping?[9]

Dozens of books have attempted to answer this question over the years, some serious, others less so. The more fanciful and conspiratorial of those have suggested there was no surprise at the highest levels of the American government on December 7. According to this view, Roosevelt—in cahoots with Marshall and his naval counterpart, Admiral Stark—not only enticed the Japanese to attack Pearl Harbor, but also knew when the attack would take place. In pursuing this strategy, the theory suggests FDR assumed a shocked and angered American public would immediately insist on war with Japan, which in turn would lead to war with Hitler. There were variations on this idea as it relates to the number of people in on the scheme (Stimson was occasionally mentioned among the accomplices), but the common narrative was that Roosevelt was the mastermind behind it.

To accept this general hypothesis, a number of questionable assumptions must be taken, a few of which seem as inconceivable now as then: First, Roosevelt had to be willing to sacrifice his beloved fleet, a couple thousand Navy men, hundreds of planes, and an Army garrison; second, he had to arrange that certain information was withheld from various commanders in Hawaii; third, he had to make sure General Marshall and his counterpart in the Navy were in on the plan or at least AWOL in the hours before the attack to ensure any information obtained through last-minute intelligence reports would not get forwarded by them to Oahu in time to properly warn the local commanders; and finally, FDR had to risk kissing off American interests in the Pacific, the protection of which was supported by his naval forces in Hawaii.

Of all the improbable arguments put forward to support this theory, the least credible one is that Roosevelt persuaded General George C. Marshall to go along with the gambit. There was simply nothing in Marshall's record or character indicating this was possible, nor any evidence uncovered that backs it up. Every major figure of the era interviewed on the subject dismissed the theory as absurd.

But this does not mean Marshall was absolved from responsibility for the disaster. On the contrary, he is one of several individuals whose actions or lack of actions during the hours, days, weeks, and months preceding the attack helped contribute to the debacle.

Most of the criticism leveled against Marshall for Pearl Harbor during the War, and in the retrospective studies following it, focused on the days and hours just before the attack. At the direction of Congress, the Army investigated Pearl Harbor shortly after it occurred and published its report in late 1944 (the Navy was asked to undertake a similar investigation). The Army report placed most of the blame on General Walter Short, the top army commander in Hawaii. But the report also censured Marshall for failing to keep General Short sufficiently informed of the Japanese threat in the weeks before the attack, and especially so on December 6 and 7 after it became apparent an attack by the Japanese was imminent somewhere in the Pacific. The Army also faulted Marshall for failing to follow up with General Short on a specific warning and instruction Marshall sent him in late November (after it became apparent Short had not fully understood the instruction nor carried it out properly).

After the report was released, Henry Stimson recruited his aides to assist him in pouring over its details. He drafted a lengthy statement supporting the report's criticism of Short but took strong issue with any recriminations on the chief of staff.[10] Despite his effort, when a Joint Committee of Congress issued its own report following the War, it agreed with the Army's view that Marshall (and his naval counterpart) could have done better in the weeks and hours before the attack in getting various warnings to the top commanders in Hawaii and following up on those warnings.

Most of the blame for Pearl Harbor can be attributed to the Army and Navy commanders in Hawaii. Their job was to jointly protect the fleet from an attack. Although a vast majority of high-ranking military and diplomatic officials believed the Japanese would first strike in the Far East, the records show that both Marshall and his naval counterpart sent proper warnings to their respective commanders on Oahu. Marshall simultaneously issued nearly identical warnings and instructions to commanders in San Francisco, the Canal Zone, and the Philippines, and all three locations promptly went on full alert.

Marshall himself believed his Hawaiian commander was culpable, and the chief of staff was not one to throw people under a bus without valid reasons. He had known Walter Short for over thirty years before assigning him command at Pearl Harbor and respected his abilities. Short's record in the First World War was excellent, he had command experience between the wars, and Marshall was impressed with his work as assistant commandant at Fort Benning. But following the War's end, when Marshall finally had enough time to carefully read all the reports, he concluded Short was derelict in not following the instructions given to him to have his troops on alert against an attack from the Japanese. More specifically, Marshall blamed him for not communicating better with the Navy, not having his planes ready and on full alert, and not running radar twenty-four hours a day.

Regarding the issue of interservice communication, most historians agree that the lack of cooperation—and therefore coordination—between the Army and Navy was one factor behind the disaster at Pearl Harbor. But this was not Short's fault alone. Although he and his naval counterpart (Admiral Husband Kimmel) got along personally, the traditional hostility between the Army and Navy would have made it difficult for these two men and their staffs to effectively share information and coordinate activities. Given what was going on in Asia, the long-standing animosity between the branches should have been set aside, and the initiative for that should have come from the top commanders in each location. Marshall specifically warned Short upon giving him command that Admiral Kimmel was known to be difficult to work with, but advised him to be the better man given the importance of the job in the existing global environment. Had Short followed this advice, the various attack warnings received would have been shared between the two services and would have been taken more seriously by both. There would also have been no mistaken assumptions about which branch was responsible for doing what during the days and hours leading up to the attack. Finally, there would have generally been a more coordinated approach to the defense of the fleet.

Although Short and Kimmel have been saddled with the lion's share of the blame for the disaster on December 7, several of the top military officials' actions or inactions during the period leading up to the Japanese attack were vulnerable to criticism from investigators during the War, congressional probers just after it, and historians since. When it comes to military preparedness and the issuing of proper warnings, it can always be argued in hindsight that more could have been done.

When it came to evaluating George Marshall in this regard, one consistent focus of inquiry related to a package sent to his attention on December 6 containing a translation of a critical Japanese intercept. The deciphered and translated communiqué was sent by the foreign office in Tokyo to its Washington-based representatives notifying them in advance of a fourteen-part answer to the "Hull Note," which would be delivered to the United States the following day (the Hull Note was a November 26 counterproposal sent by Secretary of State Cordell Hull to his Japanese counterpart outlining various conditions the United States needed Japan to meet before it could conclude a peaceful agreement with them on the issues separating both countries). The contents of the aggressive reply by the Japanese to Secretary Hull—specifically the fourteenth part of the message stating that further negotiations between the two countries were now impossible—left little doubt war was at hand.

The initial problem for Marshall (and others) was one of timing; only the first thirteen parts of the message were deciphered by 10:00 p.m. Eastern Standard Time on Saturday, December 6. The critical fourteenth part was not available until the following morning. Given this, a member of

Marshall's staff decided it was not necessary for the general to see any section of the message until it was complete.[11] By the time the fourteenth part was deciphered and translated early the following morning, Marshall was on his customary Sunday horseback ride, unaware that even the first thirteen parts had been delivered.

Unfortunately, a second Japanese intercept translated that morning was also sent to Marshall's attention while he was riding. This message from Tokyo instructed the Japanese negotiators in Washington to hold off delivering the fourteen-part message to Secretary Hull until 1:00 p.m. Eastern Standard Time. This implied that if a surprise attack were to occur, it would take place at or just before that time (which happened to be 8:00 a.m. in Hawaii).

At a time when every minute counted, Marshall's fifty-minute horseback ride helped contribute to a delay of approximately two hours between when a message could have gone out and when it was finally delivered to the office of General Short in Hawaii. The other factors were as follows: First, a security protocol put in place to protect the secret that the Japanese code had been cracked prevented several of Marshall's subordinates from reading the contents of the message themselves. Had they, they would have made it a priority to find Marshall or otherwise send out warnings themselves under his signature; second, when Marshall finally began reading the lengthy Japanese reply, one of his subordinates failed to draw his attention to the critical fourteenth part of it. Had he, Marshall would likely not have bothered to go back to read the rest of the message; third, the regular Army communication channel was not working that morning. This caused a delay, and the message was sent out by commercial telegraph instead;[12] finally, of the three locations to which Marshall directed the warning, he prioritized Pearl Harbor third (behind the Philippines and the Panama Canal Zone). This caused further delays as the Army could only send out one message at a time. The net result was that by the time the message was delivered into the hands of General Short in Hawaii, Japanese Zeros were already dropping their bombs.

Given that Marshall had been in charge of the Army for over two and a half years, he certainly shares in the blame for it being surprised at Pearl Harbor, but not necessarily for the reasons cited above. Henry Stimson's view from the start about the primary underlying failure at Pearl Harbor was straightforward: It was because neither the Army (Marshall included) nor the Navy fully understood or appreciated the extent to which airpower had developed since World War I. Stimson doubted anybody in either service anticipated that the Japanese would or could make a successful attack by air.[13] Robert Lovett said after the War that there was very little appreciation in 1941 for the strategic use of airpower within the United States military.[14]

Although Stimson and Lovett had a point, there were miscommunications, misjudgments, and mistakes within the Army, among Marshall's staff, and by the chief of staff himself that influenced the events of December 6 and 7. One of the major ones, long overlooked as a contribution to the disaster, was Marshall's delay in reorganizing the Army during the first two and half years of his tenure as chief of staff. Although he had sound reasons to delay a major reorganization, many of these smaller missteps might have been avoided if he hadn't.

War: The First Ten Weeks

With all hands on deck following the attack on Pearl Harbor, Stimson and Marshall spent the next forty-eight hours leading efforts to protect Hawaii, the West Coast, and the Philippines, locations vulnerable to Japanese attacks.

The nation had long relied on the fleet in Hawaii to protect the West Coast. After the attack, this defense strategy was dealt a huge blow. The Army needed more planes sent there to replace the losses and to protect what ships were still afloat.

The two men also organized the placement of military planes around critical aircraft plants lying between Seattle and San Diego and in Connecticut and New Jersey. In many cases, the planes being sent were coming straight off the assembly line, where they had been earmarked for the British. Believing his current needs trumped those of Churchill, Stimson met with the president to get his permission to take for himself the production of planes reserved for the Lend-Lease program. FDR acquiesced, after which Stimson advised Marshall to move ahead with the plan.[15]

With the immediate security concerns addressed over the first few days, Stimson and Marshall turned their attention to an unprecedented volume of issues that began sweeping into their offices over the next few weeks. It was not just that they were preparing to go to war on the opposite side of the world against one of the most formidable and impassioned armies ever assembled; they were simultaneously gearing up for a second war against an even more powerful army across the Atlantic (Germany declared war on the United States four days after Pearl Harbor). Despite their best efforts, they were forced by events to undertake the struggle with a wholly unprepared and inadequately supplied army against two enemies who had been arming themselves for years and had battle-tested troops in the field. And it was not just the ground on four continents Stimson and Marshall had to prepare to attack or defend, but the airspace above it as well (the Air Force was attached to the U.S. Army during World War II). The scale of problems related to the above, coupled with all the conventional issues faced when going to war, was staggering. Never before have the civilian and military heads of an army been faced with the sheer vastness and complexity of problems that confronted the two men in late 1941 and early 1942. Although both men could draw on the lessons learned from World War I, this was different. The advent of airpower, the dramatic evolution of the tank, and the adoption of new tactics related to both had changed the nature of war dramatically over two decades. Adaptation was essential.

Fortunately for America, the outstanding teamwork between Stimson and Marshall, honed over the previous seventeen months as they bonded against the common enemy of isolationism, was firing on all cylinders during the first ten weeks following the attack on Pearl Harbor. All the work related to the buildup of men and materials continued (and of course accelerated dramatically), but war immediately brought a host of new challenges to the Army they went about trying to solve together: During the first two weeks, the two men worked on establishing and maintaining harmony with the Navy (still in shock over its losses in Hawaii), amending the Selective Service and Training Act, discussing reorganization requirements, pushing for a unity-of-command concept when it came to working with both the Navy and the British, and making suggestions and decisions related to the placement of troops and equipment in Iceland, Ireland, Russia, and West Africa; during weeks three and four, they hosted Churchill and his top men in Washington for lengthy planning and coordination discussions, dealt with the continued landings by the Japanese in the Philippines, balanced the weapon requests coming from the British, the Russians, the Chinese, and their own commanders, and began contemplating the landing of their own troops in North Africa to fight the Germans; in weeks five and six, they continued to host the British (who stayed in Washington for three weeks), fought the Navy and Roosevelt for ships promised but not delivered, and grappled with the issue of African American soldiers in the Army; in weeks seven and eight, they debated organizational issues with both Great Britain and the U.S. Navy, dealt with those South American countries who wanted and needed protection, and contemplated the importance of making loans to China; and in weeks nine and ten, they balanced massive supply requirements with antitrust regulations, and began thinking of how to deal with potentially disruptive American citizens of Japanese heritage located on the West Coast. Most of these issues could not be solved overnight but were discussed continuously as the War evolved during the three months after Pearl Harbor.

No single-volume book on the wartime partnership of Henry Stimson and George Marshall could adequately cover all the issues and problems faced by both men together. Stimson's diary runs well over four thousand pages from when he joined the War Department in July 1940 to his resignation three weeks after the formal surrender of Japan (and bear in mind, his stated objective and practice during the War was to deal with only the most important issues). As the Second World War withdraws steadily back in time, it is easier for historians to separate the large issues these two men faced from the even larger ones. The remainder of this book will focus on how Stimson and Marshall worked together as a team to manage the latter.

The Philippines

On the third day following the Japanese attack, Stimson was called into the White House by FDR and asked to bring Marshall with him to join their counterparts from the Navy and a few other senior naval officers. Although a number of critical issues were discussed, the key purpose of the meeting was to decide whether a convoy heading for the Philippines by way of Australia with much-needed supplies for General MacArthur (U.S. commander of all Army forces in the Southwest Pacific Area) should have been recalled at the suggestion of Naval leaders who believed there was little chance any convoy could get past the Japanese defenses.

To the great surprise and satisfaction of both Stimson and Marshall, the president reversed the decision and ordered the convoy to continue advancing toward its destination. Neither man was under the illusion that the decision was going to save America's principal strategic possession in the Far East; Japanese dominance throughout the region in the days after Pearl Harbor confirmed it was simply a matter of time before the Philippines fell. But when it came to making decisions related to the archipelago, they believed military factors should be subordinated to political and moral considerations. Making a concerted effort was not only the right thing to do, but also necessary to prevent a decline in the overall perception and position of the United States within Asia and around the world.

In early February 1942, with the situation seemingly hopeless, President Quezon of the Philippines suggested the Islands be neutralized and made independent if no further military support could be rendered from the United States. Bitter at what he perceived to be little help from the United States and Great Britain, Quezon proposed inviting Japan and the United States to withdraw their troops from the Philippines. This proposal was worrisome enough for Stimson and Marshall, but what was worse was the apparent endorsement of the suggestion by MacArthur (Stimson wrote at the time that MacArthur went "more than half-way" toward supporting Quezon).

In MacArthur's defense, it was a difficult proposal to dismiss outright; the lives of fifteen thousand American soldiers were at stake. With the popular and politically powerful MacArthur neutral at best on Quezon's proposal, Stimson and Marshall were on edge when they brought the message to the White House on February 9. FDR read it carefully and then asked Marshall for a recommendation. Marshall deferred to Stimson to make the arguments against it.

To make his points crystal clear, Stimson decided to stand "as if before the court" and outline them carefully to Roosevelt. To his and Marshall's great relief, the commander in chief immediately and emphatically agreed that the United States should fight to the last man in the Philippines. It was at that moment, Marshall recalled fifteen years later, he first realized Franklin Roosevelt was a great man.[16]

With Roosevelt's support, the War Department did what they could for the Philippines throughout the Japanese siege of the Islands, but it was a losing proposition. By the end of February, it was decided that MacArthur was too valuable an asset to be either killed or captured, so he was ordered to leave the Philippines for Australia to take command of the U.S. forces in the Far East. MacArthur escaped by boat with his family and seventeen members of his staff on March 11. The remaining troops he left behind held out for a few more weeks before surrendering to the Japanese in early April on the Bataan Peninsula. It was these soldiers (approximately fifteen thousand Americans among them) who suffered terribly at the hands of the Japanese during the ensuing Bataan Death March.

The British Invasion of Washington (December 22, 1941–January 14, 1942)

Winston Churchill first heard about the Japanese attack on Pearl Harbor while entertaining Americans John Winant (U.S. Ambassador to the Court of St. James) and Averell Harriman (FDR's special representative) at

Chequers, the country house retreat of British prime ministers. He immediately called Roosevelt and invited himself to Washington, D.C., with his staff to discuss overall strategy. Within a week, he and his men boarded a ship bound for Hampton Roads, Virginia.

Upon arrival, Churchill and his staff proceeded to Washington for the conference (code named *Arcadia*), where FDR, Stimson, and Marshall were awaiting them, unaware they were about to receive an education on how one wages a modern war. Churchill and his men, well into their third year fighting the Germans, arrived extremely well-organized and far better prepared than their hosts for high-level strategic discussions.

It was not just the experience built up from fighting the Nazis that separated the British from the Americans during *Arcadia*; the art of war was simply more entrenched within the British psyche, having been built up campaign after campaign for more than a millennium. Leaders throughout the island's history were required to have at least a base degree of military knowledge to successfully guard against the repeated threats from both within and outside the realm. The collective learning curve only steepened for British leaders once they began building and defending their global empire toward the end of the sixteenth century. Skills in organization, communications, strategy, espionage, and constructing alliances were all honed during numerous wars and campaigns before being passed on to succeeding generations.

The Americans had no such comparable history. Yes, they fought alongside Great Britain and France during the First World War, but they arrived late into that conflict (three full years after it began) and spent less than six months actually fighting (from their first major battle at Cantigny). Before that, one had to go back to the Civil War to find a time when American military leaders were undertaking wide-scale strategic thinking.

At the very apex of the combined leadership group gathered in Washington, the British experience was also dominant. Winston Churchill was a military man to the core. At the age of fourteen, he enrolled in the Army Class at Harrow, a program designed for gaining entrance to Sandhurst, the Royal Military College (where he ended up graduating just outside the top 5 percent of his class). Churchill served twenty-seven years in the military (if one includes his years as first lord of the admiralty, minister of munitions, secretary of state for war, and secretary of state for air) and fought in two wars. When he wasn't fighting, he was writing about war, either as a correspondent or a published military historian. In his passion for the martial life, he was the British version of Teddy Roosevelt, once writing, "Nothing is so exhilarating in life as to be shot at with no result." It had to have been daunting for most of the Americans to sit across the table from a man with such a combination of enthusiasm and experience.

Stimson was quite familiar with the prime minister, a well-known international figure for many years. He and his wife read aloud Churchill's autobiography to one another in the early 1930s as well as another book the prolific writer published about one of his wartime adventures. In February 1932, while on a lecturing tour in the United States, Churchill called on then Secretary of State Stimson at his Washington office. Among the topics discussed was Japanese aggression in the Far East. Stimson wrote in his diary that Churchill, whom he noted for his pragmatic qualities, expressed a desire for the fleets of Great Britain and the United States to stand together in Asia. A natural strategist and long-term planner, Churchill explained to Stimson during that meeting that if their two nations worked together, the Japanese threat could be managed in the future.

The two men had much in common: Each came from prominent affluent families (albeit Churchill was a bona fide aristocrat); each were men of action and veterans of World War I; each had experience administering colonies; and each had managed their respective country's War Departments. More significantly, they were both committed antifascists during the late 1930s and the principal voices on either side of the Atlantic against the dangers of Hitler and Nazism. Stimson greatly admired the prime minister for the courage and doggedness he displayed against the Germans during the Battle of Britain.

George Marshall was less enamored with the prime minister. Prior to the conference organized by Churchill and the president in Newfoundland four months before Pearl Harbor, he had met the Englishman only once. Shortly after the end of World War I, Marshall was assigned as Churchill's personal escort on the London leg of the European celebratory tour that Pershing and his staff took before heading back to the United States. In that capacity, Marshall spent the entire day with the future prime minister. His first impression was not recorded, but given the contrast in the two men's backgrounds and personalities, it was likely negative. Marshall's view of Churchill at that time and between the wars was colored by the unfavorable attitude other American military officers (particularly Army intelligence officers) held for both Churchill and the British military. Although Marshall respected his fellow officers and their opinions, Stimson eventually persuaded him that Churchill was a formidable man, a fighter, and a strong leader. Given the weight Marshall gave to morale building as a key component of leadership, it is likely he would have come to the same conclusion on his own before Pearl Harbor.

Anticipating that Churchill and his top brass were going to arrive in Washington fully organized and in general agreement with one another, Marshall and Stimson were afraid to dive too deep into strategic issues with their guests. Not only were the Americans less prepared in general, but they were also far less united in their opinions on strategy. To be fair, only two weeks had passed since they entered the War, but their lack of consensus was also due to several other factors ranging from Roosevelt's command style to the history of jealousy and distrust between the Army and the Navy. With each regional theater offering different opportunities and challenges for land, sea, and air forces respectively, simply more time was needed by the Americans to get everyone on the same page.

One general issue settled quickly between the Allies was how to prioritize the two principal enemies. The British wanted to deal with Germany first. Although they thought the concept needed to be aggressively sold to their hosts (given that the Japanese had struck first blood against the United States), the Americans had come to the same conclusion long before the British arrived.[17] With little opposition, therefore, all parties agreed Germany should be defeated first before the two nations turned their full resources against the Japanese. Until then, the two Allies would maintain a defensive posture in the Pacific.

How to defeat the Germans was another matter. The Americans, led by Marshall and backed aggressively by Stimson, desired that once enough men and materials were gathered in the south of England, the Allies should go straight for the jugular and attack the Germans across the Channel in France. For Marshall, this seemed like a well-tested approach to winning a major war. For Henry Stimson, the strategy simply reflected his nature. "He was a frontal man," said John McCloy in discussing the attitude of his boss on the subject years later, "a fellow who believed in going right up to the parapet."[18]

As firm as Stimson and Marshall were for prioritizing a cross-Channel attack, the British were opposed in 1942. Churchill pushed for a plan that leaned more toward death to Germany by a thousand cuts. His ideas on how to defeat the Nazis combined a mixture of strategies, including bombardment by air, blockade by sea, espionage, and propaganda. Boots on the ground would only be deployed to fight around the edges of the Nazi juggernaut until the Third Reich was weakened enough to risk a frontal attack.

Churchill had already outlined these ideas to the Americans at the Atlantic Conference held in Placentia Bay off Newfoundland in August

1941. Sharpening his arguments in the ensuing five months, the prime minister explained in Washington that such a strategy had the ancillary benefit of giving American industry time to ramp up. He also believed executing one paramount attack in France would limit the Allies' options; he wanted to adopt a more flexible approach allowing for improvisation as events unfolded and the German military's strengths and weaknesses were better illuminated.

Glaringly behind Churchill's strategy and his opposition to a cross-Channel invasion was something else; he was frightened. For all his bellicosity and "let the muskets flame!" rhetoric, he was terrified at the thought of British corpses littering the beaches of France. He was not alone in these fears; his generation had directly experienced the appalling results of large-scale frontal assaults in a modern war. Although the American military leaders were aware of the British and French casualty statistics of World War I battles such as Passchendaele and the Somme, they could never fully comprehend, as Churchill or British officers could, the utter horror of those engagements. Hastings Ismay, a member of the British Chiefs of Staff Committee and close friend of Churchill's, said after the War the British High Command was "frankly terrified" of the prospect of a cross-Channel invasion and should have come right out and stated this to the Americans at *Arcadia*. He cited July 1, 1916 (the first day of the Battle of the Somme) as justification enough for their caution, given the sixty thousand casualties the British suffered that day.[19]

None of the American leaders had spent the last quarter century living with constant reminders of the "Lost Generation" that haunted men from the British upper class (a class that suffered disproportionally larger losses than any other class in Great Britain).[20] Churchill once remarked to John McCloy that every time he entered the House of Commons after World War I, he thought about the great many people who were not there, the best and brightest of his generation, killed during the First World War leading troops over the top.[21] This was clearly a factor driving his and his colleague's strategic thinking at *Arcadia*.

Preferring to avoid the Nazis' best troops and most secure supply lines, the British brought with them to Washington a plan code-named *Gymnast* involving a landing in French Northwest Africa together with a corollary plan code-named *Super-Gymnast* calling for an American landing at Casablanca on the Atlantic coast.

After much debate, Marshall and Stimson went along with this plan but only reluctantly; particularly Stimson, who not only disagreed with it but was appalled by Churchill's description of corpses at Passchendaele and his fears for the same in the English Channel. He told Felix Frankfurter this was no way for a war leader to talk.[22]

Roosevelt was more enthusiastic about the British initiatives. Somewhat of a savant when it came to understanding the pulse of his constituents, FDR knew they would want to see American soldiers fighting far sooner than a cross-Channel invasion could be organized and launched. Marshall, earlier than Stimson, learned not to second-guess Roosevelt's political acumen. He explained to Forrest Pogue years later that he eventually decided the president was right at *Arcadia* because in a democracy, even during war, the leader needs to "keep the people entertained." Unlike Stimson, Marshall also saw some strategic merit in Churchill's North African plan.

Despite the quick agreement by the Allies on *Gymnast*, the longer-term strategic issue of whether to attack the Germans en masse against their troops in France or continue to fight them on the outer edges remained a colossal schism between the Americans and British that lasted another two years. The gradual shift in power and deployed resources that took place during the War from the British to the Americans finally left the British with little choice but to agree in November 1943 to a full-scale invasion across the Channel in 1944. But they never embraced the idea; in fact, Churchill expressed doubts about the advisability of the cross-Channel landings right up to the eve of D-Day.

Throughout the three weeks of meetings with the British in December 1941, both Stimson and Marshall were mindful that any process established with them or action taken would set a precedent. As an experienced lawyer and diplomat—two professions that place great value on precedence—Stimson was particularly focused on this. And while Marshall also fully appreciated the risk of letting early decisions dictate future ones, neither he nor Stimson could control the bilateral discussions between the president and the British happening informally at the White House (from the start of *Arcadia*, neither man was thrilled to hear the two chief warlords were practically suite mates in the Executive Mansion). Knowing how persuasive Churchill could be, and how easily influenced FDR was on military matters, their concern was that their boss would agree to something that could trap the Americans into a general strategy or a military venture not thoroughly vetted through the proper American military channels.

It didn't take long for those fears to be realized. On Christmas Day, only three days after the British arrived in Washington, Marshall found out from the head of the British secretariat that at an ad hoc meeting between FDR and the British High Command the night before, Roosevelt agreed to consider turning over American reinforcements intended for the Philippines to the British for their possible use in Singapore.

An agitated Marshall went directly to Stimson bringing with him "Hap" Arnold and one of his newest recruits to the War Plans Division, fifty-three-year-old Dwight Eisenhower. Stimson was apoplectic upon hearing the news. He called up Harry Hopkins immediately and threatened to resign if Roosevelt planned on making decisions with the British without seeking proper advice from his military advisors.

Hopkins was as anxious as Stimson to get ahead of this behavior from his chief. He was soon able to bring the subject up to both FDR and Churchill during a meeting the three men were having together. Both leaders denied that any agreement was made. At a cabinet meeting later that afternoon, FDR sheepishly mentioned that a rumor was going around about an agreement he had made with the British but assured everyone it was not true. On certain issues Stimson might have let Roosevelt off the hook, but he felt so strongly about the president's predilection for backroom decision-making that he called him out during the meeting by reading from the notes taken by the British during the bilateral gathering. Stimson got his point across, but the incident proved to be a harbinger of the conflict to come between the War Department and the president when it came to the president's one-on-one chats with the prime minister.[23]

Formation of the Combined Chiefs of Staff

The Christmas Eve episode with FDR only served to confirm to Marshall what he believed to be the most important issue to discuss and decide during the conference: the organizational decision-making structure that should be established between the Allies. It was not just FDR's management style that drove Marshall to lead the American effort to institute a streamlined method for the Allies to conduct the war; the chief of staff was also keenly aware the British were leagues ahead of the Americans when it came to managing a war. Finding the right organizational structure would level the playing field.

Through its Chiefs of Staff Committee, including the heads of the Army, the Navy, and the Royal Air Forces, the British operated as a single unified team under the leadership of the prime minister. This structure had been in place for twenty years, and Marshall recognized its huge advantages in comparison to the American management model with no such similar committee and a poor track record of interservice cooperation.

So when the British floated the idea early on at *Arcadia* of having senior representatives stationed in Washington to represent the Chiefs of Staff at meetings with their American counterparts, Marshall moved to adopt it immediately, and the Combined Chiefs of Staff was formed. In strongly pushing his American colleagues toward accepting the concept of a joint committee, Marshall was also ensuring the creation of America's first Joint Chiefs of Staff. It was a perfect turn of events for Marshall.

Marshall worked hard to ensure that the Combined Chiefs of Staff was organized to his requirements. Realizing the committee had to be much more than an advisory group, he wanted to make sure it consisted of the men responsible for *executing* the decisions made by it as well. The British were amenable to Marshall's ideas on this subject but needed to contemplate that part of the proposal calling for all meetings to be held in Washington. Notwithstanding the fact it made sense from a practical standpoint (Washington was obviously safer than London), it was still a tough pill for the British to swallow.[24] To get them comfortable, Marshall suggested that when the British Chiefs of Staff could not attend meetings in person, they should be represented by a high-ranking member of the British military based in Washington throughout the duration of the War.

As fortune (along with aggressive lobbying by Marshall) would have it, the man chosen by the British to represent them in Washington was Field Marshal Sir John Greer Dill, whom Churchill had just decided to replace as chief of the imperial general staff (equivalent to Marshall's position as chief of staff). Although Dill was an exceptional officer with a nearly flawless service record, Churchill disliked him. To soften the blow of replacing him, Churchill assigned Dill to Washington as his personal representative.

During *Arcadia*, Marshall and Dill immediately picked up the warm relationship they had established at the Atlantic Conference five months earlier. So impressed was Marshall with Dill that he aggressively pushed Churchill to name him the senior British representative of the Combined Chiefs of Staff. Churchill agreed, and the appointment was possibly the most significant one the prime minister made during the entirety of World War II. John Dill almost single-handedly bridged the difficult relationship between the Americans and the British at nearly every turn of the War until his untimely death in November 1944 at the age of sixty-two. Churchill wrote after the War that when it came to dealing with the Americans, Dill was the "priceless link in all our business."[25] Alan Brooke, who replaced him as chief of the imperial general staff, wrote of Dill that credit was due to him "more than any other general for our final victory."

John Dill recognized that to ensure victory, an extraordinary working relationship had to exist between the two English-speaking Allies, one that could overcome suspicion, pride, and jealousy—that triumvirate of human characteristics that had tripped up military and political alliances throughout history. He worked tirelessly during his tenure to explain to the Americans what the British were thinking and vice versa. Henry Stimson, a man for whom trust was a guiding principle throughout his working life, was quick to pick up on the unusual relationship between Dill and Marshall in this regard. Writing in his diary four months after Pearl Harbor, Stimson observed that the two men "talk over all kinds of things that representatives of different countries are not apt to talk about so freely."[26]

To appreciate the contribution of Sir John Dill, one must consider that the Combined Chiefs of Staff held some two hundred meetings during the War, starting with the first one held on January 23, 1942. Alan Brooke, Dill's replacement as head of the British Army, attended less than 40 percent of these. At all the rest of the meetings, Dill represented the British side. He was hugely influential.

To effectively manage the relations between the two sides, Dill believed it was necessary to cross lines most men in his position would never consider even approaching. He did so regularly. He shared with Marshall private telegrams he received from both Churchill and the British Chiefs of Staff, trusting that the fewer secrets between the English-speaking Allies, the more effective the overall alliance would be. Dill was also able to share communications Roosevelt sent to Churchill to which Marshall was not privy, believing strongly that Marshall could not be effective if his occasionally secretive president was telling him one thing while discussing with the prime minister another.

Most importantly, Dill acted as a buffer between George Marshall and his British counterpart, Alan Brooke, each of whom represented and advocated the military views of their respective nations to the other, the latter in an overly acerbic and patronizing manner. As absorbent of such qualities as the American chief of staff was, without Dill's ability to shape Brooke's messages he might have been unable to effectively negotiate with Churchill's foremost military advisor. As a link between the two men, Dill was able to find solutions where there could have otherwise been unbreakable deadlocks.

To be successful in this role (while avoiding accusations of treason by his superiors), Dill needed a trusted partner on the American side and found an ideal one in Marshall. The two men, less than a year apart in age, shared strikingly similar professional backgrounds, temperaments, and values. For Marshall, the relationship with Dill, both personally and professionally, would be the closest of his entire life. It was an unparalleled union formed at the right time and place to keep harmony between the clashing egos and divergent priorities of the English-speaking allies. Although Churchill and Roosevelt receive most of the credit today for the "special relationship" developed during the twentieth century between America and Great Britain, the professional and personal interaction between John Dill and George Marshall represented in many ways a more compelling illustration of the strong ties that bound the two countries during World War II.

Unity of Command

Consistent with his long-held views on the subject of war, George Marshall believed unity of command in the various theaters of operation was of equal if not greater importance than integration at the top. He was determined to establish this concept during *Arcadia* as a guiding principle among the Western Allies in all theaters of action.

Marshall's efforts in this regard reflected those he made earlier in his career toward improving ties between the U.S. Army and U.S. Navy. In 1921 he worked with the Assistant Secretary of the Navy Theodore Roosevelt Jr. on a task force aimed at coordinating the purchasing activities of the two services and had proposed more radical ideas on how to improve the connections between them. Although none of his proposals got anywhere, he never gave up. He wrote to a colleague in 1936 that he was "out of step with the rest of the world" on the subject but believed it was "fundamental that the two services be effectively coordinated."[27]

With respect to working with the British, Marshall thought there needed to be a single allied commander for all land, sea, and air forces in any specific theater of action. He was convinced there was no better way to fight a modern war and had the strong backing of Stimson, who predicted that Marshall's efforts toward achieving this goal would save "a year of disaster."

At *Arcadia*, the chief of staff brought up the subject during a meeting with the British High Command on Christmas Day. Given the panic setting in with the British over Singapore at the time, he believed it was an opportune moment to propose the concept, telling the assembled group that discussions on the placement of troops in Asia were premature without first getting an agreement on who was going to run the overall show in the Pacific. Throughout the meeting, Marshall was emphatic that only one man in any region could look at the entire military picture without bias across all categories of force and draw up plans accordingly. As he often did, Marshall brought in historical precedent during his arguments, pointing out that the Allied leaders in the First World War came to the same conclusion, albeit at the tail end of the conflict. He told the group he was certain 90 percent of the problems they could expect to face during the War could be solved by adopting such an organizational structure.[28]

The British military leaders initially met the idea with skepticism. Between Australia, New Zealand, and Singapore, they had too much of their empire at stake to risk giving command to an American. Suggesting further study of the manpower requirements in other parts of Asia, they bought themselves more time to think about the proposal.

It was not just the British High Command who needed convincing; the American Navy would not commit to Marshall's plan during that first meeting either, given the differences of opinion existing among its top admirals. As all the participants broke for a joint Christmas dinner, the chief of staff knew there was a lot more work to do before they next reconvened. He immediately ordered Dwight Eisenhower to draft a letter outlining exactly what a supreme commander in the Southwest Pacific would be responsible for. The following day he strategized with Stimson, who suggested they meet with FDR on the morning of December 27 to pitch the concept and obtain his support.

The meeting took place at 10:00 a.m. in the president's bedroom, with General Arnold joining Stimson and Marshall. FDR quickly expressed his approval for the idea. Besides having great faith in Marshall[29] and appreciating the benefits of unified command, FDR saw no threat from the proposal to his own position as the ultimate decider (any proposals around organization generally got Roosevelt's approval if his power remained unaltered). Characteristically, his only condition was that Stimson needed to get Secretary of Navy Knox on board (by habit, FDR generally preferred to avoid difficult conversations). So, immediately following the meeting, the secretary of war invited Knox over to his office, explained Marshall's plan to him in detail, and received his full backing as well.

With the president, the secretary of war, and the secretary of navy supporting him, Marshall then set up a meeting at 12:00 p.m. with Admiral Stark, Admiral King, and a few other high-ranking U.S. naval officers in Stark's office. Given the high-level support he carried with him, Marshall must have thought the meeting was going to be a formality. He was mistaken; most of the admirals were dead set against the concept in general as well as Marshall's specific proposal to name a British ground commander as the supreme head in the Southwest Pacific (General Archibald Wavell).

As difficult as it was for the U.S. Navy to consider serving under a British admiral, it was just as distressing for them to contemplate taking orders from an American Army officer. But a British Army officer? That would be a double blow. Marshall was forced to confront over 160 years of fierce American naval pride when articulating the benefits of his vision. He did so by explaining to the naval brass that his suggestion to appoint Wavell (the only logical choice among British commanders) would make it easier for the British to acquiesce in the overall concept as it got rolled into other regions.

For most of the U.S. admirals, Marshall's arguments fell flat. Fortunately, Admiral King (named only a week earlier by FDR to take over full command of the Navy from Admiral Stark) was supportive of both the general philosophy behind unity of command and the specific proposal to appoint a Brit as the supreme commander in the Southwest Pacific. With the new Navy boss on board, the other admirals fell quickly in line.

Marshall was on a roll. Later that afternoon, he again brought the subject up with the British Chiefs of Staff. To his surprise, they not only came around on the proposal, but also argued for even greater powers for the regional supreme commanders (which Marshall promptly accepted). Fortunately for Marshall, General Brooke, the new chief of the imperial staff, did not attend the *Arcadia Conference* (the British cabinet requested one member of the High Command stay behind in London, and Brooke was chosen since his formal takeover of the top spot would not take place until December 25). Brooke was against the idea, but his absence reduced his ability to influence the other members of the Chiefs of Staff.

In short order, General Marshall convinced Roosevelt, the U.S. Navy, and the British Chiefs of Staff. It was time to meet with Churchill.

As a direct descendent of the first Duke of Marlborough, one of the greatest generals England ever produced, Winston Churchill would not be easily convinced to hand over military command in any region to a former colony. And without the full endorsement of the domineering prime

minister, the support Marshall garnered from the British military representatives was likely irrelevant.

Churchill had already expressed his doubts on the subject at a meeting
held the day before Christmas (the first formal meeting of the British and
United States Chiefs of Staff) and argued against it further on the night of
the 27th with the president. During these meetings, Churchill challenged
the historical argument Marshall used to support his plan by claiming unity
of command toward the end of the First World War was not a fair comparison given the proximity of troops Marshal Foch commanded in 1918. The
forces in the Pacific, he argued, would be far too scattered for one man to
adequately control.

Although the prime minister seemed firm in his opposition, Lord Beaverbrook, Churchill's close friend and minister of supply, sensed his boss
could be turned on the issue and sent a note to Harry Hopkins advising him
to continue working on him.[30]

Hopkins therefore arranged a meeting between Churchill and Marshall in the former's White House bedroom on the morning of December
28 (the prime minister generally stayed in bed until 12:00 p.m. receiving
visitors or working on papers). Churchill, aware of the number of people
who now favored the plan, might have suspected his efforts in taking on
the American chief of staff might be for naught. Nevertheless, he and Marshall debated the issue back and forth at length before the prime minister
abruptly announced he needed a break and was going to take a bath. A
puzzled Marshall remained in the room as Churchill disappeared into the
bathroom. When he walked out a short time later, he told Marshall that
the warm water did not necessarily change his mind and that he (Marshall)
would "have to take the worst with the best." He then abruptly asked his
aide to call in the Chiefs of Staff to confer with them alone.[31]

As it turned out, Marshall won the argument. Churchill advised the
president shortly thereafter that he was supporting the plan and contacted
his cabinet to recommend its approval as well as the appointment of General Wavell as supreme commander in the Southwest Pacific.

This was a huge step for the Allies and a big victory for George Marshall.
Both he and Stimson hoped it would lead to similar leadership arrangements for each theater where the Allies were going to be eventually fighting
together. Stimson credited the chief of staff fully for driving the result, and
Marshall himself believed his performance during *Arcadia* in getting consensus on unity of command was one of the greatest contributions he made
to the entire war effort.

Control over Distribution of
Weapons and Ammunition

Believing that most of the decisions made at *Arcadia* would be critical to the future outcome of the War, Marshall was particularly unyielding during the conference on those issues he judged to be most important and on which he felt there could be no benefit gained through compromise.

Thirty minutes before the last plenary session of *Arcadia* was to start (the same day the British were heading back to London), Marshall was confronted with such an issue during a discussion with the president. It involved an agreement made between Roosevelt and Churchill that the distribution of weapons and ammunition would be controlled by a civilian entity independent of the Combined Chiefs of Staff.

The manner of how the two nations would generally allocate weapons had been bandied about since the start of *Arcadia* without any conclusion. The Americans, led by Marshall, wanted control of munitions in the hands of the Combined Chiefs of Staff; the British insisted on civilian control. During the second week of January, the British made a specific proposal putting control in the hands of two committees (one each in London and Washington) reporting directly to the prime minister and president.

Marshall was dead set against the idea, believing it was inconsistent with everything else approved at *Arcadia*. Only the military, Marshall maintained, could determine what it needs and when it needs it (Pershing had insisted on such control during the First World War). It would base these decisions on the overall strategy determined by the president and prime minister. On the day before the British left, Marshall made his arguments and told his British counterparts that only Roosevelt and Churchill could settle the issue.

While meeting with the prime minister, Roosevelt decided to go along with the British plan of creating a Munitions Assignment Board split equally between London (under Lord Beaverbrook, reporting to the prime minister) and Washington (under Harry Hopkins, reporting to himself). He then invited Marshall to the White House to give him the news before the final meeting with the British was to start. With Hopkins present, FDR explained how the plan would work and then asked the general for his views. Marshall calmly proceeded to run through his well-rehearsed arguments against the scheme. Uncertain as to whether or not FDR would change his mind, Marshall concluded by telling him that to adopt the approach decided between the president and the prime minister would be a de facto vote of no confidence against himself as chief of staff, leaving him no choice but to resign.

Speechless and startled, the president turned to Hopkins. To the delight of Marshall, Hopkins told Roosevelt that Marshall was right. To emphasize his feeling on the matter, Hopkins said that if the British proposal were adopted, he would have nothing to do with it. At the meeting a few minutes later, Roosevelt broke the news to the British. After tense discussions, they acquiesced.

One will recall that Marshall made a similar threat to Stimson, less than a year earlier over the latter's insistence to draw more officers from the civilian population. In later years, Marshall expressed significant regret playing the resignation card to Stimson claiming during an interview that it was not proper, not his style, and not something he ever repeated again during the War. It seems the aging general (the interview took place more than fifteen years after these events) had forgotten about this episode with the president in January 1942. When Marshall deemed an issue critical, he eventually would use whatever leverage he possessed to get the result he wanted.

U.S. Army Reorganization

After three long weeks in Washington, Churchill and his colleagues departed on January 14, 1942. Stimson and Marshall were then able to devote a greater share of their time to handling the increasing number of problems that had piled up during the British visit. But ahead of everything, the chief of staff was determined to shake up his own house; nothing less than a complete overhaul of the Army's organizational structure was needed.

Few books about World War II cover much ground relating to the organizational issues of the U.S. Army; the subject is far less interesting than military battles. But when one considers how massive the Army was (more than eight million by the end of the War) and the sheer volume and variety of tasks to which a modern war subjected it, one can begin to grasp how challenging it must have been to organize.

Any MBA student today taking even a cursory glance at how the U.S. Army was managed in January 1942 could point out the two principal organizational problems that Marshall needed to fix at the start of the War: First, the chief of staff had too many direct reports (there were over sixty agencies reporting directly into him, and he was responsible for thirty major commands and three hundred smaller ones); and second, there were too many offices and agencies within the Army through which decisions and paper-work flowed prior to reaching Marshall and his three deputies. On its best days during peacetime, the structure was slow and inefficient. During war-time, it was unworkable.

As we learned in earlier chapters, the bureaucratic behemoth that was the United States Army when Marshall took it over had evolved since the Civil War through numerous battles between those who favored more cen-tralized executive control at the top and those who sought to keep power spread out between many agencies and departments. The latter group man-aged to keep the upper hand even after it was dealt a blow by the former in 1903, when Elihu Root undertook the last major reorganization of the Army.

Although Root's vision of the General Staff remained a sound concept in theory, thirty-eight years had passed since it was created by the time the United States entered World War II. In any large organization, time is the key ingredient required to produce an unmanageable bureaucracy. Mar-shall commented after the War that the General Staff he took over in 1939 was a "huge, bureaucratic, red-tape-ridden agency."[32]

The chief of staff was aware of these problems as soon as he took over the top job in 1939 but thought the benefits of any major reorganization would be at the expense of the buildup of the Army, something he was des-perately trying to accelerate. Resistance from within the Army would be dif-ficult enough; taking on Congress, Marshall felt, would distract the Army at a time when it needed to be focused on preparing for war.

As 1941 progressed, so, too, did the pressure on Marshall to reorganize. This pressure came not only from above (Stimson) and below (most notably Generals Henry "Hap" Arnold and Lesley McNair, head of the Air Force and chief of staff of General Headquarters respectively), but also from within (Marshall himself). In late November 1941, a month prior to the attack on Pearl Harbor, he formed a committee to start the process.

To lead the effort, Marshall relied on a recent entry into his "little black book." Needing to find an individual with the right talents and personality to force through a change as comprehensive as the one he and his staff deemed necessary, he chose forty-eight-year-old General Joseph T. McNar-ney. McNarney, unknown to Marshall before taking over as chief of staff, impressed him with his performance as a member of both the War Plans Division and the Joint Army-Navy Planning Committee.

There was one particular quality Marshall saw in McNarney that sealed the deal: candor. At their first meeting together, McNarney, an air-man, brought to Marshall's office a proposal. He sat quietly across from the chief of staff's desk as Marshall carefully read through it. After he finished, Marshall casually suggested a change, to which the airman immediately responded, "Jesus, man, you can't do that!" Marshall, taken aback by McNarney's abrupt reaction, said nothing to him in reply but realized that such a man would be useful to him in the future when a difficult assignment needed to be carried out.[33]

When describing to McNarney details concerning the bureaucratic quagmire he was stuck in, the chief of staff remarked with great frustration that he couldn't "stand it anymore" and expressed to him in simple and straightforward terms what he wanted: substantially more time to devote to high-level strategic issues. With the country at war, Marshall knew that the current structure would prevent him from satisfactorily fulfilling his two primary responsibilities: managing the Army, and strategically advising the president on military matters.[34] McNarney needed no further instructions.

The task had less to do with designing a new organizational structure from scratch as it did with forcefully and quickly refining general concepts discussed for several months by various Army and Air Force planners. This made it easier for McNarney to get results rapidly and allowed him to work with fewer of the rumors and whispers typically accompanying large-scale reorganizations.

With input from Marshall, Army planners had previously drawn up an organization that centralized power into the office of chief of staff. In theory, this would allow Marshall to delegate much of his operational responsibilities to trusted subordinates. Inspired by some of the leading corporations in the United States, the proposed changes gave Marshall more of what he most desired: time. McNarney reviewed the proposals, adjusted them to account for present realities, and began preparing a final plan.

He and his team moved quickly; within a week they put a comprehensive proposal on Marshall's desk. They had quickly figured out that it could be implemented by an executive order from FDR (a power granted to the president shortly after Pearl Harbor as part of the First War Powers Act). This meant opponents of the plan within the Army (and there would be hordes of them) could not effectively use politicians to lobby for their cause and delay implementation. This was huge. Once advised of this, and after explaining the proposed plan to a select number of senior officers, the chief of staff sent McNarney and his committee to get Stimson's support on Saturday, February 7.

As a former secretary of war, protégé of Elihu Root, counsel to large corporations, and student of U.S. Army organization in the late nineteenth and early twentieth centuries, Henry Stimson was going to have strong opinions on the subject. One will recall he labored hard during his first stint running the War Department to defend the organizational changes put in place by Root in 1903, and he still believed Root's writings on the subject were relevant. Not surprisingly, he dusted off and reread Root's reports in preparation for the meeting with McNarney's committee.

Aware Stimson held passionate views on the subject, Marshall had earlier appointed John McCloy to serve on McNarney's committee. Not only would McCloy be able to keep Stimson in the loop, but he would also be better able than McNarney to convince him of the merits of the plan. The move was characteristic of Marshall's careful planning efforts.

McCloy joined McNarney and two other Army officers at the meeting with Stimson and argued with the old man for two hours. Much of this time was spent on the largely semantic issue relating to the proposal by the committee to give the chief of staff the additional role of commander in chief of all Army forces. Stimson wanted to avoid resurrecting this concept, one Root had eliminated forty years earlier when he abolished the position of commanding general. The perception of anything less than full civilian control over the military, Stimson explained to the committee, was equally important to the reality. He acknowledged the chief of staff position had certain duties no different from those of a commanding general, but he believed firmly the chain of command from the president to the secretary of war to the chief of staff was better appreciated and understood by Americans and their representatives in Congress without confusing the issue by throwing in the term "commanding general" or "commander-in-chief."[35]

Although lacking the next-level political skills of FDR, Stimson's views on this subject revealed he was no amateur. He understood the country's deep-seated aversion to anything challenging the concept of civilian control over the military and its overall fear of giving too much power to one military man. Conceding the point, the committee went back to Stimson three days later with the revisions required to address this concern (and others) and got his agreement, but only after having to engage him in another ninety-minute debate.[36]

After explaining the changes that *would* take place to the senior brass of the Army (implying negotiation was not an option), McNarney presented the plan to the president, who fully supported it and put it in place on February 28, 1942, through Executive Order 9082. It became effective less than ten days later.

The changes were dramatic: The chiefs of arms, powerful for decades, were eliminated (this included the chiefs of infantry, cavalry, field artillery, and coast artillery); General Headquarters was eliminated; the General Staff was heavily downgraded; and the chiefs of services were placed in far more subordinate positions than they were used to. In one fell swoop, the number of officers reporting directly to Marshall dropped from over sixty to approximately six, and 95 percent of the paperwork previously passing through Marshall's desk now bypassed him (according to McNarney). It was a complete reconstruction of the American Army that only a war on the scale of World War II could bring about.

Beginning on March 9, 1942 (the day Executive Order 9082 became effective), the Army was split into an Operations Division (under Dwight Eisenhower) and three major command groups: Army Ground Forces under Gen. Lesley McNair; Army Air Forces under Gen. Hap Arnold; and Army Service Forces under Gen. Brehon Somervell.[37] Army Ground Forces was responsible for the organization, training, and administration of the ground forces. Army Air Forces had the same responsibilities for the air forces, as well as responsibility for the development of airplanes and related equipment. Anything not covered by these two groups was the responsibility of Army Service Forces. In a stroke, these three command groups absorbed the responsibilities of almost all the agencies and commands with previous direct access to the office of chief of staff.

The Operations Division (formally the War Plans Division) had broad responsibilities, including many previously held by the General Staff (a group significantly reduced by the reorganization). It provided the strategic planning and direction of all Army operations and assisted Marshall in producing and circulating orders. It was essentially Marshall's command post.

With the new structure, the chief of staff could delegate his administrative duties between the three command groups and a deputy chief of staff (McNarney). Equally important, he was able to choose his own people to fill critical positions, something chiefs of staff had previously been unable to do. His selections were mostly men he came to know, respect, and trust during his career. Although historians tend to focus on men like Dwight Eisenhower and Omar Bradley, Marshall's success in the general area of recruitment went well beyond a few key picks; he put his "little black book" to great use.

In Eisenhower, Marshall had a forceful, intelligent, confident, and decisive subordinate. Marshall had first taken notice of him twenty years earlier. It was shortly after World War I, and the two men were brought together to discuss General Pershing's memoirs. Marshall could not help but notice that Eisenhower was unafraid to forcefully and intelligently express opinions contrary to his own about the direction of the book. Shortly after becoming chief of staff, and despite meeting Eisenhower on only one other occasion, Marshall ordered him to return home from the Philippines to get command experience.

Perhaps Marshall also took a page from Stimson's recruitment playbook by reaching out to Eisenhower; after all, the young Kansan had finished first in his class at Leavenworth out of 245 officers in 1926. Whatever motivated him, Marshall would not be disappointed in his choice; beginning in March 1941, he promoted his superstar seven times over the next thirty months after seeing him perform under increasingly greater responsibilities (the first five were temporary promotions).

Leslie McNair, heading Army Ground Forces, was an officer Marshall had known since before the First World War. Marshall was aware of his talents for organization and training and put him in charge of shaking up Fort Leavenworth in 1939, before hurriedly moving him to a more critical assignment creating new divisions out of a mix of Army officers, national guardsmen, and reservists. McNair achieved results and was also relied upon by Marshall for the names of officers who needed to be either promoted or jettisoned.

Henry "Hap" Arnold (Army Air Forces) and Marshall had known one another for over twenty-five years. Arnold, one will recall, was the young officer who wrote his wife one evening while serving in the Philippines (prior to World War I) that he just met in George Marshall a future chief of staff. He made this prediction after witnessing the thirty-three-year-old Marshall dictate a series of perfect orders without notes for an attack during a large-scale maneuvers exercise. Marshall admired and respected Arnold and gave him an important role in the planning division shortly after becoming chief of staff. The two men were in total agreement when it came to their views on the potential of airpower to determine the outcome of the War.

Brehon Somervell, named by Marshall to head the Army Service Forces, was a man Henry Stimson once described simply as a "ball of fire."[38] An engineer, Somervell made his bones between the wars as head of the Works Progress Administration in New York, the New Deal program responsible for employing men to carry out public works undertakings. Working on a multitude of sizable projects (including LaGuardia Airport), the ruthless and impatient Somervell earned a reputation as a man who could deliver results. Rex Tugwell, a member of Roosevelt's first "Brain

Trust," wrote about Somervell that when it came to cutting red tape and getting things done, "there had never been anyone like him."[39] When Henry Stimson became frustrated with the lack of progress in building military camps for the growing Army in the fall of 1940, he was given the name of Somervell, then a lieutenant colonel in the Army Corps of Engineers. Stimson asked John McCloy to quietly get references about the forty-eight-year-old taskmaster from his contacts in New York. When they came back positive, Stimson asked Marshall to assign Somervell to a position in the chief of staff's office in November so that he could get "a look at him without Somervell being aware" of it.[40] The secretary of war took immediately to him, as did Marshall, and the latter put him in charge of the Army's Construction Division the following month. Marshall said after the War that Somervell was one of the most efficient officers he had ever worked with, and if he found himself in a position of authority in another war, he would start out by "looking for another Somervell."[41]

As comprehensive as Marshall's reorganization was, by no means did it solve all the Army's organizational issues. Given the haste in which it was undertaken, there were numerous kinks that needed to be ironed out after it went live. For the remaining three years of World War II, Marshall and Stimson tinkered with the structure when it needed tinkering and made more significant changes when they observed greater weaknesses in it.

Joint Chiefs of Staff

Concurrent to directing the overhaul of the Army, Marshall needed to follow up on the ideas discussed and decided during *Arcadia* concerning the newly formed United States Joint Chiefs of Staff. How the JCS operated, how it worked with the president, and how it worked with its British counterparts during meetings of the Combined Chiefs of Staff were all questions Marshall needed to answer. Nothing was put in writing at the time the JCS was created (or at any time during the War) as to what the group's remit would be or who would make up its membership. In keeping with his leadership style, FDR resisted any such attempts to do so (mainly by King); he did not like to be tied down by written rules.

As to the membership, it was informally agreed upon by FDR during *Arcadia* that it would consist of Generals Marshall and Arnold from the Army, and Admirals King (Commander in Chief, US Fleet) and Stark (Chief of Naval Operations) from the Navy. It was necessary for Marshall to push for Arnold's inclusion given the Royal Air Force's representation on the British Chiefs of Staff.

Shortly after the British left Washington following *Arcadia*, FDR sent Stark to Europe to command all U.S. Naval forces there. This left the JCS with two members from the Army and one from the Navy. Marshall knew that such an advantage for the Army would render the JCS ineffective. He therefore suggested to the president to add a new member to the group, make that new member the chairman, and fill the position with a prominent Naval man. Marshall recommended retired Admiral William Leahy, a former chief of naval operations then serving as the United States ambassador to France.[42] He trusted Leahy and thought the Navy would be keen on adding him.

Roosevelt was initially against the idea, as he feared it would limit his control, but he liked Leahy and agreed to appoint him in July 1942. He also selected him as his own military chief of staff, a move not intended by Marshall's original suggestion. Although Leahy formally presided over the JCS, his role as FDR's military chief of staff made him less an active participant than a liaison between the JCS and the president. Marshall, given the respect he commanded within the group and his natural leadership abilities, quickly filled the void and acted as the head of the JCS. This was fine with King; according to Forrest Pogue, he and Marshall came to a general understanding that King would be the point man within the JCS when it came to the war in Asia (except for the Chinese, Indian, and Burmese theaters) and Marshall would take the lead in Europe.

Roosevelt's insistence on keeping the duties of the JCS vague against the repeated calls for clarity by King was a sound decision in retrospect. It gave the JCS the ability to evolve its responsibilities as the War continued. Initially modeled after the Combined Chiefs of Staff, the JCS slowly adopted its own model and structure to fit its own specific needs. It is hard to imagine today that the Second World War could have been fought without the American Joint Chiefs of Staff. Its formation was one of Marshall's most underappreciated contributions to final victory.

12

Japanese American Internment[1]

It is a terrific problem, particularly as I think it is quite within the bounds of possibility that if the Japanese should get naval dominance in the Pacific they would try an invasion of this country; and, if they did, we would have a tough job meeting them.

—HENRY STIMSON diary entry, February 10, 1942

On February 10, 1942, the day he gave his final blessing to General McNarney concerning the reorganization of the Army (and one day after he and Marshall recommended to FDR that the Army fight to the last man in the Philippines), Henry Stimson was struggling with another high-level problem, the type of which he generally insisted was his responsibility alone to work out. The question he faced was whether to forcibly remove tens of thousands of Japanese Americans from the West Coast and intern them in camps within the country's interior, away from the naval shipyards and airplane factories stretching northward from San Diego to Seattle. For a variety of reasons, Stimson went against his initial instinct and better judgment and recommended to the president that the move be made. Stimson's pronounced role in this discreditable episode puts a significant dent in his otherwise impeccable reputation as a wise, composed, and principled public servant. As such, it is worth reviewing.

The first mention in Stimson's diary about the general issue of internment was ten days before Pearl Harbor was attacked, when he met with Attorney General Francis Biddle and several others to consider whether the Army or the Bureau of Immigration should be responsible—in the event the United States was drawn into the War—for holding in custody those "aliens" determined by authorities to be dangerous to the nation. No specific insinuation was made to the nationality of such aliens, and Stimson's only comment was that he was deferring judgment until he heard further arguments (FDR ultimately determined the issue for practical reasons; he believed the Army was the only entity within the country that could quickly carry out an evacuation and internment order of any magnitude).

Two months later, the secretary of war casually recorded in his diary that he had signed off on applications to set aside certain areas on the West Coast where the Army could place in custody Japanese "aliens" considered a threat to national security. Although he was aware at the time that certain congressmen were proposing the government lock up anyone on the West Coast with Japanese blood, there was no indication that anything was being considered in relation to Japanese Americans.[2] On the contrary, it is clear the "aliens" he was referring to in his diary were first-generation Japanese immigrants who did not have American citizenship.

A week later, everything changed. On the night of February 3, 1942, Stimson recorded in his diary that he was facing a "very difficult problem."

In late 1941 there were approximately 115,000 people of Japanese descent on the West Coast, 60 percent of whom were American citizens (generally the children of first-generation immigrants).[3] The overwhelming success of the attack on Pearl Harbor and the subsequent Japanese victories in the Far East, coupled with a general prejudice against Japanese Americans (particularly in California, where locals were jealous of the economic gains made by them over the years), created a climate perfectly suited for panic, hatred, and rumors. The increasing awareness by the general public of Japanese atrocities carried out in China in the late 1930s only fueled the flames of animosity and anxiety. The principal fear was that if the Japanese could sneak up on Hawaii undetected, they could make their way farther east to the West Coast.

In any such politically charged environment, local politicians typically like to project to their constituents that anything that can be done by them to protect the community is being done. There is little upside during war for elected officials to take a balanced approach on issues related to national security. Such was the case up and down the West Coast in the weeks after Pearl Harbor.

Several prominent local officials began aggressively calling for the relocation of *all* people of Japanese ancestry to concentration camps. Those leading the way included Congressman Leland Ford of California, Attorney

General Earl Warren of California (soon to be governor of California, and later chief justice of the Supreme Court), and Fletcher Bowron, mayor of Los Angeles. Joining these men in putting pressure on the Army brass and officials in Washington, D.C., was an ad hoc bipartisan group of House members from the Western states. This group was relentless in getting its message out that internment was the only way to safeguard the industrial assets and infrastructure on the West Coast against sabotage.

It was not only the politicians who beat the drums of alarm. The Army officer in charge of the Western Defense Command (General John DeWitt, appointed less than a week after Pearl Harbor) was persuaded in short order—albeit after initial misgivings—that anyone on the West Coast with Japanese roots was a threat to the security of the nation and should be evacuated inland. Despite evidence of any kind, DeWitt was led to believe there was a significant number of Japanese who were acting as spies, communicating with Japanese submarines offshore, and otherwise plotting to sabotage critical assets.[4] Amazingly, DeWitt and others (including Warren) used the lack of evidence as proof that the saboteurs were planning something big. This was an absurd argument, of course, and Earl Warren greatly regretted supporting it later in life (along with his role in the entire internment program).

Although General Dewitt's thinking was certainly influenced by the local politicians badgering him daily, it was two Army officials serving in Washington, D.C., who seemed most responsible for convincing him that Japanese Americans were untrustworthy and dangerous: General Allen Gullion, provost marshal general of the Army, and his assistant, Karl Bendetsen.

The provost marshal general, a position typically vacant during peacetime, was historically responsible for law enforcement within the Army during war. With the likelihood of war increasing for the country during the summer of 1941, the position was reinstated in August 1941, and General Gullion was assigned to it. He was responsible for controlling enemy aliens, running the military police, and administering security clearance. A career military lawyer, Gullion had a commendable service record and served as judge advocate general of the Army prior to taking the position of provost marshal general. He brought over with him Bendetsen, his assistant at the judge advocate general's office. Bendetsen was a civilian lawyer in Washington State until he was called into the Army in May 1940 (as a member of the Army Reserve Corps.).

From the beginning of America's entry into the War, both Gullion (friends with General DeWitt for thirty years) and Bendetsen aggressively advocated for the removal of Japanese Americans from the West Coast and worked persistently to get DeWitt to join their cause. Although supportive of relocating Japanese aliens, DeWitt did not initially think Japanese Americans should be removed, believing it was not only morally wrong but also logistically difficult. His stance did not change overnight, but between continuous pressure from Gullion and Bendetsen in Washington and the civilian authorities on the West Coast (supported by a fiery, unrelenting anti-Japanese press), DeWitt flipped by the end of January 1942.

There were very few people at the time standing up for Japanese Americans, but a handful of them were key voices in authority sitting in the nation's capital speaking loudly against taking away the rights of American citizens. Chief among them were Attorney General Francis Biddle, Assistant Attorney General James Rowe, and Edward Ennis, director of the Alien Enemy Control Unit within the Justice Department.

During a February 1 meeting to discuss the issue in detail, Rowe and Ennis got into heated discussions with Gullion and Bendetsen. The two men countered all the Army arguments thrown at them by citing the basic rights of U.S. citizens, emphasizing that moving in such an aggressive manner against them without cause would not only be unjust, but it would also make the Department of Justice obsolete as an American institution. With the lines firmly drawn and no compromise offered on either side, John McCloy—asked by Stimson to represent him during the discussions—suggested a more detailed analysis be obtained by General DeWitt regarding the military advantages, or "military necessity," of detaining Japanese Americans. Although this request from McCloy did not seal the deal for internment, it opened the door considerably to the possibility. If one emphasizes "military necessity" or "national security" to justify a certain action, it is far easier to obtain support for it.

At the time this meeting took place, there were only two people in Washington (other than the president) with the stature, position, and ability to change the thinking of the general public, its representatives, and the Army on the subject of locking up Japanese Americans: Henry Stimson and George Marshall.[5] Working alone, either man could have tempered the prevailing mood and might have persuaded the country that locking up American citizens was not only unconstitutional and morally wrong, but it was also unnecessary from a military standpoint. Working together, it is certain they could have found another way to safeguard the defense facilities located in the Western states. Neither man took on the task.

Although George Marshall did not take a public stand against interning Japanese Americans, a great majority of historians have given him a pass because he was only tangentially involved in the discussions. Three reasons accounted for this: First, Marshall was not kept in the loop on the issue by Stimson or the provost marshal general's office (critically, Bendetsen managed to arrange that General DeWitt deal directly with Gullion's office); second, the chief of staff was preoccupied at the time with pressing war-related issues (determining the fate of MacArthur's men in the Philippines; negotiating organizational, command, and strategic matters with the British; undertaking a complete reorganization of the Army; and dealing with countless other issues surfacing during the first ten weeks of war); and finally, Marshall was very careful, both before and during the War, about taking a significant role on any matter he believed was the responsibility of the secretary of war.

Marshall could have made an exception regarding this specific issue (particularly since the determining factor cited for internment was "military necessity"), but he chose not to, and he was nothing if not consistent in his approach to dividing up responsibilities between himself and Stimson to reflect their respective positions as the military and civilian heads of the Army (Stimson apparently agreed with the chief of staff regarding the matter of who should handle the relocation and internment issue as there is no evidence he spent time discussing the subject with the chief of staff).

This is not to suggest Marshall was unaware of what was going on with respect to the defense of the West Coast. He sent Lieutenant General Mark Clark there for five days in mid-January to check up on DeWitt's request for more troops. Clark reported back to Marshall on January 27, recommending that fewer men be sent, not more. Clark also explained that DeWitt's general overall panic was largely unjustified.

When Marshall later asked Clark to weigh in on DeWitt's plans to intern Japanese Americans, Clark responded that such a move was not only unnecessary but would also tie up too many troops. He suggested that key industrial assets could be protected against sabotage by placing far less men around their perimeters. Unfortunately, by the time Clark responded back to Marshall on the second question, it was too late; FDR had already approved the relocation plan submitted to him by Stimson.

A decade after the War, Marshall reflected on the episode during an interview with Forrest Pogue. He said the issue revolved around protecting the safety of Japanese Americans from angry Americans. Although recognizing it was blatantly unfair, he commented that the action was necessary to prevent vigilantism from taking hold up and down the coast.

Marshall was not conjuring up this excuse ex post facto to justify internment or his inability to stop it. The concern was real at the time. Historians have generally downplayed the question of how much the safety of Japanese Americans might have contributed to the ultimate decision to force them into camps, but there is evidence it was more than simply a minor consideration. Ten months prior to Pearl Harbor, FDR hired an associate named John Franklin Carter to build up a network of secret intelligence agents responsible for providing the president with information on several issues. In the fall of 1941, Roosevelt asked Carter to prepare a study of the Japanese on the West Coast and Hawaii. Carter handed the task to a businessman named Curtis Munson, who arrived on the West Coast in October to begin his investigation. Munson's report concluded that the Japanese threat to America was not a big concern, but the threat to Japanese Americans from the local population could become a big problem.[6]

Did the desire to protect the Japanese influence the ultimate decision? In a note written to Undersecretary of War Robert Patterson in July 1942, John McCloy suggested as much. He wrote that the Japanese Americans were "under no suspicion for the most part" but were sent away "largely because we felt we could no longer control our own white citizens in California."[7] If this were true, the Army could have warned the Japanese Americans and at least given them the freedom to decide how they would like to manage the risk of vigilantism either individually or collectively. Since this was not done, it seems that protecting the Japanese was less of a priority for authorities than trying to quickly put an end to the general panic on the West Coast.

It is possible the protection of the Japanese Americans factored in Marshall's lack of action on the matter, but it is far more likely he was simply too busy to take up the issue and confident that the responsibility for the ultimate decision rested in the qualified and experienced hands of Henry Stimson.

Stimson had no excuse; it was essentially his call to make (Roosevelt delegated that responsibility to him during a phone call in early February, when he advised him to do what he thought best). And although Roosevelt made it clear to Stimson that he was not opposed to interning Japanese Americans, that would not have necessarily influenced the secretary of war. There were plenty of occasions, both before and during the War, when

Stimson was strongly opposed to actions supported by the president and made his feelings clear to him.

So, why did Stimson, who had built a reputation for decades as someone on the correct side of nearly every major issue, drop the ball when it came to the fate of Japanese Americans on the West Coast? Many historians attribute racism as a key, if not the key explanation. There is no question racism factored into his ultimate judgment (his diary does not disguise his feelings and mistrust of the Japanese race), but it was not as pivotal a factor as several historians have theorized.

Stimson struggled considerably with the overall internment issue and was opposed to any mass evacuation for most of January 1942 and the first ten days of February. He knew taking the advice of DeWitt, Gullion, and Bendetsen would not only be unfair to Japanese Americans but also make a "tremendous hole" in the country's constitutional system.

But as much as the lifelong lawyer and patriot valued and cherished the Constitution and the rights granted within it, Stimson also considered himself a warrior. In that alternate role he so cherished, one modeled closely after his friend and mentor Theodore Roosevelt, Stimson made a distinction between the protections offered by the Constitution during periods of peace as opposed to times of war. During the former, he believed all rights within the document must be guaranteed; during the latter (particularly when he believed the cause for war was just), he understood the same rights ultimately might have to take a backseat—when necessary from a military standpoint —to the higher cause of national security.

The real question then becomes why the initially skeptical Stimson was finally persuaded that internment was a military necessity. One can only conclude that his career-long practice of meticulous fact-finding, careful deliberation, and common sense failed him. Otherwise, he would have rejected the arguments coming from certain members of the Army, sided with the attorney general, and advised FDR differently.

Again, while racism was a certainly a factor, the main reason for Stimson's failure was his reliance on Assistant Secretary of War John McCloy, to whom he had largely delegated this issue. McCloy had become indispensable to Stimson since joining his staff full-time in October 1940 and was his go-to guy on several matters, including those related to intelligence and enemy sabotage. One will recall that McCloy made his bones—and got the attention of Stimson—as *the* expert on the subject of wartime sabotage through his experience in investigating the Black Tom case (after ten years of investigation, McCloy ultimately proved German culpability in the huge ammunition explosion in lower Manhattan during World War I). Before hiring him full-time, Stimson asked McCloy in September 1940 to advise him on how to protect the country from German sabotage and was impressed with the lawyer's analysis and recommendations. From that moment forward, the secretary came to rely on the forty-seven-year-old's advice concerning the general threats from sabotage. With so much on his plate after Pearl Harbor, Stimson trusted McCloy to handle the issue and advise him accordingly.

John McCloy was a remarkably productive, energetic, and decisive can-do professional who got things done and prided himself on getting them done quickly. He earned the immediate respect of both Stimson and Marshall for this ability. But as is often the case when professionals place too high a priority on swift and decisive action, there is a cost. For McCloy, it was that he got the reputation in Washington as someone a little too clever when it came to the legality of certain actions (his legal gymnastics were influential in getting Lend-Lease legislation approved) and the morality of others (he unsuccessfully advocated for wire-tapping and other unrestricted investigative methods throughout 1941). Many respected him for this quality, but he was occasionally viewed with suspicion for it.

For men like McCloy, it was better to suffer through the consequences of a bad decision than make no decision at all. Indecisiveness, particularly during a time of war, was unacceptable. When it became readily apparent during the February 1 meeting he moderated between the Justice and War Departments that there would be no agreement between the two parties, McCloy suggested General DeWitt come back to them with a more compelling military case for internment. DeWitt must have believed that if he came back with any plausible arguments, the War Department would back him.

But McCloy was not convinced—far from it. In fact, he called DeWitt in California two days after the meeting, strongly warning him to keep his views on mass internment to himself given that his (McCloy's) current thinking (and that of Stimson) was that a more limited removal of Japanese from critical areas of industry was a better solution.[8] On the same day he made this call to DeWitt (February 3), McCloy briefed Stimson on the standoff between the Justice and War Departments. It was after this meeting that Stimson fretted about the "very difficult problem" he was facing.

Over the next seven days—until he met with McCloy to discuss the issue again—Stimson's time was occupied with a range of war-related matters: improving air defenses in Asia; overcoming logistical difficulties in Australia; fighting Congress to approve a loan to China; battling Congress and

others to relax antitrust laws for arms manufacturers; understanding the
implication of Marshall's reorganization; and deciding with Marshall and
FDR the fate of the American Army in the Philippines. Meanwhile, the Japanese military was racking up victory after victory in Asia, and "the bad news,"
wrote Stimson in his diary between his meetings with McCloy, was coming
in "from all sides of the Pacific and the situation doesn't seem to have much
light it in anywhere."

During this same week, the hysteria on the West Coast intensified with
each Japanese victory overseas. False information spread by the Army about
the cooperation of Japanese Americans was broadcast to a Western population already on edge. Both the governor of California and the mayor of Los
Angeles made speeches over the radio describing past, present, and future
activities undertaken by "our little Japanese friends."

While this was taking place, Gullion aggressively pressed McCloy telling him on both the 4th and 5th of February that if there were not mass
evacuations soon, it would be too late. Considerable pressure followed
from the media, other politicians, and the public. It seemed to finally
break him. He met with Stimson on February 10 to review possible solutions to the problems on the West Coast and convince him that mass evacuation was the best one.

In his diary following the meeting with McCloy, Stimson reviewed the
pros and cons of locking up American citizens. His only argument against
the plan was that it went against the United States Constitution. There did
not appear in his diary that day any sincere regard for the human consequences of a wholesale evacuation of American men, women, and children.
He knew these citizens were being wronged, but he seemed to weigh the
arguments strictly through the lens of a military leader at war.

In favor of the plan, and perhaps to justify it, Stimson repeated his earlier declaration that the Japanese race could not be trusted (particularly
those of the second generation living in America, a theory DeWitt convinced him of despite any tangible evidence to support it). The secretary
of war also expressed a fear, shared by many top leaders in the Army and
Navy, that the Japanese military could possibly invade the West Coast if they
achieved naval dominance in the Pacific. He knew America was unprepared
for such an eventuality, and the prior removal of thousands of Japanese
Americans from the scene would be one less distraction.

After carefully weighing all the arguments, Stimson was still not convinced by the time he finished his meeting with McCloy on February 10,

and he challenged his subordinate to find a way to create areas around key industrial facilities from which the Japanese could be removed.

By the next morning, his attitude completely changed. It was as if the persuasive McCloy had planted a seed of doubt in his boss that sprouted during the night, pushing aside any remaining objections. Not wishing to argue with McCloy any longer, Stimson requested a meeting with FDR at the White House to discuss the matter (he was uncomfortable making the decision unilaterally). Declaring himself too busy to meet in person, the president offered Stimson time on the phone instead.

After hearing the pros and cons of mass evacuation explained to him by his secretary of war, Roosevelt left an impression on Stimson that he was far less troubled than his attorney general by the constitutional considerations surrounding internment (at that moment, the Japanese military was on the cusp of taking Singapore after a two-month string of victories throughout Asia). Nevertheless, he refused to make the decision, telling Stimson instead to do "what he thought best."

That was it. Within eight days, Executive Order 9066 was issued, sealing the fate of Japanese Americans for the balance of the War. The final hurdle was cleared when Francis Biddle, FDR's attorney general, acquiesced to the decision. Although his continued opposition might not have mattered in the end, Biddle later explained that his high regard for Stimson was the reason he gave up his opposition.

After the War ended, Biddle blamed McCloy for the debacle. He did not believe Stimson was ever convinced internment was necessary from a military standpoint. Biddle felt the secretary of war, under tremendous strain after Pearl Harbor, simply capitulated to McCloy's full-court press. Had Stimson "stood firm," Biddle wrote, "the President would have followed his advice."[9]

Biddle's take seems consistent with the record. Stimson could have prevented the entire program from taking place, and he should have made the effort, since it is clear from the evidence that he never got comfortable with the concept. But his trust in McCloy—particularly in his aide's considerable experience in espionage—combined with the startling and rapid advances the Japanese military was making since bombing Pearl Harbor,allowed him to forsake his normally methodical and diligent consideration of the facts around the necessity for such action.[10] George Marshall could have been a formidable counterweight to McCloy's persistence, but like Biddle, the chief of staff's high regard for Stimson's integrity and judgment made it easy for him to focus on the bigger issues facing the United States during the frightening winter of 1942.

Ultimately, FDR put the fate of the Japanese Americans in Stimson's hands. Based on his track record and the high level of ethics for which he was renowned, one would have expected the secretary of war to rise to the occasion and use his considerable moral standing in Washington to neutralize the hysteria coming from the West. He didn't. Instead, the man who spent a career providing sound advice to the highest-ranking corporate and political chieftains failed his principal wartime client. In doing so, his legacy, and Roosevelt's, took a justifiable hit.

13

Arguing Strategy with the British

It is easy to be wise after the event, but perhaps it would have obviated future misunderstandings if the British had expressed their views more frankly. . . . I think we should have come clean, much cleaner than we did, and said: "We are frankly horrified because of what we have been through in our lifetime. . . . We are not going to go into this until it is a cast-iron certainty."[1]

—BRITISH GENERAL HASTINGS ISMAY, chief military assistant to Winston Churchill during World War II, on the British misleading the Americans in 1942 by feigning enthusiasm for a cross-Channel attack

The Disastrous Winter of 1942

While Stimson grappled over the fate of Japanese Americans in midwinter 1942, the news brought each day via telegraph to the War Department grew increasingly grim. Following Pearl Harbor, the Japanese went on a rapid run of carefully planned triumphs in Thailand, Malaya, Guam, Wake Island, Hong Kong, and the Dutch East Indies. They also took control of the Philippines (forcing General MacArthur to retreat from Manila to a narrow peninsula on the western coast and a small island just off it). The Germans, meanwhile, had crushed Churchill's hope of occupying Libya and were effortlessly picking off United States merchant vessels in the Atlantic silhouetted against the night lights of cities and towns from Florida to Maine (blackout policies were not yet mandatory).

Equally disheartening was the knowledge that there was little the U.S. Army could do. The nightmare both Stimson and Marshall had tried to avoid continued.

Following British naval losses in the Mediterranean, the fall of Singapore, and the bombing of a critical oil refinery in Aruba, a dejected Stimson wrote on February 16 that a "a somber tone pervades all conferences now." Three days later, the United States lost a destroyer, several planes, and over one hundred lives when Port Darwin in Australia was bombed. The following week, the Allies suffered their worst naval defeat of the War in the Battle of the Java Sea. And although no physical harm was done, the fact that a Japanese submarine fired shells toward a U.S. refinery in California in late February added to the existing high level of anxiety.

As disheartened as he was by the flood of bad news at this time, Henry Stimson was also incensed. Despite these well-publicized military setbacks, he was spending valuable time and energy fighting officials within the Justice Department who were aggressively applying antitrust laws against certain U.S. explosives manufacturers. Assistant Attorney General Thurman Arnold (a "self-seeking fanatic" according to Stimson) was leading the effort. Arnold had been causing trouble along this front since the previous summer.

Fortunately for Stimson, his boss had his back. Despite long being an antitrust champion, FDR understood it was hardly an opportune time to interfere with the production of war materiel. But ever cautious, he waited until early April before authorizing an announcement selectively suspending further enforcement of the antitrust laws. Roosevelt's support made it much easier for Stimson and Patterson to neutralize the Justice Department, allowing American industry to more efficiently crank out the materiel so desperately needed. The entire experience rankled the elder statesman. Somewhat similar to his thinking on the internment issue, Stimson believed antitrust matters should be viewed through an entirely different set of lenses during wartime.

Despite the negative news, the stress, and the continuing challenges he faced trying to prepare the Army, Stimson knew he must maintain a positive attitude, particularly since Marshall was hitting rock bottom and was beginning to reveal to Stimson an uncharacteristic lack of confidence.

Among the unofficial job responsibilities Stimson accepted for himself when he took over the War Department—and took as seriously as many others—was keeping Marshall fit, rested, and in good spirits. Given their frequent meetings, close proximity, and the fact that the door between their offices always remained open, it was easy for the secretary of war to monitor the chief of staff's physical and emotional well-being. Three months after Pearl Harbor, he observed Marshall's morale progressively deteriorate.

It should not have come as a surprise; Marshall was being pressured from all sides. On top of the strain related to his administrative and strategic responsibilities, the general faced a flood of demands that were fielded and passed on to him by FDR from Great Britain, the Soviet Union, Canada, Australia, and other U.S. commanders. These demands, which increased in volume and urgency with each new Allied setback, were for the usual: more men, more weapons, and more ammunition. Naturally, each request was deemed urgent by the requester, and it became increasingly difficult for Marshall to place a higher priority on one versus another and collectively against the overall requirements of the U.S. Army. It seemed during these days that the weight of the world was indeed on his shoulders.

Even if priorities could be accurately sorted out, Marshall would have agreed with Stimson when the latter wrote in early March that America was wastefully scattering its resources to simply "plug urgent ratholes."[2] Neither man thought this constituted a strategy and were anxious to get the president to commit to one. They believed (as did their newly assigned chief war planner, Brigadier General Dwight D. Eisenhower) that the American Army needed to focus on getting American bomb-laden planes into the air above Western Europe followed quickly by American boots on the ground below. The ability of the Russians to hold off the Germans once the latter resumed the offensive in the spring was uncertain. The best way to help them was to establish a second front in Western Europe.

At this early stage in the War, Eisenhower's plan was simple: In Europe, the Army would engage the Luftwaffe, bomb Germany, and invade France; in Japan, the Navy would fight defensively until the European strategy began to show results. If America wished to save the planet, it must go directly after the source of its biggest problem: Germany.

Further, Eisenhower believed the Army could start sooner than later; it could begin taking on the Germans in the air before the summer of 1942 and on the ground—in a limited capacity—before the fall.[3] And if a major buildup of men and machines could successfully take place in England, he expected that a full-scale invasion of France could be undertaken in the spring of 1943. Marshall and Stimson liked the plan and, increasingly, the planner.

It was not surprising Eisenhower was so well thought of by both men; like them, he wanted to head "right up to the parapet." But in advancing their strategy, the troika faced a formidable counterweight pacing around a smoke-filled room in London pouring over maps of North Africa. Winston Churchill's approach, as outlined at *Arcadia* at the start of 1942, remained unchanged. If anything, he was becoming more fixed in his belief that taking on the Germans directly in France would be a huge mistake. In early March, he sent a gloomy letter to FDR detailing the bad news coming in from all regions and suggested that the large-scale frontal assault desired by Stimson and Marshall would likely need to be pushed back to 1944.

Marshall, mindful of Churchill's influence with the president, was scheduled to present Eisenhower's plan to FDR over lunch on March 25 (it was the evening prior to this meeting that Marshall seemed particularly despondent to Stimson). Joining him at the meeting would be Stimson, Secretary Knox, General Arnold, Admiral King, and Harry Hopkins.

Despite receiving a characteristically professional and forceful presentation by the chief of staff, Roosevelt did not come around easily to accepting Eisenhower's plan. His attention shifted to other potential options in the Middle East and the Mediterranean before both Marshall and Stimson took turns trying to bring him around. Even with the strong pressure from these two men, FDR might not have been sold on the plan's merits without the support given to it by Harry Hopkins. On that day, the president's frail and sickly but extremely powerful advisor sided with the War Department. When Roosevelt finally relented and suggested that the strategy be further fine-tuned with the Combined Chiefs of Staff, Hopkins objected, insisting instead that once the details of the plan were drawn and agreed to by FDR, they should be presented directly to the prime minister in London. FDR was noncommittal, agreeing only to consider the plan further after he received more in-depth details.

At this point in the War, although Marshall believed Roosevelt was a great man, Stimson was far from convinced. The strategy meeting on March 25, 1942, confirmed to him that FDR was indecisive at a time when the country and the world needed decisions. In putting Stimson's feelings in context, one must bear in mind that decades earlier Stimson was a close friend, colleague, and contemporary of Teddy Roosevelt, a uniquely decisive man and one who literally stormed the parapet with guns blazing against the Spanish in Cuba nearly a half century earlier. When Stimson contrasted his hero's aggressive and decisive demeanor with the more cautious approach of FDR, the latter naturally fell short. Certain it was his responsibility to prod along the "young man," Stimson regularly tried to light a fire under the president and encourage him to show the leadership he believed the American public was yearning for. The secretary did this throughout his tenure in the War Department in person, by phone, and in writing. Two days after the March 25 meeting, the discouraged Stimson chose the latter method and fired off a letter to Hyde Park.

Stimson was characteristically direct. He followed his customary method by quoting former treasury secretary John Sherman's advice in 1877 on how to begin resuming specie payments: "by simply resuming it." "The only way to get the initiative in this war," Stimson wrote FDR, "is to take it." After continuing to lecture the president, Stimson closed his letter with a warning that if America did not come up with its own plan of action, "our forces will inevitably be dispersed and wasted."[4]

To confirm he was not alone in his thinking, Stimson showed the letter to both Marshall and Hopkins before sending it to Roosevelt. Both men approved it without changes. Although Marshall might have been more sympathetic to Roosevelt's more deliberate approach to making decisions, he regularly encouraged Stimson to put pressure on the president.

Five days later, Marshall presented to FDR the additional details of the plan that the president had requested at the close of the March 25 meeting. It was divided into three parts: In the first, the Americans would flood England with men and materiel (the code name for this project was *Bolero*); in the second, a limited cross-Channel attack (*Sledgehammer*) would be launched with up to nine divisions in the fall of 1942 if the Soviet Union appeared to be in danger of collapsing; finally, a full cross-Channel assault (*Roundup*) would commence during the first week of April 1943 with approximately fifty divisions and six thousand planes.

Both Stimson and Hopkins were again in attendance to provide support to the chief of staff. Also present were General Arnold, Admiral King, and Secretary Knox. After more than two hours of discussion, FDR approved the plan and ordered Marshall and Hopkins to London to submit it to Churchill in person. The two men arrived on April 8, 1942.

Marshall and Hopkins in London (April 1942)

The prime minister and the British Chiefs of Staff met their American guests at Hendon Airport in Northwest London. On the drive toward the city center (approximately seven miles), Marshall was impressed by the evidence of past German air attacks and even more so with the realization that London remained on high alert.[5] It brought home to him the reality that his British counterparts and the people of London were living in a war zone day in and day out. Remembering his own experiences during World War I, Marshall was fully cognizant of the courage and strength required by his hosts to stay focused on the job at hand despite the steady shelling. In later life he explained to his biographer that he tried to keep this in mind every time he sat down to negotiate with the British during the War.

After some informal meetings and a joint press conference, the prime minister put on the full charm offensive over dinner, entertaining his two guests with his celebrated personality and dazzling them with his vaunted intellect. His insights and knowledge of both the American Civil War and World War I were particularly impressive to Marshall, who was no dilet-tante on either subject. Likely taking the lead from his hosts in keeping the first day somewhat light, Marshall did not bring up the proposed United States strategy.[6]

When the general raised it the following morning to the British Chiefs of Staff (Churchill met with Hopkins separately), it was the new chairman of that group, General Alan Brooke, who formally provided Marshall with the initial British feedback. It was the first of many encounters between these two leading figures of the War and on no other issue throughout it would they be more divided.

Alan Brooke was an arrogant, cynical, and dour Anglo-Irishman who also happened to be intelligent, professional, and a first-rate soldier and military strategist. Raised in a distinguished and privileged family from West Ulster with a long-standing tradition of military service, Brooke was edu-cated in France before attending the Royal Military Academy of Woolwich. Although four years younger than Marshall, Brooke was commissioned into the British Army as a second lieutenant ten months after Marshall entered the United States Army at the same rank.

Like Marshall, Brooke's record of service leading up to the First World War was outstanding, and he won great plaudits for his skills as a planner during it. Unlike Marshall, Brooke had considerable command experience between the world wars in a variety of branches. His role in saving a sizable portion of the British Army by skillfully organizing its retreat to Dunkirk in the summer of 1940 confirmed his rising reputation and made it easier for Churchill to select him for the top spot once the prime minister became disillusioned with Field Marshal Dill. Brooke formally succeeded Dill on Christmas Day 1941 and was named chairman of the Chiefs of Staff Com-mittee less than three months later.

Marshall and Brooke were more alike than not. They were both self-less professionals committed to their respective armies; they both disliked the pomp and ceremony that went with their jobs; and they both felt more comfortable at home in a rural setting around gardens and nature than at social gatherings. Where they differed was in how they managed their temperaments; Marshall was more successful at controlling his. And although neither man suffered fools, Brooke placed almost everyone he met during the War in such a category.

Unable to attend *Arcadia* in Washington, Brooke was upset he was unable to prevent his colleagues from stopping Marshall's efforts to establish the overall concept of unity of command. Whether this early victory for Marshall influenced Brooke's opinion of him prior to their first meeting is uncertain, but in characterizing his counterpart after the first day they met, Brooke wrote in his diary that while he liked the American chief of staff, he thought he "was rather overfilled with his own importance" and added he would "not put him down as a great man."

Like Henry Stimson, Alan Brooke kept an impressive record of the Second World War through daily entries into his diary. But Brooke devoted far more ink than Stimson did to venting against those with whom he worked. Qualifying for negative entries in Alan Brooke's diary put Marshall in good company. Roosevelt, Stimson, Eisenhower, King, Hopkins, Churchill, Alexander, Pound, Mountbatten, and Eden were but a few of the major figures of the war whom Brooke railed against in his diary. In fact, one must search Brooke's diary long and hard to find any complimentary remarks regarding the military capabilities of any of his Allied brothers-in-arms (Josef Stalin, Douglas MacArthur, and Brooke's predecessor, John Dill, were notable exceptions).

One of the benefits of keeping a diary for Brooke was that it allowed him to express opinions in the blunt, condescending, and aggressive style that characterized him. It was a style he believed would be unacceptable during discussions with his American partners. Ironically, the American military leaders, particularly Marshall, were accustomed to and preferred candid language during important discussions. It was a classic clash of cultural norms. Although a completely unfiltered Brooke might have risked damaging the "special relationship" developing between the two nations, the mutual Allied cause would have been better served if Brooke had been more honest when discussing strategy with his American counterpart, particularly during the early stages of the War.

General Brooke had no problem relaying to Marshall some of his reservations concerning the plan brought to London by the Americans, but they appeared to Marshall as polite suggestions as opposed to serious objections.

Brooke suggested the Germans might be too strong for the Allies to maintain a bridgehead with only the nine divisions proposed for *Sledgehammer*; he cautioned, no doubt reflecting his experience at Dunkirk, that if the Allied troops were driven back, there would be great difficulties rescuing them; and finally, he questioned whether there would be enough landing craft to later allow fifty divisions to safely land on the French beaches in 1943.

There was a more serious concern Brooke did not share with his counterpart: He had recently lost confidence in the fighting abilities of the British army. A few years after the War, British Air Chief Charles Portal explained during an interview that the British Chiefs of Staff did not share the same trust in British troops that the American leaders had toward their own soldiers. According to Portal, a string of defeats had left the British Army's confidence so greatly shaken that its leaders thought a direct confrontation against the Germans would be disastrous.[7] Adding to their anxiety was their lack of faith in American troops as well.

As far as *Bolero* was concerned (the buildup of United States troops in England), Brooke was in favor of it. But no matter how quickly this could be achieved, he did not want the lives of any Allied soldiers risked on a full-scale invasion until the result could be all but guaranteed. He felt the Germans were simply too strong and therefore supported Churchill in his preference to engage the Germans on the periphery. But to keep his American visitor focused on fighting Germans (as opposed to Japanese), Brooke expressed only his "concerns" about the American plan to Marshall, not his opposition to it. Consequently, the straight-talking Marshall was certain Brooke was in favor of it almost in its entirety. He took note of the issues raised by Brooke and assumed they could all be addressed as the finer details emerged.

It was not only Brooke who gave Marshall a false sense of support during his visit to London; Churchill waxed eloquently both verbally and in writing on the "masterly document" and "momentous plan" brought over by Marshall and Hopkins. But the prime minister's own colleagues knew Churchill well enough to know that his praise of the plan was not to be taken seriously. For some reason they believed the Americans would be able to miraculously translate Churchill's apparent full acceptance of the plan into what was in reality a near complete rejection of it. Looking back on the April meetings after the War, Portal complained condescendingly, and with no apparent remorse, that the "matter of fact minds" of Marshall and the Americans "always took the Prime Minister seriously and literally."[8]

Hastings Ismay, Portal's colleague on the Chiefs of Staff Committee, had a different and more sensible take on the matter. He admitted after the War it was a mistake not to make it crystal clear to the Yanks that due to the collective experiences of the British High Command during the First World War, they did not wish to cross the English Channel until victory was a "caste-iron certainty."[9] Churchill himself, although unapologetic, confessed he had misled Marshall in order to keep the overall relationship with the Americans strong and to ensure they continued to cooperate with the British on all aspects of the war effort.[10] Marshall was indeed misled; before he left for home, he radioed Stimson from London that his proposal was "formally accepted."[11]

George Marshall believed Winston Churchill possessed many exceptional qualities, but he never forgot the prime minister's duplicitous behavior in April 1942. Churchill had played him, and Marshall did not think this was appropriate behavior from any wartime partner, much less one who had received as much assistance from the Americans as he had.

To criticize Marshall for being hoodwinked by the prime minster is unfair; he simply took the word of the British leader at face value. If it were any other ally (Stalin, for example), perhaps Marshall would have been more guarded. But this was Winston Churchill, the leader of the United Kingdom and the son of an American mother. It was natural that Marshall thought the command structure between the two nation's military forces—a structure agreed upon by the British three months earlier—would be reason enough to expect a candid dialogue on any issue, much less one concerning critical military strategy.

Apparently, it was not; Marshall arrived back in Washington in late April and happily confirmed to Stimson that the meetings with the British went "very well."[12] Had Marshall even expressed a modicum of doubt upon his return, it would have disappeared when Roosevelt passed on to his chief of staff the contents of a telegram he received from the prime minister detailing his enthusiasm for the plan and even suggesting that action across the Channel might be required sooner than Marshall was even considering.

Only looking back is it obvious—even without a confession from the prime minister—that Churchill and his colleagues in the British High Command were carefully balancing their need to keep the Americans focused on the Europe First strategy with their determination to put off a direct assault against the Germans as long as possible. And although Marshall was deceived in London, it did not take long for him to figure out the British negotiation tactics in this regard. For the next two years, he tried to stay focused on establishing a second front in France as soon as possible to assist the Russians and hasten the end of the Third Reich. The British fought him each step of the way.

Fighting with Roosevelt and the British in Washington

What made the cross-Channel debates even more frustrating to Marshall and Stimson was that their own commander in chief wavered on his views about the timing of the invasion. While not wanting the buildup of troops in England to slow down, FDR repeatedly made inquiries that lent support to Churchill's "death by a thousand cuts" strategy to defeat the Germans. Less than two months after giving support to the plan upon Marshall's return from London, Roosevelt began questioning the logistics of it and started to raise the prospect of *Gymnast* (the British plan to land troops in North Africa).[13]

Persuading Roosevelt alone against such a plan was challenging enough, but when Stimson and Marshall heard Churchill and Brooke were planning on coming to Washington again to present their latest reservations about the cross-Channel strategy, their anxiety levels increased. When they further learned that Churchill was going to first meet with the president privately up in Hyde Park, they started to panic. They decided to prepare a strongly worded letter to FDR outlining why the Allies should stay clear from any diversion to the plans already agreed upon in London and wanted to make sure it got into his hands before he sat down with the prime minister.

Stimson and Marshall agreed that Marshall and members of his staff would work together to draw up a draft to be cosigned by Admiral King. But during the middle of a morning horseback ride, Stimson abruptly decided he needed to put something in writing too. Pulling on the reins of his horse, he turned about and rode quickly back to Woodley to put his thoughts to paper. When he finished, he headed to the War Department and handed his draft to Marshall, who was in his office meeting with Eisenhower, Arnold, McNarney, and Clark to work on his draft. The chief of staff read it aloud to the other men while Stimson attended to other matters piling up on his desk. When he finished reading it, Marshall led the men into the secretary of war's office. Speaking for the entire group, Marshall told

Stimson his letter was a masterpiece and should be sent to Hyde Park at once.[14] Marshall must have been struck by the quality of Stimson's memorandum; as talented as his group of high-ranking military officers were both individually and collectively, they had nothing on the singular ability of the Harvard-trained veteran Wall Street lawyer to put arguments on paper in an efficient, concise, and coherent manner.

Stimson opened his memo by carefully laying out to FDR the background against which the discussions would be held and addressed the realities—as he saw them—favoring the continuation of the plan Great Britain had already accepted. He then advised the president of the importance of taking no action that might weaken the major buildup of troops and weapons in England. "When one is engaged in a tug of war," Stimson wrote, "it is highly risky to spit on one's hands even for the purpose of getting a better grip." Any pivot to North Africa, Stimson warned, would tie up shipping allocated to *Bolero* and delay the invasion of France until 1944.

To complement Stimson's letter, Marshall and King sent one to the president as well. In it, they reiterated the reasons why they believed *Gymnast* would fail (e.g., ships brought over to support the action would be threatened by German planes launched from Spain or North Africa; and cooperation from the French could not be assured). As a further precaution, Marshall called the president directly in Hyde Park by telephone, advising him to make no commitments to the prime minister without first meeting with all his advisors back in Washington.

One reality neither of the two letters addressed was FDR's strong desire to have Americans fighting as soon as possible. As time wore on during the six months after Pearl Harbor, it became less important to the president where his troops fought as long as they fought somewhere. FDR felt the American people needed to know their soldiers were doing more than simply training.

The same day the letters were sent to Roosevelt at Hyde Park (June 19, 1942), the president picked up Winston Churchill at a nearby airstrip (present-day Dutchess County Airport) where he had flown to from Washington, D.C., alone. Roosevelt drove the two men back to Roosevelt's estate less than fifteen miles away.

Once he arrived, Churchill told Roosevelt that although he was fully on board with *Bolero* (building up troops for a future cross-Channel attack) and *Roundup* (the actual attack), he was far less confident about *Sledgehammer* (the limited attack planned for September 1942 to assist the Russians).

He suggested that unless the Allies were prepared to stay in France after the landings (and neither he nor his generals thought this was possible), they should attack at a place where there would be less risk to their troops (French North Africa). The prime minister stressed that such an offensive would help the Russians (by drawing off German troops) and produce additional "strategic advantages" to the Allies.

Among the advantages Churchill did not stress to FDR in Hyde Park were those that would benefit the British Empire. Although the huge Japanese naval losses inflicted by the Americans two weeks earlier at the Battle of Midway greatly reduced the Japanese threat to India (the jewel of the British Empire), the vast British interests in the Middle East were endangered by the tremendous success German General Erwin Rommel was having that spring in pushing back British troops eastward across North Africa into Egypt. A successful Allied thrust into North Africa behind the Germans would greatly assist the British in their efforts to preserve Malta, the Suez Canal, and other associated interests in the region.

The advantages that Churchill did emphasize to Roosevelt were compelling and in many ways more convincing than those delivered to him by Stimson, Marshall, and King in defense of their cross-Channel initiatives. Showing the American people that their soldiers were fighting somewhere and contributing to the overall Allied effort was first among them. As the man ultimately responsible for the lives of these soldiers, FDR also liked the idea that French North Africa would be a good place to test inexperienced American troops in a lower-risk environment than the coastline of France.

But whatever Churchill and his own gut was telling him, the president had to consider that his advisors, to a man, were dead-set against *Gymnast* and strongly in favor of staying the course with *Bolero, Sledgehammer*, and *Roundup*. And these were not ordinary men whose opinions could be easily discounted: Marshall, King, and Arnold were career military men sitting at the top of their respective services; Stimson was a bona fide "wise man" in the eyes of Roosevelt and the country; and Harry Hopkins was an advisor whom FDR had long leaned on for quality guidance. So, despite harboring doubts about the wisdom of throwing everything at the cross-Channel initiative, FDR countered the prime minister by simply handing Stimson's memorandum to him (perhaps the president was also impressed with how Stimson had outlined the American line of thinking).

Roosevelt, respecting Marshall's request to hold off on making any commitments until he could consult with his advisors, cut off further discussion with Churchill, explaining to him that he wished to take him back to Washington on the overnight train to meet with the wider group the following day (including Alan Brooke, who had arrived in Washington a few days earlier). One way or another, the two nations needed to come to an agreement, and FDR did not wish to make the decision unilaterally without getting consensus from his team.

The discussions began the following morning in the White House. During an early break, before any measurable progress was made, Roosevelt was handed a pink telegram while he was casually chatting with Churchill, Brooke, and Ismay in his office. On it was news that Libya's British-held port city of Tobruk fell to the Germans, who captured twenty-five thousand of His Majesty's soldiers in the process. Roosevelt read the note without comment before silently handing it to the prime minister, who had been standing next to his desk.

The blow to Churchill was staggering, as heavy as any other British setback during the War. It was not just the shock or the frightening outlook for the Middle East and North Africa that devastated the prime minister; it was also the sheer embarrassment of the loss. "Defeat was one thing," he recalled later, "disgrace another." The British troops were outfought and had surrendered to less than half as many German soldiers.

More than a few historians have cited the moments immediately following the delivery of this news to Churchill as a turning point in the relationship between the British and Americans during the War. As the prime minister fully absorbed the loss, Roosevelt quietly asked him, "What can we do to help?" When Churchill suggested sending some of the new Sherman tanks to his troops in North Africa, Roosevelt turned to his chief of staff. Marshall was no less sympathetic than the president, but the Sherman tanks, designed to take on the Germans' overall superiority in tanks, had only recently begun coming off the production line and had been pledged to his own commanders. As hard as it was to renege on the promise, he immediately ordered that three hundred of them be sent off that afternoon to the British (along with other support).

Although Churchill and Brooke were undoubtedly grateful to their two American counterparts, there is no indication at the time that it led to any significant relationship breakthrough. Only after the War did Brooke write that the episode helped lay down the "foundations of friendship and understanding built up during the war" between the four men.[15] But on the day he and Churchill heard about the fall of Tobruk, Brooke failed to record in his diary Roosevelt's sympathetic words, Marshall's offer of the

Sherman tanks, or anything other than the fact that the British troops had surrendered. Given that Brooke was not parsimonious with words when making entries into his diary, the episode might not have been as consequential to the wartime friendship between the two countries as he and others suggested in later years. At that point the Americans had been providing rapidly increasing assistance to the British for over a year; the offer from Marshall that day should not have been surprising to the British High Command, nor particularly moving.

The importance of the American gesture paled in comparison to the main issue the Allies were debating when the pink telegram arrived: the next move in Europe. Toward that, FDR, Churchill, Brooke, Marshall, Hopkins, and others spent the rest of the day discussing Churchill's ideas concerning North Africa. The news from Tobruk changed the overall strategic landscape in the eyes of the British, empowering the prime minister to more aggressively shepherd the Americans away from their cross-Channel focus. Marshall, as stubborn as the British leader, stood firm throughout the remainder of the meetings in support of Eisenhower's plan. By the end of the day, he believed he had successfully parried the prime minister's arguments.

But once again it was not only Churchill with whom he had to contend. Late into the night, when the group met to discuss matters of cooperation between the British and Americans in the South Pacific, Roosevelt suddenly floated the idea of putting Americans in the Middle East on a front between Alexandria and Tehran. With that comment, Marshall stood up and told the president that his proposal undercut everything he and his team had planned. He then said it was too late in the night to discuss such matters, excused himself, and left the room.[16] He was angry and tired after a day of defending what he believed to be a superior strategy (and one to which all the participants had already agreed).

The following morning, a calmer Marshall briefed Stimson on the meetings and Roosevelt's late-night proposition twenty minutes before Stimson was scheduled to meet with the president, Churchill, and Secretary Knox at the White House. The tag-team strategy Stimson and Marshall perfected for two years would once again be put to use in hopes of getting the two leaders focused on cross-Channel initiatives.

Stimson's strong feelings on the subject were well known to both leaders as he walked into the room, no doubt with a sense of purpose. Consequently, it was not long into the discussions before FDR and Churchill brought to the seasoned negotiator their own version of the tag-team approach. Roosevelt began by criticizing the advice he had received from Marshall and King in their memorandum against *Gymnast* (knowing full well its contents were supported by Stimson). FDR claimed with derision that the two men had ventured into political considerations to defend their objections. Not taking the bait to answer directly to this accusation, the old litigator replied that *his* objections to *Gymnast* were based solely on "our shortage of shipping, our shortage of carriers, and the impossibility of getting adequate air cover over Casablanca for a movement of such magnitude."

Churchill then took over from FDR, informing Stimson that no "responsible" member of his staff believed there was a chance the Allies could successfully cross the Channel in 1942 as envisioned by *Sledgehammer*. Referencing Germany's dedicated efforts to fortify the full length of the coastal defenses, Churchill stated he did not wish to replicate the tragedy at Dunkirk. Stimson shot back, saying he was no less concerned about sending men to their deaths. He said the decision to move forward on *Sledgehammer* would be made at the time—and only at the time—when Russia looked imperiled. And if it seemed like a hazardous proposition at that point, Stimson emphasized, the Allies would think of something else. Regardless, the secretary of war continued, the Allies were preparing for a full-on invasion of France in 1943. To keep to this schedule, he warned, one should not carry out "diversions" such as those Churchill was proposing.

When Churchill countered that the troops gathered in England for a battle in 1943 could be used more profitably elsewhere in 1942, Stimson tried a different tack on the prime minister. He suggested the buildup of troops in Great Britain could be extremely convenient to His Majesty's government if Hitler made the decision to revive *Operation Sea Lion* (the German invasion of Britain). This argument was a stretch, and Stimson must have realized it as soon as the words came out of his mouth; it is likely he was simply weary of repeatedly going back at the dogged Englishman with the same arguments. But it is also possible he was trying to take advantage of the fact that the prime minister still seemed "staggered" by the contents of the pink telegram he had read just a few days earlier (which was recognizable to Stimson in Churchill's "speech and manner"). Perhaps the old lawyer in Stimson sensed vulnerability in the British leader that he could exploit.

Despite the impact the loss of Tobruk had on the overall military and political environment, and the individual and collective pressure brought to bear from Roosevelt and Churchill, it seemed to Marshall and Stimson that they had once again won the debate as the British headed back to

London.[17] Churchill saw it differently. He was determined to get the Americans on board for a North African campaign, and this was just another step in the process. To complete his goal, he needed to fully turn Roosevelt, who was still uncommitted.

A Failed Bluff

During his visit to America in June 1942, Winston Churchill sensed what Stimson and Marshall failed to sense: FDR's desperation for his troops to see action before the year was up. To the prime minister, North Africa seemed the only logical option. Accordingly, after waiting a respectable week from the time they got back to London, he once again requested the Allies reopen the discussion on *Gymnast*.[18] A message was delivered by Churchill to Roosevelt explaining that based on his most current analysis, the conditions required to make *Sledgehammer* a practical operation in 1942 were not likely to come about. As such, he hoped the United States would reconsider supporting a 1942 offensive in North Africa. Sir John Dill, who had already formed his uncommonly close relationship with Marshall by this time, shared the contents of the message with him.[19] Dill thought it was best that he be the one to absorb his friend's first reaction.

John Dill was wise; Marshall did not take the news well. In a rare display of rage, the chief of staff railed against the British High Command for its deceitful behavior. And his outburst was not for show; this latest attempt to avoid sticking with an agreed-upon plan was the last straw for Marshall. It was not only the dishonest negotiating tactics of the British that got to him, but also the consequences of such machinations, which left the Allies on a carousel of indecision when it came to the direction of the War in Europe. After weeks of giving his counterparts in London the benefit of the doubt, the chief of staff now realized they had never intended to support the American plan at all. He believed a bold new approach must be adopted by the Americans to bring their British cousins fully on board with the strategy already agreed to previously. He told Stimson it was time for a "showdown."

With Stimson's "cordial approval" (and with the surprise backing of John Dill), Marshall—joined by Admiral King—sent the president a memorandum advising him that if the British did not fully support *Bolero* in 1942, the United States should reverse the "Europe First" strategy and focus their efforts on fighting the Japanese. So emphatic was Marshall on this point that he wrote a separate note to FDR to accompany the joint memorandum.

Indicating that it was his goal to convince the British to accept a "concentrated effort" against Germany, Marshall suggested that if this was not possible, the United States should "immediately" turn to the Pacific and "drive for a decision with Japan." Support for the British in Europe would remain of course, Marshall pointed out, but be limited to air support for the bombing of the continent.[20]

The secretary of war was delighted with Marshall's initiative writing in his diary that the threat would "serve as an effective block" to the British, thereby preventing any further need for negotiations with them on the subject. But when Stimson turned his Dictaphone off that night, he did so without bothering to speculate on how the president might react to the proposal. He should have; Roosevelt was not amused.

The following morning, FDR called the War Department by telephone from Hyde Park and asked for detailed plans of the Pacific strategy, including a timeline and precise estimates of required airplanes, ships, and ground forces. Further, he requested that the consequences of such an Asian pivot on the Russian and Middle Eastern fronts be spelled out to him in detail. Finally, just in case his top officers were still curious as to how he felt about the proposition, the president asked that such plans and estimates be delivered to him *that afternoon* by plane to Hyde Park.

Roosevelt, the most skilled American politician of his era—and perhaps any era—knew a bluff when he saw one and asked his chief military subordinates to show their hands. Away on a rare day off at his home in Leesburg, Virginia, the chief of staff ordered one of his deputies to prepare a draft reply and rushed back to Washington to review it. Marshall asked Stimson and McCloy to opine on the draft before running it by King and Arnold, each of whom signed off on it.

Since Roosevelt wanted the memorandum that same afternoon and as none of the men had focused much on the Pacific theater, the two-and-a-half-page effort by the top brass was unimpressive. Probably embarrassed, Marshall, King, and Arnold began with the following statement:

> *There is no completed detailed plan for major offensive operations in the Pacific. Such plans are in process of being developed.*

The balance of the document only generally addressed Roosevelt's questions.

FDR had successfully made his point. For the avoidance of doubt, he penned the following response to his military heads (unusually signing it

"Roosevelt C in C" to emphasize to his subordinates it was the president who was constitutionally in charge of the military):

> *I have carefully read your estimate of Sunday. My first impression is that it is exactly what Germany hoped the United States would do following Pearl Harbor. Secondly it does not in fact provide use of American Troops in fighting except in a lot of islands whose occupation will not affect the world situation this year or next. Third: it does not help the Russians in the Near East.*
> *Therefore it is disapproved as of the present.*
> *—Roosevelt C in C*

Having sufficiently demonstrated his displeasure to Marshall and King in writing, Roosevelt then drafted a separate letter and asked his aide to read it over the phone to both men. In it, the message was clear. If *Sledgehammer* could not be undertaken in 1942, then the United States should fight at another location in the European theater. Acknowledging that *Gymnast* would not pack the punch of a cross-Channel attack, it would nevertheless, FDR argued, have the benefits of disrupting the Germans, assisting the British in the Middle East, providing American soldiers much-needed experience, and putting pressure on Italy by virtue of obtaining nearby airbases.

Roosevelt had spoken.

The following day, an agitated Stimson marched over to the White House uninvited and requested a meeting with Roosevelt to discuss the matter. During the meeting, Stimson handed the president a book on World War I that included a section on the disastrous Dardanelles Campaign that the then-forty-year-old First Lord of the Admiralty Winston Churchill had conceived and engineered. Begging him to read the passages he had carefully highlighted, Stimson explained that in pushing for *Gymnast*, the prime minister was essentially making the same type of mistake he had ignominiously made twenty-seven years earlier.

Roosevelt tried to calm his secretary of war by explaining he was fully behind *Bolero*. But at the same time, he remarked, he did not think threatening the British was in good form (FDR told Stimson it was like "taking up your dishes and going away").[21] Stimson told FDR he understood this but said making such a threat was the only way to "get through the hides of the British." Holding his cards close to his chest, the president had the last word, telling Stimson he was going to send Marshall and King back to

London to settle the matter with the British High Command. The secretary of war left the meeting uneasy about Roosevelt's intentions. As he walked out of the Oval Office, Marshall, King, and Arnold were on their way in.

Like Stimson, Marshall was in no mood to give in to Roosevelt. And after a lengthy and heated debate covering most of the same ground, the chief of staff felt that he, King, and Arnold had once again persuaded the president to give up thinking about North Africa or the Middle East. But the wily Roosevelt insisted that both he and King had to convince the British. They left for London the following day.

Marshall in London to Argue against North Africa (July 1942)

Like many influential men deceived by Roosevelt during his lengthy tenure in the White House, Marshall was outwitted by the masterful politician when it came to determining where American soldiers would first do battle. Although the president was determined to have his troops fighting in the European theater *somewhere* before the November elections and believed North Africa was the only viable option, he wanted to avoid issuing a direct order to make that happen. The pressure on FDR from the press alone—steadily building since the spring—was reason enough to position the Americans for combat. Only two days before his tense meetings with both Stimson and Marshall, *Time* magazine painted a grim picture of the Eastern Front, indicating that if Hitler continued to make gains, the Allies will "have lost their best chance to defeat Germany and win World War II."[22] The implied message was, "What's taking so long to fight, Mr. President?"

To help secure his goal, FDR sent along his alter ego, Harry Hopkins, to accompany Marshall and King to London. He also provided the travelers written instructions that forbade them from threatening the British High Command with an American pivot toward Japan if things did not go their way. By denying this key bargaining chip from Marshall, Roosevelt won the battle of wills between himself and the War Department and determined the outcome of the meetings in London before they began. He was certain the British would oppose any type of cross-Channel offensive in 1942 and knew Marshall could not undertake one without them. In the resulting stalemate, North Africa would emerge as the new target. It was a simple but brilliant scheme, and the normally astute Marshall seemed unaware he was being set up.

The plane carrying Marshall, King, and Hopkins landed in southern Scotland on Saturday July 18, 1942. Churchill had arranged for a special train to take the American party to Chequers for the weekend (the sixteenth-century country retreat for British prime ministers approximately forty miles northwest of London). Marshall declined the invitation, insisting he continue on to London to meet with Eisenhower (now stationed there) and hold informal discussions with his British counterparts. Churchill threw a fit, insisting to Hopkins that Marshall was trying to subvert his constitutional authority as prime minister, and to Brooke that Marshall was trying to assume Roosevelt's authority. Since the American general had no intention of going to Chequers (his first visit to Hyde Park was for Roosevelt's burial service), Hopkins agreed to go out himself on Sunday to mollify the sensitive prime minister. It was not an auspicious start to the visit.[23] It did not get better.

After three days of flogging the same dead horse, Marshall gained no ground with the British High Command. On July 23, he informed the president and Stimson by telegram that the British refused to undertake *Sledgehammer* in 1942. The best Marshall could salvage from the meetings was that the training for *Sledgehammer* would continue until the middle of September. At that time, if it was determined that his plan could not be successfully executed, he promised to immediately prioritize *Operation Torch* (the new code name given to replace *Gymnast* for the Allied invasion of French North Africa). It was the outcome Roosevelt had envisioned. The British were delighted; Alan Brooke penned in his diary at the end of the week that he and his colleagues got "just what we wanted out of the USA Chiefs." He should have thanked and credited Roosevelt.

Back in Washington, Stimson became belligerent upon hearing the news. He beat a path to the White House and once again expressed his outrage to the president that the "fatigued and defeatist government" of Great Britain had not only "lost its initiative" but was preventing the United States from leveraging its full strength. When Stimson was finished, Roosevelt disingenuously expressed to his secretary of war his disappointment in the British as well.

Not satisfied with the face-to-face meeting, Stimson decided to shoot over still another letter to the president formally protesting the decision made in London. Expressing his views like the lawyer he was, and perhaps trying to appeal to the lawyer Roosevelt once had been (albeit briefly and unenthusiastically), Stimson complained that the decision by the British was a "direct violation" of the arrangement made with Churchill earlier that summer. Worse, Stimson cautioned, *Torch* would push back the full-scale cross-Channel invasion until 1944.

There was no response from the president. When the full details of the final arrangement made between the British and Americans in London arrived, Stimson used it as an excuse to arrange yet another audience with FDR. After hearing the same arguments from his secretary of war, the president admitted that although the proposed campaign in North Africa would indeed delay the cross-Channel attack until 1944, it did not sway him from his determination to get Americans fighting in the autumn. And although Roosevelt told Stimson his decision was final, it did not stop the latter from handing over an even more detailed memorandum of protest ("for the record," Stimson explained to the president).

Marshall, although also despondent, had accepted defeat by the time his plane touched down in Washington on July 27. Stimson met him at the airport and drove him back to Quarters One. After receiving a detailed briefing from the general, Stimson concluded the British had simply lost their nerve. To him, the weak knees of an ally were an unacceptable excuse for the more powerful Americans to give up carefully-thought-out plans. Exhausted and dejected, Stimson headed off on a weeklong vacation to his beloved Adirondacks two days later.

Well rested upon his return, the intransigent warlord was not yet finished. At a shortened cabinet meeting his first day back, he listened to Roosevelt complain about reports in the papers that he and Churchill were making decisions without the advice of their military advisors. The president denied this was the case for himself.[24] Given Stimson and Knox were the only cabinet members who were advising the president in this regard and given further that Knox had far less input in the discussions than the secretary of war, the president's displeasure was clearly directed at Stimson. Although Stimson did not respond during the meeting, it frustrated him that the president was not admitting the truth and might have not even have realized it. Either way, Stimson aimed to set the record straight one last time.

After three days of catching up with department business built up during his stay in the Adirondacks, Stimson prepared a letter for the president explaining how Marshall and King went to London expecting to close *Sledgehammer* and came back with *Torch* instead. Telling FDR his military advisors were still against *Torch* and believed a heavy air attack would have more of a negative effect on German morale than any other operation,

Stimson closed the letter by challenging the president: "Before an irrevocable decision is made upon *Torch*, you should make yourself familiar with the present views of these your military advisors and the facts and reasons which underlie them."

He never sent the letter; Marshall persuaded him to leave well enough alone and assured him that if *Torch* seemed headed for certain failure, he and his staff would call it off. The president's decision was final, and the chief of staff wanted to move forward.

Stimson's stubbornness regarding the issue compared to Marshall's ultimate acceptance was partly a result of the differences in their career professions and current roles. Marshall was an Army lifer and his commander in chief had all but given him an order, albeit not a direct one. Once given, orders were to be followed in the Army, not questioned. Stimson, on the other hand, had spent fifty years as an advisor. His job was to counsel his clients (in this case, Roosevelt) to the best of his ability. FDR himself specifically confirmed to Stimson in writing his role as a military advisor to the president before approving the Marshall reorganization in February 1942. Stimson felt he was simply doing his job.

There is no evidence Stimson ever considered he might have been wrong about *Torch*. A few years after the War, while reviewing his diary in preparation for preparing his memoirs, Stimson took the time to add handwritten notes to the unsent letter he wrote to Roosevelt concerning his opposition to operations in French North Africa (which he had inserted into his diary). What "saved us from the disaster," scrawled Stimson in the margins, were three things: the unexpected success of the Russians in Stalingrad; the Allied success in destroying German submarines; and the "enormous luck" the Allies had in landing troops in North Africa. It seems he still thought crossing the Channel before going into North Africa would have been a better choice.

The current consensus among historians is that Stimson and Marshall were far too optimistic regarding the chances of successfully crossing the Channel, maintaining a beachhead, and undertaking a sustainable forward movement against the Germans before 1944. Among other factors, the ability of the Germans to quickly move divisions from the East to the West seemed too substantial to overcome. It is impossible to know conclusively what the result might have been had the Allies thrown *all* their resources into a cross-Channel attack, but given the difficulties they faced in 1944 against a weaker army and damaged infrastructure, one can assume it would have been a risky undertaking.

A final comment regarding the sincerity of the threat Stimson and Marshall wanted to make to the British about turning to the Pacific if they could not get support for a cross-Channel commitment: Stimson clearly viewed it as a bluff; his diary backs this up. The evidence is less obvious when it comes to Marshall, but it, too, suggests he was simply trying to force the British to give up on North Africa and start planning for the invasion of France. Although Marshall told Forrest Pogue in 1956 he was bluffing, and his subsequent conversations with the president indicate he was, there was a radio message he sent to Eisenhower in London during this period explaining that he and Admiral King were of the opinion that if they were not going forward with *Bolero*, "*we believe that we should turn to the Pacific and strike decisively against Japan with full strength and ample resources, assuming a defensive attitude against Germany except for air operations.*"[25] At first glance, it seems Marshall was serious, but one must consider that Ernest King was not bluffing; he had no problem pivoting America's resources to Asia. And in corresponding with Ike, Marshall was representing both himself and King.

What primarily drove Stimson and Marshall to push aggressively for an earlier invasion of France was, as Eisenhower put it, the "transcendent importance" of keeping the Russians in the War. It seemed to them that nothing short of a cross-Channel attack could accomplish this. Striking their tents in Europe and heading off to fight the Japanese would be antithetical to this goal. Bluffing FDR and the British was a last-ditch effort taken by the American High Command to ensure that the Soviet Union remained in the game. After being called on it by the president, Stimson and Marshall knew their next best option was to go along with *Torch* and hope it would draw enough Germans to accomplish the same objective.

14

Internal and External Struggles

It is essential that the size and structure of the Army for the next calendar year (1943) be fixed now in broad outline. Equipment, personnel, and construction programs have to be initiated far in advance, and already there has been too much of delay pending final decision in strategical matters which effect troop requirements.[1]

—GEORGE MARSHALL, in memorandum to
Franklin Roosevelt, dated August 10, 1942

Roosevelt's drawn-out decision to ultimately side with the British regarding North Africa had one immediate upside for both Stimson and Marshall: the disproportionate amount of time spent debating the matter (and preparing for such debates) could now be spent focused on the multitude of other problems that bombarded them each day. Marshall had complained to a friend before he left for London that:

I am pulled and tugged in so many directions, China, India, Middle East, Bolero, East Coast, West Coast, Ghormley's new command, MacArthur, Emmons in Hawaii, and now Alaska and the Aleutians in a critical situation, that it is difficult to even dream of a peaceful day in the future.[2]

As any war evolves, the assortment and volume of problems generally increase as a result of previously inaccurate estimates, poor planning, unanticipated events, and naturally recurrent changes in the military and political environments. Consequently, military leaders must continuously consult with their planners while managing the day-to-day problems coming in from their frontline commanders. Given that America was involved in two separate wars thousands of miles apart with little linking one to the other from a military perspective, the quantity of problems faced by its leaders during the Second World War was essentially double. During the summer of 1942, the U.S. Army was also expanding at a rapid rate (it grew from 1.7 million to 5.4 million people during the year), presenting even more complexity to the management challenges for both Stimson and Marshall.

As the two men sat down together after Marshall's return from London, they turned their attention to the problems facing them in each major theater: In Europe, the German Army, still a major threat to Egypt and the Suez Canal following the First Battle of El Alamein, took Rostov-on-the-Don in the Soviet Union and was rapidly advancing on Stalingrad 250 miles to the north and east; in the North Atlantic, Allied convoys were still suffering severe losses from German submarines; and in the Pacific, the Japanese had taken control of Guadalcanal, providing them air support to their own base at Rabaul and presenting a threat to Australia and Fiji.

On the homefront, there were also troubles: The procurement responsibilities of the Army were under threat by Donald Nelson (head of the War Production Board formed shortly after Pearl Harbor) just as production was beginning to surge under the guidance of Patterson; there were fairly regular shortages in critical raw materials; and it was becoming evident there were not enough men to supply the increasing labor demands from both the industrial and military sectors.

On top of everything else, since the decision was made to proceed with *Operation Torch*, there were a host of strategic and supply details needing to be worked out to get that major offensive off the ground.

Swamped from all sides, neither man was able to spend as much time as he would have liked on any one specific issue. Stimson's daily diary entries rapidly jump from one subject to another during this period, reflecting the diversity of meetings and conversations he either led or participated in (including the daily tête-à-têtes he had with Marshall).

The major issues they faced in the latter half of 1942, once *Operation Torch* was finally decided upon, reflected the changing nature of the global conflict and their desperation to turn the tables on the Axis powers.

Guadalcanal

Although the Allies had been following a "Europe First" strategy since Pearl Harbor, they could not exactly hit the pause button in the Far East against as powerful and motivated an enemy as Japan. And while the U.S. Navy took point in the Pacific given the vast expanse of water separating the various theaters of action, the Army was still responsible for the Chinese, Burmese, and Indian theaters.

And if fighting the formidable and well-entrenched Japanese Army on the other side of the world was not a substantial enough challenge on its own, George Marshall had to do so in close coordination with two of the most difficult personalities America produced during the Second World War: Admiral Ernest King and General Douglas MacArthur.

King, Marshall's counterpart in the Navy and member of the Joint Chiefs of Staff, held two positions within the United States Navy during the War: commander in chief, United States Fleet (from December 1941) and chief of naval operations (from March 1942). General MacArthur had commanded all Army forces in the Far East from his base in the Philippines until ordered by the president to leave in March 1942 (to avoid capture by the Japanese). After his dramatic escape from Corregidor Island and arrival in Australia, he was named supreme commander, Southwest Pacific Area.

Although Marshall had his hands full with both men from the beginning of the War, it soon became apparent to many key figures who worked with the chief of staff (notably Roosevelt, Stimson, Churchill, and Brooke) that there was nobody in Washington who could better manage these two recalcitrant characters.

Ernest King was one of the least liked Allied leaders during the War. Few men outside the United States Navy, or within it for that matter, got along with him, and the British particularly disliked the Anglophobic admiral almost as much as he despised them. King was a brusque individual whose default mood was angry and annoyed. King's own daughter once joked that her father was "the most even-tempered person in the Navy; he was always in a rage." Marshall, generally reluctant to criticize anyone, described him in an interview after the War as "always sore at everybody" and "perpetually mean."[3] King was extremely sensitive to any perceived slights against the Navy, or himself as head of it, and came to believe the world (particularly the British military and the U.S. Army) was out to get him.

For all these reasons, Marshall handled King with kid gloves. Shortly after King was named chief of naval operations in early 1942, he walked over uninvited to Marshall's office for a talk. When King arrived, Marshall was in the middle of a heated discussion with a high-ranking Australian official. King was therefore kept waiting in the reception area outside of the chief of staff's office. The petulant admiral did not wait long; he stormed out, visibly angry for having been stood up by his Army counterpart (despite having no appointment). Once Marshall finished his meeting, he got word from his receptionist about King's theatrical exit and immediately walked over to King's office to apologize and explain that no disrespect was intended. With King's hostility still evident, Marshall turned to the admiral and said if the two of them began fighting at this stage of the War, "what will the public have to say about us?" It was imperative, Marshall continued, that he and King "find a way to get along together." After a lengthy silence, King turned to the chief of staff and said he appreciated Marshall's "magnanimity" and added, "We shall see if we can get along and I think we can."[4]

King was right; although the two never became chummy, there was a mutual respect each acquired for the other over time that made it easier for them to work together and find compromises on the sticky interservice issues that inevitably surface during war. Marshall deserves a lion's share of the credit for this; King remained difficult throughout the conflict. The chief of staff put up with King because he appreciated the quality of aggressiveness in any military man and saw this trait in his naval counterpart. Stimson also recognized it. Although never enamored with the naval chief (in one diary entry, he referred to him as "that narrow-minded pighead of the Navy Department"),[5] when asked one day by Felix Frankfurter what he thought of the admiral, Stimson replied gruffly, "It doesn't matter what I think of King, he fights."[6]

As the War progressed, Admiral King had the opportunity to spend a lot of time observing Marshall in a variety of settings and came to appreciate the wide respect to which he was held and the temperament he possessed. During high-level meetings, King could not help but notice how Churchill seemed to fear him, Roosevelt was in awe of him, the secretary of navy respected him, and Congress trusted him. Later in the War, when Roosevelt was mulling over assigning Marshall as the supreme commander of the cross-Channel attack in 1944 (an assignment he ultimately gave to Eisenhower), King begged the president to keep Marshall in Washington, explaining that he was an indispensable presence there. He ultimately came to realize that having a good working relationship with Marshall benefited the Navy. He therefore carefully considered the extent to how any specific position he took might affect it. In this respect, he was a bit different from General Douglas MacArthur.

MacArthur was as brilliant as he was arrogant and self-righteous. Not necessarily surprising for a person with these qualities, he had some authority issues or what a doctor today might diagnose as oppositional defiant disorder. As a result, despite his legendary and hugely successful career in the Army, accusations of insubordination fell upon him from time to time. Although such allegations would normally stall a military man's career, MacArthur's intelligence, supreme confidence, excellent record, high leadership abilities, and strong political connections ensured that his climb up the ladder would be continuous. And his rise was swift; in 1919, he became the youngest general in the U.S. Army just sixteen years after joining it (nearly half the time it took Marshall to earn his first star).

As Army lifers a year apart in age, Marshall and MacArthur knew one another. As discussed earlier, the latter always associated the former with the "Chaumont crowd," the group of officers serving John Pershing at his headquarters in Chaumont, France, during World War I. That Marshall was Pershing's protégé did nothing to endear either man to the other.

MacArthur was a jealous and petty man who rarely shied away from an opportunity to humiliate those officers who worked closely with Pershing. One will recall when MacArthur was serving as chief of staff in 1933, he assigned Marshall to a teaching position with the Illinois National Guard just three months after Marshall began a coveted command position at Fort Moultrie. Marshall was so sure such an assignment would kill his chances for a senior command position in the future that he made an appeal to MacArthur to reconsider the order (the only direct appeal Marshall ever made while in the Army). MacArthur rejected it and no doubt took delight in doing so. That same year he used his position to block Marshall from getting his first star despite personal appeals from Pershing and President Roosevelt.

Notwithstanding this history and his strong distaste for MacArthur's personality, Marshall recognized his brilliance as a commander and understood how important his experience in Asia could be to the Allies if they were to go to war with Japan. Therefore, five months before Pearl Harbor, he recalled MacArthur to active duty and put him in charge of the entire U.S. Army located in the Far East (MacArthur had retired from the Army in 1935 and was serving as a military advisor to the Philippines government).

The chief of staff and secretary of war did all they could to support MacArthur in the run-up to the War by providing him as many planes as they could afford to send to support his ground forces (which did not add up to much). The War Department hoped that by strengthening the Army's presence in the Philippines, it would delay the Japanese in fully engaging the Americans in Asia (neither man thought America could prevent the Philippines from falling into Japanese hands if war began).

As soon as he took command of the Southwest Pacific theater in March 1942, MacArthur pushed his superiors in Washington for greater resources in the Pacific and insisted that the Allies adopt a Pacific-first strategy. Although he understood this flew against the Europe-first strategy agreed upon by the United States and Britain during the *Arcadia Conference* two months earlier (and adopted by the American military long before the War started), MacArthur maintained the policy was a mistaken one and lobbied to change it. During the six years he spent as a field marshal in the Philippines army, MacArthur spent a great deal of time planning how to beat the Japanese and wanted to put that knowledge to use. It would also have been inconsistent with MacArthur's personality to agree to any global strategy that put priority in a theater of operations other than the one he was commanding.

Not surprisingly, the general also wanted to be given the responsibility to drive the overall military strategy in Asia and carry out the operations with himself in overall command of the region. To justify this and all his other demands, dispatches regularly sent to Washington from Australia under MacArthur's name in 1942 implied the Japanese were concentrating their forces in his area of responsibility and anything less than immediate action would be devastating to the United States.

MacArthur's ambitions for the Army and for himself, coupled with his general arrogant and antagonistic behavior, brought him into immediate conflict with leaders of the Navy, who, almost without exception, came to despise him. It therefore fell on the broad shoulders of Marshall to regularly monitor the region and place himself between the warring parties to ensure that some semblance of unity and cooperation existed between them. This meant that he had to spend even more time with Admiral King on difficult issues created by MacArthur. It became an unending circle of hell for Marshall to keep the peace between the two men while trying to persuade them to do the right thing. Only an individual with the right combination of patience, authority, diplomacy, and sheer ability would be able to pull it off. Although it was a struggle, Marshall was ultimately able to succeed.

The challenges he faced in this respect began as soon as the basic ideas on how to organize the Pacific theater were formulated. Unable to get cooperation from either MacArthur or King, the chief of staff compromised his strongly held belief in unity of command. Consequently, the Pacific was split between the Army and the Navy; Admiral Nimitz was given the Pacific Ocean areas and General MacArthur, the Southwest Pacific area.[7]

Settling organizational matters in Asia was relatively easy in comparison to those related to strategy. Once the six-month streak of victories for Japan ended with the loss of four of its aircraft carriers to American naval pilots at the Battle of Midway in June 1942, the agreed-upon defensive strategy of the Allies in Asia was naturally reevaluated.[8] Army planners in Washington thought the victory at Midway simply meant the Europe-first strategy would now be easier to execute and therefore wished to maintain the status quo. MacArthur disagreed; he wanted to go on the attack. King, itching to get back at the Japanese for Pearl Harbor and believing he had the Japanese Navy against the ropes, also wanted to press forward. Although King and MacArthur were of the same mind regarding the need to take the battle to the Japanese, the two men held contrasting views on how to go about it.

In anticipation of the shift in strategy he wished to ultimately lead, King approached Marshall in the early spring to suggest an island-hopping strategy from the New Hebrides (current-day Vanuatu) through the Solomon Islands to the Bismarck Archipelago. Controlling this area, King believed, was key to defending the eastern coast of Australia, protecting the supply and communication lines between the United States and Australia, and establishing an Allied base for further offensive action.

MacArthur had a different idea. He wanted to take Rabaul (1,400 miles northwest of the New Hebrides), a major port on New Guinea taken from the Australians by Japan in late January 1942. Rabaul was a key forward base for the Japanese in the South Pacific and a major obstacle for any American initiatives. For this plan, MacArthur requested a task force, including a division of marines (for the amphibious landings) and at least two naval carriers.[9] Marshall favored MacArthur's plan over King's but advised MacArthur that he needed additional time to sell it to both King and to the British.

In pitching the MacArthur plan to King, Marshall once again emphasized the need for unity of command, stating it was necessary given the coordination required between land, sea, and air. King was equally consistent when he made it clear to Marshall that regardless of which plan was ultimately pursued, he was not going to allow MacArthur to control any of his carriers. As for the strategy, King reminded Marshall that he had deferred to him in the European theater and now expected reciprocity. He further hinted that he was prepared, if necessary, to go it alone without the Army (a move antithetical to everything Marshall had been pushing for).[10]

Having made his point, perhaps much of it for effect, King backed down a bit when he received the anticipated reaction from Marshall. Needing a clear strategy one way or the other, the two men sat together and hashed out a plan, incorporating parts of both King's and MacArthur's strategies. The Solomon Islands would be the first point of attack; landings by the U.S. Marine Corps on the islands of Tulagi and Guadalcanal in the southern part of the country would be followed by attacks on the rest of the islands and the northern coast of New Guinea. The Navy would be in command for this first stage until its objectives were met. Command would then pass to MacArthur, who would move on Rabaul.

Predictably, MacArthur punched holes in the compromise (not without justification), but Marshall judicously managed him throughout the entire negotiation process. It was not only MacArthur's personality that demanded careful handling; it was his fame as well. The former war hero and Army chief of staff was not only a legend within the Army (and respected if not worshipped by many officers), but he was also well known and liked by the general public. There were also several important politicians enamored by the colorful soldier. Wendell Willkie, who lost to FDR in the presidential election of 1940, suggested MacArthur be given command over the entire military forces of the United States. Other politicians had still greater aspirations for him: the presidency. As early as February 1942, high-ranking senators began making their views known regarding MacArthur's electability in 1944.[11]

Such popularity gave Marshall, Stimson, and Roosevelt additional challenges none of them needed. Each knew there was a precedent in American history for a former high-ranking Army commander challenging a sitting president for a wartime White House, and none of them wanted MacArthur to follow the example set by George McClellan when he ran against Abraham Lincoln in 1864.

Unfortunately for Marshall, he was responsible for nearly all the heavy lifting when it came to MacArthur during this period and throughout the War. Given the politics and his high regard for MacArthur's leadership skills, Marshall adjusted his normal management style. He accommodated the general when he could, and otherwise patiently put up with his constant complaints and requests.

The compromise Marshall worked out with King was the best he could get from the naval leader. When the agreement was finalized, the chief of staff made it clear to MacArthur that he expected him to play nice with King and all the other admirals. The offensive was launched on August 7, 1942.

As it turned out, both the Army and Navy once again underestimated the Japanese; the fighting in and around Guadalcanal stalled almost immediately following the successful landings by the Marines. Within a few days, the Navy lost over a thousand men and four cruisers in a naval battle off Savo Island (northwest of Guadalcanal). The Japanese viewed Guadalcanal as a critical asset for them and threw considerable resources toward keeping it from the Allies, far more than the Americans (and particularly Admiral King) anticipated. What was thought to be a short battle lasted six long months.

For the War Department, Guadalcanal became a nightmare. Still solidly entrenched in the Germany-first strategy, Stimson and Marshall had been focusing on the North African landings scheduled to begin in November 1942. But after the Battle of Savo Island, they faced a desperate and relentless campaign by Admiral King to transfer additional resources to bail him out (principally bombers, but also troops). Marshall, fearing that any shift in resources away from Europe could jeopardize *Torch* and cripple General Arnold's plan to lay waste to the industrial base of Germany from the air, offered King only fifteen groups of bombers and one infantry division. This did little to placate the demanding admiral.

Meanwhile, MacArthur continued to paint an extremely dark picture of events in Asia in regular memorandums to Washington. Using dramatic language to underscore how critical it was to swing more resources to the Pacific, MacArthur implied that if the United States failed to shift—if only temporarily—*all* of its resources to the Pacific to fight the Japanese, years could be added to the amount of time it took to vanquish them. When General Arnold stopped to visit him in Australia, MacArthur even tried to convince him the Japanese were preparing to invade Alaska.[12] Such dire prognostications and his general inability to look at strategy from a global perspective caused Arnold and several senior officers to begin questioning his fitness for the job.

Despite the high level of pressure from MacArthur and King, Marshall believed the requirements in Europe and North Africa were such that each man needed to make do with what he was given (which he thought was enough to get the job done). Stimson, Leahy, and Arnold supported him in this regard. Marshall continued to find ways to get some additional men and materials transferred to support the Guadalcanal campaign, but only a personal appeal from Roosevelt would force him to send more than he thought was necessary.

Sure enough, less than a month after Arnold returned from his fact-finding tour of the Pacific theater, a panicked Roosevelt begged the Joint Chiefs of Staff to find additional resources to divert to Guadalcanal.

Roosevelt, a Navy man at heart, paid close attention to the bad news coming from Asia, and with midterm elections coming up, wanted to minimize it.

It was a difficult request for the Joint Chiefs to consider. At this point, America had been at war only ten months. The military industrial miracle that the nation would become was still in its early stages; supply still fell well short of demand for nearly everything. There was also a shortage of shipping that made it impossible to satisfy the requests for help in the South Pacific. There never seemed to be enough ships to transport planes, tanks, or men; it was the most underrated problem the Allies faced during the Second World War.

Marshall, the logistics superstar from World War I, understood the transport shortages better than most of his colleagues. Just ten weeks after Pearl Harbor, he wrote a memorandum to FDR spelling out the critical importance of shipping to the Army. His first sentence went directly to the point: "The future effort of the Army is dependent on shipping." Using basic math, Marshall went on to explain to FDR that while there were enough men to make up a large army, a lack of merchant shipping would prevent them from assembling together in force outside of the United States.[13] Roosevelt understood and tried to address the shortage, but ships could not be built overnight. Intent on helping the Navy as the Guadalcanal campaign began to falter, the president personally arranged for the War Shipping Administration to free up twenty additional ships to support the transfer of resources to the embattled combatants. General Arnold of the Army Air Forces provided further aid when he shifted over several bombers from Europe.

The additional support helped, but it took another four months of fighting on land, air, and sea before the Americans were finally able to push the last of the Japanese soldiers off the island. While the cost to America in ships, planes, and men was considerable, the cost to Japan was far greater. After Guadalcanal, the offensive game plan of the Japanese, dazzlingly successful since Pearl Harbor, became deeply subordinated for the rest of the War to a reactive, defensive approach.

By December 1942, Stimson and Marshall realized that the Europe-first policy, as originally conceived, was dead. Going forward, the Allies would take the offensive in both Europe and Asia. With Guadalcanal in the bag, and the successful November landing of troops in French North Africa behind them, the Western Allies needed to update their strategy. They agreed to meet in Casablanca during the first half of January 1943 to do just that. Marshall would attend, leaving Stimson in Washington to sort out other important issues.

Procurement and Manpower

Problems with procurement and manpower intensified during the latter half of 1942, and Stimson took point in trying to solve the two most pressing ones: prioritizing the allocation of resources between the two major theaters and satisfying the growing demand for weapons from the British and Russians.

Stimson understood America could not afford to spread its production output too thinly, but he also knew that the British and Russian efforts would be critical to the overall success of the Allied effort in Europe. It was a conundrum that Stimson described as a "constant heavy strain" and one with which he was sure no previous secretary of war had struggled.[14]

FDR's management style made the challenging problem even worse for his secretary of war. From the start of America's participation in the War, the president sent men like Averell Harriman, Harry Hopkins, and Secretary of State Hull on special missions to Russia, Great Britain, and China to essentially take orders from the three nations for weapons and supplies. Since Stalin and Churchill were convincing and forceful individuals, these emissaries always returned home with considerable demands. Stimson believed each of Roosevelt's envoys saw but one piece of the overall puzzle and was therefore unable to properly opine on the overall distribution split between Great Britain, Russia, China, and the U.S. Army. He was convinced he was the only man in a position to do so and felt the full weight of such responsibility.

As time passed and American factories began hitting their stride, the pie got larger and the problems became less pressing. But in the latter half of 1942, Stimson complained often and forcefully in his diary about how tough it was to make such decisions. Toward the end of the summer, he was faced with a particularly difficult one. The Navy was preparing its part of the offensive campaign against the Japanese, and it became apparent to Admiral King and his staff that it needed more support from the Army than they originally thought was required. Specifically, the Navy needed air support to handle the likelihood of Japanese bombers from Rabaul being sent over to attack marines on the beach. King knew that only the Army Air Forces could provide the planes and pleaded with Marshall for assistance. Marshall conferred with Stimson.

During the same time period, the secretary of war was receiving information from General Ira Eaker of the Army Air Force that the production of planes by Germany had slowed down considerably, reducing the air protection it normally enjoyed. This meant that the Allies had an opportunity to do real damage to the Third Reich's submarine production capabilities. With German submarines still sending Allied ships to the bottom of the sea with regularity, Stimson naturally supported any plan to reduce their threat. But to do the job and do it quickly before the Germans built their production of aircraft back up, more planes were needed. This was the dilemma: Stimson had to balance legitimate needs between King and Eaker while still minding the demands from Great Britain and the Soviet Union. While all the stakeholders generally acknowledged the importance of each demand, they still thought—"as they all do," lamented Stimson—that the secretary of war could still find a way to "squeeze out a few" for their own operations. Problems such as these repeatedly plagued the War Department and kept Stimson on edge during the first year of the War.

Linked to the shortage of weapons and supplies was the shortage of manpower. Although America's population was substantial in 1942 (over 130 million), the rapid growth in military personnel coupled with the huge demand for civilian laborers to help produce and transport food, uniforms, vehicles, planes, ships, weapons, ammunition, and other general war supplies put a significant dent in the overall pool of people from which to draw. America's responsibility to produce weapons for its allies further stressed the situation.

Coordinating human with other resources during war is an underappreciated challenge; a soldier without a weapon is as useful as a weapon without a soldier. Marshall made his own thoughts clear to Roosevelt in a memorandum dated August 10, 1942, in which he requested an additional 3.3 million men in 1943 split between 37 new divisions and 109 new air groups. In the memorandum, Marshall emphasized to FDR that whatever numbers the president agreed to for the upcoming year had to be determined immediately given the time it took to turn a raw recruit into a soldier.[15] As he soon had to focus on North Africa and Guadalcanal, Marshall passed the responsibility of following up to Stimson.

With the demand for men exceeding supply, one easy fix was to simply widen the age range of men eligible to be drafted (which, until December 1941, was between the ages of twenty-one and thirty-five). Given how highly he and Marshall valued physical stamina in a soldier, Stimson's preference was to lower the minimum age from twenty-one to eighteen.

Although there was considerable civilian opposition to sending eighteen-year-old boys off to war, a greater hurdle for the War Department was Roosevelt's desire to cap the overall head count of the military. There were several reasons why FDR wanted a cap: He was sensitive when it came to the perceived or actual power of the military in the United States and wanted to control it; his instincts and experience told him that military leaders were typically conservative when it came to estimating their own needs; he wished to avoid criticism that the country was putting more men in uniform than necessary; and he was worried that the anticipated production level of weapons and supplies could fall short if too many laborers were transferred to the military.

The discussions between Stimson and the White House on this issue carried into the fall of 1942. When the War Manpower Commission hinted at limiting the requirements demanded by the Army shortly before the invasion of North Africa, Marshall stepped back into the fight. He wrote Roosevelt a strongly worded memorandum insisting it was critical to the overall war effort that the carefully calculated requirements he previously sent be approved. The tag-team approach worked again; the president relaxed his opposition.

Although FDR was ultimately successful in reducing the overall cap in the size of the Army (nine million versus the thirteen million suggested by the head of the Selection Services), the Army got what it needed for 1943: The minimum draft age was lowered to eighteen, and the maximum increased to thirty-seven.[16] This greatly reduced the War Department's anxiety about the supply of manpower sufficient to take on both the Germans and Japanese.

Given that the need to properly balance human resource requirements between the armed forces and civilian workforce was ongoing, it seemed to many that there should be one person responsible for both. Surprisingly, Stimson was not one of them; although it made sense in theory, he was firm believer in the future axiom "If it ain't broke, don't fix it." To him, the Selective Service operation, the same system that had performed successfully during both the Civil War and World War I, was working quite well. He made this point to the president during a meeting in early November after he heard that the Manpower Commission (created in April 1942 to manage civilian recruitment) wanted to take control of the Selective Service.

Roosevelt disagreed with his secretary of war but was not keen on going to battle with him. He was never fond of taking on Stimson directly and was even less inclined to do so at this point in the War. Stimson had always been fearless to those who knew him, but after two years on the job, many others took notice. A few months earlier, *Time* magazine had commented that Stimson was "afraid of no man, not even voters."[17] As many able lawyers discovered earlier in the century, and as Stimson's own staff was all too familiar with, Roosevelt and his inner circle learned the secretary of war could be downright terrorizing to debate. He was always on message, did not have any political agenda that left him vulnerable to counterarguments, and tortured people under cross-examination. Years after the war ended, Bob Lovett commented to an interviewer that Stimson loved to question people during debates and "would just tear you apart" when he did.[18]

So, when the unflinching but fatigued Stimson went on a ten-day vacation beginning on November 29, 1942, FDR cunningly, if not cowardly, issued an executive order transferring the Selective Service System to the Manpower Commission run by Paul McNutt (former governor of Indiana). Stimson was furious when he heard the news. Upon the secretary's return to Washington, Roosevelt tried to make light of his decision at a cabinet meeting by casually saying to him, "Harry, I've been robbing your hen roost while you were away." Stimson shot back sternly, "I won't go away again."[19]

Upset at the development, but always a team player, Stimson cooperated fully with McNutt. This did not temper his unhappiness with the president nor the men around him, whom he disdainfully referred to from time to time as either "the New Dealers around the throne" or the "New Deal cherubs." Like their boss, these individuals in the White House had natural suspicions about the military and believed it was their sacred duty to monitor the Army as tightly as possible to make sure it was not getting too big or taking any powers belonging to civilian authorities. Nobody was more devoted to the concept of civilian control over the military than Stimson, but there was a war going on and he believed that their actions were often over the top and counterproductive.

The Darlan Affair

Never fond of sitting behind a desk for too long, Stimson undertook an active travel itinerary during the fall of 1942 as Marshall and his Army planners were in final preparations for *Operation Torch* (launched

November 8). He visited the first African American squadron in Alabama in late October followed by two visits to Florida (to see aircraft target and bombing practices), and one each to Louisiana (to inspect B-26s), San Antonio (to observe training and psychological tests), and Nashville (to see more aircraft exercises).

Upon his return, the seventy-five-year-old was pleased to hear that the landings in North Africa had been successful, MacArthur was making headway in New Guinea, and the British had Rommel on his heels in the desert. But rarely in war does one get much time to enjoy good news before new problems surface. On the day he and Marshall moved into the newly built Pentagon in mid-November, news about the deal Eisenhower made with French Admiral Francois Darlan following the landings in North Africa went public. Darlan was the anti-Semitic commander in chief of the French armed forces under control of the pro-Nazi Vichy government headquartered in Southern France. Ike needed to deal with him to ensure the neutrality of the French troops in North Africa. The reaction in America to Eisenhower's deal with the notorious Nazi collaborator was swift and harsh.

Stimson and Marshall had no choice but to quickly divide and conquer in their effort to defend their subordinate, splitting up their time between the many high-ranking government officials and congressmen incensed and shocked that General Eisenhower had negotiated with the hated Vichy regime. Stimson walked Morgenthau, Frankfurter, and Wendell Willkie through Ike's rationale (Willkie wanted to deliver a public speech critical of the deal) while Marshall met with Secretary of State Hull and several unhappy congressmen.

The explanation both men offered was straightforward: Eisenhower thought the move was critical to ensure that French troops in North Africa (estimated to be approximately 120,000 scattered between Morocco, Algeria, and Tunisia)[20] remained neutral during *Operation Torch*. It had been evident from his intelligence officers that a vast majority of the French under arms would only take orders from Darlan. To ensure their neutrality, Eisenhower made a deal with Darlan recognizing him as the legitimate commander of French troops in North Africa and the civil head of French-controlled North and West Africa in exchange for the support of his soldiers. Darlan lived up to his end of the agreement; his troops obeyed his orders. In a press conference, Marshall estimated the deal prevented sixteen thousand American casualties.[21] This estimate, when added to the general success of the landings in North Africa, largely ended the debate, but it took a lot of time and effort to calm down those who thought Eisenhower had gone too far.

With their Army now finally engaged with the enemy, Stimson and Marshall turned their attention to a host of other issues.

A New Year and a New Building

After closing out 1942 addressing a severe fuel crisis in New England (that Roosevelt asked him to work on), Stimson met with Marshall on January 7 of the new year to have a long talk before the chief of staff headed off with the president and other officials to meet with the British at Casablanca.[22] Although only thirteen months had passed since Pearl Harbor was attacked, it must have felt much longer for the two men as they sat together in Stimson's new plush office at the Pentagon, the ridiculously massive edifice that was formally dedicated just eight days later (Stimson and Marshall had moved into the partially finished building in November). Despite the formidable challenges lying ahead for the two men, the Pentagon building was a positive daily reminder to them of how much could be accomplished in a short period of time.

The Pentagon's origins can be traced back to grumblings by Stimson about the limited, crowded, and geographically scattered office space available to the War Department when he took it over in the summer of 1940. As he approached his one-year anniversary on the job, Stimson's twenty-four thousand employees were working in twenty-three separate buildings. Although a new War Department building planned several years earlier was completed in June 1941, it still left the Department spread out between seventeen buildings. Since Stimson was adding approximately a thousand employees a month, he knew something had to be done quickly for the sake of efficiency. War seemed to be on the horizon, and he believed more than most people that it was coming soon. Marshall, another person preoccupied with efficiency, had similar issues, and their collective wheels began turning toward a solution.

What began as a plan to build a group of temporary buildings adjacent to Arlington National Cemetery evolved into a proposal to build one permanent large structure. Roosevelt approved it on July 24, 1941. When the public and press began to push back on the location (it was felt the structure would ruin the view of Washington, D.C., from the top of Arlington

National Cemetery), Roosevelt insisted it be moved to a nearby piece of property already owned by the Army about a mile southeast. Ground was broken on September 11, 1941, less than three months before the attack on Pearl Harbor. Sixteen months later it was completed.

The Pentagon was the biggest office building in the world when it was finished, and it remains one of the largest to this day. It has nearly three times the floor space of the Empire State Building. That a building of such size (6.24 million gross square feet and 3.6 million net square feet of office space) could be built in sixteen months was a testament to the power and determination of the United States and another example of how effective Stimson and Marshall were in finding the right people for the right jobs, in this case Brehon Somervell and Leslie Groves. Somervell, one will recall, was chosen by Stimson and Marshall to get the Army Construction Division back on track in the fall of 1940. Groves, a forty-five-year-old colonel with a reputation as a ruthless taskmaster, reported to Somervell and was ordered to complete the Pentagon under a phenomenally aggressive schedule.

Initially designed with the requirements it be no higher than four stories (it was decided to add a fifth shortly into the project), use as little steel as possible, and be built one wing at a time so that people could occupy it during the course of construction, the Pentagon was a truly unique building when it was unveiled. It was also efficient; although there were more than seventeen miles of corridors in the building, its pentagonal shape ensured that the longest walk from one office to another was seven minutes (albeit moving at a healthy pace).

Stimson's third-floor office, connected by a doorway to Marshall's, was magnificent. Facing the Jefferson Memorial with views of the Washington Monument and the Capitol beyond, the office contained rich wood-paneled walls, a private bathroom and shower, a wardrobe room, overstuffed leather chairs, beautiful carpeting, and twelve-by-eight-foot maps that slid in and out of a wall on tracks (the maps would be continually brought up-to-date during the War by Army cartographers). A private kitchen and a dining room that sat twenty-six was also part of the suite.

Using the same desk used by every secretary of war since Robert Todd Lincoln, Stimson did his work under the gaze of Elihu Root's portrait hung behind him.[23] Root, who passed away three years before Stimson started his second stint as secretary of war, continued to inspire his protégé a half century after hiring him to work in his law firm.

Marshall's office was not quite as big but was no less well appointed (although Marshall opted for a large globe instead of a map alcove). He worked behind a dark mahogany desk with carved lion heads adorning each of its ten drawers. His office served as a de facto conference room and had a large, beautiful matching mahogany table to host meetings. An oil painting of Pershing, his principal mentor, commanded the room. Still alive and beloved by the American public, Pershing's stature among members of the Army was even greater. Most officers who walked into Marshall's office and caught the gaze of Pershing's steely eyes were aware of the strong relationship between the two men. This undoubtedly added to the level of intimidation they already faced when called into a meeting with the chief of staff.

Marshall's formal workday began at 7:15 a.m., when he was picked up at Quarters One at Fort Myer (the home for chiefs of staff since 1910) for the short drive around Arlington National Cemetery to the Pentagon. His driver had standing orders to pick up any soldiers or war employees who seemed to have either missed their bus or were otherwise making their way by foot to the Pentagon. This presented Marshall with the opportunity on any given day to undertake his own intelligence gathering. He asked each passenger a series of direct questions about what job they did and what problems they faced doing it. The chief of staff was ahead of his time when it came to this management technique. He knew there was always information that failed to make it up the chain of command, and regular contact within the rank and file would provide him an adequate understanding of some of the specific problems that existed as well as an overall state of morale.

When he got to the Pentagon's garage, Marshall used the private elevator he and Stimson shared (the only passenger lift in the Pentagon until 2011) because he felt too much time was wasted in idle chatter when he walked through the hallways. Once he arrived at his office, he attended to the radiograms and cables that had come in overnight before rapidly dictating replies to matters of an urgent nature. He then began the first of two early morning meetings with his staff to review events occurring overnight. General Arnold attended both meetings. The first included the chief of operations (General Handy) and the head of Military Intelligence (General Strong).[24] When that ended, McNarney and Somervell walked in.

Shortly after the second meeting ended, Stimson would generally walk into Marshall's office to discuss high-level matters. The two typically met once or twice more before lunch, often alone but sometimes with one or more of their staff present. This pattern was established shortly after Stimson joined the War Department. Remarkably, the door separating their offices was left deliberately open throughout the War by mutual agreement. Any desire for privacy was offset by the efficiency of such a setup and the firm determination of both men to display to each other, their respective staffs, and any other visitors to the Pentagon that there were no secrets between the top military and civilian heads of the Army. A more powerful symbol of teamwork could not be demonstrated.

World War II historians have spent little time explaining how important it was to the overall war effort that Stimson and Marshall not only worked well together as a team, but were also seen to be working well together. It is difficult to imagine that any two other highly accomplished men under the same pressure and with the same broad responsibilities would have been able to maintain as transparent a relationship as the two did during their five years together. There is too much evidence to the contrary in the military history of America (one need not look beyond the strained relationships between Admiral King and the two naval secretaries he served under).

Both Stimson and Marshall's career experiences revealed to them two certainties: Teamwork was critical to success, and transparency was critical to teamwork. Marshall frequently lectured his subordinates that they could only be helpful to him if they were perfectly candid with him. General Albert Wedemeyer, who worked closely with Marshall in the War Plans Division until given a command assignment in Asia, recalled apologizing to Marshall for being too aggressive in his opinions during one of their meetings at Casablanca. Marshall immediately replied that he wanted the full benefit of his thinking and experience and said to him, "You would do me a disservice if you did otherwise." Stimson demanded the same throughout his lengthy career. He was famous to several generations of young lawyers who worked with him for insisting they challenge and question him relentlessly so that his clients could receive the best legal advice he could provide. There was nothing about public service that changed his style in this regard.

But it was more than their career experiences that formed these qualities (there were plenty of other men with similar backgrounds who were not team players); it was within the nature of both men to perfect themselves. They were each diligent students of behavior and saw that being candid—while often painful, awkward, and difficult—was the most effective way to get the best out of any professional relationship. That their partnership was tasked to win the War only accentuated their behaviors in this regard.

Any relationship will struggle at some point when perfect candor is the default communication style, particularly under the strain of war. Stimson and Marshall's was no exception. Two months before he moved into the Pentagon with Marshall, Stimson described in his diary a "heart to heart" conversation he had with the chief of staff that ended up "clearing the air of a very rare incident." Apparently, at one point during an earlier heated conversation between the two men, Stimson had accused Marshall of "welching" on a promise. Although Stimson did not remember the conversation, another individual told Stimson that Marshall was still upset that he had made the accusation. Stimson immediately approached Marshall and assured him that his comment was not "intended seriously" and went on to say to him that "one of the main purposes I had remaining here was to back him up." Marshall, according to Stimson, was very appreciative that he raised the issue with him, and they quickly moved on to other business.[25]

Based on reading Stimson's daily diary entries, such occurrences were extremely rare. Each man knew how critical their working relationship was to the nation, and this trumped any hurt feelings they might have acquired during the long hours spent with one another being frank under the most strenuous of circumstances.

When the seventy-five-year-old secretary of war finished up his long discussion with Marshall at the Pentagon during the first week of 1943 by wishing him luck at Casablanca, he was happy both he and the chief of staff were on the same page when it came to Allied strategy in the European theater. Like Stimson, Marshall was determined that once *Operation Torch* achieved its objectives, the Allies should storm across the Channel. Stimson mentioned that evening in his diary that the attack would take place on "one of two northwest peninsulas" but added that he did "not care to mention it yet." Reading his entry today, one senses he was certain a cross-Channel invasion was coming sooner than later. He and Marshall would have to wait another seventeen months.

15

The End of the Beginning

But I have it constantly on my mind—how much depends on keeping his physical and mental poise. On him more than anybody in the government, I think, rests the fortunes of the United States in this war.

**—HENRY STIMSON, commenting on
George Marshall in his diary on May 19, 1943**

I don't know what we would have done with someone different.[1]

**—GEORGE MARSHALL, reflecting on Henry Stimson
a decade after the end of World War II**

When George Marshall met with Henry Stimson to discuss general strategy the day before heading off to Casablanca in January 1943, he had been on the job for almost three and a half years (two and a half of them working alongside the elderly statesman). During that time, the Army grew from 170,000 to 5,400,000 men. Successfully raising, housing, and training such a volume of soldiers in such a short period of time was an astonishing achievement and a tribute to both his outstanding management skills and the uniquely close partnership he had with his civilian partner.

The two men had worked tirelessly to make sure their massive army was not only properly prepared to fight but also supplied with all the weapons and materiel required to do so effectively. Their efforts paid off. By the start of 1943, more than 30 percent of American industry was devoted to military production.[2] By comparison, this figure had been less than 2 percent in 1939. The output figures rose proportionally; during 1942 alone, the country produced twenty-five thousand tanks and twenty-four thousand antiaircraft guns.

While the future looked bright, the present was still gloomy: Despite winning a decisive battle in November 1942 that prevented Japan from reinforcing its position on Guadalcanal, American servicemen were dying in the Pacific without gaining the necessary ground to justify the casualties; despite a promising start to *Torch*, North Africa was a struggle; and merchant ships were still being sunk by German submarines at an unacceptably high rate on the Atlantic.

Painfully aware of these realities, Stimson and Marshall were greatly agitated to find that once the successful landings of troops in North Africa were made public, there was a rapid change in attitude among the American people with respect to how they saw the War progressing, one that Marshall described as going from "speculative pessimism to undue optimism." "Nothing could be more dangerous," he said in a speech to a group of manufacturers at the time.[3] The War Department worked too hard trying to alert the country that victory would only come after a long struggle and great sacrifice to let a few decent beach landings change the narrative. Managing public expectations in this respect would be a problem both men dealt with for the rest of the War. With each success trumpeted in the press, it became more difficult to convince the people and their representatives in Washington that the War was a marathon, not a sprint. The chief of staff had little time to address this problem as he slowly made his way by air to Casablanca via Puerto Rico, Brazil, and Gambia.[4] He needed the time to prepare to meet the British.

Casablanca Conference (January 1943)

Despite Roosevelt's warnings to all his military advisors that they should show up to Casablanca with a well-thought-out plan since the British would surely have one, there was little consensus among them as to what the Allies should do once the Germans were driven out of North Africa. Even within Marshall's own planning staff, there were varying opinions. The chief of staff was firm, however; he wanted to take the battle to France.

When Marshall, King, and Arnold arrived in Casablanca (Admiral Leahy was absent on the account of illness), they were caught off guard by the sheer size of the British contingent accompanying Churchill and the British Chiefs of Staff. Countless planners, specialists, and aides arrived on a British ship that had been converted to a floating command post. Given Roosevelt's preference to travel light (the American contingent numbered less than a dozen), the contrast was pronounced.

Once the meetings started, Marshall, King, and Arnold soon realized the president had been right; the British had a plan and were united behind it. Further, under the leadership of their experienced prime minister, they had carefully rehearsed pitching it to the Americans. Much like the work that goes into preparing for a modern-day U.S. presidential debate, there had been an intense planning effort undertaken by the British team before arriving at the conference. Part drill sergeant and part conductor, Churchill made sure his team had not only perfected their general arguments and counterarguments but had tailored them to the specific American officer they expected to address during any given part of the discussions. Reviewing Alan Brooke's diary, it appears such preparations began in mid-December, before the time and place of the conference had even been established. Once the date for Casablanca was chosen, efforts were only stepped up.

By contrast, Roosevelt held only one meeting with his advisors to prepare for the conference, and that was the day before Marshall left for it. This put the Americans at a significant disadvantage going into the critical negotiations over the future strategy of the War.

The British needed to be better prepared. Churchill sensed a shift beginning to take place in the relationship between the two countries. The sheer strength the United States was bringing to the collective table with respect to men, weapons, and supplies made it only a question of when the British formally became the junior member of the partnership. Perhaps by maniacally preparing his team for the discussions in Casablanca, Churchill hoped he and his colleagues could set the overall strategy for the balance of the War before the Americans started to fully leverage their superior power.

For four and a half days, Marshall, King, and Arnold sat across the table from their counterparts, General Brooke, Admiral Pound, and Air Marshal Portal, trying to reach a consensus on overall military strategy before jointly presenting a plan to Roosevelt and Churchill once the formal conference began.

Brooke opened the first meeting by laying out to the Americans what the British saw as the two principal options in Europe once the mission in North Africa was completed: cross the English Channel, or continue to attack the "soft underbelly" of Europe by invading Italy. It came as no surprise to anyone on the American side that Brooke and his colleagues strongly favored the latter option.

Adding a slightly new argument to the old ones drilled into the Americans throughout 1942, Brooke suggested that a successful bombing strategy by air against Germany coupled with a more aggressive campaign by the Allies to encourage resistance in the Nazi-occupied countries could mean that France might never have to be invaded. Marshall thought this was ridiculous (and would for the rest of his life). Bombing Germany by air would certainly *help* end the war in Europe, Marshall countered, but only foot soldiers could close the deal (he ended up being right).

Confronted with Marshall's dismissiveness, Brooke pivoted to the more conventional arguments favoring a Mediterranean strategy: It would take Italy out of the War, potentially bring Turkey into it (on the side of the Allies, of course), and force the Germans to shift troops away from the Eastern Front.

Marshall, speaking for the Americans, argued that the Russians (who had turned down an invitation to attend the conference) needed their Western Allies to open a legitimate second front, one that threatened Germany more directly in order to take pressure off Stalin's troops. The chief of staff's greatest fear at the start of 1943 continued to be the collapse of Russia, and it seemed obvious to him that it would require far less German troops to defend the movement of Allied troops up the narrow Italian boot than a broad northeastward assault through France.

Reopening arguments he unsuccessfully used against the British back in April and July of 1942, Marshall also reiterated that by remaining tied to a Mediterranean strategy, the Allies risked further delays in the cross-Channel attack. He feared landing craft and men otherwise reserved for *Roundup* (the code name at that time for the invasion of France) would be siphoned off to support a periphery engagement, providing little added value to the Allies.

As instructed to them by Churchill, the British team, led by Brooke, patiently listened to their American counterparts, letting them fully articulate their views uninterrupted. Then the British went to work just as they had rehearsed. They focused on Marshall, the man who the prime minister believed was the key figure among the Americans. First going into details about all the logistical hurdles of a winter campaign in France (the soonest realistic time the invasion could be launched) and the shortage of men and landing craft for such an operation, Brooke and his colleagues then introduced additional arguments in favor of invading Italy. Although generally aimed at convincing Marshall, a few of the advantages were meant to specifically appeal to King (the Suez Canal would get opened up) and Arnold (additional bombers would be made available for London-based attacks on Germany).

Although Marshall put up a good fight for several days, it was a losing battle. Even his own planners within the U.S. Army began telling him an invasion of France was going to be difficult to undertake in 1943. Knowing that inactivity was a nonstarter for the president, Marshall reluctantly accepted the British plan. But before doing so, he wanted to discuss the Pacific theater. Letting King take the lead, the Americans pushed hard against British efforts to restrict activities in the Pacific and limit the overall allocation of resources there.

The arguments regarding the Pacific were equally combative during the conference. The Americans and British were divided on the fundamental question of whether to take the fight to the Japanese (favored by the Americans, especially King) or maintain the defensive posture toward them agreed upon at the *Arcadia Conference* held in Washington (preferred by the British, most notably Brooke).

Marshall insisted that the conditions existing in the Pacific at the time of *Arcadia* had changed dramatically, and it was thus foolish to cling to a strategy developed at that stage of the War (an argument similar to one the British often used on the Americans when it came to European strategy). Marshall's commitment to this thinking was not simply a courtesy to Ernest King in exchange for King's support of Marshall's European goals. It did not take much for King and MacArthur to convince him that the balance of power had shifted away from the Japanese in the Pacific (particularly since the Battle of Midway in June 1942). He agreed that when it came to certain operations in that theater, the best defense was now a strong offense.

Despite Marshall's arguments and both the logic and passion that went into them, Brooke dug in his heels. It was only the effort and skill of Sir John Dill—then at the peak of his influence—that brought him to consider a compromise. The two sides finally agreed that offensive operations would be allowed in the Pacific but only if they were undertaken with the existing resources in Asia and did not deter from the primary objective of defeating Hitler first. This provided Marshall and King with enough wiggle room to exploit any opportunity presenting itself in the future.

Upon arriving back in Washington, the chief of staff formally briefed an agitated Stimson on the agreements made at Casablanca. Stimson had already received information on the central themes, but not the details. Once Marshall walked him through the entire proceedings and "brightened the picture," Stimson was less troubled. With the British dead-set against a cross-Channel operation in 1943, he, too, realized the only other logical alternative was an invasion of Sicily.

A Setback in North Africa

Despite the considerable amount of time taken up in Casablanca discussing what the next move should be *after* North Africa was taken, the Allies still hadn't taken North Africa. Quickly fortified by Hitler after the landings in November 1942, the German army, operating from its stronghold in Tunisia, held off attacks from the British (moving west from Libya) and the Americans (moving east from Morocco and Algeria). Recognizing that the overburdened Eisenhower needed assistance, Marshall agreed with the British in January to a reorganization that kept his protégé in overall command of the air, land, and sea forces but brought in British General Harold Alexander to serve as his deputy, British General Arthur Tedder to command the Allied air forces, and British Admiral Andrew Cunningham to command the Allied naval forces.

To further support Eisenhower, Marshall also decided the time was right to elevate George Patton and Omar Bradley. Both men would play crucial roles in the fighting to come and would go down in history as two of Marshall's most able recruits.

Marshall recommended Patton to Eisenhower as an officer who would make an excellent deputy for his ground forces given his talent for leadership and overall aggressiveness. When streamlining the Army as chief of staff earlier, Marshall decided against giving high-command positions to officers over the age of fifty. The fifty-seven-year-old Patton was one of the few exceptions. Impressed with his record during the First World War, particularly during the Saint Mihiel and Meuse-Argonne offensives, Marshall had noted that Patton was an officer who'd take his men "through hell and high water" and was the best tank man in the Army (prophetically, Marshall also wrote down at that time that one would need to keep a "tight rope" around his neck).[5]

Stimson loved the choice; he had known Patton for more than thirty years, going back to when the Californian served as his aide during his first stint as secretary of war. They met up again in Paris during the First World

War and strengthened their friendship. During the 1930s, the two men regularly rode horses together and had dinners with their wives.[6]

Omar Bradley was also a Marshall guy, one of the first brought over to join him when he became chief of staff. Marshall thought Bradley could act as the "eyes and ears" of Eisenhower on the ground in North Africa. He'd been preparing Bradley for such an assignment, as he liked to prepare everyone with great potential, by giving him increasingly greater responsibilities as the War progressed. Bradley would eventually command the Twelfth Army Group comprising forty-three divisions and over 1.3 million men, the greatest number of men to serve under a single commander in U.S. history.

The appointments of Bradley and Patton thrilled Eisenhower; he, too, had known both men for years. He was also pleased to hear Marshall was working to relieve him of the significant political and civil responsibilities taking up far too much of his time. John McCloy was Marshall's first and only choice for the job, but he needed to get Stimson's approval. This was anything but a given; Stimson regularly fended off requests for McCloy's services and generally expressed resentment at having to do so. But Marshall, knowing that Stimson would want Eisenhower focused solely on military matters, sent a telegram to him in Charleston (where he was taking a few days off) asking if Ike could "borrow" McCloy for "a month or two."[7]

Stimson was not happy at the suggestion but knew it was the right thing to do. After discussing it with Bundy and then McCloy (who flew down to South Carolina to talk about it in person with his boss), Stimson gave Marshall permission on the condition McCloy was back in Washington after a month.

The reorganization and the appointments of Patton and Bradley came too late to prevent the first major setback for the Americans in the North African theater, but in time to recover from it. In early February 1943, the Americans under Major General Lloyd Fredendall were driven back through the Kasserine Pass in eastern Tunisia with substantial losses in men, tanks, and artillery weapons. Bradley's reports from the field—confirmed by other American officers—suggested, among other things, there was a lack of communication between ground and air forces partly responsible for the mishap that needed to be fixed. Bradley also told Eisenhower that Fredendall had failed to provide strong leadership. The entire episode was an embarrassment to Marshall, who had been desperately trying to prove to his British counterparts that his men could fight.

Given that Fredendall was highly recommended by Marshall, Eisenhower was initially hesitant to ask the chief of staff to relieve him. But when several other officers confirmed Bradley's opinion, Ike asked Marshall to reassign him so that he could put Patton in command. Once in place, Patton immediately appointed Bradley as his deputy. With these changes, the Americans went back on the attack and recovered the lost ground by the end of the same month. After that, Rommel remained on the defensive and it became only a matter of time before North Africa was in Allied control. Realizing this, Eisenhower sent Patton to Morocco in March to begin planning for the invasion of Sicily, leaving Bradley in place to finish the Germans off. Marshall then turned his attention toward the Pacific Theater.

Troubles with the Navy and MacArthur

Notwithstanding the conventional challenges that always surface between allies during war, the working relationship between the Americans and the British began improving shortly after the Casablanca Conference. Offsetting the usual politics, clashes in ego, and legitimate differences in national interests, there were common goals and high-minded men to stay focused on them (most notably Marshall's close friend Sir John Dill, who continued to skillfully serve as a bridge between the two countries until his death in the fall of 1944).

If only the same could be said for the ongoing struggles between the U.S. Army and the U.S. Navy. Unfortunately, there was no John Dill to reconcile the long-standing differences between the rival services. It is doubtful any man could have; the mutual antipathy between the two services, passed down through the ages from cadet to cadet and midshipman to midshipman, was so entrenched that even a common enemy could not easily bring them together. One of Marshall's great accomplishments during his time as chief of staff was managing this friction. By gaining the trust and respect of senior naval leaders, he was able to craft compromises. He accomplished this despite the persistently belligerent nature of his naval counterpart, Admiral King. Integrity, something Marshall possessed in spades, went a long way toward breaking down even the most hardened of temperaments. King battled often with Marshall during the War but knew in his heart that the chief of staff had no agenda other than victory for the Allies.

Marshall also benefited by having Henry Stimson in charge of the War Department. Nobody in the Navy questioned Stimson's character or honesty either. That is not to say they liked him; several Navy men, including King, thought Stimson was self-righteous, preachy, and stubborn. But they knew he, too, had no other ambitions outside of winning the War. By earning the total trust of Secretary of Navy Knox, Stimson ensured Marshall's efforts with King and other high-ranking admirals would bring greater efficiencies to the war effort.

Despite all this, General Douglas MacArthur ensured that for every two steps forward made in the relationship, there would be a step back.

For all his greatness, MacArthur could not be relied upon to be a team player. Naturally, Admiral King did not respond well to him. Getting consensus from these two men was Marshall's cross to bear for the duration of the War. A lesser man might have been tempted to relieve himself of the constant headaches brought on by MacArthur by replacing him with an officer who acted more like Eisenhower did with the British: firm, but reasonable and amicable. But the chief of staff stood by his longtime nemesis, not out of loyalty but instead because he knew how much value MacArthur brought to the Pacific Theater. When he weighed this against the disadvantages of having MacArthur and his chief subordinates continually battle and insult the Navy, he stuck by his general, perhaps hoping that when troubles occurred, he and Stimson could smooth things over with Admiral King, Secretary Knox, and Undersecretary of the Navy James Forrestal (who became an increasingly important part of the administration as the War progressed).

Although it was difficult to maintain, Marshall's faith in MacArthur was rewarded. His successes at the Battles of Buna-Gona and the Bismarck Sea (in January and March 1943 respectively) were welcome news to the War Department. Both victories were major steps toward neutralizing the major Japanese base in Rabaul with its strategic harbor and airbases. In turn, this provided MacArthur a better chance to fulfill the pledge he made to the Filipinos to return to their archipelago and liberate it from the Japanese.

Hitting Their Stride

With positive developments finally coming from both theaters in the spring of 1943, Winston Churchill once again took the initiative to suggest another conference with the Americans. He wanted to discuss various options after Sicily was taken. The Allies had yet to launch the invasion of Sicily (that would happen during the second week of July), but it was characteristic of the prime minister to want to start the planning process early. Roosevelt agreed and proposed hosting the meeting in Washington in mid-May.

Although Marshall was focused on developing plans for Sicily and *Operation Cartwheel* (the plan to neutralize the Japanese base at Rabaul under MacArthur), he knew he had to set aside time to better prepare himself to do battle with the British Bulldog and his chief of the imperial general staff. He could be sure both men would once again lobby against the cross-Channel invasion and have all their arguments well thought out and rehearsed.

Fortunately for Marshall, he and his staff could afford to devote sufficient time to prepare for the British visit. Things were running fairly well, and he could comfortably rely on his own men and Stimson's transcendent staff to more than adequately handle the large number of issues facing the Army during the spring of 1943. Like many officials in Washington, Marshall marveled at the competence of Stimson's young team and the secretary's management of it. In a sense, it was his team, too, because the two men gave each other open access to members of their respective staffs. This allowed Stimson and Marshall not only to improve the overall efficiency of the War Department, but also to take advantage of a broader and more diverse array of talent and advice to draw upon for any specific issue. Such access also helped develop a common culture within the Army and War Departments and minimized the silo effect that can develop between civilian and military employees during peace or war. Whether directly intended by the two men, or simply a consequence of their approach to work, such silos within the War Department never took shape during the Second World War.

After almost three years working together, the partnership of Stimson and Marshall was a model of proficiency and productivity. Their division of labor was unambiguous, yet they customarily sought counsel from one another; their daily face-to-face communications were frequent, but always to the point; and they utilized each other skillfully when their combined influence was required to secure a shared objective, or when one or the other was better suited to handle a particular task by himself. Everything boiled down to the unshakable trust the two men had in each other. Neither ever questioned the motives of the other when their thinking on any given issue was not aligned. On those occasions when they had a dispute, they sat together and discussed it immediately. These discussions often got heated but rarely personal.

Considering the sheer amount of time Stimson and Marshall spent with one another and the unprecedented strain under which they worked, it is remarkable their relationship remained so resilient. Harvey Bundy, who worked closely with both men, once commented that only on one occasion during the War did he hear Marshall express frustration with Stimson. The comment, spoken lightly, related to the latter's enthusiasm for discussing military strategy (as a former secretary of war and an artillery officer during the First World War, Stimson thought he was something of a military strategist). During a discussion with Bundy, Marshall said in passing, "It would be just as well if the Secretary was a little less of a Churchillian strategist."[8]

As for Stimson, his daily diary entries during the War were full of complaints about government and military officials in Washington. But despite the countless issues he and Marshall discussed and resolved together over five years, only once did he record words that could be construed as a direct criticism of Marshall (and even this can be debated). It was the first full day of the *Trident Conference* in May 1943, and Stimson was feeling anxious that General Arnold could not attend (due to a heart attack he had suffered the day before the conference was to begin). The secretary of war wrote that the American contingent could benefit from Arnold's "fearless and undiplomatic" style, which he believed was a good counterpoise to Marshall, who was "a little over-diplomatic." In more than four thousand pages of private entries into his diary during the time the two men worked together, this was the harshest thing Henry Stimson ever said about George Marshall.

Equally important to the high regard Stimson and Marshall held for one another as individuals was the respect each man held for the other's formal position. During any meeting between the two, both men were keenly aware they sat across from not only a colleague, but one who represented a sanctioned office that had evolved over time and reflected the thinking and efforts of many prominent public servants who came before them, some of whom they knew and greatly admired. This shared conviction was another critical element to their successful partnership. Admiral King, by contrast, did not give much indication that he respected the office of the secretary of the navy, and it led to numerous problems for the Navy during the War.

With Marshall fully occupied during the spring of 1943, Stimson spent a majority of his time on a number of issues that could be divided into roughly two categories: pet projects of his relating to technology and innovation, and administrative problems he believed were the direct consequence of Roosevelt's chaotic management style.

Stimson and Technology

Regarding innovation in general within the Army, one might have expected that an old military veteran like Stimson (he was seventy-five in the spring of 1943) would remain loyal to the tried-and-tested weapons and conventional techniques of the past. Military history is full of experienced men who were punished for not keeping up with the times. British Field Marshal Douglas Haig of World War I fame is an oft-cited example. By clinging to his belief that the horse and cavalry would prevail over tanks, and dismissing the machine gun as an "overrated" threat to horses, Haig guaranteed his name would forever be associated with the carnage of the Somme and Passchendaele.

By contrast, Stimson seemed Da Vinci–like in his vision. In other parts of his life, he could be categorized as a traditionalist, but to the surprise of so many of his peers, Stimson was the exact opposite when it came to war. Far more so than Marshall and other high-ranking military officials, he was constantly and aggressively pushing for new advancements and pressing officers to open their individual and collective minds to the benefits of modern science and technology. Few people in the Roosevelt administration were as open to innovation as the secretary of war was when it came to harnessing the power of science to get an edge on the battlefield.

As soon as he joined the War Department, Stimson took the lead in lobbying Roosevelt to stay formally engaged with leading American scientists such as Vannevar Bush (director of the Office of Scientific Research and Development). He pushed for the organization of a committee to focus solely on new weapons and forcefully led the administration's efforts to stay current on developments in radar. He also spent, considering his position, an unusual amount of his time thinking about how to improve or better employ existing weapons.

It was his obsession with radar that brought most value to the American war effort. Stimson was the driving force behind the administration's efforts to develop it quickly. His interest in radar stemmed from a meeting he held in Washington in 1941 with Sir Robert Watson-Watt, the Scottish pioneer in the field. Watson-Watt, largely credited with developing the radar capabilities the English used to win the Battle of Britain, berated the United States during his visit for being so far behind in its radar defense systems. Stimson took advantage of the general excitement surrounding

Watson-Watt's visit to push for the use of radar in Panama (to protect the canal) and began fully advocating for its use on land, air, and sea in all theaters. In early 1942, he hired Edward Bowles from MIT as a consultant for such purposes, and Bowles went on to make significant contributions to the Allies in this field during the War.[9]

Why was the oldest member of FDR's cabinet the most open to new ideas and the most aggressive in creating an environment where such ideas could be nurtured? It was likely a combination of reasons: First, Stimson was a naturally creative individual with a forward-thinking personality; second, his forty-plus-year career as a legal advisor to industrial America gave him insight into how the benefits of technology could contribute to economic dominance; and finally, there was the influence of his singularly remarkable first cousin (and protégé) Alfred Lee Loomis.[10]

Franklin Roosevelt once said of Alfred Loomis that no American civilian contributed more to securing victory for the Allies in World War II. Loomis, twenty years younger than Stimson, was an unparalleled overachiever who had an extraordinary career as a lawyer, soldier, investment banker, and investor before directing his immense talents and acquired wealth to a hugely successful pursuit of scientific inventions. When the Second World War began, he turned his focus toward discoveries that could provide the Allies a winning edge.

Loomis's first job out of Harvard Law School (where he graduated cum laude in 1912) was with Winthrop & Stimson, where he immediately excelled under the guidance of his cousin and mentor. The First World War interrupted his rapid rise as a New York lawyer. Loomis volunteered and worked on ballistics at the Aberdeen Proving Ground in Maryland, where his accomplishments included inventing the first instrument in history (the Aberdeen Chronograph) that could accurately measure the muzzle velocity of artillery shells. It was during the First World War that Loomis established a lifelong love of physics through his association with renowned American physicist Robert Wood.

After World War I ended, Loomis and his brother-in-law purchased a small investment bank on the verge of bankruptcy and built it into a powerhouse on Wall Street specializing in utilities. While amassing a fortune as an investment banker, Loomis and his partner left their mark on corporate America by pioneering, among other innovations, the concept of a holding company.

Although extremely wealthy by anyone's definition during the 1920s, Loomis secured an even more formidable fortune by being one of the few individuals to anticipate both the stock market crash of 1929 and its subsequent rise. Several months before Black Tuesday, he and his partner sensed economic trends that did not square with their calculated growth projections, and therefore they converted all their investments into cash. Equally impressive, Loomis aggressively jumped back into the market just as stock prices hit rock bottom. His fortune exploded.

With enough money for several lifetimes (at one point he owned nearly all of Hilton Head Island), Loomis turned his attention and wealth to science. He established the Loomis Laboratory in his Tuxedo Park, New York, mansion, stocking it with the most expensive, state-of-the-art scientific equipment money could buy (equipment many universities could not even afford). For the next twenty years, he hosted such luminaries of twentieth-century science as Einstein, Fermi, Bohr, and Franck and conducted studies and experiments with them across a broad array of scientific disciplines.

When his operation in Tuxedo Park outgrew his mansion, Loomis moved to Cambridge, Massachusetts, where he set up a larger endeavor working jointly with MIT. It was there during World War II that Loomis and his staff began looking seriously into radar. This eventually led to his most famous invention: LORAN, a long-range radio navigational system enabling ships and planes to precisely determine their position and speed from low-frequency radio signals. Until GPS technology (based partly on LORAN) was made generally available to the public at the turn of the twenty-first century, it was the most widely used long-range navigation system on the planet.

Older cousin Henry Stimson was a father figure to Alfred Loomis (whose own father separated from his mother when he was young and died when he was in college). He idolized him and maintained close personal contact with him throughout his life. It was the Midas touch of Loomis (who handled his cousin's investments) that allowed Stimson to gain complete financial independence in the 1920s so that he could devote the rest of his life to public service. During the Second World War, Stimson and Loomis met more frequently, as the former was increasingly intrigued and influenced by the latter's enthusiasm for the promise of modern and advanced technologies.

Besides surrounding himself with all the scientific talent money could buy, and being a first-rate physicist himself, Loomis was also a visionary. Like a Steve Jobs surrounded by a group of Steve Wozniaks, Loomis possessed the talent to immediately recognize the military or commercial consequence of any specific breakthrough made in his laboratory. Stimson, having witnessed his cousin's unique abilities in law and business, assumed his intuitiveness extended into the scientific world as well, and therefore he listened closely when Loomis shared his thoughts. Writing in his diary about a lunch he shared with his cousin on New Year's Eve 1943, Stimson recorded that the subject of rockets came up. Loomis told Stimson the rocket would be "as important as the first use of the barrel for gun powder." That was enough of a tip for Stimson to immediately set up a meeting for the following night between Loomis, McNarney, and McNair so that the two generals could hear directly about the future of warfare.[11]

Stimson's efforts when it came to new technologies extended to all aspects of war. During the months between the Casablanca and Washington Conferences (held in January and May 1943 respectively), he made multiple attempts to convince both the Navy and the president to adopt better antisubmarine measures. His interest in the subject was first piqued on his visit to Panama in March 1942, when he witnessed the benefit of using bombers to successfully combat the menace of submarines. He wanted to use the same tactic in Europe by retrofitting radar equipment onto Army Air Force planes for the purpose of hunting down German submarines. He quickly asked for and was given the opportunity to test the method with several B-18 bombers being phased out. The experiment was successful and led to the sinking of several German submarines along both the North and South American coasts.

For several reasons, the Navy was not interested (perhaps one being because it did not want the Army solving any of its own problems). Stimson was incensed; although the Navy could point to its own convoy plan, it was defensive in nature, and Admiral King admitted in late March 1943 it might take up to six months to perfect.

Roosevelt understood the significance of the experiments Stimson had overseen (and similar results the British independently achieved in Europe), but he did not want to go over King's head. He therefore encouraged Stimson to convince the secretary of navy. This was a timid response from Roosevelt because he knew Admiral King paid little attention to Knox.

Frustrated, but not naïve to the realities of interservice rivalries, Stimson came up with the idea of placing the radar-outfitted bombers under joint control of the British Army, the British Navy, the American Army, and the American Navy. He believed such a structure would neutralize the U.S. Army and U.S. Navy rivalry and would therefore be acceptable to Admiral King. But Marshall, more experienced in these matters and more of a pragmatist than his boss, counseled Stimson that unless the effort was small, King would never agree to it. Feeling he could carry his special project only so far, Stimson passed the baton to Marshall and the Joint Chiefs of Staff in April and convinced Harry Hopkins to follow up closely with the president.[12]

During this same time period, Stimson took it upon himself to personally see to it that the Army update its training for the use of antiaircraft guns. Claiming old methods no longer worked for the modern weapons coming out of American factories, Stimson lobbied Marshall and other Army officers to radically change how they were teaching the skill. Stimson was embarrassed that the Navy was well ahead in its training methods and continued to badger Marshall and members of Marshall's staff until the changes were made.[13]

Stimson never stopped pushing for scientific and technical improvements or innovations both small and large. Vannevar Bush, who headed the group through which nearly all U.S. wartime military research and development was undertaken, remarked to Alfred Loomis a few days before D-Day that he found it amazing Stimson was, despite his advanced age, the most forward-looking man in either the Army or the Navy when it came to technology.[14]

Roosevelt's Management Style

When he was not pitching Marshall, the president, Hopkins, the Navy, or anyone else he could corner on the benefits of using new technologies and tactics in 1943, Stimson was spending his time on problems he believed were largely created as a result of Roosevelt's management style. He never wavered in his belief that many of the difficulties he faced before and after Pearl Harbor could have been avoided if the president was not "the poorest administrator" he had ever worked under "with respect to the orderly procedure and routine of his performance" and a poor judge of men, who also does "not know how to use them in coordination."[15] Stimson's diary entries throughout the War knocked FDR for his disorderly approach to running it. It was particularly painful for a protégé of Elihu Root—a man considered by many historians to be the greatest administrator America ever had—to be a daily witness to the consequences of poor administration.

One such issue arising before the Americans even hit the shores of North Africa involved the question of which department or agency should handle the management of occupied territories. It first came to Stimson's attention during the summer of 1942, when members of the State

Department and several of the "cherubs" surrounding Roosevelt in the White House objected spiritedly when they discovered the Army was training men for just such a task. Both Stimson and Marshall supported such training because they believed through shared experiences there was room for improvement in this regard. Stimson particularly, as a former secretary of state, thought that when one manages the affairs of an occupied territory, even if only on a temporary basis, one must have a basic understanding of economics and finance. He hoped these training schools ensured that the Army was competent in this regard in the early critical days following a military victory. Marshall was in complete agreement with him.

Once the Allies began making actual progress in North Africa, the issue of who was responsible naturally became more pressing. Characteristically, Roosevelt ensured there was a long list of possible candidates: Herbert Lehman resigned as governor of New York to accept an appointment by FDR to be the director of foreign relief and rehabilitation operations reporting to the secretary of state; Vice President Henry Wallace was chairman of the Board of Economic Warfare; Edward Stettinius, head of Lend-Lease, was also given responsibilities in regard to occupied territories overlapping those belonging to the State Department; and then there was, of course, Stimson.

The State Department believed it was the logical choice to assume such responsibilities, and many in the White House agreed. Stimson thought otherwise and spent weeks trying to make his case. He argued that the role had been in the provenance of the War Department going back to the Spanish-American War and the Army was the only logical choice given that it, unlike the State Department, had the resources already in place to get the job done once any particular town was taken over. The State Department, argued Stimson, had never been an administrative agency; its personnel—"ambassadors and ministers and consular agencies, none of which do anything except write and talk"—were not well suited for the hard responsibility. Nevertheless, pledged Stimson, the Army would eventually pass the responsibility to civilian authorities as soon as enough of them made their way toward the front lines and the recently occupied towns.

As both a former secretary of war and secretary of state, Stimson sincerely believed he was an authority on the subject. He knew how to set up such operations and explained to Roosevelt that he could ensure members of the Army followed his advice. The president, ever mindful about keeping the military from growing too powerful, disagreed.

Sure that his boss was not thinking practically about the issue, the stubborn Stimson, with help from Marshall, created a Civil Affairs Division within the War Department in March 1943 to manage the tasks that would automatically fall upon the Army until the State Department could get its act together and arrive in force to the areas of occupation. The difference between Stimson and Roosevelt on this subject was simply a matter of timing (Marshall went along with Stimson but had mixed feelings about it).

Despite telling Stimson he understood his rationale, Roosevelt was still philosophically opposed to the Army taking the lead in this area during the spring of 1943. Instead, he created a new position of assistant secretary of state to take charge. Six months later, when the U.S. Army started liberating cities and towns, the president reversed himself when he saw Stimson had been correct as to the need for the Army to take immediate charge of captured cities as they fell. He formally handed the initial responsibility to the War Department in November.[16] Stimson felt he'd wasted a lot of time for a decision that seemed fairly obvious to him.

While Stimson was attempting to introduce structure where Roosevelt had created chaos, he was also forced to work with individuals who he believed were not well suited to the jobs given to them by the president. Donald Nelson, Paul McNutt, William Jeffers, and Elmer Davis were four men who were particularly objectionable to him during the first six months of 1943. To be fair to these men, Roosevelt gave them positions either too vague with respect to their brief, too broad in their scope, or assigned too late to allow for a meaningful contribution (given other groups had been busy fulfilling many of the assigned tasks).

But even with such handicaps, Stimson believed each man fell short for a variety of reasons: Nelson was weak and indecisive (as many others in Washington believed, including Bob Patterson); McNutt was nothing more than an empire builder; Jeffers, the "Rubber Czar," was a "demagogue" with no sense of the big picture as it related to supply issues; and Davis was simply too mediocre an appointee to overcome the jurisdictional issues Roosevelt created by appointing him as head of the Office of War Information.

Even if he was inclined to agree with Stimson about these four men, the president was a man who strongly disliked firing people. In lieu of doing so, he often simply assigned another individual to a different job with similar responsibilities. This naturally created even more problems.

For Stimson, the two-week period prior to the British visit to Washington on May 11, 1943, was a microcosm of the first four months of the year with respect to both this issue and his pursuit of scientific innovations: He dined with Alfred Loomis, who briefed him over dinner at Woodley on the

progress he was making with regard to radar and other new inventions; he
was still pushing Marshall and Harry Hopkins for a solution to the German
submarine menace; and he was spending time fixing problems created by
both Jeffers and Nelson. He took a break to sit down with Marshall on May
10 to discuss how preparations were going for the visitors from London due
to arrive in Washington the following day. Both feared the prime minister
was coming over to change Roosevelt's mind about a cross-Channel attack.
They weren't wrong.

The *Trident Conference*, Washington, D.C. (May 11–21, 1943)

Churchill, the British Chiefs of Staff, and an entourage of nearly one hundred arrived in Washington by train from New York (where they had sailed
to from Scotland on the *Queen Mary*) just hours before the Allies got word
Tunisia had been taken from the Germans along with droves of prisoners
(among them General von Arnim, the replacement of Field Marshal Erwin
Rommel as head of Army Group Africa two months earlier).

Although great news, the timing did not necessarily bode well for the
Americans, who wished once again to take up the mantle of promoting a
cross-Channel attack. The British would certainly remind their hosts that
the decisive victory in North Africa proved that the strategy of hitting the
Germans on the periphery was working and the decision made at Casablanca to invade Sicily after North Africa was a correct one. They would also
leverage the good news by pushing for an invasion of the Italian mainland
once Sicily was taken. This was the master plan Alan Brooke and the British
were going to pitch to the Americans in any event, but the victory in Tunisia
gave it a greater degree of credibility.

Marshall knew the British were going to propose such a plan. All the
Americans knew. So to prepare, the Joint Chiefs of Staff agreed to ask
their respective planners to look at the option of invading Italy once Sicily was secured (the attack in Sicily was scheduled for early July 1943). It
was not that Marshall and his colleagues were any less committed to hitting
the beaches of France, but they wanted to be organized in case Churchill
was successful in convincing Roosevelt to continue the "soft underbelly"
approach to fighting the Germans.

When it came to the cross-Channel option Marshall wanted to promote,
the question of timing was one he and his American colleagues struggled

with. There was a lack of consensus whether an attack could be successfully launched in 1943. If it couldn't, Roosevelt was going to insist the U.S. Army remain active, and that meant landing troops on the mainland of Italy.

There were also several strong arguments favoring an invasion of Italy once Sicily was taken: The Italians might be inclined to give up; the Russians would benefit from the continued pressure; and the opening up of the Mediterranean would free up substantial tons of British shipping (due to the considerably shortened distance it would take their ships to get to and from India). Marshall was also conscious that a successful campaign in Italy would continue to build up both the morale and skills of the American Army in Europe that, at the time of the conference, had been fighting for only four months.

Despite seeing some merit in taking the Italian mainland, Marshall was not going to do Churchill's bidding for a strategy he believed would ultimately delay victory. On the contrary, a little more than a week before the conference began, Marshall told FDR that the Joint Chiefs of Staff were opposed to attacking the mainland of Italy after Sicily was taken. Emphasizing again that the road to victory over Hitler went through France, Marshall attempted to strengthen Roosevelt's allegiance to a French invasion before Churchill would surely chip away at it. What he wanted by the end of the conference was an ironclad commitment from the British to undertake an invasion of France at some date certain—the sooner, the better, of course.

To achieve their goals at the conference, Marshall and his JCS colleagues stepped up their preparations for *Trident* before the British arrived. Although their efforts might have fallen a little short of the standards established by Churchill and his staff (who once again used the six-day crossing of the Atlantic to endlessly hone their already-well-rehearsed arguments), the Americans were decently prepared. More importantly, they were united.

Two days before the conference began, Marshall and the Joint Chiefs of Staff got Roosevelt's agreement to push the British to commit to a cross-Channel attack and be fully prepared to launch it by no later than the spring of 1944. While happy, neither Marshall nor Stimson were sure FDR would hold steady on the pledge when faced with the incessant and persuasive arguments from the prime minister. As it turns out, they were wrong; Roosevelt proved far more resolute than either of his subordinates anticipated. As a results-oriented leader, the president was getting impatient that the predictions made by the British when pitching their plans over the past year had not come to pass: Stalin saw no considerable transfer of German troops away from his front, and the Mediterranean was no easier for

Allied ships to navigate. Perhaps the president finally believed Marshall was correct about the Mediterranean being a "blind alley."

Churchill, generally careful with his words, opened the discussions at the White House by stating his government was committed to an invasion of France but only if the odds of success were "reasonable." Until that was determined (and he doubted it would be in the spring of 1944), he suggested a successful invasion of Italy be launched instead. Among other arguments Churchill used in favor of such a strategy was that success in Italy would isolate and demoralize the Germans and cause them to shift significant troops away from the Russian Front.

Once Churchill had finished, Roosevelt spoke. Shocking the prime minister and his staff, FDR insisted firmly that the British not only needed to get on board with the decision to prioritize a cross-Channel attack, but they also needed to do so quickly. He then handed the ball off to an equally surprised but delighted Marshall, who proceeded to make a case to his counterparts. When Brooke protested and started talking up the British plan instead, Marshall pointed out to him his principal objection to it: Putting forces in the Mediterranean would only lead to the need for more forces. Citing North Africa, where the requirements were clearly underestimated by the Allies, Marshall said he envisioned the same problems in Italy, which would jeopardize any chance of attacking the coast of France, even in 1944. And this, warned Marshall, would have the added effect of stalling efforts to defeat the Japanese. Such delays, Marshall concluded firmly, were unacceptable to the Americans.

Tough talk from Roosevelt and Marshall did not deter the indefatigable Brooke. He said an invasion of France was not possible until 1945 at the earliest, and possibly not until 1946. To the Americans, this only confirmed their suspicions: The ghosts of Passchendaele and the Somme continued to haunt the British (Churchill's personal physician, a friend of Marshall's, told the chief of staff in confidence that the great loss of life suffered by the British at the Somme was indeed a key factor in the prime minister's opposition to a cross-Channel attack).[17]

At this stage of the War, the increasingly confident Americans had far less patience with their ally's continuing anxiety. They also felt they had the strength to start calling the shots. Soon after *Trident* began, this reality became painfully clear to Churchill, who had anticipated it for months (Marshall said after the War that he believed the peak of British dominance over the Americans was following their victory over the Germans in the

Second Battle of El Alamein, six months before *Trident*).[18] Power dynamics aside, the British were not going to fold easily; on the contrary, they spent most of the conference stubbornly defending their positions.

But the Americans were determined not to repeat the experience of Casablanca. While deliberating among themselves on the third day of the conference, Marshall, King, and Leahy decided that they would be prepared to draw from an old playbook by making it clear to the British that if they did not agree to prioritize an invasion of France, then the Americans would shift their resources to Japan. Roosevelt had rejected employing this threat ten months earlier, but the Joint Chiefs of Staff knew that much had happened over ten months and thought Roosevelt would likely agree to it this time.

As it happened, the threat was unnecessary. Recognizing the American strength and resolve, the British relented. They remained adamant an invasion of France was not possible in 1943 but told the Americans they thought it could be pulled off in the spring of 1944 and were willing to make that happen. Although it was a step in the right direction in the eyes of Marshall, the British continued to link the success of the cross-Channel attack with the ongoing success of the Russians. That was fine with the chief of staff; he knew he was going to ramp up bombing efforts against Germany, a strategy that would provide critical support to the Soviet Union on the Eastern Front.

Marshall, a strong believer in airpower, also believed the increased bombing of Germany would make the amphibious landings in France easier and enable the Allies to launch the assault with fewer men. A couple of years after the War ended, Charles Portal, the British chief of staff for air, credited Marshall for having the vision to see the potential of airpower more clearly than other leaders.[19] In retrospect, it seemed like an obvious strategy to get behind; at the time, however, few were certain whether it would have a significant impact or not.

Having secured the British commitment to work toward a cross-Channel operation in the spring of 1944, the Allies still needed to figure out what to do over the next twelve months in Europe (as well as discuss strategy in the Pacific). Marshall's reservations about an aggressive campaign up the Italian boot had already been registered, but Brooke and his colleagues insisted on making a more detailed presentation in favor of it. Neither man looked forward to what was likely going to be another slugfest.

After contentious meetings on both Friday, May 14, and the follow-ing morning, it was finally agreed that two sets of plans to end the war in Europe should be prepared: The Americans would focus on the buildup of troops and equipment in southern England for an eventual attack across the Channel; the British on an Italian campaign. Both plans could assume that the bombing in Germany would be intensified.

Before the conference began, Marshall had correctly anticipated that the first few days would get ugly and thought some kind of a break would be welcomed on the first weekend. As such, he thoughtfully organized an off-site, one that would enable the British and American military leaders to put aside all topics of war for a period and focus solely on relaxing and getting to know one another. He arranged for the British Chiefs of Staff (and a cou-ple other high-ranking British commanders) to join him and other mem-bers of the JCS in taking a relaxing twenty-four-hour excursion to Colonial Williamsburg in Virginia.

To successfully get the event off the ground, Marshall sought the assis-tance of the president of Colonial Williamsburg, who, in turn, recruited John D. Rockefeller Jr., the man who had recently paid for the restoration of the former capital of Virginia to its past glory. All three men threw them-selves into making the offsite a memorable one.

While Roosevelt was hosting the prime minister at Shangri-La (later renamed Camp David), the military leaders flew to Langley Field on Satur-day morning, thirty miles southeast of Williamsburg (now Langley Air Force Base). Getting in cars for the rest of the journey, the group stopped midway in order to take a quick tour of the Yorktown battlefield, where the Brit-ish surrendered to George Washington in October 1781. Marshall gambled that the historical interest from the visit would trump any lingering hard feelings among the British 161 years later. His instincts were correct; the British loved the excursion, and the historic battle was discussed at length between all members of the Combined Chiefs of Staff.

The group then jumped back into their cars and headed toward Wil-liamsburg, where John D. Rockefeller Jr. had gone out of his way to impress the military leaders and make their visit to Williamsburg special. He arranged all the menus and flew down prepared dishes from his private club in New York, fruits and cheeses from the finest upscale shops in Man-hattan, and heavy cream from his own dairy farm in Pocantico Hills, New York (hand-carried by his personal butler).[20]

By all accounts, the trip was well received by the overworked men. Mar-shall encouraged everyone to forget about the War by taking walks, playing croquet, or going for a swim. The British were more than happy to comply. Brooke spent considerable time bird-watching (an activity he periodically undertook during the War to unwind); Portal and Ismay went swimming in the cool waters running through the grounds; and Wavell took hundreds of photographs. In the evening, after enjoying mint juleps in period-fashioned silver goblets, the officers were served authentic American cuisine at the Williamsburg Inn followed by coffee and brandy. They ended the night in the Governor's Palace, the formal residence of the Royal Governors in the Colony of Virginia, meticulously reconstructed ten years earlier as part of the overall restoration of Williamsburg. The palace sparkled from the light of hundreds of candles, and the night went so well that Marshall sat down and played a small spinet he had noticed while walking around the palace (knowing very few songs, he played an old World War I–era ballad called "Poor Butterfly)."[21]

Despite the wonderful pause, it was just that: a pause. By Sunday afternoon, they were all back in Washington ready to resume the debate. Given the outing, not much progress was made by either side on the papers they were supposed to present. They went back to work, still far apart regarding their views on both the Atlantic and Pacific Theaters.

Two more days of difficult discussions led to an impasse broken only after Marshall suggested a rare "off the record" meeting between just members of the Combined Chiefs of Staff (and not the twenty to thirty additional staff normally attending the meetings). During the meeting, a compromise was struck: The Americans got from the British a commitment for a May 1, 1944, cross-Channel operation utilizing at least twenty-nine divisions; the British got American support for an operation on the Italian mainland (under the conditions that each specific operation within Italy was subject to approval by the Combined Chiefs of Staff based on Eisenhower's recommendations, and seven divisions had to be ready for transfer to England by November 1, 1943).

Although it was a compromise, General Brooke referred to the agreement as a "triumph" for the British, given that the Americans "wanted to close down all operations" in the Mediterranean after Sicily was taken.[22] Marshall did well to give that impression to Brooke. He wanted to push the British hard for a cross-Channel invasion, but he knew that attempting one in 1943 was unlikely. Given Roosevelt's lack of tolerance for idle troops, Italy was the logical choice once Sicily was taken. Marshall also recognized the benefits of taking Italy even if Brooke insisted he didn't. As the floor manager of the American Joint Chiefs of Staff during the *Trident Conference*, Marshall made sure the British clearly understood that the Allies could not expect the War to end in Europe without going through France. Marshall was certain of this; the British were not. As such, the commitment from Brooke and his colleagues to establish a western front in 1944 could be just as easily seen as a victory for Marshall.

The conference lasted another six days before the British departed Washington on May 26, 1943 (more than two weeks after they arrived). The last few meetings were not much better than the first few. The topics covered included operations in the Pacific and Chinese theaters (where the two Allies were far apart in their views), the continuing havoc brought on by German submarines in the North Atlantic, and more specific details regarding the future plans in Europe.

As *Trident* ended, so, too, did any possible doubts about the new power dynamic between the British and Americans: It had permanently shifted to the United States, and every participant understood this. After coming up short in the previous conferences, George Marshall could safely say that *Trident* was an American victory. Churchill arrived at the same conclusion, and true to his character, he was going to try his best to fix it. Toward that, he invited Marshall to accompany himself and Alan Brooke to North Africa after the conference ended to meet with Eisenhower. Marshall was opposed to going, but Churchill pressured Roosevelt to send him along (FDR might have thought it was best if his chief advisor be present in case Churchill and Brooke tried to bully Ike into agreeing on a strategy contrary to what was just decided upon in Washington). The prime minister wanted time alone with Marshall to see if he could convince him to become more enthusiastic about the Mediterranean.

The meetings in Washington took a lot out of Marshall and Brooke, each of whom carried the heaviest load for their respective sides. There were fifteen meetings held during the two weeks between the Combined Chiefs of Staff, and six others that included Roosevelt and Churchill.[23] By many accounts, the meetings were the most acrimonious of all those held between the British and Americans during the War. It was not just the fundamental disagreements they had with one another; there was also bad blood carried over from Casablanca and earlier meetings. From the American point of view, the British had pulled the bait-and-switch on them one too many times when it came to the cross-Channel initiative. As for the British, they continued to believe the Americans were strategically inept and resented that their partners could now leverage their greater overall military and industrial strength to bully them into strategies they opposed.

Ever watchful for signs the chief of staff was approaching physical or mental exhaustion, Henry Stimson sensed Marshall was on edge even before *Trident* began. Midway through it, he had no doubts. A prominent senator had suggested on the floor of the Senate that many military officers were secretly in favor of shifting the focus of the War to the Pacific. When Marshall caught wind of this, he displayed a rare burst of rage in front of the secretary of war, pacing the floor of his office and claiming the senator was trying to destroy his character and reputation. Only a stern lecture from Stimson on the impossibility of that happening calmed the general down.

Long aware of Marshall's importance to the war effort, Stimson was convinced by the middle of 1943 that he was not *one* of the key figures, but *the* key figure and the "strongest man" in the country. On the same day he talked Marshall down from his tirade, Stimson wrote in his diary that on Marshall "more than anybody in government . . . rests the fortunes of the United States in this war."[24] As the chief of staff headed off with the prime minister to North Africa, Stimson was less worried that Marshall would be vulnerable to Churchill's persuasive abilities than he was about the general's overall health.

16

Turning the Corner

I believe therefore that the time has come for you to decide that your government must assume the responsibility of leadership in this great final movement of the European war which is now confronting us. . . . We cannot afford to begin the most dangerous operation of the war under half-hearted leadership which will invite failure or at least disappointing results. Nearly two years ago the British offered us this command. I think that now it should be accepted—if necessary, insisted on.[1]

—HENRY STIMSON, in a memorandum to
Franklin Roosevelt dated August 10, 1943

The most important thing in this war are machines. . . . The United States . . . is the country of machines. Without the use of these machines . . . we would lose the war.

—JOSEF STALIN, in remarks at the Tehran Conference on November 30, 1943

Office of War Mobilization

After two tiring weeks hosting Winston Churchill in the White House, Franklin Roosevelt turned his attention to some difficult management problems at home related to the procurement and distribution of supplies and men. After neglecting for months to take the advice of most of his top advisors to give fully concentrated powers to one individual in this regard, the president finally decided to act.

The day after the British left Washington, he signed Executive Order 9347, which created the Office of War Mobilization. The OWM was formed to coordinate all government agencies involved in the war effort at that time. It was an attempt by the president to bring order to the disorder he had brought about through his piecemeal approach to managing the War and his habit of giving more than one individual or agency overlapping responsibilities.

Among other things, Executive Order 9347 brought together under one entity (and one individual) the responsibility to manage manpower as well as all the functions then carried out by the War Production Board (formed in January 1942 to coordinate procurement efforts). The formation of the War Production Board had been a step in the right direction, but it was still constrained and poorly managed according to Stimson and others. By the spring of 1943, the demand within America for factory workers, farmers, and soldiers began to exceed what the country could supply. A single authority to prioritize human resources, it was believed by many, would be far more efficient than the operating structure then in place.

The president once again turned to Stimson to be part of a committee of six men charged with running the OWM. This committee, chaired by sixty-one-year-old James "Jimmy" Byrnes, was referred to as the War Mobilization Committee. Byrnes was a Democrat from South Carolina who served in both the House of Representatives and the Senate for a combined twenty-four years before being appointed a justice of the United States Supreme Court by FDR in June 1941. He was well respected and considered to be strong, smart, competent, energetic, personable, and decisive.

Along with Byrnes and Stimson, the other members of the Committee were Donald Nelson, Frank Knox, Harry Hopkins, and former congressman and judge Fred Vinson (who was then running the Office of Economic Stabilization, the executive agency responsible for controlling inflation).

The timing of the executive order was fortunate; American factories were producing unprecedented volumes of weapons and supplies to support the war effort, but it proved challenging to prioritize the output under the multiple agencies set up by Roosevelt. Bitter disputes constantly arose between different agencies and various appointed "czars." Going forward, the Committee (and more increasingly Byrnes) would have the final say.

Stimson was greatly relieved; he had wanted something like this for three years. It turns out that he got even more than he had hoped for. When he first began to read Executive Order 9347 carefully, it occurred to him that the War Mobilization Committee was essentially responsible for guiding the economic policy of the nation. During the opening meeting of the Committee, Stimson interrupted what he believed to be an interesting if not meandering discussion to point this out to his fellow members in case they had not grasped it. Whether the president realized it or not, the Committee's principal responsibility, Stimson explained, was to determine "some of the deepest questions that confronted the government, the question of manpower, the question of labor, strikes, the cost of living, and the danger of inflation."[2] With the War going fairly well for the Allies in the late spring of 1943, Stimson thought the Committee could be far more than simply an arbitrator. He knew wars could have huge negative consequences for the victors as well as the vanquished, and he was anxious to apply whatever knowledge he acquired throughout his life to mitigate them for the United States. The OWM provided him a vehicle to do so.

Postwar Planning from the War Department

Although Stimson was relieved to be given this new assignment (he had started to worry earlier that spring that his value to Roosevelt was beginning to wane), he was concerned about the increased workload it would bring, particularly as he began spending a lot more of his time thinking about the end of the War.

As one who witnessed the challenges and consequences of sudden demobilization after the First World War, Stimson wanted to make sure the current administration was putting its finest minds to work reviewing how the nation should, when the time came, most efficiently dismantle the immense economic war machine that was firing on all cylinders in the spring of 1943. Concurrently, he was thinking about how best to reenter countless GIs back into American communities. By the spring of 1943, the Army was more than twice the size it had been at the end of World War I, and far more spread out across the globe. The secretary of war would leave the logistics of moving the men home to Marshall—the acknowledged master of such matters—and focus his efforts on the consequences of such a mass reentry of soldiers into civilian life.

To assist him, Stimson asked the newest member of his staff (George Harrison, former president of the Federal Reserve Bank of New York) to prepare a paper on demobilization outlining all the issues and recommending possible solutions. Wanting input from his entire team, and to emphasize the importance of the issue, Stimson brought together his four core advisors (Patterson, McCloy, Lovett, and Bundy) to discuss the paper with Harrison when it was completed.

Although the subject of demobilization is not within the scope of this book, Stimson's diary entries during the spring and summer of 1943 confirm the obsession he had with finding the right solutions to these problems. After what was proving to be a horrific war with increasingly higher casualties, Stimson wanted to make sure the country did not unnecessarily suffer during the transition to peace.

In this endeavor, like most others, Stimson had a true partner in Marshall. The chief of staff was also deeply concerned about demobilization and also had the foresight to begin planning for it as early as November 1942.[3] As aide-de-camp to General Pershing after the First World War, Marshall was intimately familiar with the multitude of challenges encountered in demobilizing a large army. He assigned General Somervell and some of his staff to begin working out the problems before he left for North Africa with Churchill after the *Trident Conference.*

Naturally, Marshall was more focused on logistical issues and the related problems of timing (the order by which units were shipped home). As he sat down to discuss these problems with Stimson in mid-June 1943, he estimated the number of men to be demobilized would be at least 11 million by the time the War ended compared to the 4.8 million he and Pershing had begun demobilizing in 1918.[4]

Both Stimson and Marshall encouraged Harrison and Somervell to meet together to trade notes on the subject, but the prodding was unnecessary; informal discussions between the staffs of Stimson and Marshall were a daily occurrence and had, in fact, already taken place regarding demobilization.

Teamwork

Long before their respective staffs got together to discuss demobilization, it became apparent to both Stimson and Marshall that when the efforts of highly capable individuals who spent their entire careers in the military were combined with equally capable men who labored in law offices or banks, the resulting ideas and solutions were generally of a higher quality than either group could produce on its own. Before the word *synergy* was commonly used in association with organizational structures, both men had discovered the immense power of it in practice. This gave them confidence that there were few problems their combined staffs could not handle.

This should not have come as a surprise to the duo; since the start of their partnership, each man realized there were great benefits to be realized when they brought their individual career experiences together to solve problems. And they also increasingly recognized that it was beneficial for each of them to seek opinions from members of the other man's staff. For Marshall, it was John McCloy and Bob Lovett whom he most often approached for information and advice, but he also regularly discussed matters with Patterson and Bundy, treating each of them as if they were members of his own team. For his part, Stimson often conferred with Arnold, General Somervell (head of the Army Service Forces), and Deputy Chief of Staff McNarney to see how his ideas were viewed through a military prism.

These ongoing discussions between the groups, unbridled by conventional rules of office etiquette (that generally required permission from one head to the other before approaching another's staff) were essential to the success of the entire War Department. It was only possible because of the great respect both Stimson and Marshall commanded within the Department. The unparalleled relationship between the top civilian and military heads at the Pentagon enabled trust and cooperation to flourish throughout it.

Marshall in North Africa with Churchill, Brooke, and Eisenhower

As Stimson sat in on the early meetings of the OWB in the spring of 1943, while throwing his energy into the problems around procurement and demobilization, Marshall was in North Africa with Churchill, Brooke, Ismay, and a few other members of the British High Command. Their first meeting with Eisenhower was at Eisenhower's villa in Algiers on May 29. Despite the promises made during *Trident*, the British, led by the prime minister, continued to make arguments against a cross-Channel attack in favor of maintaining pressure in the Mediterranean.

Prior to the meeting, Churchill had used all his formidable skills during the journey from Washington attempting to persuade Marshall away from a cross-Channel focus. Having failed to make an impression on the American chief of staff, he figured he'd have a go at his subordinate. But Ike toed the party line, explaining that before he could commit to an Italian mainland strategy, he wanted to see how the invasion of Sicily developed. Specifically, he wanted to determine how the Germans reacted to the landings in Sicily to better predict how they might respond to an attack on the Italian mainland.[5] In the meantime, both he and Marshall insisted the buildup of men and machines continue uninterrupted in southern England.

Although the prime minister was frustrated that he could sway neither Marshall nor his protégé, his respect for the former grew immensely following their time together in North Africa. After the War, Churchill wrote in his memoirs that prior to their meetings in North Africa, "I had thought of Marshall as a rugged soldier and a magnificent organizer and builder of armies—the American Carnot. But now I see he was a statesman with a penetrating and commanding view of the whole scene."[6]

Marshall was, indeed, a commanding figure by this point in the War. The sixty-three-year-old American impressed nearly everyone he met and was always on his game. At the close of the meetings in North Africa, he displayed his talents to the media during a press conference. Marshall began—as was his practice—by giving the reporters in attendance a sweeping overview of the War while describing to them the variety of problems the Allies faced in each theater. As usual, he did so without notes. He then took questions, but first explained to the reporters that he would only begin answering them once all the questions were asked. After patiently taking one inquiry after another, Marshall stunned the reporters by not only answering each individual question comprehensively but doing so in the order it was asked and to the specific individual who asked it. This remarkable display was widely quoted in the press at the time. When asked about it years later, Marshall did not think it was a big deal, explaining to his biographer he was fully engrossed in all aspects of the War and it was not difficult to remember which reporter asked which question.[7]

Stimson Troubleshooting for FDR

Churchill headed back to England, discouraged he could move neither Marshall nor Ike off the direct invasion of France. When he returned to London, he learned Stimson was planning a visit less than a month later. The prime minister reckoned he had another shot at nudging the American position closer to his own and must have hoped he could successfully appeal to the old lawyer's sense of logic.

The purpose of Stimson's European trip in July 1943 (he was scheduled to be gone for three weeks) was to inspect the troops and facilities in Iceland, England, Morocco, and Algeria. But before he could leave, Roosevelt gave him a few high-level issues to work out at home. Like many problems Roosevelt brought to Stimson, these were ones not necessarily the responsibility of the War Department, but once a troubleshooter, always a troubleshooter. The president trusted Stimson's judgment and knew, as his friend Henry Morgenthau had earlier discovered, that he was the guy who "made a difference in Washington."

The first crisis involved the threat of a massive coal strike organized by John Lewis, head of the United Mine Workers of America. Frustrated with low wages and emboldened by the Allied progress in the War, Lewis called for a strike in June 1943 at more than 2,500 mines representing 85 percent of the nation's coal production. Given the seriousness of the threat, Roosevelt turned to the statesman for help on June 21. One will recall that two decades earlier, Stimson spent six months studying all aspects of the coal industry on the behest of the Harding administration. He knew how important the commodity was to the nation and the war effort. The plan he helped to develop involved making it clear to the workers that if they participated in the strike, they would immediately be inducted into the Army and then ordered to return to work in the mines. Roosevelt supported this idea, and the Army began to make immediate preparations to take over the mining operations. After a few chaotic days, Lewis called off the strike.

The second crisis involved race riots taking place in Detroit during the same week Lewis was calling for a strike. Local and state officials failed to quell the violence, and after more than thirty people were killed and significant property damage was done, Stimson saw to it that six thousand troops were made available to establish order. Given the sensitivity of military overreach within the United States, it was important to undertake the effort quietly and prudently. The president was once again able to rely on his secretary of war to leverage the great respect with which he was held within Congress and around the country. The riots soon ended with little controversy.

There was one other important issue that needed addressing before Stimson went to Europe: whether the United States should still insist on an unconditional surrender of Italy once Allied troops began racing north up the boot. The concept, as it applied to Germany, Italy, and Japan, had been famously announced by FDR a few months earlier at Casablanca and would again be revisited later in the War for both Germany and Japan. With regard to Italy, Stimson and Marshall had different opinions.

As a former diplomat, Stimson was naturally hesitant to close the door on negotiations by demanding an unconditional surrender. He believed that while the American people hated the Japanese and feared the Germans, they had few problems with the Italians, making it politically easier to negotiate with them. He thought by demanding an unconditional surrender from the Italians, they would be less likely to surrender and cooperate with the Allies.

Marshall, as a pure military man, thought differently—at least on this occasion. He saw no reason why there should be any conditions attached to the surrender and did not think it wise to allow the Italians to rearm themselves after a few years (one of the conditions that could have likely been negotiated). At one point during what Stimson described as a heated debate on the subject between the two men, Marshall said to the secretary of war that the American people were getting mushy and sentimental about Italy and it seemed to be rubbing off on Stimson. "I thought you were tough," Marshall said to Stimson during the argument. Stimson replied that he was simply trying to divide and conquer.[8] In the end, the surrender of Italy was delayed because of conflicting signals sent to Eisenhower from Washington and London about terms. This allowed the Germans precious time to maneuver troops into strategic locations within Italy to continue the fight.

Once these various issues were resolved, and with his mind settled on the matters around demobilization (the details of which he had outsourced to his staff), Stimson celebrated his fiftieth wedding anniversary with his wife and some friends at Woodley on July 7 (their actual anniversary was a day earlier). The next morning, he headed by plane for Europe. His wife, Marshall, Somervell, McCloy, and Lovett were among those who saw him off at the airport.

Stimson to London

Packed with a pistol and all one could possibly need in an emergency under any weather conditions (the individual survival kits included ski goggles), Stimson and his entourage took off on July 8. After a day and night in Iceland spent inspecting troops and dining with senior American officers, Stimson and his party landed in London and spent the first evening dining with Churchill and Secretary of State for Foreign Affairs Anthony Eden at 10 Downing Street.

Churchill, with Eden's support, wasted little time in trying to convert Stimson to his side of thinking as it related to the next moves in Europe. Using the same arguments that failed to convince Marshall or Eisenhower a few weeks earlier, both he and Eden began to lay the groundwork for a prolonged siege on the American secretary of war during his stay. Stimson was well prepared. Along with the usual counterarguments the British were used to hearing, Stimson brought into the debate a new line of reasoning. He explained to the two British statesmen that further operations in the Mediterranean would not be acceptable to the American people, which in turn would not bode well for Roosevelt's prestige. It went without saying— but Stimson said it anyway—that a loss in prestige for the president could have tangible consequences for the election of 1944, which was less than sixteen months away.

Acknowledging the logic, but frustrated with it, Churchill began to lecture Stimson about the disadvantages of fixed elections and suggested such a flawed system could well end up costing Roosevelt his job. Stimson snapped back that this would only happen if "we got involved in a theater like the eastern Mediterranean."[9]

Stimson held his own in this first encounter, but he had not heard the last from Churchill. He complained in his diary that the prime minister "virtually took possession of my movements for the first week."

The secretary of war did manage to escape Churchill's clutches to visit the famed American Eighth Air Force under General Ira Eaker the following day. It was during his discussions with Eaker that Stimson learned how vitally important it was that the Allies secure air bases in Italy. Eaker explained to Stimson that bad weather in northern Europe was making the frequency of sorties difficult for the Allies. Consequently, the German air force was given time to reinforce itself. As much as Stimson wanted to forgo Italy for a cross-Channel invasion, this information from Eaker convinced him of the advantages to establishing air bases at least as far up the boot as Rome. He did not believe accomplishing this would interfere with the cross-Channel buildup.

Stimson spent a total of two weeks in England dividing his time between inspection visits, meetings with high-ranking officials, and more discussions with the prime minister (he spent a full day with him in Dover). Churchill continued to lecture him about why a cross-Channel strategy would be a mistake in 1944. He warned Stimson in Dover that even if the British put fifty thousand troops on the beaches of France, the Germans would find enough forces to push them back into the sea. Stimson, fortified by his recent conversations with Eaker and fellow Army Air Force officers Carl Spaatz and Jimmy Doolittle, countered that the Allied advantages in airpower would secure the landings. Stimson ended up being right in this respect; Allied air superiority was critical in allowing Eisenhower's troops to acquire and maintain a beachhead on D-Day.

Failing to win over Stimson with logic, Churchill resorted to emotional appeals. After one ninety-minute debate with the American statesman, he quietly suggested how terrible it would be to have British and American corpses covering the Channel and dotting the beaches of France. An unsympathetic Stimson, replying firmly to the prime minister in language ironically Churchillian in nature, barked, "We could never win any battle by talking about corpses."

The prime minister's legendary skills of persuasion once again failed to make their mark. A few days after this discussion, a dismissive Stimson told Eisenhower what he believed was actually behind Churchill's push for a Mediterranean strategy: an obsession with his overall legacy. Stimson thought the prime minister wanted to prove to future historians that his failed attempt to take control of the Dardanelles during World War I was simply one unfortunate mistake in an otherwise glorious military career.[10]

The last leg of Stimson's trip began on July 24, when his party flew to Marrakech and then on to Algiers for more inspections and a meeting with Ike. He arrived back in the United States on Saturday, July 31, after being gone more than three weeks. After a weekend recuperating at Highhold, Stimson gave a full briefing to Marshall the following Monday. He reiterated to the chief of staff his fear that the prime minister would continue to fight against *Overlord* (the new codename for the invasion of France). He was right; Churchill would come back regularly with attempts to steer the Americans away from what he continued to believe would be a disaster.

A week later, Stimson briefed the president on his trip before heading off to the Adirondacks to recover. He was exhausted. As he approached his seventy-sixth birthday, age was steadily closing the gap on him.

Quebec Conference (August 17–24, 1943)

As Stimson recuperated in the Adirondacks, Roosevelt, Marshall, King, Arnold, and Leahy got together with their British counterparts in Quebec for their third conference in seven months. Once again, Marshall was asked to do the heavy lifting. Although he was successful at *Trident* and parried Churchill's attempts to turn him in North Africa, he knew that the pressure would continue. He did not need Stimson to remind him; from the time he returned home from his trip to North Africa, Marshall saw in practically every correspondence from the British attempts to persuade him to pursue alternative options. But with the president on his side, Marshall was confident that the primary focus of the Allied effort in Europe going forward would be toward preparing for *Overlord*. As such, his goal in Quebec was less about arguing with the British for the invasion as much as it was to nail down the details of it and get them enthusiastically behind it.

One threat to that objective came about as a result of the Allied military successes in Italy following the July 10 invasion of Sicily. This hastened the collapse of the Italian government in late July, just weeks before the Conference started. Marshall knew the British would step up the pressure to remain in Italy now that the prospects for taking that country out of the War had greatly improved. Although he was prepared to offer the British flexibility in his approach to the Allied campaign in Italy, he would make it clear that the overriding priority must still be *Overlord*.

The arguments used by the Americans to make their case throughout the Quebec Conference were essentially the same ones used in every previous summit, but the force behind them was far more effective given the ever-increasing production strength of the United States, particularly as it related to aircraft. As the Allies began arriving in Quebec, planes coming off American assembly lines were pouring into the United Kingdom in accelerated volumes. This not only meant there could be a more concentrated bombing effort against German industry (one that could cripple Hitler's ability to procure additional planes, tanks, and submarines), but it could also assist the Allies in weakening the strength of the existing inventory of planes possessed by the Luftwaffe. Like Stimson, Marshall was confident that controlling the air over Europe would not only make the landings in Normandy possible, but also make victory certain for the infantry once they moved inland. With the advantage in total aircraft growing daily between the Allies and Germany, it was harder for the British to counter this line of thinking. That wouldn't stop them from trying, however.

Alan Brooke was again tasked by Churchill to convince the Americans to continue with the Mediterranean strategy he had laid out and advocated for so long. But Brooke knew he was up against it; prior to the conference, John Dill advised him that Marshall and the Americans were more optimistic coming to *Quadrant* than they had been at any of the previous conferences between the two countries. This was the last thing Brooke needed to hear. Two days before the Conference started, he went off in his diary—yet again. The Americans, Brooke wrote, "have no strategic outlook, cannot see beyond the ends of their noses, and imagine that the war can be run by a series of legal contracts based on false concepts as to what may prevail six months ahead!"[11] Brooke's opinion did not change over the course of the next week.

The Quebec Conference started off poorly by all accounts (not unlike the previous gatherings). Speaking frankly, but with his customary manners, Marshall made it unambiguous to Brooke and his colleagues during the opening meeting of the Combined Chiefs of Staff where he stood on further Mediterranean commitments. And in case the British held any possible doubts, Admiral King followed Marshall with language Admiral Leahy described as "very undiplomatic . . . to use a mild term."[12]

The British, sensing they had little choice, told the Americans they were willing to confirm their commitment to a cross-Channel attack in May 1944, but once again set conditions that were unlikely to be met. As a result, the suspicious Americans assumed, justifiably, that the British wanted to push the invasion of France back to 1945 or beyond.

Both sides spent the entire conference repeating familiar arguments. Marshall remained convinced France, not Italy, was where the Allied strength would be most effective against Hitler in the spring of 1944. He was not opposed to exploiting the gains made in Italy—in fact, he favored doing so—but insisted the major effort be made in France. For their part, the British made a more direct link between the fighting in Italy and the invasion of France. They believed the latter should only be launched when the former was finished.

While several other major issues were debated in Quebec, including strategy and command assignments in Asia, the key discussions centered on the cross-Channel versus Mediterranean strategies. In the end, Marshall got what he essentially came for: a confirmation of the commitment he had received from the British in Washington to be ready to move on Southern France by May 1, 1944.

Command of *Overlord*

Another major decision made at the time of the Quebec Conference concerned the command of *Overlord*—or more specifically, which nation would furnish the commander. Roosevelt and Churchill had conveniently put off this question during the previous two conferences, much to the irritation of Stimson. Two days before FDR hosted the prime minister at his home in Hyde Park prior to heading off to Quebec, the secretary of war strongly encouraged the president (during a private meeting and in a memorandum) to make the decision promptly and appoint General Marshall.

Stimson could have focused on any number of arguments to support his choice of Marshall, but he stressed that the appointment would go a long way in ensuring that the British did not flake on their commitment to support the cross-Channel attack (a plan Stimson said the British "rendered lip service to" but never accepted in their hearts). Stimson also told Roosevelt that Marshall was the only American the British would accept.

Prior to advising FDR, Stimson told Marshall he was going to make these suggestions to the president. Aware the chief of staff was uncomfortable even discussing the subject, Stimson deliberately signed the memorandum he planned on giving to Roosevelt before letting the chief of staff look at it. Always Washingtonian in his reluctance to proactively seek advancement, Marshall become increasingly fixated during the War with making sure nobody, particularly the president, thought he was angling for the *Overlord* command. Stimson admired George Washington as much as anyone but was frustrated that the chief of staff did not even admit to him in private that he wanted the job. He knew even the subtlest of hints from Marshall to the president about his preference for the command would have likely forced Roosevelt's hand since Marshall deserved the position and was a natural fit for it. But without one, the president felt free to weigh all the advantages and disadvantages such an assignment would entail.

The primary drawback in sending Marshall to Europe was that the superlative chief of staff would no longer be in Washington to keep all the balls in the air. It was for this reason that Roosevelt asked Marshall to make the decision himself. A keen observer of men, he knew his chief of staff would decline to do so, which would allow him to put off the decision at the very least.

Even Stimson, the loudest and strongest voice in favor of Marshall getting the command of *Overlord*, harbored serious concerns about how anyone could replace him in Washington. He did not restrict these concerns to his diary; in concluding the memorandum he handed to Roosevelt prior to the Quebec Conference, Stimson wrote, ". . . no one knows better than I the loss in the problems of organization and worldwide strategy centered in Washington which such a solution would cause, but I see no other alternative to which we can turn in the great effort which confronts us." This was hardly a convincing way to close a brief in favor of Marshall's appointment.[13]

A few days later at Hyde Park, Churchill proactively told Roosevelt that an American should command *Overlord*. This was not a painless concession for him to make. The British had been at war for four years, the Americans less than two; they had stood alone and suffered against Germany during the Battle of Britain while the Americans sat on the sidelines; and the prime minister had already promised the command to Alan Brooke and would therefore be forced to explain to him why he changed his mind. What decided the question for Churchill came down to simple math; there would be considerably more Americans and American resources involved in the invasion.[14] As persuasive as the great Englishman was, arguing for British command would have been counterproductive.

Although it seemed certain to everyone in Quebec, including Roosevelt, that Marshall would get the appointment, the chief of staff later told his biographer that the president neither promised him the job nor even discussed it with him there or during the three months following the conference.[15] Stimson likely shared the news with Marshall that he was going to be the choice (based on what both Churchill and Roosevelt separately told Stimson in Quebec), but Marshall would have been wise enough to know that anything was possible.

One month after returning from Quebec, Marshall was certain the job was his. He received a copy of a letter the president wrote to General Pershing on September 20, 1943, in response to one Pershing sent Roosevelt a few days earlier. After hearing rumors FDR was going to send Marshall to Europe, the eighty-three-year-old hero of World War I wrote Roosevelt urging him to keep his former aide-de-camp and protégé at the Pentagon. Believing a transfer of "our most accomplished officer" would be a "fundamental and very grave error," Pershing expressed hope in his message that Marshall could stay in Washington, where his "outstanding strategical ability and experience" would be crucial to concluding the war.

It is curious why the ailing Pershing seemed unable to appreciate that Marshall might have wanted to command *Overlord*. Regardless, in his reply to Pershing, a respectful Roosevelt wrote that although Marshall was "far and away the most available man as Chief of Staff," the role he was considering for the general in Europe was more expansive than Pershing might have understood. Roosevelt tried to persuade Pershing that it was "only a fair thing" to offer Marshall the job. He closed the letter by telling him he wanted the chief of staff to be "the Pershing of the second World War."[16]

Once Marshall read a copy of FDR's reply to Pershing, he realized he had to start planning. He sent Major General Harold Bull over to Europe to prepare to take over as his chief of operations of Supreme Headquarters and also put together a list of potential field commanders. He might not have been fully convinced, but his gut told him that the job was his.

Marshall's efforts were wasted; Roosevelt was apparently not yet ready to decide. Four months later, he chose Eisenhower.

Workload at the Midpoint of the War

During the four months between the close of the Quebec Conference in late August 1943 and the final day of the year, both Stimson and Marshall maintained a furious pace. Although the results for the Allies were trending in the right direction during this time, the workload remained unrelenting.

Nothing can fully prepare one for the job of managing an army during a time of war, including the actual experience of managing an army during war. By the end of 1943, both men had served two years in their respective positions since the attack on Pearl Harbor. But the dynamic nature of war—and particularly a modern and global war like World War II—meant they were regularly facing a multitude of new and distinct problems that could not necessarily be solved by drawing on their experiences during the first two years of the War or earlier experiences in other wars.

For Marshall, his involvement during World War I was useful in preparing him for his job as chief of staff, but it fell far short of giving him adequate insight into the position two decades later. Working alongside General Pershing in Chaumont was certainly educational, but Pershing was not chief of staff during World War I; he was in command of the American Expeditionary Force and had held that job for only eighteen months before Armistice Day (only the last three of which he commanded Americans in battle). Additionally, the Americans fought World War I in just one theater (as opposed to three). Finally, that war had ended twenty-five years earlier; profound changes in both how wars were fought and what they were fought with had taken place since then.

Stimson's experience counted for even less. Yes, he had previously served as secretary of war, but it was during peacetime and almost thirty years earlier (when America was still fighting Native Americans on the frontier). As for his experience during World War I, he had been too busy as an infantryman during his time in France to learn lessons applicable to his current job.

Historians who have written about men in similar roles often focus their work on the efforts and decisions made by their subjects around military strategy (this generally makes for a more interesting book). But for Stimson and Marshall, as with their predecessors during previous American wars, strategic planning was but one part of the job. During the last half of 1943, the two ringmasters worked together on a host of other critical issues.

Organization

Like other managers of vast organizations, getting the right people in the right positions within the right structure occupied much of Stimson and Marshall's time throughout the War. Although each man was confident in his ability to spot and place talent, finding the most efficient way of organizing it and making sure it continued to add value as the War progressed was more challenging.

Immediately following the Quebec Conference, General Somervell proposed reorganizing the expanding Army Service Forces. In pushing for the new reorganization, Somervell's goal was to tighten his control over various heads of supplies and administrative services. Although reporting directly to Somervell, these heads had been given considerable authority as part of the original reorganization completed by Marshall in March 1942.

Based on the strong recommendation of Somervell, in charge of the group since it was created, Marshall supported the effort despite the fact that it would have shaken up some of the existing administrative sections and divisions within ASF (e.g., Ordnance, Quartermaster, Engineers, etc.). He saw that the plan was consistent with the original reorganization.

Stimson thought differently. He understood Marshall's reasons for wanting to back Somervell but believed the disruptions of such a structural change would outweigh the benefits derived from it. Stimson recalled from his experience more than thirty years earlier as secretary of war working with his chief of staff, Leonard Wood, that trying to get behind a reorganization sponsored by a strong personality (like Wood and Somervell) could be toxic to the overall morale of the Army, and particularly to those groups or units affected (each with distinctive histories and cultures). Back in 1911–1912, Stimson forced the politically well-connected adjutant general Fred Ainsworth out of the Army in order to bring relative stability to it so that a carefully planned reorganization could successfully take place. And that was during peacetime. Stimson did not want to risk dividing the Army during the War.

Before discussing his reservations at length with Marshall, Stimson consulted with McCloy and Patterson, both of whom agreed with him. Patterson told Stimson that production and procurement activities (belonging to the ASF) were going so well that tinkering with the structure would be unsound.

Stimson and Marshall went back and forth on the issue for a few weeks in the early fall bringing in their respective staffs during meetings to weigh in on the matter. As in all of their disagreements, the two men debated the issue on the merits of it alone. Before they could resolve it, a group of senators caught wind of the proposed reorganization and began expressing their objections to it, effectively killing the initiative.

Conferences in Cairo and Tehran (November 22–December 1, 1943)

Despite Stimson's formal position as secretary of war, his opinions on military strategy were less sought out by the president as 1943 came to an end. He was still influential given his daily interactions with Marshall, but it was the chief of staff who was firmly in the driver's seat in this respect. Marshall evolved from being *a* key advisor to FDR on military strategy in Europe earlier in the War to *the* key advisor during the second half of 1943. Already aware of Marshall's leadership of the JCS, FDR would likely have agreed with Stimson's comment toward the end of the year that Marshall was "by far the biggest man" in Washington.[17] Roosevelt was going to need him as he prepared himself for meetings in the late fall of 1943 with the British and Chinese in Cairo, followed immediately by the first "Big Three" conference in Tehran with Churchill and Soviet leader, Josef Stalin.

The American contingent left Washington for Cairo on November 11, 1943, twenty-five years to the day the First World War ended. Given the important role Marshall played in that conflict, he must have noted the anniversary after boarding the battleship USS *Iowa* at the mouth of the Potomac for the long journey. Anticipating still more pressure from the British against his plans for *Overlord*, Marshall likely reflected on the fact that World War I only ended when the Allied powers focused their attack directly against the German lines.

If during the nine-day journey to Algeria (the first leg of the trip to Cairo), Marshall experienced occasional moments of optimism that the British High Command would be supportive of his cross-Channel aspirations, he would have been mistaken. The British were preparing to promote continued advances in Italy, increasing support for the partisans in the Balkans, and a postponement of *Overlord*. Believing that they could pressure the Balkan powers to break from Germany and convince Turkey to join the side of the Allies, the British once again saw few benefits in landing troops in France, and certainly not in 1944.[18]

Arriving in Cairo on November 21, the United States High Command was well prepared to state their case. So as not to be upstaged by the British as in past conferences, the Americans arrived with sixty-six planning officers and scores of others to assist Roosevelt and the Joint Chiefs of Staff with any matter of detail that might come up during the discussions.[19] They also took a page from the British by not idling their time away across the Atlantic. Six formal JCS meetings were held during the journey, two of which included the president.

The meetings in Cairo began poorly, continuing the established pattern. When the participants started debating future strategy in Asia, it soon became apparent the differences between the British and Americans in that region were no less pronounced than they were in Europe. Aside from having opposing views as to the role China should play in the War (and the support Chiang Kai-shek should or should not be given), the Americans wanted to expand efforts toward supporting the battle in Burma, a move the British strongly opposed. Brooke and his colleagues wanted more landing craft sent from the Asian theater to Europe to bolster their Mediterranean strategy.

When the discussions switched to Europe, Churchill began floating his idea about attacking Rhodes, the Greek island in the southeastern Aegean Sea. He felt this low-risk operation would not only bring Turkey into the War but also allow the Allies to dominate the Aegean Sea through their air forces.[20] Churchill broached this idea to Marshall on the night of November 23 in Churchill's villa. As the discussions became more intense after dinner, the prime minister began to dramatically lecture the American that the British military was not going to sit around and do nothing while waiting for *Overlord*. At that point, a tired Marshall heard enough and lashed out at Churchill, saying, "God forbid if I try to dictate but . . . not one American soldier is going to die on (that) goddamned beach!"[21] Marshall's rare loss of temper reflected his ongoing frustration with the continuing effort by the British—Churchill especially—to steer the Allies away from France. Because his outbursts were so infrequent, Marshall's strike against Churchill must have taken the prime minister by surprise. Robert Lovett once said, in describing Marshall at such moments, he could be the "most terrifying man you ever saw" and "could burn paint off the wall."[22]

Not surprisingly, the first day of the conference ended unpleasantly. After a break suggested by the British so that the two delegations could celebrate the Americans' Thanksgiving (the British arranged a special religious service for their counterparts at the cathedral in Cairo), discussions resumed the following day and were less acrimonious, at the start anyway.

Following further deliberations about strategy in the Mediterranean led by Eisenhower, Brooke once again suggested that the Americans should shift some resources from the Pacific to the Atlantic theater. Specifically, Brooke indicated that if the American plan to take the Andaman Islands in the northeastern Indian Ocean was postponed, and the resources allocated to it were sent to assist operations in Europe, the war could end sooner. Marshall, apparently still hot, erupted again, reminding the British how much America had contributed to the war against Germany and how many times it had sacrificed its aims to support the British. Marshall was furious that the British High Command continually attacked American plans in and around Asia and declared that the attack on the Andaman Islands (something Roosevelt insisted on) would proceed on schedule.[23]

With little progress made, the Cairo Conference closed, and the frustrated participants boarded flights to Tehran to meet Stalin and their Russian counterparts. Significant issues that had been thrashed out for months between the British and Americans would be decided quickly once the Soviet leader expressed his views.

Meeting Stalin

If the moral code of Josef Stalin and George Marshall had not been poles apart, the two men could have been mistaken for one another from a personality standpoint. Stalin's composure, ability to command attention and respect, penchant for communicating quietly and with extreme efficiency, directness, and habit of speaking without notes yet fully in command of relevant facts and statistics were traits he shared with the American chief of staff. At Tehran, these characteristics were on full display by the Soviet leader. As it happened, both he and Marshall were also on the same page regarding the major strategic issues.

After Churchill and Roosevelt took turns outlining their own strategic plans to win the war, each trying to win over Stalin, the sixty-four-year-old dictator got straight to the point. The British and Americans had to focus on *Overlord*; anything else, he stated, must be subordinate to that objective. Rejecting Churchill's strategic plans in Italy and the Mediterranean and declaring that Turkey was unlikely to enter the War anytime soon, Stalin delighted the Americans by insisting that only *Overlord*, supported by an earlier feint in southern France, was a credible plan.

Stalin was also wise enough after fighting the Germans for nearly two and a half years to know that battles cannot be planned without knowing who was going to command them. Bolstered by the heavy weight of his victories up to that date, and the immense sacrifices Russian soldiers had made to win them, Stalin told his two counterparts the Soviet Union would not take any promise of a cross-Channel attack seriously if a commander was not immediately named to execute it.

From the standpoint of military strategy, this was essentially all Stalin said in Tehran. As stingy with words as Churchill was lavish, Stalin was no less effective in getting his point across. Once he did, only the details needed to be worked out between the Americans and British (including the exact timing, strength, and location of the diversionary attack in the south of France). These issues would be discussed between the two Allies after they left Tehran and headed back for a follow-up bilateral conference in Cairo.

Final Decision by Roosevelt on *Overlord* Command

With Stalin ratcheting up the pressure to choose a commander for *Overlord*, the president knew he had to revisit all the arguments made four months earlier after the Quebec Conference and make a final decision before heading back to Washington. Although Roosevelt famously kept his thoughts to himself, it seems he was still torn between keeping Marshall in the Pentagon and sending him to London to assume command.

The president and the JCS had discussed the issue at length while on board the *Iowa* heading over to the two conferences. During these discussions, Roosevelt suggested giving Marshall command of all the Western Allied forces then fighting the Germans. To Roosevelt, such a solution would allow the proposed position to feel less like a demotion for Marshall.

It would also be consistent with the general concept of "unity of command" that Marshall had promoted for years. Everyone, correctly as it turned out, assumed the British would not accept this arrangement, so they tossed out other options that might enhance the role. Despite the efforts, they could come up with nothing.

Although no closer to a decision prior to the conference, the determined position of Stalin helped bring clarity to the issue for the president after it. Once Stalin came out hard during the debates in favor of *Overlord*, Stimson's argument that naming Marshall ensured British commitment to cross-Channel landings carried less weight; Roosevelt knew Churchill's ability to successfully take on both him and Stalin together was limited. This alone could have been enough to tip the balance toward Eisenhower. After discussions with the British on the subject during the second gathering in Cairo got nowhere, Roosevelt invited Marshall to his villa in Cairo on December 5.

Although the president, through Harry Hopkins, had already given Marshall another opportunity to express his opinion on the previous day (Marshall told Hopkins he would "go wholeheartedly with whatever decision the president made"), Roosevelt decided to give Marshall one final chance to weigh in on the decision face-to-face. Marshall recounted the conversation with his biographer, Forrest Pogue:

> As I recall, he asked me after a great deal of beating around the bush just what I wanted to do. Evidently it was left up to me. Well, having in mind all the business that had occurred in Washington and what Hopkins had told me, I just repeated again in as convincing language as I could that I wanted him to feel free to act in whatever way he felt was to the best interest of the country and to his satisfaction and not in any way to consider my feelings. I would cheerfully go whatever way he wanted me to go and I didn't express any desire one way or the other. Then he . . . evidently assumed that concluded the affair and that I would not command in Europe—because he said, "Well, I didn't feel I could sleep at ease if you were out of Washington."[24]

Ultimately, given Marshall's long-standing refusal to suggest himself for the command of *Overlord*, or even indicate that he might like the appointment, Roosevelt went with Eisenhower. Later justifying the choice to Stimson, FDR told him that if he had sent Marshall to Europe, he believed he had to replace him with Eisenhower, who knew little of what was going on in the Pacific Theater and would be far less able than Marshall to handle

Congress and the British.[25] These were arguments previously made to Roosevelt by King, Arnold, Leahy, Pershing, and the secretary of the navy.

After the War, Robert Lovett summed up Roosevelt's rationale when he said during an interview that the president "recognized that the man who ran things in Washington was bigger than the man who commanded in the field."[26] Putting aside any consideration of who deserved the appointment, it is hard to second-guess FDR's decision. Marshall himself understood that his influence in Washington and within Allied councils could not be replaced by any of his colleagues.

Nevertheless, the decision must have crushed him. It certainly came as a surprise. Only two days prior to his final meeting with the president in Cairo, Marshall wired Stimson that he expected to take command in Europe shortly.[27] Stimson was thus particularly angry when he heard about the final decision, and more than a little perturbed that FDR did not consult him about it. At the very least, the secretary believed he was owed an explanation given all he had done to get *Overlord* into "fighting shape."[28] It was left to John McCloy who attended the Conference to give Stimson the blow-by-blow of what happened when he arrived back in Washington.

After the heartbreaking decision by FDR, Marshall left Cairo to meet General Douglas MacArthur in Asia. He was still chief of staff of the United States Army and wanted to see how things were working out in the Pacific Theater before coming back to Washington to deal with all the problems likely to arise during the run-up to D-Day.

It took six months (less than three weeks after D-Day) before Henry Stimson finally acknowledged in his diary that Roosevelt might have been right. His confession followed a lengthy and productive conversation with Marshall. He wrote that the chief of staff was "keeping his hand on the control of the whole thing and his influence in driving ahead the war fast in the Pacific as well as in the Atlantic is a unique power which nobody else could render."[29]

IV

FINISHING

17

Preparing for D-Day

I was very careful to send Mr. Roosevelt every few days a statement of our casualties, and it was done in a very effective way, graphically and rather in colors, so it would be quite clear to him when we had only a moment or two to consider. I tried to keep before him all the time the casualty results, because you get hardened to these things and you have to be very careful to keep them always, in the forefront of your mind.[1]

—GEORGE MARSHALL

Marshall Sits Down with Douglas MacArthur

The lengthy journey by Marshall to Asia in early December 1943 to see General MacArthur was made almost immediately after Roosevelt tapped Eisenhower for the cross-Channel command. Marshall wanted to visit the Pacific Theater earlier but had always been pulled away by more pressing matters. He left secretly on December 8 for a tortuously long, multistop route to present-day Papua New Guinea. Not wanting to be told by Roosevelt the trip was too dangerous for him to make, Marshall informed him only after it was too late to be recalled.

Aside from wanting to provide MacArthur assurances that he and his men were not forgotten at the Pentagon, Marshall also wanted to brief the general on the discussions held in Tehran and Cairo. The chief of staff must have known his chances of getting to Asia again anytime soon were slim given what was happening in Europe. As such, he wanted to sort out as many problems as possible, get a better overall feel for what was happening on the ground, and discuss strategy.

Stopping briefly in Luxor, Egypt (for a bit of sightseeing), and Bahrain (to refuel), Marshall and his small party spent a night in Karachi and then Ceylon (current-day Sri Lanka) before undertaking a fifteen-and-a-half-hour, 3,140-mile overwater leg to Exmouth Gulf on the coast of Western Australia (more direct routes to New Guinea would have put them too close to Japanese controlled airstrips). From there, the party flew 1,800 miles to Darwin, Australia (where they spent the night), before flying another 1,127 miles northeast to Port Moresby (the current capital of Papua New Guinea), arriving on December 14. The fatigued chief of staff spent the day reviewing key military sites before flying the final two-hundred-mile leg of the journey directly east to Goodenough Island, where his celebrated subordinate awaited him.[2]

Based on the history between the two generals, any other man might have relished the opportunity to somehow stick it to MacArthur given the reversed roles they found themselves in. Marshall saw no need to; he was in charge now. Even if he were inclined to get back at his old nemesis, Marshall would not have; he knew the sixty-four-year-old general still possessed world-class leadership skills and wanted nothing to interfere with his potential to employ them for the benefit of the country. Despite all the constant headaches MacArthur induced in the chief of staff since the War began, Marshall never regretted recalling him to active duty; MacArthur generally exceeded Marshall's high expectations of him.

Unfortunately, no notes seem to have been taken by either man during their meetings together on Goodenough Island. MacArthur wrote in his memoirs that the discussions had been "long and frank." The two men headed back to Port Moresby together on December 16 before Marshall and his colleagues began the long journey home by taking a midnight flight to Guadalcanal, nine hundred miles farther east. There, Marshall was given tours of various sites in the Solomon Islands and on New Georgia Island. Continuing to fly east—visiting troops and hospitals along the way—Marshall made stops in the New Hebrides, the Fiji Islands, Canton Island (for refueling), Oahu, and Los Angeles. He arrived back to Washington on December 22, having circled the globe. He had been gone six weeks and had traveled thirty-five thousand miles. Given that the trip predated the era of the jet engine, it must have seemed to Marshall that he was in the air for a large portion of it.

Once back in Washington, aside from dealing with a few new crises brought on by the threat of a major railroad strike and an attempt by

Churchill to get General Bernard Montgomery (the hero of North Africa) named as *Overlord* commander reporting directly to Ike, Marshall spent the last week of 1943 catching up with Stimson, his staff, paperwork, and his wife. On December 31 (Marshall's sixty-third birthday), Stimson gathered the usual suspects (including Field Marshall Dill, whom Stimson regarded as "almost a part of ourselves") into his office at the Pentagon before inviting Marshall in. In a short birthday toast, the secretary of war compared Marshall to George Washington, explaining to the assembled brass that they were the only two men in American history who had led the Army during an entire war (he was obviously assuming Marshall would remain as chief of staff to the end). But what was different, pointed out Stimson, was that whereas Washington had enemies within his army working against him (mentioning General Horatio Gates as a prime example), Marshall commanded nothing but loyalty within his.

Time magazine, in naming Marshall "Man of the Year" three days later, also compared Marshall to George Washington, stating the former was the most trusted military man in America since the latter. Citizens were drawn, *Time* wrote, to both Marshall's competence and integrity and by the commonly held view that "no officer in the field suspects that the General thinks of his place in history rather than of getting tools to them in time."[3]

The brief gathering to celebrate both Marshall's birthday and New Year's Eve was a well-deserved breather. It didn't last long; both men were back in their respective offices that afternoon and the following morning (New Year's Day). The efforts to prepare for D-Day were accelerating.

Eisenhower

Fortunately for Stimson and Marshall, assisting them was fifty-three-year-old General Dwight Eisenhower. In Ike, both men were comfortable they had a commander more than fit for the huge responsibility the president had handed to him.

Marshall, as mentioned in chapter 11, gets most of the credit for this; it was he who brought the little-known lieutenant colonel back to the United States from an unhappy assignment in the Philippines in December 1939 and began giving him increasingly greater responsibilities over the next four years (and rewarding his efforts with several promotions). He trusted and respected the Kansan.

The feeling was mutual for Eisenhower, and this led to an effective partnership. Marshall was confident his subordinate could handle a vast majority of the problems that would arise in his new role (without coming to him unless there was a high-level issue that needed settling), and Eisenhower clearly understood that Marshall desired, above most qualities, officers who were candid.

Eisenhower also learned over time that the chief of staff wanted commanders who could make do with the resources they were provided. In a global war, this attribute took on an even greater importance. And if this point seemed unclear to any of his subordinates, Marshall seldom passed on the chance to get it across. In the summer of 1942, the chief of staff sent George Patton to the War College to begin training a division for desert warfare in case FDR ordered troops to the Middle East. Since Marshall had carefully communicated to Patton that it was only necessary to train a single division for any potential assignment, it was a surprise to him when the blustery general soon sent word that he thought it necessary that an additional division be given to him. Marshall immediately sent one of his staff to visit General Patton with orders to get him on a plane back to California that afternoon. After having his calls to Marshall ignored for the next couple days, Patton sent back word to him through General McNarney that after careful consideration, he could do whatever job needed to be done with one division.[4]

That was how Marshall dealt with Patton. A year later, Marshall was reviewing Eisenhower's written request for additional men and materiel prior to the invasion of Sicily. In reply, Marshall radioed to Ike that he was "wondering whether or not the figures submitted have not been somewhat based on the policy of getting whatever it is possible to obtain rather than being conservative in order to assist us in the over-all problem with which we are now confronted."[5] Eisenhower got the message and made life much easier for his boss from that point forward.

Overlord and *Anvil* versus Italy

Allied operations in Italy stalled south of Rome toward the end of 1943 due to the strength of a German resistance made more formidable by the terrain of central Italy. To counter this, Churchill convinced the Americans to land forces at Anzio (thirty miles south of Rome) that could either bypass the German troops massed along the Gustav Line (Axis military fortifications across the width of Italy seventy-five miles farther south down the coast) or draw enough enemy troops off the line to allow the stalled Allied troops to break through it.

Despite successful landings in late January 1944, the Allies were slowed down in their efforts to push north by German troops under command of General Albert Kesselring. As a result, Rome held out for nearly five months. During much of this time, Stimson and Marshall were forced to push back on relentless British efforts to double down on activities in the Mediterranean at the expense of properly building up for the cross-Channel invasion (*Overlord*), or the prerequisite landings in Southern France (*Anvil*). The ongoing battle between the Americans and the British over when or even whether to send troops across the English Channel continued right up to D-Day. Stalin's curt and forceful statements in Tehran in favor of *Overlord* and *Anvil* gave only temporary comfort to the Americans. Less than a month after they were spoken, Churchill and Brooke were up to their old tricks.

The British regularly maintained—and were not wrong—that with the conditions of war so fluid, military strategy had to be either continually tweaked or more dramatically altered from time to time. Field Marshal Brooke was particularly critical of the Americans about their predilection for treating agreements on strategy as "legal contracts" etched in stone. But Marshall felt just as much justification to complain about the British for constantly pulling back their support for a cross-Channel attack, sometimes only days after agreeing to it.

In January 1944, five months after the Americans and British met in Quebec and a month after the first Big Three meeting in Tehran, it was again events in Italy that moved Churchill to suggest to Eisenhower that the strategic situation had been altered and a stronger push there would be better than allocating resources to *Anvil*. Churchill was never sold on *Anvil*, and Stalin's insistence in Tehran that it was a necessary conjunct to the success of *Overlord* did not give him pause to reconsider. The prime minister felt that by maintaining strength in Italy, the Allies would be able to move into the oil-rich Balkans, denying the Germans their main source of petroleum (Churchill also believed that such a move would put the United States and Britain in a more favorable political position in that region vis-à-vis the Soviet Union when the War ended).

From a purely military standpoint, the immediate reason for the British opposition to *Anvil* was because Eisenhower's subordinates (chiefly British General Bernard Montgomery and British Admiral Bertram Ramsay) had just concluded that for *Overlord* to succeed, five divisions were needed on the first day as opposed to the three previously envisioned. Ramsay (responsible for delivering all Allied soldiers and equipment to the beaches on D-Day) and Montgomery (in charge of everything during the initial landings) made persuasive arguments to the newly appointed supreme allied commander. It became a question of where the Allies should get the two additional divisions along with the additional supporting resources (e.g., landing craft, naval bombing forces, etc.). They would have to be taken from *Anvil*, Italy, or some combination of both.

Not surprisingly, the British preferred that they be appropriated from *Anvil*. Equally predictable, Eisenhower concluded that they should come from Italy. It was not that Eisenhower was fully invested in a forceful *Anvil* (he could be convinced to reduce it to a strong feint), but nobody from the American High Command, most notably Stimson and Marshall, believed there were any further gains to be made by continuing to slug it out with the Germans north of Rome.

But there was one question about timing that Eisenhower struggled to answer when questioned by the British about taking resources from the Italian theater: Could the Allies easily extricate themselves from Italy in time to transfer the resources to England for *Overlord?* Ike concluded it would be challenging but possible, and he was willing to delay the Normandy landings a month (to June 1944) to make it happen. Even with that delay, Ike still agreed with his British colleagues that weakening *Anvil* was necessary. He knew Marshall would be against this and was therefore caught in a tough position between the British High Command and his boss.

Writing to Marshall in early February 1944 to lay the case out, Eisenhower explained that recent events in Italy made it difficult to conclude *Anvil* could be put on with the same strength as had been planned. Although he stressed to Marshall that the weakening of *Anvil* would not interfere in any way with *Overlord*, Eisenhower made the mistake of suggesting that a weaker *Anvil* would actually be more than offset by the fact that the Germans would continue to devote men and resources to Italy, therefore further enhancing the chances for a successful *Overlord*.

This was an argument Marshall had been hearing for months, but only from men with British accents. The following day he wrote a civil but forceful reply to Eisenhower, notably closing it by expressing his concern that "localitis" might be developing within Ike due to the pressure brought on by the British and could be causing his judgment to be "warped."

Eisenhower promptly denied this, assuring Marshall he had always given the general his own "personal convictions" and would continue to do so. But he did reiterate to his boss that the British did not like *Anvil* and "certain compromises were necessary in the conduct of coalition warfare."[6] Still upset the following day at Marshall's assertion, Eisenhower sent him another message reaffirming he was not bending to the British at the expense of his personal views.

Marshall had made his point and did not bother replying to Ike's second message; he knew his protégé would be sensitive to charges of siding with the British. He was going to let Eisenhower make the decision, but he wanted him to understand three things: First, he and Roosevelt had sent him to Europe to command all operations, not simply to coordinate them; second, Eisenhower still reported to Marshall, the chief of staff of the United States Army; and third, the United States was now providing an overwhelming majority of Allied resources and was therefore entitled to call the shots. It was this last point Marshall wanted Ike to keep in the forefront of his thoughts when he faced pressure each day from his partners in London. For two years, Marshall had watched the British cunningly get their way on major strategic decisions. There were compromises of course, but the British had squashed his attempts to cross the English Channel in 1942 and again in 1943. Marshall was not going to let them kill or weaken *Overlord* in 1944.

To be fair to Eisenhower, he was surrounded and hounded by the British in London. As a result, he might have been more mindful than Marshall of the need to find some middle ground. Fully conscious of this when attending Allied conferences, Marshall was perhaps less sensitive about it when working from within his office at the Pentagon.

In the end, the worsening situation in Italy in March 1944 caused Eisenhower, with Marshall's assent, to delay *Anvil*. Once the delay was agreed, final planning for *Overlord* went into overdrive.

By this point in the War, George Marshall had taken full command of it. For over four and a half years, all but the first ten months of it working side by side with Henry Stimson, he armed the country, designed and oversaw a brilliant training program, fought for and obtained the concept of unity of command, handpicked a vast majority of the key American personnel, and worked tirelessly with his colleagues on the JCS, the British Chiefs of Staff, Churchill, and Roosevelt to develop and implement a global strategy. While his preference was to be sitting at Eisenhower's desk at 20 Grosvenor Square in London, his power in the winter and spring of 1944 was far greater from his third-floor office at the Pentagon. He was now using it forcefully across the globe.

The British High Command could not help but notice Marshall's increased reluctance to compromise. Although he respected his British counterparts, appreciated what they had brought to the table, and admired their fighting spirit when they faced Hitler alone, Marshall believed he and his colleagues on the Joint Chiefs of Staff owed it to the American people to take responsibility for running the war given the preponderance of American soldiers and weapons making up the total Allied presence in Western Europe. And if he ever began to drift away from this thinking, he had Henry Stimson to remind him of it daily.

Stimson during the Run-Up to D-Day

In early February 1944, Henry Stimson's only sibling passed away after a brief illness. Candace Stimson, two years younger than her brother, had been a loving sister and pillar of support to the statesman. Stimson was crushed. Her passing, along with those of other friends and colleagues during the War, served as a harsh reminder of his own mortality. To take his mind off it, he stepped up his workload.

A few weeks after his sister's death, Stimson complained to Marshall he was not getting enough time to read all the materials related to military strategy and operations and therefore wanted to meet with Marshall's staff on a regular basis so he could stay updated more efficiently. With everyone on his team hard-pressed for time, Marshall thought a better solution was to simply invite Stimson into his morning staff meeting. Stimson gratefully accepted.[7]

Advising on military strategy was a task Stimson enjoyed, but one he also continued to believe was a secretary of war's duty despite the executive order issued by Roosevelt in July 1939 permitting direct access between the president and chief of staff related to "strategy, tactics, and operations." By attending Marshall's morning staff meeting, he could at least stay current with the latest strategic developments.

Although Stimson was increasingly thinking of postwar issues, he could never escape the strong pull within him to spend time solving problems directly related to winning the War. In early April 1944, he wrote in his diary:

> I recognize the importance of all this preparation for post-war work but I confess it seems a little artificial for me for I don't expect to live that long or to take much interest in carrying it out. What I'm interested in is to win the war and I am of that type of mind that, having set my mind on that, I key everything to it and

devote all my energies with that in view, and the horizon of the end of the war
pretty nearly coincides with the horizon of my own life in my thoughts.[8]

Despite his melancholy musings on that particular spring evening (two months after the death of his sister) and his stated desire to focus on winning the War, it was in fact the postwar issues of demobilization, Germany, the Philippines, and reorganization of the U.S. military that Stimson gravitated toward during the spring of 1944.

As a disciple of Elihu Root and twice head of the War Department, he thought he was uniquely qualified to offer his opinion on how the military should be organized after the War. Specifically, he believed that it was imperative that the jobs of secretary of war and secretary of navy be combined. Within the Army, there was little opposition to such a suggestion; Marshall, even more of an advocate for the change, had thrown the idea out to the JCS in November 1943.[9] But within the Navy, few if any officers supported it.

In early March 1944, Congressman James Wadsworth proposed that a committee be formed to investigate all matters related to postwar military requirements, including whether to establish a single department of the armed forces. The House of Representatives created the Select Committee on Post-War Military Policy, which was referred to as the "Woodrum Committee" (after its chairman, Clifton Woodrum). Eleven days of hearings commenced in April, giving Stimson a perfect platform on which to share his views.

Prior to making his first appearance, there was one issue Stimson needed to iron out with Marshall relating to the future of the JCS: whether it should have a direct line to the president. Marshall favored one; he had seen too many incompetent secretaries of war during his career and believed direct access to the president was a hedge against this. Stimson, believing there should be a cabinet member between the president and the JCS in the chain of command, did not; he had experiences with two presidents who did not care at all about the Army. Both men agreed that what worked out so well between them in the current structure might not work as well in the future with two other individuals.

After hashing it out between themselves and other staff members, the two came up with a compromise: Direct access between the president and JCS was fine as long as the secretary of defense was copied on the minutes of all meetings and conversations between the two and was made aware in advance of all meetings to take place between them.[10] In other words, full transparency was necessary.

Having resolved his differences with Marshall, Stimson appeared the following day before the Committee. Stimson told the members that having both a secretary of war and secretary of navy led to unnecessary duplication and inefficiencies. Addressing those who believed better cooperation between the Army and Navy was the answer, Stimson said cooperation "could never be as effective as combination." He closed by advising the congressmen that it was important to the nation that this issue be decided as soon as possible. The Committee thanked him but still needed to hear from the Navy.

One week before his appearance, Stimson had discussed his ideas with Secretary of the Navy Frank Knox. To his surprise, Knox was in full agreement. But a few days after the conversation, Knox died of a heart attack. Replacing him was fifty-two-year-old Undersecretary of the Navy James Forrestal. After being aggressively lobbied by the top navy brass shortly upon taking his new position, Forrestal began expressing reservations about consolidating the two services.

Forrestal was in a difficult position. He had already butted heads with Admiral King as undersecretary of the navy. Taking a stand on an issue opposed by King and most other senior officers of the Navy was not a great way to start off in the top job. As a result, Forrestal avoided coming out one way or another for unification during his appearance. He said the Navy wanted to study the issue closely but would make no decisions while the War was going on. Roosevelt agreed, and the issue was tabled. Three years later, the National Security Act of 1947 ended the argument by merging the two departments together and creating the position of secretary of defense (Forrestal was the first person to occupy the office).

Differences on the Issue of Manpower

Assuming he'd be tied to his desk for a while once the cross-Channel invasion was launched, George Marshall traveled as much as he could during the spring of 1944. He inspected troops, toured facilities, observed training exercises, and talked to weapons manufacturers. He always enjoyed such visits and found them highly educational.

When Marshall went on the road, he typically sent detailed instructions in advance to the host commanders outlining how he wanted the trip to go down. Besides listing the things he wanted to see and the people he wanted to meet, Marshall made specific requests on how he wanted to be received and treated during the trip. Characteristically, the chief of staff wanted to keep it simple: no honor guard or ceremony when he arrived or departed; no escort, aides, or orderlies; no advertising his visit in advance; and no posed photographs. He typically set aside time to speak to senior officers, but he made it clear that when he was meeting with the troops—which he normally did—he did not wish to see any high-ranking men milling about him.[11] He was all business when it came to such tours, and when he returned from them, his aides could expect to receive action points on any issues he uncovered.

When Marshall returned to the office after one of his trips in early May, Stimson handed him a four-and-a-half-page memorandum outlining his concerns about manpower once the cross-Channel invasion was successfully completed and American troops were making their way across France. Stimson was worried the Army would not have enough men in reserve to replace the inevitable losses once American forces began to face seasoned German divisions closer to the German border. Fearing the type of stalemate that had characterized World War I, Stimson suggested he and Marshall convince the president and Congress to get more men in training so that the advantage in numbers over the Germans would be more pronounced.[12]

This was neither the first nor the last time Stimson expressed his concerns to Marshall about manpower shortages. Before the smoke had cleared from Battleship Row in Hawaii, he had begun telling Roosevelt and others within the administration that the entire country needed to remain on a proper war footing in order to beat the Axis powers. Stimson firmly believed sacrifices had to be shared by everyone in society so that maximum force could be harnessed against the enemy. More than anyone else in the administration, Stimson promoted the mobilization of the entire adult male population for service during the War through some type of comprehensive national service legislation. As far back as July 1942, he was pushing for such a bill, much like one the United Kingdom enacted when they entered the War.[13] Such legislation, Stimson believed, would ensure that the military and industrial sectors had more than enough men to do the job.

Compared to the secretary, Marshall was relatively relaxed about the issue on the eve of D-Day. He had his reasons: First, he long believed that the quality of troops (and the weapons they brought to battle) was more important than the quantity of them. As we learned earlier, in a number of speeches promoting preparedness over the years, Marshall liked to explain to his audience that although America won the War of Independence and the War of 1812, doing so required ten times the number of troops than the enemy outfitted in the former war and thirty times the amount in the latter. This, Marshall would explain to his surprised audiences, was due to the differences in training between the two armies; second, Marshall also had greater confidence than Stimson that Allied air superiority would be a significant difference-maker, thereby reducing the need for manpower advantages. He felt that continued bombing would not only reduce Germany's industrial ability but eventually convince the Germans there was little chance they could win the War; third, Marshall was certain the massive Soviet army would continue its westward advance and tie up large numbers of German solders; and finally, Marshall devised a replacement plan for troops he believed would allow the existing divisions to remain fresh and fully stocked.[14]

The replacement plan Marshall relied upon was criticized both during and after the War as overly complex, inefficient, injurious to unit cohesion, and a cause for unnecessary casualties. As such, it is worth exploring in greater detail.

Historically, the American practice of replacing casualties during war was on an individual basis as opposed to a system whereby entire units or divisions were brought in to relieve others. This was less by design than a reflection of the nation's political system, its traditional opposition to the concept of a standing army, and how its soldiers were recruited at the start of any war.

From the Revolution through the Civil War, the U.S. Army took replacements wherever it could find them and placed them where they were most needed. This system seldom operated smoothly for a variety of reasons. Attempts were made after each war to correct for the mistakes only to be ignored when the next war came along.

During the First World War, General Pershing established recruitment depots in Europe close to the front that could quickly and efficiently provide trained men to replace troops killed, wounded, or otherwise rotated out of specific divisions. Reserve divisions (made up of approximately twenty-eight thousand men per division during World War I) also trained together with the expectation they could be used to replace other divisions as they came off the front to rest. While it seemed like a solid plan, when the pace at which soldiers were drawn from the recruitment depots exceeded the rate at which they were arriving (due to greater-than-anticipated losses), the pool became exhausted. When this happened, fresh divisions that had anticipated fighting together as one unit were broken up and scattered to replace losses on an individual basis.

Nearly a quarter century later, opinions in America on how many men were required to win World War II kept changing with the ebb and flow of the battles on all fronts, the frequent alterations in strategy, the increased quality and quantity of weapons coming out of American factories, and the ever-shifting views within the administration on how to split up human resources between the military (land, sea, and air), agriculture, and industrial sectors. As Roosevelt had set a 7.7 million ceiling on the size of the Army six months earlier, it was up to the chief of staff to decide in the spring of 1944 whether that number was still sufficient to get the job done. It was a highly complex calculation.

The safe bet was to ask for more men (which is what Stimson wanted to do), but knowing the paramount importance of the industrial production capacity of the United States to the Allied powers, Marshall opted to take a bit of a gamble instead. On the eve of D-Day, he approved a cap of ninety divisions. The risk in fixing this cap was significant. It was impossible to know what the Allies would face once they hit the shores of France, how aggressive the Soviet Union would be as the front moved farther west, and how many men were needed to defeat the Japanese. It also left few reserves in place to take advantage of any major opportunities that might present themselves in either theater or respond to any unexpected reverses.

Marshall's "90 Division Gamble," as it has been referred to, paid off for him and the Americans in the end, but only just so; there was little cushion by the time the War ended in 1945 (when it did, there were only two divisions of the ninety that failed to see action).[15] While some historians interpret this as genius on the part of Marshall, others see it as luck. In the end, Marshall was practicing what he had preached to his own commanders: make do with the resources you have. He was confident that the Russians would fight until Germany capitulated and that his air forces would play an increasingly important role going forward.

Regardless of how Marshall's gamble is perceived today, capping the number of divisions put an end to any idea of having an effective unit replacement system during the War. With the reduced number of divisions, the chief of staff was forced to revamp his system and find alternative methods to replace troops. He had earlier set up a replacement pool system based on his belief that experienced divisions with proven commanders should not let the loss of soldiers keep them from fighting at full strength. From June 1943, these pools of men were critical in keeping the American Army moving forward on all fronts.

Marshall not only believed the individual replacement system could work on its own but also saw additional benefits to it, which he explained to Stimson when he formally replied to the memorandum the secretary of war handed to him on May 11, 1944. The system, Marshall explained, ensured that active divisions could remain at full strength by inserting fully trained replacements into them in a timely fashion. The positive energy and enthusiasm of recruits would be infectious to the battle-tested veterans mentoring the new replacements. He contrasted his new plan with a division replacement scheme and suggested that to create new divisions "would mean emasculating drafts on existing divisions with a consequent lowering in their efficiency."[16]

Marshall soon learned that what made sense in theory did not necessarily pan out in practice. He could not escape the same problems Pershing faced a quarter century earlier: Casualties began piling up at higher rates than anticipated, leading to manpower shortages that stressed the overall system. The problems in Europe started as soon as the troops began negotiating the hedgerows in Normandy and continued throughout 1944. But only during the Battle of the Bulge in December 1944 did Marshall finally admit to Stimson that his unit replacement was having problems.

It was not only the fighting abilities of the Germans that caused the replacement system to go "bankrupt," in the words of General Omar Bradley. Illnesses also contributed. During a five-week stretch during the late fall and early winter of 1944, Bradley lost approximately twelve thousand men to trench foot alone, a malady caused by having one's feet exposed to dampness for too long. Although small by comparison to the sixty-four thousand battlefield casualties suffered during the same five weeks, the loss was not insignificant; a majority of those who suffered from trench foot did not return to combat.[17]

What wet feet were to the European theater, mosquitoes were to the Pacific—only far worse. Malaria crippled the U.S. Army, sometimes in unexpected ways. For example, it had long been estimated by planners in the Army Air Force that pilots would have to be replaced twice as fast as ground crews (for obvious reasons), and plans were made accordingly. But ground crews were required to work both day and night and required lighting when working in the dark. The light attracted mosquitoes. Although the army used antimalaria drugs, the side effects of the drugs made the men useless over time, causing the Air Force to adjust their replacement plans as the ground crews were rapidly depleted.[18]

Another knock against Marshall's replacement system was that the veteran soldiers fighting in existing divisions could not be replaced or even rested. Unless soldiers were killed, wounded, or fell sick, they fought until the War ended. This was a detriment to overall morale, and seasoned veterans were therefore not always in the right frame of mind to appropriately welcome new men coming into their units. Replacements were resented for several reasons: They were replacing friends who had either been killed or injured; they had not gone through the trials the veterans had experienced; or they were simply joining the party late. Even if a specific division experienced little action or hardship, the men within it had mostly gone through difficult training together, shared the experiences of getting from the United States to wherever their unit was based, and lived together on or near the front. Newcomers did not understand the culture that evolved from such experiences in any specific division, regiment, battalion, company, platoon, or squad.

Worse, the replacements were not only untested in battle but were often thrown into the front lines before they could undertake the full training planned for them (manpower shortages always lead to reduced training times). As a result, the replacements made mistakes jeopardizing their own lives and those of other soldiers (casualty rates among replacements far exceeded those of battle-tested veterans). This did nothing to smooth the process by which replacements were assimilated into existing units.

Complaints about the replacement system filtered up during the War to Marshall through his top commanders. Eisenhower, Bradley, and MacArthur were aware of the shortages of men, but they still believed the system to replace casualties was broken. Both Patton and Bradley grumbled to Marshall in the fall of 1944 that it was particularly problematic when inexperienced junior officers were placed with veteran troops.[19] Marshall was in favor of making improvements but reminded his subordinates once again that their job, like his, was to make do with what they had.

The issue of manpower was one Marshall and Stimson fought over periodically for almost all of 1944 and through the early winter of 1945. Stimson wanted more men to ensure that Germany would be defeated sooner than later; Marshall believed there were enough men to get the job done (and trying to get more would be an uphill battle). Next to their debate in the spring of 1941 over where to source leadership for the Army, this was their greatest disagreement.

Less than a week before D-Day, a tense George Marshall was in his Pentagon office when he learned that his twenty-seven-year-old stepson, Allen Tupper Brown, was killed by a sniper in Italy while leading a tank unit. The chief of staff was devastated. Allen, the youngest of Katherine's three children, was thirteen when Marshall married his mother, and the two had been particularly close over the years. He was the son Marshall never had. Upon receiving the message, Marshall abruptly left the office for home to tell his wife in person.

Having little time to console Katherine (who spent the weekend comforting Allen's widow in Leesburg), Marshall kept his focus on the target date for D-Day. Late on June 5, after a delay caused by terrible weather, he received confirmation from Ike that it was on for the following morning. Marshall immediately briefed Stimson and then went to bed. Katherine, back from Leesburg, recalled there was nothing unusual about her husband's demeanor that evening. He enjoyed a full night's sleep.[20]

By contrast, Stimson was in equal parts giddy, solemn, dramatic, and philosophical. He was also boastful, writing in his diary that he had been urging the attack since Churchill first came to America after Pearl Harbor. Excitedly, he placed a radio beside his bed that night and turned it on when he awoke at around 4:00 a.m., just in time to hear a British correspondent give a firsthand description of the parachute jumps over Normandy. He and his wife listened for an hour before falling back asleep. Although details were scant, he was relieved to hear the landings had gone well during his morning briefing with Marshall.

Race to Berlin

The end seems to be approaching on a galloping horse.

—HENRY STIMSON diary entry, August 23, 1944

Marshall's Visit to Normandy

On the day following D-Day, Henry Stimson and George Marshall gathered in Stimson's Pentagon office with their eyes fixed on the impressive twelve-by-eight-foot maps the secretary of war had installed on tracks that could slide in and out of his rich wood-paneled walls for easy viewing. With each bit of information trickling in on D-Day plus one (details on D-Day itself were sketchy), Army cartographers marked the appropriate updates on the map so the two men could follow the progress of the various landing parties in as close to real time as technology allowed in that era.

As satisfying as it must have been to see the forward movements of his soldiers in France represented on a map, Marshall longed to physically be there with them. Although he had sabotaged his own chances for leading the troops by refusing to recommend himself for command, he was not going to be denied the chance to at least witness the history he set in place on the Normandy beaches. Five days later, he was there.

It had been close to twenty-seven years to the week since Marshall last headed for France when he was part of the 1st Division sailing across the Atlantic to assist the British and French in World War I. At that time, he and his colleagues could offer their Allies little more than promises and moral support. It was an altogether different experience when he jumped off an American-made amphibious vehicle onto Omaha Beach the morning of June 12, 1944. Six days after the first wave hit the shore, American men, machines, and weapons were still landing in massive numbers against a surreal backdrop of barrage balloons hovering over the immense and unending flotilla both below and behind it. Within the short space of a week, Omaha Beach became the most active port in Europe.

There had never been a time when American power had been so prominently on display as that moment Marshall disembarked onto the shores of Normandy with King, Arnold, and Eisenhower. To those who watched the four men emerge from the waves, it must have been an extraordinary sight.

General Omar Bradley, commander in chief of all the American ground forces in France, greeted the men on the beach and gave a quick tour of the landing sites by Jeep. Bradley explained to his guests how difficult it had been a few days earlier to gain a foothold given the strong defense made by the Germans beginning with the "Belgian gates" hidden underneath the waterline and the menacing five-foot-tall X-shaped iron "Czech hedgehogs" along the shore. Once clear of those obstacles, the Allied soldiers still faced devastating German firepower (Omaha Beach suffered higher casualties than any of the other D-Day beaches).

As Marshall made his way off the beach up to the bluff, he needed no further reminders from Bradley about how ferociously the Germans defended their positions; he could see dead American soldiers atop white mattress covers still waiting to be buried next to their comrades in a temporary cemetery overlooking the sea. And before moving farther inland, he visited with some of the scores of wounded waiting to be flown to England for treatment.[1] The chief of staff, like all military leaders, knew that gains in war were rarely achieved without a cost. For this reason, it had always been his paramount goal to win the War as soon as possible. The successful landings in France were a major step toward that objective.

After lunching on C-rations and biscuits, listening to Bradley's plans to capture Cherbourg, and giving a global overview to his hosts about the progress of the War, Marshall took a ferry over to Utah Beach (fourteen miles away) to visit with Major General J. Lawton Collins. He then boarded a vessel with Admiral King back to England.[2] It was a brief trip to the front but highly rewarding. Seeing with his own eyes the established beachhead and knowing sixteen Allied divisions had already landed in France, Marshall was confident the tide had turned in Europe. There were still innumerable challenges ahead, but with the Axis powers struggling on both sides of the world, everything was trending in the right direction.

Both before and after his trip to Normandy, Marshall attended meetings of the Combined Chiefs of Staff in London. Unlike most previous meetings of the group, these were amicable. The British, relieved their long-held fears of an unprecedented massacre on D-Day did not pan out, must have been euphoric to find that everything was still going smoothly a week later. Alan Brooke, in particular, had to have been more than pleasantly surprised; he wrote down in his diary hours before the invasion began that "at the best, it will fall so very very far short of the expectation of the bulk of the people. . . . At the worst it may well be the most ghastly disaster of the whole war."[3] Churchill was no less pessimistic, telling his wife, Clementine, before he went to bed on the night of June 5 that by the time she woke up the next day "twenty thousand men might have been killed."[4]

Once Brooke fully realized that the venture had been a success (he only seemed to breathe a sigh of relief the day before he met Marshall in London), he became uncharacteristically conciliatory. He did not argue when Marshall suggested the Allies stop their advances in Italy and was even favorable to putting *Anvil* back on the table (the landings in southern France that the British had previously opposed). At the meetings held after Marshall's visit to Normandy, the progress of the invasion was the main topic of discussion along with *Anvil* (for which a late July target date was tentatively set) and the Pacific Theater (where a strategy in Burma was agreed upon).

When the conferences ended, Marshall headed back to Washington by way of Italy. There were a few reasons for this: First, he wanted to talk to Field Marshall Wilson and General Alexander to discuss the next steps in the Mediterranean (and to persuade Wilson to give up his goal of keeping as many resources as he could in Italy); second, he hoped to see Naples, Rome, and some of the fighting to the north; third, he desired to meet with General Mark Clark and his Fifth Army; and finally, he was determined to visit his stepson's grave and the precise location where he'd been killed two weeks earlier.

Marshall wanted to gather as much information as he could about Allen's death so that he could pass it along to Katherine and to Allen's widow upon his return. It was also something he needed to do for himself. After spending thirty solemn minutes at the gravesite, Marshall jumped on a small plane and had his pilot fly three hundred feet over the battlefield where Allen had died. He then insisted on interviewing some of the men who were in Allen's company. He spoke to three of them who had been right behind his stepson the moment he was killed. He wanted all the details. Comfortable he had them, he flew back to Washington by way of Casablanca, the Azores, and Newfoundland. He was back in the Pentagon on June 22.

Stimson's Turn

Although Henry Stimson was able to get a full briefing from the general upon his arrival stateside, he, too, was itching to get closer to the action and wanted to speak with the commanders and soldiers attempting to break out into Germany. Less than ten days later, he headed off by plane for France and Italy. He would be gone for three weeks.

Starting in Naples, the secretary was hosted by General Jacob Devers, who was Deputy Supreme Allied Commander, Mediterranean Theater. Devers, who six weeks later would lead the invasion of Southern France, put up Stimson and his party in a beautiful villa and was thoughtful enough to build a deck tennis court on the grounds of the property in case the secretary wished to get in exercise while based there.

Stimson's schedule did not permit much time for it. Over the course of a week in Italy moving from Naples to the north of Rome and back, Stimson held meetings with top American commanders (Mark Clark, Ira Eaker, Lucian Truscott, and Alexander Patch, among others), chatted with innumerable soldiers of all stripes, visited the wounded at hospitals, had an audience with Pope Pius XII, and stood through numerous honor guard ceremonies.

He was not only able to see evidence of the war but was privileged to be part of it when artillery units he was visiting with General Clark received firing orders. Covering his ears, the former artillery officer stood directly behind the camouflaged guns as they sent round after round toward the Axis lines. Although he looked somewhat nervous in footage taken during the exercise,Stimson must have been thrilled at the experience.[5]

On July 11, he flew to England, where his schedule was even more packed. In Southampton he inspected the docks and welcomed American troops arriving at the port. He visited armored divisions, saw training exercises, toured more hospitals, held meetings with Eisenhower and his top commanders, and dined and drank with Churchill, Brooke, and other high-ranking British officials until 2:00 a.m. On the 17th, he flew over the Channel to Cherbourg escorted by twelve P-38 fighters.

Greeted by General Bradley and his old friend General Patton, Stimson was given a tour of Cherbourg before the three men headed off to Valognes, Montebourg, Sainte-Mere-Eglise, and other Normandy towns that had witnessed recent fighting. As they drove from town to town in a Jeep, Stimson could see the infamous hedgerows used so effectively in the first few weeks by the Germans to cover their positions and fire upon the Allied troops and tanks.

At Sainte-Mere-Eglise, the secretary took time to visit the temporary grave of Brigadier General Theodore Roosevelt Jr., the oldest son of his former mentor, who had died only a few days before at the age of fifty-six. Roosevelt Jr. was the only general officer to land with the first wave of troops on Utah Beach. He died of a heart attack following a long day of fighting.

It was an emotional visit for Stimson, one reminding him of his dear friend who had passed away twenty-five years earlier. He took photographs of the grave so he could hand them to Roosevelt Jr.'s widow upon his return.[6]

After a tour of Omaha Beach and another meeting with Eisenhower, Stimson spent time with the Army's senior airmen. While visiting General Carl Spaatz (head of the U.S. Strategic Air Forces in Europe) and Lieutenant General James "Jimmy" Doolittle (commander of the Eighth Air Force), the secretary was able to see bomber groups come in from a mission to Germany. Speaking with pilots who flew the mission and visiting those who were injured during it, Stimson got a feel for the brutal nature of the job and the short lifespans of those in the air forces who undertook it.

Weary (his total trip covered fourteen thousand miles by air and over one thousand miles by cars, Jeeps, and trains) but stirred up to have fit in so much during his visit, Stimson flew back to the United States. He landed in Long Island on the morning of Friday, July 21, and was back in his office on Monday after spending the weekend recovering at Highhold. Two months shy of his seventy-seventh birthday, Stimson proved to himself that he could still maintain a punishing pace.

Problems with de Gaulle

Both Stimson and Marshall could have been forgiven if one of the motives for taking their respective trips to Normandy in June and July 1944 was to escape, if only temporarily, all the problems and headaches in Washington. Among them were those created by the presumptuous, arrogant, petty, and uniquely commanding figure of Charles André Joseph Marie de Gaulle. A nuisance to the Western Allies since France had surrendered to the Germans in June 1940, de Gaulle was making life even more difficult for them following D-Day.

The fifty-three-year-old Frenchman, a brigadier general in the French army before he escaped to London less than a week before Hitler made his famous post-victory visit to Paris, was the self-proclaimed leader of the Free French Forces. From his first days in London, de Gaulle worked tirelessly to uphold French honor and fight for its interests—and of course, for his own. He tried to accomplish this by demanding that he be treated as an equal to Churchill and Roosevelt and insisting that he be formally recognized as the head of the French government-in-exile. The longer each leader refused, the more obnoxious, insufferable, and disruptive he became.

The British, despite the great antipathy Churchill and his colleagues had toward de Gaulle personally, were more willing than the Americans to acknowledge the French general for who he was: the de facto head of the free French government-in-exile and the symbol, if not the leader, of the French Resistance. American officials—most notably President Roosevelt—had little tolerance for the Frenchman's antics and refused to believe de Gaulle was as important to the French people as he was making himself out to be. Roosevelt was also sensitive about taking any step that might provide an advantage to de Gaulle in the postwar competition for power in France. The president believed the French people should solely determine who would lead France when the time came for them to choose a leader.

Neither Marshall nor Stimson was enamored with de Gaulle either. While they respected him as a solider and had been impressed by both his refusal to surrender to the Germans and his defiance of Marshal Pétain and Vichy France, they, too, recoiled at his arrogance and pettiness. But as preparations for a cross-Channel attack were refined, they knew from discussions with Eisenhower that cooperation with the French Resistance was going to be critical once Allied troops landed on the beaches and began moving inland. Both men were therefore more willing than Roosevelt to grant some type of recognition to the French Committee of National Liberation (which de Gaulle had run since November 1943).

Regardless of their view, only that of the president mattered, and Roosevelt continued to have no interest in helping secure de Gaulle's political future. Despite acknowledging that something needed to be done from a military standpoint, the president hemmed and hawed during the spring of 1944 even after Stimson applied repeated pressure on him to send

Eisenhower instructions on how to deal with de Gaulle and the French once the invasion began.

One of the reasons Roosevelt hesitated was because the British wanted to formally recognize de Gaulle. Unlike Roosevelt, Churchill wanted France restored to "great power" status after the War and believed de Gaulle was the Frenchman most qualified to lead the country. Having witnessed Germany's resurgence after World War I, worried about the threat posed by the Soviet Union, and mindful of the possibility America could return to isolationism after the War, Churchill's determination to make France strong (and friendly toward Great Britain) was logical.

Roosevelt entertained other ideas about how the world should be policed once the War ended (that did not include France) and thus refused to back down on the issue of recognizing de Gaulle as D-Day approached. Eisenhower later wrote that the president's inaction in this regard was one of the "most acutely annoying problems" he encountered as D-Day approached.[7]

If Ike was annoyed, de Gaulle was apoplectic. He was upset at the Allies for leaving him out of the planning process, infuriated that he was not even told of the invasion until two days before it was launched, and humiliated when he learned that Americans, not the French, would be responsible for administering liberated French towns. Determined for revenge, the Frenchman decided it was time to step up his efforts to get the recognition he felt he deserved.

"Le Général" began his quest in the early hours of D-Day by holding back approximately 90 percent of the 180-plus French citizens trained by the Allies to assist them in administrative duties as they began retaking French towns from the Germans. He also delayed making a radio speech to the French people on D-Day (one specifically requested by the Allies) and then departed from the prearranged script to tell his fellow citizens to only follow instructions from the French provisional government.[8]

He wasn't finished. Once comfortable that the landings were a success, de Gaulle sabotaged the American plan to issue military currency in France on a temporary basis until a French government could be set up. Stimson likened this to stealing "our ammunition on the battlefield to turn our guns against us," and Marshall vented his rage to several of de Gaulle's officers and to Anthony Eden (the strongest supporter of de Gaulle among Allied officials).

Despite these and other affronts leading up to and following D-Day, Stimson continued pressing Roosevelt to recognize de Gaulle. He explained that it was a military necessity and politically wise to boot (because de Gaulle would likely become the leader of France after the War). Marshall left political decisions to the president but also favored recognizing de Gaulle and his followers from a military standpoint.

Roosevelt listened, but it was not until the end of August that he finally gave Eisenhower permission to deal with de Gaulle as the de facto authority in France (two months before formally recognizing his provisional government). The delay caused problems for the Army throughout the summer of 1944.

Postwar Planning

Notwithstanding the difficulties caused by de Gaulle, the news from all fronts was positive during the summer of 1944 following the return of both Marshall and Stimson from their visits to Normandy. In the Pacific, the Battle of the Philippine Sea, fought as Marshall was making his way back to Washington in June, was a huge setback for the Japanese Navy as it lost three carriers and over two hundred planes during the fighting. The decisive victory allowed the United States to more easily carry out the island-hopping strategy it began a year earlier. Guam fell the following month and the Mariana Islands in August.

On the Eastern Front, the Soviet army firmly established itself just outside of Warsaw only a few weeks after launching its summer offensive at the end of June. The broad line of troops running from Finland to the Black Sea had been pushing the Germans steadily westward for over a year. In late August, Romania switched sides to the Allies, which dealt a major blow to Hitler's access to oil for the remainder of the War.

In France, Allied troops were finally able to extricate themselves from the deadly hedgerow fighting that took place in and around Normandy during the first six weeks of fighting following D-Day. *Operation Cobra*, launched in late July under the command of General Omar Bradley, allowed the Allies to break clear into a topography where they could more easily benefit from the overwhelming number of tanks and vehicles that had come ashore since June 6. A massive carpet-bombing of German troops and equipment by Allied fighters and bombers preceding the attack gave an advantage to Bradley's troops as they pushed their way forward (although a number of bombs fell short, killing over one hundred Americans, including Marshall protégé General Lesley McNair). Once clear, the newly established Third Army, led by Patton, began its legendary dash through France, only stopping at the end of August when Eisenhower, desiring a broader front, held it back before it could make its way across the border into Germany.

Two weeks earlier, *Anvil* (renamed *Dragoon*) was launched in Southern France. Conceived and fought for by Marshall and strongly endorsed by Stalin at the Tehran Conference the previous November, *Dragoon* was an operation the Western Allies continued to bicker about throughout June and half of July before the Americans finally forced the issue by telling the British the operation was no longer negotiable.

From a military standpoint, *Dragoon* was a huge success. Marshall called it "one of the most successful things we did."[9] Launched on August 15, the operation led to the capture of the important ports of Marseille and Toulon and cleared Southern France of Germans within four weeks. Some British commanders criticized the offensive after the War, claiming it diverted forces that could have been used on the Western Front to reach Berlin before the Russians. These criticisms were made in hindsight; the issue was not brought up during meetings of the Combined Chiefs of Staff prior to the launch of *Dragoon*. Marshall's mission, as he understood it, was to win the War as soon as possible and at the least possible cost of men and materials. He was nothing if not consistent in advocating that an attack on Germany through France was the best means to achieve this. Recapturing the ports in Southern France to supply the armies moving toward Germany was critical for the overall success of that mission.

With things going well after the launch of *Dragoon*, Hap Arnold suggested to Marshall that the two of them take a brief vacation in California to fish. They were both due in Quebec on September 12 to join Roosevelt for another conference with the British, and the timing seemed right to recharge their batteries. Although arrangements were made for Marshall to have direct communication lines established to Washington, his agreement to go indicated his growing comfort over the progress of the War. In fact, less than a week before he took off with Arnold, he had already spent six days in the Adirondacks swimming, canoeing, and relaxing with his wife.[10]

The chief of staff was not the only confident figure in the Pentagon. In Stimson, Marshall was leaving behind a colleague even more bullish about the outcome; the secretary of war himself had just returned from a two-week break at his beloved Ausable Club in the Adirondacks. After getting caught up on all the war news, Stimson wrote, "The end seems to be approaching on a galloping horse."[11]

Stimson's gaining confidence during the summer of 1944 caused him to focus even harder on postwar issues. Although seemingly more concerned than his colleagues throughout the War about how the world should be structured after it, Stimson was not the only one who gave it consideration. In retrospect, it was remarkable how many Allied statesmen felt duty-bound to prepare for the end of the War well before they had even gained an edge in the fighting. Less than six months after Pearl Harbor was attacked, at a time when both Germany and Japan were running roughshod over the Allies, Stimson, Secretary of State Hull, and Secretary of the Navy Knox met together to discuss postwar reconstruction. This was before the Battle of Midway, the Battle of Guadalcanal, and the first major British victory at the Second Battle of El Alamein. By no means was the outcome of the War certain when they got together in June 1942, yet the three men were determined to get postwar ideas out on the table.[12]

Fast-forward to the summer of 1944, and no postwar question was more important to Stimson than what to do about Germany. He had been discussing the issue periodically with various members of the administration during the spring and became increasingly uncomfortable with what he felt was an overly punitive position toward Germany taken by several senior officials. No person was more extreme in his views and pushed for more draconian measures than Secretary of the Treasury Henry Morgenthau Jr. The fifty-three-year-old neighbor and longtime friend of the president's wanted to partition Germany into two different states (*after* giving part of East Prussia to Poland, the Saar to France, and putting the Ruhr under international control). He also proposed stripping the Germans of all their industrial capabilities, leaving the country essentially pastoral and its people with a standard of living no higher than subsistence levels. Finally, Morgenthau proposed shooting the top hundred or so Nazi officials without giving them the benefit of a trial.[13]

Considering the general terror that had been inflicted on the world by Germany, and more specifically the unprecedented genocide it had carried out against European Jews, Morgenthau's position was understandable. In fact, there was widespread support for much of his plan within the administration. Stimson, however, was appalled, and he made his opposition to the plan abundantly clear to both the treasury secretary and the president.

Given the passionate rebuke from his secretary of war to what was becoming known as the "Morgenthau Plan," Roosevelt agreed to establish a "Committee on Germany" to sort out the conflicting opinions within his cabinet and report back to him with recommendations before he met with the British in Quebec. He put Stimson, Morgenthau, Hull, and Hopkins on the Committee. The debate that went on between Stimson and Morgenthau, both inside and outside the formal meetings, was, in Stimson's words, "the most violent single interdepartmental struggle" of his career.

Drawing upon the full weight of his experience and expertise, Stimson tried to use pure logic when appealing to Morgenthau and other Committee members. As a leading international lawyer long connected with global economic issues, and aware of the historic importance of German industry to the economic health of Europe, Stimson stressed that the postwar recovery in Western Europe as a whole could not get off the ground without the efforts of the industrious and talented German people working in the Ruhr and Saar regions. And a strong Western Europe, Stimson maintained, was absolutely critical to both the economy of the United States as well as its security vis-á-vis the Soviet Union.

Morgenthau, a Christmas tree farmer in New York State before Roosevelt brought him into his administration, was unmoved. Although he had been heading Treasury for over a decade, his understanding of the global economy likely fell short of Stimson's. Realizing this, the secretary of war tried a different approach. As a former secretary of state who dealt directly with the consequences of "bad peacemaking," Stimson questioned why anyone would want to repeat the same mistakes made by the Allies after World War I. Yes, he exclaimed, Germany was to blame for what had gone on for the past five years, but it was up to the Committee to look past that and make the right call on what was best for the United States going forward. Methods that oppressed a country, such as those proposed by the Morgenthau Plan, would not prevent war, lectured Stimson; it would "breed" it.

His arguments did little to change any minds going into the Quebec Conference; emotions still seemed to be driving opinions. The report furnished by the Committee to the president on September 5, 1944, largely supported the thinking of Morgenthau. Stimson wrote an impassioned minority opinion (his second memorandum on the subject to FDR) outlining his principal disagreements with the plan. It was the best he could do for the moment.

In Quebec, Morgenthau was invited by the president to present his ideas to Churchill. The prime minister, although vigorously opposed to them at first, came around the following day for several reasons: First, Morgenthau convinced him of the gain to Great Britain that would follow the elimination of Germany's industrial output; and second, Morgenthau seemed to be tying the continuation of Lend-Lease support to the British after the War with its current support of the Morgenthau Plan.[14] Much to Stimson's horror, both Churchill and Roosevelt accepted much of the Morgenthau Plan in a joint communiqué they released as the Second Quebec Conference ended in mid-September (although neither man signed off on Morgenthau's plan to partition the country).

Stimson was in the process of sending a third memorandum on the subject to the president when he heard the news from Quebec. Although doubtful he could now make a difference, he decided to send it to FDR anyway to "keep the record straight." His memorandum, assisted by McCloy, was a tour de force and one of the finest examples of Stimson's statesmanship that can be found among his papers. In it, Stimson questioned whether seventy million educated Germans could be kept "within bounds" living on the subsistence levels forced on them by the Allies. Even if they could, he doubted the economic and moral rationale of making them suffer. Declaring, "Poverty in one part of the world usually induces poverty in other parts," Stimson wrote that forcing it upon the Germans was not only bad policy, but also a crime against civilization, the type the Germans would certainly commit themselves if they somehow managed to win the War. Quoting both the Declaration of Independence and the Atlantic Charter, signed by FDR and Churchill four months before Pearl Harbor (the latter document stating that both the victors and vanquished of the War would be entitled to freedom from economic want and access on equal terms to the trade and raw materials of the world), Stimson warned Roosevelt that if the goal was to prevent future wars, the Morgenthau Plan would surely fail. The question, Stimson wrote, was not about the desire to make the Germans "suffer for their sins." It was whether making that happen was good for the world from an economic or a spiritual standpoint.

Roosevelt read the memorandum and indicated to Stimson that he wanted to discuss it. Right before their meeting, someone leaked information about the strong differences of opinion within the administration on the German question and the president's support of the Morgenthau Plan. The press came out hard against both FDR and Morgenthau for their views. Under pressure, Roosevelt backtracked; he told Stimson he was not paying attention when he initialed the statement with the prime minister in Quebec and had no intention of turning Germany into a big farm. He simply wanted Great Britain to get some economic benefit from the Saar and Ruhr.[15] In retrospect, it seems Roosevelt was ambivalent about following through with the part of the Morgenthau Plan dealing with the German economy. He and Stimson did not discuss it again, and the policy discussions on postwar Germany were largely carried out at lower levels.

It took quite a bit of time, but Stimson's arguments were ultimately accepted along with the ideas he articulated to the president and his colleagues as far back as the fall of 1943 regarding the country's general economic assistance to Europe after the War.[16] His call during this time for the United States to reach a "higher level of statesmanship" sowed the seeds for what was to become the "Marshall Plan," first hinted at in a speech three years later by then Secretary of State George Marshall at Harvard University. Until that famous address, the deteriorating relationship between America and the Soviet Union had complicated the issue of how Germany was to be treated. Although Stimson had been retired for nearly two years when Marshall spoke at Harvard, it would have been fitting if the new American initiative were dubbed "the Marshall-Stimson Plan," such was the influence of Henry Stimson on the ultimate rebuilding of postwar Europe.[17]

As for Morgenthau's suggestion to execute top Nazis without trial, this, too, went unrealized, and Stimson's more tempered views prevailed. After huddling with McCloy and a few military lawyers to brainstorm, the secretary of war pushed Roosevelt—who had expressed support from time to time for trial-less executions—to support a legal action against the Nazi leaders instead of a political one. The Nuremberg trials, begun in November 1945, had the fingerprints of Stimson all over them. Controversial as they were, the trials were a far better reflection of the American values Stimson was hoping to project after the War than what was first proposed by the secretary of the treasury during it. Stimson realized America would emerge from World War II having a position of influence around the globe unlike that experienced by any other country in history. He wanted to make sure Roosevelt, and other American leaders following him, continued along the "high moral plane" that he believed characterized America's leadership before and during World War II.

George Marshall, although disciplined during the War about staying clear of political issues, was on board with Stimson, as was most of Marshall's staff. Stimson was not surprised—he thought military officers were "in many respects the best educated men of the country in regard to the basic principles of our Constitution and traditional respect for freedom and law."[18]

Allied Setbacks in Europe

When Marshall and Arnold got back from their fishing trip to the West Coast, they had to quickly prepare to meet the British in Canada for the Second Quebec Conference (code-named *Octagon*), which began on September 12. With positive news from all fronts, the meetings proved to be among the most cordial of the entire war.[19] Where differences existed, largely related to the Pacific Theater, they were sorted out amicably. During the discussions, Marshall's role was limited to trying to keep the peace between Admiral King (who insisted the U.S. Navy could finish off Japan without British assistance) and the British (who for political reasons wanted their navy to be involved in the defeat of Japan). His efforts proved moot as Roosevelt agreed to let the British take a role.

Although the British raised the prospect of launching an offensive from the Italian Theater toward Trieste and then Vienna, Marshall stayed calm. He even supported the retention of the U.S. Fifth Army in Italy in case such an opportunity presented itself. He still thought going into Vienna would be a complete waste of time from a military standpoint (as did a few of the British leaders), but since things were going so well for the Allies, it made more sense for him to avoid a confrontation and push any potential discussion on such a strategy down the road.

All told, it was an upbeat and relatively relaxed conference. Even Brooke, who normally dreaded such meetings with the "incompetent" and "shortsighted" Americans, had few complaints during his time in Quebec. Like Marshall had done before the Conference, Brooke and his colleagues went fishing directly after it, confident enough with the state of things to enjoy five relaxing days looking for trout in Canadian lakes.

As it turns out, the Western Allies were getting a bit ahead of themselves, and it was in Italy where this first became apparent. Whereas the Combined Chiefs of Staff assumed their armies would reach the northern border of that country within a month, it became clear shortly after the conference ended that they had miscalculated. In the way stood the formidable defensive position of the Germans known as the Gothic Line, which ran 170 miles across Italy from a point on the west coast approximately seventy miles south of Genoa to a town on the Adriatic Sea located more than one hundred miles south of Venice. The Allied assault on this fortified line—ordered shortly before the Second Quebec Conference got underway—got bogged down quickly by the weather, the topography, a shortage of men due to the earlier transfer of units to support *Dragoon*, and the standard tenaciousness of the German army. It was not a defeat by any definition, but neither was it the Patton-like breakthrough the Allied leaders were hoping for.

Unrelated to the struggles in Italy, Marshall decided shortly after arriving back from Quebec to meet with his commanders in Europe to determine what was really happening, whether or not the war in Europe could be won by the end of the year, and what was needed to complete the job. Before he could get on a plane, however, he had to manage an unusually difficult political issue related to the presidential campaign of 1944. Although he had avoided politics his entire professional career, the chief of staff felt he had no choice but to get directly involved. How he handled the episode was vintage Marshall, and it is doubtful if anyone else had the stature or diplomatic skill to successfully intervene in what was a highly sensitive matter in an exceedingly charged political environment.

The issue related to Pearl Harbor. Opponents of the president, facing headwinds going into the fall presidential election due to the improved fortunes of the Allies around the globe, began asking questions related to the Japanese attack in hopes of finding something they could use against him. During their quest, a few members of Congress learned that the Japanese diplomatic code was broken prior to the attack and the administration knew the Japanese would likely strike somewhere on or close to December 7. Proving Roosevelt had advance warning of Japan's intentions without properly warning the commanders of each potential military target would be political gold for the Republicans. In late September, Marshall learned that their nominee for president, Thomas Dewey, was planning to divulge this information in a campaign speech he was delivering in the Midwest.[20]

Marshall was determined to prevent this. If Dewey made the speech, the Japanese would know their codes had been broken and immediately change them, thus depriving the U.S. Army and Navy of an extremely valuable intelligence source at a time when the two services were still taking advantage of it and still preparing major offensives. The remaining length of the war and the lives of American troops depended on keeping America's code-breaking accomplishments secret.

Without informing anyone but Admiral King and his own intelligence officers, Marshall wrote a three-page letter to Dewey that was delivered by hand to the Republican candidate in Tulsa on September 26 by a trusted messenger. In the first paragraph, Marshall requested that Dewey stop reading and hand back the letter to the messenger unless he could pledge to keep secret all that he was about to learn. Dewey, assuming that Roosevelt was playing him, stopped reading and returned the letter. He was certain he already knew most of what Marshall was about to reveal to him.[21]

Two days later, Marshall sent his messenger back to Dewey with a new proposal: The candidate could disclose anything in the letter he already knew about from other sources. Dewey accepted with two conditions of his own: he be allowed to consult with one of his advisors; and he could keep Marshall's letter in his own personal files once he read it. Marshall agreed and Dewey read the full letter aloud in front of the messenger and his advisor.

In the letter, the chief of staff wrote that he was approaching Dewey because the danger of exposing the country's code-breaking success against the Japanese was "so serious" he believed "some action is necessary to protect the interests of our armed forces." He then proceeded to outline all the military advantages gained by deciphering the Japanese codes, going back to the Battle of the Coral Sea and the decisive Battle of Midway and continuing through to the present offensive initiatives. "Operations in the Pacific," wrote Marshall, "are largely guided by the information we obtain of Japanese deployments" from the intercepts. The chief of staff further explained to Dewey that breaking the Japanese code had allowed the United States to monitor German intentions (since Japanese officials communicated them to other Japanese colleagues via radio after each meeting with German officials).[22]

After asking the messenger several questions, Dewey and his advisor excused themselves to converse privately. The candidate was in an obvious pickle: He was behind in the polls and the information on Roosevelt might be able to turn former isolationists against the three-term president; on the other hand, at only forty-two years of age, the then governor of New York must have believed that he had a long career ahead of him in national politics. After twenty-two minutes of deliberation, he stepped back into the room and told the messenger to tell Marshall that he would not publicly raise the issue of the codes. It is not clear how close Dewey was to making the speech, but Marshall's personal intervention could have played a big role in his decision not to. Had it been almost anyone but General Marshall behind the request to stay quiet, Dewey might not have listened. But the chief of staff's reputation and popularity were so high in the fall of 1944 that Dewey must have felt he had little choice but to follow his advice.[23]

After silencing the Republican candidate, Marshall quickly prepared for his trip to Europe. Astutely, he invited along Jimmy Byrnes so that the increasingly influential head of the OWM could see for himself what the Army still needed in order to finish off Hitler. They left Washington together on October 5.

After meeting with Eisenhower in Paris, the two men flew off with General Bradley to meet with Patton at the latter's headquarters in northeastern France and then flew to Holland to visit British commander Bernard Montgomery (who'd been promoted to field marshal a month earlier). Predictably, Montgomery complained to Marshall about Eisenhower and the way he was running the entire operation in Europe. Marshall, believing it was just "overwhelming egotism" driving Montgomery's grumblings, held his tongue during the conversation, listening thoughtfully to the field marshal's ideas with little judgment (the British commander was not fooled, however; he knew Marshall disagreed with most of his ideas).[24]

Marshall then flew back to France and then Belgium before following a path north along the Allied front toward Holland, stopping to meet key commanders along the way (Simpson, Middleton, Gerow, Collins, and Hodges). By the time he was done, he had visited all the U.S. corps headquarters and nearly all the division headquarters. He ended the trip by returning to Eisenhower's headquarters in Versailles for a day and a night before departing for Washington on Friday, October 13.

When the chief of staff returned to the office the following Monday and briefed Stimson, he cautioned the secretary of war that the fighting in Europe was not necessarily going to end in 1944; the shortages in ammunition would likely stall the Allied advances by late fall. But he expressed confidence that Byrnes, having been by his side on the trip, would use his considerable clout to help keep the American economy cranking out what was needed to defeat the Germans in 1945 and assist in freeing up any and all bottlenecks preventing the troops from receiving what was produced in a timely manner.

Marshall was shocked to find upon his return to the United States that British Field Marshal John Dill was in critical condition at Walter Reed Hospital in Washington, D.C. Although he was aware that Dill had been having issues with his health since developing an infection following a hernia operation a year earlier, the downturn was sudden. Dill died on November 4, less than three weeks after Marshall's return. Other than the death of his stepson, nothing hit him harder during the war. It was a "cruel blow" to the general, according to his wife, and one that brought "deep grief" to their home.[25] Dill was likely the closest friend Marshall had ever had.

Anguished, the chief of staff was determined to honor the tremendous work done by his British comrade. Inspired by a precedent brought to his attention by Stimson (regarding a tablet erected by the British in Westminster Abbey after the First World War to honor U.S. Ambassador Walter Hines Page), Marshall used his considerable prestige not only to get approval to bury Dill at Arlington National Cemetery (Dill's preference), but also to find a prominent location within the cemetery to do so. There were regulations against the burial of foreign soldiers at Arlington, but Marshall was not going to be denied. Stimson knew how much Dill meant to Marshall and offered his support and stature. The secretary of war got consent from the president to issue an order to the quartermaster general that the plot of ground in which the late field marshal was to be buried should be permanently kept free of other interments.[26]

Still grieving a year later, and resolved not to let Dill's contributions be lost to history, Marshall received approval to have an impressive equestrian statue of his friend erected at the gravesite (there were also regulations against such statues within Arlington, and Marshall was forced to overcome surprising opposition by various members of the American Legion).[27] He then spent a few years leading efforts to raise funds for the statue. It was dedicated in 1950 and has been viewed and admired since by millions of Americans who have strolled by it on their way up the road to the Tomb of the Unknown Soldier or the gravesite of President John F. Kennedy.

Dill's passing was heartbreaking to those who loved and admired him, but it came at a time when his extraordinary talents were no longer needed. The big decisions on strategy, on which Dill had worked so hard to help craft compromises, had already been completed and were being executed in both theaters. For the three years up to his passing, the field marshal was the crucial connection between the Americans and the British. More specifically, he was able to explain George Marshall to Alan Brooke and vice versa in a way the two leaders could have never done on their own. After the War ended, Brooke jotted down notes alongside the original entries in his diary on the day he received word of Dill's death that credit was due to Dill "more than any other general for our final victory."

Strategic issues, the type Dill regularly discussed with the American chief of staff, were not on the forefront of Marshall's mind during the second week of November following Dill's funeral. Logistical issues were, specifically the shortages of ammunition and fuel that were threatening to stall Eisenhower's broad eastward push toward Germany. What was apparent to the chief of staff after interviewing his commanders directly in October only got worse in November. General Omar Bradley estimated late that month he had only enough supplies to continue his offensive for a couple more weeks.

The problem was not complicated. The gasoline, ammunition, and supplies that the Allies were consuming at highly accelerated rates had to be hauled to the front by trucks from the port of Cherbourg. As Eisenhower's armies moved forward, the "Red Ball Express," as the supply line was dubbed, lengthened to nearly four hundred miles and could not keep pace (although Montgomery captured the geographically more convenient port of Antwerp in September, it only became fully operational in late November).

These logistical challenges spawned sharp differences of opinion between the British and Americans during the late fall of 1944 on how best to maintain momentum. Eisenhower continued to favor a broad line of attack, but he was aggressively pitched by Field Marshal Montgomery to adopt a more focused strategy. Before these arguments could escalate to a point where Marshall's intervention was necessary, Hitler made them irrelevant in one fell swoop. On December 16, the German dictator went for broke and launched a massive surprise counteroffensive concentrated on a thinly defended sixty-mile section of the Allied lines in the Ardennes region of Luxembourg and Belgium.

Hitler's plan, a last-ditch gamble in reality, was highly ambitious at best: divide the British and American troops and recapture the Port of Antwerp in order to choke off the Allied supplies. Delusional by this time in the War, the German leader hoped that once the Allies were trapped behind his lines with their supply lines cut off, they'd sue for peace, freeing him to finish off the Soviet Union.

The Battle of the Bulge, as it was later named (due to the narrow but deep penetration made by the Germans along the broad, flat Allied lines), began with great promise for Hitler. The Allies were not able to spot the massive buildup of German troops the dictator quietly moved into position behind the dense Ardennes forest. Once the men and equipment were in place, twenty-nine divisions under German Field Marshal Gerd von Rundstedt attacked on a Saturday morning, quickly puncturing and overtaking the Allied lines. The strike was a complete surprise; in fact, it was more than two days before the Allies were able to comprehend the full extent of the offensive.

Once the news was confirmed, Stimson and Marshall huddled on December 18. Both men believed the Germans would not make it far and were taking a huge risk that might actually shorten the war. Marshall assumed Hitler's aim was simply to slow down Patton's advance into the Saar. Stimson, always looking for silver linings, expressed his hope the offensive would actually "help our cause of waking up Americans to better production."[28]

The German offensive managed to make it nearly fifty miles within the first two days before a quick and skillful response by Eisenhower's troops, along with some fortuitous weather, allowed the U.S. Army to turn the momentum in its favor by December 26. The Germans never got the breakthrough necessary for Hitler's plan to have a chance. Eisenhower's air superiority allowed him to wreak havoc on the German troops once the heavy clouds cleared. At the same time, George Patton famously marched his Third Army north from where it was positioned near the Saar and hit the Germans hard on their left flank. In turning his army around 90 degrees, marching six of his divisions more than a hundred miles over two days through snow-covered roads in bitterly cold weather, and then immediately attacking the Germans, the fifty-nine-year-old Patton cemented his legend. Omar Bradley described the achievement as an "astonishing feat of generalship."[29]

Running low on gas and having lost nearly eight hundred tanks, Hitler began withdrawing his troops back to their original positions on January 9. Approximately three weeks later, the "bulge" was closed, but it was a costly victory for the Allies; they suffered seventy-five thousand casualties, including nineteen thousand killed.

Manpower Shortages

The Battle of the Bulge brought to light within the War Department a problem that had vexed Marshall and Stimson for several months: how to find the right balance between an honest public assessment of how the War was going with the need to keep the country highly motivated to produce the weapons and supplies required to win it. It was natural for both men to want to project a picture of competence to the American people and give them a fair accounting of how the Allied armies were performing. Through his weekly press conferences, prior to which he always consulted with the chief of staff, Stimson tried to do this. When it became obvious that victory was foreseeable several weeks after D-Day, he and Marshall began receiving reports from their subordinates that production levels were dropping in the factories producing military weapons and supplies. Workers, sensing the War was coming to an end, began leaving for peacetime jobs to get a step ahead of other workers.

Those responsible within the Army for making sure the troops had all they needed—most notably General Brehon Somervell, head of the Army Service Forces—were angry with the secretary of war for making their jobs harder. Forcefully complaining to Marshall after Stimson's weekly press conference on December 28, Somervell argued he could not "command people to produce more," but he could get them to work harder if senior leaders (i.e., Stimson) shared with the people "a common understanding of our problems." Marshall, frustrated at the tone of Somervell's complaint, responded by asking him what it was exactly that Stimson "should not have been said or modified?"[30] Marshall wanted Somervell to appreciate that when communicating with the public during war in a democracy, one had to find the right balance.

Stimson regularly ruminated on this challenge in his diary throughout the War. When the Germans were finally in full retreat during the Battle of the Bulge, he noted the irony about being "distressed by our successes and good fortune." He was referring to both the general public and Congress when he said that the reaction to good news was that "everybody wants to put on his coat and stop working."[31]

After the War, Robert Patterson commented that the nation's most serious shortcoming during the conflict was its "failure to achieve genuine mobilization of manpower."[32] Consequently, he was certain the true potential of industrial output and military strength was never achieved. Patterson did not blame the general population; he believed they would have sacrificed if asked. He insisted the fault was with those officials who failed to stand up to pressure groups.

Four days before the start of 1945, Stimson began worrying about manpower again. Seven months had passed since he sent Marshall his memorandum outlining his concerns following D-Day. Although Stimson signed off on Marshall's "90 Division Gamble," it did not stop him from constantly fretting about whether the United States would fall short in its required number of troops. His worries seemed justified as 1944 came to an end.

On December 27, he met with the chief of staff for a discussion he described as "one of the longest and best talks" he'd ever had with Marshall.

At that point, neither man was aware that Hitler's troops had already hit their high-water mark in the Battle of the Bulge. Stimson asked Marshall directly if the two of them had made the right call regarding the total size of the Army and the amount allocated to the Pacific Theater. Stimson also expressed concern about fatigue in the front lines that became apparent prior to the German attack.

A confident Marshall tried to put the secretary at ease. At worst, he told Stimson, if the Germans were to win the battle in the Ardennes, there were enough troops to maintain a defensive line and the two of them could then ask Roosevelt for more to mount an offensive. But he did not think this would happen; with the massive supplies pouring into them from Antwerp combined with Allied air superiority, he told Stimson that Hitler could not hold on too much longer.

A couple of days later, Stimson got word the Germans were beginning to withdraw from the salient they had so rapidly created. This eased his concerns and allowed him to turn his attention to the other matters he had been handling.[33]

19

Defeat of Germany

Our army and people have never been so deeply indebted to any other soldier.[1]

—DWIGHT EISENHOWER to George Marshall, May 7, 1945

Pearl Harbor Investigation

Prior to the start of the Battle of the Bulge, Stimson was hoping to spend the fall of 1944 as he had spent the summer: largely focused on post-war issues. But to his frustration, "stopping ratholes" seemed to be his primary occupation.[2] The principal rathole he was referring to related to an issue that had been put on a shelf for two years: Pearl Harbor; specifically, questions asked by Congress as to whether the responsibility for the debacle might be shared by individuals more senior than the local Army and Navy commanders initially blamed.

In July 1944, a month after D-Day, Congress passed an act requiring both the Army and Navy to conduct hearings on Pearl Harbor and present its findings. Although the Roberts Commission appointed by FDR right after the attack had already issued a report less than two years earlier, largely placing the blame on General Walter Short and Admiral Husband Kimmel for "dereliction of duty," Republican members of Congress wanted to dig a little deeper to find out if anyone else deserved some of the blame (i.e., President Roosevelt).

The Army Pearl Harbor Board worked for three months up to mid-October preparing its findings. During this time, and right through the end of November, the secretary of war worked tirelessly on the investigation. Whether preparing for his own testimony, reviewing and discussing the report issued by the Board, or drafting and redrafting his own personal report, Stimson was uncharacteristically stressed. He despised the entire exercise, calling it a "wretched piece of labor which Congress has quite unnecessarily thrown on me" and the most "wearing and limping thing that I have had in the four years that I have been here."[3]

The Army report, like the Roberts Commission's findings, placed most of the blame on General Short. But the report also faulted Marshall (and General Gerow of the War Plans Division) for failing to keep General Short sufficiently informed of the Japanese threat in the weeks and critical days before the attack (particularly after it became obvious to intelligence authorities on December 6 that a strike by the Japanese was imminent somewhere in the Pacific within twenty-four hours). It also criticized the chief of staff for failing to follow up with Short on a specific warning and instruction he gave him in late November (after it became apparent Short had not fully understood nor carried out the instruction properly).

Although unrelentingly protective of the chief of staff, Stimson respected the process and believed it was his duty to come clean in his own report. He spent countless hours pouring over the Army report and working on his own. He was therefore particularly frustrated when he found out Roosevelt and Secretary of the Navy James Forrestal (heavily pressured by Admiral King) did not believe any blame should be passed to people currently serving in the War until after it was over. So, while Stimson's report was honest, extensive, and lengthy, Forrestal's first draft contained but a single sentence stating it was not in the public interest to take proceedings against currently serving naval officers.

Stimson expressed his concern to both Forrestal and Roosevelt about how poorly such a statement would be received by Congress. Forrestal agreed with much of what Stimson said, and the two men redrafted their respective reports to meet somewhere in between them. But in the end, all of Stimson's efforts were for naught. Given the necessity to keep the nation's code-breaking accomplishments secret (which factored in both reports), Roosevelt ultimately got his way, and the reports were kept from the public until after the War.

Finishing up with the investigation on the last day of November, the secretary of war headed off to Miami with his wife, Mabel, for a desperately needed ten-day break. Stimson was drained. His fatigue, a concern of his throughout the War, was not just a result of his advancing age but also a consequence of the strength of the effort he put into his work. This intensity, spoken about admiringly by his colleagues throughout his entire public and private careers, propelled him to great accomplishments, but it taxed his mind and body in the process, particularly when coupled with the self-imposed anxiety he suffered when working on issues of significance (although one must question how significant the Pearl Harbor report was considering all that was going on in the fall of 1944).

Stimson's ability to bounce back from long periods of concentrated work began to increasingly diminish as he approached the start of his seventy-eighth year, and he knew it. When he returned from Miami, he approached Harry Hopkins for a frank discussion on the subject.

Although Hopkins was twenty-three years younger than Stimson, he had been suffering from major health problems throughout the War following surgery for stomach cancer in 1939 (he ended up dying less than six months after the surrender of Japan). As such, Stimson might have felt more comfortable talking to him than anyone else about how consumed he had felt prior to heading to Miami. He explained to Hopkins that although his break in Florida seemed to restore him, he wondered if the president might prefer a younger man to take over the War Department. The question was reasonable. It was also sincere; Frank Knox (who had died earlier in the year) and Cordell Hull (who had resigned two weeks earlier for health reasons) were replaced by men twenty-five and thirty-three years younger than Stimson respectively.

Hopkins replied immediately that Roosevelt not only needed a man of Stimson's stature in his cabinet, but he also greatly valued his candor, advice, and friendship.[4] A relieved and restored Stimson got back to the grind but made sure he managed his time better and advised his staff accordingly (in an interview after the War, Robert Lovett explained that toward the end of it, Stimson had instructed him to give him nothing to work on after 4:00 p.m.).[5]

Japanese Americans

Another issue Stimson was forced to address during this period was the fate of Japanese Americans still confined in detention camps in the American West. To Stimson's discredit, he devoted far less time and emotional exertion on this matter than on the Pearl Harbor report.

The original decision in February 1942 to lock up American citizens of Japanese descent without any proof of their disloyalty was a black mark on the secretary of war, the president, and every other high-ranking public official who supported it (including the six members of the Supreme Court who upheld the constitutionality of such an action in December 1944, when they decided in favor of the government in *Korematsu v. United States*). But the length of time it took to release the innocent victims from the camps was even more ignominious. Again, fault for this rests squarely with Stimson and his boss.

If either man had any tenuously plausible excuse for overreacting to the war hysteria that swept across the nation after Pearl Harbor, they had none in the years that followed for further detaining innocent American citizens. Any potential threat of invasion from Japan (a determining factor in the original decision) declined precipitously after the lopsided loss it suffered to the U.S. fleet at the Battle of Midway in June 1942. Yet it was not until November 1944 that Stimson and Roosevelt finally discussed the matter and agreed to release the Japanese Americans from the camps.[6] It seems hardly a coincidence that they reached this conclusion just three days after Roosevelt won his fourth term in office.

Stimson might have not driven the decision to keep the Japanese Americans under lock and key for so long, but he could have stepped in to prevent it. Reviewing his daily diary entries after February 1942, it does not appear he spent much time at all thinking about the problem. Six months before his November 1944 meeting with the president, Stimson was informed that the Army saw no military reason to keep loyal Japanese Americans in camps. Although it was likely Stimson's call to make, he felt obligated to speak to FDR before considering whether to release them; he was certain that liberating them would make a "row" in California that FDR might wish to prevent. On May 17, 1944, the two men discussed the issue in the Oval Office (it was the fourth of five items Stimson wished to take up with FDR during the brief time he was given that day). The president, although implying to Stimson that he personally believed it was time to end the program, advised him to speak to California Governor Earl Warren saying he thought he was a fair man and "would take it on the right side."[7] Stimson agreed to do so, but was surprised with the suggestion, knowing that Warren was being talked about as a possible presidential candidate.

For Roosevelt to ask Stimson to bounce the idea off Governor Warren (FDR was not in the habit of clearing decisions with governors during the War) clearly suggests he thought it was politically unwise to release any Japanese Americans before the 1944 presidential election. If Stimson had been in favor of liberating them, he would have pushed the president hard, just as he had on so many other subjects of importance to him. He chose not to (it is not even clear if he ever approached Warren). The next time the subject came up in his diary was six months later (after the election), when he recounted a meeting with McCloy. During that discussion, Stimson expressed concerns to McCloy about the reaction among "radicals" on the West Coast who might attack the released Japanese Americans and suggested that the internees be released in batches over time to mitigate this. After speaking with the president again in mid-December, Stimson set the releases in motion—seven months after the Army advised him that no military reasons remained for the internees to remain in camps. His failure to act sooner was more disgraceful than the original decision and the single greatest blemish on an otherwise outstanding career in public service.

Malta and Yalta (January and February 1945)

Comfortable that the German counterattack had been thoroughly repulsed along with Stimson's repeated suggestions to him to raise more divisions (the secretary of war made one last effort in early January 1945),[8] Marshall flew to Europe in late January with other members of the Joint Chiefs of Staff to meet with their British counterparts in Malta to discuss the final steps to defeat Germany and prepare together for the second "Big Three" conference to be held with the Soviets on February 4 at Yalta on the Black Sea.

Prior to the meetings, Marshall decided it was time to have a little face-to-face talk with Eisenhower, his increasingly beleaguered subordinate. Ever since the German Hail Mary in the Ardennes was launched six weeks earlier, the supreme commander was the recipient of heavy criticism. Marshall sensed he needed to both bolster Eisenhower's confidence as well as stiffen his resolve.

The British used the setback of the Battle of the Bulge to openly question Eisenhower's strategy and his overall abilities as a commander. Field Marshal Montgomery happily took the lead in this regard. The American High Command greatly detested Montgomery due to his de Gaulle-like arrogance and utter lack of tact in dealing with superiors or peers. "Monty," as he disingenuously styled himself, had persistently complained about the supreme commander ever since Ike was given the job. The temporary reverse in fortunes suffered by the Allies in mid-December was just what he needed to further express his opinions and offer alternative views on how the Allies should reorganize their efforts in Europe (with a larger role for himself, of course). At a press conference he organized during the first week of January, Montgomery took false credit for saving the Allies during the Battle of the Bulge. The ensuing outcry from the Americans almost got him fired and caused Churchill to publicly state that the victory was an American one.

When General Omar Bradley heard rumors that Montgomery was angling to be placed between Eisenhower and himself in the chain of command, he told Ike he'd resign before agreeing to such a structure. George Patton made the same pledge.[9]

So as Eisenhower prepared to meet with Marshall, he was in a difficult position: Members of the British High Command were critical of his strategic acumen and looking to put one of their own men to take control of all Allied ground forces in Europe; Bradley and Patton were uncompromising in their refusal to serve under Montgomery or any other British officer; and both Marshall and Stimson were questioning his ability to stand up to the British (Eisenhower did not seem to be objecting to the British demands). Meeting Marshall was intimidating under any circumstances, but this meeting was going to be particularly difficult for the fifty-five-year-old general.

When the two sat down together on January 26, Marshall was curt and to the point. Given Montgomery and Brooke's resistance to continuing the broad front strategy, the chief of staff asked Ike to walk him through his plan so that he could defend it at the upcoming conference at Malta.

Eisenhower explained that while the main thrust of the attack would be led by Montgomery from the north, the other two groups (Bradley's 12th Army Group in the center and General Jacob Devers's 6th Army Group in the south) would also have active offensive roles. Reinforcements would be sent to where the most progress was made. After asking his protégé several probing questions, the chief of staff gave full support to the plan before moving abruptly to the next item on his agenda: the British request to appoint a deputy commander for ground operations sitting between Eisenhower and his three Army Group commanders.

In the spirit of Allied unity, Ike had temporarily agreed to this arrangement even though it meant effectively handing command over to the British. Marshall had previously scolded Eisenhower by telegram for even considering it. As chief of staff of the U.S. Army, the army representing an overwhelming majority of the Allied soldiers fighting in Western Europe, Marshall was not about to allow any British officer to take command of his troops, much less Monty.[10] Whether it made sense from an organizational standpoint was irrelevant to Marshall; the morale of American troops and their leaders outweighed any possible benefit that could be derived from such a change. He made it clear to Eisenhower that he would resign before accepting such a structure. Forcefully settling the matter, Marshall ended the meeting. It would be the last one held together between the two men until after the surrender of Germany.

After leaving Marseille, Marshall flew to Malta to meet up with Admiral King and the rest of the U.S. delegation before sitting together with the British High Command (General Arnold had suffered a heart attack two weeks earlier so was unable to make the trip). Since Admiral Leahy was not expected to arrive until the last day of the conference (accompanying Roosevelt), Marshall and King had to face the British alone. The principal stated goal of the meetings was to get consensus on the best strategy to end the war in Europe. For the American chief of staff, the goal was to get Ike's plan approved.

The good news for Marshall was that for the first time since the Second Washington Conference of June 1942, the British Chiefs of Staff did not press for a Mediterranean strategy. His full focus could therefore be aimed at what he and Stimson had wanted from the very beginning of the War: a frontal assault into the Third Reich. As the meetings progressed, there were still differences of opinion between Marshall and Brooke (mainly over the level of concentration of Montgomery's northern advance), but the debates were relatively calm. The civility did not last. On the third day, Brooke pushed the American chief of staff too far.

The anger and frustration from the Montgomery press conference earlier in the month, coupled with the general pressure Marshall must have felt over the Battle of the Bulge, came out as Brooke aggressively questioned Eisenhower's chief of staff, Walter Smith, about Ike's strategy. As he had often done in the past when things got heated, Marshall asked Brooke for a closed session, leaving only top advisors in the room. At some point during the ensuing discussions, Brooke continued to press for the transfer of additional American troops to Montgomery so that his men could cross the Rhine with more force. When Marshall resisted, Brooke made a comment implying that Generals Bradley and Patton overly influenced Eisenhower. At that, Marshall's legendary temper, one he so often kept at bay, got the best of him. He glared at Brooke and said that if anyone was guilty of trying to influence Eisenhower, it was Churchill and the British Chiefs of Staff. Pointing out that Roosevelt hardly ever met with Eisenhower or ever wrote to him, Marshall made it clear he did not appreciate the British prime minister and his Chiefs of Staff using their proximity to Eisenhower to relentlessly pressure him. Marshall sternly warned Brooke that "cramping" the supreme commander by issuing directives to him was something he would no longer tolerate.

Since his dander was up, Marshall continued to go after Brooke by blasting Montgomery personally (who was Brooke's protégé). Expressing what Brooke described in his diary as his "full dislike and antipathy to Montgomery," Marshall tore into the field marshal, suggesting he was overrated, conservative, and uncooperative. In making these critical statements, the implication that Brooke was complicit in Monty's behavior could not have gone unnoticed by the bespectacled chief of the Imperial General Staff. But Brooke largely absorbed the lecture for a couple of reasons: First, he was fully aware of Montgomery's "lack of tact" and "bad side" (he wrote during the war that it was "a great pity that he [Montgomery] spoils his very high military ability by a mad desire to talk or write nonsense")[11]; second, he was smart enough to realize that when push came to shove, the Americans would use their position of strength to get their way in the end.

Once the Malta meetings ended, Marshall headed to Yalta, a resort town in the Soviet Union located on the Black Sea seemingly in the middle of nowhere. Allegedly, Stalin's doctors insisted the Soviet leader could not travel greater distances for health reasons (although some speculated he had a fear of flying). To get to Yalta from Malta, Marshall had to fly for nearly eight hours to a small airfield in the Crimea. From there, he traveled nearly five hours by car over ninety miles of questionable roads.

From a military standpoint, the meetings between the Allies at Yalta largely focused on the coordination of the various ongoing ground and air operations against the Germans. The heavy discussions, along with the more important decisions made, were political in nature. Although Marshall was present for some of these talks, his role was limited.

For the vital decisions at Yalta, those later criticized by a generation of Republicans, the chief of staff and his colleagues on the JCS were literally and figuratively not in the room when they were debated and made. German reparations, the number of Soviet votes in the United Nations, the fate of Poland, and the price to be paid to the Russians for assisting in the defeat of Japan were all questions handled by Roosevelt, Stalin, Churchill, and their top non-military advisors.

More than ten years after the end of the War, Marshall was asked by his biographer, Forrest Pogue, about the attacks leveled against him during the early 1950s over his role as "King of Yalta," where he allegedly made all the key decisions in light of Roosevelt's illness. Marshall said he was "amused" by them, particularly since he attended only two of the seven sessions held between Roosevelt, Churchill, and Stalin and was not even invited to the final dinner.[12]

The only controversial decision Marshall weighed in on was related to Russian involvement with Japan once Germany was defeated. He considered Stalin's support in this regard a military matter and had been pushing for it since the beginning of the War. Given that the brunt of casualties in an Allied invasion of Japan would fall on the U.S. Army, Marshall naturally hoped the Soviet Union would send troops into Manchuria. As to the postwar criticism that he and other members of the JCS put undue pressure on Roosevelt to make heavy concessions to the Soviets to entice them to assist in defeating Japan, the record does not back this up. The question of what Stalin might get in return for helping defeat Japan was not discussed at any of the conferences Marshall attended, and there is no evidence he ever discussed it with Roosevelt. The reasons FDR agreed to the concessions might never be sorted out, but most historians have concluded that pressure from Marshall and other members of the JCS was not among them.[13]

End Game in Europe

At the time General Marshall briefed Stimson upon his return from Yalta on February 16, the war in Europe was firmly back on track. With the Allies closing in on the Rhine and the Russians less than fifty miles from Berlin, each man thought victory would be achieved by spring. When the American First Army crossed the Rhine three weeks later, General Somervell briefed Stimson on the preparations his team had been making to celebrate V-E Day. The end seemed that close.

But finishing a war is seldom easy, particularly when one is part of a coalition. In his biography of Marshall, Forrest Pogue wrote that there were three major themes that characterized the final months of the European campaign from the chief of staff's perspective: the British demand for more glory; Churchill's push to modify military strategy for the purpose of gaining a political advantage over the Soviet Union; and the Russians' increasingly rude behavior. He and Stimson had to cope with all three.

The British effort to get Montgomery's 21st Army Group into Germany and Berlin before the two American-led Army Groups was annoying and time-consuming but the easiest of the three problems to handle. Both men had the support of Roosevelt with respect to backing Eisenhower's broad front strategy, so they simply ignored the British demands.

Harder to resolve, but still controllable, was the effort by Churchill to let political considerations dictate military strategy. The prime minister aggressively pushed to get to Berlin and other cities in Eastern Europe before the Russians. He had also been advocating for strategic thrusts from Italy into the Balkans and Vienna for months and continued to push the Americans in that direction right up to the last week of the war in Europe (when he proposed to the JCS that Eisenhower make attempts to liberate Prague and as much of Czechoslovakia as possible).

George Marshall was not politically naïve, but in keeping with his philosophy of maintaining a line between military and political considerations, he was going to let Eisenhower determine the strategy based on the former unless he was otherwise ordered by the president to take the latter into consideration. Berlin was not an important military target (it was a pile of rubble). To take on additional casualties for the sake of political aims was never part of Marshall's mission, and as he wrote to Eisenhower in late April 1945, he was "loath to hazard American lives" for such purposes. Russia suffered over 350,000 casualties in its house-to-house campaign in Berlin.[14] In a dictatorship, such tradeoffs can be more easily made.

Stimson, in many respects a soldier before a politician, was in complete agreement with Marshall. Both men were criticized after the War for not making a greater effort to get British and American troops as far to the east as possible before Germany surrendered. This judgment was unfair; the president's long-standing order was to destroy Germany's military machine before going after the Japanese. If their commander in chief desired otherwise, both men would have certainly obliged him.

The most challenging of the three problems was the sudden change in behavior of the Russians. The closer Berlin came to falling, the more difficult, distrusting, and uncooperative they became. For a month beginning in mid-February, Stimson requested the Soviet Union's assistance in helping American prisoners of war make their way west after their German captors abandoned the prison camps in Poland and the eastern regions of Germany ahead of the Russian troops. The Russians ignored his requests and flatly rejected a proposal that would have had the Americans send food and aid to their men. On March 16, Stimson drafted a curt and forceful letter for FDR to send to Stalin demanding help. The Soviet dictator largely ignored it.

Things got worse later that month, when the Americans informed Russia that the Germans were making peace overtures in Italy. In reply, they received a harshly worded note from the Soviet Minister of Foreign Affairs demanding that the Soviets be present at any discussions. Stalin then accused the Americans and British of secretly concluding an agreement with the Germans behind his back. This time it was Marshall who drafted a reply for Roosevelt to send. The letter blasted the dictator's "informants" for their "vile misrepresentations of my actions or those of my trusted subordinates."[15] Although Stalin replied in a less hostile tone to Roosevelt, Soviet officials continued to be uncooperative on several fronts (during the same month, they refused to allow the United States to inspect a captured German submarine even as Allied ships continued to get sunk by U-boats in the North Atlantic). Thinking of the future, a worried Stimson wrote in mid-March that the quarrelsome behavior from the Russians was indicative of a spirit "which bodes evil in the coming difficulties of the postwar scene."[16]

A New President

There was a fourth theme Stimson and Marshall confronted toward the end of the War in Europe: Franklin Roosevelt's health. Although the president's condition had been slowly deteriorating since the Tehran Conference in December 1943, his sudden change in appearance and lack of alertness at Yalta was apparent to nearly everyone in attendance. The open mouth, gaunt and gray face, and short attention span were the common traits attributed to him during and after the weeklong conference. Churchill would later refer to the "faraway look" he observed in Roosevelt's eyes at Yalta.

On March 3, less than three weeks after the conference ended, Stimson met with the president privately for more than an hour in the White House and could not help but notice his reduced weight and lack of liveliness. Describing it further in his diary that night, Stimson wrote he was "a little bit troubled because the expression on his face has changed somewhat." With a number of important issues to take up with the president, the secretary of war met with him several more times over the next three weeks before FDR journeyed down to Warm Springs, Georgia, on March 29.

Less than two weeks later, Stimson was at Woodley when he received a call at 5:45 p.m. urging him to come to the White House immediately. Given his earlier observations, he suspected something was wrong with Roosevelt, and his fears were confirmed the moment he arrived; he was told the president had died in Warm Springs an hour earlier. A little more than an hour later, Chief Justice Harlan Stone administered the presidential oath of office in the cabinet room to the vice president of the United States, Harry S. Truman.

Following the oath, Truman spoke a few words to the cabinet before Stimson, as its senior member, told his colleagues it was time to close ranks behind the new president.[17] After the meeting, the secretary of war took Truman aside once the other members left the room and told him he had something urgent to discuss with him. It was at that moment Truman first heard about the development of the atomic bomb.[18]

General Marshall was also at home when a colleague arrived to tell him the news in person. Once he got to the White House, Eleanor Roosevelt asked him to take charge of all the funeral arrangements. This included getting her husband's remains to Washington, arranging the logistics for a White House service, and planning both the journey by train that would carry FDR's body to Hyde Park, and the final service and interment there. It was a lot to ask, given all that was going on with the War, but Marshall accepted the responsibility on the spot.

Although FDR's health had been noticeably declining, the news of his death still seemed sudden to both men. Beginning the day Stimson had joined Marshall in the War Department in July 1940, the duo had worked nearly 250 weeks with Roosevelt, first trying to prepare the country for war, and then fighting it. Marshall had never worked under any individual longer during his career, and only Elihu Root spent more time as Stimson's boss (before Root was appointed secretary of war forty-five years earlier). While Stimson was consistent in his criticism of Roosevelt's administrative abilities, he greatly admired his vision, superlative political instincts, leadership qualities, and first-rate personality. Despite their age difference, he considered Roosevelt a friend.

By contrast, George Marshall was not a friend of the president's and never cared to be, but he recognized the greatness in Roosevelt shortly after Pearl Harbor, long before Stimson came to the same conclusion.

The three days following Roosevelt's death—right up until he was laid to rest at his home on the Hudson River—were a whirlwind of activity for Stimson and Marshall. Aside from their day-to-day responsibilities, both men had to brief the new president on the current state of the War. Once back in Washington, however, it was business as usual, as if no change at all had taken place at the top. This was a testament to both Roosevelt and Truman, but even more so to American democracy. The "next man up" philosophy had never been more evident in American political history than after the death of Roosevelt. That Marshall and Stimson and their respective staffs had been operating so smoothly as a team for five years obviously made the transition that much easier. Appointing both men to their respective positions proved to be Roosevelt's most underappreciated achievement during the War.

Neither Stimson nor the chief of staff knew much about Truman or what to expect from him as president. But as a senator, Truman did not exactly ingratiate himself with the secretary of war. Nearly two years earlier, he had telephoned Stimson, questioning him about various bits of information he was receiving regarding massive expenditures for something referred to only as the "Manhattan Project." At the time, Truman headed a special Senate committee (referred to as the Truman Committee) looking into defense expenditures. The secretary of war, responsible for the project, explained that he could only tell him it was part of an extremely important secret development for a specific and unique purpose. Truman said he understood and told the secretary he wouldn't have to say another word to him. A year later and under pressure from other senators in the committee, Truman asked Stimson to let a member of his staff be taken into Stimson's confidence on the project. The secretary of war, believing Truman was a "nuisance and a pretty untrustworthy man" for going back on his pledge, refused the request and determined that he should be told nothing more.[19]

Given the intense pressure Stimson was under to keep the atomic bomb a secret, and the natural tension between a person charged with investigating fraud in defense spending and the person responsible for such spending, one can understand why Stimson might have taken umbrage at the senator's prying. But like Marshall, Stimson did not hold grudges for long, and it was water under the bridge well before Truman assumed the presidency.

Outside of a few meetings related to the Truman Committee, Marshall knew little about the new president as well. After he and Stimson sat with him the day after Roosevelt's death, the secretary of war shared his favorable impression of him to the chief of staff while the two men were driven back together to their offices at the Pentagon. Marshall responded quietly, "We shall not know what he is really like until the pressure begins to be felt."[20]

German Surrender

For George Marshall, the final week of the European war was in ways a microcosm of the previous three and half years; he had to cope with the same individuals who'd given him the biggest headaches: Winston

Churchill, never ceasing in his attempts to dictate strategy to the Americans, was urging him to move his troops into Czechoslovakia ahead of the Russians; Charles de Gaulle, steadfast as ever in his determination that France—and he—be treated as an equal, was refusing an order to remove his troops from Stuttgart, an area within the operational zone of the American Seventh Army; and Douglas MacArthur, the antithesis of a team player, needed to be strongly encouraged to stop bullying the Navy into accepting organizational changes favorable to the Army.[21]

Stimson, just a few feet away from him in the office next door, spent the week continuing to focus on those postwar issues he believed to be most important and ones to which he felt he could add most value. Hearing reports of the chaos and destitution in Germany from John McCloy (who spent more than two weeks there in April), Stimson wished he could lean on his old boss Herbert Hoover to help the administration get ahead of the famine and pestilence that would plague the region once the War ended. Hoover, one will recall, rose to fame during the First World War addressing similar issues in Belgium, and Stimson felt his experience would be invaluable. To his great disappointment, utilizing Hoover's exceptional talents was something Stimson was unable to do while Franklin Roosevelt was alive given the deep animosity felt between the two men. Truman, still a judge in Jackson County, Missouri, when the Hoover presidency ended, had no qualms about working with the seventy-year-old Republican ex-president and called him immediately after Stimson suggested it. Hoover jumped at the opportunity to assist the nation.

Between dealing with all these matters, Stimson and Marshall were trying to keep up with the rapidly moving scene in Germany as April turned to May. Two weeks after Roosevelt's funeral, Adolf Hitler killed himself in his Berlin bunker; the following day, the Soviets took Berlin while all Axis forces in Italy and Austria formally surrendered; two days after that, the Germans in the north surrendered en masse to Montgomery; and finally, on the night of May 6, Marshall received the following cable from Eisenhower:

The mission of this Allied force was fulfilled at 0241, local time, May 7th, 1945.

After three years and five months, the war in Europe was over.

Taking little time to consider the achievement, Marshall's thoughts immediately turned to the Pacific and the invasion of Japan that the Army had been planning in cooperation with the Navy. Stimson described the day of victory in Europe as not one "of exuberance or hysterical demonstrations but rather of sober satisfaction and of pulling in the belt for further effort."[22]

The secretary's lack of enthusiasm might have reflected the fact that the surrender of Germany had been well anticipated. But it also could have been because of his continuing frustration over the deteriorating state of his health. One will recall that six months earlier, Stimson's increasing fatigue had caused him to question Harry Hopkins whether Roosevelt might not want a younger man to take over the War Department. Since the start of 1945, he was feeling only worse. In March, a doctor advised him that his heart was working imperfectly and cautioned him to rest as much as he could and work just half a day for a few days each week. Given the demands of his job, Stimson did not think this was possible, but he did begin to occasionally take naps at home during the day.

On May 7, the day the Germans formally surrendered, Stimson recorded in his diary that he played deck tennis at Woodley in the late afternoon (just as he had done several times a week since he took over the War Department). It seems it was the last game he would ever play. He never explained he was retiring from the sport, but for the next four and a half months until his retirement, the physical activities in the evenings that he faithfully chronicled in his diary were limited to lawn bowling and slow walks around the grounds. Old age was no longer chasing the nearly seventy-eight-year-old Stimson; it had fully caught up to him. Ever hopeful a vacation would "refresh" him as it had in the past, Stimson headed to Highhold the week following V-E Day. He spent ten days there, the first few of which he did little but sleep.

Although he returned to Washington feeling a little better, Stimson was aware from recent experience that any boost in energy was only temporary. Resigning himself to the new normal, the secretary of war decided he was going to relieve himself "so far as possible" from all routine matters for the balance of the War in the Pacific and devote himself to the Manhattan Project, the top-secret quest to build an atomic bomb that he had been directly overseeing for more than two years, and was strongly connected with for nearly four.

The Atomic Bomb

A month before Pearl Harbor, Henry Stimson was introduced to the concept of atomic energy by Dr. Vannevar Bush, an eminent scientist who met with the secretary in his office. What he referred to that day in his diary as a "most terrible thing" would occupy a great deal of his attention for not just the rest of the War, but nearly the balance of his life.

Unbeknownst to Stimson prior to his meeting with Bush, Roosevelt had appointed him a month earlier (along with Bush, Marshall, Vice President Wallace, and Dr. James Conant) to a committee to advise the president on all questions of policy relating to the study of nuclear fission. For the next eighteen months, Stimson was directly connected with all major policy decisions regarding the development and use of atomic energy. On May 1, 1943, Roosevelt formally handed over to him administrative responsibility for the project to build the bomb.

The brief from FDR was straightforward: spare no effort to build an atomic bomb before the Germans could do so. In what became the largest scientific-industrial undertaking in history up to that time, two billion dollars was spent and two hundred thousand people were employed in the effort.[23] Assisting the secretary of war throughout his management of the project were Marshall, Bush, Conant, Harvey Bundy, George Harrison, and Major General Leslie Groves. Groves, the man responsible for getting the Pentagon built in sixteen months, was chosen by Stimson and Marshall to manage the project on the ground.

With the hard-driving Groves pushing the scientists daily in his capacity as project director, Stimson's primary responsibility was similar to his role in running the War Department: He handled the big things. Whether it was negotiating for the purchase of uranium, coordinating with the British (who had an initial head start on atomic research), or simply stepping in when a high-level policy or political issue popped up, Stimson put his skills and stature to use to keep the ball moving. Marshall was more focused on the military aspects of the bomb, but he delegated most of those matters to Groves.

Nowhere was the secretary of war's value to the project more visible than in his handling of Congress. Up until mid-1943, the Roosevelt administration managed to direct general defense funds to the Manhattan Project without congressional appropriation. But as monthly expenditures continued to increase, congressmen naturally started to ask questions. As previously mentioned, Senator Harry Truman, in his role as head of a defense spending oversight committee, peppered the secretary of war in June 1943 about the two giant facilities being built in Tennessee and Washington State. Assurances to Truman that it was a matter of the highest importance and the strictest of secrecy bought Stimson some additional time.

The following winter (February 1944), Stimson determined that he had to let congressional leaders in on the secret after Groves estimated that an additional $600 million was needed to complete the bomb. Together with Bush and Marshall, he met with Speaker of the House Sam Rayburn, Democratic leader John McCormack, and Republican leader Joe Martin in Rayburn's office. After hearing about different aspects of the project from each man, the three congressmen agreed to provide the funds and keep the secret to themselves. Four months later, Stimson and Bush (Marshall was traveling) repeated their performance to four Senate leaders in order to get the funding passed on the other side of the Capitol. They were equally successful.[24]

Keeping the project under wraps was an impressive accomplishment. It is remarkable to think today of how few people were in on the totality of the secret right up until the first bomb was dropped, and that includes the two hundred thousand people who were helping to produce it (Groves, a fanatic about secrecy, insisted that information was strictly compartmentalized and forbade different teams to speak to each other about their specific work).

Stimson agreed early on that knowledge about the Manhattan Project be shared on a exacting need-to-know basis regardless of how high up an official was in the government or military. Amazingly, until he became president, Vice President Harry Truman was clueless about the bomb (only minutes after he took the oath of office, Stimson pulled him aside and told him about it).[25] Admiral Leahy found out about the device only at the last minute, and General Arnold only when it was time to begin training his pilots to drop it (Marshall told King about it in late 1943).

Secretary of the Treasury Henry Morgenthau was another individual who was kept in the dark, even though a case could have been made for him to be let in on the secret. In October 1944, Groves advised Stimson that in order to have certain funds for the project deposited in the Federal Reserve Bank (which Grove preferred over a commercial bank), the assent of the secretary of the treasury was required. Stimson called Morgenthau to tell him he had a check given to him by Roosevelt under strict confidence concerning a secret project and he needed his permission to deposit it in the Federal Reserve Bank. A miffed Morgenthau refused, telling Stimson if he was not to be trusted with the secret, he ought to be removed from his position as secretary of the treasury. Although Morgenthau relented a week later, he did so without getting any wiser as to the purpose of the funds.[26]

At the same time that he was administratively managing the Manhattan Project, Stimson was serving as the senior advisor to the president on the military use of the bomb. Once it became clear to the scientists that the bomb might work, he began to spend a lot more time on this part of his responsibility. After returning from his vacation on May 28, 1945, Stimson was determined to devote almost all his time to it.[27]

While Stimson struggled with the moral, philosophical, and political ramifications of the bomb, a more relaxed Marshall was dreaming of retirement. He told Eisenhower shortly after the Germans surrendered that he was intending to obtain his release from active duty from Truman in the next two months.[28] This was wishful thinking; there was little chance Truman was going to replace him. First, there were too many decisions to be made about the remaining troops in Europe (regarding who stays, who comes home, and who gets transferred to the Pacific Theater); and second, Truman, like most others, viewed Marshall as the only man who could ensure that the Army and Navy would work together as a team as the nation's armed forces pivoted toward Japan.

20

Victory over Japan

The result of the bomb is so terrific that the responsibility of its possession and its use must weigh heavily on our minds and on our hearts. We believe that its use will save the lives of American soldiers and bring more quickly to an end the horror of this war which the Japanese leaders deliberately started. Therefore, the bomb is being used.

—**HENRY STIMSON**, memorandum to the press, August 9, 1945

I regarded the dropping of the bomb as of great importance and felt that it would end the war possibly better than anything else—which it did—and I think that all the claims about the bombings and all afterwards were rather silly, because we had these terrific destructions and it hadn't had these effects. I think it was quite necessary to drop the bombs in order to shorten the war. . . . There were hundreds and hundreds of thousands of American lives involved . . . what they [the Japanese] needed was shock action.[1]

—**GEORGE MARSHALL**, February 11, 1957

Planning the Invasion

On June 18, 1945, the Joint Chiefs of Staff along with Stimson, McCloy, and Secretary of the Navy James Forrestal met with Truman in the White House to discuss the proposed invasion of Japan. Marshall, who did most of the talking, summarized the plan by suggesting it was nearly identical to the one used to invade Normandy—except far more impressive in scale. Complete control of the air and sea would allow a massive bombing

439

program that would pave the way for an invasion force (the number of bombs expected to be dropped to soften Japanese resistance would have exceeded the total amount dropped on Germany during the entire War).[2]

The chief of staff had been preaching for years that wars cannot be won by air bombardment and blockades alone (a strategy for which many Naval and Army Air Force officers continued to advocate). Unless a nation was willing to put boots on the ground, it could not expect an enemy to surrender. The experience with Nazi Germany was proof of this, and Marshall had no reason to expect the Japanese government would give up without seeing U.S. troops moving up the Tokyo Plain. He expressed these views to Truman and the larger group during the meeting.

The plan for Japan, which took on the code name *Downfall*, consisted of an invasion of Kyushu (the southernmost of Japan's four major islands) followed three months later by landings farther north on the main island of Japan at a point just south and east of Tokyo. Airfields acquired or developed during the first operation, in combination with those recently secured in Okinawa, would provide ample air support to ensure success in the second. The details, finalized by the staffs of both General MacArthur and Admiral Nimitz, called for the first phase to begin on December 1, 1945.

Given the heavy losses suffered by the United States over the previous twelve months on Peleliu, Saipan, Iwo Jima, and Okinawa, President Truman was naturally interested in getting an estimate of how many casualties the country could expect from *Downfall*. The Battle of Okinawa in particular, which at the time of the meeting was winding up less than four hundred miles south of Kyushu, was yet another grim reminder to everyone in the room of how brutal it was to fight the Japanese anywhere in the Pacific, much less in locations closer to their homeland. The three-month battle cost seventy-five thousand American casualties (including 12,500 killed).

Casualty estimates for invading Japan (more than three hundred times the size of Okinawa) had been debated for several weeks. The estimates varied greatly. On the extreme end, former president Herbert Hoover estimated in a memorandum to Stimson the previous month that if the United States were to invade Japan, between five hundred thousand to one million American lives could be lost.[3] Although Marshall's staff thought this figure was "entirely too high," the chief of staff cautioned Truman during the meeting that the inconsistency in casualty figures from different battles in the Pacific Theater to date made it "wrong" to put much stock in any estimates. But he did offer the president his opinion that in the first thirty days of the operation against Kyushu, thirty-one thousand casualties could be expected. He did not even hazard to estimate the losses expected from invading the main island.

After Truman listened to estimates from King and Arnold on sea and air casualties, Stimson spoke. The secretary asserted that there was only one certainty: The enemy would fight tooth and nail to defend its homeland. This was hardly revelatory, as far back as the Battle of Guadalcanal, Americans learned that Japanese soldiers fought until they were killed or committed suicide. The Battle of Okinawa was just the latest confirmation of this reality, as ninety-five thousand Japanese soldiers and nearly one hundred thousand Japanese civilians died (many of whom killed themselves). Given this, the secretary of war was not as dismissive of Hoover's estimates as others were and suggested that a serious attempt be made to appeal to those of influence in Japan who favored peace.

Admiral Leahy followed Stimson's comments by pointing out that America was making it difficult for the Japanese to consider peace by insisting on an unconditional surrender. Leahy, like many others, believed similar terms offered to the Germans in Europe had stiffened their resistance, making the ultimate victory there more costly. With the instinct to preserve face so ingrained in the Japanese culture, Leahy knew it would likely be worse in Japan.

This was not the first time there was pushback on the demand for unconditional surrender. From the time Roosevelt first channeled Civil War hero Ulysses S. Grant by bringing up the concept of unconditional surrender at the Casablanca Conference in January 1943 (likely to keep Stalin from thinking the Western Allies would seek a separate peace from the Germans), many, including Stimson, Marshall, Churchill, and members of the Joint Chiefs of Staff, were against it. The planning team for the JCS penned a report stating that the concept was foreign to any soldier or citizen of Japan and therefore needed to be defined in a way understandable to them.[4] By not doing so, their fear was that the Japanese might literally fight to the last man, woman, and child.

Undersecretary of State Joseph Grew was a particularly strong advocate for adjusting the terms of surrender. Stimson and Marshall met with Grew a month before their June 18 meeting with Truman. Although they both fully agreed with his views, neither man thought the timing was right for the United States to approach the Japanese. They believed that with the Battle of Okinawa still raging after two months, certain hard-liners among Japanese leaders would interpret any change in terms by the Americans as a sign of weakness and use it to argue against those of their colleagues who were more willing to seek peace.[5] Four months earlier, Stimson felt the same when John McCloy mentioned to him that Admiral King suggested modifying the terms.[6]

Some historians have suggested that by delaying efforts to adjust the terms of surrender in late May 1945, Stimson and Marshall lost critical time for negotiations with the Japanese that could not be recovered during the hectic summer months. This argument is difficult to square with. Although the delay did not help the cause of those favoring an immediate modification to the terms, there was plenty of time after the Americans defeated the Japanese at Okinawa to make a deal.

Only after such matters were further debated during the June 18 meeting at the White House, along with the advantages and disadvantages of having the Soviet Union assist in the final fight against Japan, did the subject of the atomic bomb come up. John McCloy, astonished it had yet to be raised as the meeting was coming to an end, proposed giving a warning to the Japanese about the bomb that could perhaps scare them into surrendering. Initially, the group seemed nervous about talking about what had been a taboo subject of discussion throughout the War. But as everyone in the room was privy to the atomic secret, they began considering McCloy's proposal. After a short discussion, Truman decided it was currently his preference to keep the atomic bomb a secret from everyone, including the Japanese. Planning for *Downfall* would continue.[7]

Preparing for the Finish

Following the June 18 meeting, and for the next eight weeks until the surrender of Japan, Henry Stimson and George Marshall divided their responsibilities largely as they had during the previous five years: Marshall focused on military matters, Stimson on political ones. But they continued to operate first and foremost as a team, meeting regularly as they had done throughout the War.

When he wasn't directing the planning of *Downfall*, the chief of staff was spending much of the summer on issues around demobilization in Europe and troop reassignments to the Pacific Theater. After Germany surrendered in May, Winston Churchill famously declared that George Marshall had been the "organizer of victory." Unfortunately for Marshall, his organizational duties in Europe did not end on V-E Day; he was now responsible for unwinding nearly all he had put in place.

From a logistical standpoint, the transporting of troops, weapons, and equipment to the front at the start of a war is not too dissimilar from the reverse steps required when a war ends; the latter job is simply less stressful and complicated (given the reduced urgency and the fact that it is undertaken in a peacetime environment). But for Marshall, the process of demobilization after Germany surrendered was anything but stress-free and easy. Aside from the normal logistical challenges related to shipping and bases, there were many military and political considerations. How many troops should be transported home, how many should be transferred to assist in *Downfall*, and how many were needed to assist in the occupation of Germany were questions that needed to be answered. The disparate views on whether *Downfall* was even required, the uncertainty about when and if the atomic bomb would be available, and the deteriorating relationship with the Soviet Union were among the factors that needed to be considered before making any decisions.

The numbers themselves were staggering; there were approximately 5.4 million army personnel overseas.[8] Even for Marshall, the logistics wunderkind of the First World War and an officer who prided himself on his ability to solve the most intricate of logistical problems, it was a daunting task.

While trying to sort out these and other issues, the chief of staff was invited by Truman to attend the Potsdam Conference in Germany in mid-July, where many of them would be discussed. The meeting, the third held between the "Big Three," was scheduled to take place in the small suburb of Potsdam, bordering Berlin to the south and west. It was Marshall's hope that the political decisions made at this conference would help guide the military decisions he needed to make going forward.

Henry Stimson devoted what was left of his decreasing energy during the summer of 1945 to two objectives: getting Japan to surrender without undertaking *Downfall*, and making sure Henry Morgenthau's ideas on the postwar treatment of Germany were not adopted. He believed these two issues were "the largest and most important problems" he faced since joining the War Department. In both cases, he knew he was up against the passion, hysteria, and vengeance that "gets hold of a nation" after a bitter war.[9]

After intensely preparing himself during the latter half of June, the secretary sat down to discuss the two issues with Truman alone at the White House on July 2 and 3. The president, still less than three months on the job, listened carefully as Stimson explained that given all the odds stacked up against Japan, it should be possible to get its leaders to give up the fight while keeping the general spirit of an unconditional surrender intact. After hearing Stimson go into detail and explain why it was essential for the United States to have Japan exist as a peaceful and useful member of the postwar Pacific community, Truman expressed his overall support. The secretary of war then began carefully outlining his thinking on postwar Germany.

Without notes, Stimson recounted the entire debacle at the Quebec Conference the previous September when Secretary Morgenthau pitched his draconian ideas to FDR and Churchill about turning Germany into a pastoral region, where its citizens would live on subsistence levels only. He then expressed his own views, explaining to Truman that Western Europe could not be rebuilt by keeping Germany in economic handcuffs. Stimson made sure to emphasize that Roosevelt and other members of Roosevelt's cabinet—except Morgenthau, of course—agreed with his general philosophy on the subject. Germany, Stimson advised Truman, would represent the largest occupation and rehabilitation project the United States had ever taken on. As such, he stressed, "It must go right," and to get it right, any thoughts of vengeance must be set aside. To Stimson's relief, Truman indicated he was in complete agreement with his ideas on Germany as well.

When the meeting between the two men came to an end, the president told Stimson that he'd like to have him "somewhere near" when he was in Potsdam the following week. He could not be a formal member of the delegation, Truman explained, but could be there to advise him on these two issues and keep him updated with news about the bomb (still untested at this point). Stimson accepted the invitation under the condition he be allowed to bring McCloy along. Truman agreed, and the secretary of war began preparing himself.

On the same day Truman extended an invitation to Stimson to join him in Potsdam, he made an important change within the cabinet, one that had consequences on both how the war would end in the Pacific and on Henry Stimson's legacy: Jimmy Byrnes was sworn in as secretary of state, replacing Edward Stettinius.

Jimmy Byrnes was a politician Stimson highly respected and with whom he had a solid relationship. The secretary of war believed Brynes did an excellent job running the Office of War Mobilization and was impressed with his intelligence, drive, political skills, discretion, and overall competence. Referred to often as the "assistant president" while serving under Roosevelt (given his involvement in so many aspects of the War), Byrnes began to exert even more influence in the weeks after FDR's death. Given this and the general respect he held for the South Carolinian, Stimson recommended to Truman two months earlier that Byrnes be placed on a committee Stimson formed (the Interim Committee) to advise the president on all policy matters related to the atomic bomb.[10] He would come to regret making this recommendation.

Two days after Byrnes was appointed secretary of state, Henry Morgenthau resigned as head of the Treasury Department after Truman failed to invite him to Potsdam.[11] Stimson liked Henry Morgenthau and appreciated how he had graciously welcomed him to the cabinet back in July 1940, but given their divergent views on postwar Germany, the secretary of war must have been relieved to see him out of office.

Potsdam (July 17–August 2, 1945)

The Potsdam Conference was organized for the purpose of making political decisions; few military issues needed to be sorted out. George Marshall knew this would be the case and didn't even think the Joint Chiefs of Staff should attend. But as the War was still on in the Pacific, it was decided by the Big Three that their military chiefs should be there. So, four days after Stimson left for the conference by sea, Marshall headed there by air.

Since the Combined Chiefs of Staff did not attend the plenary sessions where the Big Three debated the key political issues, there was plenty of time for Marshall and his colleagues to drive around Berlin. It was a depressing sight. The principal sections of the city were destroyed, with nearly every building demolished. The homeless (mainly women, children, and the elderly) aimlessly moved about, carrying with them whatever possessions they had managed to salvage on carts, bicycles, and baby carriages. Although proud of the role they played in bringing down Hitler and his forces, Marshall and his colleagues were humbled by the human suffering they witnessed as they were driven through the streets of the Third Reich's former center of power.

When the JCS did meet up with the British Chiefs of Staff, the only significant military issues discussed involved British participation in the Pacific and related questions concerning theater command. Since these were resolved without much effort, Marshall spent most of his time in Germany continuing to oversee European demobilization and working on his biennial report.

Henry Stimson arrived in Potsdam well rested after a seven-day voyage to Gibraltar followed by quick flights to Marseilles, Nice, and then Berlin. He was thoroughly prepared and anxious to bring the full breadth of his forty years in public service to the benefit of his new boss.

Since joining the cabinet five years earlier, Stimson had always been its oldest member, but as the Potsdam Conference got underway, he was now its second-longest-serving one as well (Secretary of the Interior Harold Ickes joined in 1933). Since becoming president three months earlier, Truman had accepted the resignations of the secretary of state, secretary of the treasury, attorney general, postmaster general, secretary of agriculture, and secretary of labor. Since the replacements were mostly younger, the age disparity between Stimson and the rest of the cabinet widened. At the start of the Potsdam Conference, he was twenty-three years older than the average age of Truman's nine other cabinet members.

Having such seniority, knowing the inexperienced Truman would be looking for solid advice, believing he was on the right side of all the major issues, and accustomed to being asked opinions on matters both within and outside the War Department's realm, Stimson assumed he was going to be called upon often for guidance by the sixty-one-year-old president during his stay in Germany. So as he settled into the villa assigned to him in Babelsberg, a wooded suburb within Potsdam, he was eager to do what he had strived to do since leaving Harvard Law School: make a difference on very large matters.

What Stimson failed to fully appreciate was the rapidly rising influence of Jimmy Byrnes. The newly minted secretary of state was a highly ambitious politician who believed he, not Harry Truman, should have inherited the Oval Office after Roosevelt's death. Among the frontrunners for the second spot on the ticket in 1944, Brynes had been shocked and greatly disappointed when FDR chose the relatively unknown senator from Missouri instead. The South Carolinian's résumé (U.S. House of Representatives, U.S. Senate, Supreme Court, head of the Office of Economic Stabilization, and head of the Office of War Mobilization) far outshined Truman's, and he had worked faithfully and skillfully for the president since leaving the Supreme Court ten months after Pearl Harbor. Although Roosevelt had considered him for vice president, he ultimately decided that Brynes's more conservative views on organized labor and racial integration made him too politically risky a choice.

When President Truman offered him the State Department in early July, Byrnes accepted under the condition he be given a free rein in guiding the nation's foreign policy. He knew the position would be hugely influential as the country moved into the postwar era.

Stimson picked up on the true extent of Byrnes's ambition shortly after the meetings in Potsdam began. Writing in his diary that Byrnes was "hugging matters in this conference pretty close to his bosom," a disappointed Stimson found that although Byrnes seemed to welcome his advice, it was strictly limited to War Department issues. Further, he seemed to go out of his way to exclude Stimson from all the critical meetings held between the Big Three. The working relationship between the two men was a far cry from the one Stimson had shared with Cordell Hull for five years.

In contrast to the infrequent and "barren" discussions Stimson was having with Brynes, Harry Truman gave him time nearly every morning during the ten days the secretary of war was in Potsdam. The president would brief him on the preceding day's events, and the two would then discuss all the issues Truman was going to face during the next round of meetings. Truman was not simply acting courteous to the elderly statesman; he held a great deal of respect for Stimson that only grew once he became president. Writing in his memoirs that Stimson was a man of "great wisdom and foresight," Truman had been particularly impressed with him back in April after sitting through a detailed briefing on the Manhattan Project. In contrast to Brynes, who was solely focused on the power the bomb gave the United States in dictating terms as to how the War would end, Truman noted Stimson was equally concerned about how the bomb could shape the future history of the planet. Truman thought that having "so able and so wise a man" on one shoulder to balance the purely political and pragmatic voice of Byrnes on the other might help him make better decisions as the War wound down.[12]

Of the two big decisions Stimson was most interested in, it seemed to him the question of Germany was generally being worked out in a direction closer to Stimson's thinking than Morgenthau's original plan. Although there were many elements of the Morgenthau Plan ultimately put in place at Potsdam, they were largely watered down from the extreme versions the former secretary of the treasury envisioned (a year later, even those features were repudiated by Jimmy Byrnes in his Restatement of Policy on Germany speech).

It was the question of how to end the War in Japan that kept Stimson up at night, and the dynamics involved in making the decision kept changing while he was in Germany. On July 16, just as Stimson moved into his villa in Babelsberg and a day before the Conference started, two events occurred that were of major significance to the question: The first was a report describing, in Stimson's words, "maneuverings for peace" from the Japanese; the second was the anticipated but nevertheless startling news from New Mexico that the atomic bomb had been successfully tested.[13]

As to the "peace maneuverings," American intelligence officers had intercepted and decoded a cable from Japanese Foreign Minister Shigenori Togo to his ambassador in Moscow indicating that Emperor Hirohito had expressed an interest in negotiating the end of the War. This was big news. Earlier peace feelers coming through Switzerland, Portugal, and the Vatican did not have the apparent backing of the emperor. Although this was an important sign, there was still nothing on the table from the Japanese.

A key detail from another intercepted message from Togo implied that the only thing in the way of peace was the insistence by the Americans and British of an unconditional surrender. So just a month after the subject of softening the terms of surrender was kicked around in Truman's office, it was brought to the forefront in Potsdam, and Stimson became the leading proponent of giving the Japanese some ability to save face so that the War might end without the massive casualties that would result from either an invasion or the use of atomic bombs. Offering to allow the Japanese emperor to retain his office was a key consideration. In a memorandum Stimson delivered to Truman the day he heard about the first Togo cable, the secretary of war once again urged the president to clarify the terms of surrender. But there was immediate resistance from Byrnes, who remained the most ardent opponent to moderating any of the terms.

If the news about the intercepted Japanese cable was momentous, what Stimson received later that day was truly historic. A message arrived from George Harrison at 7:30 p.m. Harrison was Stimson's special assistant for matters related to the development of the atomic bomb. The message read:

> *Operated on this morning. Diagnosis not yet complete but results seem satisfactory and already exceed expectations. Local press release necessary as interest extends great distance. Dr. Groves pleased. He returns tomorrow. I will keep you posted.*[14]

What had been simply a theory to Stimson—albeit a promising one—when he first heard about it from scientists in November 1941 was now a reality. The atomic bomb worked, and the nuclear age had begun. Although the communication from Harrison seemed cryptic, Stimson was well aware of what the "expectations" were regarding the test at the Alamogordo Test

Range in New Mexico, and the message from Harrison clearly indicated they had been exceeded. He rushed over to the "Little White House," the villa where Truman and Byrnes were staying, to give them the good news. The following morning, Stimson briefed Marshall and Arnold.

A day and a half later, Harrison sent a second message to Stimson with a few additional details:

> *Doctor has just returned most enthusiastic and confident that the LITTLE BOY is as husky as his big brother. The light in his eyes discernible from here to High-hold and I could have heard his screams from here to my farm.*[15]

Stimson again hurried over to the Little White House. He would have explained to the president that Harrison's reference to Highhold, Stimson's estate in Long Island, meant the explosion from the test bomb in New Mexico could have been seen roughly 235 miles away (the same distance as between Washington, D.C., and Highhold). As for hearing "screams from here to my farm," this meant the test could be heard from nearly fifty miles away (the approximate distance from Washington, D.C., to George Harrison's farm in Upperville, Virginia).

It was not until Saturday morning, July 21, that a special courier hand-delivered to Stimson the full details of the test in a lengthy report prepared for him by General Groves. Stimson shared the report with Marshall before taking it over to Truman in the afternoon. The president invited Byrnes into the room, and the two men listened as Stimson read it to them for nearly an hour. Groves confirmed in the report that he would have the first of two bombs available for use between August 1 and 3. This meant that after three years of contemplating the moral, philosophical, political, and military considerations around the use of the bomb in the abstract, Stimson was now faced with an actual weapon and an accelerated timeline in which to advise the president on how best to use it. And with each passing hour at Potsdam, Stimson's desire to use the bomb on Japan seemed to diminish.

The Decision to Drop the Bombs

A policy committee chaired by Stimson had already forwarded recommendations regarding the military use of the bomb to Truman prior to the start of the Potsdam Conference. The recommendation was straightforward: drop it as soon as possible without warning on a war-related industrial facility within a city. This made Stimson's exertions in Germany to seek a peaceful end to the war in the Pacific a bit more challenging.

In his book *Atomic Tragedy*, historian Sean Malloy argued that Stimson's efforts in Potsdam were simply too late. Not only was the secretary exhausted and too deferential to the new president, but the "sheer confusion arising from the multiple vectors of policy that converged at Potsdam," Malloy wrote, "as well as the chronic irresolution over many of these issues in the preceding several years frustrated [Stimson's] last-minute efforts to shape the use of the bomb." While Malloy's analysis has some merit, the fates of Hiroshima and Nagasaki were by no means foregone conclusions at the time the American leadership gathered in Potsdam. There was enough time for Truman and his advisors to change the narrative. What was lacking was the want to do so, and one must look back over the closing three months of the War in the Pacific to see how certain events influenced this.

The considerations that went into the decision to use atomic bombs on Japan were complex, novel, and intertwined with one another, and the individuals who weighed in on them—politicians, military officials, and scientists—had varying degrees of perspectives and opinions that made finding consensus difficult. In the absence of it, it seems Truman was most persuaded by Jimmy Byrnes that using the new weapon was the quickest way to end a long, brutal war against a fanatical enemy that most people believed did not deserve any terms of surrender less than the unconditional one first demanded of it by Franklin Roosevelt more than two years earlier.

Two months prior to the start of the Potsdam Conference, the highly select and secretive committee (the Interim Committee) chaired by Stimson sat down for the first of eight meetings over a three-week period to develop policy recommendations around atomic energy. Stimson opened the meeting solemnly, telling the committee members that it was their responsibility to "recommend action that may turn the course of civilization." Although Truman formed the Committee at Stimson's request to give its opinions on matters relating to the postwar implications of atomic energy, it also deliberated on questions related to how the bomb should be used against Japan once it was ready.

The Committee was made up of eight men, including Stimson and his assistant, George Harrison. Other members included scientists Vannevar Bush, James Bryant Conant (president of Harvard and chairman of the National Defense Research Committee), and Karl Compton (president of MIT), as well as government officials Ralph Bard (undersecretary of the navy), William Clayton (assistant secretary of state for economic affairs), and Jimmy Byrnes (appointed by Truman at Stimson's suggestion). The secretary of war carefully chose the name of the Committee since he believed Congress had the right to set up a more permanent one on atomic energy after the War ended.

During each meeting held throughout May 1945, the committee members, joined on occasion by a few guests (George Marshall among them), debated several weighty issues around how to manage nuclear energy in the future. As far as how the bomb could end the war against Japan, only two principal questions were contemplated: whether a warning should be given to the Japanese prior to an attack, and what type of targets should be selected. There were no debates about whether to use the bomb or not.

On May 31, the Committee met in Stimson's office for a final two-day session, after which it agreed to present its recommendations to Truman. Stimson invited Marshall, Groves, and four top nuclear scientists (Robert Oppenheimer, Enrico Fermi, Arthur Compton, and Ernest Lawrence) to join in the discussions. Once again, the secretary of war set the tone by dramatically declaring in his opening remarks that atomic energy should not be considered "as a new weapon merely but as a revolutionary change in the relations of man to the universe." As such, he contended, the decisions about to be made could lead the world down one of two general paths, and the responsibility of the Committee was to make recommendations that would more likely lead to the perfection, rather than the doom, of civilization.

After two full days of discussions, the Committee unanimously agreed to make the following suggestions to the president about the use of the bomb against Japan:[16]

1. It should be dropped on Japan as soon as practical and without warning.
2. The specific target should be a war-related industrial facility surrounded by buildings that could be easily damaged (including civilian homes) to make as large a psychological impression on as many people as possible.

Giving the Japanese a warning about the bomb (heavily promoted by Undersecretary of the Navy Ralph Bard) was strongly opposed by General Groves during the final session for a number of reasons: It would allow the Japanese to prepare for it and possibly put U.S. prisoners of war in harm's way; it would alert the Russians to the fact that the United

States possessed a bomb when it was in the nation's interests to keep it a secret for as long as possible; and it would complicate the negotiations the United States was having with three countries for the supply of uranium. Stimson supported Groves.

As for the appropriate targets, the Committee reviewed work done earlier by a committee set up by General Groves that met three times between April 27 and May 28, 1945. The Target Committee considered several options ranging from demonstrating the bomb to an invited group of observers, using it on a city with or without warning, or using it solely against a military target. It eventually decided that a city would be the best target, one preferably spared from previous large-scale conventional bombing raids (this was because Groves and his fellow committee members understood that the bomb was going to be a "large blast" weapon and they therefore wanted to maximize damage to "most adversely affect the will of the Japanese people to continue the war)." This thinking was consistent with the policy of conventional bombing the Army Air Force conducted on Japan (and Germany earlier). Finally, it was decided by the Committee to target densely populated cities where military manufacturing was taking place.[17]

The Interim Committee largely adopted the recommendations of the Target Committee. James Conant suggested, and others agreed, that the target should be "a vital war plant employing a large number of workers and closely surrounded by workers' houses."[18] Shock and awe was the desired effect.

Stimson supported the target recommendations despite having long been opposed to the targeting of civilians (he was the only high-ranking official to question the incendiary campaigns after the firebombing of Tokyo in March 1945).[19] Two weeks before the final meeting of the Target Committee, he stressed to Truman that the country should try its best to limit civilian deaths in Japan, stating "the reputation of the United States for fair play and humanitarianism is the world's biggest asset for peace in the coming decades."[20]

Why then did the secretary of war acquiesce in the final recommendation about where to drop the bomb? There is no one definitive answer; it was a combination of reasons, including Stimson's naïve hope that the Army would be able to keep civilian deaths to a minimum (something Henry Arnold promised him), his respect for the opinions of the other members of the Committee who agreed with Groves (including the lead scientist, Robert Oppenheimer), and his awareness that the Japanese needed something extraordinary to jolt them into surrender (even more extraordinary than the March 1945 firebombing of Tokyo that killed over one hundred thousand people and destroyed sixteen square miles). But the most critical factor was the increasing political strength, aggressiveness, and skills of Jimmy Byrnes. Stimson seemed to have resigned himself to the fact it was Byrnes who now controlled the process.

He was correct. When Stimson left to attend to other business on the final day of the two-day session, Byrnes took advantage of his absence to draft the final recommendations to Truman on behalf of the Committee. He did so in such a way as to downplay the risk to civilian casualties by stressing it was a war plant being targeted. In this regard, Stimson never got comfortable with the final recommendations given to Truman, and he spent much of his time at Potsdam questioning his colleagues about the potential civilian casualties of each specific target.

One major objection of Stimson's to the Target Committee's recommendation was its selection of Kyoto as a preferred target. On this point, he was unyielding. He ordered that Kyoto be removed from the list given the significance of the city to the history and culture of Japan. The city, founded in the eighth century, was the ancient imperial capital of Japan and was home to countless historic temples and shines. The secretary of war, who had honeymooned there more than a half century earlier, believed the Japanese would never forgive the United States if the city and its structures were laid to waste. He was thinking ahead to the importance of a strong postwar U.S. alliance with Japan.

Although Stimson formally presented the recommendations of the Interim Committee to the president on June 6, Brynes had already briefed Truman at the White House immediately after the final meeting, indicating again, more than a month before Potsdam began, that he wanted to be in charge of giving advice to Truman about how the new weapon should be used. In advising the president to put Byrnes on the Interim Committee a month earlier, Stimson believed he was bringing additional stature and wisdom to the Committee. In the words of historian Richard Rhodes, he instead had "welcomed a cowbird" into the nest.

Although Stimson did not get a chance during the final meeting of the Interim Committee to discuss Japanese surrender terms, he worked hard over the following two months trying to convince Truman and other members of the administration to back off the unconditional-surrender terms first announced by President Roosevelt at Casablanca in 1943 and later confirmed by President Truman. The secretary of war raised the issue with Truman at the June 18 meeting to discuss *Downfall*, and he did so again via memorandums on July 2 and July 16. He wrote Truman that by allowing the Japanese to keep their monarchy in place, there might be a chance, even if just a small one, they'd surrender, particularly when coupled with a threat from the Russians. Stimson was not alone in this thinking; he had the support of Marshall, Grew, McCloy, and former president Herbert Hoover. But since Truman was too busy preparing for the Potsdam Conference, further conversations on the matter would have to take place in Germany and include the new secretary of state, a man with an emphatically different take on the subject.

For Jimmy Byrnes, already inclined against giving the Japanese any concessions, the news from Stimson in Potsdam about the successful test in New Mexico only strengthened his conviction. From that moment forward, he saw no reason to alter the terms of surrender (which were at that time being formalized in the Potsdam Declaration, a final ultimatum to be delivered to the Japanese). Nor did Byrnes believe the United States needed to request the Soviet Union for assistance in defeating the Japanese. He convinced Truman it would be best to delay the release of the Potsdam Declaration until the first of the two atomic bombs was ready to be deployed. If the terms were rejected or ignored by the Japanese government, Byrnes contended, an immediate nuclear response would surely wake it up. He therefore awaited further confirmation from Stimson on when the two bombs would be available for use.

That information arrived on the morning of July 24. Stimson advised Truman and Byrnes that the bombs could be ready as soon as August 1, but not later than August 10. The president thanked Stimson and told him he would use the information to time the release of the ultimatum to Japan. Taking one last shot, Stimson urged the president to reconsider giving assurances to the Japanese that they could keep their emperor and the monarchy in place. Truman was noncommittal.

Henry Stimson had failed.

Shortly after his dejected secretary of war walked out of the Little White House, Truman welcomed in the Combined Chiefs of Staff and Winston Churchill. Although no notes were taken, it is generally assumed that it was at this meeting that Truman made the final decision on using the bomb.[21]

The actual order was written up by Groves at the request of Marshall and was approved by Marshall, Stimson, and Truman. The order, to Carl Spaatz, commanding general of the U.S. Army Strategic Air Force, instructed the Air Force to drop the first bomb on one of the selected targets as soon as weather permitted but not before August 3, and the second one as soon as it was made available to them.

There was no turning back now; the order would stand unless Truman notified Stimson that the Japanese had accepted the terms of the Potsdam Declaration. Fatalistic, stressed, and frustrated, Stimson told the president he was thinking of heading to Munich to spend a couple of days with his old friend George Patton and would like to head directly back to the States from there. Truman had no objections; perhaps he was relieved to get a break from his pestering secretary of war.

The final terms to Japan issued in the Potsdam Declaration were released on the evening of July 26 without any guarantee about the fate of the emperor, any specific reference to the bomb, or any mention of Russia joining the fight. It did promise "prompt and utter destruction" if Japan did not surrender unconditionally. The Japanese government made no reply. Eleven days later, a Boeing B-29 dropped the 9,700-pound atomic bomb, dubbed "Little Boy," on Hiroshima launching the Atomic Age.

Ultimately, Harry Truman decided to follow the advice of his secretary of state, who was supported in his views by Harry Hopkins, Cordell Hull, and other prominent members of the State Department (including Dean Acheson and Archibald MacLeish). If he had any misgivings at all, the president had plenty of political cover.

Making the decision easier for Truman was his belief that if the United States attempted to soften the conditions of surrender, the Japanese would ask for a lot more than simply keeping their monarchy in place. Although there were several others besides Stimson who thought that changing the terms of surrender by offering to retain the imperial institution might have been sufficient, there is no hard evidence. On the contrary, the United States had in its hands a decrypted communication dated July 22 from Foreign Minister Shigenori Togo to Soviet Union Ambassador Naotake Sato stating specifically he would reject any such offer.[22] Additionally, it became clear from radio intercepts that the Japanese military believed it could get better terms once the Americans attacked Japan and started suffering losses. It is impossible to know one way or the other, but more than seventy-five years after the events, it seems that a promise by the Americans to retain the monarchy would have led to additional requests by the Japanese. Truman would have rejected any further demands, and the orders to drop the bombs would have been issued.

In any event, getting into a protracted series of negotiations with the Japanese and offering them anything short of unconditional surrender smelled too much like appeasement to Truman and Byrnes, both highly skilled politicians. Truman was already looking ahead to the midterm elections and the presidential election of 1948 and had no desire to be painted as soft. After Pearl Harbor, the Bataan Death March, and more than four hundred thousand American casualties in the Pacific Theater, he was convinced that the American people were in no mood to offer the Japanese anything. The fact that Stimson and Marshall both favored providing assurances about the status of the emperor, if for no other reason than he would be the only individual who could get Japanese soldiers to stop fighting, was not enough to move the dial.

As to the risk of significant Japanese civilian casualties, one must consider that the U.S. Army Air Force had been relentlessly bombing Japanese cities for over a year, killing innumerable civilians in the process (one hundred thousand in Tokyo during one night alone in March 1945). The Allies had done the same to Germany; it had been two years since forty-five thousand people (98 percent of them civilians) had died in Hamburg in what was the first firestorm in recorded history.[23] Massive civilian deaths followed similar missions in Kassel, Darmstadt, and Dresden. All told, between three hundred thousand and six hundred thousand German civilians were killed as a result of Allied bombings during the War. To many American officials, including both Stimson and Marshall, the atomic bomb was simply a safer and more efficient way to force an enemy to surrender.

In 1995, Harvey Bundy's son McGeorge (national security advisor under Kennedy and Johnson in the 1960s) suggested during an interview with historian Gar Alperovitz that had Henry Stimson been five years younger during the summer of 1945, he would have been able to put up a greater fight during the final weeks of the War and might have convinced Truman and those around him to modify the terms of surrender to the Japanese. Bundy, who coauthored Stimson's memoirs in 1947, spending three to four hours per day over eighteen months with him while he was living at Highhold, was certain Stimson's failing health in the last few weeks of the

War limited his influence on the new president. Jimmy Byrnes was political, aggressive, ambitious, and healthy. He was also fifteen years younger than the secretary of war.

In his own analysis of why the bomb was dropped, written for publication in *Harper's* magazine in 1947 at the suggestion of Harvard president James Conant and others to quell growing criticism about the use of atomic weapons on Japan, Stimson did not go into great details about his eleventh-hour efforts to change history. Although he mentioned his support for communicating to the Japanese that their monarchy could remain in place if they surrendered, Stimson matter-of-factly explained that the Potsdam Declaration failed to make any such offer. His emphasis was on the potential invasion of Japan, which he stated would have extended the War well into 1946 and "might be expected to cost over a million casualties, to American forces alone." "No man," Stimson continued in referencing the bomb, "could have failed to use it and afterwards looked his countrymen in the face."[24] General Marshall shared this view; after the War, he told his biographer that his own arguments were "very much for using the bomb."

Several historians have gone after Stimson (and Truman, who gave the same explanation) by pointing out the lack of evidence of casualty estimates nearly as high as both men suggested. Others, notably Richard Frank in his book *Downfall*, make a case that the estimates available to both men were inconclusive at best.[25] Given everything the U.S. High Command learned during the war about the Japanese soldier, and adding to that the fears of a "fanatically hostile" civilian population, nobody, Frank conjectured, could be certain about how many Americans would die during an invasion.[26]

A number of scholars have suggested that the decision to drop the bomb was also driven by the American government's desire to intimidate the Soviet Union, as relations with Stalin continued to deteriorate over the future of Europe. The record does not support this contention. Everyone involved in the decision to drop the bombs, including Henry Stimson and George Marshall, understood that the Soviets would be humbled by them, but the theory that the weapons would not have been dropped *but* for the diplomatic shot in the arm it gave to the Americans vis-à-vis Stalin simply does not stand up. At best, it was simply an ancillary benefit. Like nearly every advanced weapon developed throughout history, the atomic bomb was built with the intention that it be used. And once any new weapon is successfully employed, the nation that possesses it can derive political benefits by making its existence known to potential enemies.

Japanese Surrender

After reviewing troops and relaxing with General Patton in Munich for a spell, Henry Stimson returned to the United States on July 28 to rest. A week later, George Marshall called him at Highhold at 7:30 a.m. to advise him that the drop on Hiroshima was successful (Marshall was awakened by the news several hours earlier but was fully briefed by Groves at the Pentagon just before 7:00 a.m.). Stimson passed the message on to Truman, who was onboard a ship coming from back from Potsdam.

Back in Washington two days later, Stimson suffered what seems to have been a heart attack in the early morning hours as he was lying in bed. A few hours later, his doctor told him he needed a "complete rest." Stimson interpreted this as meaning he must leave the War Department and advised Truman later that afternoon. The president told him to take a month off if he needed it, but he wanted him by his side to see the War out.

The next day (August 9), Stimson was advised that the second bomb was successfully dropped on Nagasaki. He dragged himself to the White House to see Byrnes and pleaded with him, as he had with Truman the day before, to go easy on Japan in negotiating the final surrender. He knew that its government and military, even after two atomic bombs, would still struggle to come to terms with the concept of surrender. It was counter to a tradition dating back hundreds of years in Japan and reinforced by the army in the early part of the twentieth century.[27] Bringing with him a few letters and papers he received from others in support of a more tactful approach to the Japanese, Stimson reemphasized to both Byrnes and Truman that a solid relationship with Japan was going be critical to America's future, and how the War ultimately settled would have an impact on how that relationship developed. Having tendered what he believed was the final advice he would offer his government, a frail Stimson headed home to pack for his one-month rest in the Adirondacks.

He wasn't quite done; just as he was about to head to the airport the following morning, word arrived that the Japanese had agreed to accept the terms of surrender with one qualification: Emperor Hirohito must remain on the throne. Truman immediately summoned him to the White House to join Leahy, Forrestal, and Byrnes to determine a response.

Jimmy Byrnes made it clear from the start of the meeting that he still stood strongly against giving any ground to the Japanese. Tellingly, the secretary of state was the only nonveteran among those gathered in the

Executive Mansion. Leahy, who joined the U.S. Navy in 1897, thought the matter of the emperor was a minor one when compared to the consequences of fighting on. When it was Stimson's turn to speak, the former artillery captain agreed with Leahy and said that even if the Japanese had not made the request, the Army would have insisted the emperor remain in power under the "command and supervision" of the United States, given he was the only authority within Japan who could get all the geographically scattered armies to surrender. Unless the United States wanted a "score of bloody Iwo Jimas and Okinawas all over China and the New Netherlands," Stimson lectured, it was in the interests of America to keep Emperor Hirohito on the throne.

Truman, who had also seen action as the captain of an artillery unit during World War I, agreed with Stimson and Leahy, but Byrnes remained adamantly opposed. It was yet another sympathetic veteran who offered a compromise to bring Byrnes on board. Secretary of the Navy Jim Forrestal, a naval aviator during the First World War, suggested drafting a reply indicating to the Japanese—without any specific guarantee—that the emperor could continue to occupy the throne but "subject to the Supreme Commander of the Allied Powers." Byrnes still resisted, but Truman overruled him. After helping the secretary of state draft a reply to the Japanese, Stimson headed for the Adirondacks.

Four days later, after much internal debate and a final intervention by the emperor, the Japanese reluctantly surrendered. The War was over. Both Stimson and Marshall were greatly relieved that Japan no longer needed to be invaded. As Stimson and his wife entered the dining room of the Ausable Club that evening, fellow diners stood and applauded him.

EPILOGUE

Mabel and I entered the plane together and took off for home.

—HENRY STIMSON's final diary entry, September 21, 1945

President Truman: "General, I want you to go to China for me."
George Marshall: "Yes, Mr. President."

—MARSHALL's description of the telephone conversation he had with Truman
during the afternoon of November 18, 1945, just hours after he retired
from the Army, left his Pentagon office for good, and began
what was to be a new life of leisure in Leesburg, Virginia

Stimson Retires to Highhold

Henry Stimson spent twenty-two days recuperating up at the Ausable Club in the Adirondacks before making it back to Washington. During the first two weeks, he was "absolutely idle and useless."[1] He played no golf and was told by his doctor not to walk longer than the distance from his cottage to the Club's inn. Outside of a couple visits from McCloy (also a member of the Club) and a few phone calls (not more than four a day), little business was done. The secretary of war was intent on resting both mind and body. Although he strived to do this throughout the War, it was different during these three weeks. He was not trying to rally in order to get back to work; he was trying to recover so that he could enjoy whatever number of months or years he had left in his life.

But no matter how hard Stimson tried to relax, there was one issue he could not stop thinking about: the long-term consequences of the atomic bomb, the "Frankenstein" that had been his responsibility to bring to life. Specifically, he was struggling with the question of whether the secrets of the bomb should be shared with the world and controlled by an international organization to ensure peace.

Stimson went back and forth on the issue, coming out in favor of it early in the War and then changing his mind during the Potsdam Conference (after concluding that not all countries could be trusted with the technology). The Russians, Stimson concluded while in Germany, should have to earn their right to the secrets of the atom by adopting Western-style democratic ideals and abandoning their police state mentality.

But as the secretary of war sat around day after day on the grounds of the Ausable Club staring up at the clouds with nothing to do but think, the reality of Hiroshima and Nagasaki began to sink in, and he shifted his opinion once more. While he still felt it was important certain liberalizations were introduced within the Soviet Union, he believed they could wait. What couldn't was a healthy relationship between the two new superpowers. And he believed the relationship would never get off the ground if the United States kept the atomic bomb in its pocket during all its postwar negotiations with the Soviet Union. Once he worked through these arguments in his own head, Stimson was anxious to get his views across to Truman. He instructed McCloy to get started on a memorandum for the president.

Upon returning to Washington on September 4, Stimson immediately wrote Truman asking him to accept the letter of resignation he had sent to him back in April, when Roosevelt died. Truman requested he stop by the Oval Office the next day to discuss the matter. At that meeting, the president agreed to accept it effective September 21, Stimson's seventy-eighth birthday.

With his retirement day settled, Henry Stimson spent the next week preparing for one last chance to promote his idea of sharing the science behind atomic energy with the Soviet Union and placing control of the technology with an international organization. He got an appointment with Truman for 3:00 p.m. on September 12.

During the meeting, Stimson explained to Truman the rationale behind his change of thinking since Potsdam. He walked Truman line by line through a memorandum he had prepared for the discussion. Stimson told the president the Russians were going to develop the bomb by themselves sooner or later. Therefore, he believed it was far better to share it with them now so that the technology could be managed and controlled in a positive and cooperative manner for the betterment of civilization. Such cooperation would create an atmosphere of goodwill with the Russians that would go a long way toward keeping the peace. Stimson told Truman the United States could not simply treat the atomic bomb as a new weapon; it was too "revolutionary and dangerous to fit into the old concepts."

Knowing Truman was highly suspicious of the Russians, the secretary of war inserted into his memorandum the line for which he would become most known, and one that reflected a philosophy he had first articulated in his diary in 1932:

> *The chief lesson I have learned in a long life is that the only way you can make a man trustworthy is to trust him; and the surest way to make him untrustworthy is to distrust him and show your distrust.*

Stimson had a talent, developed over a lifetime, of acquiring the trust of people by first trusting them. It helped him succeed in his law practice and in nearly every public position he held. His accomplishments in Nicaragua and the Philippines were driven by this philosophy, and his entire management style reflected it as well. It led him to shut down the code-breaking section of the State Department when he first became secretary of state under Hoover. By famously stating, "Gentlemen do not read each other's mail," Stimson was sending a signal at that time to those within and outside of the country that the United States was going to lead by example with respect to how nations dealt with one another. Stimson hoped that Truman would adopt this thinking when it came to sharing the enormous powers extracted from splitting the atom.

After Stimson concluded his arguments, Truman told him he was in accord with every statement. With nothing more to add, Stimson moved on and discussed other issues of importance to him. In his diary that night, he expressed neither frustration nor pride regarding the outcome of the meeting, something uncharacteristic of him. One can only assume he was skeptical about Truman's response. Jimmy Brynes, after all, was strongly against the international control of the bomb (he and Stimson had discussed the issue the day after Stimson returned from the Adirondacks). But there was nothing more he could do. He was at last prepared to let others run with the issue.

George Marshall returned from his own ten-day trip to the Adirondacks five days after Stimson's meeting with Truman. Staying at one of the most luxurious Adirondack camps ever built (as a guest of Joseph Davies, former ambassador to the Soviet Union), Marshall had time to fully relax during his vacation in complete privacy. Once back, he and Stimson immediately sat down together to catch up. Although the general did not get formally involved in the debate on sharing nuclear technology with the Russians (given it was a political issue), he was sympathetic to the elder statesman's views and would have been interested to hear about how Stimson's meetings went with Truman and Byrnes.

Even if the general wished to take part in the debate, he was too busy demilitarizing Japan and sorting out the demobilization of his own armies around the world to give much thought to the subject. He was also considering several weighty issues regarding the future of the Army in the postwar period. Chief among these were the establishment of universal military training, combining the War and Naval Departments, and determining the military effects of atomic weapons going forward. In these and other issues, Marshall was looked to for leadership within the administration.

The problem was that the chief of staff, like his civilian partner of five years, was also burned out. He sent a letter to Truman four days after Japan surrendered, requesting to be relieved from duty and recommending Eisenhower as his replacement. Hoping he could be on his farm in Leesburg by the end of August, Marshall explained to the president that he had been on duty at the War Department for more than seven years, six in his current position. "Aware of the wear and tear of the job," Marshall wrote Truman, "I am certain that it would be advantageous to make a change."[2] Truman said he'd think it over but expressed his hope that he could stay on a bit longer.

Given that the War was over, Marshall's sincerity in his request to be relieved by the president was beyond doubt; he wanted out.[3] But he did seem overly optimistic about the timing of his departure. He should have given more thought to the matter before making a wager with Hap Arnold when the two discussed their mutual retirement plans in Potsdam. At that time, Arnold bet Marshall five dollars that Marshall would still be in office six months after Japan surrendered. Arnold knew Marshall well enough to know he would not push Truman for an answer and likely saw no reason why the new president would want to make a change.[4] Although he ended up winning the bet, Marshall was still on the job three months after the Japanese announced they were surrendering.

Getting back to work, the chief of staff's principal task after the War ended was to reduce the size of the Army by more than six million men within ten months in an equitable manner while leaving enough quality troops behind to properly manage the nation's occupational responsibilities in both Europe and Japan. This was a formidable undertaking, if not one of the largest and single most intricate logistics exercises in U.S. military history.

Putting aside the normal transportation challenges (exacerbated by the devastation of Europe's infrastructure), it was nearly impossible to relieve and bring home such a large quantity of scattered troops in an amount of time short enough to satisfy the public. Not long after the War ended, American families and their representatives in Congress began asking a simple question: "Why aren't the boys home yet?"

Demobilization on the scale required was impossible to accomplish without making a number of soldiers and their loved ones believe they were being treated unfairly. In most cases the complaints (passed from families to congressmen to the Pentagon) were meritless, but in others, they were justified. Although most of the injustices were unintentional, in certain situations the Army made decisions it knew were unfair. For example, men who had served longest—and therefore deserved to be sent home earliest—were often the best leaders within their units, which meant that shipping them home first would leave occupying troops with insufficiently trained leaders. When making such decisions, Marshall had to prepare himself for the inevitable backlash.

When it came, the chief of staff decided to address all the harsh criticisms and concerns at one time. On September 20, he held an informal talk with approximately 350 members of Congress in the auditorium of the Library of Congress. His speech, lasting fifty minutes and delivered extemporaneously, was so well received that the War Department transcribed it and sent it off to various newspapers around the country.

Marshall began the speech by addressing those in the audience who suggested the pace of demobilization had been intentionally slowed down so the War Department could maintain a large peacetime army. Dismissing this firmly but respectfully, Marshall explained it was simply too early to tell how many troops were necessary to effectively occupy Japan, a country that still possessed an army of 2.5 million "completely equipped and well-fed men."[5] He then went on to explain in great detail the entire demobilization effort in both men and equipment that started after Germany surrendered.

"The process of demobilization is rather intricate," Marshall understatedly told the congressmen, but he emphasized that he personally understood everyone's concerns. Informing them he had been receiving plenty of letters himself that were not exactly "light reading,"[6] Marshall then went into more details about how priorities were set, what the current timing was, how that timing was determined, how many troops the Army expected to be sending home, and what the future requirements were for troops in Europe and Asia. He concluded his remarks by inviting any and all congressmen to go overseas and observe themselves the efficiency of the process. Marshall's effort—full of facts, sympathy, empathy, and logic—helped subdue most of the congressmen and gave them logical talking points to take back home to their anxious constituents.

The day following Marshall's speech to Congress was Henry Stimson's last as secretary of war. Nearly forty years after he "crossed forever the river that separates private citizens from public men," Stimson was taking a permanent rest. He would later write that without realizing it at the time, he was on the "eve of an emotional and coronary breakdown."

The secretary began his day by preparing himself for his final cabinet meeting, to be held that afternoon. Truman had asked him to address the question of international control of the atomic bomb. Although Stimson knew the issues well, he could not break the habits of a lifetime by going into the meeting without fully preparing himself.

He would not get much of a chance. At 10:30 a.m., Patterson, McCloy, Lovett, and Bundy walked into his office along with other members of his immediate staff to present him with an antique silver tray engraved with each of their names. Stimson was moved; he was quite attached to his team, particularly the "core four" who had so ably served him during the War. These men were like sons to him, and he was extremely proud of the reputation they collectively acquired as the single best staff in Washington. The memories of countless conversations, fiery debates, energetic court tennis games, relaxing cocktails, stimulating dinners, and occasional laughter must have flooded the secretary as he shook each man's hand on their way out of his office. The five of them had literally been through war together. Stimson struggled to control his emotions in order to finish preparing for the cabinet meeting.

And then General Marshall walked in.

Three days earlier, Stimson wrote a letter to Harry Truman reminding him of a meeting they had together in which Stimson urged the president to find a proper way to recognize the services of Marshall, "the outstanding man among the English speaking soldiers of this war." After listing his accomplishments and qualities for the record, Stimson challenged Truman to show him "any war in history which has produced a general with such a surprisingly perfect record." He urged the president to get behind awarding Marshall the highest possible American decoration "bar none." Few people spent as much time with the chief of staff as Stimson did during the previous five years and got to witness his genuine greatness, indomitable patriotism, and unmatched integrity. He now had to say good-bye to him, possibly for the last time given his own deteriorating health.

Although describing his final meeting at the Pentagon with the general less than three months later as a "very deep emotional experience," Stimson could not even recall what they discussed during their hour together. They had known each other for more than twenty-seven years, and during the five years they worked side by side in the War Department, the two men developed an extraordinary relationship despite their vastly dissimilar backgrounds and thirteen-year age difference. It was not simply a wartime bond; their relationship, anchored firmly by a profound mutual respect and admiration, was elevated by the integrity each man felt was absolute in the other.

General Marshall considered Stimson as his wartime tower of strength. Referring to him during a discussion with Harvey Bundy one day, Marshall told him that Stimson's greatest power lay in the pureness of his integrity. The chief of staff told Bundy he would often respond to difficult questions or demands from politicians by simply saying, "That's a very interesting thought, but you'd better go see Mr. Stimson about it." Of course, Marshall continued, "The fellow wouldn't dare go see Stimson."[7] Marshall told many people both during and after the War how fortunate he was and how blessed the country was to have Stimson heading the War Department when he did.

General Lucious Clay, one of Eisenhower's deputies during the last year of the War, in speaking of Stimson, said he gave Marshall the kind of support "without which General Marshall could not accomplish what he did."[8] Ten years after the War ended, Marshall himself said of Stimson, "I don't know what we would have done with someone different."[9] Marshall was keenly aware he might not have succeeded without the great statesman standing firmly behind him. It would therefore have been an emotional good-bye for him that day as well.

After another difficult farewell with Harvey Bundy, his closest personal assistant and most frequent dinner companion during the War, Stimson welcomed George Harrison into his office along with Robert Oppenheimer, director of the laboratory in Los Alamos and the acknowledged father of the atomic bomb. Oppenheimer and Harrison were there to provide

Stimson with information he needed to prepare himself for the cabinet meeting later that afternoon.

Shortly thereafter, members of the larger War Department staff presented Stimson with a birthday cake. Before anyone could finish it, Stimson was abruptly called to the Executive Mansion. When he arrived, he found Truman had assembled the top commanders of the Armed Forces, members of his immediate staff, a large group of civilian staff from the White House, and his wife, Mabel, to witness him being awarded the Distinguished Service Medal.

Following the presentation, the cabinet meeting began. Stimson was given the floor. Given the interruptions during the day, he was less prepared than usual. He gave the same arguments to the cabinet that he had given to Truman earlier. He was encouraged by some of the feedback he received, but the secretary might have suspected nobody was going to be too hard on him at his final cabinet meeting. Jimmy Brynes was absent.

After saying farewell to Truman and other members of the cabinet, an emotionally spent Stimson and his wife headed to the Pentagon to quickly grab a few items from his office before being chauffeured to the airport for the one-way flight to Long Island. As the couple's car approached the airfield, a heartwarming spectacle awaited them. Greeting them on the tarmac was Stimson's staff, an Army band, and every available general officer in Washington. George Marshall had arranged it all. With more than 120 generals present, it was the single largest gathering of high-ranking officers in the history of the United States.[10] For the seventy-eight-year-old veteran, enamored with everything about the soldiering life since the turn of the century, it was overwhelming.

Given that the cabinet meeting went on for longer than anticipated, Marshall and the generals had stood in two lines opposite from one another for an hour. When his car pulled up and Stimson got out, there was a nineteen-gun salute, after which the band played "Auld Lang Syne" and "Happy Birthday" as Stimson slowly made his way down between the lines of dignitaries toward the DC-3 airplane that would fly him to Highhold.

At the end of the line, standing at the base of the aircraft's stairs, the chief of staff greeted Stimson. Removing his hat and lowering his head out of respect, Marshall extended his hand to the frail but proud statesman and bid him a final farewell. After that, as Stimson matter-of-factly noted in his diary, "Mabel and I entered the plane together and took off for home."[11] This would be the final sentence Stimson entered into his ten-thousand-page diary, one he had begun more than forty years earlier.

Marshall's Retirement from the Army

One cannot help but think that in giving the secretary of war such a grand sendoff at the airport, General Marshall was also using the occasion as a teaching moment to remind each of his generals about the proper subordination of the military to civilian authority. He long believed one of the greatest assets of the Army was the high regard and trust in which it was held by the American people. If its sole purpose continued to be to defend the republic at the direction and under the control of civil authority, Marshall believed the Army would retain that trust and ultimately, therefore, its effectiveness. So, at a moment in American history when the Army stood at its highest stature, Marshall insisted that every one of its generals stand at attention in the hot September sun to pay tribute to its departing civilian leader. It was a classic lesson in American values from one of the greatest patriots the nation ever produced.

The chief of staff must have been jealous as he saw Henry Stimson's plane take off down the runway. Even more so than Stimson, Marshall wanted to retire. He was two months from turning sixty-five and was confident he had done his duty and had earned his rest. Every evening when he came home, Katherine asked him if he'd seen the president that day regarding his departure date. Marshall's negative reply did not deter the two from making detailed travel plans each night before they turned in. Joyfully pouring over maps, the two plotted out the various routes they would take by car to different spots around the country once Truman released the general from duty.[12] It was going to be a freedom the two experienced only in fleeting intervals during their fifteen years of marriage.

For the next two months, until Truman finally granted him his wish, Marshall concentrated on demobilization, unification of the War and Naval Departments, and a universal military training program.

On the issue of unification, it was hardly a surprise Marshall was so strongly in favor of it. As the man who pushed for unity of command more than any other Allied official, he knew World War II was won *despite* the Army and Navy's difficulties communicating and coordinating with one another. It was therefore logical for the two branches to unite under the leadership of one department, and Marshall did an excellent job selling the concept to the Senate Committee on Military Affairs in October. His efforts, combined with the efforts of many, led to the National Security Act of 1947, which, among other things, abolished the positions of secretary of war and secretary of the navy in favor of a secretary of defense (a position Marshall was asked to fill in 1950).

As far as universal military training, the merits about which Marshall was even more strongly convinced, he could hardly believe the issue even needed to be debated after the experiences America had gone through twice in his career. He made countless speeches both before and during the War about the importance of preparedness and was overwhelmingly supported by Henry Stimson in this regard. Stimson spent an inordinate amount of time himself trying to convince the administration, Congress, and the American people to adopt some type of compulsory military training. Aside from the obvious benefits training accrued with respect to military preparedness, both Marshall and Stimson believed there were benefits to the individuals being trained, the economy, and American democracy itself.

During the War, there were times when Stimson and Marshall got close to securing the congressional support necessary for a bill, but the prospects collapsed after every successful turn of fortune for the Allies on the battlefield. In March 1945, the War Department gave up on any chance of getting legislation during the War, but Stimson and Marshall promised that it would be addressed when it ended.

In his final biennial report to the secretary of war issued in September, Marshall devoted the final section of it to the need for such a program. He wrote that there was an "acute revision" among Americans at the end of every war that causes the country to "confuse military preparedness with the causes of war." This has led the country to "almost deliberately" drift into the next catastrophe. In urging the country to consider the consequences of unpreparedness, he closed the report by writing, "War is not the choice of those who wish passionately for peace. It is the choice of those who are willing to resort to violence for political advantage." In late October, he presented the same message in a 3,255-word speech at a forum put on by the *New York Herald Tribune*.

Despite his entreaties, the public remained unconvinced. There was something inherent in the American psyche that equated military training with belligerency. Given that the consequences of unpreparedness in America never included losing a war, it was also easy for many to assume that the nation would continue to be able to successfully respond to any future foreign threat. Marshall and Stimson could only hope that their protégés and other successors in the Army and War Department would take up the cause after they retired from the scene.

Only after General Eisenhower returned to Washington, D.C., in November did Harry Truman finally agree to relieve Marshall. The effective date was set for November 18. On the day after he received his second Distinguished Service Medal from Truman in a short ceremony at the Pentagon (he received his first in 1919), Marshall and his wife quietly dismissed their chauffeur, got in their car as quickly as they could, and drove the forty miles separating Washington, D.C., from Leesburg, Virginia, to begin a new life at "Dodona Manor," the home they had purchased together shortly before the attack on Pearl Harbor. After nearly forty-four years of service to the U.S. Army, George Marshall was ready to relax.

Upon their arrival to Leesburg, the overjoyed couple stood together on the portico of their home taking in the fall sunlight before Katherine went up to her room to take a short nap. While she was upstairs, the phone rang. Marshall picked it up downstairs. It was President Truman, who got straight to the point: "General, I want you to go to China for me." Marshall was even shorter in his reply; he simply responded, "Yes, Mr. President," before abruptly hanging up so as not to disturb his wife's rest.

When Katherine came downstairs an hour later, she found her husband lying down on his chaise longue with the radio turned to the 3:00 p.m. news. As she approached the doorway to greet him, she heard the announcer say that the U.S. Ambassador to China had just resigned, President Truman had appointed Marshall as his Special Ambassadorial Envoy to China, and the general would be leaving to take up his new post immediately. Marshall stood up and gently approached his stunned wife, explaining that Truman had called him while she was upstairs.

Katherine Marshall was angry, but she should not have been surprised. Her husband was incapable of declining a presidential request to serve his country. Marshall had no desire to go to China; in fact, he "loathed" the thought of the entire mission. But his sense of duty trumped all other considerations.[13] Although not a graduate of the U.S. Military Academy and part of the "Long Gray Line" like so many of his mentors and protégés, George Marshall embraced its motto of "Duty, Honor, Country" as much as any former plebe. The retirement from public life he so longed for and deserved was put on hold for six long and difficult years.

Marshall ended up spending more than a year in China unsuccessfully attempting to bring together the Nationalists and the Communist Party to form a single unified government that could act as a check against Soviet expansion in Asia. It was a thankless and hopeless task, but one on which Marshall labored tirelessly (he wrote Hap Arnold toward the end of the assignment that his work in China toward finding a solution went on "interminably, rather like the seemingly never ending battle to establish *Overlord*").[14]

What was particularly frustrating to Marshall was that his chances of finding a solution were about the same as those a British diplomat might have expected coming to America in early 1861 with instructions to broker a peace between the North and South. Marshall knew the odds were stacked up against him. Prior to leaving, he reached out to Stimson for advice, and his former comrade-in-arms was no less pessimistic. Despite the low probability, he was determined to give it a shot.

Once it became certain that the mission would fail, the only solace Marshall took, as he anxiously waited for his formal recall home, was in his continuing thoughts of retirement. He was thrilled at the prospect of getting back to his gardening duties and beginning a life of pressureless leisure. But before he could even begin the long journey home from China, Truman once again interfered with his dream by asking him in early January to take over the State Department from Jimmy Byrnes (who resigned after falling out of favor with the president). Once again, Marshall was unable to turn down a presidential appeal. The announcement was made while he was en route to Washington. He was sworn in as the nation's fiftieth secretary of state on January 21, 1947.

George Marshall had reached as high an office as an American could obtain without being elected. He was now in charge of foreign policy for the United States at a time when the world had dangerously divided itself into two hostile camps. To inspire him as he prepared for the awesome civilian responsibilities awaiting him, Marshall requested that a large portrait of Henry Stimson be hung in the most prominent position in his office to the left of his desk above his conference table between two flags. In a sense, the two men would once again be working side by side.

American historian and Truman biographer David McCullough wrote that appointing George Marshall to run the State Department "was one of the best, most important decisions of Truman's presidency." Although at the helm for only two years, Marshall was able to use his considerable standing in the country, in Congress, and around the world to direct the country's foreign policy during the early and most critical years of the Cold War.

Running the State Department in the same manner as he ran the Army, Marshall put a chain-of-command structure in place to operate like an

Army chief of staff. During his tenure, he relied heavily on Undersecretary of State Dean Acheson, and then Acheson's replacement, Robert Lovett. As soon as this system was set up, Marshall began working on the massive postwar issues of the day. Starting with the problems in Greece and Turkey, followed quickly by his unsuccessful attempt to negotiate with the Soviets on coordinating the future of Germany and Austria, Marshall faced crisis after crisis and soon came to the realization—one that American diplomat George Kennan famously concluded a year earlier in his "Long Telegram"—that the Soviet Union was not interested in working together to ease postwar tensions. On the contrary, it perceived itself to be in a perpetual war with the United States and other major democratic countries. Much of what Marshall faced during his two years running the State Department reflected this new reality.

Despite the general's overwhelming accomplishments during the Second World War, it was only during his time as secretary of state that George Marshall achieved the type of lasting fame Franklin Roosevelt went to his grave believing he had forever denied him by choosing Eisenhower to command *Overlord*. The "Marshall Plan," the massive and unprecedented economic aid initiative famously hinted at during an eleven-minute speech the general made at Harvard University in June 1947, was launched by the State Department to quickly rebuild the economies of postwar Europe, bring political stability to the region, and mitigate the threat of communism. When he heard that officials wanted to attach his name to the vast program, Harry Truman, perhaps atoning for Roosevelt's *Overlord* decision, insisted the honor be given to Marshall (who never referred to it as the "Marshall Plan," but always the "European Recovery Program"). Considered by many to be one of the greatest economic and foreign policy successes of the twentieth century, the Marshall Plan built the foundation for Western Europe's expeditious postwar growth.

While preparing for his brief but seminal Harvard speech, Marshall recalled Henry Stimson's difficult battles fighting against the Morgenthau Plan three years earlier and sent for the memorandums he penned on the subject of postwar aid to Germany. It is no coincidence that in supporting and promoting the plan, Marshall was achieving the goal Stimson expressed in 1944, that America reach for a "higher level of statesmanship."

Resigning from his position as secretary of state in January 1949 for health reasons, Marshall accepted the far less taxing role of chairman of the American Battle Monuments Commission, a position he happily held right up to his death ten years later. When his health began to improve in the fall of 1949, nine months after leaving the State Department, he was happy to undertake another less challenging job as head of the American Red Cross.

But a year later, President Truman decided he needed to draw from the well one last time; he asked Marshall to take over the Defense Department less than three months after the start of the Korean War. Aside from the obvious benefits of hiring Marshall, Truman desperately needed a man of the general's stature to fix a department demoralized under the leadership of Louis Johnson (whose overly aggressive budget cutting and difficult management style alienated the upper ranks of the armed forces). Marshall agreed to serve for six months (which he extended twice at Truman's request).

Just as Truman leaned on Marshall one final time, so, too, did Marshall on Bob Lovett, asking the Stimson protégé to again leave Wall Street to be his right-hand man. Together, before Lovett took over the top spot a year later, the two men righted the ship within the Pentagon, repaired the relationship between the departments of state and defense (that fell apart during Johnson's years running the latter), presided over the difficult war in Korea, and assisted Truman in managing the insubordination of General Douglas McArthur.

On the morning of September 12, 1951, Marshall was holding his usual staff meeting at the Pentagon when he casually mentioned that as of 11:00 a.m., he would no longer be secretary of defense. He had done his job and was more than comfortable Bob Lovett could seamlessly take over his responsibilities. Six years after his "retirement," he was finally heading home.

Legacies

Henry Stimson

At the start of the Cuban Missile Crisis in October 1962, President John F. Kennedy anxiously summoned a highly select group of elder statesmen to the White House to advise him. Among the most respected of these men was Bob Lovett, to whom Kennedy two years earlier had offered the choice of any position in his cabinet (Lovett declined for health reasons). Since the end of World War II, Lovett had shuffled back and forth between his investment-banking job in New York and high public service in Washington. His impact during this time was far-reaching: In 1945, he chaired the Lovett Committee that reorganized U.S. intelligence after the War and led to the creation of the CIA; in 1947, he was asked by George Marshall to serve as his undersecretary of state, during which time he teamed with Senator Arthur Vandenberg to pass the Vandenberg Resolution, resulting in the formation of NATO; in 1950, he was recruited by Marshall again to serve as his under-secretary of defense, only to succeed the general a year later, becoming the nation's fourth secretary of defense. At the age of sixty-seven, Lovett epito-mized the respected establishment "wise man" in the Stimsonian tradition, and President Kennedy was looking for solid counsel as the crisis with the Soviet Union escalated.

When the former apostle of both Stimson and Marshall showed up to the Executive Mansion, he was ushered into the office of National Secu-rity Advisor McGeorge Bundy, the son of Lovett's fellow Stimson protégé and wartime colleague Harvey Bundy. After receiving a full briefing from Bundy on the crisis, Lovett offered up a general recommendation to the forty-three-year-old wunderkind of the Kennedy White House: "Mac, I think the best service we can perform for the President is to try to approach this as Colonel Stimson would."[15]

At the time Bob Lovett and McGeorge Bundy were seeking spiritual guidance from "the Colonel" to save the world from a nuclear Armageddon, Henry Stimson had been dead for twelve years. His march from the War Department to the grave was hastened by the poor health of his heart that began failing him during the last weeks of the War (and perhaps earlier).[16] Just one month after his retirement, Stimson suffered a massive coronary occlusion that put him in bed for five weeks. He was still in questionable shape six months later, when he was invited to address five hundred Phil-lips Academy alumni at the Roosevelt Hotel in Manhattan. It was a taxing evening for the proud alumnus; his voice faltered occasionally and when it became clear the speech took too much out of him, his wife, Mabel, began to weep. It would be Stimson's last major address.[17]

Although the aging statesman recovered enough strength to begin coauthoring his memoirs in the summer of 1946 (spending eighteen months working with twenty-seven-year-old McGeorge Bundy, who took up residence in a small outbuilding on Stimson's Long Island estate), his body continued to break down. The pain from arthritis, coupled with the normal consequences of living a physically active life, prevented him from continuing his lifelong habit of riding horses, killed any ambition to travel for leisure, and even caused him to resign as president of the Board of Trustees of his cherished Phillips Academy. "Andover," Stimson summarized to the headmaster in his letter of resignation, "is a little too far from New York for a man of my age."

Confined to a wheelchair for the last two months of his life after breaking a leg, Stimson died of a heart attack at his home on Long Island on October 20, 1950. After a simple funeral held three days later in the living room of Highhold, he was buried in a private alcove surrounded by rhododendrons at a nearby cemetery less than three miles from where his close friend and mentor Theodore Roosevelt had been laid to rest more than thirty years earlier.[18]

Death did nothing to diminish the influence of Henry Stimson. On the contrary, attracted by his high sense of ethics, love of order and laws, and undying conviction that America was exceptional in nearly every way, a generation of like-minded internationalists adopted Stimson's legalistic and moralistic approach to foreign policy and carried his interventionist principles into the second half of the American Century and beyond.

Leading the next generation of Stimsonians were men like Lovett, McCloy, Forrestal, Acheson, Harriman, George Kennan, and Charles Bohlen. From various positions of influence, these men and others— George Marshall among them—continued to strive for the more perfect world that Elihu Root and Henry Stimson first talked about at the turn of the century. Although there were times when Stimsonian thought temporarily fell out of favor in Washington, it always remained hidden in plain sight within the law offices, banking houses, and universities along the Northeast corridor until its adherents were once again called to service. And when the second generation of Stimson devotees began to retire, a third, groomed in the same internationalist traditions, was ready to take over, as Stimson would have put it, "the laboring oar."

There were two aspects of Henry Stimson's approach to foreign relations his followers found particularly compelling. The first was his pure bipartisanship; Stimson rarely if ever looked at any issue, much less one concerning foreign affairs, through partisan lenses. Few men who followed him could match this quality to the same degree as Stimson, no matter how much they admired it or wished they could. It takes tremendous courage to go against one's party, and Stimson, as this book has pointed out, was nothing if not courageous. He spent a lifetime fighting the GOP at all levels on matters both small and large: He was one of the only Republicans who supported Woodrow Wilson's efforts to join the League of Nations after World War I; he was strongly against the Smoot-Hawley tariff his boss Herbert Hoover signed in 1930; and he was vehemently opposed to the general isolationism that swept over the GOP in the 1930s. When Franklin Roosevelt tapped Stimson for the War Department in 1940, he was relieved to get tossed out of a party he believed was on the wrong side of history.

The second and equally attractive quality in Stimson's approach to foreign policy was that the former World War I artillery officer was always prepared to back up words with force. His threats were not simply tough talk from some highly educated Wall Street lawyer who never held a gun; Stimson was a soldier at heart and identified with the Army in many ways more so than the law. Thus, when he spoke about America as the only country that could successfully bring leadership and order to the world to ensure peace, and insisted that any nation that behaved badly and upset that balance should be taught a lesson, people listened.

It is not that Stimson relished war like his friend Teddy Roosevelt seemed to, but he supported it with uncommon vigor when he believed it was for a just cause. He was also single-minded in the pursuit of victory when waging it. This latter quality was probably the chief reason that the statesman acted against his better judgment when making recommendations to Franklin Roosevelt about the fate of Japanese Americans after Pearl Harbor.

During the second half of the twentieth century, aggressive interventionists who believed they were following Stimson's path did not always get it right. The Vietnam War, as David Halberstam wrote about so persuasively in *The Best and the Brightest*, was an example of how military aggression, supported by men cut out of the Stimson cloth, failed to serve the country well.

Although not a strict imperialist in the nineteenth-century mold of his mentors, Theodore Roosevelt and Elihu Root, Stimson took these two men's ideas about America's rightful role in the world and spun them together over the course of his lengthy career to craft a twentieth-century definition of the term that Stimson biographer Godfrey Hodgson described as "liberal imperialism without the brass bands." That spirit guided the leading statesmen of the postwar era as they helped build and administer an American empire. In looking at the long arc of Stimson's career against the nation's history during that period, coupled with the considerable influence of his protégés following his death, one can understand why historian Kai Bird wrote that Henry Stimson "cast a longer shadow" over the twentieth century than any other single individual.[19]

George Marshall

The last assignment entrusted to George Marshall by his country was to head the American delegation attending the June 1953 coronation of

Queen Elizabeth II in London, eight years after the Germans surrendered. As the seventy-two-year-old walked slowly but steadily alongside Omar Bradley down the aisle of Westminster Abby toward his assigned seat, Marshall began to observe row after row of prominent and notable guests rising to their feet. Curious, Marshall turned to Bradley and whispered, "Who are they rising for?" Amused, but likely not surprised by his question, Bradley responded, "You."[20]

Genuine modesty was one of the unwavering qualities possessed by Marshall during his half century of service to the United States. Of all his personality traits, many self-designed and controlled by him at an early age in order to command respect just as his hero, George Washington, had done, humility seemed to have been a gift from nature. In an interview with his biographer, Forrest Pogue, near the end of his life, Marshall was summarizing his years as chief of staff when he said matter-of-factly, "If you want to stress my contribution, it was the first two years. My commanders did the rest." Similarly, in announcing to his staff at the Pentagon that he was retiring from the Defense Department in September 1951, Marshall was equally humble, telling them he could not take credit for any successes, that he had simply "pushed a few things."[21] Nobody in American history, save Washington and Lincoln, accomplished more than George Marshall did with the same level of self-effacement.

Following his departure as secretary of defense, Marshall and his wife spent the next two years dividing their time between Virginia and North Carolina enjoying the retirement they wanted to start after the War had ended six years earlier. The general spent his well-deserved rest gardening, fishing, entertaining, visiting friends, reading, and occasionally attending golf tournaments. In the fall of 1953, Marshall caught a cold and then a bad case of the flu after returning from an extended trip to the United Kingdom around the coronation ceremony. Believing he was on the mend, he agreed to travel to Oslo, Norway, in December to accept the Nobel Peace Prize for his work on the Marshall Plan. He was mistaken; he remained sick on the voyage to Europe and the entire time he was away. For the next five years, his physical and mental health began a slow but steady decline.

On January 15, 1959, the general suffered a crippling stroke at his home in Pinehurst, North Carolina, that put him in hospitals for the remaining nine months of his life. Although he managed to receive visitors for short spells during the first few months, he stopped recognizing people by the spring (including Winston Churchill, who paid an emotional visit to him at Walter Reed Army Hospital in early May). He died on October 16, 1959.

After a short twenty-minute service at the Fort Myer Chapel near Quarters One, Marshall was buried at Arlington National Cemetery in a plot he chose himself years earlier. It was approximately five hundred feet from the Tomb of the Unknown Soldier and just a quarter mile from the equestrian statue he unveiled nine years earlier over the grave of his cherished British friend and wartime partner, Field Marshal Sir John Dill. Marshall's gravesite already contained the remains of his first wife and her mother. His modest gravestone stands today, as then, alongside neither a path nor a road, making it only visible to those who seek it out.

Before his death, Marshall gave instructions that he was not to lie in state at the Capitol, not to have his service in the National Cathedral, not to have anyone deliver a eulogy, and not to have a lengthy guest list. In a brief memorandum to an aide he penned in the spring of 1956, Marshall suggested a handful of men who might be able to serve as pallbearers. After listing a few of these, he added he'd like to have Bob Lovett serve "if convenient" and Walter Bedell Smith "if he is in town."[22]

When the great men of the World War II era looked back and spoke of George Marshall, there was little disparity in their reflections. Whether they were British or American, worked for or alongside him, were career soldiers or government officials, all spoke of his character, towering presence, and, in the words of George Kennan, "monumental integrity."[23]

From the British side, Sir Alan Brooke, who battled him incessantly throughout the War, said his integrity was "extraordinary" and "one could trust him with anything."[24] Churchill's chief aide, General Hastings Ismay, said he was "first in stature among all the personalities of World War II, a completely selfless man and absolutely trustworthy." Churchill himself wrote that Marshall was the "noblest Roman of them all" and told Robert Lovett privately he was the single greatest figure produced by the War.[25]

From his American contemporaries, all acknowledged Marshall's integrity but also spoke about his presence. "Whether he opened his mouth or not," wrote Bob Lovett, people were aware it.[26] Dean Acheson called it a "striking and communicated force" felt as soon as he walked into a room.[27] John McCloy commented he never saw a conference Marshall couldn't dominate by his presence alone. McCloy explained this was usually because he chose not to. Marshall listened more than most people, according to

McCloy, but if he saw something "going off track," he could step in, even in the presence of Roosevelt and Churchill, and take over the room.[28] There was a reason George Marshall was the only general in the world Winston Churchill ever feared; quiet integrity, when combined with logical arguments, could be greatly intimidating.

These qualities, coupled with his strong work ethic, intelligence, and serious manner, gave Marshall the power to persuade. General Henry Arnold once told a subordinate, "If George Marshall ever took a position contrary to mine, I would know I was wrong."[29] General Maxwell Taylor, who served as chief of staff after the war, wrote of Marshall, "One could never imagine questioning the accuracy of his facts or challenging the soundness of his conclusions on any subject he undertook to discuss."[30] Whether it was military officers, cabinet members, world leaders, congressmen, journalists, or the general public, Marshall's judgment was simply trusted.

Leaders can have integrity, character, and an intimidating presence but still suffer from want of decisiveness. This was not the case with George Marshall. Throughout his long career, he regularly preached to subordinates that they should "not fight problems but decide them." Believing a bad decision was better than no decision, Marshall moved constantly forward during his military career acting on the facts available to him at the time. He carried this quality into his postmilitary career as well. In his memoirs, Dean Acheson described the first meeting he had with Marshall after the general was sworn in as secretary of state. After reviewing with Acheson several problems around the world, Marshall asked if there were any matters needing a decision. Acheson replied that for more than six months the State Department had been internally torn apart about whether it should move to a new building or not. After hearing a brief description from Acheson of the reasons for and against a move, Marshall simply said, "Move," and orders were immediately issued.[31]

Some might suggest that Marshall's decision-making capabilities, along with other qualities he possessed, were largely a result of having been in the Army for most of his life. While it is true Marshall was the product of the U.S. military establishment, he greatly impressed his civilian colleagues by the "unmilitary" way he sought solutions. Although Marshall reorganized the State Department to more closely resemble how the Army was structured, Dean Acheson wrote that there was "hardly a less military mind than his" when it came to his thought process and approach to solutions.[32]

Stimson and Marshall Together

It was not the original intention for this book to be written as a dual biography; the concept was to focus solely on the five years Stimson and Marshall worked together side by side during the Second World War. But throughout the lengthy research process, it became apparent to the author how consequential their individual backgrounds were to understanding the basis for their triumphant wartime alliance. Although one could imagine this would normally be the case with any successful partnership, there was something more deeply compelling about the radically different roads each of these two men took during their life, and the synergetic benefits unleashed when they joined together as a team during the summer of 1940.

Despite the vast contrast in the education and training of Henry Stimson and George Marshall, each stop on their individual career paths seems in retrospect to have been predestined to prepare them for the joint role they would inherit together in running the Army during World War II: Manhattan and Uniontown; Yale and the Virginia Military Institute; Harvard Law School and Fort Leavenworth; Winthrop & Stimson and Chaumont; the State Department and Fort Benning. Only when one considers each man's history can one see in almost every phase of it useful lessons they collectively drew upon when they combined their individual talents and unmatched integrity to prepare the nation for war and then lead it to victory.

On the subject of greatness, Dwight Eisenhower once said George Marshall possessed "more of the qualities" of it than any other American he met in his life, with Henry Stimson a close second.[33] The two men certainly did great things individually, but it was the genuine greatness of their partnership that helped save the world.

NOTES

INTRODUCTION

1. Winston S. Churchill, *The Hinge of Fate* (Boston: Houghton Mifflin, 1950), 387.
2. Larry I. Bland, ed., *The Papers of George C. Marshall, Volume 5: The Finest Soldier*, Sharon R. Ritenour, asst. ed., May 8, 1945, 171.
3. Forrest Pogue Interview with John Martyn, George Marshall Research Library, Lexington, VA, May 21, 1959.
4. Walter Isaacson and Evan Thomas made a compelling case for Stimson's mentor, Elihu Root, being the first "wise man" in their 1986 book, *The Wise Men*. While Stimson modeled his private and public career after Root, he had the advantage over his mentor in receiving an earlier and greater exposure to international issues during his legal career by virtue of the increasingly global nature of business and law during his years of practice.
5. *Time*, March 29, 1948; Forrest Pogue Interview with Robert Lovett, George Marshall Research Library, Lexington, VA, June 28–29, 1973.
6. Andrew Roberts, *Masters and Commanders: How Four Titans Won the War in the West, 1941–1945* (New York: Harper, 2009), 80.
7. *Time*, December 23, 1946.
8. Kai Bird, *The Color of Truth: McGeorge Bundy and William Bundy* (New York: Simon & Schuster, 1998), 23.
9. C. H. Cramer, *Newton D. Baker* (Cleveland: The World Publishing Company, 1961), 274.
10. Elting E. Morison, *Turmoil and Tradition: A Study of the Life and Times of Henry L. Stimson* (History Book Club by arrangement with Houghton Mifflin Company, 2003), 560.
11. Forrest Pogue Interview with Robert Lovett, George Marshall Research Library, Lexington, VA, October 14, 1957.
12. It is no coincidence that Washington happened to be one of Marshall's personal heroes, the other being Robert E. Lee. At his home in Leesburg, Virginia, he had portraits of both men prominently on display.
13. Stephen E. Ambrose, *Eisenhower the President* (New York: Simon & Schuster, 1984), 223.

CHAPTER 1: The Education of a Wall Street Lawyer

1. Henry L. Stimson and McGeorge Bundy, *On Active Service in Peace and War* (New York: Harper & Brothers, 1947), xii.
2. In 1941, a British doctor visiting Stimson to discuss issues related to wartime medicine told Stimson that he was well acquainted with his father's books.

3. Woodley Mansion today is part of the Maret School, a private school less than a half mile east of the National Cathedral. Phillips Academy sold the property to the school in 1950.

4. *The Phillipian*, February 24, 1961.

5. Stimson and Bundy, *Active Service*, xiv.

6. Elting E. Morison, *Turmoil and Tradition: A Study of the Life and Times of Henry L. Stimson* (History Book Club by arrangement with Houghton Mifflin Company, 2003), 26.

7. Ibid.

8. Ibid., 27.

9. Ibid.

10. Ibid., 43.

11. In the spring of 1887, Stimson won the Junior Exhibition Prize, sufficiently important to be covered by the *New York Times* (*New York Times*, April 1, 1887). One of his fellow competitors was Irving Fisher, who later achieved fame as an economist.

12. Morison, *Turmoil and Tradition*, 34.

13. *Boston Daily Globe*, February 15, 1887.

14. Ibid., 41.

15. In 2001, the firm became part of Pillsbury, Winthrop, Shaw, Pittman after a merger.

CHAPTER 2: Uniontown, Pennsylvania, to the U.S. Army

1. Forrest C. Pogue, *George Marshall: Education of a General, 1880–1939* (New York: The Viking Press, 1963), 41.

2. William Frye, *Marshall: Citizen Soldier* (Indianapolis: Bobbs-Merrill Co., Inc., 1947), 24.

3. Auguste Levasseur, *Lafayette in America in 1824 and 1825*, Alan Hoffman, trans. (Manchester, NH: Lafayette Press, Inc., 2006), 455.

4. Larry I. Bland, ed., *George C. Marshall, Interviews and Reminiscences for Forrest C. Pogue*, 3rd edition, Joellen K. Bland, asst. ed. (Lexinton, VA: George C. Marshall Foundation, 1996), 86.

5. Ibid., 40.

6. Ibid.

7. Frye, *Marshall*, 50.

8. Larry I. Bland, ed., *The Papers of George C. Marshall, Volume 1: The Soldierly Spirit, December 1880–June 1939*, Sharon R. Ritenour, asst. ed. (Baltimore and London: The Johns Hopkins University Press, 1981), 8; Pogue, *George Marshall: Education of a General, 1880–1939*, 53.

9. Robert L. Beisner, *Dean Acheson: A Life in the Cold War* (New York: Oxford University Press, 2006), 50.

10. Forrest C. Pogue, *George Marshall: Organizer of Victory, 1943–1945* (New York: The Viking Press, 1973), 325.

11. Pogue, *George Marshall: Education of a General, 1880–1939*, 63.

12. Ibid., 85.

CHAPTER 3: Wall Street Lawyer to Public Servant

1. Elting E. Morison, *Turmoil and Tradition: A Study of the Life and Times of Henry L. Stimson* (History Book Club by arrangement with Houghton Mifflin Company, 2003), 47.

2. Ibid., 83.

3. Ibid., 96.

4. Henry L. Stimson and McGeorge Bundy, *On Active Service in Peace and War* (New York: Harper & Brothers, 1947), 7.

5. Ibid., 8.

6. Morison, *Turmoil and Tradition*, 104.

7. In a letter to his wife during World War I, Stimson wrote that he would not make a good staff officer because he had long trained himself "to throw details onto others and keep my mind clear for the big decision" (*Henry L. Stimson Diary*, March 31, 1918). He maintained this style of leadership for his entire career in the law and in public service.

8. Morison, *Turmoil and Tradition*, 132.

9. *Henry Lewis Stimson Diaries*, microfilm ed., Manuscripts and Archives (New Haven, CT: Yale University Library, January 7, 1909), accounted by Stimson years after the event.

10. Morison, *Turmoil and Tradition*, 144.

11. Stimson and Bundy, *Active Service*, 22.

CHAPTER 4: The Making of an Army Legend

1. Forrest Pogue Interview with Dwight Eisenhower, George Marshall Research Library, Lexington, VA, June 28, 1962.

2. Forrest Pogue Interview with George C. Marshall, April 4, 1957; Larry I. Bland, ed., *George C. Marshall Interviews and Reminiscences for Forrest C. Pogue*, 3rd edition, Joellen K. Bland, asst. ed. (Lexington, VA: George C. Marshall Foundation, 1996), 160.

3. George C. Marshall letter to Colonel Bernard Lentz, October 2, 1935; Larry I. Bland, ed., *The Papers of George C. Marshall, Volume 1: The Soldierly Spirit, December 1880–June 1939*, Sharon R. Ritenour, asst. ed. (Baltimore and London: The Johns Hopkins University Press, 1981), 45.

4. Forrest Pogue Interview with George C. Marshall, April 4, 1957; Bland and Bland, eds., *Marshall Interviews for Pogue*, 157.

5. Ed Cray, *General of the Army: George C. Marshall, Soldier and Statesman* (New York: W. W. Norton & Co., 1990), 41.

6. Pogue Interview with Marshall, April 4, 1957; Bland and Bland, eds., *Marshall Interviews for Pogue*, 173.

7. William Frye, *Marshall: Citizen Soldier* (Indianapolis: Bobbs-Merrill Co., Inc., 1947), 110; Dik Alan Daso, *Hap Arnold and the Evolution of American Airpower* (n.p.: Smithsonian Institution Press, 2000), 77.

8. Larry I. Bland, ed., *The Papers of George C. Marshall, Volume 4: Aggressive and Determined Leadership, June 1, 1943–December 31, 1944*, Sharon R. Ritenour, asst. ed. (Baltimore and London: The Johns Hopkins University Press, 1996), 173.

9. Frye, *Marshall*, 119.

10. Ibid., 127.

11. Pogue Interview with Marshall, April 5, 1957; Bland and Bland, eds., *Marshall Interviews for Pogue*, 196–198; Forrest C. Pogue, *George Marshall: Education of a General, 1880–1939* (New York: The Viking Press, 1963), 152–153.

12. In June he wrote to the adjutant general requesting to be assigned to troops. Explaining that he had been in a staff position for more than three years, Marshall wrote that he "was tired from the incessant strain of office work" (Bland and Ritenour, eds., *The Papers of George C. Marshall, Volume 1*, 144).

CHAPTER 5: Secretary of War to Colonel in the Artillery

1. Henry L. Stimson and McGeorge Bundy, *On Active Service in Peace and War* (New York: Harper & Brothers, 1947), 35.
2. *Congressional Record*, Sixty-Third Congress, Third Session, 493.
3. Louis Smith, *American Democracy and Military Power: A Study of Civil Control of the Military Power in the United States* (Chicago: The University of Chicago Press, 1951), 19.
4. Merrill D. Peterson, *The Great Triumvirate: Webster, Clay, and Calhoun* (New York and Oxford: Oxford University Press, 1987), 87–88.
5. Irving H. Bartlett, *John Calhoun: A Biography* (New York: W. W. Norton & Co., 1993), 92.
6. Fletcher Pratt, *Stanton: Lincoln's Secretary of War* (New York: W. W. Norton & Co., 1953), 164.
7. Smith, *American Democracy*, 119; Philip C. Jessup, *Elihu Root, Volume 1: 1845–1909* (Hamdon, CT: Archon Books, 1964), 240.
8. Jessup, *Elihu Root, Volume 1*, 240.
9. Ibid., 215.
10. It took over three years before he accomplished the goal through the passage of the General Staff Act in 1903. During those years, Root succeeded in winning small battles that slowly chipped away at the existing structure until the time was right to make the big changes.
11. Townsend Hoopes and Douglas Brinkley, *Driven Patriot: The Life and Times of James Forrestal* (New York: Alfred A. Knopf, 1992), 137, 170.
12. Keith E. Eiler, *Mobilizing America: Robert P. Patterson and the War Effort, 1940–1945* (Ithaca: Cornell University Press, 1997), 209.
13. Elting E. Morison, *Turmoil and Tradition: A Study of the Life and Times of Henry L. Stimson* (History Book Club by arrangement with Houghton Mifflin Company, 2003), 152.
14. Jack McCallum, *Leonard Wood: Rough Rider, Surgeon, Architect of American Imperialism* (New York: New York University Press, 2006), 253–256; Morison, *Turmoil and Tradition*, 156.
15. Forrest C. Pogue, *George Marshall: Education of a General, 1880–1939* (New York: The Viking Press, 1963), 112.
16. Donald Rumsfeld later served twice as secretary of defense (the position created after World War II that combined the offices of the war and navy secretaries), the first time under Gerald Ford and the second time under George W. Bush.
17. Stimson recorded in his diary that Roosevelt indicated to him over lunch one day that the seeds of trouble between the two men were planted as far back as the summer of 1908, when Roosevelt sensed a hint of ingratitude from Taft despite everything he had done to get him elected.
18. *Henry L. Stimson Diary*, Reel 1, 125.
19. Stimson and Bundy, *Active Service*, 51.
20. Morison, *Turmoil and Tradition*, 91.
21. Ibid., 206.
22. Cited from an *Andover Bulletin* provided by Paige Roberts, the archivist at Phillips Academy.
23. Morison, *Turmoil and Tradition*, 212.
24. Ibid., 213.
25. *Henry L. Stimson Diary*, January 23, 1918.
26. *Henry L. Stimson Diary*, March 24, 1918.
27. Marshall thoughtfully turned him down, explaining that if he became an aide yet again, the Army would see him as an aide and "never a commander" (Larry

I. Bland, ed., *The Papers of George C. Marshall, Volume 1: The Soldierly Spirit, December 1880–June 1939*, Sharon R. Ritenour, asst. ed. [Baltimore and London: The Johns Hopkins University Press, 1981], 322).

28. *Henry L. Stimson Diary*, Reel 1, V76.

CHAPTER 6: The Slow Climb

1. Larry I. Bland, ed., *The Papers of George C. Marshall, Volume 1: The Soldierly Spirit, December 1880–June 1939*, Sharon R. Ritenour, asst. ed. (Baltimore and London: John Hopkins University Press, 1981), 351.

2. Larry I. Bland, ed., *The Papers of George C. Marshall, Volume 4: Aggressive and Determined Leadership, June 1, 1943–December 31, 1944*, Sharon R. Ritenour, asst. ed. (Baltimore and London: The Johns Hopkins University Press, 1996), 175.

3. Bland and Ritenour, eds., *The Papers of George C. Marshall, Volume 1*, 705.

4. An excellent source for information on Fort Benning and Marshall's time there can be found in Peggy Stelpflug and Richard Hyatt, *Home of the Infantry: The History of Fort Benning* (Macon, GA: Mercer University Press, 2007). It has been relied on heavily for this section.

5. George C. Marshall, letter to Pershing, October 14, 1927; Bland and Ritenour, eds., *The Papers of George C. Marshall, Volume 1*, 315.

6. Bland and Ritenour, eds., *The Papers of George C. Marshall, Volume 1*, 415.

7. Eric Larrabee, *Commander in Chief: Franklin Delano Roosevelt, His Lieutenants and Their War* (New York: Harper & Row, 1987), 111.

8. George C. Marshall, letter to Pershing, January 30, 1925; Bland and Ritenour, eds., *The Papers of George C. Marshall, Volume 1*, 273.

9. In 1920, Marshall wrote an essay for the *Infantry Journal* warning officers that the U.S. Army had no experience fighting the first phase of a modern war and should not therefore rely on conclusions drawn from World War I; Bland and Ritenour, eds., *The Papers of George C. Marshall, Volume 1*, 205.

10. Forrest C. Pogue, *George Marshall: Education of a General, 1880–1939* (New York: The Viking Press, 1963), 256.

11. Ibid., 255.

12. Katherine Tupper Marshall, *Together* (Chicago: Peoples Book Club, 1946), 3.

13. Ibid., 6.

14. George C. Marshall, letter to Major General George Moseley; Bland and Ritenour, eds., *The Papers of George C. Marshall, Volume 1*, 423.

15. Katherine Tupper Marshall, *Together*, 13.

16. Bland and Ritenour, eds., *The Papers of George C. Marshall, Volume 1*, 446.

17. Ibid., 468.

18. Ibid., 513.

19. George C. Marshall memorandum to the General George Grunert, December 5, 1938; Bland and Ritenour, eds., *The Papers of George C. Marshall, Volume 1*, 659.

20. Katherine Tupper Marshall, *Together*, 24.

21. Felix Frankfurter credited Edwin "Pa" Watson, another top aide and close friend of the president, with being the major influence on FDR's decision. Throughout his career, FDR famously kept his decision-making close to his chest, which led many to believe that they were responsible for some decision of his or another; Forrest Pogue interview of Felix Frankfurter, February 20, 1958.

22. A Survey of the Army Program Since July 1939. Statement by George Marshall to the Senate Special Committee Investigating the National Defense Program, April

22, 1941; Major H. A. DeWeerd, *Selected Speeches and Statements of General of the Army George C. Marshall, Chief of Staff, United States Army* (Washington: The Infantry Journal, 1945), 101.

23. Forrest C. Pogue, *General George C. Marshall: Ordeal and Hope, 1939–1942* (New York: The Viking Press, 1965), 5.

24. Later that month, Marshall asked General Pershing to send a letter to FDR making a few of the same arguments as they related to the need for armament. Marshall took the liberty of drafting the letter (George C. Marshall, letter to Pershing, November 23, 1938; Bland and Ritenour, eds., *The Papers of George C. Marshall, Volume 1,* 654).

25. George C. Marshall, address at Brunswick, Maryland, November 6, 1938; Bland and Ritenour, eds., *The Papers of George C. Marshall, Volume 1,* 644–648.

26. George C. Marshall, address to the American Legion Convention, Milwaukee, Wisconsin, September 15, 1941; DeWeerd, *Selected Speeches and Statements,* 168.

27. Statements on the Purposes and Advantages of Army Maneuvers before the House of Representatives Subcommittee, Committee on Appropriations, 76th Congress, 3rd Session, November 30, 1939; Larry I. Bland, ed., *The Papers of George C. Marshall, Volume 2: We Cannot Delay, July 1, 1939–December 6, 1941,* Sharon R. Ritenour, asst. ed.; Clarence E. Wunderlin Jr., asst. ed. (Baltimore and London: The Johns Hopkins University Press, 1986), 644–648.

28. *Franklin D. Roosevelt Day by Day,* a project at the Pare Lorentz Center at the FDR Presidential Library that provides FDR's daily appointment calendar.

CHAPTER 7: Wise Man

1. *Time,* July 1, 1940.

2. Elting E. Morison, *Turmoil and Tradition: A Study of the Life and Times of Henry L. Stimson* (History Book Club by arrangement with Houghton Mifflin Company, 2003), 268.

3. Loomis continued to successfully manage Stimson's assets for many years, pulling him out of the markets before the 1929 crash and persuading him to remain in cash even when Stimson believed it was time to reinvest; *Henry L. Stimson Diary,* November 2, 1931, December 29, 1932.

4. *Henry L. Stimson Diary,* April 26, 1926.

5. Henry L. Stimson and McGeorge Bundy, *On Active Service in Peace and War* (New York: Harper & Brothers, 1947), 117.

6. Larry I. Bland, ed., *The Papers of George C. Marshall, Volume 1: The Soldierly Spirit, December 1880–June 1939,* Sharon R. Ritenour, asst. ed. (Baltimore and London: The Johns Hopkins University Press, 1981), 322.

7. Morison, *Turmoil and Tradition,* 289.

8. Stimson and Bundy, *Active Service,* 156.

9. Ibid., 162, 196.

10. Ibid., June 1, 1931.

11. Although Woodrow Wilson was against an excessively high number, he believed it was a European problem that should be sorted out by Europeans; August Heckscher, *Woodrow Wilson, A Biography* (New York: Charles Scribner's Sons, 1991), 560.

12. Stimson and Bundy, December 16, 1931. Stimson attached to his entry a thirteen-page letter he wrote to the chairman of the House Ways and Means Committee that provided an excellent summary of the crisis and the justification for Hoover's actions.

13. William Starr Myers and Walter H. Newton, *The Hoover Administration: A Documented Narrative* (New York: Charles Scribner's Sons, 1936), 101.

14. *Henry L. Stimson Diary,* November 7, 1931.

15. Ibid., January 2, 1932, January 3, 1932.

16. The *New York Times* commented two days after the letter was delivered that Stimson was "laying down doctrines" (*New York Times,* January 9, 1932).

17. Stimson and Bundy, *Active Service,* 277.

18. *New York Times,* October 19, 1932.

19. *Henry L. Stimson Diary,* December 22, 1932, December 23, 1932, January 1, 1933, January 4, 1933.

20. Ibid., January 9, 1933, January 10, 1933.

21. During one of these meetings, FDR commented to Stimson, "We are getting so that we do pretty good teamwork" (Ibid., January 19, 1933).

22. Ibid., November 9, 1932.

23. The Woodley Mansion still stands today. In his will, Stimson bequeathed the house and property to Phillips Academy. Phillips Academy, in turn, sold it to the Maret School, which has preserved the mansion and still owns much of the land that surrounded it at the time of Stimson's death.

24. Stimson and Bundy, *Active Service,* 156.

25. *Henry L. Stimson Diary,* May 17, 1934.

26. Godfrey Hodgson, *The Colonel: The Life and Wars of Henry Stimson, 1867–1950* (New York: Knopf, 1990), 216.

27. *Henry L. Stimson Diary,* June 25, 1940.

28. *New York Times,* June 21, 1940. Chairman John Hamilton said that Stimson and Knox "are no longer qualified to speak as Republicans or for the Republican organization."

29. Woodring was certain that Marshall had something to do with his departure when, in fact, Marshall was not even consulted.

30. Larry I. Bland, ed., *The Papers of George C. Marshall, Volume 2: We Cannot Delay, July 1, 1939–December 6, 1941,* Sharon R. Ritenour, asst. ed., Clarence E. Wunderlin Jr., asst. ed. (Baltimore and London: The Johns Hopkins University Press, 1986), 252.

31. Ibid.

CHAPTER 8: Together in Washington

1. Forrest Pogue Interview with George C. Marshall, February 11, 1957; Bland and Bland, eds., *Marshall Interviews for Pogue,* 420.

2. Forrest Pogue Interview with Robert Lovett, August 28 and 29, 1973.

3. Frank Freidel, *Franklin D. Roosevelt: A Rendezvous with Destiny* (Boston: Little, Brown & Company, 1990), 125.

4. *Henry L. Stimson Diary,* February 18, 1916.

5. Ibid., April 22, 1941, May 24, 1941.

6. Ibid., November 14, 1941.

7. Jonathan W. Jordan, *American Warlords: How Roosevelt's High Command Led America to Victory in World War II* (New York: Penguin Group, 2015), 19.

8. George C. Marshall, letter to Brigadier General Asa L. Singleton, November 22, 1939; Larry I. Bland, ed., *The Papers of George C. Marshall, Volume 2: We Cannot Delay, July 1, 1939–December 6, 1941,* Sharon R. Ritenour, asst. ed., Clarence E. Wunderlin Jr., asst. ed. (Baltimore and London: The Johns Hopkins University Press, 1986), 108.

9. *Henry L. Stimson Diary,* November 7, 1940, January 8, 1941, November 7, 1941, November 12, 1941.

10. Ibid., April 2, 1941, September 17, 1941.

11. Forrest C. Pogue, *General George C. Marshall: Ordeal and Hope, 1939–1942* (New York: The Viking Press, 1965), 21.

12. Elting E. Morison, *Turmoil and Tradition: A Study of the Life and Times of Henry L. Stimson* (History Book Club by arrangement with Houghton Mifflin Company, 2003), 490.

13. *Franklin D. Roosevelt Day by Day*, a project at the Pare Lorentz Center at the FDR Presidential Library that provides FDR's daily appointment calendar.

14. *Henry L. Stimson Diary*, July 23, 1940, July 29, 1940. Apparently, the air-conditioning unit was a pain to install, but when it was completed, he could get the rooms cold "whenever we want it."

15. It was well known around Washington that when Knox or his assistant secretary of the navy, James Forrestal, wanted information that was not available to them, Forrestal would have lunch with Stimson aide John McCloy, who had the reputation as the most informed man working in the Pentagon.

16. *Henry L. Stimson Diary*, May 27, 1941.

17. John Morton Blum, ed., *From the Morgenthau Diaries: Years of Urgency, 1938–1941* (Boston: Houghton Mifflin Co., 1959), 166.

18. Author's (Edward Farley Aldrich) interview of Robert Morgenthau, March 27, 2014.

19. Larry I. Bland, ed., *The Papers of George C. Marshall, Volume 5: The Finest Soldier, January 1, 1945–January 7, 1947*, Sharon R. Ritenour, asst. ed. (Baltimore and London: The Johns Hopkins University Press, 2003), 434.

20. *New York Times*, January 30, 1946.

21. Kenneth S. Davis, *FDR: The War President, 1940–1943* (New York: Random House, 2000), 101.

22. Pogue, *Ordeal and Hope*, 131.

23. C. H. Cramer, *Newton D. Baker* (Cleveland: The World Publishing Company, 1961), 169.

24. Forrest Pogue Interview with Harvey Bundy, October 7, 1959.

25. *Henry L. Stimson Diary*, November 22, 1932.

26. Forrest Pogue Interview with Robert Lovett, August 28 and 29, 1973.

27. J. Garry Clifford, ed., *The World War I Memories of Robert D. Patterson: A Captain in the Great War* (Knoxville: The University of Tennessee Press, 2012), 40–44.

28. Edward S. Greenbaum, *A Lawyer's Job: In Court—In the Army—In the Office* (New York: Harcourt, Brace & World, Inc., 1967), 128.

29. Author's (Edward Farley Aldrich) Interview with Robert Patterson Jr., March 4, 2014.

30. Keith E. Eiler, *Mobilizing America: Robert P. Patterson and the War Effort, 1940–1945* (Ithaca: Cornell University Press, 1997), 282.

31. For this section, I have relied almost exclusively on Kai Bird's excellent biography of John McCloy, *The Chairman: John McCloy, The Making of the American Establishment* (New York: Simon & Schuster, 1992).

32. Stimson tried to get the State Department to hire McCloy during the summer of 1940, but when they took no action, he brought him into the War Department. By the fall, Stimson knew McCloy would be a huge asset to his department.

33. *Henry L. Stimson Diary*, January 13, 1943.

34. Author's (Edward Farley Aldrich) Interview with Robert Morgenthau, March 27, 2014.

35. Walter Isaacson and Evan Thomas, *The Wise Men: Six Friends and the World They Made* (New York: Simon & Schuster, 1986), 112.
36. Ibid., 192.
37. Kai Bird, *The Color of Truth: McGeorge Bundy and William Bundy* (New York: Simon & Schuster, 1998), 83.
38. Ibid., 25.
39. McGeorge Bundy coauthored Stimson's memoirs after World War II, spending nearly two years living on the ground of Highhold and working daily with the former secretary of war.
40. Larry I. Bland, ed., *The Papers of George C. Marshall, Volume 1: The Soldierly Spirit, December 1880–June 1939*, Sharon R. Ritenour, asst. ed. (Baltimore and London: The Johns Hopkins University Press, 1981), 202.
41. Thomas E. Ricks, *The Generals* (New York: The Penguin Press, 2012), 25.
42. The others were Marshall, MacArthur, Eisenhower, and Arnold from the Army, and Leahy, King, Nimitz, and Halsey from the Navy.
43. Alan Axelrod, *Bradley* (New York: St. Martin's Griffin, 2008), 66.
44. Omar Bradley, *A Soldier's Story by Omar Bradley* (New York: Henry Holt and Co., Inc., 1951), 20.
45. Andrew Roberts, *Masters and Commanders: How Four Titans Won the War in the West, 1941–1945* (New York: Harper, 2009), 29.
46. Forrest Pogue Interview with George C. Marshall, December 7, 1956; Larry I. Bland, ed., *George C. Marshall Interviews and Reminiscences, for Forrest C. Pogue*, 3rd ed., Joellen K. Bland, asst. ed. (Lexington, VA: George C. Marshall Foundation, 1996), 267.
47. Less favorable opinions of Baker's performance were from civil leaders (including those industrial leaders who were tasked with bringing efficiency to the Army and to general procurement efforts). Some historians have suggested that the military loved Baker because he largely left them alone during the War.
48. Forrest Pogue Interview with George C. Marshall, December 7, 1956; Bland and Bland, eds., *Marshall Interviews and Reminiscences for Pogue*, 269.
49. Cramer, *Newton D. Baker*, 98.
50. Ibid., 96.
51. Pogue, *Ordeal and Hope*, 16.

CHAPTER 9: Playing Catch-up

1. George C. Marshall, letter to Mrs. John Singer, July 23, 1940; Larry I. Bland, ed., *The Papers of George C. Marshall, Volume 2: We Cannot Delay, July 1, 1939–December 6, 1941*, Sharon R. Ritenour, asst. ed., Clarence E. Wunderlin Jr., asst. ed. (Baltimore and London: The Johns Hopkins University Press, 1986), 275.
2. *Henry L. Stimson Diary*, August 26, 1940.
3. C. H. Cramer, *Newton D. Baker* (Cleveland: The World Publishing Company, 1961), 274.
4. In 1931, Stimson added lighting to the court so that he could play during those months when it got dark early (*Henry L. Stimson Diary*, November 30, 1931).
5. *Henry L. Stimson Diary*, May 10, 1943.
6. He consulted Felix Frankfurter and another lawyer, each of whom told him that while the *Time* story was libelous, it was not worth his time pursuing it.
7. George C. Marshall, letter to FDR, July 17, 1940; Bland, Ritenour, Wunderlin Jr., eds., *Marshall Papers, Volume 2*, 268.

8. George C. Marshall, letter to Matthew Ridgway, August 24, 1936; George C. Marshall, letter to Matthew Ridgway, August 24, 1936; Larry I. Bland, ed., *The Papers of George C. Marshall, Volume 1: The Soldierly Spirit, December 1880–June 1939*, Sharon R. Ritenour, asst. ed. (Baltimore and London: The Johns Hopkins University Press, 1981), 505.

9. George C. Marshall, letter to Mrs. John J. Singer, July 23, 1940; Bland, Ritenour, Wunderlin Jr., eds., *Marshall Papers, Volume 2*, 275; George C. Marshall, letter, to Admiral Harold Stark, June 18, 1942; Larry I. Bland, ed., *The Papers of George C. Marshall, Volume 3: The Right Man for the Job, December 7, 1941–May 31, 1943*, Sharon R. Ritenour, asst. ed. (Baltimore and London: The Johns Hopkins University Press, 1991), 240.

10. Katherine Tupper Marshall, *Together* (Chicago: People's Book Club, 1946), 67.

11. George C. Marshall, letter to John Pershing, June 15, 1942; Bland and Ritenour, eds., *Marshall Papers, Volume 3*, 238.

12. Forrest Pogue Interview with George C. Marshall, February 14, 1957; Larry I. Bland, ed., *George C. Marshall Interviews and Reminiscences for Forrest C. Pogue*, 3rd ed., Joellen K. Bland, asst. ed. (Lexington, VA: George C. Marshall Foundation, 1996), 450.

13. *Henry L. Stimson Diary*, October 10, 1940.

14. In 1997, Keith Eiler wrote *Mobilizing America, Robert P. Patterson and the War Effort, 1940–1945* (Ithaca: Cornell University Press, 1997). It is an exceptional book, and I have borrowed heavily from his efforts to write this section.

15. Ibid., 117.

16. *Henry L. Stimson Diary*, July 24, 1940. Stimson hints in his diary that he was already on top of this general issue after two gentlemen came calling on him to press upon him the seriousness of the problems.

17. Eiler, *Mobilizing America*, 115.

18. *Henry L. Stimson Diary*, July 22, 1941.

19. Ibid., February 14, 1941.

20. David Kaiser, *No End Save Victory: How FDR Led the Nation into War* (New York: Basic Books, 2014), 99.

21. Eiler, *Mobilizing America*, 44.

22. Stimson referred to DuPont as an example of a company that required a significant push when gunpowder was in such short supply during the summer of 1940.

23. *Henry L. Stimson Diary*, August 26, 1940.

24. Like Stimson, Patterson liked to hire the best and the brightest, and he brought five members of the Harvard Law Review to Washington to work on contracts for him (Eiler, *Mobilizing America*, 50).

25. Ibid., 164.

26. *Henry L. Stimson Diary*, October 17, 1940.

27. Ibid., April 3, 1941.

28. Eiler, *Mobilizing America*, 200.

29. Andrew Roberts, *Masters and Commanders: How Four Titans Won the War in the West, 1941–1945* (New York: Harper, 2009), 28.

30. Statement before the Senate Committee on Military Affairs, July 12, 1940; Major H. A. DeWeerd, ed., *Selected Speeches and Statements of the General of the Army George C. Marshall, Chief of Staff, United States Army* (Washington: The Infantry Journal, 1945), 60–65.

31. Henry L. Stimson and McGeorge Bundy, *On Active Service in Peace and War* (New York: Harper & Brothers, 1947), 346.

32. *Henry L. Stimson Diary*, September 27, 1940.

33. Ibid., February 14, 1932.

34. Godfrey Hodgson, *The Colonel: The Life and Wars of Henry Stimson, 1867–1950* (New York: Knopf, 1990), 51.

35. Author's (Edward Farley Aldrich) Interview with Robert Patterson Jr., March 4, 2014.

36. Marshall's Statement before the Senate Special Committee investigating the National Defense Program, April 22, 1941; DeWeerd, *Selected Speeches and Statements*, 101.

37. *Henry L. Stimson Diary*, July 8, 1941.

38. Ibid., July 11, 1941.

39. Martin Gilbert, *Winston S. Churchill: Volume VI, Finest Hour* (Boston: Houghton Mifflin Co.,. 1983), 996.

40. Even years after the War ended, Marshall was extremely reluctant to express opinions about the political matters related to the War. Through a series of interviews with Forrest Pogue, he generally refused to comment on them.

41. Forrest Pogue Interview of George C. Marshall, January 22, 1957; Bland and Bland, eds., *Marshall Interviews and Reminiscences for Pogue*, 303.

42. Stimson's first mention in his diary about requests from Stalin's government was on July 21, 1941.

43. *Henry L. Stimson Diary*, July 21, 1941.

44. Forrest Pogue Interview of George C. Marshall, January 22, 1957; Bland and Bland, eds., *Marshall Interviews and Reminiscences for Pogue*, 302.

CHAPTER 10: Running Out of Time

1. Major H. A. DeWeerd, ed., *Selected Speeches and Statements of General of the Army George C. Marshall, Chief of Staff, United States Army* (Washington: The Infantry Journal, 1945), 119.

2. Ibid., 169.

3. Benjamin Fletcher Wright, ed., *The Federalist: The Famous Papers on the Principles of American Government, Alexander Hamilton, James Madison, John Joy* (n.p.: Barnes and Noble Books in arrangement with the Harvard University Press, 1996), 212.

4. Address before the Joint Meeting of the American Military Institute and the American Historical Association, December 28, 1939; DeWeerd, ed., *Selected Speeches and Statements*, 35–39.

5. During World War I, Stimson grew tired of "kow-towing to regulars," believing that for the most part they lacked the "natural capacity" that some of the "citizen soldiers" subordinate to them had (*Henry L. Stimson Diary*, June 13, 1918).

6. Marshall claimed after the War that it was the first subject Stimson brought up at their first meeting together in Long Island after Stimson was appointed secretary of war; Larry I. Bland, ed., *The Papers of George C. Marshall, Volume 2: We Cannot Delay, July 1, 1939–December 6, 1941*, Sharon R. Ritenour, asst. ed., Clarence E. Wunderlin Jr., asst. ed. (Baltimore and London: The Johns Hopkins University Press, 1986), 265; Forrest Pogue Interview with George C. Marshall, January 22, 1957.

7. *Henry L. Stimson Diary*, August 8, 1940.

8. Statement before the House Committee on Military Affairs, April 9, 1940; DeWeerd, ed., *Selected Speeches and Statements*, 44–48.

9. Forrest Pogue Interview with George C. Marshall, January 22, 1957; Larry I. Bland, ed., *George C. Marshall Interviews and Reminiscences for Forrest C. Pogue*, 3rd ed., Joellen K. Bland, asst. ed. (Lexington, VA: George C. Marshall Foundation, 1996), 300.

10. Interestingly, when it came to training pilots, the positions taken by both the Army and the War Department switched. Major General Hap Arnold, whom Marshall put in charge of the Army Air Corps, insisted that his flyers have at least two years of college before learning to fly. Bob Patterson, seeing that such a requirement was limiting the ability to fill the ranks, wished to relax the standard. Eventually, the standards were loosened, but the Army always insisted that education be a determinate in selecting officers for the Army Corps. Stimson backed General Arnold and Marshall on this.

11. Forrest C. Pogue, *General George C. Marshall: Ordeal and Hope, 1939–1942* (New York: The Viking Press, 1965), 106.

12. DeWeerd, ed., *Selected Speeches and Statements*, 96.

13. *Henry L. Stimson Diary*, March 11, 1941.

14. DeWeerd, ed., *Selected Speeches and Statements*, 122.

15. Eric Larrabee, *Commander in Chief: Franklin Delano Roosevelt, His Lieutenants and Their War* (New York: Harper & Row, 1987), 143.

16. *Henry L. Stimson Diary*, March 11, 1941.

17. Pogue, *Ordeal and Hope*, 116.

18. *Henry L. Stimson Diary*, September 15, 1941.

19. Ibid., November 5, 1941.

20. Ibid., April 25, 1941.

21. Marshall did not think the fall of Britain would be quite as disastrous for the United States as Stimson believed.

22. *Henry L. Stimson Diary*, December 19, 1940.

23. Ibid., December 29, 1940.

24. Ibid., April 17, 1941.

25. Ibid., June 6, 1941.

26. Henry L. Stimson, letter to FDR, June 23, 1941; *Henry L. Stimson Diary*, June 23, 1941.

27. *Henry L. Stimson Diary*, July 2, 1941, July 4, 1941.

28. Ibid., August 29, 1941.

29. Ibid., July 22, 1941.

30. The Soviets refused to allow U.S. mechanics into the country given Stalin's obsession with secrecy.

31. *Henry L. Stimson Diary*, October 21, 1941, September 23, 1941.

32. Ibid., October 13, 1941.

33. Ibid., November 28, 1941.

34. Ibid., December 7, 1941.

CHAPTER 11: Pearl Harbor and the First Ten Weeks

1. Mark Perry, *Partners in Command: George Marshall and Dwight Eisenhower in War and Peace* (New York: The Penguin Press, 2007), 55.

2. Katherine Tupper Marshall, *Together* (Chicago: Peoples Book Club, 1946), 99.

3. *Henry L. Stimson Diary*, March 2, 1932.

4. By Sunday morning, Washington time on December 7, intelligence gathered through intercepts from the Japanese pointed toward an attack likely happening at or just before 1:00 p.m. EST.

5. Forrest C. Pogue, *General George C. Marshall: Ordeal and Hope, 1939–1942* (New York: The Viking Press, 1965), 172.

6. George C. Marshall, letter to General Walter Short, February 7, 1941; Larry I. Bland, ed., *The Papers of George C. Marshall, Volume 2: We Cannot Delay, July 1, 1939–December 6, 1941*, Sharon R. Ritenour, asst. ed., Clarence E. Wunderlin Jr., asst. ed. (Baltimore and London: The Johns Hopkins University Press, 1986), 411–413.

7. Forrest Pogue Interview with Harvey Bundy, October 7, 1959 (to match October 7, 1959, given in the bib entry, p. 512; n. 24 on p. 490; n. 8 on p. 499; n. 7 on p. 509).

8. In maneuvers put on by the Navy in 1932 to test the defense of the fleet at Pearl Harbor against an air attack, the attack was successful.

9. *Henry L. Stimson Diary*, December 7, 1941.

10. Roosevelt did not think it was wise to publicize Stimson's lengthy retort during the War but allowed Stimson to issue an abbreviated statement.

11. Roosevelt read the first thirteen parts that evening (all of which rejected the various Hull proposals). His gut feeling was that war was imminent, and he placed a call to Admiral Stark. When told Stark was at the theater, Roosevelt did not think it important enough to risk raising the alarm of others at the theater (Stark read the report later that night). The secretary of the navy also read the incomplete report that evening and tried to reach Stark but made no further attempt when he found he was not at home. Stimson did not see the message until the next day.

12. Many people, including the undersecretary of the navy, James Forrestal, could never understand why Marshall did not use the telephone that was available on his desk. His excuse was that he did not want to risk the Japanese intercepting the call, which might have jeopardized the secret that the United States had cracked their code. This excuse falls short for those, like Forrestal, who believed that the commercial telegraph he used was just as vulnerable.

13. *Henry L. Stimson Diary*, January 25, 1942.

14. Forrest Pogue Interview of Robert Lovett, October 14, 1957.

15. Henry L. Stimson, memorandum to George C. Marshall, December 9, 1941; *Henry L. Stimson Diary*, December 9, 1941.

16. Pogue, *Ordeal and Hope*, 247–248.

17. The "Europe First" strategy dated back to late 1940, when Admiral Stark's "Plan Dog" memo was generally accepted by the U.S. military as doctrine. The British and Americans also agreed to the concept at their first meeting in Placentia Bay the previous August.

18. Forrest Pogue Interview with John McCloy, March 31, 1959.

19. Forrest Pogue Interview with Lord Ismay, October 18, 1960.

20. Although Churchill was forty years old when the First World War started, more than 10 percent of his class at Harrow died during the conflict.

21. Forrest Pogue Interview with John McCloy, March 31, 1959.

22. Forrest Pogue Interview with Felix Frankfurter, February 20, 1958.

23. *Henry L. Stimson Diary*, December 25, 1945.

24. Alan Brooke officially took over the role of Chief of the Imperial General Staff during *Arcadia* but was absent from the Washington meetings. He was the member of Churchill's inner circle most hostile to the idea of having the meetings in Washington.

25. Winston S. Churchill, *Their Finest Hour* (Boston: Houghton Mifflin Co., 1949), 20.

26. *Henry L. Stimson Diary*, April 29, 1942.

27. Larry I. Bland, ed., *The Papers of George C. Marshall, Volume 1: The Soldierly Spirit, December 1880–June 1939*, Sharon R. Ritenour, asst. ed. (Baltimore and London: The Johns Hopkins University Press, 1981), 594.

28. Pogue, *Ordeal and Hope*, 270.
29. FDR was in awe of Marshall, having seen him in action over two years. Six months earlier, Harry Hopkins confided to Stimson how high an opinion FDR had of Marshall (*Henry L. Stimson Diary*, June 23, 1941).
30. Pogue, *Ordeal and Hope*, 279.
31. Forrest Pogue Interview with George C. Marshall, October 5, 1956; Larry I. Bland, ed., *George C. Marshall Interviews and Reminiscences for Forrest C. Pogue*, 3rd ed., Joellen K. Bland, asst. ed. (Lexington, VA: George C. Marshall Foundation, 1996), 595.
32. Pogue, *Ordeal and Hope*, 289–290.
33. Forrest Pogue Interview with Joseph McNarney, February 2, 1966.
34. Ibid.
35. *Henry L. Stimson Diary*, February 7, 1942.
36. Stimson learned from Marshall only three months later that he had felt demoted to some degree when Stimson removed the responsibility of command from the chief of staff position. Stimson felt badly, but he greatly admired the general for his honesty in telling him and his selflessness for agreeing to the changes made (*Henry L. Stimson Diary*, May 13, 1942).
37. This group was initially referred to as Service of Supply.
38. *Henry L. Stimson Diary*, February 27, 1942.
39. Steve Vogel, *The Pentagon: A History: The Untold Story of the Wartime Race to Build the Pentagon—and to Restore It Sixty Years Later* (New York: Random House, 2007), 253.
40. Ibid., 5.
41. Forrest Pogue Interview with George C. Marshall, February 11, 1957; Bland and Bland, eds., *Marshall Interviews and Reminiscences for Pogue*, 445.
42. Forrest Pogue Interview with George C. Marshall, February 14, 1957; Bland and Bland, eds., *Marshall Interviews and Reminiscences for Pogue*, 431.

CHAPTER 12: Japanese American Internment
1. For this section, I have relied heavily on the work of two excellent historians who covered the issue of Japanese American internment during the War extensively: Greg Robinson and Roger Daniels. Greg Robinson wrote *By Order of the President: FDR and the Internment of the Japanese Americans* (n.p., MA: Harvard University Press, 2001) and *A Tragedy of Democracy: Japanese Confinement in North America* (New York: Columbia University Press, 2009). Roger Daniels authored *The Decision to Relocate the Japanese Americans* (Malabar, FL: Robert E. Krieger Publishing Co., 1975).
2. On January 16, Stimson received a letter from California congressman Leland Ford requesting that Japanese Americans be moved to concentration camps away from the West Coast (*Henry L. Stimson Diary*, January 16, 1942).
3. Approximately 75 percent of the 115,000 resided in California. There were another 15,000 scattered throughout the United States.
4. Japanese submarines sank the merchant ships and engaged a few more off the West Coast in mid- to late December.
5. Roosevelt could have acted, but as an elected official with a fourth presidential campaign ahead of him, FDR was under the same wartime pressure as other politicians, and it would not have been out of character for him to avoid looking soft on the issue of Japanese Americans and national security.
6. Robinson, *By Order of the President*, 66.
7. Robinson, *A Tragedy of Democracy*, 102.

8. Daniels, *The Decision to Relocate the Japanese Americans*, 41.
9. Robinson, *By Order of the President*, 116.
10. The Japanese took Hong Kong in late December 1941, and Manila in early January 1942. When Stimson sat down with McCloy and FDR, the situation in Singapore was hopeless—it fell on February 15, 1942.

CHAPTER 13: Arguing Strategy with the British
1. Forrest Pogue Interview with Lord Ismay, October 18, 1960.
2. *Henry L. Stimson Diary*, March 8, 1942.
3. Forrest C. Pogue, *General George C. Marshall: Ordeal and Hope, 1939–1942* (New York: The Viking Press, 1965), 305.
4. Henry L. Stimson, letter to FDR, March 27, 1942; *Henry L. Stimson Diary*, March 27, 1942.
5. Pogue, *Ordeal and Hope*, 309.
6. Alex Danchev and Daniel Todman, eds., *War Diaries, 1939–1945: Field Marshall Lord Alanbrooke* (Berkeley and Los Angeles: University of California Press, 1957), 244.
7. Ibid., 149.
8. Ibid., 147.
9. Pogue, *Ordeal and Hope*, 319–320.
10. Winston S. Churchill, *The Hinge of Fate* (Boston: Houghton Mifflin Co., 1950), 139.
11. Radio from Henry L. Stimson to George C. Marshall, April 15, 1942; Larry I. Bland, ed., *The Papers of George C. Marshall, Volume 3: The Right Man for the Job, December 7, 1941–May 31, 1943*, Sharon R. Ritenour, asst. ed. (Baltimore and London: The Johns Hopkins University Press, 1991), 134.
12. *Henry L. Stimson Diary*, April 20, 1942.
13. Roosevelt had long expressed an interest in French North Africa. Stimson sometimes referred to the plan condescendingly as FDR's "baby."
14. *Henry L. Stimson Diary*, June 19, 1942.
15. Danchev and Todman, eds., *War Diaries*, 269.
16. *Henry L. Stimson Diary*, June 22, 1942.
17. Given Roosevelt's lifelong passion for the United States Navy, naval history, ships, and all things related to the sea, coupled with his past experience as the assistant secretary of the navy, the president tended to seek and take less advice from Secretary Knox and his top admirals than he did from Stimson and Marshall.
18. *Henry L. Stimson Diary*, July 10, 1942.
19. David L. Roll, *The Hopkins Touch: Harry Hopkins and the Forging of the Alliance to Defeat Hitler* (n.p.: Oxford University Press, 2013), 208.
20. George C. Marshall to FDR, July 10, 1942; Larry I. Bland, ed., *The Papers of George C. Marshall, Volume 3: The Right Man for the Job, December 7, 1941–May 31, 1943*, Sharon R. Ritenour, asst. ed. (Baltimore and London: The Johns Hopkins University Press, 1991), 271.
21. *Henry L. Stimson Diary*, July 15, 1942.
22. *Time*, July 13, 1942.
23. Roll, *The Hopkins Touch*, 213.
24. *Henry L. Stimson Diary*, August 8, 1942.
25. George C. Marshall radio to Dwight D. Eisenhower; Bland, Ritenour, eds., *Marshall Papers, Volume 3*, 274.

CHAPTER 14: Internal and External Struggles

1. George C. Marshall, letter to FDR, August 10, 1942; Larry I. Bland, ed., *The Papers of George C. Marshall, Volume 3: The Right Man for the Job, December 7, 1941–May 31, 1943*, Sharon R. Ritenour, asst. ed. (Baltimore and London: The Johns Hopkins University Press, 1991), 298.
2. George C. Marshall to Admiral Start, June 18, 1942; Brand, Ritenour, eds., *Marshall Papers, Volume 3*, 240.
3. Forrest Pogue Interview of George C. Marshall, October 5, 1956; Larry I. Bland, ed., *George C. Marshall Interviews and Reminiscences for Forrest C. Pogue*, 3rd ed., Joellen K. Bland, asst. ed. (Lexington, VA: George C. Marshall Foundation, 1996), 593.
4. Ibid., 434–436.
5. *Henry L. Stimson Diary*, August 2, 1943.
6. Forrest Pogue Interview with Felix Frankfurter, February 20, 1958.
7. The Navy split its command further into a South Pacific Theater led by Admiral Robert Ghormley, and a Central and North Pacific Theater led by Nimitz (the more senior of the two men).
8. While the Battle of the Coral Sea in May 1942 was a strategic victory for the Allies, it was considered a tactical victory for the Japanese Navy.
9. Forrest C. Pogue, *General George C. Marshall: Ordeal and Hope, 1939–1942* (New York: The Viking Press, 1965), 379.
10. George C. Marshall to Ernest J. King, June 29, 1942; Bland, Ritenour, eds., *Marshall Papers, Volume 3*, 254.
11. Pogue, *Ordeal and Hope*, 374.
12. Ibid., 389.
13. George C. Marshall to FDR, February 18, 1942; Bland, Ritenour, eds., *Marshall Papers, Volume 3*, 106.
14. *Henry L. Stimson Diary*, January 1, 1942.
15. George C. Marshall, letter to FDR, August 10, 1942; Bland, Ritenour, eds., *Marshall Papers, Volume 3*, 298.
16. *Henry L. Stimson Diary*, October 2, 1942.
17. *Time*, September 14, 1942.
18. Forrest Pogue Interview with Robert Lovett, August 28 and 29, 1973.
19. *Henry L. Stimson Diary*, December 11, 1942.
20. Jonathan W. Jordan, *American Warlords: How Roosevelt's High Command Led America to Victory in World War II* (New York: Penguin Group, 2015), 206.
21. Ibid., 218.
22. *Henry L. Stimson Diary*, January 7, 1943.
23. *Life*, December 21, 1942; Steve Vogel, *The Pentagon: A History: The Untold Story of the Wartime Race to Build the Pentagon—and to Restore It Sixty Years Later* (New York: Random House, 2007), 271.
24. Larry I. Bland, ed., *The Papers of George C. Marshall, Volume 4: Aggressive and Determined Leadership, June 1, 1943–December 31, 1944*, Sharon R. Ritenour, asst. ed. (Baltimore and London: The Johns Hopkins University Press, 1996), 173.
25. *Henry L. Stimson Diary*, September 9, 1942.

CHAPTER 15: The End of the Beginning

1. Larry I. Bland, ed., *George C. Marshall Interviews and Reminiscences for Forrest C. Pogue*, 3rd ed., Joellen K. Bland, asst. ed. (Lexington, VA: George C. Marshall Foundation, 1996), 622.

2. Jonathan W. Jordan, *American Warlords: How Roosevelt's High Command Led America to Victory in World War II* (New York: Penguin Group, 2015), 210.

3. Major H. A. DeWeerd, ed., *Selected Speeches and Statements of General of the Army George C. Marshall, Chief of Staff, United States Army* (Washington: The Infantry Journal, 1945), 219.

4. George C. Marshall, letter to Mrs. John Singer, February 1, 1943; Larry I. Bland, ed., *The Papers of George C. Marshall, Volume 3: The Right Man for the Job, December 7, 1941–May 31, 1943*, Sharon R. Ritenour, asst. ed. (Baltimore and London: The Johns Hopkins University Press, 1991), 257.

5. Carlo D'Este, *Patton: A Genius for War* (New York: Harper Collins, 1995), 377–378.

6. Ibid., 130; *Henry L. Stimson Diary*, January 15, 1931.

7. *Henry L. Stimson Diary*, January 13, 1943.

8. Forrest Pogue Interview with Harvey Bundy, October 7, 1959.

9. *Henry L. Stimson Diary*, March 23, 1942, April 1, 1942.

10. For my description of Loomis, I relied heavily on Tuxedo Park, Jennet Conant's fantastic biography of Loomes published in 2003.

11. Ibid., December 31, 1943.

12. It took another four months before the Army and Navy finally came to an agreement on how the two services would work together utilizing the strategy Stimson had worked so hard to adopt.

13. *Henry L. Stimson Diary*, February 8 and 9, 1943.

14. Ibid., June 3, 1944.

15. Ibid., January 23, 1943, March 28, 1943.

16. Ibid., November 12, 1943.

17. Forrest Pogue Interview with George C. Marshall, October 5, 1956; Bland and Bland, eds., *Marshall Interviews and Reminiscences for Pogue*, 588.

18. Andrew Roberts, *Masters and Commanders: How Four Titans Won the War in the West, 1941–1945* (New York: Harper, 2009), 291.

19. Forrest C. Pogue, *George Marshall: Organizer of Victory, 1943–1945* (New York: The Viking Press, 1973), 202.

20. Today the dairy farm is part of the Stone Barn Center for Food and Agriculture and home to Blue Hill at Stone Barns, one of the top restaurants in the world and a leader in the farm-to-table movement.

21. Pogue, *Organizer of Victory*, 202–204.

22. Alex Danchev and Daniel Todman, eds., *War Diaries, 1939–1943: Field Marshal Lord Alanbrooke* (Berkeley and Los Angeles: University of California Press, 1957), 407.

23. Roberts, *Masters and Commanders*, 359; Winston S. Churchill, *The Hinge of Fate* (Boston: Houghton Mifflin Company, 1950), 808.

24. *Henry L. Stimson Diary*, May 19, 1943, May 25, 1943.

CHAPTER 16: Turning the Corner

1. *Henry L. Stimson Diary*, August 10, 1943.

2. Ibid., June 8, 1943.

3. George C. Marshall Memo to FDR, June 21, 1943; Larry I. Bland, ed., *The Papers of George C. Marshall, Volume 4: Aggressive and Determined Leadership, June 1, 1943–December 31, 1944*, Sharon R. Ritenour, asst. ed. (Baltimore and London: The Johns Hopkins University Press, 1996), 257.

4. *Henry L. Stimson Diary*, June 18, 1943.

5. Winston S. Churchill, *The Hinge of Fate* (Boston: Houghton Mifflin Co., 1950), 825.

6. Ibid., 813.
7. Forrest C. Pogue, *George Marshall: Organizer of Victory, 1943–1945* (New York: The Viking Press, 1973), 218–219.
8. Ibid., 223.
9. *Henry L. Stimson Diary*, August 4, 1943.
10. Harry C. Butcher, *My Three Years with Eisenhower* (New York: Simon & Schuster, 1946), 373.
11. Alex Danchev and Daniel Todman, eds., *War Diaries, 1939–1945: Field Marshal Lord Alanbrooke* (Berkeley and Los Angeles: University of California Press, 1957), entry dated August 12, 1943, 440.
12. Pogue, *Organizer of Victory*, 245.
13. Stimson was not the only one from the High Command who expressed this fear to Roosevelt. Admiral King and General Arnold both lobbied against the appointment, recognizing how difficult it would be for anyone to replace Marshall in Washington.
14. Winston S. Churchill, *Closing the Ring* (Boston: Houghton Mifflin Co., 1951), 85.
15. Pogue, *Organizer of Victory*, 262.
16. Ibid., 272.
17. *Henry L. Stimson Diary*, December 16, 1943.
18. Pogue, *Organizer of Victory*, 300.
19. Bland, Ritenour, eds., *Marshall Papers, Volume 4*, 187.
20. Churchill, *Closing the Ring*, 346.
21. Pogue, *Organizer of Victory*, 307.
22. Forrest Pogue Interview with Lovett, October 14, 1957.
23. Pogue, *Organizer of Victory*, 308.
24. Forrest Pogue Interview with George C. Marshall, November 15, 1956; Larry I. Bland, ed., *George C. Marshall Interviews and Reminiscences for Forrest C. Pogue*, 3rd ed., Joellen K. Bland, asst. ed. (Lexington, VA: George C. Marshall Foundation, 1996), 344.
25. *Henry L. Stimson Diary*, December 18, 1943.
26. Forrest Pogue Interview with Lovett, October 14, 1957.
27. *Henry L. Stimson Diary*, December 3, 1943.
28. Ibid., December 17, 1943.
29. Ibid., June 22, 1944.

CHAPTER 17: Preparing for D-Day

1. Forrest Pogue Interview of George C. Marshall, February 11, 1957; Larry I. Bland, ed., *George C. Marshall Interviews and Reminiscences for Forrest C. Pogue*, 3rd ed., Joellen K. Bland, asst. ed. (Lexington, VA: George C. Marshall Foundation, 1996), 416.
2. Ibid., 199.
3. *Time*, January 3, 1944.
4. Forrest Pogue Interview of George C. Marshall, November 19, 1956; Bland and Bland, eds., *Marshall Interviews and Reminiscences for Pogue*, 545–546.
5. Larry I. Bland, ed., *The Papers of George C. Marshall, Volume 4: Aggressive and Determined Leadership, June 1, 1943–December 31, 1944*, Sharon R. Ritenour, asst. ed. (Baltimore and London: The Johns Hopkins University Press, 1996), 45.
6. George C. Marshall to Eisenhower, February 7, 1944; Bland, Ritenour, eds., *Marshall Papers, Volume 4*, 272.
7. *Henry L. Stimson Diary*, February 28, 1944.
8. Ibid., April 12, 1944.
9. Bland, Ritenour, eds., *Marshall Papers, Volume 4*, 416.

10. *Henry L. Stimson Diary*, April 24, 1944.

11. Forrest C. Pogue, *George Marshall: Organizer of Victory, 1943–1945* (New York: The Viking Press, 1973), 353–354.

12. *Henry L. Stimson Diary*, May 11, 1944.

13. Ibid., September 17, 1942.

14. George Marshall, memorandum to Henry L. Stimson, May 16, 1944; Bland, Ritenour, eds., *Marshall Papers, Volume 4*, 447–450.

15. Eric Larrabee, *Commander in Chief: Franklin Delano Roosevelt, His Lieutenants and Their War* (New York: Harper & Row, 1987), 145.

16. George Marshall, memorandum to Henry L. Stimson, May 16, 1944; Bland, Ritenour, eds., *Marshall Papers, Volume 4*, 447–450.

17. Omar Bradley, *A Soldier's Story by Omar Bradley* (New York: Henry Holt and Co., Inc., 1951), 444.

18. Forrest Pogue Interview of George C. Marshall, October 4, 1956; Bland and Bland, eds., *Marshall Interviews and Reminiscences for Pogue*, 599.

19. Bland, Ritenour, eds., *Marshall Papers, Volume 4*, 622.

20. Pogue, *Organizer of Victory*, 389.

CHAPTER 18: Race to Berlin

1. Forrest C. Pogue, *George Marshall: Organizer of Victory, 1943–1945* (New York: The Viking Press, 1973), 395.

2. Omar Bradley, *A Soldier's Story by Omar Bradley* (New York: Henry Holt and Co., Inc., 1951), 289–291.

3. Alex Danchev and Daniel Todman, eds., *War Diaries, 1939–1945: Field Marshall Lord Alanbrooke* (Berkeley and Los Angeles: University of California Press, 1957), 554.

4. Andrew Roberts, *Masters and Commanders: How Four Titans Won the War in the West, 1941–1945* (New York: Harper, 2009), 487.

5. Stock footage of Stimson taken when these artillery rounds were being fired can be assessed at criticalpast.com.

6. Ted Roosevelt Jr. happened to be a good friend of George Marshall's going back to the First World War. When Eisenhower proposed posthumously awarding Roosevelt a Distinguished Service Cross, both Marshall and Stimson overruled him and awarded him the Medal of Honor instead.

7. Dwight D. Eisenhower, *Crusade in Europe: A Personal Account of World War II* (New York: Doubleday & Co., 1948), 218.

8. Pogue, *Organizer of Victory*, 399.

9. Forrest Pogue Interview of George C. Marshall, October 29, 1956; Larry I. Bland, ed., *George C. Marshall Interviews and Reminiscences for Forrest C. Pogue*, 3rd ed., Joellen K. Bland, asst. ed. (Lexington, VA: George C. Marshall Foundation, 1996), 613.

10. George C. Marshall, letter to Mrs. John J. Singer, August 17, 1944; Larry I. Bland, ed., *The Papers of George C. Marshall, Volume 4: Aggressive and Determined Leadership, June 1, 1943–December 31, 1944*, Sharon R. Ritenour, asst. ed. (Baltimore and London: The Johns Hopkins University Press, 1996), 549.

11. *Henry L. Stimson Diary*, August 23, 1944.

12. Ibid., June 2, 1942.

13. Ibid., August 21, 1944, August 25, 1944.

14. David L. Roll, *The Hopkins Touch: Harry Hopkins and the Forging of the Alliance to Defeat Hitler* (n.p.: Oxford University Press, 2013), 345.

15. *Henry L. Stimson Diary*, September 27, 1944, October 3, 1944.

16. Ibid., September 8, 1943, November 22, 1944.
17. When researching the topic of aid to Germany prior to his famous Harvard speech in the spring of 1947, Marshall—recalling Stimson's efforts three years earlier—asked for a copy of Stimson's memorandum to FDR on the subject and shared it with Dean Acheson, the undersecretary of state and one of the Marshall Plan's most staunch supporters.
18. *Henry L. Stimson Diary*, September 7, 1944.
19. Roberts, *Masters and Commanders*, 515.
20. Forrest Pogue Interview with George C. Marshall, February 11, 1957; Bland and Bland, eds., *Marshall Interviews and Reminiscences for Pogue*, 409–411. Marshall goes into greater detail on this in his February 11, 1957, interview with Pogue.
21. George C. Marshall, letter to Thomas Dewey, September 25, 1944; Bland, Ritenour, eds., *Marshall Papers, Volume 4*, 605.
22. George C. Marshall, letter to Thomas Dewey, September 27, 1944; Bland, Ritenour, eds., *Marshall Papers, Volume 4*, 607.
23. Richard Norton Smith, *Thomas E. Dewey and His Times* (New York: Simon & Schuster, 1982), 425–430.
24. Viscount Montgomery of Alamein, *The Memoirs of Field-Marshall Montgomery* (n.p.: Pen & Sword Books Ltd., 2005), 254.
25. Katherine Tupper Marshall, *Together* (Chicago: Peoples Book Club, 1946), 214.
26. *Henry L. Stimson Diary*, November 17, 1944.
27. Dill's is one of only two equestrian monuments at Arlington National Cemetery (the other one being of Civil War hero General Philip Kearny).
28. *Henry L. Stimson Diary*, December 18, 1944.
29. Bradley, *A Soldier's Story*, 472.
30. Pogue, *Organizer of Victory*, 489.
31. *Henry L. Stimson Diary*, January 15, 1945.
32. Keith E. Eiler, *Mobilizing America: Robert P. Patterson and the War Effort, 1940–1945* (Ithaca: Cornell University Press, 1997), 467.
33. Stimson, still worried about manpower issues, raised the issue with Marshall again in early January. In a heated discussion, an impatient Marshall insisted to the secretary of war again that the country had enough men to finish the job.

CHAPTER 19: Defeat of Germany

1. Larry I. Bland, ed., *The Papers of George C. Marshall, Volume 5: The Finest Soldier, June 1, 1945–January 7, 1947*, Sharon R. Ritenour, asst. ed. (Baltimore and London: The Johns Hopkins University Press, 2003), 169.
2. *Henry L. Stimson Diary*, November 17, 1944.
3. Ibid., November 11, 1944.
4. Ibid., December 12, 1944.
5. Forrest Pogue Interview of Robert Lovett, October 14, 1957.
6. *Henry L. Stimson Diary*, November 10, 1944.
7. Ibid., May 17, 1944.
8. Ibid., January 9, 1945.
9. Omar Bradley, *A Soldier's Story by Omar Bradley* (New York: Henry Holt and Co., Inc., 1951), 483–489.
10. Mark Perry, *Partners in Command: George Marshall and Dwight Eisenhower in War and Peace* (New York: The Penguin Press, 2007), 352.

11. Alex Danchev and Daniel Todman, eds., *War Diaries, 1939–1945: Field Marshall Lord Alanbrooke* (Berkeley and Los Angeles: University of California Press, 1957), 19, 638, 653, 669.

12. Forrest Pogue Interview of George C. Marshall, February 4, 1957; Larry I. Bland, ed., *George C. Marshall Interviews and Reminiscences for Forrest C. Pogue,* 3rd ed., Joellen K. Bland, asst. ed. (Lexington, VA: George C. Marshall Foundation, 1996), 403.

13. Forrest C. Pogue, *George Marshall: Organizer of Victory, 1943–1945* (New York: The Viking Press, 1973), 523–535.

14. Perry, *Partners in Command,* 355.

15. Jonathan W. Jordan, *American Warlords: How Roosevelt's High Command Led America to Victory in World War II* (New York: Penguin Group, 2015), 433.

16. *Henry L. Stimson Diary,* March 17, 1945.

17. David McCullough, *Truman* (New York: Simon & Schuster, 1992), 348.

18. Harry S. Truman, *Memoirs by Harry S. Truman, Volume 1: Year of Decisions* (New York: Doubleday, 1955), 10; *Henry L. Stimson Diary,* April 12, 1945.

19. McCullough, *Truman,* 289; *Henry L. Stimson Diary,* March 13, 1944.

20. *Henry L. Stimson Diary,* April 13, 1945.

21. Bland and Ritenour, eds., *Marshall Papers, Volume 5,* 161, 163; E. B. Potter, *Bull Halsey* (n.p., MD: Naval Institute Press, 1985), 378–379.

22. *Henry L. Stimson Diary,* May 8, 1945.

23. McCullough, *Truman,* 278.

24. *Henry L. Stimson Diary,* February 14, 1944, February 18, 1944, June 9, 1944, June 10, 1944.

25. McCullough, *Truman,* 348.

26. *Henry L. Stimson Diary,* October 14, 1944.

27. General Groves told Stimson and Marshall in December 1944 that the first bomb would likely be ready by August 1, 1945.

28. George C. Marshall, radio to Eisenhower, May 16, 1945; Bland and Ritenour, eds., *Marshall Papers, Volume 5,* 192.

CHAPTER 20: Victory over Japan

1. Forrest Pogue Interview with George C. Marshall, February 11, 1957; Larry I. Bland, ed., *George C. Marshall Interviews and Reminiscences for Forrest C. Pogue,* 3rd ed., Joellen K. Bland, asst. ed. (Lexington, VA: George C. Marshall Foundation, 1996), 424–425.

2. David McCullough, *Truman* (New York: Simon & Schuster, 1992), 401.

3. Larry I. Bland, ed., *The Papers of George C. Marshall, Volume 5: The Finest Soldier, January 1, 1945–January 7, 1947,* Sharon R. Ritenour, asst. ed. (Baltimore and London: The Johns Hopkins University Press, 2003), 232; Gar Alperovitz, *The Decision to Use the Atomic Bomb and the Architecture of an American Myth* (New York: Alfred A. Knopf, 1995), 520; McCullough, *Truman,* 400.

4. Richard B. Frank, *Downfall: The End of the Imperial Japanese Empire* (New York: Random House, 1999), 35.

5. Henry L. Stimson and McGeorge Bundy, *On Active Service in Peace and War* (New York: Harper & Brothers, 1947), 628.

6. *Henry L. Stimson Diary,* January 22, 1945.

7. Kai Bird, *The Chairman: John McCloy, The Making of the American Establishment* (New York: Simon & Schuster, 1992), 246–247.

8. Frank, *Downfall,* 123.

9. *Henry L. Stimson Diary,* July 2, 1945.

10. Ibid., May 3, 1945.
11. McCullough, *Truman*, 404.
12. Harry S. Truman, *Memoirs by Harry S. Truman, Volume 1: Year of Decisions* (New York: Doubleday, 1955), 87.
13. *Henry L. Stimson Diary*, July 16, 1945.
14. Richard Rhodes, *The Making of the Atomic Bomb* (New York: Simon & Schuster, 1986), 686.
15. Alperovitz, *The Decision to Use the Atomic Bomb*, 241.
16. The other principal recommendation concerned the future of atomic energy and whether it should be shared with the rest of the world and controlled through an international organization.
17. Rhodes, *The Making of the Atomic Bomb*, 627.
18. Sean L. Malloy, *Atomic Tragedy: Henry L. Stimson and the Decision to Use the Bomb against Japan* (Ithaca: Cornell University Press, 2008), 114–115.
19. Warren Kozak, *Lemay: The Life and Times of General Curtis Lemay* (Washington, DC: Regnery Publishing, Inc., 2009), 225.
20. *Henry L. Stimson Diary*, May 16, 1945.
21. McCullough, *Truman*, 442.
22. Frank, *Downfall*, 238–239.
23. Ibid., 41.
24. *Harper's*, February 1947, 106.
25. Frank, *Downfall*, 143–146.
26. Ibid., 188.
27. Stimson was correct. Even after the news of Nagasaki was confirmed, Japanese leaders could not agree to surrender after eight hours of meetings. It was only after they took the unprecedented step of having the emperor voice his opinion that they accepted the Potsdam Proclamation. Even then, they added the condition that the emperor would remain on the throne.

EPILOGUE

1. August 21, 1945, letter to the headmaster of Phillips Academy, reprinted in the *Andover Bulletin*. Made available by Paige Roberts, director of archives and special collections for the school.
2. George C. Marshall, letter to Harry S. Truman, August 20, 1945; Larry I. Bland, ed., *The Papers of George C. Marshall, Volume 5: The Finest Soldier, January 1, 1945–January 7, 1947*, Sharon R. Ritenour, asst. ed. (Baltimore and London: The Johns Hopkins University Press, 2003), 281–282.
3. Although Truman had still not responded to Marshall three weeks after receiving the letter, the chief of staff was carefully planning his transition with Eisenhower; George C. Marshall, letter to Eisenhower, September 4, 1945; Bland and Ritenour, eds., *Marshall Papers, Volume 5*, 293.
4. Bland and Ritenour, eds., *Marshall Papers, Volume 5*, 288.
5. Ibid., 307.
6. *New York Times*, September 21, 1945.
7. Forrest Pogue Interview with Harvey Bundy, October 7, 1959.
8. Jean Edwards, *Lucious Clay, An American Life* (n.p.: Henry Holt & Co., Inc., 1990), 197.
9. Larry I. Bland, ed., *George C. Marshall Interviews and Reminiscences for Forrest C. Pogue*, 3rd ed., Joellen K. Bland, asst. ed. (Lexington, VA: George C. Marshall Foundation, 1996), 622.

10. Sean L. Malloy, *Atomic Tragedy: Henry L. Stimson and the Decision to Use the Atomic Bomb against Japan* (Ithaca: Cornell University Press, 2008), 3.

11. *Henry L. Stimson Diary*, September 21, 1945.

12. Katherine Tupper Marshall, *Together* (Chicago: Peoples Book Club, 1946), 259–260.

13. Forrest Pogue Interview of Robert Lovett, October 14, 1957.

14. Bland and Ritenour, eds., *Marshall Papers, Volume 5*, 723.

15. Godfrey Hodgson, *The Colonel: The Life and Wars of Henry Stimson, 1867–1950* (New York: Knopf, 1990), 4.

16. Former President Hoover, in an official statement on Stimson's death, spoke of his courage given that to his knowledge, Stimson had a heart ailment that needed attending as far back as 1930; *New York Times*, October 22, 1950.

17. *Andover Bulletin* made available to the author by Paige Roberts, director of archives and special collections at Phillips Academy in Andover.

18. If it were not for Mabel's poor health, Stimson would have been honored with a state funeral. Her preference was to have it held at Highhold.

19. Kai Bird, *The Color of Truth: McGeorge Bundy and William Bundy* (New York: Simon & Schuster, 1998), 23.

20. Gerald M. Pops, *Ethical Leadership in Turbulent Times: Modeling the Public Career of George C. Marshall* (n.p.: Lexington Books, 2009), 73.

21. Forrest C. Pogue, *General Marshall: Statesman, 1945–1959* (New York: The Viking Press, 1987), 491.

22. George C. Marshall, memorandum to Colonel George, March 27, 1956. On display at the Marshall Museum in Lexington, Virginia.

23. Pops, *Ethical Leadership*, 67.

24. Andrew Roberts, *Masters and Commanders: How Four Titans Won the War in the West, 1941–1945* (New York: Harper, 2009), 390.

25. Forrest Pogue Interview of Robert Lovett, October 14, 1957.

26. Pogue, *General Marshall: Statesman*, 514.

27. Dean Acheson, *Present at the Creation: My Year in the State Department* (New York: W. W. Norton & Co., 1969), 140.

28. Forrest Pogue Interview of John McCloy, March 31, 1959.

29. Eric Larrabee, *Commander in Chief: Franklin Delano Roosevelt, His Lieutenant and Their War* (New York: Harper & Row, 1987), 254.

30. Pops, *Ethical Leadership*, 69.

31. Acheson, *Present at the Creation*, 214.

32. Pogue, *General Marshall: Statesman*, 148.

33. Stephen E. Ambrose, *Eisenhower the President* (New York: Simon & Schuster, 1984), 222–223.

GENERAL SOURCES

SELECTED BIBLIOGRAPHY

Acheson, Dean. *Present at the Creation: My Years in the State Department.* New York: W. W. Norton & Co., 1969.

Alperovitz, Gar. *The Decision to Use the Atomic Bomb and the Architecture of an American Myth.* New York: Alfred A. Knopf, 1995.

Ambrose, Stephen E. *Eisenhower the President.* New York: Simon & Schuster, 1984.

Ambrose, Stephen E. *Eisenhower: Soldier, General of the Army, President-Elect.* New York: Simon & Schuster, 1983.

Ambrose, Stephen E. *The Victors: Eisenhower and His Boys: The Men of World War II.* New York: Simon & Schuster, 1998.

Anderson, Judith Icke. *William Howard Taft: An Intimate History.* New York: W. W. Norton & Company, 1981.

Andrew, Christopher. *For the President's Eyes Only: Secret Intelligence and the American Presidency from Washington to Bush.* Harper Collins Publishers, 1995.

Axelrod, Alan. *Bradley.* New York: St. Martin's Griffin, 2008.

Bartlett, Irving H. *John Calhoun: A Biography.* New York: W. W. Norton & Co., 1993.

Beisner, Robert L. *Dean Acheson: A Life in the Cold War.* New York: Oxford University Press, 2006.

Beran, Michael Knox. *The Last Patrician: Bobby Kennedy and the End of the American Aristocracy.* New York: St. Martin's Press, 1998.

Bergamini, David. *Japan's Imperial Conspiracy: How Emperor Hirohito Led Japan into War against the West.* New York: William Morrow and Company, Inc., 1971.

Beschloss, Michael. *The Conquerors: Roosevelt, Truman and the Destruction of Hitler's Germany.* New York: Simon & Schuster, 2002.

Bird, Kai. *The Chairman: John McCloy, The Making of the American Establishment.* New York: Simon & Schuster, 1992.

Bird, Kai. *The Color of Truth: McGeorge Bundy and William Bundy.* New York: Simon & Schuster, 1998.

Black, Conrad. *Franklin Delano Roosevelt: Champion of Freedom.* New York: BBC Public Affairs, 2003.

Blum, John Morton, ed. *From the Morgenthau Diaries: Years of Urgency, 1938-1941.* Boston: Houghton Mifflin Company, 1959.

Bradley, Omar. *A Soldier's Story by Omar Bradley.* New York: Henry Holt and Company, Inc., 1951.

Butcher, Harry C. *My Three Years with Eisenhower.* New York: Simon & Schuster, 1946.

Calhoun, Mark T. *General Lesley J. McNair.* Kansas: University Press of Kansas, 2015.

Camp, Charles Wadsworth. *History of the 305th Field Artillery*. Garden City, NY: The Country Life Press, 1919.

Chase, James. *1912: Wilson, Roosevelt, Taft & Debs—The Election That Changed the Country*. New York: Simon & Schuster, 2004.

Churchill, Winston S. *Closing the Ring*. Boston: Houghton Mifflin Company, 1951.

Churchill, Winston S. *The Gathering Storm*. Boston: Houghton Mifflin Company, 1948.

Churchill, Winston S. *The Grand Alliance*. Boston: Houghton Mifflin Company, 1951.

Churchill, Winston S. *The Hinge of Fate*. Boston: Houghton Mifflin Company, 1950.

Churchill, Winston S. *Their Finest Hour*. Boston: Houghton Mifflin Company, 1949.

Churchill, Winston S. *Triumph and Tragedy*. Boston: Houghton Mifflin Company, 1953.

Clifford, J. Garry, ed. *The World War I Memories of Robert P. Patterson: A Captain in the Great War*. Knoxville: The University of Tennessee Press, 2012.

Conant, Jennet. *Tuxedo Park: A Wall Street Tycoon and the Secret Palace of Science That Changed the Course of World War II*. New York: Simon & Schuster, 2002.

Cooper, John Milton Jr. *Woodrow Wilson: A Biography*. New York: Alfred A. Knopf, 2009.

Cramer, C. H. *Newton D. Baker*. Cleveland: The World Publishing Company, 1961.

Cray, Ed. *General of the Army: George C. Marshall, Soldier and Statesmen*. New York: W. W. Norton & Co, 1990.

Danchev, Alex, and Daniel Todman, eds. *War Diaries, 1939-1945: Field Marshal Lord Alanbrooke*. Berkeley and Los Angeles: University of California Press, 1957.

Daniels, Josephus. *The Wilson Era: Years of Peace*. North Carolina: The University of North Carolina Press, 1944.

Daniels, Roger. *The Decision to Relocate the Japanese Americans*. Malabar, FL: Robert E. Krieger Publishing Company, 1975.

Daso, Dik Alan. *Hap Arnold and the Evolution of American Airpower*. Smithsonian Institution Press, 2000.

Davis, Kenneth S. *FDR: The War President, 1940-1943*. New York: Random House, 2000.

Davis, Richard G. *Carl A. Spaatz and the Air War in Europe*. Washington DC: Smithsonian Institution Press, 1992.

D'Este, Carlo. *Patton: A Genius for War*. New York: Harper Collins, 1995.

DeWeerd, Major H. A., ed. *Selected Speeches and Statements of General of the Army George C. Marshall, Chief of Staff, United States Army*. Washington: The Infantry Journal, 1945.

Dorwart, Jeffery M. *Eberstadt and Forrestal: A National Security Partnership, 1909-1949*. College Station: Texas A&M University Press, 1991.

Dower, John W. *War without Mercy: Race & Power in the Pacific War*. New York: Pantheon Books, 1986.

Dutton, David. *Anthony Eden: A Life and Reputation*. London: Arnold, 1997.

Edwards, Jean. *Lucious Clay, An American Life*. Henry Holt & Co., Inc., 1990.

Eiler, Keith E. *Mobilizing America: Robert P. Patterson and the War Effort, 1940-1945*. Ithaca: Cornell University Press, 1997.

Eisenhower, Dwight D. *Crusade in Europe: A Personal Account of World War II*. New York: Doubleday & Co., 1948.

Frank, Richard B. *Downfall: The End of the Imperial Japanese Empire*. New York: Random House, 1999.

Freidel, Frank. *Franklin D. Roosevelt: A Rendezvous with Destiny*. Boston: Little, Brown & Company, 1990.

Frye, William. *Marshall: Citizen Soldier*. Indianapolis: Bobbs-Merrill Co., Inc., 1947.

Gilbert, Martin. *Winston S. Churchill: Volume VI, Finest Hour*. Boston: Houghton Mifflin Company, 1983.

Gilbert, Martin. *Winston S. Churchill: Volume VII, Road to Victory*. Boston: Houghton Mifflin Company, 1986.

Goodwin, Doris Kearns. *No Ordinary Time: Franklin and Eleanor Roosevelt: The Home Front in World War II*. New York: Simon & Schuster, 1994.

Goodwin, Doris Kearns. *Team of Rivals: The Political Genius of Abraham Lincoln*. New York: Simon & Schuster, 2005.

Grant, James. *Bernard Baruch: The Adventures of a Wall Street Legend*. New York: John Wiley & Sons, 1975.

Greenbaum, Edward S. *A Lawyer's Job: In Court—In the Army—In the Office*. New York: Harcourt, Brace & World, Inc., 1967.

Halberstam, David. *The Best and The Brightest*. New York: Random House, 1969.

Hamilton, Nigel. *The Mantle of Command: FDR at War, 1941-1942*. New York: Houghton Mifflin Harcourt, 2014.

Heckscher, August. *Woodrow Wilson, A Biography*. New York: Charles Scribner's Sons, 1991.

Hewes, James E., Jr. *From Root to McNamara: Army Organization and Administration*. Washington, DC: Center of Military History, United States Army, 1974.

Hodgson, Godfrey. *The Colonel: The Life and Wars of Henry Stimson, 1867-1950*. New York: Knopf, 1990.

Hoopes, Townsend, and Douglas Brinkley. *Driven Patriot: The Life and Times of James Forrestal*. New York: Alfred A. Knopf, 1992.

Huston, James. *The Sinews of War: Army Logistics* 1775-1953. Washington, DC: Center of Military History, United States Army, 1997.

Isaacson, Walter, and Evan Thomas. *The Wise Men: Six Friends and the World They Made*. New York: Simon & Schuster, 1986.

Jackson, Julian. De Gaulle. Cambridge, MA: Harvard University Press, 2018.

Jessup, Philip C. *Elihu Root, Volume I, 1845-1909*. Hamdon, CT: Archon Books, 1964.

Jessup, Philip C. *Elihu Root, Volume II, 1905-1937*. Hamdon, CT: Archon Books, 1964.

Jordan, David M. *FDR, Dewey and the Election of 1944*. Indiana University Press, 2011.

Jordan, Jonathan W. *American Warlords: How Roosevelt's High Command Led America to Victory in World War II*. New York: Penguin Group, 2015.

Kabaservice, Geoffrey. *The Guardians: Kingman Brewster, His Circle, and the Rise of the Liberal Establishment*. New York: Henry Holt & Co., Inc., 2004.

Kaiser, David. *No End Save Victory: How FDR Led the Nation into War*. New York: Basic Books, 2014.

Kozak, Warren. *Lemay: The Life and Times of General Curtis Lemay*. Washington, DC: Regnery Publishing, Inc., 2009.

Lacouture, Jean. *DeGaulle: The Rebel 1890-1944*. New York: W. W. Norton & Co., 1990.

Larrabee, Eric. *Commander in Chief: Franklin Delano Roosevelt, His Lieutenants and Their War*. New York: Harper & Row, 1987.

Lerwill, Leonard L. *The Personnel Replacement System in the United States Army*. United States Army, 1954.

Levasseur, Auguste. *Lafayette in America in 1824 and 1825*. Translated by Alan Hoffman. Manchester, NH: Lafayette Press, Inc., 2006.

Lyons, Eugene. *Herbert Hoover*. Garden City, NY: Doubleday & Company, 1964.

Malloy, Sean L. *Atomic Tragedy: Henry L. Stimson and the Decision to Use the Bomb against Japan*. Ithaca: Cornell University Press, 2008.

Manchester, William. *American Caesar: Douglas MacArthur, 1880-1964*. Boston: Little, Brown & Company, 1978.

Marbury, William: *In the Catbird Seat*. Baltimore: The Maryland Historical Society, 1988.

Marshall, George C. *Memoirs of My Service in the World War, 1917-1918*. Boston: Houghton Mifflin Company, 1976.

Marshall, Katherine Tupper. *Together*. Chicago: Peoples Book Club, 1946.

McCallum, Jack. *Leonard Wood: Rough Rider, Surgeon, Architect of American Imperialism*. New York: New York University Press, 2006.

McCullough, David. *Truman*. New York: Simon & Schuster, 1992.

Meacham, Jon. *Franklin and Winston: An Intimate Portrait of an Epic Friendship*. New York: Random House, 2003.

Meiertöns, Heiko. *The Doctrines of US Security Policy: An Evaluation under International Law*. Cambridge: Cambridge University Press, 2010.

Millis, Walter, ed. *The Forrestal Diaries*. New York: The Viking Press, 1951.

Morison, Elting E. *Turmoil and Tradition: A Study of the Life and Times of Henry L. Stimson*. History Book Club by arrangement with Houghton Mifflin Company, 2003.

Morris, Edmund. *Colonel Roosevelt*. New York: Random House, 2010.

Myers, William Starr, and Walter H. Newton. *The Hoover Administration: A Documented Narrative*. New York: Charles Scribner's Sons, 1936.

Neal, Steve. *Harry & Ike: The Partnership That Remade the Postwar World*. New York: Scribner, 2001.

Nofi, Albert A., ed. *The War against Hitler: Military Strategy in the West*. New York: Hippocrene Books, 1982.

Patterson, James T. *Mr. Republican: A Biography of Robert A. Taft*. Boston: Houghton Mifflin Company, 1972.

Perry, Mark. *Partners in Command: George Marshall and Dwight Eisenhower in War and Peace*. New York: The Penguin Press, 2007.

Peterson, Merrill D. *The Great Triumvirate: Webster, Clay, and Calhoun*. New York and Oxford: Oxford University Press, 1987.

Plokhy, S. M. *Yalta: The Price of Peace*. New York: The Viking, 2010.

Pogue, Forrest C. *General George C. Marshall: Ordeal and Hope: 1939-1942*. New York: The Viking Press, 1965.

Pogue, Forrest C. *George Marshall: Education of a General, 1880-1939*. New York: The Viking Press, 1963.

Pogue, Forrest C. *George Marshall: Organizer of Victory, 1943-1945*. New York: The Viking Press, 1973.

Pogue, Forrest C. *George Marshall: Statesman, 1945-1959*. New York: The Viking Press, 1987.

Pops, Gerald M. *Ethical Leadership in Turbulent Times, Modeling the Public Career of George C. Marshall*. Lexington Books, 2009.

Potter, E. B. *Bull Halsey*. Maryland: Naval Institute Press, 1985.

Pratt, Fletcher. *Stanton: Lincoln's Secretary of War*. New York: W. W. Norton & Company, 1953.

Preston, Andrew. *The War Council: McGeorge Bundy, the NSC, and Vietnam*. Harvard University Press, 2006.

Rhodes, Richard. *The Making of the Atomic Bomb*. New York: Simon & Schuster, 1986.

Ricks, Thomas E. *The Generals*. New York: The Penguin Press, 2012.

Roberts, Andrew. *Masters and Commanders: How Four Titans Won the War in the West, 1941-1945*. New York: Harper, 2009.

Robertson, David. *Sly and Able: A Political Biography of James F. Byrnes*. New York: W. W. Norton & Co., 1984.

Robinson, Greg. *A Tragedy of Democracy: Japanese Confinement in North America*. New York: Columbia University Press, 2009.

Robinson, Greg. *By Order of the President: FDR and the Internment of Japanese Americans.* Massachusetts: Harvard University Press, 2001.

Roll, David L. *The Hopkins Touch: Harry Hopkins and the Forging of the Alliance to Defeat Hitler.* Oxford University Press, 2013.

Schmitz, David F. *Henry L. Stimson: The First Wise Man.* Wilmington, DE: SR Books, 2001.

Service, Robert. *Stalin: A Biography.* The Belknap Press of Harvard University Press, 2005.

Sherwood, Robert E. *Roosevelt and Hopkins, An Intimate History.* New York: Grosett & Dunlap, 1948.

Smith, Gene. *Until the Last Trumpet Sounds: The Life of General of the Armies John J. Pershing.* New York: John Wiley & Sons, 1998.

Smith, Louis. *American Democracy and Military Power: A Study of Civil Control of the Military Power in the United States.* Chicago: The University of Chicago Press, 1951.

Smith, Richard Norton. *Thomas E. Dewey and His Times.* New York: Simon & Schuster, 1982.

Stelpflug, Peggy, and Richard Hyatt. *Home of the Infantry: The History of Fort Benning.* Macon, GA: Mercer University Press, 2007.

Stimson, Henry L., and McGeorge Bundy. *On Active Service in Peace and War.* New York: Harper & Brothers, 1947.

Truman, Harry S. *Memoirs by Harry S. Truman, Volume 1, Years of Decision.* New York: Doubleday, 1955.

Truman, Harry S. *Memoirs by Harry S. Truman, Volume 2, Years of Trial and Hope.* New York: Doubleday, 1956.

Tuchman, Barbara W. *Stilwell and the American Experience in China, 1911-1945.* New York: The Macmillan Company, 1970.

Unger, Debi, and Irwin Unger, with Stanley Hirshson. *George Marshall: A Biography.* HarperCollins, 2014.

Viscount Montgomery of Alamein. *The Memoirs of Field-Marshal Montgomery.* Pen & Sword Books Ltd, 2005.

Vogel, Steve. *The Pentagon: A History: The Untold Story of the Wartime Race to Build the Pentagon—and to Restore It Sixty Years Later.* New York: Random House, 2007.

Weintraub, Stanley. *15 Stars: Eisenhower, MacArthur, Marshall, Three Generals Who Saved the American Century.* New York: Free Press, 2007.

Whitaker, Brigadier General Denis. *Dieppe: Tragedy to Triumph.* Toronto: McGraw-Hill Ryerson, 1992.

Wright, Benjamin Fletcher, ed. *The Federalist: The Famous Papers on the Principles of American Government, Alexander Hamilton, James Madison, John Jay.* Barnes and Nobles Books in arrangement with the Harvard University Press, 1996.

MANUSCRIPT COLLECTIONS

George C. Marshall Papers, Marshall Research Library, Lexington, Virginia.

Henry Lewis Stimson Papers, Manuscripts and Archives, Yale University Library, New Haven, Connecticut.

Henry Lewis Stimson Diaries, Microfilm edition. Manuscripts and Archives, Yale University Library, New Haven, Connecticut.

Larry I. Bland, Editor, Sharon R. Ritenour, Assistant Editor. *The Papers of George C. Marshall, Volume 1: The Soldierly Spirit, December 1880–June 1939.* Baltimore and London: The Johns Hopkins University Press, 1981.

Larry I. Bland, Editor, Sharon R. Ritenour, Assistant Editor; Clarence E. Wunderlin, Jr., Assistant Editor. *The Papers of George C. Marshall, Volume 2: We Cannot Delay, July 1, 1939–December 6, 1941.* Baltimore and London: The Johns Hopkins University Press, 1986.

Larry I. Bland, Editor; Sharon R. Ritenour, Associate Editor. *The Papers of George C. Marshall, Volume 3: The Right Man for the Job, December 7, 1941–May 31, 1943.* Baltimore and London: The Johns Hopkins University Press, 1991.

Larry I. Bland, Editor: Sharon R. Ritenour, Associate Editor. *The Papers of George C. Marshall, Volume 4: Aggressive and Determined Leadership, June 1, 1943–December 31, 1944.* Baltimore and London: The Johns Hopkins University Press, 1996.

Larry I. Bland, Editor; Sharon R. Ritenour, Associate Editor. *The Papers of George C. Marshall, Volume 5: The Finest Soldier, January 1, 1945–January 7, 1947.* Baltimore and London: The Johns Hopkins University Press, 2003.

NEWSPAPERS AND MAGAZINES
Boston Daily Globe
Chicago Tribune
Harper's Magazine
New York Times
The Phillipian
The Phillips Bulletin
Time Magazine

AUTHOR'S INTERVIEWS
Robert Morgenthau. 27-Mar-2014
Robert Patterson, Jr. 21-Aug-2012 and 4-Mar-2014
Stephen Bundy. 23-July-2019

ORAL HISTORIES AND INTERVIEWS BY OTHERS
Forrest Pogue Interviews with George Marshall. Recordings (nearly forty hours) along with Pogue's notes made available by the George C. Marshall Foundation.

Larry I. Bland, Editor, and Joellen K. Bland, Assistant Editor. *George C. Marshall Interviews and Reminiscences for Forrest C. Pogue*, 3rd edition. Lexington, VA: George C. Marshall Foundation, 1996.

Forrest Pogue Interviews from the George Marshall Research Library, Lexington, VA.
Field Marshal Viscount Alanbrooke, 5-May-1961
Harvey Bundy, 7-Oct-1959
Dwight Eisenhower, 28-Jun-1962 and 4-Jun-1964
Felix Frankfurter, 20-Feb-1958
Leslie Groves, 7-May-1970
Hastings Ismay, 18-Oct-1960
Robert Lovett, 14-Oct-1957, 17-June-1964, and 28/29-Jun-1973
John Martyn, 21-May-1959
John McCloy, 31-Mar-1959
Joseph McNarney, 2-Feb-1966
Harold Stark, 13-Mar-1959

Eleanor Gamble James Oral History Interview, 15-Nov-1975 by Donald R. Lennon. Digital Collections, East Carolina University.

OTHER
Nomination of Henry L. Stimson. Committee on Military Affairs, United States Senate, July 2, 1940. United States Government Printing Office: 1940.

INDEX

Acheson, Dean, 4, 35, 455, 473, 476; on Marshall, G. C., Jr., decisiveness, 480; on Marshall, G. C., Jr., integrity, 479
AEF. *See* American Expeditionary Forces
African Americans: in Army, 254; in Army Air Force, 326; draft and, 211–13
Ainsworth, Frederick, 76, 86, 87–90, 373
aircraft production, 126–27, 200, 204, 240, 253; balancing needs for, 323; in Germany, 323
airpower, 353
Alamogordo Test Range, 448–49
Alcoa. *See* Aluminum Company of America
Alexander, Harold, 337, 401
Algeria, 374
Alien Enemy Control Unit, 281
Allied troops: ammunition shortages of, 415; Europe setbacks of, 412–18; extricating from Normandy, 406
Alperovitz, Gar, 456
aluminum: production of, 198; shortages of, 197
Aluminum Company of America (Alcoa), 199
America First Committee, 217
American Battle Monuments Commission, 473–74
American Expeditionary Forces (AEF), 70, 133
American Red Cross, 474
Americans: British differences of opinion, 375, 412, 417; Stalin statements in Tehran and, 387
American Sugar Refining Company, 50
antiaircraft guns, 347
anti-draft postcards, 217
antifascism, 258
anti-submarine measures, 346
antitrust law, 136, 198–99; explosives manufacturers and, 290; wartime and, 290

Anvil, 401, 407; British opposition to, 387; versus Italy, 386–90; weakening, 388. *See also Dragoon*
Anzio, Italy, Americans landing forces in, 386–87
Arcadia Conference, 242, 257–65, 269, 276, 277, 316, 336; war plans at, 291
Argonne Forest, 72
Arlington National Cemetery: Dill burial in, 416; Marshall, G. C., Jr., in, 479
Army and Navy Munitions Board, 206
Army Construction Division, 328
Army Corps of Engineers, 275
Army Pearl Harbor Board, 421–22
Army Service Forces, 275, 373
Army War College, 61, 85, 100; Marshall, G. C., Jr., teaching at, 108–9
Arnold, Henry, "Hap," 180, 262, 266, 292, 362, 407, 472, 494n10; as Army Air Forces head, 274, 275; atomic bombs and, 437, 449, 452; at Casablanca conference, 333–34; heart attack, 190, 342; JCS and, 276–77; MacArthur and, 320; on Marshall, G. C., Jr., 480; meeting Marshall, G. C., Jr., 66; Normandy arrival, 400; reorganization and, 271; on state of air force, 200; strategic bombing plans, 320
Arnold, Thurman, 290
"Arsenal of Democracy" speech (FDR), 234
Aruba, bombing of, 290
Atlantic Conference, 259–60
atomic bomb, 6, 181, 435–38, 461–63, *O*; decision to use, 449–57; first use of, 455; message about working of, 448; political benefits from dropping, 457; range of, 449; secrecy of project, 437
Atomic Tragedy (Malloy), 450
Augusta, USS, 239

513

ABOUT THE AUTHOR

Edward "Ted" Aldrich is an international banker and commodity specialist by trade who has held senior banking positions in New York, London, and Zurich. He holds degrees from Colgate University and Boston College. He and his wife Susie have three grown children and reside in Westport, Connecticut. Although Aldrich is a lifelong student of history, *The Partnership* is his first book.